Richard B. Peiser and David Hamilton
with Sofia Dermisi, Nick Egelanian, and Suzanne Lanyi Charles

FOURTH EDITION

T0350832

PROFESSIONAL
REAL ESTATE
DEVELOPMENT

The ULI Guide to the Business

Urban Land Institute
2001 L Street, NW
Suite 200
Washington, DC 20036

About the Urban Land Institute

THE URBAN LAND INSTITUTE is a global, member-driven organization comprising more than 45,000 real estate and urban development professionals dedicated to advancing the Institute's mission of shaping the future of the built environment for transformative impact in communities worldwide.

ULI's interdisciplinary membership represents all aspects of the industry, including developers, property owners, investors, architects, urban planners, public officials, real estate brokers, appraisers, attorneys, engineers, financiers, and academics. Established in 1936, the Institute has a presence in the Americas, Europe, and Asia Pacific regions, with members in 80 countries.

The extraordinary impact that ULI makes on land use decision-making is based on its members sharing expertise on a variety of factors affecting the built environment, including urbanization, demographic and population changes, new economic drivers, technology advancements, and environmental concerns.

Peer-to-peer learning is achieved through the knowledge shared by members at thousands of convenings each year that reinforce ULI's position as a global authority on land use and real estate. In 2021 alone, more than 2,700 events, both virtual and in person, were held in cities around the world.

Drawing on the work of its members, the Institute recognizes and shares best practices in urban design and development for the benefit of communities around the globe.

More information is available at uli.org. Follow ULI on Twitter, Facebook, LinkedIn, and Instagram.

Project Staff

Trey Davis
Vice President, Marketing & Membership

Lori Hatcher
Project Manager and Editor

James A. Mulligan
Senior Editor

Karen Coda and Sara Proehl
Publications Professionals LLC
Manuscript Editors

Brandon Weil
Art Director

John Hall Design Group
Book and Cover Designer
www.johnhalldesign.com

Craig Chapman
Senior Director, Publishing Operations

Urban Land Institute
2001 L Street, NW
Suite 200
Washington, DC 20036-4948

Library of Congress Control Number: 2022947192

Recommended bibliographic listing:
Peiser, Richard B., David Hamilton, Sofia Dermisi, Nick Egelanian, and Suzanne Lanyi Charles, *Professional Real Estate Development: The ULI Guide to the Business*. Fourth Edition. Washington, DC: Urban Land Institute, 2023.

ISBN: 978-0-87420-477-3

Front cover photos, from top: Roman Babakin/Shutterstock; Mike Mareen/Shutterstock; i viewfinder/Shutterstock; Suzanne Lanyi Charles
Back cover photos, from top: Talon Private Capital; Storybuilt; Steiner + Associates; Matthew Milman

About the Authors

RICHARD B. PEISER, PHD, is the first Michael D. Spear Professor of Real Estate Development in the Department of Urban Planning and Design at the Harvard University Graduate School of Design (GSD). He founded and served as the first director of the university-wide Real Estate Academic Initiative as well as the university's highest-level real estate executive training curriculum, the Advanced Management Development Program. He is past director of the Master in Design Studies concentration in real estate and past director of the Urban Planning program at GSD. Before coming to Harvard, he founded the Master of Real Estate Development program and the Lusk Center at the University of Southern California.

Professor Peiser's primary research focuses on developing an understanding of the response of real estate developers to the marketplace and to the institutional environment in which they operate, particularly in the areas of urban redevelopment, affordable housing, and suburban sprawl. His current research focuses on mixed-use development, urban sprawl, property technology, and new towns. His latest book, *New Towns for the 21st Century*, with Ann Forsyth was published by the University of Pennsylvania Press in 2021. His book, *Professional Real Estate Development: The ULI Guide to the Business*, is one of the Urban Land Institute's all-time best sellers.

Professionally, he has developed housing, apartments, land, and industrial properties in Texas, California, and China, and has served as the lead expert witness in a series of high-profile cases on affordable housing, apartment investments, real estate investment trusts, golf courses, master-planned communities, and most recently a major fraud case prosecuted by the Federal Trade Commission on a resort community in Belize.

Peiser was born in Houston and grew up in Dallas. He received a BA from Yale University, an MBA from Harvard University, and a PhD in land economy from Cambridge University. He has held teaching appointments at Stanford and Cambridge universities and at Southern Methodist University in Dallas; he has also been a Visitor to Seoul National University, the University of Ulster, the University of Regensburg, Tsinghua University, and Ardhi University in Tanzania. He is a governor and trustee of the Urban Land Institute and former coeditor of the *Journal of Real Estate Portfolio Management*. He served on the board of the publicly traded Berkshire Income Realty and currently serves on a number of advisory boards for private equity companies as well as the Board of Trustees for Mount Auburn Cemetery and the Board of Councilors for the Native Plant Trust.

DAVID HAMILTON is a principal at Geobarns and a visiting professor at the Harvard University Graduate School of Design. Trained as an architect, Hamilton has managed innovative real estate development projects at a variety of scales, ranging from medical and university campuses to award-winning high-tech office and R&D spaces. As a codirector of the Cambridge Innovation Center, he managed the design and construction of a model coworking and incubation space for technology-related businesses. As a principal of Qroe Farm Preservation Development, Hamilton led project design, entitlement, and construction efforts for conservation development projects in New England and the mid-Atlantic. At Geobarns, he advises teams on the development of agricultural-residential communities. His primary research interest is the future of productive and ecologically valuable landscapes under development pressure. To that end, he has led teams developing rural hospitality and agritourism destinations and designing facilities for wine, distilling, and other artisanal food and beverage businesses.

Hamilton has contributed to various ULI publications on topics ranging from inner-ring suburban regeneration to land use regulation and conservation development. He teaches real estate finance and development courses at Harvard's Graduate School of Design (GSD) and introductory courses on the built environment at Middlebury College. He is a graduate of Middlebury College (BA) and Harvard GSD (MArch). He lives in Middlebury, Vermont, where he is active in local land use, governance, economic, and affordable housing issues.

DR. SOFIA DERMISI is the Lyon and Wolff Endowed Professor of Real Estate in the Runstad Department of Real Estate, professor of Urban Design and Planning, and director of graduate real estate programs at the University of Washington's College of Built Environments (UW-CBE). Before joining UW in 2014, she was the Pasquinelli Distinguished Chair at Roosevelt University's Heller College of Business where she developed the MBA-RE curriculum and established the MSRE program.

At UW, she formed and chaired an interdisciplinary group of faculty (across UW and Seattle colleges), advisory board members, staff, and students. She restructured the MSRE, which brought more students to the program, thus allowing a major expansion in personnel and the establishment of a department.

Dermisi has multiple publications, 10 best manuscript awards, a best practice award, and the prestigious Kinnard Young Scholar Award. Her research has been funded by the National Science Foundation, Real Estate Research Institute, Building Owners and Managers Association of Chicago, Council on Tall Buildings and Urban Habitat, Illinois Department of Transportation, and others; her focus is on office market analysis in major downtown locations and the effect of internal and external shocks, with an emphasis on disasters (terrorism, life/safety issues) and sustainability. Professionally, she worked as a market analyst/consultant, which included undertaking two economic impact studies for BOMA/Chicago (2006 and 2013).

Dermisi was born and raised in Thessaloniki, Greece. She received her diploma in Planning and Regional Development Engineering from the University of Thessaly and her master's and doctoral degrees from the Harvard University Graduate School of Design. She also served as the American Real Estate Society's conference program chair (2018) and president (2019–2020).

NICK EGELANIAN is an industry thought leader and frequent speaker and writer on retail trends and the evolution of the retail and shopping center industries. He coined the phrases "post-department store era," "department store deconstruction," and "convergence era"; and in his numerous articles in industry publications, he pioneered the segmentation of retail into commodity and specialty genres.

Egelanian has spent nearly 35 years in the shopping center industry. As president of SiteWorks, he has advised a wide array of retail clients and shopping center owners and developers throughout North America,

including a stint as chief retail adviser (with master planning firm Elkus Manfredi) to Sagamore Development, the developer of Port Covington, a planned 275-acre, 10 million-square-foot mixed-use waterfront development in Baltimore. He also developed merchandising and site plans for three Amazon HQ2 contending sites, including the winning site in Crystal City in Virginia.

Egelanian recently completed his eighth year teaching graduate-level retail theory and development as an adjunct professor in the Colvin Real Estate Development program within the University of Maryland's School of Architecture, Planning & Preservation in College Park. He earned his BS in finance at the Smith School of Business at the University of Maryland and his JD at the George Washington University National Law Center.

DR. SUZANNE LANYI CHARLES is an associate professor of city and regional planning and of real estate at Cornell University. She serves as acting chair of the Rubacha Department of Real Estate and director of graduate studies in real estate at the university.

In the Baker Program in Real Estate at Cornell, Charles teaches courses on commercial and residential real estate development, the form of the built environment, and housing policy. Her research examines infill redevelopment and "mansionization," the financialization of housing, and single-family rental housing. Charles's academic research has received grants from the U.S. Department of Housing and Urban Development, Harvard University's Joint Center for Housing Studies, the Institute for the Social Sciences at Cornell, the President's Council of Cornell Women, and the Cornell Center for Cities. She was a 2021–2022 Fulbright Scholar to Belgium during which she was a visiting professor at Katholieke Universiteit Leuven in Leuven, Belgium.

Charles is trained as an architect. She was vice president of Booth Hansen Architects in Chicago, as well as a real estate consultant at the Weitzman Group in New York City. She holds undergraduate and graduate degrees in architecture and received her doctorate from the Harvard University Graduate School of Design.

Authors

PRIMARY AUTHORS

Richard B. Peiser
Michael D. Spear Professor of Real
 Estate Development
Harvard University Graduate School of
 Design
Cambridge, Massachusetts

David Hamilton
Principal
Geobarns
White River Junction, Vermont

CONTRIBUTING AUTHORS

Sofia Dermisi
Lyon and Wolff Endowed Professor of
 Real Estate
University of Washington
Seattle, Washington

Nick A. Egelanian
Founder and President
SiteWorks Retail Real Estate
Annapolis, Maryland

Suzanne Lanyi Charles
Associate Professor, City and Regional
 Planning; and Real Estate
Cornell University
Ithaca, New York

OTHER CONTRIBUTORS

Wynne Mun
Chief Financial Officer
Metropolitan Properties Inc.
Boston, Massachusetts

John W. Loper
Associate Professor of Real Estate
 (Teaching)
Sol Price School of Public Policy
University of Southern California
Los Angeles, California

Lesley Deutch
Managing Principal, Consulting
John Burns Real Estate Consulting LLC
Boca Raton, Florida

Beau Arnason
Executive Vice President, Asset
 Management
Stelner + Associates
Columbus, Ohio

David Lobaugh
Founder and Principal
August Partners
Atlanta, Georgia

James McCandless
Vice President
MPC Colorado
Denver, Colorado

All Members of SWA Affiliates
SiteWorks Advisory Group
Annapolis, Maryland

STUDENT ASSISTANTS

George Zhang, Harvard Graduate
 School of Design
Julian Huertas, Harvard Graduate
 School of Design
Andrew Mikula, Harvard Graduate
 School of Design
Maya Kazamel, Harvard Graduate
 School of Design
Katherine Selch, Cornell University,
 Baker Program in Real Estate

PRIMARY CONTRIBUTING AUTHORS, PREVIOUS EDITIONS

Ken Beck
Sierra Madre, California

Anne B. Frej
Real Estate and International
 Development Consultant
Santa Fe, New Mexico

Adrienne Schmitz
Washington, D.C.

Dean Schwanke
Vice President, Multifamily Housing
National Association of Home Builders
Washington, D.C.

Frank Spink
Annandale, Virginia

REVIEWERS

Dan Biederman
President
Bryant Park Corporation/Biederman
 Redevelopment Ventures
New York, New York

Arthur Danielian, FAIA
Founder and Chairman
Danielian and Associates
Irvine, California

Barry DiRaimondo
Chief Executive Officer and Chairman
Steelwave
San Francisco, California

Phillip Hughes
President
Hughes Investments Inc.
Greenville, South Carolina

Howard Kozloff
Founder and Principal
Agora Partners
New York, New York

Christopher Kurz
President and CEO
Linden Associates Inc.
Baltimore, Maryland

Randall W. Lewis
Executive Vice President
Lewis Management Corporation
Upland, California

Matthew Mowell
Senior Economist
CBRE Econometric Advisors
Boston, Massachusetts

Vicki Mullins
Executive Vice President
Brookfield Properties
Dallas, Texas

H. Pike Oliver
Founder
Urbanexus
Seattle, Washington

Contents

Contents (continued)

For supplemental materials, see americas.uli.org/PRED

Preface

REAL ESTATE DEVELOPERS face an awesome responsibility. The communities and buildings they create become the fabric of our civilization. They influence people's lives in a multitude of ways. What they build affects whether or not people can realize the lifestyle of their dreams. Developers play a key role in determining the financial health of cities and the everyday experiences of their inhabitants. Where people play, work, and shop; how long it takes them to get there; and the quality of the amenities and environment they find all depend to a large extent on the work of developers.

Thirty years have passed since this book was first published in 1992. This edition is the fourth, and much has changed—even since the last edition in 2012. Developers face a more complex world than they did 30 years ago. Everyone has a stake in their activities. The days are past when a developer could unilaterally decide what to build and then build it without consulting community leaders, neighbors, and others affected by the development. The political, environmental, and financial context is changing just as rapidly as the market itself. In the 1990s, because of overbuilding in virtually all segments of the industry as well as the collapse of the savings and loan industry, the development industry went through its biggest adjustment since the Great Depression. Next, in the wake of the global financial crisis of 2008–2009, the real estate industry once again endured wrenching changes as commercial mortgage–backed securities and other securitized financing vehicles collapsed, 8 million homes went through foreclosure, unemployment rates soared, and burgeoning debt forced enormous cutbacks in government spending and private debt. Then, beginning in March 2020, the COVID-19 pandemic forced shutdowns throughout the economy. Although life is returning to normal, COVID's impacts are still being felt as this edition goes to press—and will likely be with us for years to come.

Three major changes have occurred over the past 30 years that have affected the development industry dramatically: globalization and institutionalization of ownership, securitization in the financial markets (notwithstanding the 2008 collapse), and the technological revolution. These changes create both opportunities and obstacles for beginning developers. Entrepreneurial development is harder now than

it was 30 years ago: it requires more capital to get started and more time to get projects off the ground. Today, we are seeing a reverse in some aspects of globalization, while climate change and the push for greater diversity in the real estate industry are forcing major changes in how development gets done.

At a time when the development industry is undergoing such rapid change, why do we need a book on how to develop real estate? First, if all the developers of real estate who lost their buildings in recent downcycles had practiced sound development principles, much of what was built would have never been conceived, let alone financed. Second, developers face important new challenges that affect all aspects of the development process. Third, qualified developers will always be necessary, and they should have the best possible training. Development is not for amateurs. When projects go bankrupt or are poorly designed, the whole community loses, not just the developer and its financiers. Tenants should not have to put up with poorly designed spaces. And communities should not have to suffer the tax losses of ill-conceived projects and unoccupied buildings.

Successful development requires understanding not only how to develop good real estate projects but also how to determine their impacts on neighborhoods and cities. The increasing importance of environmental, social, and governance (ESG) issues not only affects how equity and debt providers decide where to invest their money but also how developers get projects approved. Developers must demonstrate how their projects meet ESG criteria and objectives and add to their communities. Long-term real estate values are directly tied to the quality of the urban areas where they are situated. Developers must take an active role in protecting and enhancing the long-term economic health of the cities in which they build.

Although this book was conceived as a practical guide for developing five major real estate types—land, residential, office, industrial, and retail—it is intended to do much more. Successful developers must have a thorough understanding of urban dynamics, of how and why cities grow. They must be informed critics of architecture; they must be knowledgeable about law, public approvals, and public finance; and they must possess fundamental real estate skills in finance, market analysis, construction, leasing and sales, and property management. Real estate development is the art—and, increasingly, the science—of creating real estate value by managing development risk. Development expertise can be applied to much more than building new buildings and subdivisions. Development talents are essential for such activities as buying empty office buildings and leasing them, renovating older warehouses, repositioning shopping centers by changing the tenant mix, securing development entitlements for raw land, and buying distressed debt and workout properties from banks and turning them around.

Development is exciting because it is dynamic. The conditions that enabled developers to be successful in the latter part of the 20th century are different from the ones that govern the 21st century. This book presents the collective wisdom of developers of both successful and unsuccessful projects, acquired throughout their careers. It is organized by property type to emphasize the different risks and concerns particular to each. The steps in the development process, however, are the same.

The challenge of building more livable cities can only be met by qualified developers working together with other real estate professionals, public officials, and neighborhood representatives. Perhaps the greatest challenge is to build a fairer and more efficient development process—one that reflects the needs and aspirations of all groups while reducing the many hurdles that raise the costs of development without providing commensurate benefits. Of one thing we can be certain: the expertise that developers require will be different tomorrow from what it is today. This book is intended to help tomorrow's developers meet the challenge.

Acknowledgments

THE FOURTH EDITION of *Professional Real Estate Development: The ULI Guide to the Business* is the culmination of four years of work begun in 2018. As in the previous three, this fourth edition benefits from well over 100 new interviews, all-new case studies, and new spreadsheets reflecting current rents, costs, and taxation. The previous edition came out just after the world had gone through the global financial crisis and the United States experienced the deepest recession since the Great Depression. Interestingly, the first edition in 1992 dealt extensively with the savings and loan crisis of the late 1980s. A theme of this new edition—emphasized by many of the contributors—is how they have dealt with the enormous consequences for real estate of the economic cycle as well as the COVID-19 pandemic.

In every sense of the word, this book is a cooperative effort. I have been blessed with wonderful students over the years, both at Harvard and previously at the University of Southern California. This edition is the collaboration of three of the best from Harvard: David Hamilton, Sofia Dermisi, and Suzanne Lanyi Charles. David Hamilton is fully my coauthor. The two of us cowrote chapters 1 and 8. David also revised chapters 2 and 3, chapters to which he contributed significantly in the two previous editions. I focused on chapter 4, multifamily residential development. Sofia Dermisi revised chapter 5 on office development. And Suzanne Lanyi Charles wrote chapter 6 on industrial development. Nick Egelanian, a retail consultant who wrote the retail chapter in the previous edition, revised chapter 7 on retail development. I would also like to acknowledge Wynne Mun's work on the spreadsheets in chapter 4. He brought his extraordinary talents to bear on both the programming and the presentation of the five stages of analysis.

David and I are forever grateful to Lori Hatcher, who not only is the official ULI editor of the book but also has guided the book's development at every step of the way. We are also especially thankful for the extremely careful editing of Jim Mulligan, Karen Coda, and Sara Proehl. The current edition stands on the shoulders of the three previous editions. The handiwork of my previous ULI editors and coauthors—Adrienne Schmitz, Anne Frej, and Dean Schwanke—is evident throughout the new book. They bear no responsibility for errors or omissions in the latest edition, but the new edition would not be what it is without their enormous contributions.

The help of research assistants drawn from among our best students at the Harvard Graduate School of Design has also been invaluable. George Zhang and Julian Huertas conducted most of the interviews for chapter 4 and wrote drafts of the case studies and market analysis; they also drafted the industry-wide survey presented in chapter 1. John Loper wrote the section in chapter 1 on how three developers got started. Andrew Mikula and Maya Kazamel helped conduct the interviews in chapter 3.

David is also profoundly grateful to the many professionals who contributed their expertise and experience to this book. Roger and Kristin Glover and Kirsten Nease of Cornerstone Homes were particularly generous in sharing the story of the development of an award-winning "agrihood," Chickahominy Falls, in Virginia. Michael Padavic and the team at StoryBuilt also contributed the lessons of their terrific infill development project, North Bluff, in Texas.

Sofia Dermisi wishes to thank Tajal Pastakia and Mark Craig for their background material on chapter 5's first and third case studies, respectively, and Bill Pollard for his insightful interview and detailed material for the chapter's second case study. Additionally, she extends her thanks to the following industry professionals interviewed: Murphy McCullough, David Yuan, Chris Hellstern, Sakriti Vishwakarma, Gregg Johnson, Julianna Plant, Gabe Reisner, Jeff Jochums, Laura Ford, and Lisa Stewart. The comments of Matt Mowell and Christopher Kurz were especially helpful.

Nick Egelanian is grateful to Beau Arnason, Roy Higgs, Nick Javaris, David Lobaugh, James McCandless, and all the members of SWA Affiliates for pulling together information and offering their guidance and expertise.

Suzanne Lanyi Charles would like to thank Paul Rubacha and Meredith Azar at Ashley Capital for their generous help in preparing the case study for the industrial development chapter. She would especially like to thank Katherine Selch for her research assistance. In addition, she extends her thanks to the following industry professionals who contributed their expertise: Ryan Bandy, Barry DiRaimondo, Mel Fish, Howard Freeman, John Morris, Somy Mukherjee, Jessica Ostermick, Spencer Papciak, Mark Seltzer, Gayle Starr, and Dennis Williams.

Acknowledgments (continued)

As in previous editions, I owe a tremendous debt to friends and mentors from the Urban Land Institute. Some of them are no longer with us—Charlie Shaw, Harry Newman, Bob Baldwin, Joe O'Connor, Stan Ross, and most recently, Gerald Hines, who was a life-long friend and mentor. I have relied tremendously on the advice and input of other ULI friends, including Jim DeFrancia, Jim Chaffin, Buzz McCoy, Jerry Rappaport, Tony Green, and Phil Hughes. I would also like to thank the Steering Committee: Karen Abrams, Chris Akins, Karen Alschuler, Joe Azrack, Phil Belling, Dan Biederman, Lucy Billingsley, Toby Bozzuto, Daryl Carter, Aaron Conley, Michael Covarrubias, Art Danielian, Larry Ellman, Calvin Gladney, Richard Gollis, Pam Herbst, Leslie Himmel, Phil Hughes, Larry Johnson, Ladd Keith, Steve Kohn, Leanne Lachman, Randall Lewis, Todd Mansfield, Vicki Mullins, Jeremy Newsum, Bob Ruth, Ellen Sinreich, Gayle Starr, and Jeff Swope. Many of them are close friends who also happen to be experts on individual property types. In addition, I would like to acknowledge several close personal friends who not only are great companions but provide sounding boards for my ideas: Jim Perley, Peter Jungbacker, Chris Kurz, and Ted Raymond. I am grateful to my colleagues at Harvard and USC who have helped forge my views about urban development over the years—Ann Forsyth, Alan Altshuler, Alex Krieger, Peter Gordon, Eric Heikkila, Dowell Myers, Rahul Mehrotra, Jerold Kayden, Carl Steinitz, Tony Gomez-Ibanez, and Bing Wang—as well as colleagues from other schools—Jim Berry, Alastair Adair, Karl Werner-Schulte, Tobias Just, and Glenn Mueller. Sadly, my lifelong mentor from Yale, Alex Garvin, recently passed away.

I have leaned shamelessly on former students, many of whom are now at the height of their careers, as well as participants in the Advanced Management Development Program—Harvard GSD's advanced executive education program for senior managers and entrepreneurs. The great benefit of teaching at universities like Harvard is the incredible students one gets to work with along the way.

All these people deserve credit for helping make this fourth edition a reality. They are absolved of any mistakes, the full responsibility for which falls to David and myself.

Last but not least, my wife Beverly has endured my absences and preoccupation as I worked to get the book finished. I cannot thank her enough for all that she does for me. It is to my children, my grandchildren, and my students that this book is dedicated, in the hope that the knowledge and practice of real estate development, in its fullest meaning, will be better tomorrow than it is today.

Richard B. Peiser
Cambridge, Massachusetts

PROFESSIONAL
REAL ESTATE
DEVELOPMENT

The ULI Guide to the Business

1 Introduction

RICHARD B. PEISER

What Is a Developer?

Few job descriptions are as varied as that of real estate developer—or as impactful on society and the environment. Though practitioners may come from finance, design, sales, or construction, development is a multifaceted business. Development can encompass activities ranging from the acquisition, renovation, and re-leasing of existing buildings to the purchase of raw land and the sale of improved parcels to others. Developers conceive, initiate, and coordinate these changes to our built environment. They lead teams of professionals, coordinate competing visions, and apply ideas to real property, shaping the urban fabric and the experiences of generations to come. On a ground-up, new project, developers may control the process from beginning to end, or they may specialize in a phase or type of work. They often take the greatest risks in a project, and they can receive the greatest rewards.

Developers are also in a position to influence debate and policy, on issues from environmental responsibility to social and racial equity. Developers must think big; but this is a detail business, and oversights can have serious consequences. Though all development is a team effort, developers are ultimately accountable—for both their projects and their impact on society.

Good developers are flexible managers who can adapt to rapidly changing conditions. During the approval process, for example, they may have to negotiate with multiple stakeholders, each promoting conflicting visions of a neighborhood or project. The developers must not only navigate those conflicts, but, crucially, they must come out with a project that satisfies investors, fulfills regulatory requirements, and matches the capability of their team. Most important, they must find personal satisfaction in the process, finding ways to improve their work by engagement with many other stakeholders.

Developers are experts in managing risk and dealing with uncertainty. Sharif Mitchell, principal at Dantes

Community Partners, sums it up this way: "It always takes longer than expected to deliver a construction project. You can't predict the timing of the capital markets."[1]

Successful developers usually have strong opinions, but they cannot possibly be authorities on all the different fields of expertise involved in a project. Their success depends on the coordinated performance of many other parties and on the developers' judgment and skill in putting those inputs together in a coherent way.

Developers must be able to work with a range of professionals with diverse perspectives. Most obvious are the building professionals, including surveyors, planners, architects and other designers, technical consultants, contractors, and tradesmen. Next are buyers and tenants with varied preferences and busi-

Truax Lofts in San Diego is a small-scale multifamily property featuring studio floor plans and single and double mezzanine lofts. Sustainable materials and solar panels were used to offset electric power usage.

ness needs. And at various points in the development process, developers must work closely with attorneys, bankers and investors, planners, elected and appointed officials at all levels of government, and sometimes overlapping layers of regulators and inspectors. In addition to professionals, the successful developer must communicate effectively with citizens groups, homeowners associations, and community organizers. From financial management to human resources, to construction administration, developers need to know how to find and retain expertise. Success requires familiarity with best practices and rules, knowing whom to call with each question that arises, and the ability to sift and evaluate conflicting advice and information. When the topic is furthest from their own expertise, developers must still know how to incentivize and motivate the team.

Development is often creative—in design, financing, or marketing—and a creative spark can distinguish one developer from the competition. As in any creative business, management of an innovative team is a balancing act. Too much guidance may stifle creativity; too little oversight may lead to a chaotic process and lack of direction. Obtaining good work from the team without exceeding the budget is one of the fundamental challenges of managing the development process; it requires a framework of rigor and accountability, with intentional space and time for flexible exploratory work on design and construction options when appropriate.

Development of communities is an organic, evolutionary process. No two projects are exactly alike because each one responds to its site, users, and neighbors and because the circumstances in a development change constantly. Development is also harder than it looks. Most beginning developers report having to work twice as hard as seasoned professionals to keep their projects moving in the right direction. At some point in almost every deal, the complications make the developer wonder if the project was ever a good idea. At these critical moments, developers discover how badly they want the deal.

Solving problems as they occur is the essence of day-to-day development, but carefully preparing for key moments, anticipating the unexpected, and attentively managing risks are the keys to a long, lower-stress career. Preparation before an important meeting, arranging an introduction to the best prospective lender, creating the best possible setting for negotiations, and knowing as much as possible about the prospective tenant's or lender's needs and concerns before meeting with them help to ensure success.

The Book's Approach and Objectives

This book is specifically directed to beginning developers and to professionals who work in or around the real estate industry. Readers are assumed to be familiar already with at least one or two segments of the industry, through either professional work, academic training, or personal investment. The hope is that even seasoned professional readers may gain a better understanding of the role their companies play in the development process: What are the rules of thumb concerning the way developers do business with them? What are the critical elements affecting the success of the development?

The book addresses the five major types of development that beginning developers are most likely to undertake: land subdivision, multifamily residential, office, industrial, and retail. Single-family housing is only addressed insofar as land developers conceive their communities to sell subdivided lots to homebuilders. Each of the five product types is described from start to finish: selecting sites, performing feasibility studies, considering alternative approaches, identifying the market and designing a product specifically for it, financing the project, working with contractors, marketing the building or subdivision, and managing the completed project through operations or disposition.

The development process, although similar for each product, is different in important ways. For example, pre-leasing is not necessary for apartment development and not meaningful in for-sale land development, yet it is critical for both office and retail development. And the way a developer analyzes the market for industrial space is unique to that product and crucial for designing and marketing industrial buildings.

The book contains three main parts: an introduction to the development process, discussions of individual product types, and a look at trends in the industry. Chapters 1 and 2 provide an overview of the development process, entry into the business, and ways to select and manage the development team through common challenges and changing environments. Chapters 3 through 7 describe development of the five main product types: land development (chapter 3), multifamily residential development (chapter 4), office development (chapter 5), industrial development (chapter 6), and retail development (chapter 7).

Chapters 3 and 4 provide detailed step-by-step summaries of the core processes for development and serve as valuable references for the other product types. Chapter 3 focuses on land development, illustrating analysis of for-sale property types, including subdivisions. Land acquisition, approval, and entitlement issues, which are common to all property types, are given particular attention in this chapter because they are so critical to land development. Chapter 4 (multifamily residential) provides a detailed introduction to income property development. Many steps are the same for all four income property types, and chapter 4 describes those steps in detail, for example, how to calculate financial returns for the overall project and for individual joint venture partners. After reading chapters 3 and 4, readers seeking more granular detail should then turn to the sections of the book that concern the particular product types that interest them.

Because real estate exists primarily to serve society, readers will also benefit from zooming out to larger issues, such as ecological responsibility, diversity and equity in organizations and in communities, and rapid technological change. The book's final chapter outlines historical and current industry trends and identifies emerging professional and social issues likely to drive changes in development and investment in coming years.

The breadth and detail of this book should not be considered a substitute for remaining up to date with market and regulatory conditions. Every community and jurisdiction is unique, and over the long history of real estate development, one constant has been change. New regulatory approaches, social prerogatives, construction innovation, and even court rulings can upend long-standing best-practices and standards presented in this book. So, while this book is intended to be a primer covering all aspects of development, it is no substitute for expert local advice from experienced developers, attorneys, consultants, brokers, lenders, and others involved in the process.

Information is as specific as possible, with costs, rents, and financing information included for each product type. The figures indicate the magnitude of individual items and the approximate relationship of one item to another, but they are not appropriate for use in estimating or project modelling. Costs may be two or three times higher in cities like New York and Los Angeles than they are in rural areas, and material and labor costs can rise and fall dramatically, sometimes day to day. In some cases, figures presented here may be useful for initial crude estimates, but local sources should be consulted for information specific to particular projects. A wealth of information is now available online to facilitate every step of development—from market analysis and local

Understanding the Real Estate Industry

The real estate industry is divided into five main product types: residential, office, commercial, industrial, and land. Other businesses, such as hospitality and energy, are also closely dependent on real assets. The market for each product type can differ dramatically by region and by access to employment centers, transit, or other location factors. These relationships are not always simple or obvious, as when suburban locations, for a variety of self-reinforcing reasons, achieve higher values than their center cities. Understanding these patterns requires continuous study and an open mind.

Property markets are also segmented by density and design. Each combination represents a different building type and cost structure. For example, high-rise apartments with structured parking cost much more to build and operate than garden apartments, so rents must be higher. For a project to be successful, the developer's market study must demonstrate sufficient unmet demand for the proposed type of units in that location.

demographics to environmental conditions, government approvals, and financing. The wide availability of information and opinion is itself a trend, and analytical components shown in this book should be a framework for filtering, understanding, and acting on this torrent of information.

Requirements for Success

Developers take risks. At the low extreme of the risk spectrum, developers may work for a fee, simply managing the development process as agents for other owners or investors. In this role, they might incur a small degree of risk from investing some of their own money in the venture or having an incentive fee that depends on their bringing the project in on schedule or meeting leasing or budget targets. At the other extreme, developers can undertake all the risk, investing the first money in the project, taking the last money out, and accepting full personal liability. Failure can mean bankruptcy. (See figure 1-1.)

Developers can take risks because they specialize in managing risk. They minimize, delay, share, hedge, or eliminate risk at each phase of the development process—at least getting it down to an acceptable level relative to potential returns—before moving forward. They attempt to minimize risk at early stages, so that the level of investment at risk rises along with the likelihood of success. Beginning developers usually must accept greater risk than experienced developers do, because beginners lack a strong bargaining position to transfer risk to others. They often must begin with projects that, for whatever reason, more experienced developers have passed over. Beyond this basic truism, though, Phil Hughes of Hughes Investments argues that beginning developers often take on more risk than they have to.[2] They need to look harder to find the right opportunity. Many developers study 10 or 50 projects for each actual investment, but every project includes opportunities to reduce risk.

Many people are attracted to some aspect of this business because of the perceived wealth and glamour associated with successful developers. To be sure, development can offer rewards, both tangible and intangible. Besides economic considerations, many developers relish their roles in creating lasting contributions to the built environment. The feeling of accomplishment that comes from seeing the result of years of effort is, for this type of person, worth the trouble and the inevitable anxiety along the way.

Development's biggest risks, however, require a certain kind of personality. Individuals must be able to wait a relatively long time for outsized rewards. Three or more years often pass before the developer sees the initial risk money again, not to mention profit. Generally, this delay is growing longer as projects and approvals become more complicated. When appearing before a zoning board or negotiating an anchor lease, developers risk losing everything they have invested; such turning points may happen two or three times during the course of a development project, so developers must live with uncertainty. Events almost never go as planned, especially for beginning developers or those moving into new product types or markets, and projects almost always seem to take longer and cost more than initially expected.

Development also can be extremely frustrating. Developers depend on people outside their organization to complete a variety of tasks at every stage of development, and many events, such as public approvals, are not under the developer's control. Some team members' work can only be completed after another prerequisite task is done, so delays can pile up. One developer recalls that when he started developing single-family houses, he often became frustrated when work crews failed to show up as promised. Only after he learned to expect them not to show up and was pleasantly surprised when they did, did building become fun. Developers are also increasingly being held accountable for issues extending far beyond their projects' boundaries, or over which they exercise little control. In addition to stormwater or public safety, de-velopment proposals may be evaluated against more subjective criteria like environmental justice, gentrification, and inclusion, or with reference to global issues like decarbonization. The public approval process has become much more time-consuming and costly over the past two decades. It is also more accommodating to interested stakeholders, reducing the developer's control over the process and adding considerably to risk, especially in the early stages when risk is already highest.

Development requires considerable self-confidence. Until beginners gain sufficient confidence in their skills and relationships, they might work for another developer and learn about the process without incurring the risk. Even when they are ready to undertake their own project, beginning developers often start with a financial partner who bears most of the financial risk.

Perhaps the most effective way to limit risk is to start on projects that involve leasing or rehabilitation risk but do not involve all the risks, such as government approvals, that are required in a completely new development. An alternative is to begin with single-family houses or small infill commercial buildings on existing, fully entitled lots ready for building. In any event, a beginning developer should start on projects where the at-risk investment can be lost in its entirety without causing undue stress.

Even the smallest projects today commonly require $100,000 cash up front, often called "*pursuit capital*," to get a project to the point where equity and construction loan funding can be raised. A developer should never begin a project without having at least twice as much cash in hand as seems necessary to get the project to the point where other funding is available. The upfront cash is only part of the total cash equity that a developer will need to complete a project. Most lenders today require a developer to invest cash equity to cover 20 to 50 percent of total project cost. Total cash equity need not be in hand or even sufficient to purchase the land, but it should carry the project through to a point at which the developer can raise other funds from investors, lenders, or—eventually—operations.

One important way to reduce risk is through the terms of the land purchase (chapter 3 discusses this method in detail). Developers can limit risk substantially by having the right kind of contract to purchase land. For example, closing on land should take place as late in the process as possible. If 60-day or 90-day closings are typical in a community, beginning developers should look for a land seller who is willing to allow 180 days (likely with options to extend beyond the normal closing date). If public approvals such as zoning changes are necessary, developers can make the necessary approvals a condition of purchasing the land. The land might cost more, but the extra time and certainty is often worth the difference. This is one kind of "risk shifting"—from the developer to the seller—and it will also align seller and buyer interests in the approval process. If public approvals or financing fall through, developers will avoid spending their precious risk capital on sites that cannot be developed profitably. Options on property that provide control over a site without having to purchase it immediately are one of the best tools for developers. They reflect the developer's ability to negotiate and to satisfy the owner's needs at the same time.

Raising equity for their first deal is perhaps the biggest hurdle for beginning developers. In general, developers want equity that is available immediately. If developers must raise equity before they can close on a property, the seller will likely become nervous about their ability to close and less willing to let them tie up the property in the first place. Options may overcome many financial obstacles with creatively constructed purchase agreements, but developers must be able to convince the seller that they have the necessary financing in place before they spend pursuit capital.

Beginning developers often do not have established sources of equity unless they have sufficient funds in their own pocket or close family or business connections. Even if the equity funds are not guaranteed, the developer must have them at least tentatively lined up before entering into a purchase contract. In most cases, investors want to see what they are investing in before they commit funds. They should, however, be precommitted to the extent possible. The developer secures such commitments by speaking to potential investors in advance and soliciting their interest in investing in the type of property, location, size, and market strategy that the developer plans to pursue, often with a target rate of return appropriate to the risk. Investors want to know that developers have done their homework. The message for prospective investors is straightforward and may

FIGURE 1-1 ## The Partnership Continuum

	ADVISORY	PARTNERSHIPS			ACQUISITION
	Developer is hired by owner as consultant to provide advice and project management services	Owner retains possession of land with developer managing process and sharing in profits	Property is transferred to a new entity jointly owned by developer and owner	Owner gives developer option to acquire property, which closes following completion of planning and permitting	Developer acquires property from owner "as is" at agreed-on fixed price
ROLES/CONTROL					
Owner	Planning direction and approval of all aspects	Planning direction and approval of major project components	Early planning direction and share of major decision-making	Early planning direction	Very limited role
Developer	Management of process subject to owner approval	Management of process subject to owner approval of plan, budget, and major decisions	Management of process provided certain benchmarks are being met	Management of process if meeting milestones; complete responsibility after acquisition	Complete responsibility for development process
CONTRIBUTION					
Owner	Land and all project costs, including developer fees	Land and project costs	Land and share of project costs	Seller note to finance portion of acquisition cost	None
Developer	Expertise and experience	Partial deferral of fees	Share of development costs	All project costs, land deposits, and required acquisition equity	All acquisition and project costs
COMPENSATION					
Owner	All sales revenue (including "profit")	Most profits from project	Land value; priority return on land value and capital contribution; split of profits	Land value	Land value, discounted for entitlement risk
Developer	Fees for time, paid current	Fees for time, partially paid current; percentage-based incentive fee	Agreed-on fee for management role; priority return on capital contribution; split of profits	Development fees and project profits	Development fees and project profits

ULI members who were identified as development professionals were surveyed about their experiences in the field of real estate development in August and September 2020 and in March and April 2021. The following summary, based on the 129 completed surveys, gives an idea of the background of people in the development industry who are active in community and building development.

A PROFILE OF DEVELOPERS

All respondents are actively engaged in real estate development. Figure A shows the breakdown of the types of positions represented. Figures B and C break down respondents' developments over the previous 10 years by property type and geographical location. In addition to development activities, respondents were also involved in the purchase of land and existing residential, office, retail, industrial, mixed-use, hotel, self-storage, and parking projects (figure B).

CAREER PATH TO DEVELOPMENT

Respondents identified their professional backgrounds, representing experience in business administration, accounting, brokerage, construction, lending, real estate consulting, and law, among others (figure D). Other than development, business administration was the most common step on the development career path. The responses indicate that project management, investment, finance, and construction offer good entry points to development. Numerous respondents also spent time in the fields of accounting, brokerage, lending, architecture, and law.

The most popular product type for respondents' initial project was residential development, with land development following up as the second most popular (figure E). Respondents' second and third projects were also weighted toward

residential development, but they included office, industrial, retail, and mixed-use development as well. The most popular product type for the developer's third project was evenly split between office and industrial development. The increase in office development involvement likely occurred in part because, by their third project, respondents had gained enough experience to tackle office and industrial development.

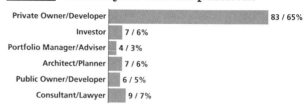

FIGURE A What is your current position?

Position	Value
Private Owner/Developer	83 / 65%
Investor	7 / 6%
Portfolio Manager/Adviser	4 / 3%
Architect/Planner	7 / 6%
Public Owner/Developer	6 / 5%
Consultant/Lawyer	9 / 7%

Note: Positions that received just one response are not illustrated in the figure. Positions receiving one response include affordable housing tax syndicator and lender, broker, marketer, professor of planning and design, and city department head of business and economic development.

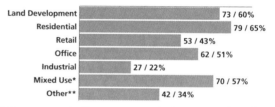

FIGURE B What types of projects have you bought/built during the past 10 years for each listed product type?

Product Type	Value
Land Development	73 / 60%
Residential	79 / 65%
Retail	53 / 43%
Office	62 / 51%
Industrial	27 / 22%
Mixed Use*	70 / 57%
Other**	42 / 34%

* Three or more significant revenue-producing uses; significant functional and physical integration; and conformance to a coherent plan
** Hotel, self-storage, parking

even be formalized with a strategic partnership or memorandum of understanding: if the developer can find a property that meets certain already-identified specifications, then the investors are willing to fund the deal. Equity requirements and rules of thumb on terms for outside equity are discussed in detail in chapters 3 and 4, but this area is particularly prone to change. It has been said that markets experience only two emotions: greed and fear. In particularly hot markets, developers may find a sense of urgency among potential equity partners, desiring to get in on a prospective deal. In a downturn, investors retreat to safety, and equity terms become more dear, and sometimes investment may not be available under any terms. Aside from market fluctuations, though, the development process generally becomes easier as

developers gain experience and undertake successive projects with the same team. Instead of waiting for a bank to provide a loan, developers with a track record may discover that lenders are calling them to offer to do business.

The most difficult project is the first one, and if it is not successful, a beginning developer may not get another chance. Beginners must choose a first project that will not lead to bankruptcy if it fails. Because of increasing difficulty in obtaining public approvals and financing, beginning developers should not be surprised if they have to attempt five or more projects before one gets underway. For larger, experienced development teams, with good feasibility criteria and methods, dozens or even a hundred projects may have to be screened to find an attractive deal.

In running their businesses, respondents devoted their primary attention to the front end of the development process: site acquisition, procurement of regulatory approvals, market analysis, and design and planning (see figure F). Site acquisition, the regulatory and approval process, and design and planning were the phases of development in which respondents had most commonly been engaged.

FIGURE C In what geographic markets have you bought/built projects during the past 10 years?

- New England 21 / 17%
- Mid-Atlantic 41 / 34%
- Midwest 33 / 27%
- South 44 / 36%
- Southwest 30 / 25%
- West 57 / 47%
- Outside the U.S. 20 / 16%

FIGURE D What is your professional background?

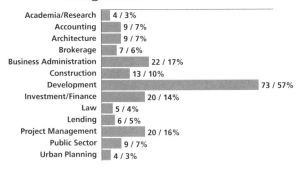

- Academia/Research 4 / 3%
- Accounting 9 / 7%
- Architecture 9 / 7%
- Brokerage 7 / 6%
- Business Administration 22 / 17%
- Construction 13 / 10%
- Development 73 / 57%
- Investment/Finance 20 / 14%
- Law 5 / 4%
- Lending 6 / 5%
- Project Management 20 / 16%
- Public Sector 9 / 7%
- Urban Planning 4 / 3%

Note: Professional backgrounds that received two or fewer responses are not illustrated in the chart. Backgrounds receiving two or fewer responses include consulting, economics, economic development, marketing, appraisal/valuation, landscape architecture, capital markets, engineering, and students.

FIGURE E What product type was your first, second, and third project?

	First	Second	Third
Land Development	32	7	9
Residential	46	46	31
Retail	11	17	14
Office	13	19	21
Industrial	13	19	21
Mixed Use*	9	15	16
Other**	4	8	13

* Three or more significant revenue-producing uses; significant functional and physical integration; and conformance to a coherent plan
**Hotel, self-storage, parking, etc.

FIGURE F Please select one or two phases that you have concentrated on in your business.

- General Advice 23 / 18%
- Operations and Maintenance 20 / 16%
- Marketing and Leasing 28 / 22%
- Construction 18 / 14%
- Joint Venture Structure 41 / 32%
- Permanent Financing 11 / 9%
- Construction/Development Financing 37 / 29%
- Design and Planning 56 / 44%
- Market Analysis 29 / 23%
- Regulatory and Approval Process 56 / 44%
- Site Acquisition 48 / 37%

Note: For figures A, B, C, D, and F: the bar shows the number of respondents/percent share.

Paths for Entering the Development Field

With such varied responsibilities and skills, there is no single path to a career in development. Developers come from a variety of disciplines—property sales and leasing, mortgage banking and commercial lending, consulting, construction, architecture, planning, and law, among others. Most people want to learn the business by working for another developer. Jobs with developers, however, are the most competitive in the real estate industry, with many people looking for relatively few jobs. Moreover, many of the jobs available with developers do not provide the broad range of experience needed. Larger developers usually hire people for a specialized area, such as property management, leasing, sales, or construction. The ideal entry-level job, however, is to work as a project manager with full responsibility for one or more small projects, or to work for a small firm that provides the opportunity to see and do everything.

Some positions in the real estate industry make it easier to move into development. Many developers start as homebuilders, then move naturally to developing the land subdivisions on which their homes are built. Or, they might expand laterally into apartment or commercial development. Others begin by constructing projects for other developers and then for their own investors. Developers might start as commercial brokers, putting together a deal with a major tenant as an anchor in a new office building or finding a site to develop for a build-to-suit tenant. Developers also might start as mortgage brokers or in private equity; by controlling a source of funding, they could make the transition to development by overseeing the financial side of a joint venture with an experienced developer. Whatever the partner's area of expertise, many experienced developers will undertake joint ventures with a new partner if the partner brings a deal that strategically expands their business.

Finding the First Deal

One of the most famous teachers of development, James Graaskamp, emphasized that to start, beginning developers must control at least one of four assets: land, knowledge, tenants, or capital. If they control more than one, the task becomes easier. If developers control land, then the task is driven by supply—a site looking for a use. If developers control knowledge or tenants, then the task is driven by demand—a use looking for a site. If they have capital, they have a choice (see figure 1-2).

A USE LOOKING FOR A SITE

Investable projects are not built to satisfy the developer's desire for monuments. Nearly all development must ultimately be driven by demand. Determining who needs space—potential buyers or tenants—and what type of space they need is the starting point for all development projects. The initial market analysis should define the gaps in the market and the product or products that will fill them.

Knowledge can take several forms. Many developers capitalize on their familiarity with a particular local market gained from their previous experience in the field. Knowledge of the marketplace can give beginning developers a competitive edge—knowing where space is in short supply and which tenants are looking for space, for example. The ability to tell this story, to convince potential lenders and investors that a market opportunity exists, is a core competence of development professionals. The case must include supporting evidence, such as market data or letters of intent from prospective tenants, especially for beginning developers without a long track record to prove their instincts.

For commercial developers, whether beginners or seasoned, finding the tenant or end user is the most important task. Commitments from quality tenants can help draw lenders or investors, and an especially appealing end user can overcome resistance from neighboring homeowners or government agencies.

Many developers enter the business through contacts with potential tenants, perhaps by developing a new building for a family business or for a company with space needs. Knowing a tenant, understanding that tenant's needs, and controlling the decision about location might enable the beginning developer who works for a firm to participate as a principal in the deal. Knowledge about sources of financing is another way to break into the business. Assisting an established developer who needs money or a friend who has control over a tenant to find a lender or investor can enable a beginner to become a principal in his or her first deal.

All these cases start with a use looking for a site, and the use defines requirements for the site. The developer's task is to find the site that best fits the demand.

A SITE LOOKING FOR A USE

Another possible starting point is controlling—not necessarily owning—a well-located piece of property. Many developers start by developing family-owned or company-owned land. Others begin by convincing a landowner to contribute the land to a joint venture in which the developer manages the development. In both cases, development is driven by supply.

The first question developers must answer is, "What is the highest and best use of the land?" Beginning developers commonly decide to develop a type of product that appears to offer the highest return (condominiums, for example) without diagnosing a demand for that product. Unless demand is sufficient, the site will not produce a financially attractive return. Thus, the beginner's first step is to perform a market analysis to determine the highest and best use and to estimate absorption (units sold or square feet leased per month) for the site.

At any given point in time, every site has a highest and best use that will maximize its value. Every potential buyer should analyze a property's highest and best use and diligently compare it to other potential uses, before presenting an offer for a property. In fact, a property's selling price is determined by many buyers computing the highest and best use under different assumptions and bidding accordingly. The owner can then determine whether it makes more sense to accept a buyer's offer or to wait.

Whether to proceed immediately or to wait depends on an assessment of possible changes in use or density in the future. This calculation involves an understanding not only of market demand, but of town planning, infrastructure development, and the political and regulatory process. A tract at the corner of two highways on the edge of town, for example, might eventually make a good site for a shopping

FIGURE 1-2 You Must Control One of These to Get Started

Land	Capital
Knowledge	**Tenants**

center; but if current demand for retail space does not yet justify a shopping center, the most profitable current use may be single-family lots. Waiting five years may offer a higher profit because the shopping center could then be justified, but of course carrying costs, price changes, and regulatory risk might mitigate this differential. This decision requires judgement, but current and accurate information, organized properly, can increase the owners' conviction.

Many buyers base their bids on the maximum number of units or square footage allowed under the current zoning. One of the ways to increase the development value is to change the zoning or increase the density. Rezoning, however, takes time and money and depends strongly on current council members as well as neighboring property owners' attitudes and concerns. Rezoning also depends on the attitudes of neighborhood groups and other residents toward traffic congestion, school overcrowding, and infrastructure capacity. Some cities are lenient toward rezoning while others are highly restrictive, in which case it may take years to change the zoning. Beginning developers are cautioned to avoid rezoning unless they can determine it is feasible and will not take too much time or money.

When the developer already owns the site, the market study should indicate what to build, how much to build, the expected sale price or rental rate, and the amount of time that sales or leasing will likely require.

While the market study is underway, the developer should investigate site conditions (how much of the land is buildable, what percentage contains slopes, whether environmentally sensitive areas are present, whether areas are prone to flooding, and so forth) and find out what public approvals are necessary.

Once the developer has acquired information about the market, engineering, and a pathway through environmental and public approvals, the development strategy can be created. A large site does not necessarily need to be developed all at once. Financing capacity is usually limited by the combined net worth of the developer and any partners, including the unencumbered value of the land (land value net of loans).

IMPROVING THE CHANCES OF SUCCESSFUL DEVELOPMENT

Selecting the location and type of the first development project should not be left to synchronicity, nor should beginners necessarily grab the first opportunity they see. The first deal is the most difficult and among the most important that the developer will ever undertake. Failure will make it that much harder to obtain backing for another opportunity. The first deal establishes the developer's track record; sets the tone for the quality of future developments; establishes a reputation in the marketplace; creates a network of consultants, brokerage, and other business relationships for future deals; and builds relationships with bankers and investors. Still, every beginning developer makes mistakes. The goal should be to deliver a high-quality project that serves the needs of the local market. The beginner should get the best advice possible but not be afraid to make a decision and move on.

A maxim of development is that it takes just as long and is just as difficult to undertake a small deal as it is to undertake a large one. By this logic, developers should look for the largest deals they can confidently execute. But this maxim is not true for beginning developers.

The absence of a track record is perhaps beginning developers' greatest handicap. Getting one success "under their belt" should be the priority, so selecting the right-size project is critical. The major guidelines are these: look for a project that can be put together in, say, six months, and look for one that is within your financial capabilities—personal resources plus those that can be raised through family, friends, or other currently identifiable partners. A general rule of thumb is that the combined financial net worth of the partners must be at least as large as the project's total

The Concept of Present Value

Because most projects require investment now, for returns in future months or years, an understanding of *present value* is essential for developers.[a] Present value analysis equalizes the *time value* of money. Because one can earn interest on money, $100 today will be worth $110 in one year at 10 percent interest and $121 in two years with annual compounding. Ten percent interest represents the *opportunity cost* if one receives the money in, say, two years rather than now. Meaningful comparison of sums accruing at different times requires discounting each to comparable present values.

The present value of $121, received in two years, is $100. That is, the *discounted value* of $121 at a 10 percent discount rate, received in two years, is $100 today. If the discount rate (opportunity cost rate) is 10 percent, then it makes no economic difference whether one receives $100 today or $121 in two years. They represent the same value.

The formula for calculating present value is as follows:

$$PV = FV \left[\frac{1}{(1+r)} \right]^n$$

where **PV** is present value, **FV** is future value, *r* is the discount rate, and **n** is the number of years. Thus, the present value of $121 received in two years at 10 percent discount rate is

$$PV = \$121 \left[\frac{1}{(1+0.10)} \right]^2 = \$100$$

The landowner's dilemma about developing the land immediately into single-family lots or waiting five years to develop a shopping center is solved by applying present value analysis. Suppose, for example, that land for single-family development today is worth $100,000 per acre, whereas land for a shopping center would be worth $200,000 per acre in five years. If the personal discount rate is 10 percent, then $200,000 to be received in five years is worth $124,184 today—clearly more than the value of the land if it is developed for single-family houses. The best option is to wait. In this example, if the discount rate is 20 percent rather than 10 percent, then the present value of $200,000 is only $80,375. At the higher discount rate, the best decision is to develop the land for single-family lots today.

Which discount rate—10 percent or 20 percent—is appropriate? The answer depends on risk. Generally, land development (except for single-family houses) is considered the riskiest form of development because of uncertainties about entitlements and market absorption. Building development risk depends on local market conditions. Office development is considered riskier than industrial or apartment development because the lead time is longer, and space has been oversupplied in many markets.

Because of the high rates of return and high risk associated with development, most developers have personal discount rates of at least 20 percent. That is, they expect to earn at least 20 percent per year on their investment during times when expected inflation is 5 percent. Inflation is a component of the discount rate:

Real return rate + Inflation + Risk = Discount rate premium

or 3% + 5% + 12% = 20%

If inflation increases to 10 percent, then a developer's required return increases to 25 percent. The risk premium depends on the particular property and might range from as low as 4 percent for a completed office building to 15 to 20 percent for unentitled land development.

[a]Any introductory textbook on principles of real estate finance describes present value. One such text is William B. Brueggeman and Jeffrey D. Fisher, *Real Estate Finance and Investments,* 17th ed. (New York: McGraw-Hill, 2022).

cost and preferably double the cost. In times of tight money, net worth requirements may be even greater. For example, suppose the developer has $50,000 cash and a personal net worth of $100,000. To undertake a $2 million project would require bringing in a partner with at least a $2 million net worth. Finding partners with a financial statement verifying that much net worth may be difficult—especially those who are willing to sign personally on the construction loan.[3] But finding partners with $2 million financial statements is much easier than finding those with $50 million financial statements. Further, most projects require substantial cash equity. If lenders require 40 percent equity, for example, raising $800,000 equity for a $2 million project is much easier than raising $4 million equity for a $10 million project. If the developer has created value over and above the project cost, it may be possible to reduce the amount of cash equity required by the bank. *Value* is a function of signed leases and market rental rates: the income streams that will accrue to the investors. For example, if the appraised value of a property costing $10 million to develop is $12 million when completed, then a 60 percent loan will provide $7.2 million, leaving only $2.8 million that the developer needs as cash equity.[4]

In addition to preferring *smaller* deals, beginning developers should search for *simple* deals—deals that require fewer steps to bring to fruition. Smaller buildings can be developed in less time, incurring less risk, and involving fewer steps. They also can be leased more quickly.[5] Although small buildings can be just as complex as larger ones, the criteria for selection should emphasize projects that do not require a lengthy and uncertain process of public approvals, uncertain construction scope, or complicated financing.

One exception to arguments in favor of simple deals is that smaller "problem" deals that experienced developers have passed over may offer opportunities for beginning developers. For example, larger developers may decide that a site requiring special attention to cure problems with easements, boundaries, or flooding is not worth the necessary time and effort. A beginner, however, might be able to tie up the property at little cost while working out the problems, with less pressure to get to marketable lots than a major homebuilder. Another opportunity can be found with sites owned by local and state governments and redevelopment agencies, because large developers may prefer to avoid government entanglements. Unless the site is simply put up for auction, however, beginners might need to demonstrate a track record to convince government officials to work with them. Nonetheless, keeping officials aware of their continuing interest in a project as the government works through various procedures and public hearings can give beginners an edge when the agency finally issues a request for proposals or advertises the property for sale.

In most cases, beginning developers must sign personal guarantees to secure financing, especially for construction. Banks typically look at the net worth of the developers and partners in the deal before granting a construction loan. In some instances, however, a major tenant's credit on a long-term lease may take the place of the developer's.

Developing a small part of a larger tract of land can be another way to get started. One advantage is that the rest of the land can be used as collateral for financing the first project. Defaulting on the loan, however, might entail loss of the entire site: once the land is pledged as collateral, the bank can foreclose on it after default to collect any balance owed.

Development projects that begin with a site looking for a use provide an attractive way for beginning developers to start, because they will not be required to locate and tie up land until a deal can be put together. Although such projects are perhaps the easiest way to get into development, the major problem is that land already owned may not be the best location to develop at a given time.

When capital is more readily available, beginning developers have an easier time finding financing. In such times, there is often more money available than "good deals"—projects that are likely to generate significant profit—and lenders and equity investors feel pressure to put their capital to work. Another successful strategy for beginning developers who have extensive local relationships is for them to meet in advance with potential financial partners (especially local private investors) to determine what kinds of deals they are looking for. Armed with this information, beginning developers can look for deals that meet the profile of the investor's preference, such as land for small single-tenant industrial properties worth $2 million to $4 million. If a suitable property is found, the developer can tie it up and present it to the financial partner quickly. Time is critical: often the developer must *go hard* on the land purchase within 30 to 60 days, so having the financial partner ready and waiting to review deals and commit quickly is very important.[6]

In the final analysis, a developer's strongest assets are a reputation for integrity and an ability to deal in good faith with a multitude of players. A large developer may be able to outlast the opposition in a contentious deal, but the best advice for a beginning developer is to avoid such situations altogether and find clearer paths to execution.

Managing the Development Process

No generally accepted definition exists to determine who is a developer and who is not, but a developer can be defined as the person or firm that is actively involved in the development process and takes the risks and receives the rewards of development.[7] Developers may take on different degrees of ownership and risk depending on their ownership structure and the complexity of the project. In the following discussion, developers who operate alone and invest only their own money are said to be *100 percent owner/developers*. They furnish all the cash equity, accept all the risk and liability, and receive all the benefits. The concept of a 100 percent owner/developer is useful for quickly analyzing development opportunities; if a project does not make economic sense in its entirety (as viewed by someone who has all the risks and rewards), it will make even less sense as a joint venture or other form of partnership.

Development is distinct from investment in operating properties (commonly referred to as income-producing properties) because it involves much more risk. Many firms and individuals invest in operating properties with existing cash flow, buying assets and managing them as investments. Investors may incur some risk in leasing and may make renovations that entail some construction or market risk, but there is a base of income-derived value from the moment of acquisition. Developers, on the other hand, take on the full set of risks associated with entitlement, construction, and leasing. Nonetheless, buying existing properties that need minor renovation or re-leasing is a good way for beginning developers to get into the business. It entails less time, less risk, and easier financing. Another distinction is between a developer and a broker: an individual or firm that receives a commission for performing a service, such as finding tenants or money, is a broker rather than a developer.

Many people involved in a development project may incur risk. Those who design, build, and lease a building for a landowner for a fee are agents of the owner and are developers insofar as they are engaged in the processes of development, but they incur little risk if the fee is fixed. Of course, they may be exposed if the owner goes bankrupt. If work for hire is well documented, they at least have legal recourse. But if the fee depends on the project's success, the individual accepts some performance risk associated with development.

Development risk is associated with delivery of the entire project and thus may be distinguished from performance risk associated with individual tasks (such as contractors who accept construction risk when they have a fixed-price contract). The major rewards in development are for the risk taken on. Experienced developers are able to transfer some or most of the risk to others by using other people's money or finding a lender who will give them nonrecourse financing (lending without personal liability). They still carry the burden of delivering a successful project, however. In almost all cases, developers will have something at risk somewhere along the line, such as front money for feasibility studies, investment in preliminary designs, earnest money, or personal liability on construction financing.

Development companies increasingly serve as development managers for major institutions or corporations. In this role, they perform all the normal functions of developers except that they bear little or no risk. The institution—a bank, investment group, insurance company, foreign corporation, or major landowner—bears the risk. The developer works for a management fee and usually a percentage of the profits (10 to 20 percent) if the project is successful. Historically, developers have preferred to own real estate rather than to manage it for others, because ownership has enabled them to leverage completed projects into new deals as they build wealth. Nevertheless, major developers increasingly have accepted roles as managers, either to keep their staff busy during slow periods or to enter new markets with minimal risk. This approach was especially important during the real estate crash of the early 1990s, and firms who succeeded in finding this type of opportunity during the Great Recession of 2008–2010 benefited from steady, though less spectacular, cash flow.

Property management, brokerage, tenant representation, construction management, and other tasks in the skill set of developers can become valuable, or at least sustainable, as service businesses at any time. Developers building an organization should know, however, that in times of distress, competition for service contracts increases dramatically, and banks and other property owners will find themselves in excellent bargaining position for these services. Firms that specialize in these service businesses stand a better chance of providing cash flow in such periods.

REAL ESTATE CYCLES

The adage "timing is everything" is especially applicable to real estate development. The importance of real estate cycles cannot be overemphasized. Like other large, capital-intensive purchases, real estate is highly sensitive to changes in interest rates, as well as to macroeconomic conditions such as employment and internal migration. Income properties (office, industrial, and retail space, and apartments) provide insufficient cash flow to be financed when interest rates move above certain levels. For-sale developments, such as housing subdivisions, office buildings, or residential condominiums, suffer from higher financing costs and from the effect of rising interest rates on the amount of money that potential purchasers can borrow. When rates are high, buyers tend to wait for them to come back down before buying a property. The development industry is further affected by high interest rates because development firms typically are smaller than most corporate bank customers. When money is scarce, lenders tend to prefer their non–real estate customers. Even very sound projects can be difficult to finance because lenders fear the unknown development risks.

Supply and demand are constantly shifting in most markets. Lenders often appear to exhibit a herd mentality, all seeming to prefer the same type of product or geographic area at the same time. Following the

STARTING IN PHASE I—RECOVERY, at the bottom of a cycle, the marketplace is in a state of oversupply from previous new construction or negative demand growth. At this bottom point, occupancy is at its trough. As excess space is absorbed, vacancy rates fall and rental rates stabilize and even begin to increase. Eventually, the market reaches its long-term occupancy average where rental growth equals inflation.

IN PHASE II—EXPANSION, demand growth continues at increasing levels, creating a need for additional space. As vacancy rates fall, rents begin to rise rapidly, pushing rents to cost-feasible levels. At this stage, demand is still rising faster than supply, and there is a lag in the provision of new space. Demand and supply are in equilibrium at the peak occupancy point of the cycle.

PHASE III—HYPERSUPPLY commences after the peak equilibrium point when supply is growing faster than demand. When more space is delivered than demanded, rental growth slows and eventually construction slows or stops. Once the long-term occupancy average is passed, the market falls into Phase IV.

PHASE IV—RECESSION begins as the market moves past the long-term occupancy average with high supply growth and low or negative demand growth. The extent of the down cycle is determined by the difference between supply growth and demand growth. The cycle eventually reaches bottom as new construction and completions slow or as demand begins to grow faster than new supply added to the marketplace.

FIGURE 1-3 Physical Real Estate Cycle Characteristics

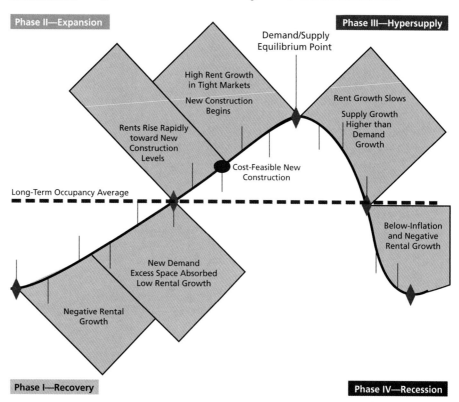

FIGURE 1-4 National Property Type Cycle Locations

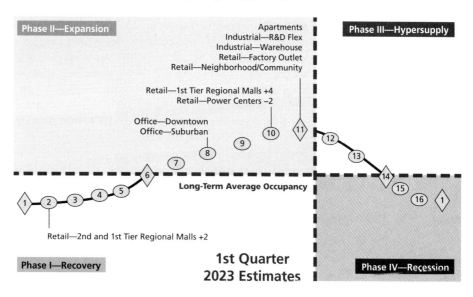

1st Quarter 2023 Estimates

Source: Glenn Mueller, Legg Mason Real Estate, Baltimore, Maryland.

Note: The diamonds mark the four main turning points: the bottom (1), the transition from recovery to expansion (6), the peak (11), and the turning point from hypersupply to recession (14). The numbers mark different periods in the market cycle. The National Property Type Cycle Locations graph shows the relative positions of the subproperty types in each phase. The +/- numbers indicate changes since the previous report.

herd is a convincing story to tell investors, but it can be dangerous when market opinion turns. Development takes time, but markets—and regulations—can change quickly. With the widespread availability of market data and business news, one consequence seems to be that such turns in opinion can happen faster than ever before; the shift from robust growth to pullback can turn on a few indicators, government decisions, or opinion leaders.

Selecting the right time to enter the business is crucial. Most beginning developers plunge ahead, regardless of the general economic climate, and often their success in financing the first project depends on their timing with respect to the cycle. Ironically, financing a project toward the end of a customer's preference for it (when many lenders are enthusiastic about a particular geographic area and product type) is often easier. Toward the end of the positive cycle, however, risk increases as the competition for tenants or buyers intensifies. If supply becomes excessive, those who were the last to enter the market will usually be the first to get in trouble: their costs are higher and competition for tenants is fierce.

Even in a period of relatively stable overall economic growth, real estate markets are cyclical as a result of the lagged relationship between demand and supply for physical space. Professor Glenn Mueller divides the market cycle into four phases: recovery, expansion, hypersupply, and recession (see figures 1-3 and 1-4). Each phase is characterized by different changes in vacancy and new construction as well as changes in rent. The position of property in the market cycle differs by property type and location. This type of analysis is helpful for understanding market timing—when the market is most favorable for new development.

A project launched early in the positive cycle means less competition for the developer. The long lead times required for finding the right site, designing the project, and receiving zoning and other public approvals mean that developers must be able to perceive new market opportunities before others do—often before they have become popular among lenders.

During the early stage of the development cycle, land is cheaper, terms are softer, and there is less entitlement and market risk. During later stages, landowners push more risk onto the developer. Developers may be required to take land down outright, with increased entitlement and market risk, as well as carrying costs. Closing times are shorter, and free-look periods are shorter or even unavailable for due diligence before contingencies are removed on purchase contracts.

How does a developer determine where a city is with respect to the economic cycle? General economic indicators, such as unemployment rates and business failures, provide information on general economic conditions. Local conditions are much more relevant than national data, although since capital is highly mobile, national and even international conditions determine fluctuations in interest rates and credit availability. As the local market starts to approach the top of the economic cycle, rent increases slowly, if at all, and the supply of new space increases faster than absorption of that space. The peak of the cycle passes when new supply exceeds absorption, causing vacancy rates to increase.

Real estate cycles create windows of opportunity for financing and strong market demand in advance of additional supply. If beginning developers can synchronize their development efforts with the cycle, they can improve their chances of success. If they try to develop against the cycle, the odds against them will only increase. The biggest problems for beginners are (1) finding a suitable project, and (2) completing it within the window of time during which the market is favorable. The favorable window (Phases I and II in figure 1-4) may be three or four years; the chances for success decline significantly in Phase III when oversupply exists, occupancy is weakening, and rents may be declining; and finding money may be almost impossible in Phase IV. Unfortunately, it is hardest to raise money at the bottom of the cycle, when the prospects for leasing the project during the recovery and expansion phases are better than starting a project at the top of the cycle when raising money is easier, but the project may be finished and in the leasing phase when hypersupply is at its worst.

GETTING STARTED

The first step in the development process for beginning developers who do not already own the land is to select the target market, in terms of both geographic area and type of product. Staying close to the area where a developer has previously done business provides a major advantage because success often depends as much on personal relationships as on skill. All real estate is local, and knowing the market is critical to getting started. (Of course, having a specific tenant or ultimate buyer is a powerful way to begin—anywhere.) Nationally recognized developers may have an edge in competing for major projects (e.g., high-rise office buildings, shopping malls, major business parks), but otherwise local players have significant

advantages over outsiders. They understand the dynamics of the local area. They know from observation the directions in which the area is growing and how buyers, tenants, and lenders feel about various neighborhoods. They know a good price and where prices have been changing rapidly. They know whom to call when they need information. A newcomer may need a year or more to begin to understand these factors.

Newcomers can *become* insiders, however, even if they are recent arrivals. The best way is to bring in a local partner who is well connected in the community—an especially important move if public approvals are required. Another way is to use banking connections from home to open doors in the new community. Whatever the approach, newcomers have to work harder—to overcome the natural suspicion of outsiders and to equalize the competitive advantage of local developers who have better information and more contacts.

After deciding *where* to do business, the next question is *what* to develop. For beginning developers, the answer is simple: develop a product with which you are familiar—provided that equity and debt are available for it. Even developers with no previous development experience can sell potential investors and lenders on their experience with the product type if they study the local market to determine rents, competition, the regulatory environment, local tastes, local construction methods, and the types of units or buildings in greatest demand. Although beginners can successfully branch out into a new product type, they lack the background to fine-tune information about design and construction costs or to predict potential pitfalls. Beginners who do branch out cannot work alone; they will probably have to bring in an experienced partner to get financing.

POPCourts! is part of a Chicago-area program to help revitalize underused land along neighborhood retail corridors in communities with limited access to open space. The colorful plaza invites the community in and is flexible in its design—accommodating basketball courts and "pop-up" events such as farmers markets, entertainment, and festivals. The city of Chicago provided significant funding for the project's development and construction.

Identifying a product that the market lacks can make a project successful: finding that niche is the developer's challenge. Market niches are defined geographically and by product type. They can be as narrowly defined as, say, an apartment complex that has more two- and three-bedroom units than do other projects in the area or a multitenant warehouse building with specific upgrades. The phrase "designing for a specific market" is used often in this book, because that is how developers create a competitive advantage. Finding that special market, however, usually requires more than a good market study. It requires a perception of the market that other developers do not have because, if a market opportunity is obvious, another developer is probably already building to satisfy the demand. Thus, the beginner must understand the market well enough not just to act, but to do so before other developers see the opportunity.

STAGES OF DEVELOPMENT

The six main stages of development—feasibility and acquisition, design and approvals, financing, construction, marketing and leasing, and operations and management—are described for each major product type—land, apartments, offices, industrial space, and retail space—in chapters 3 through 7.

Figure 1-5 shows the timeline of development for an apartment building or small office building. The

How Three Developers Got Started

JEREMY HUDSON

Jeremy Hudson started off studying construction management in college. After graduation, he went into the residential brokerage business and for several years worked with first-time homebuyers to purchase homes in Fayetteville, Arkansas. Over time, he noticed a lack of good property managers that would work on smaller properties, so he decided to enter the property management business.

After managing 100 duplexes for individual owners and banks, Jeremy saw a 1970s 96-unit apartment complex come up for sale. It was only 70 percent occupied and needed redevelopment. In 2010, he was able to purchase the property on a 7.0 capitalization rate for $11,000 per unit. The problem with the complex was that rents were $470 per month but the landlord was paying $200 per month for the utility costs and other expenses of running the building. The tenants were mainly students from the University of Arkansas.

The goals of the redevelopment included
- energy efficiency;
- water efficiency (potable water and stormwater);
- creating a sense of community; and
- improving health (air quality, natural light).

Jeremy raised the capital to purchase the units at $11,000 per unit and then borrowed, through a construction loan, $60,000 per unit to rehabilitate the complex. He installed new insulation; removed the old gas boiler heating system and installed efficient "mini-split" heating and cooling systems; and installed new windows, a stormwater capture system, and a solar hot water system. Together these improvements reduced the energy costs to the owner by more than 50 percent. The finishes included low volatile organic compound (VOC) cabinets and solid floorings instead of carpet to provide healthy air quality.

The renovation was done in four phases so the existing tenants could be moved around over the course of the school year. Students moved out of each building in May, the renovations took place during the summer, and students moved back in time for fall semester.

The project was geared to two markets: upper class/graduate students and young professionals who wanted to live close to downtown Fayetteville. All of the units are 600-square-foot (56 sq m) studios. About 40 percent of the tenants are students. Rents rose from $470 to $695 per month while utility costs were cut in half, increasing the net operating income and the value.

Because this was Jeremy's first development and he did not have the necessary capital, he contacted one of his property management clients to see if they would partner with him and provide the capital to purchase the property. The client knew Jeremy understood the market and so was interested in doing so. The partners were able to get a construction loan because the main investor in the project had a portfolio of properties. However,

securing the loan was made more difficult by the lack of good comparables at the original rent level in the neighborhood. In addition, construction was started on the first phase before the loan was secured, which caused issues with mechanics liens. Ultimately, though, they got the loan with 60 percent leverage.

The project, named Eco Modern Flats, was successful and won several awards, including 2015 Green Good design award, 2013 ULI Global Awards for Excellence finalist, 2012 LEED for Homes Outstanding Multifamily Project, AIA of Arkansas Chapter Merit Award, and LEED Platinum certificate.

LIZ DUNN

In high school Liz Dunn wanted to be an architect. Her career path changed in college when she interned for Microsoft. After several years at Microsoft, she felt burned out and left to get a master's degree in business administration, and then enrolled in architecture and urban planning courses at the University of Washington. She realized that she had the foundational skills to be a developer. And she was happier to be able to conceive the whole project as the developer than to be only the designer.

While in graduate school, Liz sold her Microsoft stock options to fund school and purchase her first property. She bought a 3,200-square-foot (297 sq m) lot zoned for a six-story structure in the Capital Hill area of Seattle, Washington, for $300,000. Her first project became an industrial loft condo project on this postage stamp lot. She saw a need for urban condos and named the project East Union Lofts. The eight-unit project was built out of steel and concrete, which was unusual for a residential condo project in Seattle at the time. To provide parking for the units, she found a unique German-built stacked-garage system.

She had two presales when the economy fell apart in the dot-com bust of 2001. She lived in three different units while she tried to sell the remaining units. When the project was featured in Metropolitan Homes Magazine, she was able to get more traction with sales. She did not make money on her first deal, but she was able to pay back her bank loan—at a time when many loans were defaulting. This relationship led the same bank to finance her next project.

Her second project was more ambitious. She met an owner of several automotive buildings in Seattle that he wanted to sell. They were two-story concrete, steel, and heavy timber buildings with 20-foot (6 m) ceilings, built as an automotive repair shop. The lower story faced one street, and the upper story was level with a second street. Liz named this project Chophouse Row. Chophouse Row morphed into a multiphase project. The project included renovating the existing buildings and building a new multistory loft office building and residential units.

This project was a jigsaw puzzle, as Liz redeveloped several different buildings. An important goal was not to displace locally owned businesses. One of the existing tenants was a family-owned hardware store; Liz worked with the family to update the store's merchandising, and it became an integral tenant in the development. She moved other tenants around to keep them in the project and brought in new tenants to complement them. She created a courtyard and renovated an alley to create unique outdoor spaces, and provided restaurants, offices, and residential uses in both the renovated and the new buildings. The outdoor spaces provide room for entertainment and outdoor restaurant seating and allow for gathering spaces within the project. Chophouse Row was nominated in 2016 for the ULI Global Award for Excellence.

The work was done in phases so the project could be financed incrementally. The seller even helped her convince the bank to provide financing for the first acquisition. As one building was redeveloped, she could place permanent financing on the building and pull funds for the next phase. Fortunately for Liz, commercial values were rising, which made the refinancing process a little easier. By moving slowly and incrementally, she was able to put together a mix of retailers that created a vibrant community space. She has become the successful developer she envisioned when she started her first project.

ROD MULLICE

After a obtaining a degree in political science and economics, Rod Mullice spent eight years working on the water infrastructure in Atlanta, Georgia, with a private engineering and construction company. He wanted to broaden his career, so he took a Certified Commercial Investment Member (CCIM) class and transitioned to become a broker at Newmark Knight Frank. One of his jobs at the firm was to perform consulting work for the city's transit agency (MARTA), determining the transit-oriented development (TOD) and retailer strategy for 38 train station sites. He understood that TOD development is an important tool to reduce energy and water usage.

This consulting work led Rod to the town of College Park whose Economic Development Department asked him to sit on a steering committee to study opportunities for TOD development. In that capacity, he helped develop a plan for residential and commercial uses at the last station on the line before the main airport in Atlanta.

A couple years later, in 2013, College Park was able to convince the Federal Aviation Administration (FAA) to stay in a 217,000-square-foot (20,160 sq m) office building and even expand its use, adding 400 new employees to the TOD. Across the street from the FAA, within the TOD, the city owned nine parcels of an 11-parcel site. Only two of the parcels could be built on due to various restrictions. Because Rod knew the TOD regulations, the market, and the players in the city government, he decided to develop a proposal for the site. He was able to purchase the two sites not owned by the city and got an agreement to purchase the nine parcels owned by the city as well.

What made this site so complicated was that only two parcels could be built on. Rod designed a five-story building that fit on the 0.87-acre (0.35 ha) buildable area and used the remaining 10 acres (4 ha) for surface parking and water retention. The site fit 109 units, and the surface parking helped make the economics work, since the parking spaces were very inexpensive compared to structured parking. Because the site is only one stop from the Atlanta airport, Rod designed a unit mix that would appeal to airline workers. Since most of the flight attendants had roommates, the project was designed with 70 percent two-bedroom units, 20 percent one-bedroom units, and 10 percent studios. The design included a top-floor lounge with views over College Park. The unit mix worked well for the market, but it was unconventional and had to be explained to the lenders because it didn't fit the normal parameters of other apartments in the market.

The nearest competitor with a dense project was over four miles away, with structured parking which made it difficult to prepare the market analysis. Since Rod had helped prepare the original MARTA study and had worked on the Economic Development Department steering committee, he knew the market and the demand generators. He thought that, in addition to the airline employees one stop away, the expansion of the FAA would generate demand. The city was supportive and approved the project in about two months, in November of 2014. Rod managed the project, while keeping his brokerage business going to generate income for living expenses.

One of Rod's clients owned a construction company that also had a portfolio of 5,000 apartments. Rod approached his client, explaining that he wanted to be a developer and had a site tied up. He asked the client to contribute all the predevelopment money and to cosign the construction work. Rod contributed 10 percent of the money and between friends and family and the one major investor, he was able to come up with $5.9 million for the equity. He needed a $10.6 million construction loan for the $16 million project.

Rod used his brokerage skills to prepare a presentation book about the project and the market and met with several lenders. The lender that came through on the project had a business relationship with Rod's largest investor (the construction company), which helped cement the deal. Having low leverage on the project was crucial to getting his first project financed.

Rod admits that he made lots of little mistakes along the way on his first project. Construction ran late, and the dates for leasing were too early—before units could be delivered. It took 14 months to lease the project, and it was delivered in February 2017. Ron was able to finish the project and pay off the construction loan five days before it was due.

After operating the project for five years, Rod sold the project in 2021 and was able to pay off all his partners. Despite the delays and a recession, he was able to make a profit on his first development and the development was a success. His second development was also in College Park, which allowed him to use his connections and knowledge to develop a for-sale townhome development.

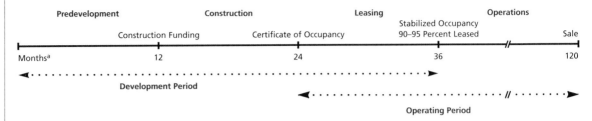

FIGURE 1-5 Timeline for Development of an Apartment Building or Small Office Building

ᵃTime varies widely according to a project's size, complexity, and location. Predevelopment may take two to four years or more in California but require only 90 days in some other parts of the country.

development period runs from the signing of the purchase contract for the land through lease-up of the building (Month 36). The development period covers all the major development risks, including financial, construction, and marketing. The operating period technically runs from the certificate of occupancy (when the building is ready for occupancy) until the building is sold. The stabilized operating period runs from the time the building is fully leased until it is sold. Stabilized operating period is the time frame used for standard appraisals of the building's value.

The six stages of development can overlap considerably. In the timeline, *predevelopment* covers the period from first identification of the development site to the start of construction. In the figure, predevelopment is shown as the first 12 months. Ideally, this period would be reduced to four to six months, allowing the developer to start construction at the same time the land deal is closed. That time frame is difficult to achieve, especially for beginning developers, but the shorter the predevelopment period, the lower the cost and risk.

Four of the six stages of development occur during predevelopment: feasibility studies, design, financing, and marketing. In fact, a developer should be reasonably confident about the prospects for success on a project before signing the initial purchase contract. Developers rarely go hard (remove contingencies) on the purchase contract until they are very confident they can obtain all necessary public approvals to build what they want and can raise all necessary financing for it. The primary purpose of predevelopment is to give the developer the necessary confidence to move forward. Before closing on a new project, a developer should be almost absolutely certain that the proposed project can be developed profitably according to the plans and objectives.

Figure 1-6 summarizes one view of the steps common to developing most types of property—determining a project's feasibility, design, financing,

construction, marketing, operation, and management. It illustrates a fundamental principle of development: Development is an iterative process in which the developer obtains more and more precise information in each iteration, until gaining enough confidence in the information to make a go/no-go decision. The process contains many moving parts, and knowing when they are moving in the right direction is critical. As figure 1-6 shows, certain steps can be taken simultaneously, whereas others must be taken sequentially. For example, active pre-leasing for an office building begins as soon as preliminary design drawings are ready to show to prospective tenants. Pre-leasing occurs throughout the development period, from financing through construction. With an apartment project, leasing usually begins during construction, but it also occurs simultaneously with other steps.

Analysis of the numbers becomes more detailed and more sophisticated at each step. The initial contract for earnest money may require only a simple capitalization analysis to see whether land cost yields the desired overall return (net operating income divided by total project cost). Before the earnest money contract becomes final, however, an annual cash flow pro forma is necessary, at least for the operating period. It should reflect the actual square footage planned, projected rents (based on the market analysis), and estimated construction costs. For the next iteration, a monthly cash flow during the construction period is necessary to convince the lender that enough cash will be available to complete the project. It will be based on still more accurate information about costs (from detailed design drawings) and revenues (including rent concessions and tenant improvement allowances). Finally, for a joint venture or equity syndication, a cash flow statement is necessary that combines both construction and operating periods and illustrates the timing of equity requirements, distributions of cash, tax benefits, and proceeds of sales (see chapter 4). The level of detail should correspond to the quality of information available at each stage. Preparing a monthly spread sheet for 60 months before reasonably accurate construction costs and market data have been assembled is a waste of time and money, yet developers need enough information to make a good decision at each stage. The information should be comparable in quality for all the different parameters, and it should be as comprehensive as possible for a given level of risk money.[8]

At each stage of analysis, certain items must be completed before moving to the next stage. For example, before lenders consider a mortgage application, the developer usually must provide conceptual drawings, a boundary survey, title information, information about the site's feasibility, market surveys, personal financial information, and an appraisal. (Because different lenders have different requirements for appraisals, it may be wise not to order an appraisal until a promising lender has been identified. Otherwise, another appraisal—by someone the lender approves—might be necessary.)

The sequence of steps to be taken and even the steps themselves change frequently in development. The rate of change in the development world is one of its major sources of excitement. It also gives beginning developers a better chance to compete with experienced developers because all developers must adapt to, and keep up with, changing conditions—or they will fail.

Financing methods and sometimes even the sequence of financing steps may change over time. One major change, for example, occurred in the aftermath of skyrocketing inflation in the early 1980s. Developers traditionally obtain a commitment for a permanent loan first and then use that commitment (the takeout commitment) to obtain a construction loan. When inflation reached double digits in the early 1980s, however, developers suddenly could not obtain takeout commitments. Instead, they went directly to construction lenders, who started giving "miniperm" loans—five-year loans that covered both the construction period and the initial operating period. By doing so, lenders and developers gambled that interest rates on permanent mortgages would come down (which they did) within five years. They were also prepared to extend the loans (roll them over into new loans) if rates did not fall. Once inflation receded, developers and lenders reverted to the traditional system, though miniperms remain a useful tool.

Another innovation is mezzanine financing, which provides higher loan-to-value ratios and reduces the amount of equity a developer needs. The mezzanine piece is a form of equity and may carry interest rates ranging from 11 to 13 percent or higher. Although expensive, this type of financing is still cheaper than equity financing, which often carries an implicit cost of 20 percent or more.

Over the past 40 years, real estate financial markets have matured and become increasingly institutionalized for both debt and equity. Large developers now have a wide variety of financing alternatives available to them. For example, they frequently establish credit

FIGURE 1-6 **The Go Decision**

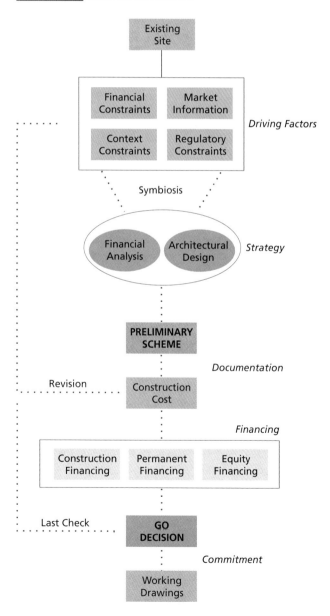

Advice for Beginning Developers

Advice was provided by many ULI members and industry leaders, including Benjamin Cha, Mackenzie Makepeace, Jeff Hines, Roy March, Owen Thomas, Peter Rummell, Tom Bozzuto, Phil Hughes, Jerry Rappaport, and the late Gerald Hines.[a] Three themes emerged: be well prepared at all times; work with experienced people, even if they are more expensive; and anticipate delays throughout the development process.

Managing Your Team

- Ask a lot of questions and seek out mentors who will help you identify potential pitfalls, bringing together the right project team. Your ability to assemble the team and manage them is paramount.
- Surround yourself with great people. Make sure they have the skills, assets, network, and authority to be successful. You can spread your wings because you can do more. Trust in them. It takes trust and integrity, transparency, honesty, and partnership.
- Team members learn who the jerks are before the president does, and they watch how s/he handles it. Deal with it quickly. You can't do anything until you have assembled a group that complements your skill set and each other.
- Plan well ahead for succession and the time to pass leadership on to the next generation or owner.

Site Acquisition

- Correctly analyze the purchase price of a site to include usable, not total, square footage.
- Anticipate problems with sellers who are not familiar with real estate and delays while a disputed estate is being settled.
- Analyze the site's physical constraints, including the availability of utilities.
- Conduct a soils test and check for hazardous waste.
- Identify the site's legal and political constraints, such as the availability of the required zoning or the existence of a moratorium on building.
- Research the market before purchasing the site.

Regulatory Process, Obtaining Approvals

- Be prepared to work with the community to resolve concerns and challenges to the project.
- Take time to understand the local political climate.
- Prepare for the local regulatory process and public hearings.
- Use qualified and experienced consultants, lawyers, and architects to give your project added credibility.
- Anticipate and do not underestimate delays in the approval process.

Product Selection, Market and Economic Feasibility

- Remember that when an opportunity is obvious, it is obvious to everyone—resulting in a great deal of competition.
- Choose a respected market consultant with a strong reputation in the city where your project is located.
- Decide how much time to allocate for the feasibility study. Some developers consider this step to be vital and maintain that the study should be thorough; others feel it should not be belabored.
- Make sure that extensive primary research accurately identifies all competition, whether under construction or still on the drawing board.

Design, Site Planning, Engineering, and Construction

- Do not complete the design until you have thoroughly reviewed the market study.
- Work closely with the architect and the contractor.
- Do not ignore important information, even if it entails redesign or additional approvals.
- Use a flexible design that can be easily adapted to different tenants' needs.
- Accept the design and recognize that it will never be perfect.
- Spend sufficient time and money to check all references before retaining contractors and subcontractors.
- Remember: "You always need to have the proper documentation. You need to have a mutually agreed upon retainer, reliable base map with topography, land dedications or easements, and identified unbuildable areas or areas that must be preserved. You also need an ALTA report (American Land Title Association), a market research study, architectural guidelines (when applicable), full design criteria from the builder/client, and a reasonable work schedule."[b]

Construction and Development Financing

- Establish relationships with several lenders to eliminate lengthy delays.
- Deal with experienced lenders.
- Make adequate allowances for contingencies.
- Remember it could take three to four months to process a $10 million loan—even if the lender says it will take only six weeks.
- If the market softens, be able to cover interest out of your own pocket until the market comes back.

Permanent Financing

- Establish good communications with the lender.
- Prepare a detailed, professional presentation package for the lender.
- Secure the permanent loan before beginning construction. (Beginning developers might be forced to do so, even if they would prefer to wait until after the project is built and leased.)
- Be aware of trends in interest rates.

Equity Financing

- Watch the market and signals about downturns. Just because the money is there does not mean you have to spend it.
- Investigate the financial records of sources of equity.
- Find two or three compatible partners who can provide or raise equity for the project.

- Do not give away too much equity position to secure funds, because nothing may be left to give if you come up short.

Operations, Management, and Maintenance

- Pay close attention to building management and operations. Find a first-rate building manager.
- Budget properly for postconstruction maintenance.

In General

- Stick to geographic areas and product types with which you are familiar.
- Think small. Find a first project that is within your financial capabilities and can be developed in a reasonable amount of time. Don't start with mixed use—condos, hotels, townhouses—or a big site. Start with a project that is manageable, like a six-unit condo down the street.
- For your first or second deal, make sure you have a generalist background that takes you through all the stages of development, from site acquisition, construction, organization, and finance to marketing and sales. Make sure you are comfortable with a generalist hat.
- Find a specialty and a niche where you can have some expertise above someone else.
- Never begin a project just because you have financing available.
- During the feasibility stage, keep investment in the project low to maximize your flexibility.
- Do your homework. Know what the holes in the market are and how to plug them—quickly.
- Never enter a negotiation that you are not prepared to leave.
- Attend to details. Whether you are designing a building or negotiating a lease, you personally must be on top of every detail. You must rely on your professional consultants, but if you do not understand the details, you should arrange for someone else to help you.
- Do not be afraid to make a nuisance of yourself. The people you are dealing with are usually very busy and hard to reach. You may have to make several telephone calls or personal visits before you talk to them. Learn to be tenacious—nicely.
- Do not deceive yourself by ignoring facts and warning signs as they are presented to you. Be aware that self-deception occurs most often with evaluation of the market.
- Increase the time you think you need to develop a project— perhaps by twice as much.
- Do not promise cash payments to investors by a certain date. Be neither overly optimistic nor overly conservative in your assumptions.
- Be able to turn on a dime and switch your strategy instantly.
- Follow up everything. Never assume that something has been done just because you ordered it.
- If you promise something to a lender, a professional consultant, a tenant, or a purchaser, deliver.

- Communicate honestly and often with your lenders and investors. Avoid deals that show early signs of being contentious.
- Recognize that the buck stops with you. A million excuses can be found for things that go wrong in a development project, but you have the ultimate responsibility for ensuring they go right.
- Recognize brokers with incentives such as dinners and awards.
- Don't become isolated: Join trade associations and attend education conferences.
- Don't forget: This is a long-term journey. It is a long gradual climb with occasional breakthroughs.
- If things are going well and you're comfortable, do not overextend yourself. Development is a risky business.

Joint Ventures and Partnerships

- Find partners that share your values.
- Structure a fair deal so that no partner is burdened with excessive risk and meager profits.
- Make clear who is in charge of the project.
- Avoid establishing goals that conflict with those pursued by other partners.
- Have agreements ready to cover dissolution of the partnership.
- Monitor changes in tax legislation that could affect returns.
- Establish a record of regular, honest communications with partners.

Marketing and Leasing

- Be prepared for unanticipated changes or a weakening market.
- Find a broker you trust and can work with.
- Understand the importance of marketing the project yourself.
- Create a suitable tenant mix for commercial projects.
- Be specific about tenant improvements and tenants' responsibilities in the lease, and include escape clauses for your own protection.
- Be creative about concessions. Consider buying stock in a tenant's startup company, paying moving expenses, or providing furnishings.
- Understand the implications of leasing versus sales on tenants' earnings and balance sheets.
- Advertise that you have made a deal or signed a lease.

[a]Interviews by Richard Peiser, December through February 2022: Tom Bozzuto, chairman and CEO, The Bozzuto Group, Baltimore, Maryland; Daryl Carter, chairman and CEO, Avanath Capital Management, Irvine, California; Benjamin Cha, chief executive, Asia Pacific, Grosvenor, Hong Kong; James DeFrancia, principal, Lowe Enterprises Inc., Steamboat Springs, Colorado; Jeff Hines, president and CEO, Hines, Houston, Texas; Mackenzie Makepeace, director of development, RMS Investment Corporation, Shaker Heights, Ohio; Roy March, CEO, Eastdil Secured, New York; Jerry Rappaport, director, New Boston Fund, Boston, Massachusetts; Peter Rummell, principal, Rummell Company, Jacksonville, Florida; Ron Terwilliger, chairman, Terwilliger Pappas Multifamily Partners, Atlanta, Georgia; Owen Thomas, CEO, Boston Properties, New York; Edward Walters, global CEO, The Urban Land Institute, Washington, D.C.

[b]Art Danielian, founder and chairman, Danielian Associates, interview by Julian Huertas, 2019.

lines at banks to provide capital for site acquisition and even construction financing. The credit line takes the place of development and construction loans on individual properties. While credit lines are invaluable for financing on the front end, cyclical downturns as well as major crises can cause banks to reduce or eliminate credit lines very quickly.

The development process resembles the construction of a building. The foundation must be level if the walls are to be straight. The frame must be square if the finish is to be attractive. Each step in the process depends on the quality of previous steps. Badly negotiated or poorly written agreements with lenders, contractors, tenants, or professionals will come back to haunt the developer. At best, they will be costly to correct. At worst, they might halt completion or occupancy of the project. In the typical real estate development, where interest costs and promised returns tick away with time, lawsuits and their associated delays are losers for everyone involved. When disputes involve government agencies or the interpretation of public approvals, "you can't beat city hall" proves true in most cases.

Because each stage depends on the preceding one and because the developer must depend on other people to do much of the work, an adequate monitoring system is essential. Each development should have a "critical path chart," showing not only the events that must occur before others can be accomplished but how much time each step should take. The chart also shows which events are on the critical path (those requiring the shortest time) and which events have

Located in Vancouver, Ironworks is Canada's first stacked mixed-use commercial industrial project. The overall form of the project consists of two primary buildings—140,000 square feet (13,000 sq m) of light-industrial development and 70,000 square feet (6,500 sq m) of office space. The project offers functional and flexible space for industrial, office, cultural, technological, and culinary uses.

some slack time. Critical path analysis allows the developer to calculate the cost to shorten the path, for example, by paying workers overtime or paying extra freight charges to receive materials more quickly. This monitoring system is the best way to reinforce the written documents. For example, when an issue arises and the monitoring system has three or four written confirmations of the contract, the parties can more easily find a solution.

The early stages of development are especially important, involving many iterations of planning and analysis before the architectural plans and other arrangements are finalized. A common mistake at each phase of analysis is to go into too much detail too soon. For example, obtaining detailed working drawings before a market feasibility study is completed is a waste of money. First, the market study should influence the design. Second, if the market is not as healthy as it appeared or if financing is unavailable or too expensive, the developer may want to abandon the project.

Projects go through several stages of risk. Developers' *at-risk capital* is the total amount of money that can be lost at any point in time. During the period in which the developer makes preliminary assessments of the market and the site, the risk money typically is limited to what is spent on feasibility studies—analyses of soils and the floodplain, regulatory analysis, market studies, and conceptual design. As soon as the developer goes hard on the land purchase contract, then the nonrefundable earnest money is also at risk. The money at risk escalates dramatically when the developer closes on the land, pays for financing commitments, or authorizes working drawings. These events should be delayed as long as possible, while the developer answers remaining questions and assembles the information needed to proceed or to abandon the project. Developers' most precious asset is their risk capital—the money they have to spend on projects upfront to obtain control of property and to determine project feasibility. The last thing a developer wants is to have risk capital tied up in land that cannot be

FIGURE 1-7 Developer Exposure over Time

The money that a developer can lose if a project fails is illustrated here for a 160-unit apartment project using housing revenue bonds guaranteed by Fannie Mae for the mortgage. Exposure is greatest just before bond closing when the developer has invested $540,000 in a project that could still fall apart if the bonds fail to close.

[a]The inducement is transferable but has a one-year limit.
[b]The land value has increased by an amount sufficient to cover sales commission costs if it has to be resold.
[c]At the time of closing on the land, the earnest money ($30,000) is recovered.
[d]The Fannie Mae commitment adds value only if bonds can be sold.
[e]Most legal costs have no value if the bonds are not closed.
[f]At bond closing, the risks are substantially eliminated, as all financing parameters are fixed.
Source: Stages of investment for August Park Apartments, Dallas, Texas, developed by Peiser Corporation and Jerome Frank Investments.

Month	Activity	Cost	Total Investment to Date	Current Value to Date	Exposure
1	Land optioned	$30,000	$30,000	$0	$30,000
	Extensions	$42,000	$0	$0	$0
	Architecture	$20,000	$0	$0	$0
	Inducement	$20,000	$0	$0	$0
7	Inducement received	$0	$112,000	$0[a]	$112,000
9	Land closing	$776,000	$888,000	806,000[b]	82,000[c]
	Architecture	$20,000	$0	$0	$0
	Appraisal and market study	$20,000	$0	$0	$0
10	Fannie Mae commitment	$48,000	976,000[d]	$806,000	$170,000
	Architecture	$30,000	$0	$0	$0
	Engineering	$40,000	$0	$0	$0
	Equity syndication	$100,000	$0	$0	$0
	Bond costs	$200,000	$0	$0	$0
15	Bond rate secured	$0	1,346,000[e]	$806,000	$540,000
16	Bonds closed	$676,000	2,022,000[f]	$0	$0

FIGURE 1-8 Typical Months Elapsed for Development of a Small Office or Apartment Building

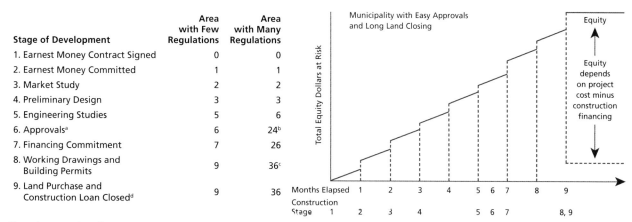

Stage of Development	Area with Few Regulations	Area with Many Regulations
1. Earnest Money Contract Signed	0	0
2. Earnest Money Committed	1	1
3. Market Study	2	2
4. Preliminary Design	3	3
5. Engineering Studies	5	6
6. Approvals[a]	6	24[b]
7. Financing Commitment	7	26
8. Working Drawings and Building Permits	9	36[c]
9. Land Purchase and Construction Loan Closed[d]	9	36

[a]Assuming no zoning changes are necessary.
[b]Environmental, political, design review, and other approvals can take two to five years.
[c]Building permits can take six to nine months after working drawings are finalized.
[d]Most sellers require closing on the land sooner than nine months, but the deal should not be finalized without tentative financing commitments and approvals in place.

Introduction

Lessons Learned

Developers and industry leaders were surveyed and interviewed to provide lessons learned that could benefit those new to development.[a] Many respondents highlighted mistakes made at the front end of their projects that came back to haunt them. The most salient points are presented here.

SELECTING THE RIGHT TEAM

During planning and construction, the majority of respondents cited the importance of selecting competent, experienced team members and effectively coordinating them. As Charles Rulick, executive vice president of development for CenterCal Properties, notes: "Real estate development is multidisciplinary by nature, and it is the job of the developer to lead and assemble the best team for a given project. You can't conduct the orchestra and also play the instruments. Hire the best and let them do their jobs with the right guidance and leadership."

Having partners that understand your operations and vision is essential, and many respondents highlighted the importance of thoroughly vetting team members and joint venture partners. "Select contractors who understand that change is not just an opportunity for a change order, but it is an inevitable part of the creative process," recommends Peter Rummell. "Find contractors who will be partners who will not gouge you for every change order, who view the relationship as a long term one." Ben Cha says, "Build quality product." He observes that many developers have built shoddy product—that is, with poor workmanship, little attention to the public realm, poor design. "You won't be successful today. Unlike previous generations when [if] you built it, they would come; not so today." Roy March says, "Have humility—grace and gratitude. From that comes generosity of spirit, kindness, and all the rest. Humans need humans."

NAVIGATING THE APPROVAL PROCESS

Another major point is being skilled at the intricate details of the approval process to avoid resource-draining delays. Many spoke of the importance of forming strong relationships with local regulatory bodies and bringing in the community early in the process. Anne Cummins, COO for Gattuso Development Partners, echoes this sentiment: "Know the municipality and have relationships with the folks giving approvals. Know the local master plans and build relationships with reliable general contractors willing to stand behind their committed estimates and delivery dates." "Building trust and good will with the city and community is key," says Mackenzie Makepeace at RMS Investment Corporation. She observes that a huge reason for the success of Forest City's Stapleton Airport redevelopment was the ability to tie up all the land at a prenegotiated price but take it down only when it was needed. Mackenzie says

that getting a development from concept design to groundbreaking always takes longer than expected. "Give yourself some breathing room on carrying the land." She emphasizes that developers must understand the local landscape: the council people, the city itself, the community development corporations. Daryl Carter, at Avanath Capital Management observes, "All can be great advocates, or huge roadblocks. Everyone wants to feel that the project is theirs." He adds that the opposition is never who you think it is.

PERFORMING DUE DILIGENCE IN ACQUISITIONS

Another dominant concern pertains to thorough due diligence in acquisitions. Acquisition terms can be as important as price. Paying more for entitlement contingencies, phased takedowns, or lease-up contingencies can be well worth the cost, reducing risk.

Many successful developers made their profits from the acquisition and entitlement phases, but they agree that a bad acquisition is almost impossible to rectify. Land value comes through entitlements, so developers should ensure that their acquisitions have approval strings attached. Understanding the market through extensive preliminary study alleviates the risk of getting stuck with an unworkable project. Developers should use the market to shape their decisions, think about the end user, and not seek to impose a use on a site. "Don't try to build your way out of a bad market. Follow the economy and be flexible as to market demands and what you buy, sell, or invest in," writes Charles Wathen of Pier Investments LLC.

DEALING WITH OBSTACLES

Recognizing which obstacles are immediate, short term, and temporary—and which ones are deal breakers—is crucial. Many survey respondents addressed the importance of maintaining a critical distance from the project and allowing research and a conservative pro forma to generate a commitment to the deal—not an emotional excitement for the building or site. Linda Congleton, principal at L.S. Congleton & Associates, writes, "Do your market study and financial pro formas with optimistic and worst-case scenarios before buying property, before [the] entitlement process, and before securing loans."

Knowing when to walk away is also important. David Farmer, managing principal at Keystone Development Advisors, says, "Always plan for delay and cost overruns." Knowing when to cut their losses differentiates successful developers—despite the difficulty in letting go of a project.

PLANNING FOR CHANGE THAT CAN AFFECT FINANCING

Respondents noted several lessons with regard to financing. Leverage works both ways. The developer should stress-test debt service going into a deal. And they should know their "burn rate." Cash is king. As Stewart Fahmy of California Land Development LLC noted amid the crisis in 2009, "Builders' market positions are entirely based on their liquidity."[b] Refinancing, hibernating, building your way out, and pursuing consulting business—all strategies for surviving a downturn—require ready cash. A developer's coveted "institutional finance partnership" should not be mistaken for a guarantee. In a crisis, rock-solid partners can decline a capital call, and banks can become insolvent. "Don't take money just because the banks will lend it," says Ron Terwilliger of Terwilliger Pappas Multifamily Partners and former chairman of Trammell Crow. "You will have to guarantee it. At one point, we would never close unless the land was zoned and they had a financial partner to go vertical." Later, that rule changed. If they had a partner, they would close on the land. The partner put up 20 percent for the land and Crow borrowed the rest. When land values dropped 50 percent, they took huge losses. "If you do buy land," he advises, "don't leverage it beyond 50 percent." Roy March agrees. "Taking people's money because it's available is the biggest pitfall—as opposed to investing people's money because it is a worthwhile project." Don Killoren of Celebration Associates, notes that managing inventory is managing risk. "Don't get stuck with a lot of standing inventory."

STAYING ON TOP OF TRENDS

Staying on top of trends is also important. Jim DeFrancia says, "We could have anticipated some things that would have created enhanced value. We were constantly looking ahead five to seven years. Three years into it, you must look at it again." He laments that his firm was sometimes slow to see innovative changes in the marketplace (e.g., product development, community governance, the character of the buyer). "I was not as sensitive as I should have been in monitoring those changes." Owen Thomas says, "When I look back, I think more about things we did not do that we should have done. I wish we had gone to Seattle 10 years ago. We knew about life science and tech but did not see Cambridge going up 5 to 6 percent per year. If you see the trends, believe in them and be aggressive to win deals. Whatever you believe in, do it and get the assets because you will be rewarded." He adds that every 10 years, something goes wrong, and it is always something different. "Make sure you are not over-levered." Jeff Hines says, "Don't make the mistake of chasing yield when things become too pricey." He notes that Hines did that before the financial crisis of 2009–2010. "We went to more commodity-type real estate and more commodity locations. We invested too late in the cycle and too much in those products. Before, our decisions were always very bottom up. We relied on local partners. After [the financial crisis], we formed a research department that is more top down." He says the macroeconomic research gives them more ability to play the cycle. "It helps us avoid doing bad deals at the top of the market."

KNOWING WHEN TO SELL

Tom Bozzuto advises, "Don't count the other guy's money. Look at how much you're getting. In 2006, someone offered us $30 million for our homebuilding subsidiary. We had made a deal with a partner who would get half of the sale price. Our biggest mistake was not selling our homebuilding company— we held on and ended up writing off a lot more. Don't let greed get in the way." One mistake people make is keeping every asset in the company. Tom has made a point of segregating some assets—having liquidity events: "Sell properties, take some money out, so you can put it into other assets."

[a]The survey was conducted and collated by Julian Huertas, MDES Real Estate student at Harvard Graduate School of Design, 2021. Interviews were conducted by Richard Peiser, December through February 2022: Tom Bozzuto, chairman and CEO, The Bozzuto Group, Baltimore, Maryland; Daryl Carter, chairman and CEO, Avanath Capital Management, Irvine, California; Benjamin Cha, CEO, Asia Pacific, Grosvenor, Hong Kong; Linda Congleton, principal, Linda S. Congleton & Associates, San Juan Capistrano, California; James DeFrancia, principal, Lowe Enterprises Inc., Steamboat Springs, Colorado; David Farmer, managing principal, Keystone Development Advisors, Naples, Florida; Jeff Hines, president and CEO, Hines, Houston, Texas; Don Killoren, principal, Celebration Associates LLC, Hot Springs, Virginia; Mackenzie Makepeace, director of development, RMS Investment Corporation, Shaker Heights, Ohio; Roy March, CEO, Eastdil Secured, New York; Peter Rummell, principal, Rummell Company, Jacksonville, Florida; Ron Terwilliger, chairman, Terwilliger Pappas Multifamily Partners, Atlanta, Georgia; Owen Thomas, CEO, Boston Properties, New York; Edward Walters, global CEO, The Urban Land Institute, Washington, D.C.

[b]Steward Fahmy, CEO, California Land Development LLC, Los Gatos, California, interview by Kristen Hunter, 2009.

RMA PHOTOGRAPHY INC.

developed as planned. Experienced developers know that it is worth paying a little more upfront to extend the closing on land until they are certain they can proceed with development.

Because each deal has its own distinctive characteristics, limiting risk as much as the developer would like is not always possible. In very hot markets, for example, a free look may not be possible and earnest money may be forfeitable from the first day, or the developer might have to close on the land in 60 days, before securing a firm commitment for financing the future development. Two general principles apply:

- Recognize that development is an iterative process in which each iteration brings more accurate information and puts a greater amount of money at risk.
- Spend enough money to get the quality of information needed, but do not risk more than is necessary for each level of commitment.

Conclusion

Real estate development requires many different talents and skills for managing people and managing risk. Development is fundamentally a creative process, and managing creative people and motivating them to do their best work are two of the elements necessary for success. Development involves solving numer-

EPIC—Netflix's newest campus in Hollywood, California—is a new model of creative office space. It is the first office project in Los Angeles to implement a building facade that is integrated with solar photovoltaic technology to offset electricity consumption. The building features 26,000 square feet (2,400 sq m) of exterior patios and open space.

ous problems. No matter how well planned a project is, unexpected events arise that the developer must overcome.

Beginning developers may come from all facets of the real estate industry. They face a much harder road than experienced developers do: not only are they going through the steps of development for the first time; they must also establish many new relationships with advisers, consultants, professionals, financiers, and others involved in the process. For that reason, a simple, more straightforward project is preferred at the outset. The first project should not set a new precedent or require difficult public approvals or new forms of financing. Beginning developers have enough problems simply delivering a successful project. They should not take on additional burdens that even experienced developers shy away from.

Phil Hughes recommends that beginning developers look for problems and missed opportunities: "Problems are my biggest friend: they give me the opportunity to see a solution that others haven't seen.

Everyone's out there looking for the shiny perfect deal, but the most value is created when there's a (fixable) problem."[9] Tom Montelli advises, "Think of development as a multiphase process. The more you understand that there is potential disruption in any one of those phases, the better off you will be."[10]

Jerry Rappaport offers the following advice to beginning developers:[11]

- Become an expert in one part of the process (e.g., entitlements), then branch out to other phases of development.
- Use your competitive advantage, whatever it is, to *source* deals. Off-market is much better than widely marketed deals. If you find a high-quality opportunity, the money will come.
- Joint venturing with a landowner or a business is a creative way to access deals with lower need for equity.
- Take a long view of the business.

The key to successful development is serving the needs of a particular segment of the market in a particular location. In almost every instance, it also means serving the needs of particular stakeholders (whether a mayor, regulator, business owner, landowner, neighborhood activist, or homebuyer) who must have their needs met in a particular manner. Above all, it requires understanding what the local market is missing. No one—not even the most experienced developer—has a monopoly on this knowledge. Beginning developers will face obstacles that they cannot envision in advance, but perseverance, hard work, and integrity will increase their chances of success.

NOTES

1. Respondent to the Beginning Developer Survey: Getting into the Business, 2020.

2. Phil Hughes, president, Hughes Investments, interview by Richard Peiser, April 2019.

3. The issue of net worth is significant for construction lenders, who need to be satisfied that the developer has sufficient financial resources to pay the bank back if the project goes sour. Although they may consider the total net worth of all general partners, they are more likely to prefer that one partner has net worth equal to the maximum loan commitment, because it is likely to cost more in legal fees to collect from several partners with smaller net worths than from one high-net-worth individual.

Underwriting criteria for lenders are discussed in detail in chapter 4. In most cases, the developer must be personally liable on the construction loan, meaning that the developer's fortune, to the limit of the loan, is at risk in the event of a default on the loan. Banks have different criteria for determining sufficient net worth. Some banks may look at total assets minus total liabilities, giving real estate full value in the computation of net worth. Other banks may require liquid net worth in excess of the loan amount in the form of cash, stocks, and bonds. This hurdle can be difficult even for experienced developers, most of whose net worth is often tied up in property.

4. Construction lenders often require the developer to provide cash equity equal to (1 − LTV) times the development cost rather than the appraised value when completed unless there is a firm permanent mortgage commitment based on the appraised value.

5. Operating risk may be higher for smaller projects than for larger projects, however, because the loss of one tenant can jeopardize the project's cash flow. Further, a small apartment or small office project costs more to operate per dwelling unit or per square foot. Nevertheless, total development risk is lower for a smaller project.

6. When money is widely available, the market is likely to be hot, with lots of activity. In such times, sellers are more likely to demand shorter closing times and shorter free-look periods during which the buyer does feasibility studies before putting up nonrefundable deposit money (going hard). The customary amount of deposit, or terms of diligence, may increase in severity as well.

7. Phil Hughes adds that the definition of a developer ought to include the ability to control the process. He distinguishes between full developers and fee developers: the latter face many of the same risks and rewards but do not control the project because they work for somebody else. "This is also true for 'corporate developers,' who are not satisfying themselves personally but satisfying committees and others. The whole of the corporate committee and the development manager make up the 'developer.' A developer has risk/reward and control. Otherwise, he is someone's employee," notes Hughes. (From Hughes, interview.)

8. Accuracy is measured by how narrow the range is around an estimate. Statistically, it is defined by the standard deviation of the estimate. For example, a construction cost estimate of $100,000 with a standard deviation of $10,000 means that actual costs should range from $90,000 to $110,000 68 percent of the time. A standard deviation of $20,000 means that the costs should range from $80,000 to $120,000 68 percent of the time.

9. Phil Hughes, president, Hughes Investments, interview by George Zhang, 2019.

10. Tom Montelli, developer, Post Road Residential, interview by Julian Huertas, 2020.

11. Jerry Rappaport, director, New Boston Fund, interviews by Richard Peiser, 2022, and Julian Huertas, 2020.

2 Organizing for Development

DAVID HAMILTON

All developers seek high-quality sites with potential for creating value, and they all require reliable access to capital. Small developers can face challenges on both fronts, so their success may rely particularly on the quality and organization of the development team. A strong partnership with complementary skills, supplemented with appropriate consultants, improves decision-making and efficiency. Well-managed small teams can execute projects more nimbly, solving problems and addressing complicated sites that big competitors cannot.

The cyclical history of real estate development has proven repeatedly that a lean central organization is key to surviving downturns. One way to stay lean is to use consultants for many noncore tasks. Small developers can often use some of the same professional consultants as larger developers. Although small developers may be a lower-priority client, using consultants has advantages. In addition to gaining the project expertise that top consultants can bring, beginning developers can acquire credibility by engaging a respected professional. That borrowed credibility can smooth interactions with approval authorities and other stakeholders, and it can reassure investors and lenders. Even experienced developers, moving into new markets or product types, often find that engaging local firms experienced with that market or product can mitigate developers' concerns about pursuing innovation.

Assembling a great team takes time. From their first day in business, beginners should solicit names of prospects and meet with them. Development often follows a "hurry up and wait" pattern, so slow times between tasks are an opportunity to assemble the kind of network that experienced developers have already established with consultants, contractors, and professionals. Building a permanent team will take more than one project. Nonetheless, time spent finding the best possible team is a good investment.

Smart developers put as much effort into building relationships as they do seeking investment capital and land. Very often these relationships can bring potential projects to the developer's attention.

The best assembly of professionals, of course, is only the beginning. Great development teams are well-managed. That means developers must establish and coordinate their lines of communication. John Loper, professor at the University of Southern California, advises, "Stay on top of your consultants, get out and talk to your people. Firms have personalities, and when you're starting out, it's yours."[1]

Forming Partnerships

Even more important than assembling the team is structuring the development or operating partnership. The result of a hastily assembled partnership can be heartache and financial risk. The safest partnerships are those in which the partners have come to know each other through a long history of working together. Over time, the partners come to understand each other's strengths and develop confidence in their

Half Moon Village, in Half Moon Bay, California, is an innovative, high-quality community for seniors. It provides 160 affordable rental homes to low-income seniors in the nation's most expensive rental housing market. Residents have access to amenities such as community gardens and an adjacent health and social services center.

BRUCE DAMONTE

integrity. Beginning developers, of course, seldom have such long-standing relationships, though they may have some. The beginner must remedy this limitation by making good strategic partnership choices and being diligent in the legal structuring of the development entity.

Partnerships frequently form around specific projects, and developers may have different sets of partners for various projects. Partnership arrangements can evolve over time. Early deals might involve several partners, each filling a major function, such as financing or construction. In subsequent deals, the number of partners might diminish as the developer learns how to obtain the needed expertise without sharing control or equity.

Landowners are often partners in a developer's early projects. Even if they are not able to contribute critical analytical or management skills, landowners' involvement can be valuable. They may contribute their property to the partnership as equity, which is always scarce for the beginning developer, and they may supply debt, via seller-financing, at terms unavailable through financial institutions. Even if they do not materially participate, landowners can agree to tie up land while financing and approvals are obtained. In contentious approvals processes, keeping the landowner involved and incentivized can add a local ally in discussions with neighbors. Likewise in situations involving income property, key tenants may be offered partnerships to induce them to lease space in the project, particularly if the project can be designed around a tenant's specific needs. Both landowners and tenants, however, generally prefer to limit their liability, and developers are reluctant to cede control of project decisions. Often a contractual framework is developed

Good strategic partnerships are critical. A common mistake is to choose partners with similar rather than complementary skills. Typical complementary pairings include capital and development experience or construction and management experience.

to provide certainty, for example, a phased purchase agreement for landowners or a guaranteed completion and occupancy schedule for tenants. Landlords or tenants are most often limited partners, with the developer as general or managing partner.

A common mistake in forming partnerships is to choose partners with similar rather than complementary skills. Typical complementary pairings include capital and development experience or construction and management experience. Whatever the match, partnerships work best when everyone shares equitably in risks and returns and is equally able to weather potential losses. In most partnerships, however, one person is wealthier than the others and will understandably be concerned about ending up with greater risk, even if the partnership agreement allocates this burden equally. This concern may be overcome in several ways, beginning before the partnership is formalized. The first step is selecting an appropriate liability-limiting structure. The partnership agreement should then specify how additional capital might be required, who must contribute, and how partners who decline to contribute might lose or dilute their interest. From the start, the wealthier partner can be given more of the return, a quicker return, or less of the management workload to compensate for any greater potential liability.

A major source of problems in partnerships, especially general partnerships in which everyone has equal interests, is uneven distribution of the workload or inadequate compensation for the partners who handle the day-to-day work of creating and implementing a project or projects. Successful developers think of compensation primarily in terms of incentive, rather than fairness. Key areas of responsibility must be determined in advance, and types of compensation should be defined appropriately to incentivize each. For example, one partner might receive a greater share of the development fee, with another receiving more of the leasing fee. Partners may also outline different compensation goals in the agreement, preferring regular cash flow or payment at exit. To conserve cash, accruing fees might be preferable to paying them as earned—so long as funding is adequate to meet expenses and provide a living wage to the working partners. Even if accrued compensation is not part of the initial deal, variation in cash flow may make it necessary, and the agreement should clarify who decides. Accounting for partners' interests in a *capital account* is good practice, offering an ongoing check on the appropriate equity investment of each partner and allowing management to address imbalances at each distribution.

Partnerships can last for years, so the choice of partners is critical. Large developers that bring in less experienced partners for specific deals generally enjoy a rather one-sided partnership, ensuring them management control. Beginning developers do not have the same negotiating power and must carefully consider whether to add partners who dilute their equity interest and management flexibility. Key points of project control include pricing, selection of contractors and consultants, operations and disposition, and marketing strategy.

Working out the partnership arrangement in advance, with legal advice, is essential for anticipating and avoiding conflict. A written agreement that defines each partner's role, responsibilities, cash contributions, tax needs, and share of liabilities and that sets out criteria for the dissolution or modification of the partnership is an essential document. Many members of general partnerships formed casually, based on verbal assurances, have been shocked to discover that they are liable for their partners' debts unrelated to the partnership's purposes. Those types of liabilities are often the default condition of a general partnership constructed without good legal advice.

The most basic unit of partnership combines someone with extensive development experience and someone whose credit is sufficient to obtain workable financing. The financial partner should have net worth at least equal to the total cost of the project under consideration, and preferably twice that amount. When economic conditions or outlook are soft, banks might require a higher multiple. If the partnership does not include someone with sufficient credit, then the partners will have to find someone to play that role before they can proceed. In the past, many savings and loan associations and some life insurance companies had subsidiaries that engaged in joint ventures with developers who could demonstrate a track record. Today, other developers or builders, high-net-worth individuals, or syndicates of investors are more promising candidates for partnerships with beginners.

The full requirements for cash equity and credit guarantees should be known before any financial partner is brought in. Say, on the one hand, the financial partner is asked to provide the necessary financial statement and $800,000 cash equity for 50 percent of the deal. If the developer later finds that an additional $100,000 cash equity is needed, he may have to give up an unnecessarily high portion of ownership. On the other hand, if the developer has no financial partner waiting in the wings, a prospective lender or seller will likely lose interest while the developer is locating one. Ideally, the developer can line up one or more prospects in advance, with a general understanding of the types of projects being pursued and a "soft" commitment to invest in deals that meet agreed-upon criteria of scale, location, investment duration, risk, and return. The firmer this relationship is, the better. In the absence of significant cash and a strong balance sheet at the start, beginning developers will almost always need a financial partner to cosign construction loans and provide cash equity.

The Firm's Organization and Management

Development is always a team effort, but the team can be assembled in several ways. At one extreme, a large company might include many services, from design and permitting to construction management and leasing. If the firm has enough work to invest in a robust organization, the advantages will be obvious. The most critical services can be performed in-house, presumably with better communication and quality control than outside vendors would offer. Developers must, however, beware of "mission creep," expanding into activities too far from the core competencies of the principals. Managing a design firm or brokerage uses a different skill set, it takes time, and owning those services requires continuous overhead even when work is intermittent.

Arrangements on the lean end of the spectrum are more common: a development company of one or two principals and a few staff members that hires or contracts with other companies and professionals for each service as needed. A critical first staff hire is an accountant to file taxes, run pro formas, document past performance, and put together investor packages. A second key hire is a project manager to close acquisitions and financing, oversee construction, and manage the sales or leasing process. That person can also put together presentations and handle investor relations and quarterly reporting. A construction manager, initially outsourced, could be hired after two to three projects are completed. Although a lean organization requires more contract management and external communication, the advantages are substantial. This lesson is relearned at every market downturn when firms with limited overhead are able to remain viable with low or no operating income. Limiting the "burn rate" of the development firm is good practice in a strong market, and it becomes an essential survival skill in a serious downturn. Lean structure has the side benefit of bringing in key consultants earlier in projects. "Input from marketing, for example, ideally starts at the 'blank piece of paper' phase, and should be fully engaged by entitlement," says Amy Levi of Strada.[2]

From the perspective of organization, development can be a low-cost business that is relatively easy to enter—for those with the credibility and relationships needed to access investment capital. A single person can start a development company with little fixed investment beyond an office. Small developers are often able to compete effectively against larger organizations, using technology and consultants to leverage the capabilities of the principals. Although larger developers might obtain better prices in some areas and certainly have easier access to money, they also tend to have higher overhead expenses and are usually slower to respond to market changes.

ORGANIZATIONAL LIFE CYCLES

Like most enterprises, development firms typically pass through four stages—startup, growth, maturity, and transition—and each stage is characterized by distinct risks and transition opportunities.

STARTUP. The startup stage is characterized by work toward two short-term goals—successfully developing a track record with the first few projects and establishing consistent sources of revenue to cover overhead. During this stage, firms are more likely to be *merchant*

builders, selling their projects to free up capital after they have been completed and leased, rather than *investment builders*, holding them for long-term investment. "During the startup period, the developer's entrepreneurial skills are the critical ingredient. The developer has to develop contacts—with investors, lenders, political leaders and staff, investment bankers, major tenants, architects, engineers, and other consultants. Eternal optimism and the ability to withstand rejection are essential."[3]

A common startup pitfall is overexpanding before the company has developed the staff and procedures to handle greater activity and new types of business. When tenants or buyers sense that a developer is not responding to their needs quickly enough, the developer's reputation suffers. A growing developer must build staff and establish procedures for accounting, payable and receivable processing, leasing, tenant complaints, reporting to investors and lenders, construction administration, property management, and project control. Successful developers know that accountability for functions handled by consultants is just as important as it is for in-house services.

A related mistake is hiring too many people too quickly. A startup business seldom has enough cash to pursue every line of business, and those that watch the overhead closely during startup tend to survive. Many development firms have been built with a professional staff of three to five key people.

GROWTH. A firm in the growth stage has achieved a measure of success. It has instituted procedures for running the business and has assembled a team of staff and consultants to cover all the major development tasks. With more systems and a track record, it is less vulnerable to one underperforming project. This firm is in a position to make strategic decisions about its future: what kinds of projects to pursue, in what markets, with what sort of capital structure and partners?

Maintaining the mission and entrepreneurial energy of the founders and inculcating that spirit into new team members are always challenges for growing firms. The firm must implement controls and procedures, without bureaucratic sclerosis. Development at any scale requires quick decision-making. The key is to maintain direct involvement of the firm's principals through this growth phase. Adding capacity and processes must always be undertaken to leverage principals' time, not to replace their judgment and expertise.

Employees accustomed to the flexible roles and atmosphere of a startup sometimes resist increased structure and oversight by senior management. Thus, in the growth phase, a firm may find itself with a new problem: retention of key players. The firm must maintain an entrepreneurial environment that motivates qualified, aggressive people. A one-person firm succeeds because that one person accepts risk, understands the incentives, and controls every aspect of the process. When staff becomes necessary to handle the workload, the transition to greater hierarchy can be difficult. Not only must the right staff be in place, but the founders must also be able to delegate.[4]

The right staff for a startup organization is not necessarily right for an organization in the growth phase.

MATURITY. Firms reach maturity after they have established a track record of successful projects and have built an organization that handles them effectively. Mature development companies have a network of relations with financial, political, and professional players and have cash flow and assets that confer stability. These firms can focus on larger, more sophisticated projects that tend to be more profitable and that allow more efficient oversight than multiple smaller, less predictable projects. With higher barriers to entry, they usually face less competition.

As firms and their projects increase their footprint, both can attract attention from regulators, investors, and the public. Compliance becomes more important for preserving the firm's reputation. This starts with formalizing processes to ensure compliance with land use and building safety requirements but must also include careful attention to human resource issues, worker's insurance, and project bonding commitments. Investors and lenders will require more information, reported in formats that agree with their risk management, as well as their environmental, social, and governance (ESG) or other portfolio requirements. Investors and public regulators may insist on particular certifications of environmental responsibility that require tests or audits. Adam Weers, chief operating officer at Trammell Crow, notes increasing attention to diversity, equity, and inclusion (DEI) coming from investors, particularly public pension funds, and from employees.[5] Although beginning developers are less likely to attract institutional capital from pension funds and insurance companies, they should note that capital providers are increasingly looking at ESG and DEI criteria as important when deciding whether to invest with a developer. A team with diverse perspectives

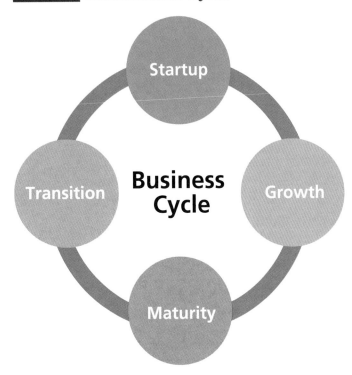

FIGURE 2-1 The Business Cycle

Startup

Business Cycle

Transition

Growth

Maturity

Firms experience risks and opportunities during each of the four stages in the business cycle: startup, growth, maturity, and transition to new owners.

brings internal benefits and can improve external communication as well; but admittedly, implementing ESG and DEI criteria can be difficult in parts of the industry that have historically had few women or people of color in leadership roles.

"Externally, municipal and redevelopment [requests for proposals] often include 'supplier diversity' requirements, and pension funds are definitely interested in DEI in their investments," notes Weers. But recently, tenants and development clients, particularly in the tech industry, "are asking questions about representation in firm and building management. Internally, employees and key partners want to see progress, which is a two-part problem: attracting and retaining talented employees. Retention is the hard part, requiring that managers think about what makes their employees feel like they 'belong' in the organization." Weers recommends a high-level commitment to DEI initiatives, such as a management committee that sets goals and standards, with flexibility for organic "bottom-up" organization, such as affinity groups and formalized mentorship arrangements.

TRANSITION. Many development firms are, at least at the beginning, family businesses. The difficult transition in this case is often generational. Family dynamics can complicate the transfer of management control, and—even after the transfer—the founding parent may remain in the background, giving directions that may not match the firm's new model. Many firms never make it through this transition.

ORGANIZATIONAL STRUCTURE

The importance of organizational structure increases with each phase of growth. In the early years, most developers resist formalized organizations. Everyone reports directly to the owner, who makes all the major decisions. As firms grow, the delegation of authority, especially in financially sensitive areas, becomes essential because the owner's time and availability are limited. Sometimes an outside consultant or new chief executive is needed to instigate necessary change.

In most firms, the principals control the same few decisions: site acquisition, partnership and financing arrangements, terms of major leases, and timing and terms of the sale of a project. A common practice among even very large firms is for the principals to retain responsibility for making deals, initiating and maintaining strategic relationships, hiring, and compensation—the activities most reliant on personal contacts, reputation, and strategic vision—and to delegate tactical responsibilities.

Development firms are organized by function (e.g., construction, sales), project, or some combination of the two. Smaller firms are more often organized by project, larger ones by function. That is, owners of small firms tend to put one individual in charge of each project, and the group working on that project advances and reports on all aspects of it—financing, construction, marketing, leasing, and general management. In contrast, large firms may have one group responsible for each key function across all projects,[6] with project managers coordinating the effort. In some organizations, employees report to two different managers, one responsible for function and the other for geographic area or product line. Increasingly, firms use a hybrid model, in which partners, who may have expertise in leasing, construction, or deal structure, each take on direct responsibility for general management of a project, drawing in the other partners on project tasks for which their expertise falls short. With different skill sets driving different projects, standardized compliance policies for legal, human resource, and quality concerns become more critical. A firm's organi-

zational structure often reflects how it has grown and evolved over time. Some of the largest firms maintain a project-manager structure because they have grown by giving partners responsibility for specific geographic areas, product types, or both. Regardless of what structure a firm began with, that structure should be evaluated periodically as the firm grows, to maintain partners' comfort with the framework as their responsibilities change.

COMPENSATION

Manager compensation is a major issue facing owners who want employees to align with the firm's mission. One answer is to give key individuals equity in the firm. According to John O'Donnell, chair of the O'Donnell Group in Newport Beach, California, "The reason you give employees equity is you can't pay them what they would command on the open market. Instead, you give them a stake in the future."[7] Senior executives might be afforded true partnership equity, whereas key personnel at the project level might receive *phantom equity*.

Phantom equity, computed from firm or project profits like a bonus, is an incentive for project managers, encouraging them to think like entrepreneur-owners. Unlike real equity, however, the individual does not legally own an interest in the project and is not liable for capital contributions. The project manager's signature is therefore not required for transactions; this point is important because junior staff turnover is common in this cyclical business. Also, if a partnership includes more than one property, phantom equity in the firm avoids the accounting difficulty of project-specific interest, which can complicate operating agreements or joint ventures. O'Donnell's firm measures the performance of each property each year and contributes the appropriate share of the manager's profit to a phantom equity account. For example, if the property makes $100,000 and the manager has a 5 percent interest in it, the account is credited $5,000. If the property loses $100,000, the manager does not have to cover the 5 percent share of the loss out of pocket; but paper losses do accrue to the account and must be "repaid" before future profits are distributed. In this way, the employee does not have to worry about raising cash to cover potential liabilities but participates materially in both the upside and downside potential of the business.

Many firms provide for a period of five to 10 years before an employee's phantom equity becomes vested. O'Donnell's firm, for example, might give an employee 2.5 percent of a project's earnings after three to five years of employment. Each year after the employee becomes vested, he or she receives an additional 0.5 percent, up to a limit of 5 percent. If a vested employee leaves the company, O'Donnell retains the right to buy out that person's interest at any time based on a current appraisal of the property, and he retains the right to select the appraiser. If an employee leaves the company without notice, O'Donnell might buy out that employee's interest immediately. In other circumstances, employees—say, a longtime secretary who leaves to start a family or a manager who gives advance notice (e.g., three months)—might receive profit distributions for years, thus enjoying the project's potential to the extent that their tenure vested those rights.

No formula exists for determining how much equity a developer should give away to attract top managers. Beginning developers may have to pay experienced project managers 15 percent or more of a project's profits, whereas established developers may need to pay only 1 to 5 percent depending on the size of the project. Employees' risks, and profit shares, are typically lower with a more established developer. One major developer, for example, has three levels of participation, which are given not as rewards but as career paths. The lowest level is *principal*. Project managers who are star performers are eligible. They receive up to 10 percent (5 to 7.5 percent is typical) of a project in the form of phantom equity. The next level is *profit and loss manager*, someone in charge of a city or county area. Project and loss managers are responsible for several projects and principals; they receive 15 to 20 percent of the profits from their areas, also in the form of phantom equity. The top level is *general partner*, reserved for managers of a region, state, or several states. General partners receive real equity, are authorized to sign documents on the firm's behalf, and incur full risk.

Real estate is a cyclical business. In each downturn, a substantial portion of capable junior and middle managers leave the industry. As a result, even in relatively weak markets, professionals with more than 10 years of experience can be in relatively short supply. Firms respond with creative and highly motivating compensation packages to attract and, more important, to retain these experienced hires. Compensation for top performers is usually paid through bonuses rather than salary and can range from 10 percent of salary, at the project level, to well over 100 percent for executives.

Personnel costs are typically 60 to 80 percent of most operating budgets, and they are the most critical component of a management or operating company. Benefit costs, especially for health care, continue to rise; and as in every industry, managers are increasingly sharing those increases with employees. Firms are also downsizing core teams, shifting to consultants for third-party and back-office functions. The 2008–2009 financial crisis solidified the model of a lean payroll with flexible, on-demand contract labor, which is commonly used across many industries.

STRATEGIC PLANNING

Most beginning developers—and even many large ones—do not have a formal strategic plan. Rather, they may focus on a specific demographic market, or a neighborhood, or a property type. Within those parameters, the firm will respond to opportunities as they arise—and more opportunities tend to arise within a well-chosen market. In that way, developers build expertise and a track record of success.

As firms gain maturity, size, and diversity, they may benefit from more formal strategic planning. A strategic plan gives junior team members a sense of the direction of the business and helps them understand how to contribute at the deal or project level. The effect of a good strategic plan, then, can be counterintuitive: encouraging more decentralization of the day-to-day activity of the firm. The plan should include budgets, a master schedule tied to the budget, and processes for approving decisions and tracking projects. The accompanying feature box summarizes the major issues that strategic planning should address.[8] Just as important is the inclusion of the assumptions, identified trends, and external dynamics that underpin elements of the strategy, so that they may be reevaluated in future revisions of the plan.

The strategic plan helps the company achieve its objectives faster, because everyone understands the firm's immediate goals and longer-term objectives. Such plans are most effective when prepared with broad participation and when the resulting strategy flows into clearly defined tasks. Whereas the business plan is strategic, the budget is tactical; that is, the budget lays out the specific approach that will be used to follow the broad strategy of the plan. The strategic plan culminates in an action plan, which should establish specific protocols for managers to follow—for example, policies for evaluating the competition and an area's long-term economic outlook, or for evaluating individual deals, contractors, or joint ventures against the criteria of the strategic plan.

Evaluate the present situation.

- What are the company's accomplishments? How do they compare with previous goals?
- Where is the company headed? How should it get there?
- What are the owner's or founders' interests and expectations?
- What is the external environment?
  - » Market changes and trends
  - » Changes affecting products and services
  - » Opportunities from changes
  - » New and old risks and rewards
  - » Political environment
  - » Reputational pressures on organization (ESG)
- Who are key competitors? Where do they excel?

Analyze the company's strengths and weaknesses.

- What properties has it developed, bought, marketed? How successful have they been?
- How has the firm done in the past?
  - » Management capabilities
  - » Threats
  - » Opportunities
- What past decisions would be changed?

Specify goals for the strategic plan.

- What is the financial strategy?
- What is the firm's strategy regarding products?
  - » Quality and market segment
  - » Investor or merchant builder
- Does the company need to diversify or simplify its product offerings?

- Does the company need to diversify its location?
- What is the company's strategy regarding land?
  - » Land banking versus carrying land in slow times
  - » Developed land versus raw land
- What is the marketing strategy?
- What is the strategy regarding production and construction?
- What key roles are needed, and what is the strategy to attract and retain candidates?
- What is the management and organizational strategy?

Specify an action plan—programs, steps, or tasks to be carried out—concerning risk, reward, and reality.

- What activities is the company engaged in now?
- What is the state of financial reporting and planning?
- Where do equity and debt come from?
- How reliable are financial suppliers? Are there unknowns?
- What will be the financial needs in the next 24 months, the next 36 months, or longer to meet strategic goals?
- What are the company's objectives? What metrics is it committed to achieving?
- How will lines of communication and internal controls function?
  - » Financial results
  - » Acquisition and development
  - » Operations: property management, leasing, tenant improvements, customer relations
  - » Controls and measurement
  - » Recruiting, training, and retention
  - » Responsibilities and budgets

Source: Sanford Goodkin, president/chief executive, Sanford R. Goodkin & Associates, San Diego.

Choosing Consultants and Contractors

Assembling a team of professionals to address the economic, physical, and political issues inherent in a complex development project is critical. A developer's success depends on its ability to coordinate the completion of a series of interrelated activities efficiently and in the appropriate sequence.

The development process requires the skills of many professionals: architects, landscape architects, planners, and engineers to address project design; market consultants and brokers to determine demand and a project's economics; multiple attorneys to handle agreements and government approvals; environmental consultants and soils engineers to analyze a site's physical and regulatory limitations; surveyors and title companies to provide legal descriptions of a property; contractors to budget and supervise construction; and lenders to provide financing.

Even the most seasoned developer finds that staying on top of all a project's technical details is difficult. For beginners, a key is to find consultants and partners who can help guide the development process, as well as provide technical knowledge. Art Danielian recommends a team approach,[9] in which the full range of consultants are available throughout the project and kept abreast of progress before and after their primary input. "Total compensation will be about the same whether they are brought on individually, or at the beginning," but "synergistic effects" happen when an entrepreneurial team is assembled early. Regardless of experience, most developers can benefit from continuing investment in their own training and in updated software and communications tools to leverage their personal project-management abilities. Developers may find that small subcontractors lack technologies and communications tools which they take for granted; that disparity can complicate efforts to integrate those subcontractors as the firm grows and takes on more complex projects.

LOCATING A CONSULTANT

To begin the search for a consultant with particular expertise, developers should first seek the advice of successful local developers who have completed projects similar to the one under consideration. They should ask about the consultants they use and their level of satisfaction with the consultants' work. Beginners should also remember, however, that established developers may consider newcomers the competition, and some time may be needed to build the trust necessary for a frank exchange of opinions. Another avenue to pursue is to find out which consultants typically work together. Often, the same sets of consultants work on multiple jobs together, so a planning firm can often suggest a civil engineer or wetland scientist. Beginning developers might take advantage of networking opportunities by joining associations of local developers or builders, or finding national organizations geared toward their real estate product, be it residential, shopping centers, or business parks. The key is to be active: serve on committees and attend events.

Public officials and their staff are often prohibited from recommending professional service firms, but developers can often get an informal opinion. Certain approvals might hinge on the reputations of specific team members; indeed, part of consultants' value can lie in the connections they maintain with the public sector. A look at public meeting minutes or documents posted for public comment will reveal which consultants represent each developer and builder going through the process. Because governments sometimes rely on certifications of outside professionals for approvals, many tasks that were once performed by public servants may now be performed in the private sector by the very same people. A common example is soil evaluation, a function of departments of public health, which is commonly performed by "authorized evaluators"; these are typically former department employees who retain both the knowledge of their field and relationships with the approving agency.

Associations of architects, planners, and other development-associated professionals are another source of potential consultants. Such organizations usually maintain rosters of members, which are useful as a screening tool because most professional and technical organizations have defined standards for their members. Those standards might include a certain level of education and practical experience, as well as a proficiency examination. Most associations publish trade magazines or referring directories online.

SELECTING A CONSULTANT

Strategies for selecting consultants vary according to the type of consultant being sought. The most common approach is a series of personal interviews because, aside from the work product, a cordial and responsive relationship is the most important factor. Beginners should not hesitate to reveal their inexperience with the issues being addressed or to ask potential consultants to explain their duties and the process of working together. Consultants will profit by working with a developer, so they should take the time to explain the fundamentals.

A proper interview should address the developer's concerns regarding experience and attitudes. The developer should look for experience with similar projects. An architect or market consultant who has concentrated on single-family residential development would be the wrong choice for a developer interested in an office or retail project. Domain expertise is becoming more important with the growth of technically oriented "innovation hubs focusing on life sciences or nanotechnology," says urban designer Jim Stickley of WRT, "and we have to demonstrate value."[10] Ideally, the project type or jurisdiction should be new to only one or two, hopefully minor, team members.

The developer must ask for references and contact those references personally. The point is to learn about the consultant's quality of work and business conduct, ability to deliver on time and within budget, interest in innovation, tolerance for clients' direction, and professional integrity.

The developer may also inspect some of the consultant's work—marketing or environmental reports, plans and drawings, and finished projects. The developer should be comfortable with the design philosophy of a prospective member of the creative team and satisfied with the technological competence of a potential analytical consultant.

The developer must be certain that the chosen firm has the personnel and facilities available to take on the assignment. This balance is difficult to achieve: the developer is likely to be attracted to small firms'

Who Is Involved, and When, in the Development Process?

Site Selection
- Brokers
- Title companies
- Market consultants
- Transactional and land use attorneys

Feasibility Study
- Market consultants
- Economic consultants
- Construction estimators
- Surveyors
- Mortgage brokers and bankers
- Land use attorney
- Engineers

Design
- Land planners/landscape architects
- Road and infrastructure engineers
- General contractors/construction managers
- Surveyors (pre- and post-design)
- Soils engineers

- Architects
- Specialty engineers (structural, mechanical, acoustic)
- Environmental consultants (wetlands, wildlife, historic preservation)

Marketing
- Brokers and on-site sales/leasing employees
- Public relations firms and advertising agencies
- Graphic designers, web and social media service firms

Financing
- Mortgage brokers and bankers
- Construction lenders and appraisers
- Permanent lenders and syndicators
- Title companies
- Appraisers

Construction
- Architects or construction managers
- General contractors
- Engineers
- Landscape architects
- Surety companies
- Authorized inspectors

Operations
- Property managers
- Specialty and amenity maintenance teams

Sale
- Brokers
- Appraisers

Throughout the Process
- Attorneys (title, transactional, land use, litigation)

---

personal attention, but sensibly wary of an organization without capacity or staying power. If a consultant appears to be struggling to keep up with current responsibilities, the proposed project is likely to suffer from neglect. A good rule of thumb is that the proposed project should represent no more than a third of the consultant's overall business, and the consultant should have been in business for much longer than the projected timeline of development to come.

Having ascertained the overall fitness of the consulting group, the developer should establish who will manage the project, request a meeting with that person, and examine several projects for which that manager was responsible. Then, specific personnel and time allocations can be delineated in the professional services agreement. Toward that end, the developer should ask what subconsultants ("subs") the firm is likely to hire and how the scope of work will make each sub accountable to the project timeline and performance standards. The developer may choose to speak with key subs, to map out a plan for completing the assignment together. The project scope should be divided into three parts: the scope that must be completed, hopefully at a guaranteed price; the work that is needed but is of unknown difficulty or duration; and optional additional services. For the undetermined

items, the developer should negotiate a framework for how such work will be approved and how costs will be calculated. Successful completion of the assignment requires coordination between the consultant and the subs; the developer, who is dependent on those individuals, should know who is responsible for what.

The hiring process is a two-way street. While the developer is sizing up the consultant, a similar process is going on across the table. Thus, displaying a positive attitude about the project and the consultant's potential contribution is important. Beginning developers should not be offended when a consultant asks about their experience and ability to complete a development project, their financial resources and accounting capacity to pay the bills, the feasibility of the proposal, the decision-making process, and what happens if the project is delayed or aborted.

Many consultants view working for a developer—as opposed to less cyclical institutional clients, the government, or end-users—as risky. Consultants need to be confident about a developer's ability to meet obligations and should know when they are working "at risk." This last consideration has become especially important as cash flow difficulties for developers and owners of real estate have trickled down and become crises at firms offering development services. An experienced consultant will appreciate an honest conversation about when work will be compensated and will be cautious about releasing work if pay is uncertain.

Finally, developers should judge whether they have established a rapport with the people being considered during the preliminary interview. Rapport is not simply personal comfort; the developer may have goals for the project—such as environmental quality or diversity and inclusion—that require a shared commitment. Thinking ahead to the long timeline of some development projects, the developer may wish to consider whether the consulting firm has the same culture at the junior level as at the executive level. Compatibility is key, and most communication will be between project and job managers.

If, after checking references, the developer feels uncomfortable with any aspect of the consulting firm, eliminating the firm from further consideration may be the most sensible move. If the developer's view of the firm is generally favorable but less so about the particular person being assigned to the project, that concern should be raised with the firm's principals. A larger firm likely has another staff person available; a smaller firm may not. The developer must be assured that the most qualified people will be assigned to the project and (to the best of their knowledge) available until the project is complete. Turnover is natural, so the developer should set expectations for how decisions, submittals, and communications will be archived. A legible record of decisions and legal justifications is particularly important if the project is delayed or a team member leaves. Regardless, all team members should be aware of protocols for communication. Any communication must be considered as it might be viewed in a future regulatory action or litigation. Developers must be able to trust their team and should train them accordingly.

RATES

Consultants should willingly quote a fee for their services, presenting a written proposal reflecting the costs for delivery of the desired product. Depending on the consultant's expertise, the quotation may be a simple lump-sum bid, an hourly rate, or a menu of services and associated costs. The developer benefits from having as much information in writing as possible. Although cost is an important factor, it must be balanced by experience and the quality of the consultant's past work. The most experienced consultants in some fields are the least likely to put

guaranteed fixed fees on their work, understanding that the process is unpredictable. Developers should be careful not to choose simply the lowest price. If detailed proposals are available, developers should compare the proposed budgets to see how the money is allocated and to identify the differences in proposals to judge whether the numbers are reasonable. They should also ensure that the prices reflect comparable services. A lower quotation may exclude services that will later be required, necessitating additional charges. It may also exclude a contingency to cover unforeseen scope. The issue of unforeseen costs is a hazard of the development business. Often, changes to the scope and cost of services ultimately amount to more than the differences in initial quotes. Thus, any professional services agreement must spell out clearly the types of events that could trigger additional costs (inadequate base drawings, new regulatory requirements), the process by which the scope may be changed and the notice required to do so, and the specific unit prices for additional work.

Once they have selected a firm, most developers prefer to employ a fixed-price contract, using the figures quoted in the proposal. Payment can be made in several ways, depending on the nature of the product to be delivered. Most typical is milestones: the delivery of a specified work product triggers an agreed-upon payment. For projects with a long timeline, developers might simply allocate a monthly payment for an agreed scope to advance the project. Smaller jobs might require a deposit and a payment upon completion.

Some consultants, such as lawyers, work according to a *time-and-materials* (T&M) agreement, with the client billed according to a schedule of hourly rates and the cost of materials used to complete the task. Materials include reimbursable expenses, such as printing or shipping, which may receive a markup for management time. For new (i.e., unknown) clients, many consultants prefer T&M arrangements. However, developers must constantly monitor T&M agreements to verify the amounts that are being billed and to understand them in relation to the overall project scope. Less experienced developers lack benchmark information about appropriate costs for handling specific tasks, making these agreements inherently risky. When constructing T&M agreements, the developer should be clear on a dollar value that may be billed each period without prior approval, so that a casual approval to "take care of that" does not turn into an unanticipated receivable at the end of the month. Regardless of careful construction and monitoring, T&M agreements require trust, and clear communication of common expectations for the work to be performed.

Retainer agreements that pay the consultant a flat monthly fee should be avoided because such arrangements can be very costly in the long run. Delays may stop work on an aspect of the project, but the billing continues apace. Not only is cash flow impaired, but the incentives of developer and consultant may become warped when 50 percent of the work is completed, but 90 percent of payment has been received. Retainer agreements are usually appropriate only for elements of a project that are truly ongoing (such as public relations management during the lease-up period) or for services that are more like insurance against possible eventualities (such as land use counsel during the development period).

Regardless of the chosen method of compensation, both the developer and the consultant must negotiate a mutually agreeable performance contract. The contract must explicitly list each duty the consultant is expected to complete. The developer should expect that services not explicitly included in the agreement will probably require future negotiations and likely lead to additional costs for the developer. The contract should clearly spell out a schedule for the delivery of services, including the expected turnaround for major steps in the process and a definitive date for delivery of the final product.

WORKING WITH CONSULTANTS

After the parties sign the agreement, the working relationship begins. The developer must communicate regularly with the consultant to ensure that everything proceeds according to schedule. The development team is made up of a group of players whose tasks are interrelated, and the tardiness or shoddy work of a single firm could set off a chain reaction and cause costly delays.

As the team leader, the developer must ensure that each consultant is provided with accurate information and that information from one consultant is relayed to the others as soon as it is available. Changes should be reviewed carefully and distributed immediately upon approval, which is usually best handled by making one consultant the steward of drawings and specifications. This key person, often the architect or planner, provides the base documents that all subs

Assembling a team of professionals to address the economic, physical, and political issues inherent in a complex development project is critical.

follow (numerous software tools address this coordination and communication). The developer should know where this information resides and how it is secured. As client, the developer must be sensitive to the effect that changes in the project will have on the consultants' analysis, altering criteria for the design, environmental requirements, or parking, for example. Alterations can be costly. Consultants may demand extra compensation to address the changing elements of the project, and alterations typically get more expensive as the project gears up with more interrelated consultants. Setting a firm project concept early, with some diligence to confirm feasibility, will help provide a logic for all the decisions that need to be made over the timeline.

A developer must have the management skill necessary to coordinate consultants' efforts while ensuring that all parties respect the developer's ultimate authority to make decisions. There is no room for outsized egos. A good developer knows when to listen to and accept the advice of others.

The Design/Construction Team

The design/construction team includes an array of consultants and contractors who perform tasks ranging from site and regulatory analysis and planning to cost estimating, building design, and construction management. The work that they perform or manage represents the bulk of the project's total *soft costs*. These expenditures receive the most scrutiny from investors; they are also riskier than direct construction investments because their completed value is less tangible. Effectively managing these contributions and costs is critical.

ARCHITECTS AND URBAN DESIGNERS

Both beginning and experienced developers depend on architects and urban designers (possibly a single firm) for advice and guidance. If the two are in separate firms, they should have a record of working together. Some developers appoint the architect to head the design portion of a project, and sometimes the construction period as well. Most developers, however, prefer to be their own team leader, both to maximize their influence on the design and to expedite time-critical processes. Beyond building and site design expertise, architects usually offer extensive experience with the regulatory and physical constraints placed on development and provide valuable help in locating and communicating with other consultants and in coordinating the design process with others

during construction. Galina Tachieva of DPZ emphasizes that new preferences and household types mean that the design team must be familiar with demographics and with new models of development that might not yet be common in every market.[11]

The search for an architect must be thorough. Only firms whose experience is compatible with the proposed project should be considered. Crucially, the architect must be focused on delivering a workable product at a reasonable cost that can be evaluated at various points along the way. Specialists in high-end custom homes may not be suitable for a development of production homes, where every cost is multiplied and supply chains must be considered. Beginning developers especially may lean on the project experience of the architect. A brilliant but inexperienced architect is likely a better match for a more seasoned developer. The developer should always check a firm's credentials and ensure licensure in the state where the project will be built. A call to the building department will confirm the requirements for stamps of a state-admitted architect or engineer.

The developer and the architect should share a common philosophy of design, though the developer will often benefit from the broader experience of a design professional. A good architect respects the client's opinions and can work through disagreement. At the same time, the developer must consider the architect's knowledge and experience. Some developers prefer to hire an architect whose work has withstood the test of time; others look for an architect known for innovative designs that make a distinctive statement and may give the developer a competitive advantage or a boost in public relations or approvals.

Once the developer finds an architect, the next step is to reach a written agreement. The American Institute of Architects (AIA) provides a set of standard contracts that form the basis for defining the relationship between developer and architect. AIA Document B151, "Agreement between Owner and Architect," clearly outlines the architect's duties in the development process and is widely used in real estate development. Developers should remember, however, that this agreement was written from architects' perspective and seeks to protect their interests.[12] In some circumstances, modifications to the AIA agreement form are appropriate; however, both parties should be aware that a body of opinion and case law exists for interpreting this standard document, and changes may introduce uncertainty. Whatever the agreement, most developers prefer to keep direct contractual relationships with subdisciplines, such as engineers, rather than ceding contractual authority to the architect.

The design phase runs from the initial concept to the completion of the final drawings. The design is based on a program that outlines the project's general concept, most notably its identified uses and amenities, and initial allocations of floor area, volume, or acreage for each. It is increasingly common for planners or architects, or even branding and sales consultants, to participate in the programming phase, particularly in urban, mixed-use locations where the allocating program can be very complex. Defining the scope of the project is critical, says Woo Kim of WRT. "There can be so much to be done in the neighborhoods where we work. Too much weight is put on the project to solve every issue. Clarify the achievable goals for the project."[13]

Initially, the architect prepares schematic drawings that include general floor and site plans and propose basic materials and physical systems. A construction cost estimator or contractor should review the design and assess its economic implications at least at the conclusion of each design phase. These schematic drawings are an important component in presentations to lenders and should include a basic set of presentation images, such as rendered elevations or a physical or digital three-dimensional model.

Upon approval of the schematic drawings, architects typically move into a "design-development" phase, in which the original concept begins to be fleshed out into construction systems and a more precise division of functional spaces. Most major design decisions are made in the schematic and design-development drawing stages; changes to the design become more difficult and expensive as the project proceeds. Even under the inevitable time constraints, it is nearly always better to address design concerns as they arise than to table these issues assuming they can be fixed later. This is the time for other members of the design team to review preliminary drawings, so that proposed changes, and potential conflicts, can be handled at once. The design team should include not only the contractor or construction manager but also marketing, leasing, and property management representatives. If those team members are not yet named, then the developer should ask potential contractors, brokers, and property managers to review and critique the drawings. Beautiful but unmarketable projects can lead to finger-pointing later.

After approval of the design-development package, the developer typically has the first real handle on the potential cost of the project. At this point, the developer should review estimates against the design drawings and resolve major budget issues before going forward. Upon approval of the design and cost, the architect produces specification drawings, also called *working drawings*. Specifications include detailed drawings of the materials to be incorporated with the mechanical, electrical, plumbing, and heating, ventilating, and air-conditioning (HVAC) systems. Generally, drawings pass through several iterations before the final plans and specifications are deemed finished. The developer should review the interim drawings, referred to as 25 percent, 50 percent, 75 percent, or 95 percent complete. After addressing all the developer's concerns, the architect completes final drawings and specifications.

Because most developers are interested in the project's image and feel, they often spend their time reviewing drawings at the expense of specifications, which is a mistake. The quality, durability, and safety of a structure are as dependent on "the spec" as on the drawings. The spec is typically organized around the Construction Specifications Institute's *MasterFormat*, which groups construction materials into categories consistent across all types of projects; a master specification defines not only materials but also precisely how and by whom each material should be installed.[14] The spec is therefore an incredibly important document for the long-term operation of the building because it governs the warranty and regulatory compliance of nearly every material in the building. In reviewing partially completed designs—both drawings and specifications—the developer should pay particular attention to the implications for potential users by visualizing how commercial tenants or residents will react to the design. Brokers, tenants, and other developers can be consulted to help identify the needs of the target groups, and real estate professionals' comments on the design drawings can be solicited as they progress.

The next phase of the architect's duties involves compiling the construction documents, including the package used to solicit bids from contractors. This package includes the rules for bidding, standard forms detailing the components of the bid, conditions for securing surety bonds, detailed specifications identifying all components of the bid, and detailed working drawings. The developer also relies on the architect's experience to analyze the bids and to help select the best contractor for the job. Although the architect is best suited to understand the components of bids on a design, the developer is the one who will have to live with those bids, and with missing or misunderstood scope or cost during the development phase. For this reason, developers must thoroughly understand the bids, and they may wish to introduce special format requirements so that bids dovetail with the development and operating budgets they will be administering on the project.

Once construction begins, the architect is responsible for monitoring—but not supervising—the work site. The architect is expected to inspect the site periodically to determine whether contract documents are being adequately followed. Constant monitoring is beyond the scope of the architect's responsibility, requires additional compensation, and is more effectively achieved with a construction manager, who may be compensated by percentage or by a fixed scope and cost.

The developer also relies on the project architect—or project engineer, in the case of infrastructure development—to confirm that key milestones have been satisfactorily completed. The approval involves a *certificate of completion,* which must be approved by the design professional to permit disbursement of the contractor's fee. Certification may also be required by lenders, in addition to their own inspection of installed value. The AIA provides another standard certificate, limiting the architect's liability resulting from this role; it notes that the architect's inspections are infrequent, defects could be covered between visits, and the architect can never be entirely sure that construction has been completed according to the plan.

The relationship between architect and developer commonly follows one of two models. The *design/ award/build* contract is most traditional in the United States; it breaks the project into two distinct phases, with the architect completing the design phase before the developer submits the project for contractors' bids. The alternative, the *fast-track* approach, involves the contractor during the early stages of design because the contractor's input at this stage could suggest ways to save on costs, making the project more economical and efficient to construct.

The fast-track method is primarily a cost-saving device, as it uses time efficiently to reduce the holding costs incurred during design. The developer is able to demolish existing structures, begin excavation and site preparation, and complete the foundation before the architect completes the final drawings. One risk is that the project is under construction before costs have been determined and before necessary approvals are finalized.

Several methods are available for compensating architects for their services. Most developers avoid T&M agreements, preferring a fixed-price contract with a more open-ended "additional services" clause. These specify the amount that the architect will receive for completing the basic services outlined in the performance contract; any duties not listed in the contract are considered supplementary and require additional compensation. Other methods calculate architectural fees as a fixed percentage (usually 3 to 8 percent) of a project's hard costs, or even a fee per square foot (which varies widely between project types). Architects contend that these methods can fairly account for a project's complexity, but they provide no incentive to the architect to economize in building area or cost. Developers often have to engage the architect and other professionals on the basis of either T&M or a short-term retainer during project conceptualization, because the project scope remains unclear, and then shift to a fixed-price arrangement when the project is more defined and subject to better quantification. Hybrid models of compensation are also popular. For example, a particular milestone will be priced as "not-to-exceed," with hourly billing against the maximum, and no costs authorized beyond that number. In this way, the architect offers the client protection against overruns but is paid within an established range for work performed.

Regardless of the mode of calculating compensation, the architect is entitled to additional reimbursable expenses—travel, printing, photocopying, and other out-of-pocket expenses. Beginning developers should be aware that, on a project with even a fairly simple path through public approvals, printing costs alone for the many dozens of required drawing sets can rise well into five figures, so getting an estimate up front is wise.

LANDSCAPE ARCHITECTS

Landscape architects do much more than plant trees and flowers. Landscape architects work with existing conditions—topography, soil composition, hydrology, and vegetation on a site—to create a functional setting and a sense of place for the project. Their responsibilities include collaborating with the architect to produce an external environment that enhances the development, devising a planting and hardscape plan, and incorporating components into the project, such as plants, trees, furnishings (benches, for instance), walkways, artwork, and signs. Landscape architects can also help reduce energy costs by selecting plants that provide shade and solve drainage problems with grading and plantings.

It is becoming increasingly common for landscape architects to take a leading role in entitling projects. Communities commonly demand that new projects include open space and expect to have a say on landscaping of public roads and views. In land development projects, landscape architects may take the lead; their drawings are often the most instructive to the community and, with emphasis on the green and natural, sometimes the most appealing design vision of the project.

Landscape architects first develop preliminary plans and then manage the completion of those plans. They obtain bids, complete working drawings and final specifications, prepare a schedule, and inspect the site to verify that the contractor is implementing the plan correctly. Expertise in other kinds of construction does not necessarily translate into landscape construction and installation. Many very expensive installation problems in landscapes can be virtually invisible to the untrained eye (e.g., inadequate soils testing or preparation, or poor subsurface drainage). The developer is well advised to have someone with specific expertise inspect the project at least upon completion, if not periodically through construction.

The architect may be responsible for hiring the landscape architect, but developers should inspect the chosen landscape architect's work to be sure they are comfortable with the design philosophy. The American Society of Landscape Architects maintains rosters and certifies its members. Landscape architects typically work through conceptual planning on a T&M basis, then bid a lump sum to complete working drawings and specifications, then generally return to working on an hourly basis to supervise completion of the plans. A monthly or weekly retainer may also be used for construction administration.

LAND PLANNERS

With land development projects and larger building projects, land planners translate the developer's desired uses into a plan to maximize the site's potential. They allocate those uses to best use the site and determine the most efficient layout for adjacent uses, densities, and infrastructure. Individual building projects usually rely on the judgment of the architect and market consultants. The land planner's goal is to produce a plan with good internal circulation, well-placed uses and amenities, and adequate open space. Land planners typically prepare several schemes that expand on the developer's proposal and discuss the pros and cons of each with the developer. The developer coordinates the land planner's activities with input from marketing, engineering, economic, and political consultants to ensure that the plan is marketable, efficient, and financially and politically feasible. On land development projects, the land planner is the principal professional consultant and likely coordinates engineering. Reputation and past projects are the best indicators of a land planner's ability. A key characteristic to look for in a land planner is the ability to work well with the project engineer and architect. Because the activities of a land planner vary widely, many architects and landscape architects offer "planning" on their menu of services. The skill sets do overlap, and some architects are certainly capable of high-quality site planning. However, professional planners often bring more to the table than simply their skills. When evaluating a planner, developers should be aware of the office's connections and reputation within the approvals process, as well as its relationships with infrastructure contractors and landscape construction firms.

ENGINEERS

Engineers play a vital role in the development of a building. Several types of engineers with specific expertise—structural, mechanical, electrical, civil—are essential to ensure that the design can accommodate the required physical systems. They sometimes are engaged by the project architect and sometimes contract directly to the owner or developer. Regardless of the relationship, they must maintain a very close relationship with the architectural staff as the project design unfolds. For this reason, the developer should seek the architect's input when selecting all the project engineers. Larger architectural firms may have an in-house engineering staff, which can expedite coordination but limit competition; smaller firms prefer to hire individual engineers project by project.

Although the architect may make recommendations or offer a list of candidates, the developer should reserve the right to select engineers after inspecting their qualifications; reviewing previously completed projects of the same scope and property type, including interviewing the project's proponent; and checking their working references with various general contractors and local building inspectors. Contractors may have strong opinions about engineers that they have worked with in the past. Although these opinions should be considered, the developer should also understand that projects often place engineers and contractors on opposite sides of the process, and contractors can resent the oversight of an engineer.

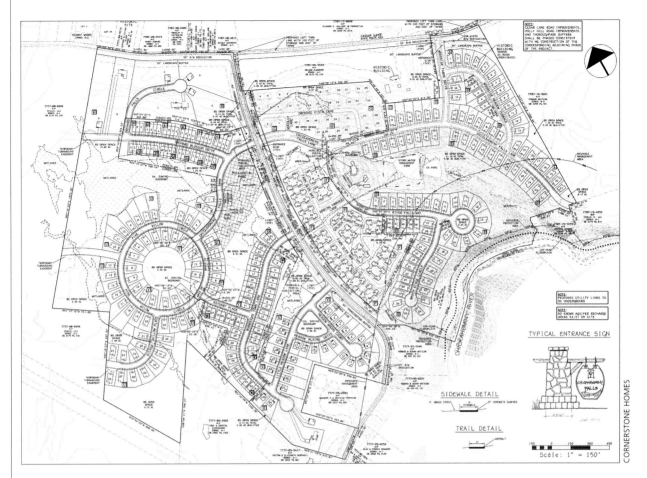

CORNERSTONE HOMES

Engineers must be licensed by each state in which they operate, and plans cannot receive approvals unless signed by a licensed professional engineer. Developers should clarify which submittals require stamps from which kinds of engineers.

The architect may hire certain engineers as subcontractors and in that case is responsible for subcontract deliverables, schedule, and budget. Engineers are generally required on all substantial construction projects, including new developments, renovations, or additions to existing structures. The engineer's fee schedule is usually included in the architect's budget and generally ranges from 4 to 7 percent of the overall soft cost. When engineers subcontract to architects, evidence of payments to subs should be required in the architectural contract; nonpayment or default by the architect can sometimes result in a *mechanics lien*[15] on the property.

During the initial design phase, the architect works with the engineers to develop and modify working drawings to accommodate the project's structural, HVAC, electrical, and plumbing systems. Each engineer then provides a detailed set of drawings showing

The planner creates the master plan to integrate survey information with proposed lots, structures, and infrastructure, keying to detailed drawings of the elements of the site plan.

the physical design of the systems for which the engineer is responsible. The architect is responsible for coordination of each successive drawing set and for instructing the engineers to resolve any conflicts.

Structural engineers help the architect design the building's structural system to efficiently provide the spans and spaces in the plans. They work with soils engineers to determine durable and cost-effective foundation systems. And they produce a set of drawings for the general contractor explaining their design in detail, especially the structural members' sizing and connections. Structural engineers can range from sole practitioners who produce framing plans for single-family homes to large professional practices that can engineer steel-framed high rises. Developers of specialty buildings for medical offices, labs, and the like should be aware that these building types require specialized expertise beyond the professional engineer credential.

Organizing for Development

Specialty buildings should only be undertaken with an engineer experienced in the type and jurisdiction.

Mechanical engineers design the building's HVAC systems, including mechanical plant locations, air-flow requirements for climate control and public health, and any special heating or cooling requirements, such as computer rooms in office buildings or isolation wards in hospitals. Many firms offer a combined mechanical, electrical, plumbing (MEP) practice, allowing them to take responsibility for the building's plumbing design. Developers should not feel obligated to lump all engineering specialties together in one firm, but doing so can improve coordination, as mechanicals need power and water connections.

Electrical engineers design the electrical power and distribution systems, including lighting, circuitry, and backup power supplies and specifications for inbound site electrical utilities. Civil engineers design the on-site utility systems, sewers, streets, parking lots, and site grading. Wise project managers clearly delineate where each engineer's jurisdiction ends: for example, "site utilities" may extend to within three feet of the building envelope, while "building electrical" may be within this boundary.

Effective project coordination relies on upfront communication, and engineers should be included early in the design process. Experienced developers generally facilitate a series of meetings with all architectural and engineering project personnel to define scope and communication channels and to discuss each discipline's goals and objectives in depth. For example, if the goal is to construct a high-efficiency building with systems that result in lower operating costs—digital thermostats, automated or remotely monitored off-site HVAC system controls, automatic water closets—those project aims need to be spelled out early in the process. Often, developments now aim for performance certification—such as Leadership in Energy and Environmental Design (LEED), Passive House, or at a minimum Energy Star—and such goals magnify the importance of early engineering and cost-estimating coordination. Costs of LEED certification, for example, vary widely by product type and by the strategic choices made to get to certification. Increasingly, developers report that the "green premium" for more sustainable construction is falling: payback is faster as utility costs rise and many of the techniques become mainstream. Developers should be aware of cost tradeoffs between higher development costs and lower ongoing operating expenses and should furnish engineers with the criteria needed to make decisions on their behalf. Just

as important, developers should investigate incentives, often through state advisory or utility programs, that can offset costs of these investments.

Ronald Stenlund, president of Central Consulting Engineers, advises developers and their engineers to insist on two-year warranties on all installed mechanical systems.[16] It is vital that each component, particularly a building's heating and cooling systems, go through a full season of startup and shutdown to be evaluated. Unfortunately, a one-year guarantee is the industry standard, and this period generally begins on the *shipping* date rather than the *installation* date. Further, maintenance people must be properly trained in the nuances of each system and gain familiarity with the operations. Developers should insist on well-organized manuals and training for building personnel, during or following building commissioning.

One concern of all developers is soft costs coming in over budget. According to Stenlund, "Failure to achieve effective communication among the developer, architect, and engineering staff early in the process is the single most common cause for project delays, redesigns, and cost overruns. Coordinating the team early, defining expectations, and developing a congruent project vision are the three keys to minimizing this risk factor."

SOILS ENGINEERS

Experienced developers recommend completing at least basic soil tests on a site before purchasing the property. Soils engineers can conduct an array of tests to determine a site's soil stability, the presence and concentrations of common toxic materials, and any other conditions that will affect construction. Geotechnical engineering is not an exact science, so scoping requires understanding the role of proposed tests in different phases. Sampling for toxics begins at acquisition, with informed guesses on test locations, and expands in area and intensity if initial results cause concern. This testing is a kind of due diligence to understand and reduce risk. Geotechnical analysis for structural characteristics is more targeted. To fully understand factors like load-bearing capacity, water level, or compaction for roads or excavation, testing is directed to areas identified in the design process, such as foundations, roads, and bridges. These factors inform design and budget, but even a well-tested site will invariably yield some unexpected soil conditions. Many jurisdictions require, and good construction managers will recommend, as-built analysis, whereby cores are taken of installed materials at key locations (such as road subgrades) to determine construction quality.

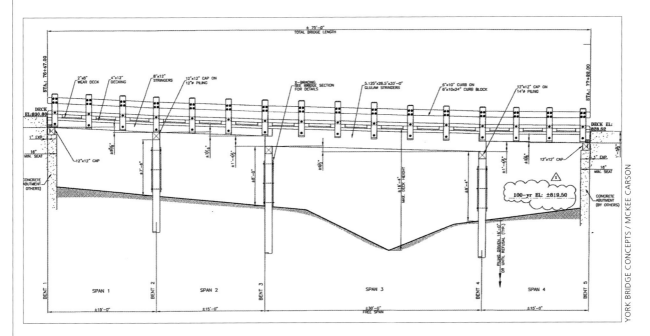

ENVIRONMENTAL CONSULTANTS

Increasing environmental regulation has resulted in substantial growth in specialty environmental consulting for real estate. Nonetheless, two basic types of environmental consultants remain: one, engaged during the feasibility and approvals stage, analyzes the project's ecological, economic, social, and cultural effects on the surrounding built environment; the other, engaged in the design phase, determines strategies and, in conjunction with soils engineers, mitigation for impacts associated with the development. Impacts can range from intrusion on streams or wetlands to increases in traffic, noise, and emissions. Planning and budgeting for environmental consultants require solid understanding of the regulatory process. Land use attorneys and planners are good sources of information, and they should be consulted early. Some aspects of on-site evaluation require long lead times, and some can only be accomplished during certain times of year. Emergent wetlands, for example, might only be identifiable when wetland-associated plants are visible in the spring, and some surveys cannot be conducted in winter. The developer must come up with a sequenced plan for these tasks and understand at what point in the approvals process formal environmental reviews are required.

Environmental reviews are often necessary for development projects of significant size and scope, and they are generally required and administered by state environmental quality agencies. Reviews usually focus on impacts to the immediate surroundings caused by

Engineering plans detail key elements of the infrastructure package for permitting, bids, and construction. Beginning with topographic grading plans, engineering plans may be required for stormwater, roadways and bridges, water and sewer connections, and electrical and data service.

the proposed development, such as increased traffic, reduced air quality or land fragmentation, sunshine and shading, and infrastructure requirements.

The environmental approval process varies widely based on state and local regulations and attitudes. Increasingly, these reviews encompass regional or even global issues, such as the assessment of climate impacts from land use change. Under California's Environmental Quality Act, greenhouse gas emissions must be calculated as a baseline, then specific strategies for reduction must be proposed in the development plan. These reviews are often politically sensitive and require diplomacy and persistence on the developer's part. No developer wants to be perceived as an environmental threat. However, developers should respond to requests clearly and promptly and insist that statutory timelines and requirements are followed; many developers have found that project opponents abuse the environmental review process as a way to delay legitimate and low-impact projects.

The financial outlay, time, patience, and perseverance required to successfully navigate an environmental review and secure final building permits must not be underestimated. The process starts with determinations of jurisdiction. Usually, the local zoning authority leads and requires sign-off from the state and federal authorities that have jurisdiction. Authorities first determine whether the project requires a formal environmental analysis and which tier of study is indicated by the project. This process is triggered if a project exceeds various size or scale thresholds or affects environmentally sensitive areas, such as wetlands or an endangered species' habitat. Empowered by federal legislation, including the National Environmental Policy Act of 1969, each state and locality has created its own environmental laws to which developers must adhere, and these laws vary widely. Early consultation with a land use attorney is essential to understand these risks and the rights of applicants.

Very minor projects with minimal disturbance, such as renovations, may proceed with a simple affidavit asserting compliance with regulations. For substantial development, the least stringent type of required analysis is usually an environmental impact statement (EIS), or an environmental site assessment. A more stringent environmental impact report (EIR), based on state and local legislation, may be ordered when a project is expected to pose substantial alterations to the built or natural environment. Developers are well-advised to analyze the legislation to understand the various thresholds that trigger a partial or full EIR; in some situations a small change to design can eliminate the need for a full EIR. For example, sensitivity analysis can show whether additional density might be worth the time and expense of the necessary additional study.

An EIR not only describes the proposed development, the site, the overall design parameters, and the project's effect on the local community; it also proposes appropriate mitigation measures. Once a draft of the EIR has been prepared, it is submitted to various state and local agencies, circulated to concerned parties, and made available to the general public; each is allowed a specific period to submit comments. These comments may lead to significant design changes; at a minimum they will require some sort of response, usually in writing. At this point, a developer must be extremely careful of making promises or statements beyond the facts at hand.

Thereafter, the developer's environmental consultant must produce a final EIR that responds to all comments. Any mitigation measures recommended by the consultant must be feasible for the developer to implement. Agencies that regulate environmental impacts typically offer multiple methods of mitigation for those impacts and often allow cash payment to a state-administered fund in lieu of specific perfor-

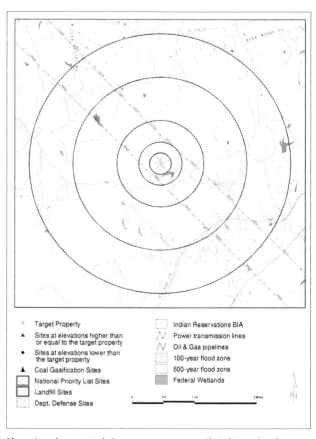

☆ Target Property	▢ Indian Reservations BIA
▲ Sites at elevations higher than or equal to the target property	⋏ Power transmission lines
◆ Sites at elevations lower than the target property	⋏ Oil & Gas pipelines
▲ Coal Gasification Sites	▨ 100-year flood zone
▢ National Priority List Sites	▨ 500-year flood zone
▢ Landfill Sites	▨ Federal Wetlands
▢ Dept. Defense Sites	

Phase I environmental site assessments compile information from public databases, land records, on-site surveys, and interviews to provide an overview of potential environmental issues, such as potential contamination, regulatory jurisdictions, and sensitive features that may warrant additional investigation.

mance. The timing and magnitude of these measures can vary greatly, so the developer must insist on analysis of the potential avenues for mitigation and make an informed decision. Public bodies, usually the planning commission, the city council, or both, generally include mitigation measures in their conditions for project approval, or at least as a condition for the release of completion bonds. These conditions are sometimes referred to as *exactions*, which are burdens placed on the developer to make financial payments or complete on-site and off-site improvements to mitigate the project's environmental effects.

Any change to the development plan requires simultaneous changes to the consultant's analysis and will sometimes require an informal check with regulators to ensure continued compliance with the rules as understood before. A sound development strategy is to secure input from all concerned parties as early as possible, even before submission of the draft EIR, and to incorporate as many of those changes into the proposed design as possible. Regulators, for the most part, understand this strategy, and many are willing to meet informally, before submittals or review, to answer questions and outline the process ahead. Developers should take advantage of such an offer but should be wary of releasing information in a public process before the design is complete. And they must be aware that many regulations include a line like "… and any other information requested by the authority," allowing expansion of original scope. Best practice is to start by discussing the rules, rather than simply presenting the project and asking if it is compliant.

The environmental review process can be a moving target and, if not managed effectively, can lead to skyrocketing development costs and delays that wipe out returns. Because new attitudes and criteria are occasionally added, a jurisdictional determination is only as good as it is recent. For complex urban projects, a developer could even have to change the entire project, including use, height, and overall square footage. As this process unfolds, keeping an eye on the market is important; the time needed to secure permits is independent of economic and market cycles and may cause the developer to miss the market or the financing window altogether.

The cost of hiring an environmental consultant varies according to the size and complexity of the project analysis. Most consultants work on a lump-sum basis, with payment schedules tied to performance milestones. Developers should consider that the contract scope of an environmental consultant likely assumes typical regulatory jurisdiction and action, but environmental regulation is a relatively new field. As Matt Kiefer of Goulston & Storrs says, "We are entering a phase of regulatory experimentation. As the public sector has pulled back from direct involvement [in development], the emphasis has moved to performance-based measures."[17] Compliance with these standards can be notoriously difficult to determine. Surprising regulatory interpretations are to be expected, and they will often result in changes to the scope of the consultant.

The consultant's contractual obligations usually end with the production of the final report, although the developer might additionally require the consultant to make presentations and answer questions from municipal staff or from the public at hearings. The contract with the consultant must be reviewed to determine what is and is not included in the initial scope of responsibilities. Once the contract expires, the con-

sultant's compensation is based on a T&M agreement. Note that, at the point of completion of the contract, the developer will be deeply bound to the consultant because of prior work on behalf of the project, so T&M rates should be negotiated up front.

Developers may need to engage another type of environmental consultant as well, one that specializes in detection, containment, and removal of hazardous materials. Hazardous materials have become a major concern for developers and a significant source of litigation and liability, as well as delays and increased costs for containment and soil removal. Consequently, environmental analysis, including soils analysis, should incorporate tests to determine the presence of toxic materials, particularly heavy metals and known or suspected carcinogens. Ascertaining a property's previous use(s) is important, as particular uses connote the potential presence of different materials. Developers should be aware that brownfield sites with known or perceived contamination are not the only sites that warrant caution. Greenfield sites that appear the picture of cleanliness and health at the time of acquisition may, for example, have supported commercial orchards in the 1930s, when the pesticide of choice was powdered lead arsenate. In this example, the appropriate testing might only be ordered if historic aerial photos have been analyzed.

Environmental reports consist of three phases of analysis. Many lenders require a Phase I analysis for almost any kind of project; it simply involves a title search of previous users to determine the likelihood of toxic contamination. If the Phase I report finds potential contamination from, say, a gas station, dry cleaner, or industrial user, a Phase II report may be required to determine the extent of any perceived problem. Phase II usually includes analyzing soil samples, and it always includes at least a cursory examination of the property for clues to the location and potential extent of any problems. If the Phase II analysis finds possible off-site contamination or a serious threat of contamination of the water table, a Phase III analysis will be required.

Inspection of every development site for the presence of hazardous materials is vital. Liability for any future cleanup falls to any and all parties named on the chain of title and may result in personal recourse to the developer—even if the contamination predated the developer's acquisition of the site. A verdant green landscape does not obviate the issue: beautiful farmland can be seeded with decades of pesticide or fuel contamination. Because hazardous waste contamination can involve millions of dollars in cleanup costs,

Organizing for Development

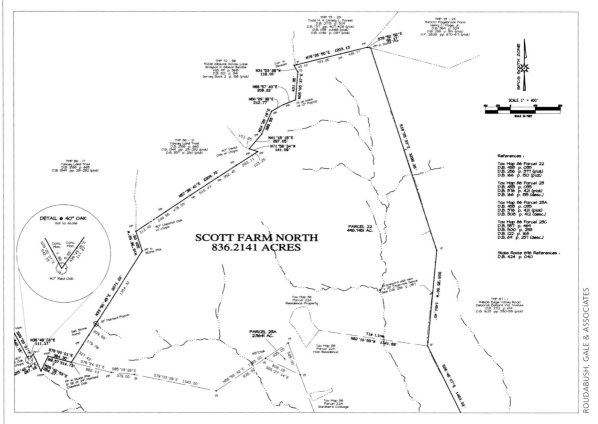

SCOTT FARM NORTH
836.2141 ACRES

PARCEL 22
448.7451 Ac.

PARCEL 23A
23.641 Ac.

years of delay, and potentially expensive litigation, prudent developers perform the necessary environmental analyses, and learn the history of the site, before they acquire a property.

SURVEYORS

Surveyors determine a property's physical and legal characteristics—existing easements, rights-of-way, and dedications on the site—and prepare a site map plotting the characteristics, delineating how much of the site can be built out and the allowable square footage and densities. Surveyors are among the first consultants hired, typically well before nonrefundable money is committed on a purchase. Developers should note that some critical services, such as aerial topographic mapping of slopes, can only be done at specific times of the year.

Developers commonly use four types of survey services: *boundary survey*, *construction survey*, *construction stakeout*, and *as-built survey*. The boundary survey determines the boundaries of the site (easements and other legal requirements affect ownership of the property being plotted on a map). The construction survey plots the location of relevant infrastructure—water, sewers, electricity, gas lines, and roads—to assist in planning connections to utility services and

The survey precisely locates property lines, physical and topographic features, and important legal aspects, such as easements, setbacks, and tax parcels. Every design and sales document refers to the geometry and legal research done in the survey phase.

physical characteristics related to development, such as flood zones, watershed areas, and existing improvements. Surveyors also augment the work completed by soils engineers, analyzing a site's topography, likely runoff and slope, and the implications for civil engineering of the building's proposed location. The surveyor will typically return once the project design is complete to perform a construction stakeout, which involves physically setting out annotated stakes that will direct the grading, excavation, and paving crews in construction. The precision of the construction staking directly affects the quality of construction on site. Finally, when all major construction is complete, a surveyor may be brought back to the site for an as-built survey. Approval authorities often require as-built drawings, which precisely indicate building corners, utility locations, public and private roadways, and drainage improvements critical to off-site uses.

The American Land Title Association (ALTA) has defined standard survey types for various kinds of real estate transactions. Developers should find out early which level of survey will be required by their lender and buyers and commit to at least that level of detail. An ALTA survey can cost three to four times as much as a simple property-line survey, but it may be required by lenders. In addition, municipal, state, and federal regulators may require differing levels of survey accuracy, particularly in topographic surveys. Developers should inquire about these requirements and contract for the most stringent that will be required by any agency during the development period.

Surveyors may work on a lump-sum contract, but most projects will require some T&M agreement for later work as needed. Generally, someone who has surveyed the property in the past will be faster and less expensive because they have baseline work. Even if the previous firm is out of business, its surveys may still be available: many retiring surveyors convey their work to other firms for follow-on work. On simple projects, surveyors perform many land planning functions, proposing and documenting divisions, setbacks, and development zones.

PARKING AND TRAFFIC CONSULTANTS

Parking and traffic capacity are often major limiting factors for real estate development. High land values and restrictive local parking ordinances require a well-devised parking plan. A qualified parking consultant considers all the significant factors involved in designing the optimum parking for the site. The parking consultant should be included early in the design process so that the architect can incorporate parking recommendations in the overall design.

Parking consultants may be responsible for many aspects of a project: (a) evaluating the economics of a surface lot versus a parking structure, (b) designing an efficient parking configuration, (c) discovering whether local municipal codes can accommodate the estimated parking demand, (d) determining whether parking should be provided free or at a fee, and (e) deciding where the points of ingress and egress will be.

Parking is an expensive undertaking, costing tens of thousands per space for a structured garage, and many jurisdictions are implementing substantial changes in their parking requirements. Many municipalities are finding ways to reduce or waive parking requirements to promote walkability and housing density in some districts. Consequently, the services of a well-qualified and local consultant are often essential to project economics. Referrals from the architect and other developers can provide a list of potential con-

sultants, but regulators' trust is the key issue. Public officials must be confident that the proposed solution will not generate unmanageable off-site impacts. Parking consultants usually work under a lump-sum contract or at an hourly rate.

Traffic consultants are included here because their firms' capabilities often include parking consultation, but the range of issues they can address is much wider. Traffic studies, for example, are commonly required in the EIR process. In many jurisdictions, the developer must prove that the proposed development is adequately served by existing roads and transit; inadequate infrastructure is a prime justification for delay and denial by approval authorities. Increasingly, trip generation is being included in environmental impact review, with a preference for walkability and housing/job colocation.

While developers usually prefer to have the lowest number of parking places possible to reduce costs, lenders, marketing consultants, and brokers want to be sure the parking is sufficient to attract tenants. Unknown future requirements might warrant extra investment in "future-proofing." Providing parking that can be converted to other uses is costly, but it is an increasingly attractive option, as is providing a sufficient number of electric charging stations to accommodate future demand.

ASBESTOS ABATEMENT PROFESSIONALS

Renovation or adaptive use of a building constructed between 1920 and 1976 is likely to uncover asbestos contamination. Pricing for abatement is competitive in major construction markets. The industry has developed efficient methods of service delivery, and the amount of asbestos requiring removal is declining. Asbestos was commonly used for fireproofing and insulation in the United States until 1973, when federal legislation prohibited its future use for those purposes. Asbestos is found in pipe and duct insulation, but it can also be an additive in materials such as shingles, making it hard to detect. Because it is most dangerous when disturbed, the U.S. Environmental Protection Agency closely regulates activities, such as demolition, that could release asbestos into the air. The reconfiguration of interior spaces may also require some form of asbestos abatement, with associated expense.

Asbestos removal requires the services of qualified professionals and permits for disposal; the hazards inherent in abatement could lead to legal repercussions if inexperienced firms are hired. Asbestos abatement occurs in two stages: inspection and removal.

Inspectors should be state-licensed, and abatement firms should be bonded. Consultants charge by the hour or by the square foot. Surveys for a typical 20,000-square-foot (1,860 sq m) building, for example, might be priced around $5,000 for the physical inspection. Costs can escalate rapidly if work must be done in an occupied structure, with isolation measures to protect adjacent spaces.[18]

CONSTRUCTION CONTRACTORS

Construction contractors are required to complete an array of services (both before and during construction) on time and, ideally, on budget. They can provide a reality check on such critical matters as construction materials, structural and architectural design, local construction practices, and pricing information and can help establish a realistic budget when brought in early on a project.

Developers can select a contractor through negotiations with a particular firm or through open bidding. To find a good contractor, developers should solicit several contracting firms, asking them to submit proposals or general statements of qualifications. Responses should include descriptions of past projects, references from clients and lenders, résumés outlining the experience of key employees (particularly the proposed project engineer or manager), and, possibly, verification that the company is bondable. Payment histories from business credit-reporting agencies, such as Paydex, and audited financial statements should also be reviewed. These submissions can be used to select a company for direct negotiation.

In open bidding, developers send out a notice requesting bids and statements of qualifications. The problem with this approach is that contractors are reluctant to spend time bidding on a project unless they think they have a good chance of being selected. As a result, the developer may not attract an adequate number of responses from which to choose, especially if the developer is new to the business and proposing a relatively small project in a hot market. Even in slow markets, contractors will need two to four weeks to return satisfactory responses. A comprehensive bid on a complex project will take longer, but the time can be accelerated by involving likely bidders as the project goes through design.

The most effective way to limit the number of bidders but still ensure that the targeted firms will respond is a combination of a request for qualifications (RFQ) and competitive bidding. After reviewing several contractors' qualifications, developers may ask the best three, four, or five contractors to prepare a bid for the project. A preference for one contractor could result in direct negotiations with a particular firm. Developers should not feel obligated to conduct protracted bidding if they have already found the best contractor for the job. Developers who wish to continue working in a market must respect the time of major contractors. Contractors should not be brought into a bidding process in which they have no chance of success, simply to "keep the other guy honest."

Jonathan Rose, principal of Jonathan Rose Companies, suggests keeping in mind three points when choosing contractors:[19]

1. Find someone who is experienced in the product type being considered for the project. A specialist in assisted-living facilities will likely not be an appropriate choice for multifamily housing.

2. Be certain that your project amounts to no more than one-third of the contracting firm's total workload, a good benchmark for organizational and financial stability. That is, if you have a $20 million project, look for a contractor with at least $60 million in total business at the time the contract is signed.

3. Ask for and check references to understand how the contractor has performed for past clients.

During the design stage, a contractor working for fees or a construction price estimator (also called a *quantity surveyor*) should check the architect's drawings and formulate an estimated budget for completing the project. A permanent contractor, once hired, is responsible for completing a construction cost estimate based on the architect's completed construction drawings. If the developer chooses to put the project on a fast track, the contractor should be a helpful source of creative and cost-effective suggestions during preliminary design.

One of the contractor's tasks is to set up a projected schedule for disbursing loans, which should be coordinated with and agreed to by the construction lender. The contractor's major responsibility, however, is the project's physical construction. The tasks include soliciting bids from and then hiring all the subcontractors—construction workers, plumbers, painters, and electrical and mechanical contractors. The contractor is legally responsible for building a safe structure and must hire the best-qualified employees and subcontractors for the job.

Two basic methods are used to determine the

contractor's compensation: bids, typically in the form of a lump sum, or some derivative of a cost-plus-fee contract. A lump-sum bid is more common when the design is already established and the construction drawings are completed before the contractor is selected. This option is rarely feasible for beginning developers, however, because they are probably not willing or able to underwrite the cost of complete drawings until the decision to construct is finalized.

Contractors' fees are based on the size of the project, the number and amount of anticipated change orders, and so on. On a $10 million project, a contractor would be expected to charge a fee equivalent to 5 percent of total *hard costs* (costs of installed construction, not excluding design and consulting fees) in addition to project overhead and on-site supervision costs. On smaller jobs, a 12 to 15 percent *overhead-and-profit* share is common.

A cost-plus-fee contract is a preferable means of compensating experienced contractors with excellent reputations. Under this option, all costs—labor, salaries of accountants and other such employees, travel, construction materials, supplies, equipment, and fees for all subcontractors—should be explicitly set forth in the contract. The costs should not include overhead and administrative expenses for the contractor's main or branch offices, and they should not include full costs for assets that are used only partially for the job being bid. Costs that cannot be accurately estimated before contract should be negotiated on a unit basis, such as price per cubic yard of fill, leaving only the quantity to be accurately recorded during construction.

The contractor must calculate the time required to complete the project as a basis for a fixed or percentage fee. Most developers avoid a percentage fee because it does not incentivize the contractor to minimize costs, but these concerns can also be addressed with performance bonuses.

Often, the construction lender requires the contractor to guarantee a maximum cost, or gross maximum price, when the cost-plus-fee method is used. In such cases, the architect is responsible for providing drawings with sufficient detail to allow the contractor to solicit quotes from subcontractors to calculate the maximum cost. Guaranteed maximum cost contracts can include an incentive to save costs; perhaps 25 to 50 percent of the developer's savings could be shared with the contractor if total project costs are less than the guaranteed maximum. Another model splits the contingency fee; that is, the developer and the contractor split every dollar saved under budgeted costs, which

CORNERSTONE HOMES

As sales proceed, new construction phases and amenity projects are begun in individual neighborhoods to limit capital at risk and to limit construction impacts on existing residents.

could amount to 5 to 10 percent of a project's costs.[20]

If a bonus is to be paid, the developer must make sure that the contractor does not sacrifice quality to receive the bonus. Maintaining high quality is accomplished by detailed attention to project specifications and construction documents. Other types of incentive bonuses can also save costs. A bonus for early completion pays a defined amount for completing the work by a specific date; some contracts pay a fixed amount for each day that work is completed before the deadline. By the same token, bonus clauses can be used to penalize the contractor for being late. Some contracts include a liquidated damage clause or a penalty clause to cover late completion. Not surprisingly, contractors dislike such clauses, which, they argue, undermine teamwork.

Bonus and incentive clauses are a tool for guaranteeing the contractor's performance, but they must be clear about how to handle prerequisite work that is late, timely provision of key information, and weather and other uncontrollable factors. The developer incurs costs, however, most notably in the necessary monitoring of the contractor's performance.

Real Estate Service Firms

A variety of service firms can provide a wide range of real estate services that are critical in the development process. These firms are usually brought into a project to perform specific, short-term tasks.

MARKET CONSULTANTS

Successful real estate decisions hinge on the availability of reliable and accurate information. A market consultant provides a professional assessment of the proposed project's appeal to various quantifiable groups or types of buyers and tenants. The deliverable, the *market study*, analyzes the proposed project's feasibility based on current and projected market conditions. Lenders, investors, design professionals, and sales staff all use the market study at various points in the development process.

Some developers complete their own market studies, and lenders may accept a well-documented study by a developer, particularly for a small project. But a third-party perspective on the market from a professional market analyst is always worthwhile. One of the most important decisions made during the predevelopment period is which market consultant to hire. Developers may ask other developers for recommendations; however, lenders' recommendations are particularly important because their decisions depend on the market data proving the project's feasibility. Although a few national consulting firms offer real estate market studies, market intelligence is a highly localized business. Developers in a well-documented geographic area who work with a common product—bought, sold, or leased frequently—may be well served by a nationally known firm. For niche products, in secondary markets, local knowledge is irreplaceable.

"Real estate hasn't been data driven, but instinct and local-knowledge driven," says data scientist James Chung. "But in the last year we've gone from a few startups to hundreds of data scientists looking at real estate, and major investors increasingly demand data analytics." With rapidly increasing preference and mobility data, the application of machine learning to market analysis is becoming an important subspecialty.[21]

The market consultant's databases are useful indicators of the consultant's approach. Aside from being technically proficient, the consultant must be able to understand the subtle nuances of the market that may not be readily apparent. A good market consultant can identify the proposed competition and thoughtfully analyze the political situation.

Developers should ask to see several market studies that the consultant has produced and make sure that they are comfortable with the assumptions and techniques used. The style of writing and presentation of the report should be carefully examined as well, as the material will be presented to investors, lenders, and marketing staff.

The market consultant is responsible for producing a final study that addresses all factors affecting the proposed project's feasibility. As a client, the smart developer looks for a comprehensive study that provides independent evidence about the marketability of the development proposal. (The specific features of the process for various property types are discussed in the appropriate sections of chapters 3 through 7.)

The study should include a profile of tenants or buyers to be targeted and the amenities and lease terms to be offered. Many marketing professionals define these target groups in "psychographic" terms, defined by preferences and attitudes, rather than simply demographic and income criteria. As such, a well-conceived market study may go beyond identifying the buyer and begin to suggest ways of reaching, vetting, and converting leads to sales. The architect should use the market information to help determine the project's design, unit sizes, amenities, and so on to appropriately address the market.

After the feasibility and business-planning phase, a good market study provides a foundation for sales and marketing decisions and can be particularly useful when multiple brokers or sales agents must cooperate on a single project. The market study can provide the framework for a sales narrative about the project, its neighborhood, and qualitative aspects of the project's "lifestyle."

A market consultant's fee is based on the level of detail that the developer requests. Preliminary information may be obtained for less than $5,000, while a detailed report may cost $25,000 to $100,000 or more, depending on the complexity of the study. For a preliminary analysis or a quick inventory of the market, the consultant may work on an hourly basis, but larger, more complex studies require a fixed contract.

APPRAISERS

The appraisal report should state the property's market value and offer supporting evidence. Three methodologies can be used to complete an appraisal: the *income approach*, *market approach*, and *cost approach*. The income approach is preferred for all income-producing property (commercial, industrial, office, and rental apartments). Value is determined by dividing the project's net operating income by an appropriate capitalization rate. Value depends on the definition of net income used, so investors must be clear on what is included. The market approach uses recent information about sales of comparable properties to determine a market value. This approach is used most often with single-family residential properties, condominiums, and land. The cost approach estimates the cost to construct a project similar to the one under consideration. It is used to determine the value of recently completed buildings or of buildings without a deep and liquid market, such as specialized industrial facilities.

Banks rely on competent appraisals to set loan terms and leverage, so appraisers should carry an MAI (Member, Appraisal Institute) credential or other certifications. They should produce a legible, standardized report, for which they may charge from $2,000 for a detached home to $10,000 or more for commercial buildings.

ATTORNEYS

Many facets of real estate development—taxes, land use, leases, and joint venture partnerships, for example—require separate legal specialists. No single attorney can be an expert in all these areas. For zoning and other activities involving public hearings, an attorney with a proven success rate in cases involving a particular public body might be the proper choice. The ability to work behind the scenes with the local planning staff and politicians may be an attorney's greatest asset in such cases, getting straight answers on the application of complex and intersecting rules. Developers of the type of project under consideration can often recommend good land use attorneys.

Attorneys are essential for producing partnership or syndication agreements and contracts for consultants, acquiring property, writing up loan documents and leasing contracts, and negotiating the public approval process. The process of obtaining public approvals can be an intimidating maze for a beginning developer without an experienced attorney and may lead to costly delays or outright rejection.

Attorneys generally bill clients by the hour, although fixed prices for certain transactions are not uncommon. The developer should obtain an estimate of the total cost for a job before authorizing it and should reach an understanding early on about what constitutes "approval" for work done on the developer's behalf. Developers who are not lawyers themselves must also admit that they do not necessarily know how long certain tasks will take, and they must be open with their attorney about their fee expectations.

Leonard Zax of Latham & Watkins real estate group, gives the following tips for getting the best work from one's attorneys:[22]

- The development firm's general counsel is the best person to ensure legal continuity for a project. Without a general counsel, overlap among attorneys' responsibilities can cause gaps and allow details to slip through.
- Attorneys should clearly distinguish between legal advice and business comment.
- Developers need to understand the context in which their legal counsel is operating, for example, knowing what other matters the attorneys have before public bodies that have influence over the developer's project.
- The most effective lawyer is not always the tough table pounder and doesn't always agree with the developer. The most effective lawyer takes time to listen and formulate a candid opinion of the legal elements that need to be addressed.
- Developers should have patience and listen to their attorney's advice.

TITLE COMPANIES

Title companies certify who holds title to a property and guarantee the purchaser and lender that the property is free and clear of unexpected liens that may cloud the title. Title companies will defend any future claims against properties that they insure. The type of title policy determines the extent of the protection. Most policies follow a standard format, but many real estate investors fail to read and understand what protection their title policy provides, and to whom. That failure can lead to problems if claims are asserted after closing and costly litigation ensues.

When selecting a title company, developers should make sure that the company has the financial strength to back any potential claims—they are rated like other insurance companies—and should research its record to find out how long a company takes to obtain a clean title.

Title companies often provide additional services. They provide, free of charge, both current and potential customers with a profile of a property in which the customer is interested. The profile details ownership, property taxes paid, liens, easements, size of lot and improvements, grant and trust deeds, notes, and most recent sale price. Title companies also provide local data, such as comparable sales information and plat maps.

A preliminary title report can be prepared for a fee. This preliminary document is not an insurance policy, but it is a close reading of the existing title, which highlights potential problems a future owner may need to clear before title is transferred. Standard title policies do not usually cover material that does not appear in public records (e.g., family members' interests in property, which have not been recorded but which might be asserted by statute). An ALTA policy offers extended coverage that does cover such unrecorded claims; it requires the kind of in-depth survey that commercial purchasers usually demand.

Title fees can be obtained from any representative of the company and are usually applicable statewide. They are commonly quoted on a scale that slides according to the sale price of the property being insured. More often than not, the seller pays for title insurance, though terms of the purchase and sale agreement can address this question directly. Costs associated with ALTA title insurance vary but are nationally competitive and are usually under $1 per $1,000 of asset value.

SURETY COMPANIES

Developers need insurance to guard against a consultant's or contractor's failure to perform an agreed-upon task, and municipalities often require similar guarantees for a developer's performance in completing promised improvements. Such a failure may have serious economic and legal consequences for the development project, and potentially for the community. For instance, a contractor's failure to meet obligations could result in a lien on the property, delaying if not stopping sales altogether. All public works projects must, by law, be bonded for performance because liens cannot be placed on public property. Most private projects include some form of bond, and bonding of infrastructure can allow developers greater flexibility in constructing improvements at a pace consistent with sales. Attorneys can clarify whether, in a given jurisdiction, bonding is required or advisable. Contractors are generally required to be *bondable*, meaning they qualify for surety coverage appropriate to the amount of their contracts.

General contractors deal directly with a surety company to obtain performance and payment bonds. The developer must inform all contractors that bonds will be required before bids are submitted, and contractors pass their bonding costs through in their bids. A surety bond is a three-party contract in which a surety company joins with a principal, usually the contractor, in guaranteeing the specific performance of an act to the developer or municipality, also referred to as the *beneficiary*.

The three main types of bonds are *performance*, *payment*, and *completion*. Performance bonds guarantee the developer that if the contractor fails to complete the agreed-upon contract, the surety is responsi-

ble for seeing that the work is finished. The agreement allows the surety to compensate the developer with an amount equal to the money needed to complete the project or to hire a contractor to finish the job. Lenders sometimes insist on bond coverage for their own protection. The general contractor, either at the developer's request or on its own, requires subcontractors to purchase performance bonds and may be requested to provide evidence of this bonding to the client.

Payment bonds guarantee that the surety will meet obligations if the contractor defaults on payments to laborers, subcontractors, or suppliers, protecting the property against liens that might be imposed in response to nonpayment. Developers, lenders, or both often require the general contractor to purchase these bonds to protect them against any future claims of nonpayment made by subcontractors or suppliers. Payment bonds are usually issued concurrently with performance bonds; both bonds often appear on the same form.

Completion bonds, often referred to as *developer off-site* or *subdivision bonds*, ensure local municipalities that specified infrastructural improvements will be completed. Many states require local municipalities to secure the bonds as assurance that the developer will complete the improvements. Bonding expensive infrastructure, rather than accelerating construction timelines ahead of sales, can greatly improve project cash flow as phases are released.

In most states, surety companies must charge uniform rates. For performance and payment bonds, the rate charged is the same regardless of whether 50 or 100 percent of the contract price is guaranteed; therefore, developers should ask for 100 percent coverage. Rates are based on the contract price and are calculated on a graduated payment scale. The rates for completion bonds are generally higher because they involve additional underwriting, but they may be quite low when negotiated across multiple projects with an established development partner.

Opinion is divided about the need to secure the various forms of surety bonds. Performance and payment bonds cost roughly 1 percent of the construction costs, so it is up to the developer to decide whether or not bonding is worth the abated risk.

BROKERS/LEASING AGENTS

Real estate brokers and leasing agents are hired to sell or lease a project to prospective tenants and buyers. Developers can benefit greatly from the services of a skilled salesperson who is able to quickly and completely lease or sell a project at or near the pro forma pricing. Developers must decide whether to sign an agreement with an outside real estate broker or to place an agent on the payroll. The decision usually depends on the type and magnitude of the project. Building in-house sales is a major investment, which is usually only recouped over a large volume of sales, or over multiple projects. The return on this investment is not primarily a savings of commissions, but more control over telling the story and negotiating sales.

Retaining outside brokers with local knowledge may be a more sustainable option for small development firms. Brokers are usually aware of potential tenants with existing leases that are about to expire; brokers from large brokerage houses may have information about regional or national tenants. In residential and resort sales, a regional or national firm may have relevant experience selling similar products in other markets and may offer creative ways to approach out-of-town relocation buyers.

An essential step is to interview representatives from several firms. The goal is to find one with relevant experience and without conflicts due to competitive listings. The working relationship between developer and broker is defined in a contract referred to as a *listing agreement*. Under an open listing agreement, the developer may recruit several brokers but pays a commission only to the one who sells or leases the property. If the developer completes a transaction without the broker's assistance, no commission is necessary. An exclusive listing agreement involves, as the name suggests, a single broker.

The most common form of agreement for developers is an *exclusive right-to-sell listing*, in which the developer selects one broker, who automatically receives the commission no matter who sells the property, including the developer. If another broker brings a buyer to the listing broker's property, the two of them are usually responsible for negotiating a split of the commission. To prevent conflicts that might scuttle sales, developers may wish to specify the split in the listing agreement. Predictability and fair treatment are essential. Brokers must spend substantial and uncompensated time learning about properties, with hopes of someday being compensated by matching a buyer to the product. Respect for brokers' time and business needs is important and so is listening to their input on early design and marketing decisions. Brokers bring buyers to projects they admire and business to people they respect.

In leasing, the broker's responsibility is to negotiate leases with prospects while keeping in mind the devel-

FIGURE 2-2 Typical Real Estate Sales Commissions

Product type	Percentage of total price
Raw land	5–10
Single-family houses	3–6
Apartment building	3–6
Office building	3–7
Industrial building	4–6
Shopping center	4–6
Hotels	3–6

FIGURE 2-3 Typical Lease Commissions
(Percentages by Year)

Property type	1	2	3	4	5	6–10	10+
Shopping center	6	5	4	4	3	3	3
Office building	6	5	4	4	3	3	3
Industrial building	5	4	3	2	1	1	1

Note: Sales and lease commissions are subject to negotiation and vary widely depending on location, market conditions, type of lease, and property value. Typically, percentages are lower for large assets.

oper's goals regarding rates of return and preferred type of tenant. The developer should establish lease guidelines for the broker to follow and should readily accept leases presented by the broker within those guidelines to maintain credibility with the brokerage community. Once the project is leased, the developer may retain the broker to lease space as it becomes available.

Real estate brokers work almost exclusively for commission. The broker and the developer negotiate the rate of compensation, which varies according to the type, size, and geographic location of the project, and is typically based on a percentage of the total price for sales (see figure 2-2).

Lease commissions payable to the broker are calculated as an annual percentage of the value of a signed lease for each year of the lease. Over the term of the lease, the percentages paid to the broker are scaled down (see figure 2-3). Half the aggregate commission is typically paid upon execution of the lease and half is paid at move-in.

The developer should negotiate a schedule for commissions that will provide incentives to lease or sell the building as quickly as possible—for example, by providing higher commission rates or bonuses for tours and contracts early in the project to gain momentum.

PUBLIC RELATIONS AND ADVERTISING AGENCIES

Promotion spreads the word about the project to the community and differentiates it from the competition in the minds of potential users. Developers often neglect promotion, hoping that the project will sell itself. Although the best press is editorial, not paid, leaving public relations to chance is a mistake. Nowadays, as many first impressions are gained online, through platforms with their own algorithms and norms, expertise has become more valuable to developers who want their product or brand to stand out.

Public relations firms not only produce news releases, press kits, newsletters, and personal communications conveying information about the project but also can create opportunities for the project to gain positive exposure in the community. Different projects and product types require custom approaches to attract interest from potential buyers, builders, and end-users, and the agency chooses the tools that are most appropriate for a given project. The agency should also have creative ideas to market the project effectively, and it should be involved as early as possible in the conceptual design phase. Aesthetic and programmatic choices, typically made to satisfy concrete demand illustrated in market studies, may also have implications for the project's branding and identity. Simple and inexpensive choices like street names, palette, and landscape, as well as amenity location and types can also be important to advertising strategy, and the input of professionals with these concerns in mind can be invaluable.

Public relations and advertising services are often bundled in one firm, but clients can and should unbundle them if one side is the true competency of the group. Marketing plans may include print publications, broadcast media, and outdoor signs, but most real estate developments receive the majority of inbound traffic via real estate apps, direct internet searches, and social media. Project marketing investments have followed the traffic, so for most categories, developers target 90 percent or more of their budget to online platforms or digital communications. Paid internet search is still a cost-effective way of gathering potential buyers and tenants, but the key benefits of all digital methods are actually prequalification, priming, and segmentation of leads. Marketing professionals can know very early whether potential clients can afford the purchase, how far along they are in the process, and which leads might respond to different types of appeal. Sales teams are now armed with much more

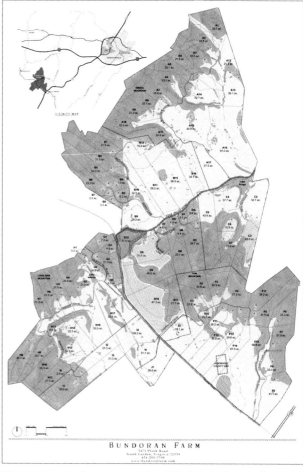

Watercolor renderings or expressive digital methods can refine the site plan for clarity and visual appeal, making the plan usable at different scales, for communications ranging from approvals to marketing.

information about leads, even before personal contact is initiated.

Both content and methods of communication about a project may benefit from demographic research, which may be its own subspecialty. Helen Foster of Foster Strategy notes that "ideas like wellness and health, that appear in communications, connect differently with age cohorts and regional differences"; they need to be shaped in early partnership with the design team to be effective later in sales.[23]

SPECIALTY PUBLIC RELATIONS AND MARKETING

New media platforms, as well as changing demographics and political values, have driven the development of several subspecialties in public relations and marketing. While a traditional agency usually takes the lead, development teams may now include specialists in some phase or aspect of the project. "Creating an early sense of community, unfolding stories about a place," is key, says Stuart Rosenberg, director of Public Content.[24] The flexibility of digital work means that, in some cases, these team members are able to work remotely.

At the very first stage of feasibility, the traditional knowledge of the real estate agent or consultancy is at work, keeping tabs on the strength of various neighborhoods, product types, and buyers or tenants. Often, that effort is being supplemented by more advanced data science. The firms providing this information are not necessarily local, but they have invested in large data sets and, sometimes, predictive algorithms to make quantitative judgments about trends and needs in real estate markets. In the early stages of commercialization, these firms offer a supplemental view of real estate as one of many commercial transactions that can be tracked and analyzed.

In the design and approvals phases, increased deference to neighborhood and environmental stakeholders has prompted many development teams to take on a separate consultant, under the umbrella of public relations, to manage predesign community outreach. In a community concerned about gentrification, for example, the consultant might arrange community meetings and interactions with the design team via software and direct communication to address concerns, tailor the project to the site, tell the story, and get to the approval process with allies rather than opponents. Sandra Kulli of Kulli Marketing describes this strategy as creating "collective effervescence," developing human relationships to reach and understand stakeholders.[25]

The swirl of digital communication in the sales and leasing space has, surprisingly, made in-person events and programming even more important. Some developers contract with consultants to program new developments, such as workspaces and apartment buildings, with food, culture, education, and entertainment. This extended version of a "launch party" can last for the duration of lease-up and fold into the operational plan of the property. For most agencies, the investment in time and networking to create "buzz" around a new property, using events to drive social media, driving more events and visits, requires a dedicated specialist.[26]

Charles Adams of Thrivemore Advisors concludes that "jaded millennials and bombarded eyeballs

Marketing graphics simplify the plan and enhance legibility with color, text, and callouts to highlight key features of the project for use in sales and marketing, to accompany tours and sales presentations.

Healthy living comes naturally with over 73 acres of farmland, wooded preserves and green space.

The Barn
A working barn with a seriously playful side, this signature amenity will feature a professional demonstration kitchen and indoor/outdoor gathering spaces designed for neighborhood socials and private parties.

Woodside Farms
The 10-acre heart and soul of the community, this four-season, professionally managed farm will grow a curated mix of fruits, vegetables, herbs and flowers selected for their health and wellness benefits for people 55 and better.

Walking & Biking Trails
Staying active is easy with miles of trails and outdoor fitness stations winding throughout the community and alongside the Chickahominy River.

Demonstration Kitchen
Local chefs, caterers, and of course, Chickahominy Falls' own homeowners will love using this professionally curated space to host farm-to-fork cooking demonstrations, happy hours and more.

Fishing Pond
From the Chickahominy River to the community pond, water adds a splash of tranquility to this vibrant, farm-inspired community. Great moments and memories await around every corner.

The Clubhouse & Pool
This 5-star amenity overlooking manicured lawns and the pond will feature shaded decks and patios, a fire pit, swimming pool, fitness center, game room, library, entertaining kitchen, bar and so much more.

– HANOVER COUNTY –
chickahominy falls

Woodside Meadows
Carriage Homes By Cornerstone Homes
SOLD OUT!

River Falls
Carriage Homes By Cornerstone Homes

The Farmstead
Villa Homes By Cornerstone Homes

The Orchard
Cottage Homes By StyleCraft Homes
SOLD OUT!

Little Meadows
Custom Carriage Homes By Boone Homes

Upton Woods
Townhomes By StyleCraft Homes
SOLD OUT!

*All renderings are for illustrative purposes and are subject to change without notice.

CORNERSTONE HOMES

FIGURE 2-4 Developing a Marketing Strategy

- Market Analysis — Before Going Hard / Before Land Closing
- Target Analysis
- Marketing Strategy
  - Leasing
  - Market Analysis
  - Advertising
  - Merchandising
  - Brochures
  - Public Relations
  - Property Management Personnel
  - Leasing Personnel

require new approaches to penetrate."[27] With Deven Spear of Overabove, he has invested in "branded content"—essentially sponsored film productions. For example, a short film about farming, "signal-boosted by influencers," is appealing enough to spread widely for purely entertainment or information value, but it links back to a farm-lifestyle development concept. Bringing these sorts of customized new-media products into a marketing plan requires expertise in the systems that spread digital content, a concept far more complicated than choosing magazines based on their circulation.

Regardless of how many entities make up the team, assembling a comprehensive marketing and public relations plan, with the developer's input, is essential and should occur early in the project, preferably at least a year before sales or leasing begin (see figure 2-4). Advertising and public relations firms, as well as associated professionals in digital media, generally work on monthly retainers plus expenses to cover radio, television, online, newspaper, billboard, and magazine advertising.

PROPERTY MANAGEMENT

Following construction and lease-up, the developer's outlook shifts from visionary to operational, focusing squarely on maximizing value at the time of sale. The two overriding goals are to maintain rental rates and high occupancy rates. As such, this phase of the project calls for sustained property management.

Property management can be handled by in-house staff or through a skilled outside service provider. The decision rests squarely on the development firm's internal organizational skills, whether property management can be a profit center, the amount of time the activity will command, and the opportunity costs inherent in managing this activity as opposed to pursuing other revenue opportunities. Each situation is unique, and the developer should reflect on the overall vision for the company and how it meshes with this activity. Keeping property management in-house provides certain advantages:

- direct property oversight and quality control;
- granular knowledge of operational cost and efficiency;
- constant tenant contact;
- a diversified organizational revenue stream that can be a side business; and
- insight into changing tenant operational and maintenance issues, which can lead to future development opportunities and higher project quality.

But in-house property management also has some disadvantages:

- Time cost may be high compared with other revenue-producing activities.
- Organizational skills, staffing, and experience with the property type are limiting factors.
- Economies of scale place smaller developers at a competitive disadvantage compared with professional property management firms.
- Property management can end up becoming a cost center as opposed to a profit center.

The manager should provide a comprehensive short-, medium-, and long-range strategic plan for the property, specifying the frequency of physical inspections, maintenance needs, and a replacement schedule. Developers should insist that these schedules be outlined during building commissioning and turnover. This plan is particularly important for large capital expenditures, such as roof maintenance and replacement, HVAC systems, and other physical and structural issues. In certain projects with repeated units, even very small expenditures, such as window washing, can add up and severely affect cash flow. Budgeting and planning for the year ahead will reduce unforeseen operating costs and diminish the likelihood of emergency repairs. As frontline personnel, property managers need training to address all aspects of the developer's relationship with tenants. Initially, managers should supervise the tenant improvement and move-in processes, making sure everything proceeds smoothly. Ensuring that tenant relationships start off on a high note is important. A clear understanding of what tenants should expect—including priorities such as diversity and inclusion initiatives, energy or environmental priorities, specific training for building staff—is helpful up front.

Effective managers maintain communication with tenants so that any problems can be quickly resolved with a high degree of customer satisfaction. The manager must keep in mind that the developer's reputation is at stake; complaints from tenants directly to the developer are a signal that the property manager is not performing effectively.

Some contracts call for the property manager to also serve as the leasing agent. This arrangement can be beneficial, as the management firm has the most intimate relationship with the property. A property with a large number of vacancies, however, may need a more aggressive leasing strategy or the expertise of a leasing broker with broader market knowledge. Each situation is unique, and the developer must decide who is more capable of filling vacancies that arise. High turnover rates are a sign that something—physical, managerial, or both—is amiss, and the developer should take action to determine the causes and remedies.

Operations run more smoothly when the management company is authorized to sign contracts within agreed-upon parameters, to release budgeted funds for scheduled maintenance, and to implement capital improvements when required to meet operational guidelines. The agreement between developer and property manager should specify dollar limits on what the manager can spend before the owner's approval is required, with the owner's approval necessitated in all instances of projected capital expenditures.

For tax, audit, and tracking purposes, funds belonging to the property owner and to the management entity should be maintained in separate accounts. The management firm should set up a trust account to protect the owner's funds and to prevent any commingling of funds between properties and entities. Audit reports should be prepared regularly (twice a year is recommended) so the developer can verify rental collections, deposits, occupancies, vacancies, management expenses, and capital expenditures.

Property management services are generally priced as a percentage of the property's gross revenue. Very high-end residential units with concierge services are an exception, where the fee might be a fixed dollar amount per unit. Property managers typically negotiate a fee ranging from 1 to 5 percent of gross revenue. The fee is predicated on the amount of management activity and degree of difficulty the project presents. When comparing bids from management firms, the developer should be careful to determine which costs are included in the fee and which are additional billable expenses to the property (management and maintenance salaries are most notable). This fee does not include maintenance labor and material costs provided by outside vendors.

Some management firms offer to perform property management at break-even cost or at a loss in exchange for securing the right to all potential leasing or sales fees generated by the project. And some brokerage firms offer management services. Developers should proceed cautiously. The two services require different skill sets, and developing scale and efficiency in either business is easier than in the two combined.

Most larger developers manage their own properties through dedicated in-house staff or a wholly owned subsidiary, which may do custom work for other property owners for a fee. Beginning developers generally choose to use an outside source. Property management represents an enormous commitment of human resources to the project, and many management tasks become profitable only when personnel, equipment, and purchasing can be amortized over multiple properties.

The third-party property management firm should be evaluated on the basis of its experience with the type of project under consideration. A careful evaluation will examine a list of all properties under its management, a client contact list, and the résumés of staff assigned to the project. Visits (preferably unannounced) to representative properties currently under management can provide a sense of maintenance quality, staffing, and overall tenant satisfaction. An additional selection criterion is the buying power of the management firm, which generally is a function of its size: larger firms can purchase services less expensively by employing economies of scale, leading to lower operating costs.

A good source for locating a third-party property management firm is the local chapter of the Institute of Real Estate Management, which is part of the National Association of Realtors.[78] A property manager's job begins in earnest once tenants begin to occupy the property. Daily functions include collecting rents from tenants and paying recurring expenses, maintaining common areas, and ensuring that necessary repairs are carried out by soliciting bids, selecting vendors, and overseeing the quality of workmanship.

Lenders

The developer's most important relationship is with the lenders, due to their unusual legal rights in the property. Lenders have two major concerns: the developer and the project. First, they evaluate the developer's experience and credibility. They learn whether the developer has ever defaulted on a note, how much the company is worth, whether the developer will personally guarantee the note, and whether the developer has the ability to deliver the project on time and within budget. Lenders then analyze the project, assessing the location, the pro forma, and whether it is sufficiently pre-leased if already constructed.

Among the most important qualities that a lender looks for in a developer are honesty and organization. Demonstrating those qualities is especially important for developers without a track record or reputation in a given community.

Construction lenders lend money to build and lease a project. Permanent lenders finance the project once it is built through long-term mortgages. In both cases, the developer's potential gain is less important than the lender's potential loss. Lenders will ask, can the developer withstand fluctuations in the interest rate during the development period? Does the developer have sufficient equity to cover extra costs if interest rates go up during the construction period or if more time is needed to lease the project? Underwriting success does not guarantee a great project. It does confirm that the loss of principal is unlikely.

Relying on their knowledge of the area, lenders weigh the developer's potential for success against their own fees and exposure. For a construction loan, lenders usually require the developer to supply a market feasibility study and an appraisal. Permanent lenders are concerned about a project's long-term potential.

The amount of pre-leasing that lenders require depends on the type of project and whether the loan is for construction or permanent financing. Apartment buildings require little pre-leasing for either type of financing. Office projects must be 50 to 75 percent pre-leased, or more in soft markets or shaky economies. Pre-leasing requirements for retail and industrial projects fluctuate dramatically with the market.

Lenders study a project's tenant mix carefully. Strong anchor tenants with high credit ratings and a diversity of other tenants are desirable in both retail and office projects. Construction lenders are concerned about tenant mix because they depend on the permanent lender to take out the construction note. Thus, determining the criteria for tenant mix before leasing begins is a critical step. Special project types, such as mini-warehouses and auto marts, are harder to finance: they are considered riskier than conventional retail and industrial projects, having a very limited pool of buyers in the event of foreclosure action. Some lenders finance them, but at higher loan rates than conventional projects.

Even experienced developers need to convince lenders about the economic viability of their projects. Beginning developers, or those lacking a reputation in the community or real estate industry, must sell themselves and their firms as well.

To find a lender, developers can begin by making a list of prospects. They may want to start at the bottom of the list and practice their presentations before introducing the project to a lender with which they really want to work.

To build a reputation, developers need to avoid common mistakes. In addition to understanding the local market and demand for their product, they must have a well-developed, thorough, and realistic budget; set a realistic timeline with milestones; and have money in reserve or access to capital. The developer must also demonstrate competency in construction, sales, and leasing.

Lenders often base fees on the size of the deal. For projects under $10 million, they typically assess between zero and one point (0 to 1 percent of the total loan amount) for the service of providing the loan.[29]

Each lender receives a fee as well as coverage of certain expenses, such as appraisals. In addition, if loan brokers are involved in finding a lender, they too will be paid a fee, typically 1 percent of the loan amount. If a project is seen as unusually risky, an additional one to two points may be added. If the project is larger than $10 million, the fee may not increase proportionally; the net fee may actually be less.

Lenders consider the following factors when evaluating a potential borrower.

FINANCIAL BACKING/EQUITY

Both permanent and construction lenders are interested in the sources of excess capital. Does the developer have enough resources to carry the project, or will the lender be expected to do so (unacceptable for lenders)? Many developers fail because they do not plan cash flow and are unable to finance unexpected costs. Lenders want evidence that the developer has cash available or at least the ability to raise capital if interest rates go up during construction, if leasing is slower than expected, or if extraordinary cost overruns occur.

Lenders also want clear evidence that the borrower understands the financing needs. For example, does the borrower want to find the cheapest loan, one with flexibility, or one with the highest loan proceeds?

MANAGERIAL CAPABILITY

Lenders also want assurances that the developer understands real estate—in particular, how to work with the local government, subcontractors, and leasing agents. The developer must assemble a team that satisfies these concerns. A catalog of the economic results of transactions the developer has been involved in can be helpful. It should include items such as cash in and cash out, time period, and internal rates of return. The developer may also want to include a description of both the good and the challenging aspects of past development projects. An organized, thorough, and internally consistent application with necessary photos, maps, plans, and financial information creates a good first impression and demonstrates a developer's managerial capabilities.

CHARACTER

Lenders look for developers who share their values regarding development quality, marketing, and management. Is the developer open and honest about the obstacles and challenges associated with the development? Does the developer repay debts and keep promises? Is the developer litigious?

Developers should answer all lenders' concerns, recognizing that lenders' greatest fear is that they will be left with an unviable project. Developers must demonstrate their commitment, resolution, and professionalism and anticipate problems before lenders point them out.

Sources of Financing for Real Estate Projects

Several types of financial institutions are potential sources of real estate loans.

COMMERCIAL BANKS

Commercial banks are a principal source of both construction and miniperm loans, which can fund multiple phases in one loan. They usually prefer to lend money for a short term—one to three years— through the construction and leasing period, at which time the permanent lender pays off the construction lender. For larger developers, commercial banks may grant miniperm loans up to five years. These loans are especially attractive during periods of high inflation

when developers expect permanent mortgage rates to fall. One hundred percent financing is sometimes available on a superior project, although 60 to 70 percent financing is more common. Beginning developers are more likely to find a local bank than a larger national bank willing to fund their first few projects. Construction loans are usually made by local and regional banks because those banks are familiar with local conditions. Moreover, they have the ability to oversee and properly manage the loan during the construction phase and to monitor the process and progression of construction. After a developer has completed three or four successful projects, larger national banks, which tend to lend greater amounts of money, show more interest. Banks are reluctant to participate in joint ventures but sometimes will take part in participating mortgages; this type of mortgage offers the developer higher loan-to-value ratios while giving the bank higher yields through participation in project cash flows.

INSURANCE COMPANIES

Life insurance companies fund large projects with long-term loans, typically 10 years, and provide both construction and permanent financing. Loans may have fixed rates, unlike those from most construction lenders. Beginning developers with a limited track record will have difficulty attracting an insurance company to a project. For merchant builders, though, the requirements for insurance companies may be worth investigating, as they can provide a source of funding for institutional buyers of completed and stabilized projects.

PENSION FUNDS

Pension funds have become a major source of financing for real estate as they have sought to diversify their investments. Their large and increasingly diverse portfolio targets have made them attractive financing prospects for developers. They finance both construction loans and longer-term mortgages, usually at fixed rates. Generally, they finance large projects undertaken by experienced developers. Pension funds often employ advisers who perform all the functions that a traditional real estate owner or lender performs. They evaluate the project's location, market potential, projected cash flow, the developer's reputation, and the project's quality. Pension fund investments can take longer to finance because decisions do not rest with an individual but are made by a committee in the organization.[30]

FOREIGN INVESTORS

Global money markets, including foreign investors and foreign banks, play a role in real estate, both in the United States and abroad. Both private capital and sovereign funds poured into U.S. markets during the boom of the early 2000s. The increasingly globalized financial system will likely continue to attract capital from abroad. Just as important, real estate developers and owner/managers will have to contend with high-growth foreign economies as competitors for investment capital that was once reluctant to accept the risk of overseas investment. Although most foreign investors prefer to buy developed properties, usually employing low rates of financial leverage, they also have been important sources of development capital for larger firms.

SYNDICATIONS AND REAL ESTATE INVESTMENT TRUSTS

Syndications and real estate investment trusts (REITs) provide a way to carve up real estate ownership into small pieces that many people can afford. They have been used to raise equity capital and mortgage financing for development projects. Both vehicles limit investors' liability and provide pass-through tax benefits that flow directly to the investor, thus avoiding the additional layers of taxation associated with corporate ownership. Public syndications are no longer a significant source of capital; private syndications, however, remain the best source of capital for small developers through limited partnerships and

The St. John in San Antonio is the adaptive use of the former St. John's Seminary College. Located in one of the poorest, oldest, and ethnically concentrated areas of the city, it is now home to 228 apartments. The property is within walking distance of the San Antonio River Walk as well as employment and commercial centers.

joint ventures with a local or regional investment outlook.

REITs have become a significant mechanism for raising capital to fund development projects, and they are dominant players in the acquisition of medium-to-large, completed development projects. REITs are entities that combine the capital of many investors to acquire or provide financing for all forms of real estate. A REIT serves much like a mutual fund for real estate, in that retail investors obtain the benefits of a diversified portfolio under professional management. Its shares are freely traded, usually on a major stock exchange, and the REIT's assets are assembled by sector, with an eye toward specific investment goals, such as capital appreciation, current cash flow, or value potential. The acquisition criteria of REITs are important even to developers who never deal directly with them. Their size within the market for debt and equity financing makes their criteria important benchmarks for any real estate investment, and developers must contend with the presence of public REIT stocks as an alternative, diversified vehicle for investing in real estate. In any potential investor's mind since the late 1980s must be the question, "Could I just get the upside, with far less risk, by investing in a REIT?"

PRIVATE INVESTORS AND JOINT VENTURES

The most likely financial partner for a beginning developer is a private investor, who can be almost anyone with sufficient net worth and sophistication to invest. Besides putting up the necessary equity, the private investor may be willing to sign a personal guarantee on the construction note—something that beginning developers often require to obtain their first construction loan, or a loan for a project substantially larger than their track record. Occasionally, a private investor funds a project's total cost. The profit split with private investors may range from 80/20 (80 percent to the investor) to 50/50, but regardless of the split, the return to the investor will be privileged over developer profit. When building a track record, each equity partner should be approached and treated in a way that inclines them to come back for the next deal. John Loper advises, "Be realistic with equity partners, never over-promise."[31]

To align the partners' incentives, the developer should always make some cash investment. On small deals, this investment ranges from 5 to 33 percent of the total equity, but in larger deals it may be as little as 1 or 2 percent. The developer may also be required to take on the first assignment of risk, that is, cover losses up to a certain amount. Because the investor risks a greater percentage of the equity but takes less than its pro rata share of profit, the investor will need to have complete confidence in both the project and the developer's reputation before pursuing a deal.

Investment firms also assemble equity capital from multiple investors to fund new development or to buy existing real estate. Many of these firms work with Wall Street to match up investment funds with developers that provide desired program uses or desired markets in particular locales. Beginning developers who work hard to develop the track record to attract Wall Street money are often surprised at the prohibitive cost of this sort of equity capital. They should note that reporting requirements and other administrative costs rise at least as quickly as the amount financed. Once they make the jump to institutional financing, developers may recall fondly the simpler arrangements of small deals with high-net-worth individuals.

THE BOND MARKET AND COMMERCIAL MORTGAGE–BACKED SECURITIES

The issuance of commercial mortgage–backed securities (CMBSs)—the sale of bond-like interests in portfolios of mortgage-backed loans backed by commercial real estate and sold through the capital markets to individual and institutional buyers—gained market share in overall holdings of real estate debt in the 1990s. CMBSs grew from less than 0.5 percent of the value of outstanding commercial real estate mortgages in 1989 to almost 14 percent in 2000. The sector ground to a halt in the 2008–2009 financial crisis and the forced receivership of the government-sponsored entities like Fannie Mae. Even 10 years later, by 2020, annual CMBS issuance was a fraction of precrisis volume. The growth of securitized debt has deeper roots in the institutionalization of real estate lending, so developers of quality large-scale projects should anticipate a return of these financing sources.

CREDIT COMPANIES

Some large U.S. corporations use their power in financial markets to establish *credit companies*, which can provide development financing outside the parent companies' business. Compared with banks, credit companies are subject to less federal government regulation, although the 2008 crisis increased scrutiny of such "shadow banking." Credit companies are more likely to invest in more complex deals, typically with higher interest rates and stronger recourse measures than commercial banks.

CONSTRUCTION LENDERS

Several different types of lenders finance construction loans. The specific institution funding a project depends on the development team's level of experience and the type and size of the project. Most construction loans have interest rates that float with the prime rate. Construction loan interest rates typically run 150 to 300 basis points (1.5 to 3 percent) over prime, depending on the developer's size, experience, and credit rating. Thus, if the prime lending rate (to a bank's best customers) is 6 percent, construction loan rates will be 8 percent, assuming a 200–basis point spread over prime.

Beginning developers should start their search for construction financing with a banker they know. They should ask for referrals and choose half a dozen potential lenders. They may also solicit the advice of other developers in the field.

Once the construction loan is closed and the construction lender begins to fund construction of the building, the developer should be vigilant about the lender's concerns and try to address them before they become problems. If a project is falling behind schedule or going over budget, the developer should inform the lender quickly and not allow the lender to hear the news from its inspector or from third parties. All experienced real estate lenders understand the complications that can arise during the development process. They can often advise the developer about financial strategies that can be employed while the obstacles are being overcome. Regardless, the developers absolutely must keep lenders informed to maintain their confidence and trust.

Developers must recognize and address the varied concerns of construction lenders:

- **Design**—Lenders are increasingly concerned about a project's design. The general trend is toward better-quality projects, and national trends toward sustainability or preferred project types (rentals versus condominiums, for example) may be built into lending officers' guidelines for approval.
- **Permits**—Developers must prove that all permits and entitlements are either in place or forthcoming so that the project is not subject to delays or moratoriums.
- **Environmental factors**—Most lenders require a borrower to indemnify and hold them free and harmless of any liability resulting from toxic or hazardous waste located on a site. Lenders typically require at least a Phase I environmental assessment before closing.
- **Insurance**—The builder's risk and general liability insurance must be in place, usually with lenders named as an additional insured. As new contractors join the project, certificates may be required of each.
- **Developer's capacity**—Lenders evaluate whether the developer's associates or partners can complete the project if the developer is suddenly injured or they must bring in another individual.
- **Credibility/integrity/cash**—Lenders analyze the developer's credibility and integrity and the status of the firm or principals' cash flow—anything that may prevent the completion of the project.
- **Disbursements/inspections/lien releases**—Most lenders inspect the site monthly to verify requests for payments. If a lender has problems with lien releases (i.e., if suppliers or contractors file a mechanics lien against the property because they are not paid), the lender may write joint checks to the developer and contractor. A joint check must be endorsed by all payees. That helps a lender ensure that the contractor and suppliers are paid and that the collateral is unencumbered. The check endorse-

ment by the contractor serves as proof of payment and protects the lender (and the developer) against frivolous mechanics liens.

- **Standby commitments**—Construction lenders are not in the permanent mortgage business. They require assurance that their loan will be repaid when construction is completed or soon thereafter. Standby commitments provide that assurance when permanent financing has not yet been arranged. The standby commitment is rarely exercised because developers find permanent financing before their construction loans expire. Standby commitments are available from certain banks, insurance companies, credit companies, and REITs. Fees for a standby commitment run 1 to 2 percent of the total loan amount each year that it is in force but remains unfunded (the developer has not borrowed any funds under the standby commitment). If the standby loan is actually funded, interest rates typically run 5 percent or more over the prime rate. Although standby commitments are expensive, they allow developers to proceed when a construction lender demands some form of *takeout* (repayment) commitment before it will fund the construction loan.

Once the loan agreement is operational, the developer must make prompt and punctual payments, maintain the project in good operating order, and keep all insurance and taxes up to date. If problems arise, the lender should be informed immediately. By being candid, a developer will retain the lender's confidence and find it easier to obtain financing the next time.

Colin Niedermeyer, of Umpqua Bank in Oregon, states that the bank wants even young and new borrowers to have completed a similar project—or have a guarantor who has—before a loan will be granted.[32] In the absence of a track record, the bank may require the borrower to hire an owner's rep to help manage the general contractor. The bank's requirements include a 1.2 to 1.25 *debt service coverage ratio* (annual net income divided by debt service) for new developers (see chapter 4). Although the firm Trammell Crow maintained that its target premium for market cap rates over construction cap rates was 2 percent, Niedermeyer says he has seen deals with less than a 1 percent premium. His bank also offers construction loans with a permanent loan option whereby the permanent loan rate is fixed at the initial construction loan closing. Niedermeyer states that virtually all construction lenders want to see the full equity in a collateralized

restricted reserve account even though they may allow a staging of equity investment in proportion to the debt as costs are incurred. They look to the borrower to have in place a guaranteed maximum (GMAX) construction contract before closing that includes at least a 5 percent contingency. If cost savings occur, they will allow reallocation of the budget. Banks normally require the borrower to have liquidity equal to 20 percent of the loan amount and a net worth of three times the loan amount. For underwriting new borrowers, they look at contingent debt and will discount the value of vacant land on the borrower's balance sheet. Niedermeyer states, "If you are a beginning developer, keep yourself financially fit. Don't stretch yourself too far. It's a relationship business. A warm introduction through a relationship gives us comfort in working with you. Loan brokers are helpful."

MORTGAGE BANKERS AND BROKERS

Both mortgage bankers and mortgage brokers help developers obtain financing for their projects. In some cases, the broker assists the developer in getting financing but does not have direct access to funds; the banker has direct access to funds and usually services the loan as well.[33] The relationship between the banker and the client differs somewhat from the broker/client relationship. The banker has a fiduciary relationship with the client, whereas a broker acts as an intermediary and merely looks for the best combi-

The Cottages on Vaughan is located in an ethnically diverse area of Clarkston, Georgia. This pocket neighborhood includes eight micro-cottage homes within walking distance to community retail and amenities. The site is laid out intentionally to foster community interaction, including a common green area with a fire pit. The development has many sustainable features and four of the homes have achieved net zero.

nation of funding for the client. A developer may use a single broker or hire different brokers to help find mortgage financing and equity financing. Brokers assist the borrower in preparing a summary package for the deal, which includes underwriting and research; marketing the loan to many lenders using their established relationships; and negotiating, processing, and closing complex deals and transactions.

Some developers believe that using a mortgage broker adds an unnecessary middleman; others say it is necessary because loans can be very complex and a financial specialist such as a broker can help find more creative solutions to financing. Some developers also believe in giving bankers or brokers exclusive rights to assemble the capital, to maintain their full attention, rather than spreading this responsibility among multiple parties. In such cases, the developer may want to require the intermediary to seek other investors and split fees if necessary or to go to other bankers to access their exclusive list of lenders. In some instances, a developer may ask the banker or broker to work with the developer's own established contacts for lenders, which may reduce the broker's fee.

Not every banker or broker is suited for every project. Developers should not be afraid to ask brokers and bankers for their credentials and references and should find out what projects they have financed and how well-versed they are in the real estate business. Developers should also question how a prospective lender's specific system works: How do the developer and contractor request draws? Will the lender allow a land draw up front? How often will the lender visit the site? How and when are interest, points, and origination fees paid? At the same time, developers can indicate their readiness to use a lender's services again if they prove to be satisfactory this time. Eventually, developers may want to approach lenders with the idea of starting a long-term relationship. Once a relationship with a banker or broker is established, a developer can get the most out of the association by considering the entity as an integral part of the team whose function is to bring expertise about the capital market to the table. And as at other stages in the borrowing process, the developer should fully disclose both the strengths and weaknesses of the deal to the banker or broker.

Mortgage brokers' fees vary. The standard fee is 1 percent of the loan amount. The lender also charges fees for the application, the appraisal, and all the other costs of a loan.

PERMANENT LENDERS

The permanent loan provides the takeout for the construction loan. Banks, insurance companies, and pension funds make permanent loans. Increasingly, permanent loans are securitized on Wall Street, where they are sold to investors in the CMBS market.

Traditionally, a developer must have a permanent loan in place to obtain construction financing. Larger, more experienced developers with strong balance sheets may be able to get a construction loan without a permanent loan commitment, but beginning developers most likely will need that commitment before they can begin construction. Permanent financing usually has fixed interest rates, and although the loan is typically amortized over 30 years, the term of the loan is often limited to 10 years. After 10 years, the note is renegotiated or refinanced by a new permanent loan.

Most of the concerns listed for construction lenders apply equally to permanent lenders. Permanent lenders look to the property more than to the borrower for assurance that they will not lose their investment. In most cases, developers do not sign personally on permanent loans. Thus, a strong and fully leased property owned by a financially weak party will obtain financing more quickly than an unleased property with a strong owner.

A developer should thoroughly understand the lender's criteria, such as the percentage that must be pre-leased, and should compare effective borrowing costs on different mortgages. Chapter 4 discusses this computation in greater detail. In brief, it takes into account interest rates, fees, points, prepayment penalties, and other costs, as well as anticipated holding time until the developer sells or refinances the property.

MEZZANINE DEBT

Mezzanine debt is as an intermediate funding mechanism that has been available since the 1980s. It usually supplements the equity investment and first mortgage. Any of the lenders already identified may use it. Typically, deals with mezzanine debt are structured with a 70 percent mortgage, 5 to 20 percent mezzanine debt, and the remainder from the developer's equity. Unlike a mortgage, a partnership interest is assigned in case the developer defaults on the loan, making mezzanine a convertible debt-equity instrument. Its pricing typically reflects that hybrid position. As such, mezzanine financing must always be compared with preferred equity investment. These loans are typically short term, anticipating takeout by lower-rate debt or sale, and have higher fees: 2 to 3 percent is common.

For permanent loans, mezzanine rates from debt funds or hedge funds in early 2022 had interest rates from 7 to 9 percent and combined loan-to-value (LTV) ratios up to 75 percent, with a senior permanent loan in the 60 to 65 percent range. Steve Bram at George Smith Partners states that banks will do construction loans up to 65 to 70 percent LTV with interest rates of LIBOR (London Interbank Offered Rate) plus 250 basis points, or prime plus 100 basis points. Debt funds will do combined construction loans up to 80 percent LTV. Interest rates may be as low as 4 to 5 percent for bridge financing (two- to three-year loans with one or two extensions) for projects that are built but have leasing risk, or 6 to 9 percent for rehab and construction. Debt funds will sell off the A piece (the first 60 to 65 percent) to investors at low rates and keep the B piece (the mezzanine portion) in-house. Bram says that buildings with credit tenants or presale may have higher LTVs. Participating loans from life insurance companies are rare but may go up to 90 percent LTV with the lender receiving 20 to 25 percent of the upside.[34]

Conclusion

Development is always a team effort. The lenders, contractors, professional consultants, and other specialists described in this chapter represent the major players with whom developers must be familiar, but they are not the only ones. Regional characteristics sometimes require unusual specialties, and as development becomes increasingly complex, new talents must be integrated. For example, permitting and political consultants were only rarely employed as recently as 20 years ago. Today, in some jurisdictions, they commonly lead the early phases of development.

Successful projects depend on the developer's ability to manage the many participants with divergent experience in the process toward a common goal. In this complicated and expensive business, simply gathering and sifting through the relevant information can be a herculean—and critical—task. The developer must be able to recognize high-quality work in many disparate disciplines and must know when to ask questions, whom to ask, and what to ask. The developer must strike a delicate balance between trust in the decisions of the players on the team and constant oversight of work on the critical path of the development timeline. If mistakes are made, the developer is ultimately responsible: to investors, to lenders, and to the community.

NOTES

1. John Loper, professor, USC Price School for Public Policy, interview by author, September 2021.

2. Amy Levi, CEO, Strada, Denver, Colorado, interview by author, 2021.

3. Richard Hardy, "Strategic Planning in Development Firms," *Journal of Real Estate Development* (Spring 1986): 29.

4. Peter Inman, Inman and Associates, Irvine, California, interview by author, 2010.

5. Adam Weers, COO, Trammell Crow Co., Washington, DC, interview by author, 2021.

6. Small homebuilding firms and industrial developers also tend to be organized by function because their business is repetitious by nature. Repetition, especially in leasing and construction, lends itself to more functional organization, in which activities are more specialized.

7. John O'Donnell, chair, the O'Donnell Group, Newport Beach, California, at the USC Lusk Center for Real Estate Development spring retreat, Desert Hot Springs, California, interview by author, 1989.

8. For more information, see Christopher Bettin and Kenneth Reyhons, *Strategic Planning for the Real Estate Manager* (Chicago: Realtors National Marketing Institute, 1993); George S. Day et al., eds., *Wharton on Dynamic Competitive Strategy* (New York: Wiley, 1997); Colin Eden and Fran Ackermann, *Making Strategy: The Journey of Strategic Management* (Thousand Oaks, CA: Sage, 1998); Arnoldo C. Hax et al., *The Strategy Concept and Process: A Pragmatic Approach*, 2nd ed. (Upper Saddle River, NJ: Prentice Hall, 1996); Jay R. Galbraith, *Designing Organizations: An Executive Briefing on Strategy, Structure, and Process*, Management Series (San Francisco: Jossey-Bass, 1995); and Anthony W. Ulwick, *Business Strategy Formulation: Theory, Process, and the Intellectual Revolution* (Westport, CT: Quorum Books, 1999).

9. Art Danielian, chairman, Danielian Associates, Irvine, California, interview by author, 2022.

10. Jim Stickley, principal, WRT Design, San Francisco, California, interview by author, 2021.

11. Galina Tachieva, managing partner, DPZ CoDESIGN LLC, Miami, Florida, interview by author, 2021.

12. See the AIA website for more information: www.aia.org.

13. Woo Kim, principal, WRT Design, San Francisco, California, interview by author, 2021.

14. For more information about *MasterFormat* and how to subscribe to the service, see the Construction Specifications Institute's website (https://www.csiresources.org/standards/masterformat).

15. A mechanic's lien gives a contractor the right to retain the property if payment is not made.

16. Ronald Stenlund, president, Central Consulting Engineers, Green Bay, Wisconsin, interview by author, November 2010.

17. Matthew Kiefer, attorney, Goulston & Storrs, Boston, Massachusetts, interview by author, 2020.

18. Douglas Hahn, senior environmental scientist, URS Corporation, Los Angeles, California, interview by author, March 2002.

19. Jonathan Rose, principal, Jonathan Rose Companies, interview by author, May 2002.

20. Patrick Kennedy, owner, Panoramic Interests, Berkeley, California, interview by author, March 2002.

21. James Chung, president, Reach Advisors, and cofounder, StratoDem Analytics, Cambridge, Massachusetts, interview by author, 2021.

22. Leonard Zax, Latham & Watkins LLC, Washington, DC, interview by author, December 2001.

23. Helen Foster, Foster Strategy, New Orleans, Louisiana, interview by author, November 2021.

24. Stuart Rosenberg, director, Public Content, Houston, Texas, interview by author, September 2021.

25. Sandra Kulli, real estate marketing strategist and president, Kulli Marketing, Los Angeles, California, interview by author, August 2021.

26. Rosenberg, interview.

27. Charles Adams, founder, Thrivemore Advisors, Jacksonville, Florida, interview by author, 2020.

28. See www.irem.org.

29. *Points* are expressed as percentages (1 or 2 percent), whereas *basis points* are expressed as hundredths of a percent (100 basis points = 1 percent).

30. Pension fund real estate advisers belong to the National Association of Real Estate Investment Managers (NAREIM; see www.nareim.com). Member organizations represent a very important class of financing sources for developers, as well as jobs for real estate students.

31. Loper, interview.

32. Colin Niedermeyer, vice president, Umpqua Bank, Roseburg, Oregon, interview by author, December 2021. Construction cap rates are the ratio of net operating income to total construction cost; market cap rates are the ratio of net operating income to market value.

33. *Loan servicing* involves collecting loan payments and sending them to the current holder of the loan. The originator often sells loans to another lender. The servicing agent does not necessarily change if the loan is sold.

34. Steve Bram, president, George Smith Partners, Los Angeles, California, interview by author, 2022.

3 Land Development

DAVID HAMILTON

Overview

Subdivision of land is the initial mechanism by which communities are developed. Technically, *subdivision* describes the legal and physical steps a developer must take to convert raw land into developable land. This chapter examines those steps, which may apply to tracts of any size or use, using the development of residential subdivisions as an example. Subdivision is a vital part of a community's growth. It is a critical decision point that defines major elements of the community's appearance, its mix of land uses and densities, and basic infrastructure, including roads, drainage systems, water, sewerage, and utilities. In parallel, subdivision often establishes rules of governance to guide future development and operations. Subdivision regulations are regularly updated by jurisdictions, as performance requirements and design preferences evolve for streets, utilities, and building types. The subdivision process also offers a key point of input to many stakeholders, where developers must coordinate their proposals with community interests, such as protecting ecological and cultural resources and promoting affordability and inclusion.

Developers and planners have often led the way toward better regulation, with their projects demonstrating how improved standards can lead to superior development patterns. But developers must be mindful of the impact that their projects may have on communities. Even when their projects conform to approval requirements, developers frequently must justify them in terms of beneficial (or at least not adverse) effects on the environment, traffic, tax base, schools, parks, and other public facilities. The list of potential impacts for consideration is growing, to include social goals like equity and affordability. Developers must offer a value proposition, not only to investors and end users, but to the communities where they build.

utilities extended to the edge of the property); and developed or subdivided land, platted into individual homesites and 1.5- to 10-acre (0.6–4 ha) commercial parcels, ready for building. The latter is typical for large projects on previously undeveloped parcels. Smaller projects and infill and redevelopment sites typically skip the second phase. The process of converting raw land to semideveloped land differs by region, depending on the pattern of landownership, terrain, the capacity of local developers and financial institutions, legal frameworks of local and state authorities, and the institutional mechanisms—public and private—for providing roads and utilities.

SUBDIVIDING LAND

The subdivision process generally takes place in three stages: raw land; semideveloped land (usually divided into 20- to 200-acre [8–80 ha] tracts[1] with roads and

Investment in public and green spaces, and carefully designed infrastructure define this central neighborhood redevelopment in Carmel, California. The details of "complete streets" and attention to the public realm create value and sponsor activity throughout the neighborhood.

HADLEY FRUITS, RUNDELL ERNSTBERGER

To coordinate required infrastructure, some states, such as California, Texas, and Florida, rely on special districts—independent layers of government created to finance utility services by levying taxes and fees or by issuing debt. Special districts go by different names and may serve multiple functions to facilitate the shared investments that are required to start development. Where districts cannot be created, developers must wait for the community or utility company to extend service, reach out to make agreements to pay for the extension of roads and utility lines themselves, or form nongovernmental partnerships with other landowners to fund and manage these investments.

The conversion of raw land to intermediate steps tends to be a project best suited to larger, well-capitalized developers, with long time horizons. Such developers typically work with 200- to 1,000-acre (81–405 ha) tracts of land, which they subdivide into smaller 20- to 100-acre (8–40 ha) parcels. They provide the major infrastructure, including arterial roads, utilities, and drainage systems for the smaller parcels so they can subsequently be subdivided into buildable lots. Figure 3-1 shows the structure of the land conversion industry and the roles of typical players.

Land does not become available for development in a smooth pattern. Rather, farmers, timber interests, and other landholders may sell individual parcels for various reasons, such as a death or retirement, an impending change of law or zoning, or simply in response to an attractive offer. In suburban fringe areas where neighboring parcels are already converted, the developer may skip a stage and convert raw land directly to subdivided lots with approvals for building. Direct conversion is more common in slower-growth areas and in places where municipal utilities or cooperatives install primary utilities. Large regional and national homebuilders, whose business depends on steady inventory, typically take land development in-

Opportunities are increasingly found in infill sites, such as Solis, a quarter-acre corner lot in Seattle. The development team created a strong identity for the property by designing an exuberant ground-floor streetfront and achieving "Passivhaus," the highest standard of energy efficiency, for the units above.

house, with an acquisition and development division feeding their homebuilding operation.

Because large contiguous tracts of land rarely become available at one time, developers must sometimes assemble multiple parcels in separate deals. If they cannot, then so-called leapfrog development, which pushes development farther away from the city center, can create sprawl.[2] Sprawl results in inefficient use of infrastructure and creates densities of potential users too low to finance municipal services, including transit, public safety, and utilities. Leapfrogging can, however, be an opportunity for small developers. Parcels that were passed over during the first wave of development can be affordable opportunities for infill projects. These sites can be complicated, as key decisions about infrastructure are already locked in, and there may be more organized stakeholders (potential opponents to development) than first-wave developers face. But such sites are often better located and may offer more market potential than greenfield sites farther from jobs and amenities. The complexity of developing such parcels can also serve as a barrier

FIGURE 3-1 Types of Land Investors

	Raw Land Buyer	Land Speculator	Predeveloper	Land Developer	Builder/End User
Major function	Begins conversion	Holds; waits for growth to approach	Analyzes market; clears regulatory hurdles	Installs utilities; completes subdivision	Buys lots; builds structures for sale, rent, or own use
Typical financing	Noninstitutional, cash or local banking		May attract institutional investment	May attract construction loans and long-term investors	
Typically sells to	Land speculator	Other speculator; last in line sells to developer	Land developer or end user	Other (smaller) builders or end users	
Typical length of tenure	10+ years	8–10 years	2–5 years	1+ years	Indeterminate

to entry, reducing competition from larger firms that often place value on scale and predictable processes.

DEVELOPERS AND POLICY

Developers must understand the dynamics of both market and regulatory forces. They must be politically astute, if not connected, because unlocking value in land usually depends on permission that can only be granted or denied by governmental agencies. Residents tend to resist change and oppose new development unless it offers them a tangible benefit, and increasingly broad groups of stakeholders expect a voice in approvals. Developers must gain the support of those who play major roles in determining local land use: elected officials, planning and zoning boards, utilities, regional commissions, public works, environmental regulators, local institutions, press and other opinion leaders, and well-organized citizens groups and neighbors who pursue influence in environmental or land use policies.

Developers should also be adept in coordinating across multiple government jurisdictions. Most sites are subject to overlays of local, state, and federal rules. Sometimes, particularly in rural unincorporated areas, the controlling jurisdiction may be unclear and/or the site may be subject to conflicting policies and regulations.

Historically, developers could safely assume a right to develop land as long as they met current zoning and other land use requirements, but nowadays a presumption of development rights can be risky. Even when a project conforms to existing zoning, development rights may be subject to reduction, phasing, or outright moratorium, depending on the attitudes of neighboring residents and the political environment surrounding growth and community change. Obtaining necessary approvals in a timely fashion is one of the major risks that developers must evaluate before committing themselves to a project. Developers should be well versed in local politics and cultivate personal alliances, as even uncomplicated tracts may require a lengthy approval process. Critically, developers must also have the team and financing in place to survive the process, as returns to capital may not appear until long after investment begins. The difficulty of the approval process can be as much about sequence and timing as cost. Poor coordination among reviewing agencies can substantially increase timelines, increasing not just cost but risk of a market turn. Even a well-conceived project can fail if getting to market takes too long, so strategies that accept modest risk

to compress the approval timeline may be worthwhile.

Developers must be involved in designing regulatory policies and should help educate their communities about the effect such policies may have on creating a sustainable community. Poorly conceived antigrowth measures can have unintended consequences, such as raising housing prices or exacerbating sprawl. In many states, "smart growth" ideas have influenced planners and developers to find ways to accommodate growth pressures while preserving the environment and limiting impacts, by directing growth toward urban centers with efficient infrastructure, employment opportunities, and public amenities.[3] In exurban areas, some developers have advanced concepts of "conservation development" to harmonize lower-density development with agriculture and conservation goals. Developers can and should advocate for their city and region. From affordability and ecology to equity, development professionals can help policymakers understand how to achieve community goals.

LAND DEVELOPMENT VERSUS BUILDING DEVELOPMENT

This chapter focuses on small-scale land development, typically involving 20 to 100 acres (8–40 ha). Although the techniques described here apply to any form of land development, new developers are most likely to become involved with small residential or mixed-use subdivisions, or potentially light-industrial or small retail centers.

Many developers engage in both land development (horizontal development) and building development (vertical development). When they perform both activities on the same tract, as many homebuilders do, they often view the two activities as a single project. However, the two are distinct businesses, and each should be analyzed on its own merits. This requires some accounting, as finished lots are "sold" from a development process into a building process, but it is essential for understanding where in the process most value is created.

Complications can arise when a developer oversees both land and building development on the same property. Risk is greater in the first process, and debt and equity often come from different sources, with different expectations for each phase. Further, independent homebuilders may be reluctant to buy lots because of the competition from the developer's own building activities. The land developer has a cost advantage, controls leads and marketing to potential buyers, and is already mobilized on site. Builder partners might be

brought in successfully to offer a specialty product or to target a complementary market segment, creating a healthy mix of aesthetic and product types.

Norms for developing small subdivisions vary by region. In some areas, homebuilders typically subdivide the land and build the houses, using a single construction loan—especially for tract houses in communities that require public hearings on architectural plans as well as on subdivision.[4] Elsewhere, land developers more commonly sell finished lots to multiple homebuilders, diversifying the end product with a variety of specialists.

In general, land development is riskier but potentially more profitable than homebuilding. Land development depends on the public sector for both approvals and infrastructure and may involve a long investment period without cash flow. Assuming this combination of risk and investment must be rewarded by superior returns—yet another reason to consider the two businesses separately.

Project Feasibility

Although opportunities exist for many types of land, new land developers are advised to search for comparatively simple parcels under single owners: land that is already served by utilities and is appropriately zoned or requires only administrative public approvals. Although raw land may be available, the resources and time required to entitle and bring utilities to a tract are

The provision of an outdoor "living room" and redesign of surrounding streets is the ultimate amenity for the Van Aken District, in Shaker Heights, Ohio. Recentering the neighborhood on both outdoor public space and indoor attractions like the Market Hall ensures street activity. The "local first" retail strategy makes the district unique and appealing to visitors.

beyond the capabilities of most small developers. "Hit some singles and doubles, don't go for home runs," advises Joe Barnes, development director of NEOM in Saudi Arabia. "Build a track record."[5]

MARKET ANALYSIS BEFORE SITE SELECTION

Market analysis should occur at least twice during land development—before and after site selection. The objective of the first market analysis is to identify which segments of the market are underserved and which sorts of buyers might be lured by a competitively priced and appropriately designed development. The goal is to identify opportunities across a market. Large developers have the luxury of investigating several markets, even internationally, to select the most promising niches for their products. Beginners lack the resources for open-ended exploration, and they usually want to remain in familiar territory with their local knowledge and personal connections. Local planning boards and regulators tend to view local developers less suspiciously than they might view out-of-towners. And even the ability to regularly check in on site,

Professional Real Estate Development

without travel expense or a paid site manager, is helpful for a lean organization.

Telepresence and technological tools for project management make more remote projects possible, but new developers have enough difficulties to overcome without the additional hurdles of distance and unfamiliar markets, processes, and construction practices. Moreover, beginning developers' primary concern, aside from developing stable cash flow, should be the cultivation of their reputation, which is more easily accomplished with multiple projects and a regular stable of players in one market. Geographic focus also increases the network effect of reputation, as developers with a track record are often shown parcels early, when owners are considering selling.

A developer's primary market decisions concern the proposed project's use, location, and size. Use preferences might arise from market conditions, such as a perceived shortage in one type of housing or commercial space, or from expertise in a particular type of construction that offers functional or price advantages. If a developer has no preference for a specific use, then each potentially permittable segment of the market—residential, industrial, commercial, or mixed use—should be analyzed for "highest and best" use. Real estate markets are highly segmented, so a developer cannot infer from residential demand that retail development is also in demand (see chapter 1 for an overview of market cycles by type). Similarly, a developer should not assume that demand for the same product type extends across multiple submarkets.

Historically, many developers specialized in a use, then searched for a suitable site. Today, with developable sites at a premium in so many metropolitan regions, developers more often select the site first, possibly even "tie it up" with a contract and deposit, and then undertake market analyses to identify ideal uses and refine the market analysis. If the developer has already identified the land use for which excess demand exists, the purpose of the market analysis is to identify the particular market segment (for instance, mid-priced, single-family houses for move-up families) and the location where demand is greatest (a side of town, or a school district). This formulation simplifies the task, although many developers prefer to pursue multiple potential opportunities at once, often in the same community.

Major sources of information are brokers, lenders, and especially, builders to whom the land developer will market the developed sites. Because homebuilders are prospective clients and want to ensure their own inventory, they are usually eager to share their intelligence. Some caution is advised, however, because some of these builder-clients will also be competitors with their own projects. Leading brokerages often compile quarterly trend reports on their market segments and distribute this research to potential clients. Regional economic and market data are abundant online, particularly on for-sale housing, which is served by the Multiple Listing Service and other commercial listing apps. Assembling this information and analyzing it can take considerable effort, so hiring a market consultant—or at least soliciting brokers for their interpretation—may be more efficient. The most important questions to be answered concern the market for the proposed product type.

Major homebuilders look at recent history to project demand throughout their metropolitan area, which they call *absorption*. They break down the number of sales by market area and by price intervals. Starting with 1,000 annual sales, they might find that 50 percent were sold in one neighborhood, and 25 percent of those sold at around $400,000; thus, the annual absorption in that neighborhood and price band is (1,000 × 0.5 × 0.25 = 125 units). Brokers can help compare these demand numbers with historical averages, and a safe assumption, unless job growth or other factors have substantially changed, is an eventual reversion to the historical pace. Analysts should also be cautious when defining market areas: is the whole neighborhood drawing demand, or is it a particular street or school district? Geographic information systems (GIS) make this detailed analysis of submarkets possible for the developer, and search filters in sales platforms make it increasingly common for buyers.

After estimating demand, developers should ask how much of that demand they can expect—the *capture rate*. Capture projections should be based on conservative assumptions to avoid overly optimistic projections—which are common. A rational capture rate depends on the number of similar projects selling in the market and on how competitive the proposed development is likely to be. Developers must consider how their project compares in attractiveness, access, and amenities. If, for example, five developers are pursuing the absorption of 125 annual sales from above, each starts with a pro rata share (25 sales in each project). This share might be improved with a superior product or with marketing incentives, but any increase will take share from competitors. In the long run, the competitors will respond, cutting prices or improving marketing or amenities to be competitive again.

Site Evaluation Factors

Market Area and Competition
- Existing inventory
- Pipeline expected during sales/leasing
- Similar products that may compete
- Price points or ranges by type

Location and Neighborhood
- Proximity to key metro locations
- Quality of surrounding environment
- Existing housing stock, other buildings
- Schools and churches
- Parks, clubs, and recreational facilities
- Other amenities
- Shopping and entertainment
- Public improvements (existing and planned)

Utilities
- Water and sewer/septic (capacity and expense)
- Electricity (availability and quality)
- Data services/cable TV
- Wireless coverage

Physical Conditions
- Visibility and accessibility
- Slopes and required grading
- Vegetation, forestry, and agriculture
- Existing structures/infrastructure
- Soils and hydrology
- Toxic wastes and nuisances
- Wildlife and ecological features

Legal Constraints
- Utility and private easements
- Covenants and deed restrictions

Regulatory Environment
- General climate toward development
- Exactions and impact fees
- Future infrastructure work/takings
- Approval process and timeline
- Process of stakeholder participation
- Administrative versus board approvals
- Upcoming elections and rule changes

Land developers must remember that their product is an intermediate good used to produce an end product. The demand for finished lots rises and falls with the demand for houses in the price range that justifies the lot price. The ratio of lot price to retail house price varies from about 20 to 50 percent. This ratio has risen steadily, particularly in high-income cities and areas with difficult land use approvals. Historically, many builders look for lot inventory priced around 25 percent of the finished lot-home package price, though such rules of thumb are no substitute for individual analysis of the specific market.

Suppose the absorption rate is 10 units per month for $600,000 houses, compared with 15 units per month for $500,000 houses. Builders of the $600,000 houses will pay $150,000, rather than $125,000 per lot for the lower cost houses. Developers that invest under the assumption they can sell lots nearer the higher rate may be in trouble if the market turns out to favor the less expensive houses. Even if they are willing to lower their prices, the lenders may base loan covenants on the originally projected prices, requiring additional approvals that delay sales at prices below those rates.[6]

Market research is a critical first step, not only for selecting a site but also for assembling a list of builders to approach, and for understanding their terms. Smart developers use this process to generate interest among builders. One might focus on smaller builders who build five to 50 houses per year and are likely to purchase a few lots at a time in a subdivision. The builders will tell the developer where they want to build and what the ideal lot size, configuration, and amenity package are. If the developer can meet their requirements, builders may even precommit to purchasing the lots by a letter of intent. If the builder has good credit, such commitments, while seldom legally binding, can help to secure financing for a first deal.

SITE SELECTION AND ACQUISITION
In selecting a site, new developers face several limitations that can be overcome only with diligent research. To overcome the limitations,

- choose a manageable geographic area for the search—a good guideline is "no air travel";
- set an appropriate time frame for investigating market conditions;
- do not depend exclusively on brokers to find sites; and
- do not look for "home runs"—build a reputation on smaller projects.

Because beginners lack reputation and contacts, they are less likely to hear about deals firsthand. But deals that have been "on the street" are not necessarily bad. A property may have been passed over for many reasons. For example, it may be too small or otherwise uneconomical for a large firm but may be suitable for the beginner. In addition to working with a network of brokers, developers should not be afraid to talk to landowners whose land is not currently for sale. Direct contact may generate a deal or lead to a possible joint venture or favorable terms of purchase. Large landowners know one another, and even a "no" may eventually lead to a referral.

SITE EVALUATION. The relative importance of various factors of subdivision development depends on the end user of the lots. The major site evaluation factors are summarized in the accompanying feature box, and greater detail regarding site evaluation for residential development can be found in chapter 4.

Many physical, legal, and other factors must be considered before finalizing terms and conditions for land acquisition. Among the more important items, the developer should

- make sure all easements are plotted on a map, any easement problems are cleared up, and any purchase arrangements for required easements are made before closing;
- check for drainage problems and ascertain the level of the water table, which affects sewer lines, septic tanks (if not connecting to a sewer system), and building foundations;
- check seismic hazard maps to make sure that faults do not cross the land or that their presence can be designed around or mitigated;
- check flood insurance and Flood Hazard Area maps;
- check local and Federal Housing Administration (FHA) requirements concerning width of roads, culs-de-sac, and other design features;
- investigate whether any parties are likely to delay or stop the sale; pay particular attention to the seller's family and/or other parties with a financial interest in the property;
- make sure that utilities such as water, sewer, gas, electricity, and communication lines are available and can be extended at reasonable cost;
- check with planning/zoning and engineering departments about off-site requirements;
- check permit costs, impact fees, and exactions, and consider statutory accelerations or upcoming changes;
- check for appropriate zoning and research actual— not statutory—approval timelines for similar projects;
- determine whether all necessary development approvals will be granted, or make closing of property acquisition contingent on approval;
- make sure that builders will be able to obtain building permits in a timely fashion;
- check for environmental issues—especially if a body of water lies on the land; avoid wetlands, as they usually involve a time-consuming approval process;

The affordable housing and support services offered at Casa Arabella in Oakland, California, are enhanced by coordination of the development with the adjacent rapid transit station. Walkability may be essential to affordability, and the promise of a less car-dependent life is increasingly desirable in many types of new home communities.

- check for fire hazards and availability of fire protection;
- beware of unusual soil chemistry or composition, such as sulfates or high clay levels;
- check for radon, a harmful derivative of uranium that is present in many areas;
- check historical aerial photos that may show evidence of toxic waste, such as storage tanks on the site;
- check construction lenders' requirements for environmental site assessments;
- check for landfills and other nuisance-generating sites close by, including illegal sites;
- look for smoke, fumes, and other odors and for noise, vibration, and light pollution; and
- always walk the land, preferably at many different times on weekdays and weekends.

The developer should also carefully consider the surrounding environment. What is the overall political climate with regard to growth, and does it vary by neighborhood? Is the planned development compatible with the surrounding neighborhood or with approved comprehensive plan goals? If so, is the plan up for review soon? Are shopping, schools, and parks nearby? If schools are an issue for buyers, what is their reputation and in what direction is that reputation moving? If schools and other infrastructure are important for approvals, are capacities adequate to permit a new project, or might developers be asked to subsidize capacity?

Particularly on infill and redevelopment sites, with established neighborhood patterns, developers

Land Development

Checklist for Buying Land

Market Area and Proposed Product

Product type, target markets, competition, resale market, neighborhood, commercial and industrial developments, military and government installations, employment base and growth, schools, shopping, transportation, daycare, advice of experts

Entitlements and Environmental Approvals

Approvals required at local, regional, state, and federal level, sequence and requirements, politics

Purchasing Agreement Data

Ownership information, environmental statements, improvements, buildable area, price, real estate agent, seller financing, escrow agent and fees, deposits needed

Condition of Title

Title report, lawsuits, heirs and claimants, existing loans, taxes, judgments or mechanic's liens, building restrictions, assessments, easements, crops, other agreements, leases, licenses currently in place

Physical Aspects

Topography, drainage, survey, special zones, environmental conditions (including soils, flood areas, potential wetlands and habitats, toxics)

Development Costs

All on-site improvement and off-site infrastructure costs, all building and subdivision fees, overhead and soft costs for design and engineering, refundable utility and hookup costs, cost per lot

Financial Projections

Based on realistic, conservative assumptions, including post-closing and operational costs

---

must be attentive to additional stakeholders. Several hot-button issues can directly affect public debates on development, and prospective developers should know going in how a project might become a focus of debate on gentrification, displacement, or affordability. Along with decarbonization, these larger social issues present unique challenges to development. Addressing concerns about traffic or wetlands may be difficult, but at least the answers are clear (e.g., designing roads and buffers). Less clear is how to address concerns of historic and systemic discrimination, or how to approach a global emissions problem. Knowing whether and how these larger debates are framed in the community is key, as applicants must enter the process with a clearly defined scope of what they can accomplish, and what benefits and costs are appropriate to the project.

SITE ACQUISITION. In land development a three-stage contract is customary: a free-look period, a period during which earnest money is forfeitable, and the closing of the transaction. If land use entitlements and/or regulatory approvals must be sought, developers may negotiate modest option payments until those approvals can be finalized. Time is a key point of negotiation, as important as price: purchasers want as much time as they can to close with as little money at risk as possible. Sellers want the reverse. The agreed-on terms depend on the state of the market and the

needs of each party, and each can change rapidly.

In slow markets, favorable terms of purchase are more likely. With fewer buyers, sellers are typically more willing to give a potential purchaser more time to investigate the property without requiring hard earnest money. In a hot market, sellers are less afraid of losing any particular deal and are more concerned about tying up their property when another buyer—and possibly a better offer—may be just around the corner. When conditions in the marketplace shift toward seller-dictated terms (requiring cash offers without financing contingencies, short due diligence periods, and high prices), the market is likely nearing its apex; the new developer who is having trouble competing as a buyer may just be better off waiting.

If the site consists of multiple parcels under separate ownership, progress is further complicated by the need to acquire all the parcels first. Land assembly is a tricky business and usually requires sophisticated negotiation and acquisition techniques to ensure that the owner of the last or other key parcels does not insist on an exorbitant price.

The terms of acquisition set the stage for everything else, and an overpriced or complicated takedown of land can doom an otherwise well-conceived project. When buying land, developers are chiefly concerned about whether they can build what they want, whether they have time to study all site conditions affecting feasibility, and whether they will be able to assemble market data, obtain financing, and assess project economics in a business plan before the required closing.

Sites with special problems, such as easements or contamination, may be attractive but must be approached with caution because they may be more difficult than a beginner can handle. Beginning developers are usually thinly capitalized, leaving little room for unanticipated costs or delays. Before deciding to tackle problem sites, developers must determine whether the problem can be solved within a reasonable time frame and cost. If they cannot answer that question with a high level of confidence, they should probably look for another site. However, sometimes they can convince a landowner to work with them to solve such problems without having to close on the property until the problems are solved.

Because of possible legal complications, developers generally use an attorney during land acquisition, no matter how straightforward a transaction might appear to be. Each part of the country has its own terminology for the sequence of steps in property acquisition. In Texas, for example, the first step is called *signing the earnest money contract*; in California, it is *going into escrow* on the purchase contract; and in New England, it is an *offer to purchase* agreement. In most cases, these actions initiate a free-look period during which various contingencies have to be resolved. This agreement is binding and contains all the contingencies, at least in summary form. It stipulates that on or before a certain date, the parties will enter into a *purchase and sale agreement*, which enumerates and records all aspects of the transaction.[7]

Even before submitting a purchase contract, purchasers may discuss or submit a *letter of intent* or term sheet to sellers that sets out the business terms for purchase of the property. The letter of intent specifies the property to be purchased, its price, payment terms, timing, and other major business points. In the case of seller financing, terms and timing of lien releases are also critical. Letters of intent are especially helpful when the purchaser or seller plans to use a long, specially written legal purchase agreement rather than a standardized broker's form. The letter of intent saves time and unnecessary legal expense in the beginning because it clarifies the primary aspects of the transaction. If the buyer and seller cannot come to agreement on the major business terms, there is no point in exchanging full legal documents. The letter of intent is nonbinding, but it does call for signatures by both parties to signify agreement on the major transaction points. The term sheet may be appended to the purchase contract or other documents to clarify the intention of deal points in the event of future disputes.

The *offer to purchase* must spell out all contingencies and any penalties other than specific performance (compelling the parties to consummate the agreed deal) for failure to close. Contingencies typically include physical inspections, environmental assessments, regulatory approvals, title checks, or financing approval. A common mistake is for purchasers to assume they can negotiate more contingencies or other issues in the purchase and sale agreement. The latter cannot be more restrictive than the offer to purchase unless both parties agree to the changes. Three items make the offer to purchase binding: (1) specific consideration, enough to entice the seller to take the property off the market for a given period; (2) proper identification of the property; and (3) a time to close or to enter into the purchase and sale agreement. The offer to purchase should include a provision for prompt return of the purchaser's deposit if a purchase and sale agreement is not signed.[8]

Purchase Contract or Earnest Money Contract. Whether or not a letter of intent is used initially, the *purchase contract* (also called purchase and sale agreement, or *earnest money contract*) is the primary legal document for purchase of property. It sets out all terms of purchase, indemnities, responsibilities for delivering title reports (usually the seller) and other documents, performing due diligence, and remedies in the event that the sale does not close. Signing of the final purchase agreement may happen immediately in the case of a simple purchase contract for one or several lots, or it may drag on for weeks or even longer if buyers and sellers haggle over individual provisions. Although purchase contracts are almost always negotiated following due diligence, the purchaser may use the time delay in signing to begin to line up financing, to recruit builders, or to advance project design. Until the purchase contract is signed, however, the buyer is at risk of the seller accepting another offer. Complicated purchase contracts are appropriate in complex transactions of larger properties, but new developers should keep it simple. Overly complicated legal paperwork may signal to the seller that the buyer is litigious or looking for reasons not to close.

Contingencies. Contingencies in the purchase contract refer to events that must occur before the purchaser "goes hard" on the earnest money. Beginning developers often make the mistake of including many unnecessary contingency clauses that only complicate the negotiations. The most all-encompassing clause is

Steps for Site Acquisition

Before Offer

1. Verify that a market for the property type exists.
2. Determine the price you can pay by running preliminary financial pro formas.
3. Determine whether the seller can sell the property for the price you want to pay. (Estimate the seller's basis and outstanding mortgages on the property.)
4. Find out why the seller is selling the property. (Is the sale necessary, or can the seller wait for a better price?)
5. Check the market for comparable properties. Research price trends in the property type.

Due Diligence Period

1. Ask for at least 60 days for due diligence. If a broker brought the developer the deal, the developer might expect that the broker also contacted other developers and that 60 days for due diligence may therefore not be acceptable to the seller.
2. Place a refundable deposit, or earnest money. Customary percentages vary widely by region and by deal size.
3. Request specific due diligence that must be provided by the seller, such as surveys, soils reports, environmental clearances and certifications, preliminary design and engineering studies, preapproved plans, development rights determinations, or agency approvals.
4. Negotiate terms and fees for unilateral extension of closing (monthly fee, number of months available). Extension fees should not be punitive but based on market interest for the capital.

Conditions for Closing

1. If zoning must be changed for the project, ask that closing be contingent on zoning approvals; if not approved, the earnest money is refunded. Be sure to state in the offer exactly what constitutes approval, for example,
   » general plan approval or rezoning;
   » conditional use permits (variances or waivers);
   » development agreements;
   » tentative tract or parcel map;
   » final tract or parcel map;
   » site plan approval;
   » design approval; or
   » issuance of building or disturbance permits.

2. Answer other questions:
   » Can a good title be secured?
   » How much of the site is buildable, how soon? What are the existing leases, easements, slopes, soils, floodplain, drainage, and geological conditions? (These issues may be addressed not only in subdivision ordinances but also in engineering and other standards.)
   » Can you build what you want to? How many units, of what size and at what density, can be built? Can parking and amenities be built and accessed by users and emergency services?
   » Can financing be obtained not only for land but also for the improvements you envision?

3. Complete as much of the following as possible before closing on the land:
   » preliminary design drawings outlining building envelopes, property divisions, access;
   » conceptual estimate of construction costs;
   » mortgage package preparation;
   » commitments from permanent and construction lenders;
   » receipt of regulatory approvals or assurances that they can be obtained (zoning opinion or development rights determination); and
   » selection of construction manager and property manager (who should assist in designing the project).

4. If the analysis indicates more time is needed to create a buildable site, ask for it. If the seller refuses, ask for the deposit money back and pull out of the deal.

Closing

1. Closing typically occurs 60 days after due diligence is complete, although longer periods can often be negotiated.
2. Closing can be made dependent on a variety of factors, including the availability of financing and the removal of toxic wastes.

---

one that makes the sale "subject to obtaining financing." If, for whatever reason, financing is not available, then earnest money is returned. Another encompassing clause is "subject to buyer's acceptance of feasibility studies." The contract may spell out those studies to include soils, title, marketing, site planning, and economic feasibility. As long as the clause gives the buyer

discretion to approve the reports, it effectively gives the buyer a way out of the contract. As soon as the buyer goes hard, though, the earnest money paid to the seller can be forfeited if the sale is not completed.

Most sellers will not give a blanket contingency for more than 30 to 60 days. In strong market conditions, sellers may not allow them at all, preferring to keep the property on the market for a highly committed cash buyer.

One important contingency in the purchase agreement is that the seller must support the developer in obtaining zoning and other necessary approvals. In areas where extensive public approvals make the allowable building density uncertain, developers may purchase sites on the basis of the number of units approved. In this case, the seller has a strong incentive to assist in the approval process. For example, if the price is $50,000 per unit and permission is given to build 100 units on the site, then the purchase price would be $5 million. If the developer receives approval for only 80 units, the price would be $4 million. Having the seller on the developers' side can be valuable in a tough approvals environment, where developers may have less credibility than longtime landowners. Be aware that having a contingency like this means having another interested party on the team, who may have input on decisions that will be made in approvals.

As a general rule, 2 to 5 percent of the total purchase price or a payment of $10,000 to $100,000 for smaller deals is required as earnest money for a 90- to 120-day closing. Because the earnest money theoretically compensates the seller for holding the property off the market, the earnest money usually bears some relation to the seller's holding cost or the opportunity cost of interest on the sales price. The amount is negotiable but has to be large enough that the seller believes the buyer is viable and serious about closing. Financing land is expensive—usually at least two points (2 percent) over prime. For example, if the prime rate is 5 percent and the land loan is 7 percent, then a four-month closing would incur holding costs of 2.3 percent (4/12 × 7 percent).

In hot markets, sellers sometimes try to get out of a sale because they have received a higher offer. Although each state has its own property law, buyers generally control a purchase contract as long as they strictly observe its terms. Land is legally unusual in that it is not considered fungible, and therefore specific performance (closing on that specific site) may be compelled. Most contracts state that a clause is waived if the buyer does not raise concerns in writing before the expiration date of the clause or contingency. If the clause (such as buyer's approval of title reports) is not automatically waived according to the contract, however, the seller may argue that the buyer failed to perform in a timely fashion and that the contract is therefore null and void. If the seller tries to get out of the contract before the expiration date, the threat of litigation is usually sufficient to bring the seller back to the table. Pending litigation makes it very difficult to sell the property to anyone else and can tie up a property; it is a last resort on the part of the buyer.

Release Provisions on Purchase Money Notes. One of the most important areas of negotiation concerns the release provisions on purchase money notes (PMNs)—seller financing used to purchase the property (also called *land notes*). Release provisions refer to the process by which developers remove and unencumber individual parcels in larger tracts from the sellers' land notes. Release provisions are also a major part of the negotiation with the developers' lenders (discussed in the Financing section later).

Lenders require a first lien on the developer's property. Lien priorities are determined by the date a mortgage is created, so land notes from the seller automatically have first lien position, unless sellers specifically subordinate land notes to land development loans, which they rarely do. Developers must therefore release parcels from the land note before they can obtain development financing from lenders. The unencumbered land constitutes their equity. Even if developers finance development costs out of their own pockets, land must be released from the land note for the developer to deliver clear title to builders or other buyers of the lots. Buyers need clear title (free of liens) before they can obtain their own construction financing. Buyers usually view land note financing favorably during the predevelopment period before they take down the construction loan, as long as they have the option of paying it off at any time.

Land sellers' main economic concern is that they will be left holding a note with inadequate underlying value in the "security parcel." As landowners, they also do not wish to have a large remaining property fragmented by a failed development. They therefore want strict release provisions that require the developer to pay down more on the land note than the actual value of the land to be released, leaving more land as security for the unpaid portion of the note. Additionally, they may wish to preserve their unreleased parcels in a contiguous piece. The developer's objective, on the other hand, is to achieve maximum flexibility in the location and acreage of land to be released. Ideally, the developer wants to be able to release the maximum amount of land for the minimum amount of money; this flexibility is particularly important early in the project's life, when costs have exhausted a large proportion of the developer's capital and getting to positive cash flow is critically important.

Suppose a developer purchases 100 acres (40 ha) for $1 million with an eight-year land note for $800,000, or $8,000 per acre ($20,000/ha). The note is amortized at the rate of $100,000 per year. Suppose the developer also negotiates a partial release provision that calls for a payment of $12,000 per acre ($30,000/ha). To sell 25 acres (10 ha) to a builder, the developer must pay the seller $300,000 (25 ac × $12,000 or 10 ha × $30,000) to release the land. Without clarifying language, the developer's $300,000 payment reduces the seller's note from $800,000 to $500,000. Instead of reducing the note principal balance immediately, this specific language permits the developer to pay interest only on the note for the next three years. The clause "all prepayments are credited toward the next principal installments coming due" means that the next three principal installments are paid by the $300,000 payment, but that repayment of the note is not accelerated. The developer will not have to make another principal payment for three years. Without the clause, the seller would probably construe that the $300,000 payment simply shortens the remaining life of the note from eight to five years. The developer, of course, wants the flexibility of the full term, so that it will not be necessary to sell the land prematurely or to find other financing sources to pay off the land note. For retail lot sales, release payments are usually negotiated as a simple and predictable percentage of net sales price, subject to review against developers' initial representations of lot pricing. In this case, the release percentage is set to fully pay off the note well before the last lot is sold. This "acceleration" ensures that the note will be paid even if price targets are not met, and it will be negotiated, as the developer wants it low and the seller wants it high.

Developers never want to release more land from the note than is necessary at any one time, because seller financing is usually their lowest-cost source of money. Thus, they should try to avoid release provisions that call for releasing land in strips or in a sequence of contiguous parcels.[9] If releases have to occur on contiguous properties, then developers will be forced to release the entire property to develop or sell a tract at one end. Such an arrangement is especially concerning for developers of subdivisions with distinct subneighborhoods, because they will want to have a variety of products on the market at once, to increase absorption. Sellers will rightfully be concerned if developers can "cherry-pick" the most desirable land and then abandon the rest of the proj-

ect. To get around this problem, the release provision can assign values to parcels or strips in the property that reflect market values. Thus, prime land may have a release price that is significantly higher than that for less desirable land. Alternatively, the provision may call for the developer to release two acres (0.8 ha) of less desirable land for every acre (0.4 ha) of desirable land, or the release may be spelled out in a predetermined

Tips for Land Acquisition

Conversations with successful developers have produced a number of useful tips regarding land acquisition.

- Make sure the owner is actually willing to sell the land. Sellers may use your bids to negotiate with others or just to check on their asset's value.
- Do not let the seller dictate the use of the property after the sale.
- Beware of appraisals of sites that have not been physically analyzed for hazardous or other undesirable conditions.
- When rezoning is necessary, attempt to buy the land on a per-unit basis, giving the landowner an incentive to help obtain approvals.
- If a conditional use permit or variance will be needed, ask the current owner to sign a waiver to allow you to act as his or her agent in dealing with the city or county before closing.
- If you obtain seller financing, make sure the seller frees up some of the land immediately so that you can build on it. You need to be able to give the construction lender a first lien on the land.
- In some states, such as California, use a *deed of trust* for purchase-money mortgages so the seller cannot claim a deficiency judgment against you if you default.
- Concerning "no-waste" clauses, be sure to read the fine print on the trust deed form because you may not be able to remove trees or buildings on the property until the note is paid off.
- Make sure you select a title company that is strong enough to back you up if you need to defend a lawsuit involving title. Some nationwide title companies enfranchise their local offices separately so that you do not have the backing of the national company.
- Make sure that the seller's warranties survive the close of escrow. Consult your attorney for the current state law on this topic.
- Beware of commissions, and be clear with brokers when you are—and are not—engaging their services. Mentioning a property in passing may create a claim for an eventual commission.

sequence of parcels coinciding with the phasing plan of the development. In short, a variety of structures can be employed to assuage sellers' concerns, but developers must maintain the ability, within reason, to change direction.

KEY POINTS OF A PURCHASE CONTRACT. A variety of clauses and provisions should be included as part of the initial purchase contract to minimize later renegotiations with the seller:[10]

- **Supplementary Note Procedure**—This clause allows the sale of subparcels (parcels within the original tract) to builders and other developers without paying off the underlying first lien. This provision, which must be specifically negotiated, allows the developer to pass on seller financing to builders through a supplementary note, which gives builders more time before they need to pay the full lot cost. Nevertheless, unless the seller is willing to subordinate seller financing, the supplementary note has first lien position, which means that builders who purchase subparcels must pay off the note before they can obtain construction financing, as construction lenders also require a first lien position. In fact, builders usually pay off the supplementary note with the first draw on the construction loan.
- **Out-of-Sequence Releases**—This clause satisfies the developer's need to release certain parcels out of sequence for roads, major utilities, or amenities or to change phasing.
- **Joinder and Subordination**—This clause provides for the seller to join within 30 days any applications for government approvals made by the developer. It also provides for the seller's subordination agreements, required by any government authority for the filing of subdivision maps or street dedications.
- **Transferability**—This clause protects sellers from having the deal they negotiated transferred to another buyer, presumably giving the buyer the benefit of appreciation during his or her ownership. Nontransferable contracts may give the seller unreasonable influence if the buyer needs to bring in a partner at a later point, and they may be narrowly tailored to allow for additional financing.
- **Subordination of Subparcels**—Most sellers are unlikely to allow subordination of their note to development lenders. They may be willing, however, to allow subordination on one or two subparcels. This action can help the developer obtain the development loan without paying off the land note.

- **Seller's "Comfort Language"**—The seller is not required to execute any documents until he or she has approved the purchaser's general land use plan.
- **Ability to Extend Closing**—This clause permits the purchaser to extend the closing by 30 or 60 days by paying a prenegotiated amount of additional earnest money.
- **Letters of Credit as Earnest Money**—The developer can greatly reduce upfront cash requirements if the seller will accept letters of credit as earnest money. Letters of credit can be cashed by the seller on a certain date or if certain events occur—for example, if a purchaser fails to close. The clause might say, "Purchaser may extend the closing for 60 days by depositing an additional $50,000 letter of credit as additional escrow deposit."
- **Property Taxes**—This clause clarifies which party pays taxes accruing before and after the purchase, which will not coincide with a tax due date. Many municipalities and counties have categories such as "open space" or "agricultural land" that reduce taxes. When the land is developed, the owner must repay the tax savings for the previous three or five years. This "rollback" can amount to a major unexpected cost to the developer if it is not provided for in the purchase agreement. For example, such a provision might say, "Seller agrees to pay all ad valorem tax assessments or penalties assessed for any period before the closing as a result of any change in ownership or usage of the property." In addition, some areas with agricultural-use taxation will only guarantee these favorable tax rates to landowners who enroll their parcels in voluntary restrictive-use agreements. These agreements can run five or 10 years, and because they are not easements, they will not necessarily be visible in the recorded history of the parcel deed.
- **Title Insurance**—The seller usually (though not always) pays the title insurance policy. Many title insurance policies have standard exception clauses, however, such as a survey exception.[11] The party responsible for paying the insurance premium for deleting these exceptions is subject to negotiation.
- **Seller's Remedy**—If the purchaser defaults, the seller's sole remedy is to receive the escrow deposit as liquidated damages. This clause prevents the seller from pursuing the purchaser for more money if the sale falls through.

What Makes a Good Market Study

Proper Delineation of the Market Area

The geographic area where competing subdivisions are sampled should be large enough to include the entire quadrant of the city where your project is located, but small enough to exclude areas that derive their economic value from proximities the subject site does not share.

Appropriate Market Segmentation

Markets seldom reflect a smooth gradient from cheap to expensive. Different types of buyers are more commonly clustered in specific price bands, with associated preferences and needs. Analysis can reveal how demographics and economics propel demand from these segments at different rates.

Proper Delineation of the Competing Market Product Types

A market should not be defined so narrowly that it omits relevant competition, which leads to underestimated supply. For example, low-cost single-family houses compete with condominiums, and large-lot subdivisions may compete with rural parcels for buyers.

The Capture Rate

The capture rate of lots for the subdivision should take into account both the total demand in the marketplace and the number of other subdivisions. In metropolitan areas with populations greater than 1 million, capture rates in excess of 5 percent for *any* project, are suspect. Capture rates greater than 30 percent may be appropriate for very specialized products (which should connote a small overall market as well) or within a severely supply-constrained market. The case for a supply-constrained market must also look at the development pipeline for the duration of proposed sales or lease-up.

Employment and Absorption Rates

Projections of demand should be based both on employment projections and on long-term (five- or 10-year) historical absorption rates in the area. Large increases relative to historical absorption rates are always suspect. A developer's claim that growth is changing substantially and sustainably should be supported by an explanation of the underlying regulations, infrastructure, or consumer preferences that are driving the change.

These clauses constitute only a small fraction of all those included in a standard purchase contract. They are highlighted here because they represent items that the purchaser should try to negotiate with the seller. Experienced developers use a specially prepared standard form that includes such clauses. Sophisticated sellers may insist on using their own custom contract, to which these clauses will probably have to be added. An experienced real estate attorney should always assist in the preparation of contracts.

MARKET ANALYSIS AFTER SITE SELECTION

After tying up a site, the developer should reexamine the target market for the proposed project. Special features of the selected site, as well as changes to the overall economic climate, may indicate a different market from the one identified during the preliminary market analysis undertaken before site selection. Land uses change slowly, but markets can change quickly.

At this stage, analysis should concentrate on location, neighborhood, and amenities. For example, suppose a developer's initial target market is buyers of move-up houses selling from $500,000 to $600,000. If sales in that price range are moving steadily, the developer may want to continue with such a program, even if several other developers are competing at the same price point. But if that market is saturated, with forward indicators such as building permits or presale

deposits beginning to soften, the plans can be modified—for example, to develop a lower-priced community or to diversify the offering to appeal to multiple price points.

The market analysis at this stage helps the developer advance physical planning. Iteration between design and market data helps determine the specific target market and therefore the size and configuration of lots, amenities, and other fundamental aspects of the design. Marketing professionals should be involved in this stage of design. This analysis also informs the appropriate documentation (e.g., a development appraisal) to obtain a loan and refine a business plan for investors. A convincing market study also supports marketing to prospective builders. The conclusions and statistical backup will be essential in communicating the value of the proposed community and explaining choices of design, amenities, and structure that build that value.

Unless a subdivision is very small or the developer has already secured informal commitments from builders, a local market research firm that specializes in subdivision development should be hired. Ideally, the market research firm should already have a database covering all the competing subdivisions. From its analysis, the market research firm should be able to help the developer determine the best market for the lots and the total number of lots the developer can sell per month, grouped by lot size and price range. The report should document total housing demand and supply for the market area and, from that number, forecast demand and supply for the specific product type and submarket area the developer's project will serve (see the accompanying feature box). The bottom line of the market study should be a projection of the number of units that can be sold each month by product type and the projected sales price. For example, suppose demand for $400,000 to $450,000 townhouses is 200 houses per year (16 per month) in the submarket, and two subdivisions are competing for buyers. Expected sales would be approximately eight per month, assuming that each subdivision captures its share of total demand. However, this figure should never be assumed to be the pace of sales. Demand is never precisely met by the product that is actually developed. Many potential buyers will not purchase what is offered because it is too expensive or not to their taste, or for any number of other reasons. Projections of the pace of sales must be tempered by observation of market reality. Regardless of what demand statistics show, if developers of similar projects in the general area are selling only two or three units per month, then others—particularly a newcomer—will not likely sell twice as many. Developed lots are an intermediate factor, not the only factor, in the production of housing; other factors include construction and financing. It is possible for a shortage of housing and a surplus of lots to exist simultaneously. Therefore, the market study should examine demand and supply for both the final housing product and the developed lots.

Generally, a homebuilder purchases (*takes down*) more than one lot at a time. A lot sale may include four or five or as many as 100 lots, depending on the type of project, size of builder, and market conditions. *Rolling options* are a popular method for master developers to control builders' takedown of lots. These options provide for the builder to take down a designated number of lots every quarter or year. The option gives the builder an assured supply of lots, at a predictable wholesale price, while giving the land developer an out from the contract if the builder cannot sell as many houses as anticipated. The rolling option typically has a built-in escalation in the lot price—perhaps a 2 to 4 percent increase per year. Rolling options can be structured to protect the interest of the master developer, the builder, or both.[12] Master developers want some assurance that builders will meet or exceed the takedown schedule and not tie up future option increments if they are not performing. Builders

want to ensure continued availability of lots—but do not want to pay before the lots are needed. Builders want to carry as small an inventory of lots as possible and want the ability to decline future options with as little notice or penalty as possible.

Builders may pay option fees, which are usually based on the value of the unexercised options. Paying option fees is a tradeoff against a reduction in the price escalation: when option fees are paid, the price escalation is lower. Higher option fees encourage the builder to take down the option sooner (to avoid paying the option fee). Option fees are paid even if the future increments are not acquired. For example, suppose a master developer has 200 lots. The deal may provide that the builder has an option to purchase annual increments of 50 lots under an agreed pricing framework over a four-year period. If the builder fails to take down a scheduled increment, he may lose his option rights to future increments. The builder may pay value escalations and/or option fees on unexercised options. Incentives other than cash may appeal to builders. If the community is unique, access to custom-home clients through an "approved builder" list may attract good builders, and favorable land subordination terms may be more enticing than well-priced options.

REGULATORY PROCESS

A project's feasibility is determined by regulations at the local, state, and federal levels. Developers need to understand these regulations and be able to navigate the approval process efficiently. The goal should be to clarify approval risks early, then to reduce risk at every step in the process.

ZONING AND PLATTING. The process of subdividing land is called *platting* or mapping. Platting usually involves a zoning change, typically from a low-density designation to a density one or two steps up the zoning spectrum. In suburban fringes, land is often zoned "agriculture" or some other nearly nondevelopable designation that must be rezoned to allow lot subdivision and development. Every locality has a different procedure for zoning,[13] though there are common elements. In the Northeast and Mid-Atlantic, zoning is administered at the township level or by the city in urban areas. In the South and West, the process is controlled by county or municipal government. Vast differences in the professionalism of staff and officials exist among jurisdictions. Rezoning applications are formal proposals to the regulatory agency, typically an appointed planning commission or its delegated staff, to modify the jurisdiction's zoning map to allow a different use or greater density on specific parcels. The applicant must make the case that the proposed changes, though not consistent with the existing map, are consistent with goals of the jurisdiction's comprehensive plan and are beneficial, or at least not detrimental, to the infrastructural and fiscal environment. In reality, the process is politically fraught; the concerns of "abutters"—ranging from traffic to property values to noise and other nuisances—as well as larger issues of urban structure and infrastructure are likely to dominate the discussions.

The process can take from several months to many years, depending on the environmental and political sensitivity of the site. Many sites are also subject to the approval of special agencies or commissions, which adds costs and time. For example, land in California that is located within 1,000 yards (915 m) of the ocean is subject to the California Coastal Commission's jurisdiction. Fulfilling the commission's requirements may add years to the time necessary to secure subdivision approvals. Because even many experienced developers lack the staying power to pilot a site through the commission's process, new developers are well advised to avoid jurisdictions that involve lengthy and expensive approval processes.

Platting Process. Platting is the official procedure by which land is subdivided into smaller legal entities. It is how cities and counties enforce standards for streets and lots and record new lot descriptions in subdivisions. The legal description of a house lot typically follows this form: "Lot 10 of Block 7143 of Fondren Southwest III Subdivision, Harris County, Texas." The legal description parallels the platting procedure. The developer submits a plat of the property showing individual blocks and lots. In some areas, platting requires a public hearing, even if the intended use conforms to the zoning. In other areas, no public hearing is required as long as the platted lots are consistent with zoning and all other subdivision regulations. Even when platting is legally an administrative process, the developer may be drawn into a public process by companion ordinances to the subdivision law, such as water protection or critical slope protections.

The number of units permitted to be built on a given parcel usually depends on a combination of several factors, including minimum lot width and depth, setbacks, alley requirements, and street rights-of-way. The target market determines whether a developer plats the greatest possible number of lots, creates larger lots for more expensive houses, or includes a mix of types. Platting also commits parcels to community or amenity use and potentially to conservation uses. A developer should avoid going for the highest allowable density unless previous experience has shown that the resulting density and smaller lots are consistent with target market demand. That being said, developers often enter the process proposing density near the maximum allowable, knowing that the process will almost always result in a reduction from the initial proposal. In areas with transferable development rights (TDRs), this action can have additional benefits, as the developer may be able to monetize any surplus of rights beyond the business plan by selling the right to increase density to other developers through the TDR market. Even in areas without formal TDRs, the developer may want to consider donating unusable land to a conservation trust, which will provide immediate tax deductions for the value of the land. Both processes are complex legal arrangements, and a land use attorney should be consulted before acquisition to ensure that the development's structure allows these kinds of transactions.

Replatting a previously platted area can present unexpected difficulties, especially if the developer must *abandon* (that is, remove from official maps) old streets or alleys. In Dallas, Peiser Corporation was investigating a site when it unexpectedly found that *all* abutting property owners had to agree to abandon a mapped but never built alley. With 50 homeowners involved, the likelihood of unanimous agreement was almost zero. The developer passed on the site, despite having invested considerable time and money.

In addition to platting requirements, the subdivision may be subject to restrictive covenants imposed by the seller or a previous owner. Restrictive covenants should show up in the initial title search and, even if their enforceability is questionable, they may have a profound influence on the type of development allowable.

Developers should be aware of opportunities and pitfalls caused by multiple, overlapping regulatory jurisdictions. Massachusetts, for example, is a "home rule" state, meaning that local authorities overlay many state approvals with their own, and vice versa. In home rule states, major land use changes can happen quickly, certainly within the timeline of even a modestly scaled development. In "Dillon's Rule" states, such as Virginia, major regulatory change must often be authorized by state legislators, which usually means a developer will have a one- or two-year warning before such changes are enacted. A land use attorney can advise the developer on such issues. The public dissemination of land use information is improving with the advent of GIS technology. However, deployment of good resource mapping is uneven, and many critical requirements are not available online—or if they are, their amendments are not. Some relevant codes are not even published in the commonwealth's general laws. Developers should invest early in local expertise to

- identify all necessary approvals;
- provide realistic timelines in light of local customs; and
- advise on the likely content (and expense) of conditions or necessary mitigation.

Filing a Subdivision Application. Every jurisdiction has its own procedure for obtaining subdivision approval. Most jurisdictions have at least a two-stage process that requires approval from the planning commission and then the city council or county supervisor. California, for example, has a two-tier process. The first tier is the *general plan*, which defines land use for all parts of the city and is reviewed every five years. Most important for new subdivisions, it defines which areas are encouraged for development and which are not. General plans may also be linked to the municipality's capital budget, which prioritizes planned public expenditures for utilities, roads, parks, and other infrastructure improvements. The significance of the general plan is that it makes obtaining permission for zoning changes that are in accord with the general plan relatively easy. Changes that are contrary to the general plan—such as development in an agricultural zone or apartments in an area designated for single-family residences—may be almost impossible to get approved. Land that is designated for agricultural use must be changed to urban use, specifying property type and density, in the general plan before a specific plan (the second tier) can be created to develop the property. This step takes considerable lead time since general plans are revised only every five years.

Specific plans spell out the actual zoning, density, and, in some cases, footprint, street access, and other details of the proposed development. Specific plans are even more detailed than zoning and, once achieved, may tie the developer to a particular development scheme. Changing a specific plan often requires a new round of public hearings and subjects the developer to the full risks associated with regulatory change. These risks have grown substantially in recent decades as more and more communities have attempted to curtail growth. Any public review can be highly politicized, giving the planning commission and city council the opportunity to impose new restrictions, require more investment by the developer (exactions), or lower the allowable density of development.

Phasing. Most subdivisions larger than about 200 lots are divided into phases. Even a much smaller development may be phased if the developer's company is small and has limited resources, or if a portion of the land remains unavailable until later. Each phase typically involves a single filing of the plat and subdivision restrictions. Developers finance and construct utilities, roads, and other improvements necessary to create finished lots for each entire phase. Therefore, phases should not be so large that they cannot be financed or absorbed by the market in a reasonable time frame—usually within 18 to 24 months, or one economic cycle. Delineation of phases is a balancing act because developers usually want the critical mass of a substantially complete development project as quickly as possible, to reassure buyers skittish about new communities. At the same time, communities may demand to review every aspect of a multiphase project at once, to assess impacts of the whole. Jo Anne Stubblefield, president of Hyatt and Stubblefield in Atlanta, advises developers not to file more than the first phase of a project at the outset, especially for larger properties. Once plans are recorded, the developer may be held to them for a phase that is years away, limiting the ability to change with market conditions. Moreover, most of the regulatory process makes it advantageous to plat in smaller portions, again to preserve flexibility later if the market changes.[14] Of course, owners must be watchful to protect rights allocated to future phases, as future approvals might fall under increasingly stringent conditions or political opposition as the city council changes over time.

REGULATORY CONCERNS. An entire book would be needed to describe the many different forms of regulation that a developer can encounter. Staying on top of new local ordinances is not enough. A developer must know which regulations are about to come into force, which are still under discussion, and which are only vague proposals. The lead times required to get a development off the ground are often long—and they are growing longer. The more agencies involved, the longer it takes. Projects in environmentally sensitive areas have been known to take 10 years or more to secure approvals. Litigation over public approvals for larger tracts is becoming the rule rather than the exception.

"Political involvement," says Scott Smith of Oakwood Homes in Colorado Springs, "is no longer just a good idea; it's critical. Good relationship building with the city planner, city manager, and water/sewer officials is obviously necessary, but don't forget larger issues. We work hard at developing relationships with state and national political parties—a move that may have seemed unjustified until now—when we face a ballot initiative that could kill development even of existing projects."[15]

"What has changed . . . is really the intensity of competition for land entitlement. As competition for land entitlement (and associated costs) heats up, political involvement is becoming more critical," according to Al Neely, chief investment officer at Charles E. Smith Co. in Arlington, Virginia. "If you are not a consensus builder, you just won't make it. That means consensus at all levels, not just three or four government agencies, but community activists and advocacy groups as well. You have to engage people and get them on board."[16]

Tim Edmond, CEO of the Edmond Group in Tallahassee, Florida, adds, "Make sure you understand fully the cost and time required for entitlements, and then add 30 percent to your estimate."[17]

Roger Galatas, of The Woodlands, Texas, advised that credibility with regulatory agencies is built with words *and* actions. "That means, do what you say you'll do. Successful developers engage regulators themselves or send their most senior people. What does it say about you if you send someone junior to make your presentation to the planning board?"[18]

Four major regulatory issues affect most land developers today: vesting of development rights, growth controls, environmental issues, and traffic congestion.

Vesting of Development Rights. Historically, if developers could obtain zoning, they had the right to build what the zoning allowed. If they owned or bought a property that was already zoned, they were entitled, without public hearings, to develop the property within the limits established by the zoning. But this is no longer true in many parts of the country. If a court decides that the right to develop was not *vested*, the developer may be denied the right to proceed. Standards for vesting vary widely. In development-friendly areas of the Southeast, vesting may be assumed at the "preliminary plat" (analogous to a general plan) and is secure at the "final plat," subject to administrative renewals. In California, vertical construction may be required to prove vested development rights.

Development agreements have become a popular solution to the problem of securing vested development rights for larger projects. They are negotiated between the developer and the municipality and ensure that the ground rules under which a developer builds are the same as those that were in effect at the time the agreement was signed. These formal contracts protect the developer's right to build a specified density of uses, referring to fairly detailed plans, in exchange for providing certain facilities to the community. While these documents resolve an important uncertainty for big projects, the sequence and costs laid out in them represent major commitments, and a specialist attorney should be involved. Development agreements are common in California, and a growing number of states have passed enabling legislation to allow them.

Growth Controls. Effective growth management schemes focus on guiding community development and responding to development proposals comprehensively, rather than piecemeal as applications are submitted. They are used to ensure a level of quality in development, including conservation of open space, and ensure that infrastructure is in place to support new development as it occurs.

Growth management provisions are often incorporated in local zoning ordinances. They typically include

- linkage of zoning approvals to capital budgeting investments in infrastructure and services;
- establishment of growth boundaries or other policies to limit the supply of developable land and direct density to urban centers and transit nodes;
- ceilings on the number of housing units or square feet of space that can be constructed in the jurisdiction, or even quotas on building permits;
- linkage of development and availability of water supply, sewage capacity, or, conceivably, any limited natural resource; and
- linkage of projects and specific public facilities, such as schools, transit, or road improvements.

Growth management is not new. Communities have been able to limit the number of building permits they issue annually ever since the *Ramapo*[19] and *Petaluma*[20] decisions in the 1970s. Over time, growth management has become more sophisticated and more widespread.

Communities adopt antigrowth or smart-growth measures for two main reasons: first, as a reaction to the changing character of the community; and second, in response to overburdened infrastructure—

schools, sewers, parks and open space, and, most commonly, local roads. Traffic and parking congestion, both real and perceived, drive many antigrowth measures. The capacity of roads and intersections has become the primary criterion in many communities determining where and how much new development will be allowed. Developers are often required to build additional traffic lanes, install new traffic lights, and even build new freeway interchanges to offset their projects' effects. As public-sector investment has stagnated, municipalities have ironically become more dependent on these exactions and proffers by private developers.

Well-informed and serious debate about growth and development can lead to positive changes in land use regulations. A growing number of local and state governments provide incentives to developers of environmentally or socially responsible projects, including density bonuses, waived fees, fast-track reviews, and infrastructure improvements, such as parks, roads, and pedestrian links.

Environmental Issues. Since the early 1970s, developers of larger projects in some jurisdictions have been required to submit environmental impact statements (EISs) and reports (EIRs) to receive project approval from federal and state agencies. Over time, the size of projects that require an EIR steadily decreased, and enforcement has become more rigorous. In areas with growth concerns, almost all development projects are required to produce some form of environmental impact analysis, if only an engineer's certification of compliance. The requirements are increasingly coming from local zoning and companion codes, such as groundwater or slope protection ordinances. Formal EISs cover all potential impacts of new development on a community, including impacts on water, biodiversity, vegetation, animal habitat, archaeology, and public facilities, such as roads, schools, utilities, and community services. In smaller projects, EIRs may address only the external impacts of the project beyond the site boundaries; in projects of 500 acres (200 ha) or more, the most consequential impacts may be within the site. Some environmental issues requiring extensive due diligence include location in a 100-year floodplain, wetlands, and the presence or potential presence of endangered species, cultural resources, or toxic waste. Each of these items should show up on an EIS, but the developer should not assume that an EIS protects the investment completely. Financing typically requires a Phase I environmental site assessment (ESA), which is a cursory review intended to highlight areas of concern for additional tests. Recommendations in an EIS/ESA for additional study will send a wise developer immediately to an attorney. Responsibility for the results of such investigation is complicated, and prudent developers will be sure they know their responsibilities before moving forward on a Phase II study.

EISs are circulated to interested parties, with comments invited. Reviewers' responses are then appended to the statement, which may be modified after comments. Federal legislation allows litigation over the adequacy of an EIS, which can lead to huge costs and delays.[21] This type of litigation is one method that well-funded adversaries use to stop undesirable projects. Developers should never assume that compliance with federal law translates to compliance with state law. State laws often conflict with similar federal laws, so developers should consult an attorney to clarify obligations. Although the developer may ultimately be right in a court of law, the time and cost of litigation could break an undercapitalized developer.[22]

One of the most sensitive aspects of EIRs concerns hazardous waste. For land developers, sites that encompass brownfields present both constraints and opportunities. The U.S. Environmental Protection Agency (EPA) defines brownfields as "abandoned, idled, or underused industrial and commercial facilities where expansion or redevelopment is complicated by real or perceived environmental contamination." Although many of these sites are problematic because of their industrial locations and the potential cost of cleanup, well-located brownfields are often attractive infill locations. Amendments to the Superfund law in 1997 hold lenders harmless when financing the redevelopment of brownfield sites, and at least 35 states have enacted legislation to limit cleanup liability. As a result, insurance companies are writing policies to limit the developer's liability, and financial institutions are making loans for the development of brownfields.

State and local agencies are becoming increasingly knowledgeable about cost-effective cleanup methods and are frequently willing to provide federally funded grants or local tax incentives and, where possible, to cap or reduce liability for cleanups.

Value can be added to a project in the course of solving some of these environmental problems if the developer is flexible enough in acquisition. "We've had success in these situations by creating land trusts, environmental trusts, conservation easements, and other structures to deal with endangered species, wetlands, and cultural resources, which can then

be carefully marketed as amenities for the overall development project. This matter has to be dealt with up front, however, incorporating risk in the acquisition program and acquiring enough land to allow the developer to give up parcels to these kinds of structures without serious damage to the project's economics."[23]

Traffic. Traffic congestion in many suburbs is as bad or worse than congestion in urban centers, typically with fewer transit options. As a result, concerns about traffic are often at the root of antigrowth movements. Traffic studies are a standard part of environmental impact reviews. Localities often require developers to pay for major off-site road improvements to receive approvals. Legal precedent in these matters requires "rough proportionality" and "a reasonable nexus" for exactions, meaning that the required contribution may not be unreasonably large, relative to the economic value of the approval, and that some connection must exist between the exaction and the impact of the approved project.[24]

FINANCING INFRASTRUCTURE. Regulatory uncertainty is integrally tied to the time and cost of providing or obtaining necessary infrastructure facilities, including utilities, roads, and drainage and potentially parks, schools, treatment plants, and fire and police stations.

A variety of methods for financing infrastructure are available:

- **General Taxes**—Historically, street and utility improvements have been financed by bonds that were repaid by general property tax revenues.

Careful attention to environmental assessment is always important, but it is essential on former industrial sites. The volunteer-led Wild Mile project, in Chicago, also shows how ecological resources can be respectfully programmed, sometimes in multiple ways, to connect visitor and environment.

- **Federal and State Grants**—Historically, federal and state grants have assisted local communities in building water treatment facilities, sewage treatment plants, highways, and other infrastructure. Since 2008, the regular funding process has been supplemented with irregular, large packages of infrastructure, social, and environmental investment intended as economic stimulus.
- **Impact Fees**—These fees are imposed on the developer at the final plat or building permit and are usually computed per unit, per square foot, or per dollar value of finished construction.
- **User Fees and Charges**—Such fees and charges are a traditional means of obtaining revenues. Monthly fees (water and sewer fees, for example) are pledged as revenue streams to repay bonds issued to finance the facilities and to pay operating and maintenance expenses.
- **Assessment Districts**—These districts can issue bonds and levy a special tax on property owners who benefit from specific public improvements in the district.
- **Special Districts**—Special districts are similar to assessment districts, except that their governing bodies are separate from the local government. They can issue bonds and levy taxes on property owners in their jurisdiction. They may exist for many purposes or to finance one narrowly defined public good.

- **Tax Increment Financing Districts**—Increases in tax revenues that result from new development in a specified area are earmarked for public improvements or services in that area, rather than using the general fund.
- **Developer Exactions**—The developer is required (officially or unofficially) to install or pay directly for community facilities in return for approvals.

Developers must thoroughly understand public and private infrastructure financing. After the cost of the land itself, infrastructure accounts for the largest portion of land development costs. Developers must understand how their development will affect the revenues and costs of the local jurisdiction where they want to build. Increasingly, development approvals depend on whether the proposed development will have a positive impact on local finances. The calculation of fiscal effect can be subjective, as large costs must be allocated per capita, or per area, and revenues must be projected far into the future.

The legal test for impact fees is that a rational nexus can be proved to exist between the fees charged and the benefits received by the future residents of the development: The fee and the impact must be related and proportional. The developer should not be expected to pay the entire cost of facilities that benefit other residents of the community.

Ironically, growth moratoriums and building permit caps are motivated, in part, by the lack of adequate impact fees. Promoters of moratoriums claim that developers are not paying their full share of the cost that they impose on a community. Developers may find that supporting "pay to play" impact fees is in their own best interest. In that way, the necessary infrastructure funding can be linked to development patterns.

As development fees have become popular and developers have accepted them, many communities have come to resist general tax increases. As a result, local governments have looked to developers to provide an ever-increasing share of the costs of services—so much so that in some cases, new residents are subsidizing existing residents. Many cities now require developers to pay for half the cost of major arterials that abut their property.[25] Further, developers typically must pay for some or all of the new utility lines required to serve their property, although a portion of these installation costs may be recoverable once the development is occupied with paying customers. These off-site requirements have a major impact on the location of subdivisions. Even for very large developments, the cost of bringing in water and sewer services from more than a mile away is prohibitive. Unless the municipality can underwrite the cost directly or share it through some form of special district, the amount that developers can afford to pay for off-site facilities is limited. The first developer is often required to install infrastructure—notably roads, sewers, water, and drainage—to serve a new area. Many cities require other property owners who benefit from that infrastructure to reimburse the developer later, when those owners subdivide their own property. This procedure gives the developer the potential to recoup the cost, albeit on an uncertain schedule.

AVOIDING PITFALLS. Many regulations serve vital functions—protecting the environment, reducing flooding, controlling traffic, and ensuring that adequate infrastructure is built. From the developer's point of view, however, increasing government regulation adds considerably to the time, expense, and risk of land development.

The larger the land development project, the more likely it is to be a target of special regulatory concern. One way to minimize the impact of regulation is to choose infill areas located in older jurisdictions that have more established regulations. They may present other problems, however, as infill tracts are typically surrounded by existing development; developers may have to deal with established advocates for homeowners and neighborhoods.

In general, developers can reduce the regulatory risk by following these suggestions:

- Stay closely in touch with local planning staff, and document all correspondence.
- Know and respect local representatives. Planning boards will often listen to the local delegate when projects affect their constituents.
- Monitor pending ordinances and referenda.
- Join and be active in the local building industry association.
- Once a concern has been identified, consult the regulatory agency's staff and, if necessary, an attorney to find out how to protect or exempt the project.
- Consider working with redevelopment agencies, which often have the power to expedite approvals or at least to outline a clear path.
- Consider using a development agreement on larger projects to protect development rights.
- Select local architects, engineers, and zoning and other consultants who have worked extensively in the community.

Maintaining Flexibility. The development value of land is tied to the number of units or square footage that can be built on a site. That relationship shifts the approval risk, in part, from developers to sellers, because the purchase price is lower if developers are not confident of required approvals. Most land sellers are unwilling to accept regulatory risk after closing, but Matt Kiefer of Goulston & Storrs advises that due diligence must include a clear path to approval, certainly before closing and preferably before hard deposits. "Managing the process of approvals is still the highest value add of a developer."[26] The developer must either accept this risk or find a seller who is willing to defer the closing until zoning or other approvals are completed. The land price will reflect which party takes on the entitlement risk, being far lower if the developer closes without the entitlements. Developers are advised to share the risks, when possible, with the seller—even if that means less profit—unless they are very confident they can obtain zoning approval for enough units to make the project profitable.

At the same time that government approvals are becoming harder to obtain, planning commissions and city councils are requiring developers to meet specific timetables. Developers are often required to build roads and community facilities by a specific time, often in advance of selling lots. In some cases, developers must commit to building a specified number of units per year. The cyclical nature of the real estate industry, however, makes periods of boom and bust inevitable. Developers must retain the flexibility to build more units when times are good and to reduce production (and infrastructure installation) when times are bad.

Developers should also retain the flexibility, when possible, to program the mix of units for each development phase. Because of the frequent delay between approvals and construction, developers must be able to respond to current market conditions when deciding on their final unit mix. Otherwise, they may be forced to sell lots to homebuilders to meet a market that is no longer in demand and may be precluded from selling lots for houses in a price category that is in demand. For larger projects, developers should work in increments or stages that are small enough for them to vary the product mix as the market indicates. Many communities now require approval of specific plans that lock the developer into specific unit sizes and finishes. Such a requirement adds substantially to the developer's risk, as a change in the market requires a new series of public hearings to update the specific plan.

Working with the Community. Good relationships between a developer and neighboring homeowners have always been critical to a developer's success. Recent national debates about inequality and affordability have propelled a new skepticism of developers' proposals. The most common objection raised by neighborhood groups to a proposed subdivision is that it will reduce the quality of the neighborhood—exacerbating traffic problems or introducing lower-cost homes that will affect property values. In gentrifying neighborhoods, the concern can be precisely the opposite—that new development will be expensive and push out long-term residents. In fact, both pressures can apply to the same project. In urban fringe development, opposition tends to focus on spillover costs and inadequate infrastructure.

Most experienced developers prefer to talk to homeowner groups themselves instead of hiring someone to represent them. Developers must convince the community that they will keep their promises, and this trust is more likely to be gained in person. However, some professionals and tools can help structure community engagement on a development proposal. A good foundation for soliciting and synthesizing community input needs structure, starting with a clear scope of what the project can and cannot address.

The developer of a small project may not be compelled to talk with homeowner groups if few public approvals are required, but any hope of flying under the radar is usually wishful thinking. Almost every public action in land use requires notification of at least the abutting property owners. Homeowner groups become particularly intransigent when they believe they are being ignored—especially if they do not learn about proposed projects until the public hearing.

A better approach is to identify in advance the groups that may have concerns about the project and to seek them out. Developers should also be careful to identify the most influential leaders in a local community. Peiser Corporation, for example, lost a zoning case because it met with the president of the local homeowners association but not with another community leader, a minister, who came out against the project in part because he was not consulted initially.

When a public hearing is required for approval, the following approach is recommended:

- Start by collecting data; let stakeholders know you want to hear from them. Particularly for historically marginalized groups, do not assume that public documents correctly incorporate their desires for their neighborhood.
- Clearly communicate project facts to potentially affected members of the public. Try not to communicate ideas that are not yet fixed, to maintain a trustworthy consistency.
- Talk to planning departments early in the process to explore options and compare them to stated community goals and policies, such as a Comprehensive Plan.
- Be aware that the public hearing process is not adequate for addressing all opposition. Serious concerns need to be addressed in side-meetings, beginning at least 90 days before the hearing.
- Keep an open mind. In addition to regulated aspects of land use, communities may have other interests. Concerns about gentrification directly involve housing but may also be addressed with space for local retailers or services, opportunities for startups, and community wealth building.
- Be proactive: talk to the city council or legislators to get in touch with citizen groups, develop contacts with them, and keep them informed. Think of them as ambassadors.
- In contentious environments, enlist a trusted third party as an ally and mediator. A strategic partnership with a hospital, school, or employer can bring local credibility and knowledge.
- Use press relationships and a clear online and social media presence to communicate plans to those who are not at the public hearing. If the project is very complex, consultants can solicit input from, and facilitate continuous outreach to, concerned parties.
- Be certain that all plans are clearly explained and all numbers (density, unit count, traffic studies) are accurately illustrated. Most people understand pictures, not plans, and certainly not engineering plans. Invest in visualization to tell the project's story.
- Allocate time for the development staff to communicate with the public.

Much opposition to growth is motivated by the belief among existing homeowners that they pay an unfair portion of the cost of facilities that will be used by future residents. But each new generation of residents benefits from previous generations' investment in infrastructure. Major infrastructure investment—typically, streets and utilities—is characterized by debt payments over 20- to 30-year periods, slow deterioration, and periodic replacement. When the financing life is shorter than the economic life of a facility and when a community's growth rate is more than 3 percent per year, the residents of that community pay for benefits faster than they receive them. When taxes to pay for growth rise faster than property values, dissension between current residents and future residents (represented by the developer) soon follows.

The main justification for impact fees and other development charges is that they will alleviate the burden that growth imposes on existing homeowners. Theoretically, impact fees are imposed for the developer's share of facilities from which the developer benefits, including those that have been installed and paid for earlier. In some cases, such facilities may be off site and may benefit other parties as much as they directly benefit the developer's project. Attempting to share these costs equitably is usually better achieved by outreach and mediation than by litigation.

FINANCIAL FEASIBILITY ANALYSIS

Financial feasibility analysis for land development is performed in two stages. The first stage is a "quick-and-dirty" pro forma that summarizes the project's sales revenues, expenses, interest, and profit. The second is a multiperiod discounted cash flow (DCF) analysis that provides a detailed projection of cash flows, equity and loan needs, profits, and basic return measures, including internal rates of return (IRRs). Developers should perform both stages of analysis before they commit earnest money to a project. From the first analysis, note which variables (price, financing and construction costs, etc.) are the most uncertain, and prioritize them for due diligence research. Each projected cost should include an adequate contingency to cover unforeseen issues; this contingency can be reduced as uncertainty is resolved. The cash flow analysis should be regularly updated during the feasibility period as the team establishes sales, price, and cost information with greater accuracy. The DCF analysis feeds into the investor return analysis, which provides a picture of the returns to the different parties that furnish the equity for the project—the investors and the developer—under proposed deal structures. The DCF analysis and the investor return analysis are the developer's primary spreadsheets for evaluating a project's financial prospects, obtaining a land development loan, and raising equity from investors. Lenders and investors will ask the developer questions that cannot be credibly answered without these analyses. Although software tools allow small developers to use a variety of analytical techniques, a basic spreadsheet can do this work; most important is a conceptual understanding of project cash flow.

BASIC CONCEPTS. Financial analysis for land development differs from that for other property types, and developers should be aware of some basic concepts for this type of analysis.

For-Sale versus Income Property. The fundamental difference between financial analysis for land development and other property types is that land is for-sale property, whereas apartments, offices, retail stores, and warehouses are income properties. For-sale property is analyzed over the development period, which depends on how long it takes for the market to absorb the land for homes or other property types: one or two years for a small subdivision, three to five years for a larger one, and two to three decades for new town-scale development. For-sale projects are typically financed by a combination of equity and a land development loan, though multiple loan types may be employed. As lots are sold to homebuilders, subdevelopers, or end users, the land developer's profit is the difference between revenues from land sales and the costs of purchasing the raw land, planning the project, acquiring approvals, installing infrastructure, and marketing the land to end users, including the operational and carrying cost of all those expenditures. In contrast, financial feasibility of income-producing properties focuses on computing the capitalized value of the completed and fully leased property using an analysis that includes permanent financing and, typically, a five- to 10-year holding period. The development profit is the difference between the value of the stabilized property and the total cost (including financing) of developing it.

Gross versus Net Developable Acreage. Developers must understand the distinction between gross acres, net developable acres, and net usable acres.[27] *Gross acreage* refers to the total acreage at the time of purchase. *Net developable acreage*, or net acreage, omits major streets, open spaces, floodplains, and major easements that are significant to the entire project. *Net usable acres* omits interior street rights-of-way, alleys, and any other areas that are not actually for sale from net developable acres. Total net usable acres should equal the total area actually sold—the aggregate total area of building lots plus multifamily, commercial, industrial, and office sites. These distinctions become important in analysis, as developers need to

FIGURE 3-2 Approximate Residential Lot Yield per Acre

Lot Size (sq ft)	LOT YIELD/ACRE	
	With Alleys	Without Alleys
10,000	3.0	3.3
8,500	3.6	3.8
7,500	4.1	4.4
6,500	4.7	5.0
6,000	5.1	5.4
5,000	6.1	6.5
4,000	7.0–8.0	7.5–8.5

know their cost, sales price, and margin on any given transaction, as well as on the whole project.

Most rough calculations are performed on the basis of net developable acreage, which includes interior streets. When developers investigate a new piece of property, they must know how much land *cannot* be developed because of floodplains, easements, major road rights-of-way, or dedications for schools, parks, or other community facilities. The remaining acreage is used to calculate the number of lots and the number of acres of apartments or commercial sites to be sold separately.

Yield formulas provide a reasonably good estimate of the number of lots that can fit on a specified property. (See figure 3-2.) For example, 7,500-square-foot (697 sq m) lots typically yield four lots per acre (10 lots per ha). Such lots may be called *quarter-acre* lots because of the yield, even though they are smaller than a quarter acre, which is 10,890 square feet (1,012 sq m). Thus,

4 lots × 7,500 square feet per lot = 30,000 square feet (0.28 ha)
Estimated street right-of-way = 12,000 square feet (0.11 ha)

Total = 42,000 square feet (about 1 acre) (0.4 ha)

The yield may differ, depending on the standard street rights-of-way and whether alleys are required. Most planners allow for some waste because, for example, corner lots are larger and irregularly shaped sites are difficult to develop efficiently.

The developer should check with a local planner for lot yield, but the following rules of thumb may serve as starters. Deduct 25 percent of the acreage for streets (30 percent if alleys are required), and then divide the remainder by the lot size. (Representative densities for residential development are shown in figure 3-3.) The rough yield estimates shown here should not be confused with the formal process of yield calculation. Many systems of zoning require a "yield plan" to illustrate the actual buildable density under a set of zoning rules. That number is then used as the unit count under another, alternative zoning rule. A formal yield plan must conform strictly to the governing code, and this calculation may bear little relation to an accurate yield estimate.

Land Use Budget. The allocation of total net developable acreage into different land uses is called the *land use budget*. Including all product types, roads, open space, and community facilities, this budget should add up to total developable acreage. The most profitable (optimal) land use budget is determined by the marketplace, based on the product types that are being absorbed most quickly and reliably and at the highest prices. To get started, a rough estimate of cost may be obtained from other developers, civil engineers, and contractors. With this information, plus sales prices and marketing, tax, and administrative cost estimates, a developer can produce a quick-and-dirty analysis. Figure 3-4 gives an example of the land use budget for a 100-acre (40 ha) site.

The land use budget should be roughly established before meeting with the land planner. The land use mix should be primarily an economic decision based on market absorption and pricing, within regulatory constraints. Planners and engineers should shape and enhance the allocations, but not invent them, because they will become the major initial input into the financial feasibility analysis. Serious planning or engineering of the project cannot be undertaken until these factors are known.

The absorption rate for the land is expressed as the number of acres that can be sold each year. In the example shown, four years is needed to sell out the 7,500-square-foot (697 sq m) single-family lots, more than three years for the 5,000-square-foot (465 sq m) lots, two years for the apartment land, and three years for the retail land (all selling simultaneously, which, it should be noted, is an assumption). These relatively high absorption rates for the retail component are based on a high-visibility location, for example, fronting on a new freeway.

The ideal land use budget maximizes the value of the property by allocating as much land as possible to high-value uses within the constraints of absorption. Developers often mistakenly allocate too much land to high-value uses, such as office or retail, which command higher prices or lease rates, but have slower absorption rates. In addition, land absorption for higher-density projects, such as high-rise apartments,

takes longer than it does for lower-density projects because more units must be sold to absorb each acre. Longer absorption times increase risk of a market downturn during the sellout.

Another difficulty is distinguishing between land sales to builders and other developers and those to end users. In larger projects, if enough land for 20 or 30 years of absorption has been reserved for office and retail use, the developer may be tempted simply to assume that the unsold inventory will be sold to "land investors" at the end of the development life— say, three or five years later. However, the developer must assume a very significant discount (25 to 50 percent or more) in the retail sales price of lots to end users. Investors who buy the unsold inventory will have to wait until demand from end users warrants building out the site, so they will not pay retail prices. Such a large difference between retail and wholesale price points up an obvious difficulty in land use budgeting: absorption and price are not independent. As the analysis proceeds, developers should evaluate

FIGURE 3-3 Densities by Residential Types

Product Type	FAR	Net Density (units/acre)	Gross Density
Single-family detached	0.2	8	5
Zero-lot-line detached	0.3	8–10	6
Two-family detached	0.5	10–12	4
Rowhouses	0.8	16–24	4
Stacked townhouses	1.0	25–40	4
Three-story walkup apartments	1.0	40–45	4
Three-story walkup over parking	1.0	50–60	4
Six-story elevator apartments	1.4	65–75	4
13-story elevator apartments	1.8	85–100	75

Source: Kevin Lynch and Gary Hack, *Site Planning*, 3rd ed. (Cambridge, MA: MIT Press, 1985), p. 253.

Note: Density ranges for apartments have been adjusted upward.

FIGURE 3-4 Land Use Budget for a 100-Acre Site

Uses	Land Use Budget (acres)	Absorption (acres/year)
Residential		
Single-family detached (7,500-sq-ft lots)	40.0	10
Single-family detached (5,000-sq-ft lots)	20.0	6
Apartments (30 units/acre)	10.0	5
Retail	15.0	5
Community facilities	2.0	0
Parks and open space	8.0	0
Subtotal	95.0	26.0
Arterial (highway dedication)	5.0	
Total	100.0	

Land Development

ABOVE: The smaller, urban-scale single-family homes of North Bluff cluster around pedestrian and green spaces, allowing living spaces to open to this shared landscape. RIGHT: The North Bluff project in Austin, Texas, includes a variety of detached homes and townhouses on a small infill site. Careful consideration of vehicular and emergency access allowed the developer, StoryBuilt, to orient most units adjacent to pedestrian connections and outdoor space, rather than to parking areas.

how much absorption could be improved by aggressive pricing or by pricing strategies. Periodically, they may also consider whether an early exit, even at a discount, better fits their risk and return goals. A good financial model, regularly updated with market data, enables owners to fully understand these "sell or hold" decisions.

Optimal Land Use Planning. Clearly, the relative value of high-value-per-acre land and fast absorption must be established, and some factor must be applied to recognize the time value of these sales. Figure 3-5 illustrates the computation of land value and the allocation of land uses for a 35-acre (14 ha) tract of land. Suppose that retail land can be sold for a net profit of $200,000 per acre ($500,000/ha), whereas 7,500-square-foot (697 sq m) single-family lots bring $20,000 each, or $80,000 per acre ($32,400/ha). Suppose also that demand is one acre per year for retail land versus 40 lots (10 ac, or 4 ha) per year for single-family lots. Note that retail absorption is much slower than single-family lot absorption. Figure 3-5 shows the present value of land sold for retail use each year for

eight years. To compare the value of retail land sold today with that sold in seven years, the value may be discounted at a hefty 15 percent per year—a discount rate that reflects both the high holding cost of land and the high risk associated with land development. A retail acre sold in seven years is worth only $75,000, compared with $200,000 today. By comparison, an acre of single-family land sold today is worth $80,000. In this example, therefore, the sale of an acre of single-family land today is more advantageous than the sale of an acre of retail land in seven years. These present values are ranked, in the figure, in order of each acre's present value.

The developer should allocate land to the highest-value use as long as the present value of that year's absorption rate is greater than the next highest-value use. Figure 3-6 shows the resulting allocation. The developer allocates the first seven acres to retail use (seven years of absorption of retail land at one acre per year), because the present value is greater than that for single-family land sold today, even though it will not be consumed by the marketplace for up to six years (allocations 1 through 7, indicated in parentheses in the figure). The next 10 acres go to single-family land (allocation 8) because the present value ($80,000) is higher than the value of the retail land sold in seven years ($75,000). Ten acres—one year of absorption—are allocated to single-family use. The next acre goes to retail use (allocation 9). The next 10 acres go to single-family lots (allocation 10), and then one more acre to retail (allocation 11). At that point, 20 acres are assigned to residential use and nine acres to retail use. The last allocation (allocation 12) goes to residential. Because only six acres are left to bring the total to 35 acres, the third year's allocation of residential absorption is not completely used. The final budget is 26 acres of single-family lots and nine acres of retail use.

This procedure for allocating land is an application of linear programming to real estate.[28] It works for any number of uses and can be done by hand or very quickly with common spreadsheet functions. The only information needed is net developable acreage, sales price, development cost, and absorption rate for each land use or product type. A good starting discount rate—representing opportunity cost—is 5 percent above the current interest rate for development loans. The resulting land use allocation is only a guideline for the land use budget and will probably be modified by zoning, political, or environmental constraints. Nevertheless, a market-based land use allocation is the only accurate and reliable method for determining the land use budget. It should determine the land use plan, not vice versa.

QUICK-AND-DIRTY ANALYSIS. The developer analyzes financial feasibility several times during the course of a project. The first analysis is performed before tying up the property; as the deal progresses, the analysis becomes successively more thorough and complex. A good financial feasibility analysis becomes the basis for managing the project once construction begins; therefore, the categories in the analysis should coincide with the project manager's chart of accounts.

The financial analysis illustrated here is from North Bluff, an infill project in Austin, Texas. The land development component of the project includes 67 finished lots, permitted for three phases of for-sale housing, including single-family detached homes and townhouses in a walkable, dense community plan. As recommended in this chapter, StoryBuilt (which is both the developer and the homebuilder) analyzed the land and homebuilding businesses separately. Revenue, in this example, refers to sales of lots from developer to

builder, whether in-house or to other builders. Costs include acquisition, carrying costs, entitlement, and soft and hard costs of site development, through sales and marketing. An "inside" sale to the home-building division requires dividing costs between the two businesses, sometimes artificially. For example, expenses attributed to marketing the overall community are charged to this land development analysis, while marketing of finished homes is assigned to the homebuilding business. In reality, these costs may be contracted together, and their timing may overlap.

A "quick-and-dirty" analysis is an initial estimate of financial performance. It summarizes projected revenues from the sale of lots, land and development costs

FIGURE 3-5 Effect of Present Value Factors on Land Allocation for Multiple Uses

Project Years	Present Value Factor at 15%	Profit on 1 Acre of Retail Land	Rank	Profit on 1 Acre of Single-Family-Detached Land	Rank
0	1.000	$200,000	1	$80,000	8
1	0.869	$173,800	2	$69,520	10
2	0.756	$151,200	3	$60,480	12
3	0.657	$131,400	4		
4	0.571	$114,200	5		
5	0.497	$99,400	6		
6	0.432	$86,400	7		
7	0.375	$75,000	9		
8	0.327	$65,400	11		

Note: Fifteen percent represents an estimated opportunity cost. Values are computed by multiplying Year 0 value by the factor for the year in question. For example, $200,000 × 0.869 = $173,800.

FIGURE 3-6 Allocation of Land for 35-Acre Tract

Using Present Value Rankings from Figure 3-5

Project Years	Retail Use in Acres (Rank)		Single-Family Use in Acres (Rank)	
0	1	(1)	10	(8)
1	1	(2)	10	(10)
2	1	(3)	6	(12)
3	1	(4)	0	
4	1	(5)	0	
5	1	(6)	0	
6	1	(7)	0	
7	1	(9)	0	
8	1	(11)	0	
Total	**9**		**26**	

Note: Assume absorption of one acre per year retail and 10 acres per year single-family land.

and interest, and expected profit. All figures are aggregated for the entire project life. No time dimension for development or sales is considered. Quick-and-dirty analysis represents the starting point for evaluating the deal. It does not, however, give the developer all the information needed to make proper decisions.

Figure 3-7 shows the quick-and-dirty analysis for North Bluff. StoryBuilt developed the property in three phases. Sales prices for the lot types vary by the size of allowable home in each phase. The average lot price is $110,075, for total revenue of $7,375,000.

Land for the project costs $1.25 million. Development costs include on-site land improvements, with hard costs of $2.65 million, soft costs before sale of $578,646, and allocated general and administrative costs of $737,500. Total development costs are estimated at $5.6 million, including land. Financing costs are estimated by assuming that StoryBuilt invests $2 million in equity and borrows the rest at 6.5 percent. In actuality, the development loan did not reach the maximum shown in this preliminary analysis, because early lot sales provided revenue to offset costs. In this simplified method, interest is estimated by assuming that the project can be developed in one year. Starting at zero, and borrowing all costs by month 12, the analysis assumes an average monthly loan balance during development of $1.8 million. Profit is $1,678,854, or about 29 percent of total costs. Traditional rules of thumb suggest that this ratio should be at least 20 percent. Such simple rules, however, do not provide any estimate of return on equity, and they do not take into account the holding period. In fact, in any project with unentitled land, the holding period is an essential factor and thus a limitation of this type of analysis. For example, a 30 percent return on equity in one year would be good, whereas a 30 percent return over three years would be only 10 percent per year uncompounded and 9.14 percent per year compounded.[29] Developers should keep in mind that expected returns are determined by the market. The risk of land development means that investors will require returns that exceed those obtainable in other, less risky investments. Over the long term, the appropriate discount rate should track, with a premium, long-term returns from stocks, bonds, and other asset classes. Developers can never assume that last year's rule of thumb will be appropriate to attract investment capital this year.

Because the time value of money is not included in the quick-and-dirty calculation, comparing it with other investment alternatives is difficult. This analysis has other shortcomings:

- It gives no indication of how quickly lots are sold.
- It has no means of introducing inflation.
- Computation of interest on the development loan is grossly simplified.
- It gives no information about when funds are needed or the amounts needed.
- It has no means of computing present values or internal rates of return.

The loan calculation is the weakest part of the quick-and-dirty analysis. In the North Bluff example, the loan amount is chosen so that it covers all the costs, including loan interest, which can usually be borrowed. In reality, the size of the loan at any moment depends on how quickly the lots are being sold. Whether or not the loan amount will cover 100 percent of the costs depends on the raw land appraisal, the development cost and schedule, the borrower's creditworthiness, and current lending standards and business outlook in the market. Most land development projects require some form of real equity—cash investment or significant appreciation in land value above the developer's basis.

The main advantage of the quick-and-dirty analysis is that it forces the developer to make explicit assumptions concerning land uses, site planning, sales rates, prices, costs, and financing. These assumptions can then be tested against market data. This exercise provides a rough indication of whether the deal makes economic sense, sets up key ratios that experienced developers will have in mind, and serves as the foundation for all subsequent investigation.

MULTIPERIOD DISCOUNTED CASH FLOW ANALYSIS. Multiperiod DCF analysis is an application of the capital asset pricing model to real estate. The cash flow analysis assigns revenues and expenditures from the quick-and-dirty analysis to specific periods of time, tracking the resulting net cash flows through the project life. In the quick-and-dirty analysis, project returns are simple multiples; in the DCF, they reflect the present value of all predicted cash flows in and out of the project. Note that the cash flows in figure 3-7 reflect the funding and repayment requirements of equity investors and lenders available to land developers. (Common financing terms are discussed later in this chapter under Financing.) The multiperiod DCF analysis for the 67-lot development at North Bluff is shown in figures 3-8a through 3-8c. Its principal purpose is to compute (1) returns to the overall project (as if 100 percent owned, without financing), (2) loan

FIGURE 3-7

North Bluff Quick-and-Dirty Analysis

#			Price/Lot	Revenue	Total	Per Lot	% Cost	% Revenue
1	**Revenue (inside sale to building company)**							
2	Lots							
3	Phase I	19	$100,000	$1,900,000				
4	Phase 2	33	$125,000	$4,125,000				
5	Phase 3	15	$90,000	$1,350,000				
6		67			$7,375,000	$110,075		
7	**Expenditures**							
8	Land Cost				$1,250,000	$18,657		
9	Soft Costs Allocated to Horizontal Development							
10	Capital Fees (estimate)				$144,690	2.5%	$2,160	
11	Survey and Land Planning				$82,182	1.4%	$1,227	
12	Environmental Studies				$41,092	0.7%	$613	
13	Soils Study and Engineering				$7,235	0.1%	$108	
14	Utilities Studies				$20,618	0.4%	$308	
15	Landscape Architect				$20,795	0.4%	$310	
16	Engineering and Consultants				$107,071	1.9%	$1,598	
17	Permits and Fees (incl. printing)				$10,273	0.2%	$153	
18	Loan Fees and Interest Expense				$144,690	2.5%	$2,160	
19	**Subtotal Soft Costs**				**$578,646**	**10.2%**	**$8,637**	
20	**Hard Costs: Horizontal Development**							
21	Fees and Permits				$43,000	0.8%	$642	
22	Site Preparation				$55,000	1.0%	$821	
23	Clearing, Excavation, and Grading				$267,000	4.7%	$3,985	
24	Erosion Control				$45,000	0.8%	$672	
25	Sanitary Sewer System				$315,000	5.5%	$4,701	
26	Storm and Water Quality				$925,000	16.2%	$13,806	
27	Domestic Water System				$288,000	5.1%	$4,299	
28	Electric, Gas, Phone Utilities				$250,000	4.4%	$3,731	
29	Street Improvements				$315,000	5.5%	$4,701	
30	Common Area Landscaping				$145,000	2.5%	$2,164	
31	Subtotal Hard Costs				$2,648,000	46.5%	$39,522	
32	Community Marketing	2%	of sales		$147,500	2.6%	$2,201	
33	Sales, General and Administrative	10%	of sales		$737,500	12.9%	$11,007	
34	Contingency				$250,000	4.4%	$3,731	
35	**TOTAL Development Costs**				**$4,361,646**	**$65,099**		
36	**Subtotal Including Land**				**$5,611,646**	**$83,756**		
37	Interest Calculation							
38	Equity			$3,611,646	64.4%			
39	Debt			$2,000,000	35.6%			
40	Avg. Bal.		65%	$1,300,000				
41	Duration		1 year					
42	Rate		6.5%		$84,500			
43	**Total Expenditures**				**$5,696,146**	**$85,017**		
44	**Land Development Profit**				**$1,678,854**	**$25,058**	**29.5%**	**22.8%**

Note: This analysis is based on data provided by the developers of North Bluff, but it is intended for educational use. Specific items may be changed to respect trade secrets, and generally, the land development analysis has been removed from the larger land-and-homebuilding analysis on which the developer evaluated this project.

Spreadsheets in figures 3-7 and 3-8 a–e are available online in supplemental materials at americas.uli.org/PRED.

requirements, and (3) returns to joint venture participants. It is a before-tax computation.

Land development financing is similar to construction financing during the development period of income property (Stage 3 analysis in chapter 4). No permanent mortgage is arranged, because the purpose of land development is to sell developed lots to homebuilders and other users. Another important difference from income property analysis is that the development loan is retired by the sale of lots rather than by funding of the permanent mortgage, which for income property takes out (pays off) construction debt with a long-term loan supported by operating cash flow. Land development DCF analysis is used to determine the building program, phasing, and expense budget that the project can support. Like Stage 2 analysis for income properties (see chapter 4), land development DCF analysis is rerun many times as assumptions change during the feasibility period and over the life of the project. The land use budget, cost, and sales timing are fine-tuned as more accurate information becomes available. The cash flow analysis for land development is used for both planning the design of the project and obtaining financing.

Several key items should be noted about the methodology of the DCF analysis for land development.

Time Periods. Intervals should be selected that provide five to 12 total time periods of analysis. For example, for a sale of 120 lots at the rate of 30 lots per quarter, plus 12 months for development, the total time required is about two years. Quarterly time periods (three months per period) would provide eight total periods, a good starting point for analysis. For larger projects that require, say, 10 years to be fully developed, annual periods would be appropriate at the start, though finer detail is useful later. Projects with a natural cycle, such as office leases, should include a full cycle. The time from acquisition to sellout for North Bluff was just under three years, so the analysis shows 10 quarters.

Level of Detail. The purpose of the early runs of the DCF analysis is to obtain a picture of the total project. Beginners often go into too much detail at first, forgetting that every item in the spreadsheet is subject to change. Because the developer has not yet done a detailed site plan, and sales and cost estimates are, at best, rough approximations, a monthly cash flow analysis would be meaningless. The spreadsheet can always be enhanced by adding more periods and more line items as more information becomes available. Usually, the developer should wait to prepare a monthly cash flow forecast until the site plan has been adopted, the market study has been completed, contract bids are available, and a monthly forecast of construction draws for loan approval is needed.

Construction of the Analysis. Keeping in mind that nearly every input may be subject to change, cash flow models should, when possible, aggregate all variable inputs in one place, or in one column and one row, clearly marked as "inputs" or "assumptions." Where these numbers are needed in the analysis, the analyst can refer to the input cell, so that the model recalculates automatically when inputs are changed in one location.

Time Period Zero. Time period zero represents the starting period of analysis and can be set for any date. It should always be included in cash flow analysis. When analyzing existing projects, the recommendation is to set time period zero three to six months earlier than the present, at a point for which the exact amount of money spent to date and a monthly burn rate are known. When money has already been spent on the project, a line item on the spreadsheet, "costs to date," should be added that aggregates the total money spent, including carry costs, as of time period zero. For new projects, time period zero is normally the closing date on the land. Any costs incurred before closing are simply included under the land cost or costs-to-date category. If development activity starts immediately after closing, it is possible that retainers, deposits, and other predevelopment expenses may need to be allocated to time period zero.

Timing of Sales. Enough time should be allocated to develop the property and to investigate the effects of slower than anticipated sales. One model run should assume half the expected sales pace. This study can compute the maximum loan amount needed for this downside case, and the impact on returns.

Inflation. DCF models typically include three different inflation rates—sales price inflation, cost inflation, and the inflation rate implicit in the interest rate. These rates are correlated but not necessarily the same. A 3 percent inflation rate in sales prices, for example, indicates a development loan interest rate of 7 to 11 percent (3 percent inflation plus 2 to 3 percent real rate of return plus 2 to 5 percent risk). Higher inflation assumptions can make a project look better than it probably is. Lenders are rightfully cautious of overly high inflation assumptions and may insist on a DCF analysis run with zero inflation in sales prices. Even if inflation is included, a common mistake in DCF modeling is setting price appreciation at a higher rate than cost increases. In mature markets, this assumption is seldom justifiable, though it may be in developing countries or special cases. Costs can be assumed not to escalate if they are fixed by contract at the beginning of the project.

Development Loan Borrowings. The development loan provides bank financing for all borrowing needs after the equity. Once the loan has been reduced through the release and sale of lots, developers are usually not allowed to return to borrow additional money (as they would be able to with a revolving line of credit) because the collateral for the loan—namely, the land—has been partially sold off. In the North Bluff development loan (figure 3-8c, lines 80–83), the loan balance varies as successive phases are developed and then sold. In actuality, additional borrowing might have to involve separate loans on each phase, or a revolving line of credit for improvements only, separate from the land-secured financing. Borrowing for a phase might be conditional on substantial completion of a previous phase, or on selling some percentage of inventory in the currently financed phases.

Loan Repayments. Loan repayments (releases) represent the amount by which the land note and/or the development loan must be repaid as property is sold. Every time a lot is sold, the land that was pledged as collateral for the development loan must be "released" from the construction loan or land loan lien by the lender. These releases are shown as *cash out* or repayment items (development loan repayments and land note repayments, lines 46–48, in figure 3-8b).

Before-Tax Computation. Before-tax rates of return may be used for evaluating the economic feasibility of a land development project as long as they are compared with before-tax returns from other investment opportunities. Unlike the development of income property (see chapter 4), in which tax benefits are an important part of the return, land development offers no special tax benefits (such as deductions for depreciation and current interest). The Internal Revenue Service (IRS) treats the land developer as a "dealer in land," and as such, the developer must pay ordinary tax on reported profits. For example, if the developer's tax rate were 33 percent, the tax would be $333 on each $1,000 of profit.

Return Measures. The unleveraged internal rate of return (figure 3-8a) assumes that all cash requirements are financed from cash equity. IRR is the discount rate that makes the present value of all future income equal to the initial investment, so it is a way to view irregular cash flows as a simple rate of return across

the entire investment. This simple rate can then be compared to other investments. It is computed on line 110 in figure 3-8d, which refers to the results of line 74, "profit before interest," exclusive of all financing. The unleveraged return varies from year to year but should be at least 12 to 18 percent.[30] It should exceed the cost of borrowing money so that the developer can obtain positive leverage. If, for example, the unleveraged IRR is 12 percent and the interest rate on the development loan is 8 percent, then the developer's return on equity will be higher than 15 percent. Negative leverage exists when the return is less than the loan rate. Positive leverage means that as the developer borrows more money, the return on equity

FIGURE 3-8A DCF Results

Profit before interest	$1,471,824	Cash flow after financing	$2,779,518
Less interest	92,306	Less repayment of equity	1,400,000
		Less unpaid loan balance	—
Profit	**1,379,518**	**Profit**	**1,379,518**
UNLEVERAGED RETURN[a] (CASH FLOWS BEFORE INTEREST & FINANCING)		**LEVERAGED RETURN ON EQUITY[b] (NET CASH FLOWS AFTER FINANCING)**	
Net present value @ 15%	547,133	Net present value @ 15%	651,124
IRR	27.7%	IRR	36.8%

Year	Net Profit	Year	Equity	Cash Inflows
0	(1,920,836)	0	1,400,000	479,164
1	(448,000)	1	—	(463,000)
2	(174,330)	2	—	(16,164)
3	7,380	3	—	—
4	216,140	4	—	—
5	666,627	5	—	—
6	658,879	6	—	313,555
7	549,457	7	—	549,457
8	772,790	8	—	772,790
9	558,341	9	—	558,341
10	585,375	10	—	585,375
11	—	11	—	—
12	—	12	—	—
13	—	13	—	—
14	—	14	—	—
15	—	15	—	—
16	—	16	—	—
Total	**$1,471,824**	**Total**	**$1,400,000**	**$2,779,510**
			Profit	**$1,379,518**

[a]The unleveraged return is computed on the cash flows before financing. Thus, it is an all-equity rate of return. The unleveraged return should be significantly greater than the interest rate on financing. Otherwise, no profit will be left over after financing costs are paid.

[b]The return on equity is computed on cash flows after financing. A leveraged rate of return gives the IRR on equity for the entire project (the owner/developer provides all necessary equity).

FIGURE 3-8B North Bluff Assumptions
Sales Timing, Prices, Development Costs, Land Note

| 1 | Number of Time Periods Per Year: | | | | 4 | (1=annual, 2=semi-annual, 4=quarter[ly]) | | |

2						Q2 2017	Q3 2017	Q4 2017	Q1 2018
3	Sales (Lots)[d]				Total	0[c]	1	2	3
4	Phase 1			19	19	—	—	4	7
5	Phase 2			33	33	—	—	—	—
6	Phase 3			15	15	—	—	—	—
7	Total			67	67	—	—	4	7

8	Sales Prices[e]	Price Esc. Annual	Price Esc. Annual	Price Per Sq Ft	Price Per Lot	1	2	3
9	Phase 1[f]	3.00%	0.75%	—	$100,000	$100,000	$100,750	$101,506
10	Phase 2	3.00%	0.75%	—	125,000	125,000	125,938	126,882
11	Phase 3	3.00%	0.75%	—	90,000	90,000	90,675	91,355
12	Miscellaneous	3.00%	0.75%	—	—	—	—	—

13	Sales Revenues[g]	Total	0	1	2	3
14	Phase 1	1,931,675	—	—	403,000	710,539
15	Phase 2	4,298,715	—	—	—	—
16	Phase 3	1,438,891	—	—	—	—
17	Total Revenue	7,669,281	—	—	403,000	710,539

18	Costs[h]	Inflation	Total	0[i]	1	2	3
19	Land		1,250,000	1,250,000			
20	Site Preparation		55,000	10,000	25,000	20,000	
21	Excavation and Grading		267,000		30,000	100,000	100,000
22	Erosion Control		45,000		5,000	5,000	5,000
23	Sanitary Sewer		310,000				60,000
24	Storm and Water Quality		925,000		125,000	250,000	200,000
25	Domestic Water		288,000		40,000	48,000	50,000
26	Electric, Gas, Phone Utilities		250,000				50,000
27	Street/Common Landscape		460,000				60,000
28	Fees and Permits		43,000		23,000	10,000	
29	Financing Fees		144,690	144,690			
30	Soft Costs		578,646	478,646	100,000		
31	Indirect Land Development		737,500	37,500	100,000	100,000	100,000
32	Subtotal Development Cost		4,103,836	670,836	448,000	533,000	625,000
33	Interest Per Period (decimal)	0.075/year		0.0188	0.0188	0.0188	0.0188

34	Land Note[j]	Data Input	Total	0	1	2	3
35	Total Land Cost	1,250,000		1,250,000			
36	Lots Sold (enter release price/lot)	50,000	67	—	—	4	7
37	Down Payment		250,000	250,000			
38	Beginning Lots Released	50,000		5.0	5.0	5.0	3.0
39	Ending Lots Released				5.0	1.0	—
40	Lots to be Released			—	—	—	4.0
41	Land Note		1,000,000	1,000,000			
42	Repayment Terms					10.0%	20.0%
43	Minimum Land Payments			—	—	100,000	200,000
44	Max Land Note Balance			1,000,000	1,000,000	900,000	700,000
45	**Starting Balance**			**1,000,000**	**1,000,000**	**1,000,000**	**900,000**
46	Land Note Releases	50,000	900,000	—	—	—	200,000
47	Remaining Balance			1,000,000	1,000,000	1,000,000	700,000
48	Additional Note Payments			—	—	100,000	—
49	Ending Balance			1,000,000	1,000,000	900,000	700,000
50	Additional Lots Released	50,000				2.0	—
51	Interest Per Period	1.5%	58,500		15,000	15,000	13,500
52	**Land Note Total**		**$58,500**	**($1,000,000)**	**$15,000**	**$115,000**	**$213,500**

Q2 2018	Q3 2018	Q4 2018	Q1 2019	Q2 2019	Q3 2019	Q4 2019
4	5	6	7	8	9	10
8	—	—	—	—	—	—
—	9	8	7	8	1	—
—	—	—	—	—	7	8
8	9	8	7	8	8	8
4	5	6	7	8	9	10
$102,267	$103,034	$103,807	$104,585	$105,370	$106,160	$106,956
127,834	128,792	129,758	130,732	131,712	132,700	133,695
92,040	92,731	93,426	94,127	94,833	95,544	96,260
—						
4	5	6	7	8	9	10
818,135	—	—	—	—	—	—
—	1,159,132	1,038,067	915,121	1,053,696	132,700	—
					668,807	770,084
818,135	1,159,132	1,038,067	915,121	1,053,696	801,507	770,084
4	5	6	7	8	9	10
37,000						
5,000	5,000	5,000	5,000	5,000	5,000	
60,000	60,000	60,000	60,000	10,000		
50,000	50,000	50,000	50,000	50,000	50,000	50,000
100,000	50,000					
50,000	50,000	50,000	50,000			
100,000	100,000	50,000	50,000	50,000	50,000	
10,000						
100,000	50,000	50,000	50,000	50,000	50,000	50,000
512,000	365,000	265,000	265,000	165,000	155,000	100,000
0.0188	0.0188	0.0188	0.0188	0.0188	0.0188	0.0188
4	5	6	7	8	9	10
8	9	8	7	8	8	8
—	—	—	—	—	—	(8.0)
—	—	—	—	—	—	—
8.0	9.0	8	7	8		
35.0%	35.0%					
350,000	350,000	—	—	—	—	—
350,000	—	—	—	—	—	—
700,000	**300,000**	—	—	—	—	—
400,000	300,000	—	—	—	—	—
300,000	—	—	—	—	—	—
—	—	—	—	—	—	—
300,000	—	—	—	—	—	—
—	—					
10,500	4,500	—	—	—	—	—
$410,500	**$304,500**	—	—	—	—	—

Spreadsheets in figures 3-7 and 3-8 a–e are available online in supplemental materials at americas.uli.org/PRED.

[c]Each period is a quarter (line 2). The number of periods per year should be chosen to produce five to 15 periods overall. A 10-year project is best analyzed with annual periods (10 periods), a 20-year project with two-year periods (10 periods), and a three-year project with quarterly periods (12 periods).

[d]Sales by product type are entered for each period. Units of measurement do not have to be the same. Thus, residential sales may be expressed as number of lots sold per period (lines 3 through 7); office space is expressed in acres sold per period.

[e]Sales prices are expressed in the same units as are sales. Thus, if residential sales are expressed in lots, sales prices should be expressed in price per lot (lines 8 through 11).

[f]Lot prices may be escalated at a given rate per period (lines 9 through 11).

[g]Sales revenue is computed from the number of acres or units sold per period times the price per period (lines 13 through 17).

[h]Costs are entered by category and period. Detailed cost breakdowns for individual categories, such as utilities, are best handled in supporting spreadsheets (see lines 18 through 32), since an overabundance of detail makes the analysis more difficult to follow.

[i]Time 0 should be treated as a separate period. Typically, Time 0 is the time of closing. Costs incurred prior to Time 0 should be lumped together as "startup costs."

[j]The land note defines the terms, if any, of the land purchase from the land seller. The release price negotiated in the land note is $50,000 per lot (note that the release price often differs for different lots). Given a downpayment of $250,000, five lots (line 38) are released immediately from the note. The land note also defines the repayment terms (line 42). If sales are slower than the terms of the note, then the developer must pay additional money to satisfy the land note (line 48), which releases additional lots (line 50). If lot sales occur faster than the note repayment terms require, then additional lots must be released (line 50) in order to sell the lots. In the example, the sales pace is slower than the terms of the note. If releases from sales are slower than those required under the amortization terms of the land note, then the shortfall is covered by the development loan or additional equity.

FIGURE 3-8C North Bluff Cash-Flow Summary

		%	Total	0	1	2	3
53	Cash-Flow Summary[k]		Total	0	1	2	3
54	Income						
55	Sales Revenue		$7,669,281	—	—	$403,000	$710,539
56	Total Income		7,669,281	—	—	403,000	710,539
57	Expenses (from above)[l]						
58	Land[m]		1,250,000	1,250,000	—	—	—
59	Site Preparation		55,000	10,000	25,000	20,000	—
60	Excavation and Grading		267,000	—	30,000	100,000	100,000
61	Erosion Control		45,000	—	5,000	5,000	5,000
62	Sanitary Sewer		310,000	—	—	—	60,000
63	Storm and Water Quality		925,000	—	125,000	250,000	200,000
64	Domestic Water		288,000	—	40,000	48,000	50,000
65	Electric, Gas, Phone Utilities		250,000	—	—	—	50,000
66	Street/Common Landscape		460,000	—	—	—	60,000
67	Fees and Permits		43,000	—	23,000	10,000	—
68	Financing Fees		144,690	144,690	—	—	—
69	Soft Costs		578,646	478,646	100,000	—	—
70	Indirect Land Development		737,500	37,500	100,000	100,000	100,000
71	Community Marketing[n]	5.0%	383,464	—	—	20,150	35,527
72	Admin. and Contingency	6.0%	460,157	—	—	24,180	42,632
73	Total Expenses		6,197,457	1,920,836	448,000	577,330	703,159
74	Profit Before Interest[o]		1,471,824	(1,920,836)	(448,000)	(174,330)	7,380
75	Less Development Loan Interest		33,806	—	—	2,585	7,170
76	Less Land Note Interest		58,500	—	15,000	15,000	13,500
77	Net Profit		1,379,518	(1,920,836)	(463,000)	(191,915)	(13,290)
78	Financing[p]						
79	Plus Equity		1,400,000	1,400,000			
80	Plus Development Loan Borrowings		704,214	—	—	275,751	213,290
81	Plus Land Note Borrowings		1,000,000	1,000,000	—	—	—
82	Minus Development Loan Repayments[q]		(704,214)	—	—	—	—
83	Minus Land Note Repayments		(1,000,000)	—	—	(100,000)	(200,000)
84	Cash Flow After Financing		2,779,518	479,164	(463,000)	(16,164)	—
85	Cumulative Cash Position		$1,635,802	$479,164	$16,164	—	—

FIGURE 3-8D North Bluff Cash and Loan Calculations and IRRs

		Total	-	1	2	3
86	Cash Account and Loan Calculation					
87	Cash Account	Total	-	1	2	3
88	Starting Cash Balance		$0	$479,164	$16,164	$0
89	Additions to Equity	1,400,000	1,400,000	0	0	0
90	Profit Before Interest	1,471,824	-1,920,836	-448,000	-174,330	7,380
91	Land Note	(58,500)	1,000,000	-15,000	-115,000	-213,500
92	Subtotal	2,813,324	479,164	16,164	-273,166	-206,120
93	Amount to be Financed Before Interest	673,646	0	0	273,166	206,120
94	Cash Available for Loan and Interest		479,164	16,164	0	0
95	Loan Repayments	704,214	0	0	0	0
96	Interest	3,237	0	0	0	0
97	Ending Cash Balance	$1,635,802	$479,164	$16,164	$0	$0

4	5	6	7	8	9	8
$818,135	$1,159,132	$1,038,067	$915,121	$1,053,696	$801,507	$770,084
818,135	1,159,132	1,038,067	915,121	1,053,696	801,507	770,084
—	—	—	—	—	—	—
—	—	—	—	—	—	—
37,000	—	—	—	—	—	—
5,000	5,000	5,000	5,000	5,000	5,000	—
60,000	60,000	60,000	60,000	10,000	—	—
50,000	50,000	50,000	50,000	50,000	50,000	50,000
100,000	50,000	—	—	—	—	—
50,000	50,000	50,000	50,000	—	—	—
100,000	100,000	50,000	50,000	50,000	50,000	—
10,000	—	—	—	—	—	—
—	—	—	—	—	—	—
—	—	—	—	—	—	—
100,000	50,000	50,000	50,000	50,000	50,000	50,000
40,907	57,957	51,903	45,756	52,685	40,075	38,504
49,088	69,548	62,284	54,907	63,222	48,090	46,205
601,995	492,504	379,187	365,663	280,907	243,166	184,709
216,140	**666,627**	**658,879**	**549,457**	**772,790**	**558,341**	**585,375**
11,096	9,718	3,237	—	—	—	—
10,500	4,500	—	—	—	—	—
194,545	**652,409**	**655,642**	**549,457**	**772,790**	**558,341**	**585,375**
205,455	9,718	—	—	—	—	—
—	—	—	—	—	—	—
—	(362,127)	(342,087)	—	—	—	—
(400,000)	(300,000)	—	—	—	—	—
—	—	313,555	549,457	772,790	558,341	585,375
—	—	$313,555	$863,012	$1,635,802	$2,194,143	$2,779,518

Spreadsheets in figures 3-7 and 3-8 a–e are available online in supplemental materials at americas.uli.org/PRED.

[k] The cash-flow summary presents the net cash flows from the land development (lines 53 through 85).

[l] Expenses summarizes the cost entries in lines 58 through 72. Figures in the summary are higher in most categories because they include inflation.

[m] Even if land is contributed to the deal, its cost should be included as an expense (line 58).

[n] Some cost categories, such as marketing, are typically calculated as percentages of sales revenues (lines 71 and 72).

[o] Profit before interest is derived from line 74 which sums the differences between total income and total expenses. This line gives the unleveraged cash flows, before financing, found in the results (figure 3-8a).

[p] A primary purpose of the analysis is to determine the amount and timing of development-loan requirements (lines 80 through 83). Cash equity (or land equity that is considered "cash" if it is contributed to the deal) is infused into the project initially (line 79). As money becomes available from sales, it is used to retire the development loan.

[q] Development-loan repayments, called "releases," are typically a negotiated ratio, usually 1.1 to 1.3 times the loan amount per lot (line 82). Release prices are usually assigned to each lot, depending on its relative value. In this analysis, all positive cash flows are assumed to go toward paying down the development loan until it is fully retired.

4	5	6	7	8	9	10
$0	$0	$0	$313,555	$863,012	$1,635,802	$2,194,143
0	0	0	0	0	0	0
216,140	666,627	658,879	549,457	772,790	558,341	585,375
-410,500	-304,500	0	0	0	0	0
-194,360	362,127	658,879	863,012	1,635,802	2,194,143	2,779,518
194,360	0	0	0	0	0	0
0	362,127	658,879	863,012	1,635,802	2,194,143	2,779,518
0	362,127	342,087	0	0	0	0
0	0	3,237	0	0	0	0
$0	$0	$313,555	$863,012	$1,635,802	$2,194,143	$2,779,518

CONTINUED

FIGURE 3-8D North Bluff Cash and Loan Calculations and IRRs | CONTINUED

98	Loan Account						
99	Beginning Balance				0	0	0	275,751
100	Loan Draws				0	0	273,166	206,120
101	Loan Repayments				0	0	0	0
102	Trial Ending Balance				0	0	273,166	481,871
103	Average Balance				0	0	136,583	378,811
104	Interest Rate				0	0	0	0
105	Interest				0	0	2,585	7,170
106	Interest Paid from Cash				0	0	0	0
107	Ending Balance				0	0	275,751	489,041
108	Borrowings After Interest				0	0	275,751	213,290
109	**NPV and IRR Calculations[r]:**	**Quarter IRRs**						
110	(1) Unleveraged Return (from line 74)	27.66%	1,471,824	-1,920,836	-448,000	-174,330	7,380
111	(2) Return on Equity (from line 84)	36.85%	1,379,518	-920,836	-463,000	-16,164	0
112	Cumulative Return on Equity			-$920,836	-$1,383,836	-$1,400,000	-$1,400,000

FIGURE 3-8E North Bluff Investor-Return Analysis

113	**Investor-Return Analysis[s]**						
114	**Cash Flows to Investors**	Data Input	Total	—	1	2	3
115	Cash In-Cash Out		$2,779,518	$ 479,164	$(463,000)	$(16,164)	—
116	Starting Equity Balance				1,400,000	1,428,000	1,456,560
117	Equity Investment		1,400,000	1,400,000	—	—	—
118	Subtotal		1,400,000	1,400,000	1,428,000	1,456,560
119	Cumulative Preferred Return/Period[t]	2.0%		—	28,000	28,560	29,131
120	Noncumulative Preferred Return[u]	—		—	—	—	—
121	Preferred Return Paid		70,953	—	—	—	—
122	Preferred Return Accrued		145,713	—	28,000	28,560	29,131
123	Subtotal			1,400,000	1,428,000	1,456,560	1,485,691
124	Reduction of Equity		1,545,713	—	—	—	—
125	Ending Equity Balance			1,400,000	1,428,000	1,456,560	1,485,691
126	Cash for Distribution[v]		1,162,851	—	—	—	—
127	Equity Partner	50%	581,426	—	—	—	—
128	Developer	50%	581,426	—	—	—	—
129	**Rate of Return Calculation**						
130	Equity Partner Investment		(1,400,000)	(1,400,000)	—	—	—
131	Preferred Return		70,953	—	—	—	—
132	Reduction of Equity		1,545,713	—	—	—	—
133	Cash Distribution		581,426	—	—	—	—
134	**Total Cash Flows to Investor**		**$798,092**	**$(1,400,000)**	—	—	—
135	Net Present Value	3.0%	$333,591				
136	IRR[w]		23.8%				

489,041	694,496	342,087	0	0	0	0
194,360	0	0	0	0	0	0
0	362,127	342,087	0	0	0	0
683,401	332,369	0	0	0	0	0
586,221	513,433	171,044	0	0	0	0
0	0	0	0	0	0	0
11,096	9,718	3,237	0	0	0	0
0	0	3,237	0	0	0	0
694,496	342,087	0	0	0	0	0
205,455	9,718	0	0	0	0	0
216,140	666,627	658,879	549,457	772,790	558,341	585,375
0	0	313,555	549,457	772,790	558,341	585,375
-$1,400,000	-$1,400,000	-$1,086,445	-$536,988	$235,802	$794,143	$1,379,518

[r]IRRs are calculated on the profit before interest (line 110) and cash flows after financing and interest (line 111). Both lines restate information from above for the purposes of calculation.

4	5	6	7	8	9	10
—	—	$313,555	$549,457	$772,790	$558,341	$585,375
1,485,691	1,515,405	1,545,713	1,263,073	738,877	—	—
—	—	—	—	—	—	—
1,485,691	1,515,405	1,545,713	1,263,073	738,877	—	—
29,714	30,308	30,914	25,261	14,778	—	—
—	—	—	—	—	—	—
—	—	30,914	25,261	14,778	—	—
29,714	30,308	—	—	—	—	—
1,515,405	1,545,713	1,545,713	1,263,073	738,877	—	—
—	—	282,641	524,196	738,877	—	—
1,515,405	1,545,713	1,263,073	738,877	—	—	—
—	—	—	—	19,135	558,341	585,375
—	—	—	—	9,568	279,171	292,687
—	—	—	—	9,568	279,171	292,687
—	—	—	—	—	—	—
—	—	30,914	25,261	14,778	—	—
—	—	282,641	524,196	738,877	—	—
—	—	—	—	9,568	279,171	292,687
—	—	$313,555	$549,457	$763,222	$279,171	$292,687

[s]The investor-return analysis is a before-tax computation of cash flows to the developer and investors in a joint venture (lines 113 through 136). If the landowner contributes the land to the deal, the land value is treated as cash equity for purposes of this calculation.

[t]Preferred returns are priority returns of cash flow to the investors. Cumulative preferred returns are accumulated into succeeding periods whenever the amount of cash available is insufficient to pay the preferred return in the current period (line 119).

[u]Noncumulative preferred returns are not accumulated into future periods. If the amount of cash from the current period is insufficient to pay the noncumulative preferred return, it is forgotten (line 120).

[v]The cash distribution percentages are negotiated between the developer and the equity investors (lines 127 and 128).

[w]The investors' IRR is computed on line 136. The IRR is that discount rate at which the present value of future cash flows equals the initial equity investment ($1.4 million in Period 0). Since the periods are quarters, the IRR is multiplied by 4 to give an annualized rate of return.

Note: Due to rounding, some totals may not add exactly.

increases. The unleveraged return in figure 3-8a is 27 percent per year for this project. Acceptable unleveraged IRRs go up as the risk of the project goes up. While 10 percent may be acceptable for a small subdivision with no entitlement risk and available utilities, a large piece of unentitled raw land would require an unleveraged return of 20 percent or more.

Return on Equity. The return on equity is also an IRR calculation. In contrast to the unleveraged IRR, the return on equity takes financing into account. The developer's cash investment, plus any in-kind equity, such as the value of land contributed to the deal, is represented as a cash outflow. Cash flow after financing (figure 3-8c, line 84) shows cash inflows to the developer. Sometimes, no net cash inflows occur until the development loan is fully retired, although that depends on the lender's loan release provisions; higher release prices will prioritize debt paydown over developer returns. The return on equity should be higher than the unleveraged IRR because the amount of equity is usually only a fraction, say 20 percent, of total project cost. The return on equity should always be higher than the loan interest rate because equity investors have lower priority for access to cash flows than mortgage holders and thus incur more risk. If the project is financed by 100 percent equity (no debt), the return on equity is the same as the unleveraged IRR. In figure 3-8d, line 111, the IRR on $1,400,000 equity is 36.8 percent per year. The rate of return that constitutes an acceptable return on equity varies, but by any criteria, the land component of this analysis is strong. Most developers require a return on equity that is 12 to 15 points higher than what they could obtain on risk-free government bonds. If, for example, one-year Treasury bills (T-bills) are paying 5 percent, most developers want a return on equity of 15 to 20 percent.

If no equity is invested (that is, the project is 100 percent financed), then the return on equity is infinite. But that does not necessarily mean the project is economically feasible. Even if the project equity is zero, the *unleveraged* IRR should be on the order of 10 points above the T-bill rate and preferably should be around 15 points for taking the risk of land development.

Evaluating feasibility involves aggregating multiple return measures. IRRs are often paired with investment (or equity) multiples (the ratio of cash received in the future to cash invested today) and with net present value (NPV). The calculation of NPV offers an alternative method of ranking projects than IRR because it provides the value in today's dollars of the wealth that a project will generate in the future; it uses as a discount rate the developer's opportunity cost rate—the rate that can be earned in alternative investments of similar risk. Evaluating opportunities with an investment goal in mind, the project with the highest NPV is preferred. If only one project is being considered, then the NPV should be sufficient to justify the time and risk of development, even if the developer has no equity invested in the project. For example, suppose the NPV on a four-year project with $1 million equity, discounted at 15 percent, is $200,000. Thus, the developer would earn the equivalent of $200,000 in today's dollars over and above a 15 percent return on the initial investment. The developer must then determine whether the project is worth the time and risk involved. If it would be necessary to work on the project full time for four years or sign personally on a $5 million loan, it probably is not.

Even very experienced developers must often extend personal guarantees on loans or substitute a corporate guarantee backed by a strong balance sheet. Some developers treat their guarantee as a component of equity and compute an IRR on that basis. Because the guarantee is a contingent liability (neither the necessity nor the actual size of the investment is known) rather than a cash investment, the appropriate return on the guarantee is not comparable with the IRR on equity when the equity is in the form of hard cash.

Relationship between Returns, Inflation, and Risk. All returns move with inflation. Return on equity has three components—a real, riskless rate of return (2 to 3 percent), an inflation premium, and a risk premium.[31] If expected long-run inflation (over the life of the investment) is, say, 4 percent and the risk premium is 10 percent, then the required return on equity would be 16 to 17 percent. The risk premium depends on the status of the real estate—whether it is fully leased, under construction, or in predevelopment—as well as on the amount of leverage (all equity versus 60 to 95 percent or more financing), the property type, location, and other factors that bear on the likelihood of success or failure (such as neighborhood opposition, competition, and market and economic trends). The risk premium alone may range from 10 to 20 percent or more depending on the amount of perceived risk. The earlier the stage of development, the greater the risk. Unentitled property is considered the riskiest of all forms of development; there is no assurance that the developer can entitle the land to build, and failure means the land has only agricultural or conservation value, typically a fraction of the proposed development value. A high "hurdle rate" of return is associated with this risk.

Although required rates of return change quickly depending on economic and capital market conditions and are hard to generalize, some rules of thumb apply. For example, pension funds making all-equity investments in fully leased, investment-grade income properties (large shopping centers, office buildings, apartments) may look for returns as low as 10 percent. Projects that have entitlements but are not yet built typically should offer at least a 15 percent unleveraged before-tax IRR or a 20 to 25 percent leveraged before-tax IRR. Because land with entitlement risk is considered the riskiest form of real estate, leveraged returns on equity have historically ranged from 15 to 30 percent or more. These figures may be appropriate for times of expected 3 to 4 percent inflation; if inflation is higher, required return rates rise as well. The Great Recession and ensuing housing market turmoil obscured these historical relationships, as did the sudden re-emergence of pandemic-associated inflation. When riskless rates are near zero, traditional investment capital for land development is unavailable in many markets, and the discount price of existing land deals indicates that investors are seeking double their typical average returns for their effort.

One of the most common misunderstandings in real estate is the relationship between IRRs, inflation, and capitalization rates (cap rates). As noted earlier, hurdle IRRs (required returns on equity) go up with inflation. This situation occurs because inflation and risk are two components of the required rate of return. Capitalization rates, however, tend to go down as inflation goes up. Because capitalization rates are simply the ratio of current net operating income (NOI)[32] to the purchase price for income property, buyers are willing to pay more for property because inflation is expected to increase—causing capitalization rates to go down and prices to go up for the same NOI. However, as risk goes up, cap rates go up as well because buyers are willing to pay less money for property if they perceive the risks to be greater.

Design and Site Planning

Land planning begins with target buyers or end users and a marketing concept for the buildings that will ultimately be built on the finished lots to attract these customers. The primary components are established by the relative values. The end product—the size, style, and quality of building—dictates how the land should be subdivided.

Good subdivision design involves much more than an engineer's efficient layout for streets and utilities. Historically, developers favored the most cost-efficient plan—the rectangular grid. Beginning in the mid-20th century, however, developers began to prefer curved streets and culs-de-sac that took advantage of natural features. Today, the grids of towns and cities are once again favored over the organic forms of suburbia. In the best plans, natural features are considered as well, and the grid may bend and curve to accommodate hills and valleys, streams, wooded areas, and other important features.

SUSTAINABILITY CONSIDERATIONS

Increasing environmental awareness has touched all aspects of the real estate development industry, including community and housing design. Environmental concerns in many communities have led to stricter open-space and conservation requirements, more comprehensive planning reviews of subdivision infrastructure design, and increasing restrictions on building practices in environmentally sensitive areas. The most obvious effect of these concerns has been to substantially restrict the amount of developable land and its permissible uses. A secondary effect is to dramatically increase the soft costs associated with engineering and environmental permitting.

All development puts stress on land, but even simple practices can reduce impacts. Zoning and comprehensive planning give guidance, but developers must ultimately decide how they will manage or mitigate these impacts on each parcel. First, developers should carefully consider the location of their projects. Increasing regional planning and widespread use of GIS mapping mean that valuable ecologies are less and less subjective, and features are more likely to be well defined and documented before development pressure arrives. Developers must know from the outset which kinds of environmental assets to avoid. Parcel-scale mapping of unfragmented wildlife habitat, watersheds, and prime agricultural lands is often available from planning offices or state environmental agencies. Experts such as wildlife biologists or field ecologists can be hired to analyze data in the preliminary site search and to quantify risks. For the beginner, a site that does not conform to the general plan is usually not a good choice. That said, an otherwise developable parcel with a manageable complication might be worthwhile—if purchased at the right price—as tract builders may pass over the opportunity, looking for more yield or a simpler plat.

Once a parcel and use have been identified, developers should quickly establish a strategy for developing that parcel at a reasonable profit without violating its natural features. If the natural features are of particular value as amenities, developers should determine which development practices, if any, will complement what exists and consider whether these assets can be enhanced by improved stewardship. Developers do not just react to regulatory policy; they help create it by their actions. Innovative developers can outperform regulatory requirements, which are usually a minimally acceptable standard.

Homebuyers increasingly place value on more sustainable development. But Roger Glover of Cornerstone Homes says, "It's not generally their environmental values, it's the value of the environment."[33] His point is that buyers are attracted to views, open space, and trails along streams, but they do not often dig into the developer's stormwater practices. Though sustainability is seldom a primary motivation of buyers, developers must be able to address both buyers' needs and regulatory requirements, and sales can benefit from good decisions made early. Integrating ecological principles is easiest when considered from the very beginning, rather than attempting to "greenwash" a conventional development. Conservation can be incorporated into projects in many ways. For example, developers can

- reserve open spaces that enhance natural features, such as stands of trees or watercourses;
- legally and physically protect areas of natural beauty and reserve areas for outdoor recreation or agriculture, designing managed access that protects these resources;
- integrate stormwater features and water retention areas into the site plan, which, properly designed, can become amenities, or at least open-space features;
- create varied landscaping, including permaculture and native planting areas that enhance a project's appearance and biological function with less intensive maintenance;
- construct, landscape, and maintain to minimize soil erosion, particularly on slopes;
- actively manage erosion, air and water quality, noise, and traffic during construction; and
- provide community opportunities for residents to engage with the landscape.

DECARBONIZATION, RESILIENCE, AND REGIONAL PATTERNS. The developer's first decision within a market is where, on the urban–rural spectrum, to look for opportunities. Since the postwar suburban boom, the consistent answer for new developers was to look to the fringe of suburbia. There the development issues were simpler, land was more easily priced and lightly regulated, and the supply of exurban migrants was as certain as the job growth of the metro area. In some fast-growing areas this is still true enough, but in many places perpetual outward growth is reaching its limits. Smart-growth policies are limiting regulatory approvals, and a growing portion of buyers seem to value walkability and connection to urban amenities. Plus, another objection has begun to be codified in law: emissions reduction.

Historically, California has been an early adopter of regulations that subsequently become common across the United States. Greenhouse gas (GHG) emissions are one example: they are now a routine part of large land use decisions there, recognizing that where and how homes are built are part of the carbon economy. As part of statewide climate goals, which include industrial and utility rules, environmental review for land use changes now includes a required emissions calculation, and applicants must demonstrate their development's reduction from an emissions baseline, by implementing various practices. California planner Steve Kellenberg suggests, "This is surprising to people, but it's just part of a comprehensive quantification of everything that goes in and out of the development, which is becoming an expectation."[34] Kurt Culbertson of Design Workshop suggests that, along with diversity, equity, and inclusion (DEI), carbon is becoming a major point in most large requests for proposal (RFPs), particularly in projects with a public or institutional component.[35] In addition to emissions, as a function of vehicle-trip generation and building efficiency, climate policies require attention to resilience. Because under any plausible scenario for global carbon reduction, some amount of climate change is already happening, developers can expect increasing concern from both regulators and investors about the long-term prospects of their projects in an era of changed weather, potentially including less predictable rain events and drought, as well as the obvious risk of rising sea levels in coastal areas. At the time of this writing, some climate effects are already visible, and others will almost certainly manifest during the economic life of communities being developed today. Designing above standards for flood and fire hazards, as well as planning for energy transitions demanded by regulation or by market forces, are all becoming more commonly required. Even if buyers do not ask, developers and designers—at least—need to have an answer for how they think about climate resiliency and emissions strategy. As major investors' environmental, social, and governance (ESG) requirements influence land investments, carbon accounting is likely to be a required part of investor reporting, creating pressure from both sides.

CONSERVATION, INNOVATIVE PLANNING, AND PUD. Among the key planning concepts with which a developer should be familiar are conservation development, cluster development, new urbanism, and planned unit development (PUD).

Conservation development is an approach to exurban community development that proposes sensitive landscapes and development can coexist. Conservation communities can range in size from a few acres to thousands, but they generally share several concepts. They usually include legal protections—such as a conservation easement—for some areas of the plan. They also typically control housing design and building practices to a greater degree than comparably located subdivisions.

Clustering is the most common zoning-approved method of conservation development. In cluster development, higher densities in certain areas permit protected open space elsewhere on the site. Following traditional zoning, overall, gross density usually remains the same for cluster developments as for traditional tract housing where housing is spread more uniformly over the entire tract. Clustering demands closer attention to natural features and more design detail on individual homesites.

New urbanism offers another alternative to conventional subdivision design, emphasizing traditional neighborhood planning based on grid street patterns more associated with preautomotive suburbs and towns. These plans feature narrower streets with sidewalks, small public squares and parks, narrower lots with rear garages to manage car traffic, and more walkable town centers.

New developers aspiring to these characteristics should be advised that they are not as simple to achieve as they may sound. First, the more comprehensive design vision of a master-planned community requires substantially more attention and expense in the design phase, which can be tough for a small firm to sustain. Second, the consistent vision of a master-planned community requires legal structure, governance documents and boards, and operational funding for common area maintenance, as well as ongoing design review and builder oversight. This "software" is just as complex as the actual construction. Third, the concept of conservation development is a more complicated story to tell in marketing. That said, demographics clearly support more of this type of development, particularly in light of the aging of the U.S. population, an increased interest in walkable places, and the increasing diversity of household types that are poorly served by conventional suburban houses.

Whereas conservation and new urbanist development are design and governance concepts, PUD is a legal concept. PUDs are alternative zoning classifications typical in many jurisdictions. The names vary (e.g., planned residential development or planned residential unit), but the purpose remains the same. Instead of traditional zoning classifications, PUDs favor a more flexible approach that considers the project in its entirety, as a response to the specific parcel. Certain zoning map areas are usually allowed to submit plans as a PUD, and special uses such as schools or infrastructure are likely to use this channel as well. The PUD is approved as an entity and is like a customized rezoning for a desirable project, though it may carry over key density criteria from its previous zoning overlay. It may combine commercial and residential uses, include several types of residential products, and provide open space and common areas with recreational and community facilities. Specific proposals for access, open space, and parking may be advanced, rather than prescriptive standards.

In a PUD, residential areas may be outlined and a certain number of units designated, but limited detail regarding the specific site plan is required for approval. Most jurisdictions require later public review of the specific site plan; some treat that review as cursory, if the plan is being followed. Developers have the right to build a certain number of units or a certain number of square feet of commercial or office space as long as they conform to the stipulations of the PUD ordinance. Long-term development may require periodic updates of the PUD plan, as it changes.

SITE PLANNING PROCESSES

After the site investigation has been completed and base maps prepared, the land planner should present the developer with a site plan that describes a number of different approaches toward developing the site. The site plan, which combines information regarding the target market with the base map, must consider many different items:

- topography at intervals that will be required by regulators;
- geology, drainage, and known environmental features;
- natural vegetation and tree calipers if required;
- vistas and sightlines;
- private and public open spaces;
- neighboring uses;
- setbacks, easements, and other restrictions;
- roads and utilities;
- waste, recycling, and maintenance spaces;
- patterns of pedestrian, bicycle, and other vehicular circulation—ingress and egress, sidewalks, alleys, and parking for dwelling and community uses;
- market information;
- sales office location, visitor parking, and other temporary operational concerns;
- buffers for noise and privacy; and
- building types.

Design is an iterative process. It can quickly spiral out of control and over budget without a dedicated project planner to keep the project focused on future users and their relationship to every aspect of the site. The site planner first produces a diagram showing constraints and opportunities with all the site's relevant features—undevelopable slopes and wetlands, neighboring uses, view corridors, arterial roads, access points, streams, forests, and special vegetation. Next, using the developer's land use budget from the market analysis, the site planner prepares alternative layouts showing roads, lots, circulation patterns, open space, amenities, and recreation areas, reconciling lot sizes, setbacks, and access to parcel features.

Throughout the schematic planning phase, developers must ensure that the plan will meet their marketing and financial objectives. They should mentally drive down every street, examining traffic patterns, and consider such aspects as attractive vistas, landscaping, and homeowners' privacy. They should also envision the entrance to the subdivision, playgrounds, and street crossings. Sequence and the sense of arrival are key elements that the developer should always keep in mind.

A team approach usually works best, and the contractor, civil engineer, political consultant (if needed), and especially sales and marketing staff should be involved as early as possible. Rough drawings of alternative schemes should be reviewed at regular intervals.

KAUFMAN

In Columbus, Ohio, Gravity, a project incorporating both adaptive use and new mid-rise construction, offers a carefully curated environment for urban living. The project is integrated with on-site health and wellness spaces and providers, while interiors and park spaces alike are enlivened with public art.

Another way to develop a plan is by holding a *charrette,* during which the land planners work with the public, community leaders, and other representatives to incorporate their concerns and ideas. This model of public participation, if handled correctly, allows stakeholders to feel they had a say in shaping the proposal. If handled poorly, it is a recipe for disappointment and expense. Charettes are work sessions with the public, but decisions should never be announced in this environment. The project design team is ultimately responsible for fulfilling the development's objectives. The desires of other stakeholders should be considered but only adopted if they add value to the proposal.

When the developer is satisfied with the schematic plan, the planner produces the final version. The final plan also goes through several iterations. Because it will ultimately be submitted to the city for plat approval, the final plan must show the boundary lines, dimensions, and curvatures of every lot and street. Jurisdictions typically offer detailed guidelines for these submittals, but the guidelines often include a troubling, open-ended line: ". . . and other information that may be requested for departmental review." Developers must meet with reviewers early on and obtain a clear list of what documentation, including engineering calculations or modeling, are required for review and approvals.

Design guidelines provide an important tool for land developers in setting the tone and overall appearance for a subdivision. In master-planned communities, detailed urban design guidelines can cover all aspects of design, from the streetscape and landscaping to individual house sites, materials, setbacks, and architecture. Although guidelines that are too severe can create monotonous subdivisions where everything looks alike, well-crafted guidelines can help establish an attractive subdivision. Creating design guidelines is a skill that may not be within the capability of the project planner. Some firms specialize in coding and guidelines, but developers should coordinate such documents closely with the attorney drafting the governance documents for the property owners' association; the association, or its agent, will need the legal authority, design support, and operational budget to follow through for many years. Developers should also be sure to retain the right to modify guidelines if buyers react negatively to the initial approach; they can convey this right in some form when owners take over design control duties. Architectural guidance should be framed positively: "How porches can create an active streetscape" rather than "all porches must be eight feet deep and painted white."

SITE INFORMATION

The design process begins with a base map that delineates the parcel's relevant physical and legal features. All subsequent design schemes are drawn on the base map, so accuracy is paramount (though it is more easily adjusted with computer aided design). Zoning and other resource mapping and aerial photos are often available for download from planning departments or from private companies. Aerial photos are invaluable for understanding and engineering the property, as well as for marketing the project later. Land developers should be cautious when committing to a timeline for due diligence: in areas with tree cover and slopes, accurate aerial photogrammetry is seasonal and best accomplished when deciduous trees are bare. City halls, local libraries, utility agencies, state highway departments, and local engineering firms are sources for topographic maps, soil surveys, soil borings, percolation tests, and previous environmental assessments. Title companies and the development attorney are the sources for existing easements, rights-of-way, and subdivision restriction information.

TOPOGRAPHIC SURVEY. Site planning begins with the topographic map that shows the contours of the property, rock outcroppings, springs, marshes, wetlands, soil types, and vegetation. Although topographic maps are available for many counties, a custom-drawn topographic survey is invaluable for sites with significant grading. Finding the firm that did a previous survey of the same parcel, or a neighbor,

will often save time and money because key reference markers will already have been located. In tight subdivisions, or on sites with substantial vegetation, on-site micro-surveys are often needed to obtain more accurate information in specific areas.

SITE MAP. Developers should prepare a vicinity map at a small scale that shows the surrounding neighborhood and the major roads leading to the site. The map can be adapted later for marketing, loan applications, and government approvals. In addition to location information, the map should show

- major land uses around the project;
- transportation routes and transit stops;
- comprehensive plan designations;
- existing easements;
- existing zoning of surrounding areas;
- location of airport noise zones;
- jurisdictional boundaries for cities and special districts, such as schools, police, fire, and sanitation; and
- lot sizes and dimensions of surrounding property.

BOUNDARY SURVEY. The boundary survey shows bearings, distances, curves, and angles for all outside boundaries. In addition to boundary measurements, it should show the location of all streets and utilities and any encroachments, easements, and official county benchmarks from which boundary surveys are measured or triangulation locations near the property. It is important to know which elements the lender will require—typically the American Land Title Association standard—and also to think ahead to requirements of the final plat and engineering review.

The boundary survey should include a precise calculation of the total area of the site, reconciled with other legal descriptions, as well as flood areas, easements, and subparcels. Calculations of area are used to

- determine the number of allowable units based on zoning information;
- determine net developable area (the size of this area serves as the basis for both site planning and economic analysis of the project);
- determine sales prices—often, sales price is calculated per square foot or per square meter (for instance, $10 per net developable or gross square foot [$107.60/sq m]) rather than as a fixed total price; and
- provide a legal description of the site.

UTILITIES MAP. The utilities map is prepared at the same scale as the boundary survey. It shows the location of

- all utility easements and rights-of-way;
- existing underground and overhead utility lines for telephone, electricity, and street lighting, including pole locations;
- existing sanitary sewers, storm drains, manholes, open drainage channels, and catch basins, and the size of each;
- rail lines and rail rights-of-way;
- existing water, gas, electric, and steam mains, as well as underground conduits, and the size of each; and
- police and fire alarm call boxes, fire hydrants, or any other public safety equipment.

CONCEPT DEVELOPMENT. Once base maps have been prepared and gross and net developable acreage calculated, the true design process begins. Before the planner begins drawing, the developer should define the target market, the end product (including lot sizes), and the approximate number of units needed to make the project economically feasible.

Base maps outline developable areas as well as features such as lakes, stands of mature trees, and hills on the site. The developer determines which features should become focal points for the design based on the site's physical condition and specific market. For example, although a creek and its floodplain are often excluded from the developable area because of potential flooding problems, it may be the site's best feature when used as a focal point for public open space or as a private amenity for certain lots. Most likely, it also performs a vital drainage function that may be expensive and destructive, if not illegal, to alter.

The goal of site planning is to maximize the value of the property subject to market absorption and zoning constraints. Lots with views, or that adjoin open space or water, sell at a premium, as do lots protected from future change, such as end lots or lots adjoining conserved areas. Developers may achieve high returns by placing higher-density products such as townhouses, multifamily housing, or zero-lot-line homes next to valued features or built amenities. Lots that do not front on these features will sell for more if the plan gives them physical and legal access. The best plans create value by using a desirable feature as a generator of lot premiums—for example, a town square with houses fronting it. The public has access

to the square and its surrounding streets, while the houses that front on it have special views. A lake, golf course, or other active or passive recreational amenity could similarly enhance value. Many developers have noticed that trail systems are a particularly valued use which requires little land allocation and hard construction but can touch many if not all lots.

If the development's use is perceived as incompatible with adjacent uses, the project may be contested by local residents. For example, if single-family houses face a developer's property, any non-single-family use is likely to draw objections from the neighbors. Although different uses on adjoining properties are appropriate in many situations, the burden falls on the developer to demonstrate the reason for not maintaining consistency in use or density. Reference to the jurisdiction's own Comprehensive Plan can be a good argument for additional density or new types.

Many residential tracts border major streets. Because such commercially suitable frontage usually sells for three to five times the value of single-family land, the developer may wish to consider placing retail, office, or multifamily uses with ground-floor commercial space at these locations. A realistic plan for developing and leasing these spaces becomes very important, as the commercial vitality of this frontage informs the image of the project.

STREETS AND STREET HIERARCHY

In the design of street systems for a new development, a street's contribution to the neighborhood environment is as important as its role as a transportation link. The street system should be legible to visitors so that the intended function of a particular street segment is readily apparent.

Although debate over the appropriate functions and definitions of street types persists, the concept of a hierarchy of streets remains practical. The commonly used functional classification of streets includes, in ascending order, local streets, collectors (sometimes called "boulevards" or "avenues"), and arterials (including freeways).

- **Arterial Streets**—Arterial streets are seldom created as parts of new subdivisions. The primary purpose of arterial streets is mobility—the movement of as much traffic as possible as fast as is reasonable—and the mobility function of arterials therefore overshadows their function of providing access to fronting properties, such as residences or commercial uses.

- **Collector Streets**—Collector streets serve as the link between arterial streets and local streets. Typically, they make up about 5 to 10 percent of total street mileage in new developments. Increasingly, new collector streets are fronted by active properties, such as neighborhood commercial centers, institutions, and multifamily residences.
- **Local Streets**—Local streets usually account for around 90 percent of the street mileage in new communities and are intended to provide access to the residential properties fronting them. As the preponderant class of streets in terms of mileage, they contribute much to the signature of their neighborhoods. They also constitute the backbone of neighborhood pedestrian and bicycle networks.

When designing streets for a new development, designers should begin with the minimum width that will reasonably satisfy traffic needs. On most local streets, a 24- to 26-foot-wide (7.3–7.9 m) pavement is appropriate. This width provides two parking lanes and a traffic lane or one parking lane and two moving lanes. For lower-volume streets with limited parking, a 22- to 24-foot-wide (6.7–7.3 m) pavement is adequate. For low-volume streets where no parking is expected, an 18-foot-wide (5.5 m) pavement is adequate. Widening small streets a few more feet does not increase capacity, but it does encourage higher driving speed, unless the width is demarcated for cycling or other use. A wide access street also lacks the intimate scale that makes an attractive setting. Designers should consider the viability of bicycle traffic to evaluate whether any widening might be better used for bike lanes, which can expand the nonmotorized domain on the street and are sometimes preferred by regulation.

A residential collector street should be designed for higher speed than access streets, permitting unrestricted automobile movements. Residential collector streets 36 feet (11 m) wide provide for traffic movement and two curbside parking lanes. When parking is not needed, two moving lanes of traffic are adequate, with shoulders graded for emergency parking.[36] Designers should keep in mind that a street section, once chosen, need not remain constant for the length of the street. In fact, changes in the street design, such as expanding sidewalk area periodically to allow outdoor dining or allowing nose-in diagonal parking to alternate with traffic-calming landscape elements, are powerful signals that something special is happening in those locations.

Residential streets should provide safe, efficient circulation for vehicles and pedestrians and should create positive aesthetic qualities. The character of a residential street is influenced to a great extent by its paving width, its horizontal and vertical alignments, and the landscape treatment of its edges. Residential streets are community spaces that should project a suitable image and scale. For example, much of the character of older neighborhoods is derived from the mature street trees that form a canopy over entire streets, whereas a neighborhood with wide streets devoid of trees conveys an entirely different image. Vertical elements, including not only trees but light posts, shading structures, bollards, and signs, can be more important than the surface of the street in communicating pedestrian safety and insulating lower-floor building programs from the effects of traffic.[37] The rise of e-commerce, as well as the prevalence in urban areas of ride-sharing services, have emphasized the importance of service drop-off and short-term parking, particularly on commercial streets, and designers should pay attention to this public service area.

Straight streets with rectangular lots give a more urban ambience, whereas curvilinear streets tend to create irregularly shaped lots and provide a more pastoral feel. A minor problem for the developer is that irregular lots may have to be resurveyed when the builder is ready to start construction because the iron pins that mark lot corners tend to get moved or lost during construction of other houses.

SITE ENGINEERING

Adequate grading and the optimal provision of utility services are important elements of site design, and the cost of providing them is critical to a project's bottom line. Developers should never leave the decision about these elements to the civil engineers; the lowest-cost site engineering is rarely the most profitable subdivision design. The developer's objective is to maximize the sale value of the lots subject to efficient site engineering, but this value may also derive from a harmonious relationship between built and natural landforms.

GRADING. The grading plan must contain precise details and take into consideration such factors as the amount of dirt that will be excavated, the finished heights of lots, steep areas that may require retaining walls, and graded areas that may be subject to future erosion (developers are liable for erosion even after they have sold all the lots on a site). Grading is also used as an engineering tool to correct unfavorable subsoil conditions and to create

- drainage swales and retention areas;
- berms and visual and noise barriers;
- solid subgrade for roads and driveways, plazas, and recreational spaces;
- topsoil at a proper depth for planting;
- circulation routes for roads and paths; and
- suitable subsoil conditions and ingress for facilities.

Grading also serves aesthetic purposes to provide privacy, create sight lines, emphasize site topography or provide interest to a flat site, and connect structures to the streetscape and planting areas. Grading plans should be done, if possible, in coordination with the site contractor, who may have preferences for the manner of marking for later work.

STORM DRAINAGE AND FLOODPLAINS. Storm drainage systems carry away stormwater runoff. In low-density developments with one-acre (0.4 ha) lots or larger, natural drainage may suffice, and generally, natural approaches are more cost-effective. In denser developments, however, some form of storm drainage system is always needed, and the best design may be a hybrid of conventional and low-impact techniques.

Gently rolling sites are the easiest and cheapest to drain; flat sites and steep sites are more difficult and expensive. As with other environmental issues, drainage problems can come back to haunt a developer long after the lots have been sold, and these issues can be difficult to predict.

If a property contains any hint of wetlands, this is among the first studies a developer should commission before buying a site. Developers should understand where the property lies in relation to floodplains. They can start by obtaining the Federal Emergency Management Agency's flood hazard boundary maps (see www.fema.gov) or flood hazard GIS data from the municipality. Land that is within the 100-year floodplain— that is, the area that is expected to flood once every 100 years—is usually not developable except for uses such as golf courses, parks, or storage of nontoxic materials. Even if uses are permissible, developers should consider whether they make sense, and whether the resulting structures will be insurable. Developers should ask their engineering consultant whether the mapped floodplain is consistent with recent experience and trends. Flood maps are periodically updated, and over time, climate change is expected to expand some areas vulnerable to 100-year flooding.

In some localities, land within the 100-year floodplain *is* developable, albeit with restrictions, and structures can be mortgaged by federally insured institutions only if the structure carries flood insurance. To alter floodplain areas, developers must apply for a permit from the EPA, U.S. Army Corps of Engineers, or other body, such as state environmental or natural resources agencies, with authority over the local wetlands or creek system. The Army Corps of Engineers designates floodways as well as 100-year floodplains. A floodway is that portion of a stream's floodplain designated to provide passage of the 100-year flood, as defined by the Corps, without increasing elevation of the flood by more than one foot (0.3 m). Developers may not build within floodways. Floodways must retain the same or better rate of water flow after development as before it; otherwise, floodplain elevation is likely to rise upstream from the development, causing increased flooding in those areas. Developers can alter the floodway, but any changes must be engineered properly to preserve water flow and must be permitted by the appropriate authorities, including the Corps of Engineers.

Climate change is affecting floodplain regulations. Houston's Harris County recently passed a regulation requiring the finished floor of all new homes to be above the 500-year floodplain elevation *plus 36 inches (91 cm)*. This change is dramatically impacting how much land is developable for new homes.

Irrespective of the frequency with which they flood, areas within a property may be defined as wetlands and thus come under the jurisdiction of the EPA as well as other federal, state, and local agencies; these include the corps and the U.S. Fish and Wildlife Service or, more commonly, the state department of environmental quality. Often, all agencies must be informed and satisfied before the Corps of Engineers will issue a permit to disturb a wetland.

Wetlands come in many forms, including ephemerally wet swales, intermittent streams, hardpan vernal pools, and volcanic mudflow vernal pools. Regulatory streamlining has encouraged coordinating agencies to adopt standard definitions of these features. But ultimately, delineation is done by an individual field biologist or hydrologist on site, who makes a representation to the governing agency, and jurisdictional determination is subjective.

In evaluating a site that contains potential wetlands, developers should hire an experienced consulting biologist to conduct a preliminary wetlands evaluation study, to map potential wetland sites on the property, and to suggest mitigation measures and alternative approaches to the design of the property.[38] Developers should be aware that some features, such as vernal pools, may be only seasonally visible, meaning that a project that is ready to go in September may be delayed by six months for a complete wetland delineation. At the same time, the required flagging of wetlands degrades over time, so the delineation should not precede development activity by much more than a year.

LOW-IMPACT DEVELOPMENT. Several aspects of land development can adversely affect site hydrology in multiple ways. Expansion of impervious surfaces and changes in vegetation can concentrate and accelerate surface stormwater flow. The introduction of vehicles, new uses, and landscape maintenance regimens can increase pollutant discharge, and the combination of increased water use and reduced permeability can impair the recharge of aquifers on which the development and surrounding uses depend. Low-impact development (LID) water quality management strategies can make up an integrated approach to improve water quality.

Integrated LID methods can result in better environmental performance while reducing development costs when compared with traditional conventional stormwater management approaches.[39] LID techniques are a simple yet effective approach to stormwater management that integrates green space, native landscaping, natural hydrologic functions, and other techniques to generate less runoff from developed land. These processes can also remove pollutants, such as nutrients, pathogens, and metals from stormwater.[40] In short, LID is used to maintain—as closely as possible— the benefits of natural site hydrology and to mitigate the adverse effects of stormwater runoff and nonpoint source pollution associated with some conventional stormwater management methods.

Common LID practices include the following:

- **Conservation Design and Impervious Surface Reduction**—Following conservation design methods, such as clustered housing, shared driveways, and narrower roadways, as well as rainwater collection systems on buildings, can reduce the overall impervious surface and decrease stormwater management costs.
- **Bioretention (Rain Gardens)**—A bioretention cell is an engineered natural treatment system consisting of a recessed landscaped area constructed with a specialized soil mixture and site-appropriate vegetation. Slightly recessed, the cell intercepts runoff, allowing the soil and plants to filter and store runoff; remove petroleum pollutants, nutrients, and sediments; and promote groundwater recharge through infiltration. These rain gardens can be relatively inexpensive to build and can become site amenities.

- **Temporary Erosion Control**—More ecologically sensitive approaches are not limited to permanent installations. Up to a quarter of stormwater management costs can be expended on temporary measures of erosion control during construction and landscape establishment. Filter-fabric and compost constructions are now commonly deployed in lieu of silt fences and check dams in these applications. Typically, these measures cost more to install, but they can be deployed so that they remain in place permanently, making the life-cycle cost comparable with conventional measures.
- **Vegetated Swales, Buffers, and Strips**—Constructed downstream of a runoff source, a vegetated or grassed swale is an area that slows and filters the first flush of runoff from an impervious surface. From both a budget and an environmental perspective, swales are nearly always preferable to culverts.
- **Permeable Pavement**—This type of pavement allows stormwater to infiltrate the soil. Materials and maintenance costs are substantially more expensive than conventional pavements, but their use can radically reduce impervious surface over the whole site, a metric that is increasingly evaluated by local and state approval authorities.
- **Low-Impact Landscaping**—Increasingly, native plants may be specified for site landscaping. These varieties are often more expensive, but they reduce operational cost and impact and require less water and maintenance. They also tend to be resilient to known pests.
- **Green Roofs and Rainwater Collection**—Capturing rainwater for reuse and slow discharge reduces concentrated runoff. Green roofs capture rainwater while improving buildings' thermal performance in several ways.

As demonstrated by multiple EPA case studies, the use of LID practices can be both fiscally and environmentally beneficial to developers and communities. These systems can often substitute for more expensive elements such as curbs and gutters; sometimes they can reduce requirements for intensive site engineering, such as flood-control structures.[41] In case studies, capital cost savings have ranged from 15 to 80 percent when LID techniques were used.[42] The best examples of LID use functional features as landscape amenities in ways that increase value, and studies have shown that attractive implementations of these systems can result in developments that appreciate at a higher rate than conventionally designed subdivisions.[43]

SANITARY SEWERS. The layout of the sanitary system is determined by the topography of the site and the location of the outfall point—that is, the point of connection to the sewer main. Sewers are primarily gravity driven, so if the sewer main that connects the subdivision to the treatment plant is not located at the low point of the site, the developer may have to provide a pumping station, which brings both construction and operational expense.

New developers should avoid tracts of land for which nearby sewage and water services are not available because the cost of bringing these services in from off-site locations can be prohibitive. When major off-site utility improvements are necessary, developers usually require a minimum of 200 homes to recoup their investment and risk. Creating a utility district to provide service or building a plant where none exists typically takes two years or more, as well as significant front-end investment, and can entail substantial operational and legal entanglements. It is usually only feasible on even larger developments in desirable areas.

One option available to developers whose sites do not have sanitary service is to buy or lease a package treatment plant, a small self-contained sewage treatment facility, to serve the subdivision and to design the system to tie eventually into the community's system. This option can work in rural areas and in communities that are accustomed to working with package treatment technology.

Septic tank systems are usually feasible only in rural areas. Their use depends on soil conditions, and in most areas, they are allowed only on lots of at least one-half acre (0.2 ha). If a well is included on the same site as a septic tank, even larger lots are sometimes necessary to prevent contamination of the well water; health depart-

Natural and engineered systems can be combined in low-impact development. For this redevelopment of an industrial waterway at Riverfront Park in Spokane, Washington, the development team softened and diversified the channel's edges, creating space for water, for pedestrians, and for public and private programs. Together they form a resilient but active waterfront.

ment approvals will be contingent on an adequate physical separation of the two, usually both by distance and by extending the well casing's grouted seal.

In planning a sewer system, the developer should investigate

- sewage capacity requirements, which may vary (100 gallons per day [379 L/day] per person is a common standard; for houses the standard is often framed in terms of number of bedrooms);
- available capacity and cost of the treatment plant and connector lines;
- number of hookups contracted but not yet installed;
- the municipality's method of charging for sewer installation; and
- the people responsible for issuing permits and establishing requirements for discharging treated sewage into natural watercourses.

Sanitary sewer lines are normally located within street rights-of-way but not under road pavement, so they may be maintained without cutting expensive pavement or landscape. House connections to sewers should be at least six inches (15 cm) in diameter to avoid clogging; all lateral sewers should be at least eight inches (20 cm) in diameter. Sanitary lines and waterlines should be laid in different trenches where possible, although some cities allow a double-shelf trench that contains the sanitary sewer on the bottom and the waterline on the top shelf. Except in very high-density communities, these "wet" infrastructure elements should not be colocated with power and communications services.

WATER SYSTEM. A central water system is standard in urban communities. As with the requirements for sewage capacity, those for water supply vary, but 100 gallons per day (379 L/day) per person is common. Requirements can vary greatly in their calculation of occupant load: jurisdictions may count bedrooms, bathrooms, or habitable square footage.

Water mains should be located in street rights-of-way or in utility easements. Residential mains average six to eight inches (15–20 cm) in diameter, depending on the water pressure. Branch lines to houses are three-quarter-inch or one-inch (2 or 2.5 cm) pipe connected to a five-eighths- or three-quarter-inch (1.5 or 2 cm) water meter, respectively. Because waterlines are under pressure, their location is of less concern than that for sewer lines, which rely on gravity flow.

Developers should consult the fire department about requirements for water pressure and the placement of fire hydrants. The fire department is likely to restrict the depth and slopes of culs-de-sac and the maximum distance between fire hydrants and structures. Fire department requirements, like road requirements for emergency services, are increasingly used as "backdoor" development restrictions, and developers should be aware very early of these requirements. Emergency services may require a secondary access to sites with more than a certain number of homes, in case the primary road system is blocked.

Water, sewer, and drainage lines should be installed before streets are paved. If installation before paving is not possible, developers should install underground crossing sleeves where the lines will cross the streets so that the utility contractor can pull the lines through later; otherwise, streets will have to be torn up to install and maintain lines.

UTILITY SYSTEMS. Electricity, gas, telephone, and data services are typically installed and operated by private companies—although in the case of underground electrical service, the site contractor may act as the utility's agent. Designating the location of utility easements is an essential step in the process of land planning. If the land planner does not specify a location, the utility company may do so with little regard for aesthetic considerations. Usually, easements run with the street right-of-way, and along the back

FIGURE 3-9 Typical Designs for Bioretention Basins

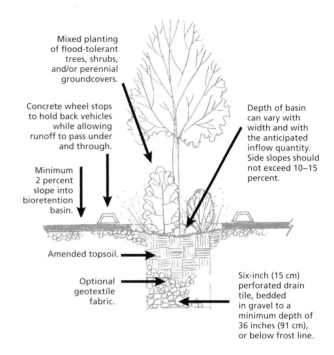

Mixed planting of flood-tolerant trees, shrubs, and/or perennial groundcovers.

Concrete wheel stops to hold back vehicles while allowing runoff to pass under and through.

Depth of basin can vary with width and with the anticipated inflow quantity. Side slopes should not exceed 10–15 percent.

Minimum 2 percent slope into bioretention basin.

Amended topsoil.

Optional geotextile fabric.

Six-inch (15 cm) perforated drain tile, bedded in gravel to a minimum depth of 36 inches (91 cm), or below frost line.

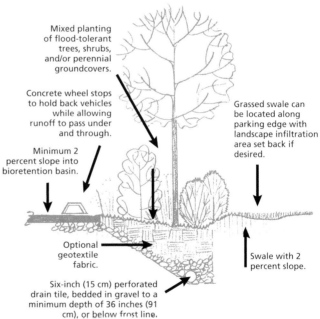

Mixed planting of flood-tolerant trees, shrubs, and/or perennial groundcovers.

Concrete wheel stops to hold back vehicles while allowing runoff to pass under and through.

Grassed swale can be located along parking edge with landscape infiltration area set back if desired.

Minimum 2 percent slope into bioretention basin.

Optional geotextile fabric.

Swale with 2 percent slope.

Six-inch (15 cm) perforated drain tile, bedded in gravel to a minimum depth of 36 inches (91 cm), or below frost line.

Source: Martin F. Quigley and Timothy Lawrence, *Multi-Functional Landscaping: Putting Your Parking Lot Design Requirements to Work for Water Quality*, Ohio State University Extension: CL-1000-01, 2002.

or side lot lines, within five or 10 feet (1.5 or 3 m) of each lot. Most planners prefer to place all electrical power transformers underground or in semi-exposed secure cabinets; however, local custom and ordinances may dictate whether lines are above- or belowground. Local power companies often communicate their preference with prohibitively high costs for the less preferable option. The installation of transformers underground can be done at a reasonable cost and can prevent vandalism and the need for frequent maintenance. Transformers located aboveground can be hidden and protected from vandals by wooden lattices or painted metal cabinets with thorny shrubs or similar landscaping devices. Landscaping for these areas should closely follow the utility's operational guidelines, as major work will almost certainly occur here as homes are built in the development.

Although electricity, gas, telephone, and data services tend to play a smaller role in site design than do public utilities, such as water, sewer, and drainage, they still determine where structures can be built on each lot. Because the rapid development of data infrastructure has reshaped so many aspects of domestic and work life, many developers have made major investments in fiber-optic network installation for their communities. The value of these networks to retail lots or homebuyers over time is not yet established. Developers of communities must think beyond the year or two of the development period and consider both the function of the utility service and the durability of the "deal" they have made for their customers by committing to providers. Developers have, in some cases, saddled their communities' residents with long-term contracts in an effort to get affordable and high-quality service, only to find that falling costs make their packages unattractive in just a few years. The safest approach is to attempt to "future-proof" development projects by installing additional empty conduit and equipment space during development, when unit costs are low. In this way, additional technology can be accommodated at modest cost later as long as it fits in the pipe.

The developer should talk to each utility provider as early as possible. Utilities are by nature uncompetitive, and within their concession area, providers may have little incentive to move quickly or improve service. Delays in obtaining services are common and can easily throw off the developer's schedule and hold up final sales.

PLATTING

Lot size and layout should reflect the nature of the surrounding community. In an infill site, matching the character of the new development with its surroundings is especially important. A developer should not try to suburbanize an urban community with deep setbacks, wide lots, and side garages. Alternatively, a compact development in a rural setting may not be appropriate or marketable.

Two determinants of a community's layout are lot width and garage placement. Many postwar suburban subdivisions were designed with wide lots—some up to 100 feet (30.5 m) to accommodate a house and a two-car garage and driveway. More recently, 25- to 40-foot (7.6–12.2 m) widths have become more common. The new urbanist approach embraces the concept of narrower lots, smaller front yards, and garages at the rear of lots, typically accessed by a vehicular and service alley. This layout creates a better streetscape because the view is not dominated by garage doors. For developers, this approach can be desirable because it allows the placement of more houses on the same length of street, saving per-unit infrastructure costs.

In the past, attached townhouses tended to be sited in rows surrounded by parking lots. Today's townhouses often include individual garages that are tucked under the living space at the front or rear or in separate, dedicated buildings at the rear. Garage townhouses can be very cost-effective for builders and developers because they use less land and cost little more to construct. They can also make good use of lower-lying land where ground-floor residential space might not be valued.

Sidewalks, curbing, planting strips, and catchment basins must all be adjusted to the density and price point of the development. A single-family subdivision of 20,000-square-foot (1,860 sq m) lots on minor streets need not be developed with the same street improvements required for a higher-density subdivision of 2,500- to 4,000-square-foot (230–370 sq m) lots.

If the development adjoins a busy street, that edge must be handled with great care. Ideally, the community should not turn its back on the street but should take advantage of the traffic and activity and turn it into an asset. If the project is a mixed-use development, this location could be ideal for intensive uses, such as a retail or service district. Or it could be the site of neighborhood facilities, particularly if they are shared with the greater community, such as schools, libraries, or parks. If houses must be sited along a busy street, visual and sound buffering may be needed, which could take the form of service streets, landscaping, or site walls, or potentially upgrades to the building envelope. If sound isolation is required, developers are advised to retain acoustic consultants, as landscape effects on noise can be highly unpredictable.

Because lots facing busy streets may yield lower prices than interior lots, the developer should consider ways to boost their appeal or possibly use them for lower-priced units. Experienced developers, like good architects, understand which items can create value. But even experienced developers should spend time in the field investigating why people react more favorably to one design element than to another. The need for market research cannot be overemphasized. Successful developers always review the competition, use focus groups, and collect exit data from potential buyers who stop at sales offices or visit community websites or events.

HIGHER DENSITIES

Throughout the country, land cost as a percentage of house value has risen steadily since the 1960s, from 15 to 25 percent on average. In certain areas of major cities, land costs may exceed 50 percent of the house's value. As of this writing, pandemic relocations have completely scrambled these relationships as people sought more space to accommodate working from home. But the long-term sustainability of this change is unknown.

In response to rising land values and other demographic factors, traditional housing types are being rescaled and redesigned for modern use. Bungalows and cottages on small lots are particularly suited to move-down empty nesters, single parents, and others who make up today's smaller households. Townhouses are popular in both urban and suburban areas, offering an alternative to those who do not want the maintenance of a single-family house but are not interested in multifamily living. Townhouses are not always lower-priced options; they can be as upscale as any other housing.

Large estate houses in exclusive communities remain an American icon that appeals to certain market segments. In many areas, estate-style houses are now being rescaled to fit on quarter-acre (0.1 ha) lots. These houses (called small-lot villas or, pejoratively, McMansions) typically have highly articulated two-story facades that face the street, giving an impression of height, volume, and quality.

ZERO-LOT LINE OR PATIO HOMES

Traditionally, local zoning codes have established minimum side yard setbacks ranging from three feet (0.9 m) to 10 percent of the lot width. Three- or five-foot

FIGURE 3-10 Lot Yield Analysis for Different Zero-Lot-Line Configurations

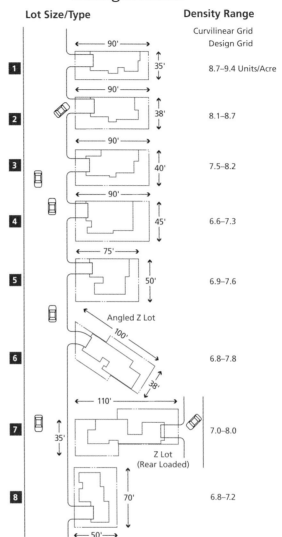

Lot Size/Type	Density Range
	Curvilinear Grid Design Grid
1 — 90' × 35'	8.7–9.4 Units/Acre
2 — 90' × 38'	8.1–8.7
3 — 90' × 40'	7.5–8.2
4 — 90' × 45'	6.6–7.3
5 — 75' × 50'	6.9–7.6
6 — Angled Z Lot 100' × 38'	6.8–7.8
7 — 110' × 35'	7.0–8.0
8 — Z Lot (Rear Loaded) 50' × 70'	6.8–7.2

Density ranges are based on

- **representative, relatively flat 10-acre irregular site with both curvilinear and grid layouts;**
- **comfortable, achievable densities;**
- **no recreation centers or common open space;**
- **50-foot dedicated street right-of-way;**
- **32-foot private street system—can increase density by ± one-half unit per acre; and**
- **individual characteristics and constraints of each site.**

Actual densities obtained will vary up and down from these generalized guidelines.

Source: Richardson-Nagy-Martin, Newport Beach, California.

(0.9 or 1.5 m) side yards result in unusable spaces. Windows from one house often look into windows of the next house, only six feet (1.8 m) away. To make side yards more usable, zero-lot-line lots, which allow densities up to nine units per acre (3.6/ha), were created. Today, most major cities and high-growth counties have modified their zoning codes to allow them.

A zero lot line means that the house is left or right justified; that is, one side of the house is built on the lot line so that the opposite side yard can occupy the total width available (10 feet [3 m] is considered the minimum width for usable space). The side of the house on the lot line is usually a mostly windowless, but not shared, wall. Each lot must take care of its own drainage. If builders design a roof that drains water onto the next property, they must obtain a drainage easement from the owner of that property. In addition, a maintenance agreement, which can be made before construction while the builder or developer owns all the lots, must be recorded if the neighbor's lot is needed to maintain the wall on the lot-line side of the house. Creative architects have mastered the challenge of designing zero-lot-line homes (also called patio homes) by making good use of the outdoor space and developing floor plans and elevations that maximize light and space (see figure 3-10 for various zero-lot-line configurations and associated densities).

Small-lot, high-density housing must be carefully coordinated with scattered-lot or multiple-builder land sale programs. The land plan, in fact, should be drawn up concurrently with the house plan. The lot layout should seek to achieve a variety of goals:

- a site that does not require excessive grading or unusually deep foundation footings;
- sufficient usable area for outdoor activity (one or two larger areas are preferable to four small areas);
- adequate surface drainage away from the house, with slopes running toward the front or rear of the house; land developers should grade the lots so that they all drain toward the storm drainage system;
- minimum on-lot grading and maximum retention of specimen trees; and
- a minimum number of adjoining lots—preferably no more than three (one on each side and one along the back).

With creative site planning and unit design, greater densities can be achieved without sacrificing privacy and livability. Increased densities are one tool to be used in solving the crisis of affordable housing in areas with high land costs. Community acceptance of higher densities is more likely if developers are careful to design attractive, livable communities that enhance their surroundings.

Financing

The major difference between the development of land and the development of income property is that land is usually subdivided and sold rapidly, whereas income property is usually held and operated over a period of years, even if sale is the eventual goal. The holding period is the key to deciding the appropriate type of financing. Land development is financed by a short-term development or construction loan, which is paid down as sales occur. Income property development is financed by both a construction loan and a permanent mortgage, the latter of which is known as a *takeout loan*. For income property development, the construction lender depends on the permanent lender to replace (take out) the construction loan with the permanent mortgage. For land development, the construction lender relies on the developer's ability to sell the finished lots within the agreed-on time frame and at the projected price.

Success in land development—and the developer's ability to repay the development loan—thus depends on the successful marketing of the lots. Because no takeout exists for construction lenders, they must be satisfied that the developer will be able to sell enough lots fast enough to pay off the loan. Often, construction lenders require other collateral, such as letters of credit, in addition to a mortgage on the property. The amount of the loan is usually limited to 30 to 50 percent of the projected sale proceeds to provide a cushion in the event that sales occur more slowly than projected. Slower sales translate into greater interest costs because the balance of the development loan is reduced more slowly than the developer initially projected. Initial pro formas should contemplate a base case, and faster and slower sales paces, and confirm the serviceability of project debt in the slow case.

OBTAINING FINANCING

The most difficult task for beginning developers is obtaining financing. Most developers will need to convince lenders to provide them with financing. In many situations, developers must contribute equity and sign loans personally. A developer's equity can be furnished in cash or in land. Suppose, for instance, that a developer purchased land for a project for $100,000 and the market value of that land after entitlement and planning rose to $400,000. If the total cost of the developer's proposed project is $1 million ($600,000 for development costs plus the market value of the land), the developer could probably find lenders willing to lend 70 percent of that amount. In other words, the lenders require $300,000 equity. Because the market value of the land is $300,000 greater than the original land cost, the developer should be able to use the land equity to satisfy the lender's requirement for $300,000. In fact, the loan would cover the developer's original $100,000 land cost because the $700,000 commitment exceeds the development cost of $600,000 by $100,000.

PURCHASE MONEY NOTES. The terms of the purchase money note can play a vital role in financing the project. PMNs automatically have first lien position and must be paid off before the developer can get a development loan because the development lender must hold a first lien position on the land. If the developer can get the seller to *subordinate* the PMN to the development loan, however, the need to raise outside equity—the hardest money for any new developer to obtain—can be reduced or eliminated.

Finding a seller who will subordinate the PMN is difficult but not impossible. Beginning developers should look for sellers who do not need cash immediately and who are willing to accept the risk of subordination in return for more money. The developer should expect to pay a higher land price, higher interest rate on the PMN, or both in exchange for subordination. Because a subordinated PMN can be crucial for covering a thinly capitalized developer's equity requirements, it may even be worth giving the seller a percentage of the profits as added incentive to subordinate. This arrangement merely recognizes the reality: the seller is, by virtue of this loan, a secured partner in the deal.

Even with subordination, the developer will have to negotiate with the development lender to treat the subordinated PMN as equity. Subordinated or not, the PMN's *release provisions* are among the most important business points for negotiation with the seller. The release provisions provide for removing designated subparcels of land as collateral from the PMN so the developer can give the development lender a first lien (when the PMN is unsubordinated) or a buyer can get construction financing to build a home.

The release provisions designate which subparcels of land are to be released from the first lien of the PMN. They have two main parts: (1) initial land released concurrent with the downpayment and (2) land released by future principal payments on the PMN. On larger tracts, the downpayment on the land provides

for the release of the first subparcel the developer plans to develop. The land that is to be released first must be designated specifically in the purchase contract and the PMN mortgage to avoid any conflict or confusion. The unencumbered parcel provides the initial collateral for the development loan, although the developer may have to provide additional collateral, such as a personal guarantee, letter of credit, or other assets, including other real estate. The development loan can be extended to cover other subparcels as they are released from the PMN, thereby providing construction money for development.

The land development contractor will be able to build improvements on only those parcels for which the development lender has a first lien. If the contractor begins work on any part of the land before the lender has *perfected* the lien (recorded it), the lender may halt construction until possible lien conflicts are cleared. Clearing lien conflicts can take several months because all suppliers who have delivered material to the property and all subcontractors who have worked on the property must sign lien waivers indicating that they have received full payment. If anyone is unhappy for any reason (a common occurrence in building), that person may use the developer's need for a signature on the lien waiver as leverage to get more money.

BUILDERS' PRECOMMITMENTS. In the market feasibility stage, the developer obtains from local builders indications of interest in purchasing the lots. Next, the developer must secure commitment letters from those builders, which become part of the documentation the developer will have to submit to the lender to obtain a loan commitment. The commitment letter specifies the number of lots each builder will buy in the project.

Ideally, the developer will have commitments for most of the lots on a site before approaching potential lenders. Although commitments help reduce the market risk, they do not guarantee that the lots will be sold unless they are backed by letters of credit (LCs). LCs provide guarantees to the developer that the builder's unpaid balance on the lots will be paid off by the bank that issues the LC. Developers that intend to build on all the lots themselves rather than selling to other builders, may find the financing to be more complicated. The lender will look at equity and financing needs for the entire project, including the homes.

Builders are often reluctant to guarantee that they will purchase the lots. The developer must convince the lender that builders' commitments are solid or must provide proof with the LCs. The developer should know the type of documentation that lenders will require before talking to builders. If the lender requires firm commitments backed by LCs, then the developer must address that requirement as part of the deal with the builders.

BUILDERS' PURCHASE TERMS. The purchase terms that builders require for lots vary according to local market conditions. Downpayments range from a nominal amount of earnest money to 10 percent—or even 20 percent—of the purchase price. Builders pay the earnest money when they reserve the lots. The balance is covered by a note that typically sets the interest rate beginning the day the developer delivers finished lots. The contract for purchasing lots usually defines "lot delivery" as the date on which the city accepts public street dedications or the engineer certifies that the project is substantially complete. The contract may stipulate a list of conditions that must be satisfied to convey the finished lot.

In slow markets and in workout situations (when the developer has defaulted on the loan), builders hold a stronger position than the developer. To generate interest from builders, developers sometimes subordinate to the construction lender some portion of the land note on builders' model houses, allowing builders to reduce upfront costs, or they may provide seller financing to builders. Another approach that developers use to generate interest from builders in slow markets or workout situations is to discount the initial lots. Any concessions should be cleared well in advance with lenders and investors and preferably presented as a marketing cost in the business plan.

TIPS FOR DEALING WITH LENDERS. Although each deal with a land development lender is unique, several guidelines usually apply:

- The developer should borrow enough money at the beginning of the project; the developer should not think that a loan can be renegotiated later or that lots can be sold faster.
- The developer should allow enough time on the loan to complete the project or to provide for automatic rollover (extension) provisions, even though the lender will charge for the rollover option.
- If working with a lender on multiple projects, the developer should consider that terms on one project may become open to renegotiation if progress on a second project is not going according to plan.

- Typical points for the land development loan are two points up front and one point per year, starting in the third year. Points are calculated on the total loan request, not on the amount drawn to date. For example, two points on a $1.5 million loan request amount to $30,000.
- The loan can be structured as a two-year construction loan with three automatic renewals.

Development loans are a form of construction loan. The amounts by which the developer pays down the loan cannot be borrowed again later. If possible, developers should structure the development loan as a revolving line of credit that allows borrowing up to the maximum limit of the credit line, regardless of repayments already made. Doing so will likely require the provision of additional collateral as the lots are sold.

The development lender holds a first mortgage on the entire property and must release its lien on individual lots so that the purchaser (the builder or end user) can obtain construction financing. The *release price* is thus a major item for negotiation between the developer and the lender. The lender wants to ensure that the loan is paid off faster than the land is released from the mortgage, which protects the lender's security in the event that the developer defaults on the loan. The developer, on the other hand, prefers that the release price simply be a prorated share of the development loan. For example, if the development loan is $1 million for 100 lots, the sale of one lot would retire the loan by $10,000 (1 ÷ 100 × $1 million). Most lenders set the release price at 1.2 to 1.5 times the prorated share (called the multiple). For a multiple of 1.2, the release price is 1.2 times $10,000, or $12,000 per lot. Thus, every time a lot is sold, the developer pays down the loan by $12,000. The lender often wants a high multiple—1.3 or greater—for releasing lots. The developer wants a multiple as low as possible—1.2 or lower—to maintain cash flow. In return for a low multiple, the lender may require some form of credit enhancement, such as an LC or second lien on other property. Particularly in developments with widely divergent lot prices, the lender may simply set release prices as a percentage of an agreed-on lot price list, but the same acceleration of loan repayment (a higher percentage) will be the lender's goal.

JOINT VENTURES

In the cash flow analyses shown earlier in this chapter, the developer was assumed to own 100 percent of the deal, investing 100 percent of the equity and receiving

100 percent of the cash flow. The developer would also have 100 percent of the downside risk and liability. All or any part of a land development project, however, may be packaged as a variety of *joint ventures*.

The various legal forms of joint ventures are described in chapter 2. In this chapter, the business side of joint ventures is the focus. Most joint ventures involve three major points of negotiation for distributing cash flow from the venture:

1. preferred returns on equity;
2. priorities of payback of equity, fees to the developer, and cash flows from the venture; and
3. split of the profits.

In addition to dividing the returns of the venture, the joint venture specifies how risk is shared among the parties—the timing and amount of equity contributions, fees to the developer and other parties, personal guarantees on notes, and management control of the development entity and other operating entities and associations (see chapter 6).

DEVELOPER AND LANDOWNER. A common approach for new developers is a joint venture between developer and landowner. The land is put into the deal at a negotiated price; land value commonly covers in full the equity that the developer may need to obtain development financing, although partners may demand some additional cash as "skin in the game." The landowner may hold a purchase money mortgage subordinated to the development loan or a first priority for receipt of positive cash flow. The order in which cash flows are distributed (the order of *cash distribution priorities*) might be as follows if land value equals total equity:

- **Priority 1**—The landowner is returned the equity land value allowed by the lender.
- **Priority 2**—The landowner receives a preferred return (cumulative or noncumulative) on the equity (see chapter 4).
- **Priority 3**—The developer receives a development fee, some of which may be paid during the construction and leasing periods.
- **Priority 4**—The developer and the landowner split the remaining profits; priorities and fees are subject to negotiation.

When required equity is less than land value, the landowner receives some value out of the first loan draw. If equity is greater than land value, a two-tiered partnership provides for additional equity investment.

If the landowner has a subordinated PMN on the land, that loan agreement provides for releases similar to those in the development loan agreement. Both liens must be released before homebuilders or other buyers of the lots can obtain free and clear title, which they need to obtain construction financing. For example, suppose a subdivision has both bank financing and a subordinated PMN from the seller. Suppose also that the PMN calls for repayment of $10,000 to release a lot from the note and that the development loan calls for $20,000 repayment. If the developer sells 10 lots that net $35,000 each, the cash flow would be

Sales revenue: 10 × $35,000 =	$350,000
Minus repayment of development loan: 10 × $20,000 =	$200,000
Minus repayment of PMN: 10 × $10,000 =	$100,000
Cash available for distribution:	$50,000

Most joint venture agreements provide for the venture to retain *cash available for distribution* as working capital until the development loan is retired. The cash provides a safety net to cover future equity needs in the event that sales slow or costs increase. Alternatively, such cash could be given to the landowner until the land equity has been fully recovered, or it could be considered profit and divided among the joint venture parties. The landowner would prefer, of course, to receive first priority on all cash flows until recovering the value of the land equity. Customarily, the developer receives a small development fee—3 to 5 percent of the hard cost—during the development to cover direct management costs. This amount is paid currently, not subordinated to the lender's or landowner's repayments.

Sometimes, the revenue from land sales does not cover the required loan release payments for a given parcel or series of lots. In that case, the joint venture's partnership agreement would require the partners to invest new equity to cover the deficit. The development loan agreement may require the lender's approval for sales below a certain price, although the developer would prefer to have full control over pricing decisions. Such pricing approval, while common, can be a recipe for disaster if the lender will not approve prices lowered to match market conditions. A common middle ground is for the developer and lenders to agree on a base price and an allowable maximum discount, which are preapproved and can be executed quickly by the sales team.

One benefit for landowners of putting their land into a joint venture is to save on taxes, especially when they have owned the land for a long time and their basis is well below the current market value. If they sell it outright, they must pay taxes immediately on the full capital gain. If they put it into a joint venture, they can defer paying taxes until the property is sold by the joint venture and capital is returned to them. A tax accountant should be brought into the negotiations early with the landowner to understand IRS requirements for "installment sales." Taxes on the gain are paid as principal payments on the PMN are made. In a joint venture with a subordinated PMN, the principal payments are usually timed to occur when lots are sold to homebuilders or according to a prenegotiated schedule (typically three to 10 years), whichever comes first. For example, suppose land originally purchased for $100,000 is put into a joint venture at the current market value of $1 million, with a PMN for $750,000. One-quarter of the $900,000 gain is taxed initially because the downpayment is one-quarter of the sales price—$250,000 of $1 million. The rest of the gain is paid as the PMN is retired. Note that this structure works with any PMN, even if no joint venture is created with the land seller. Taxes are deferred longer, however, if the PMN is subordinated. If it is unsubordinated, it must be paid off as soon as the developer obtains a development loan.

DEVELOPER AND INVESTOR. Joint ventures between the developer and third-party investors are simpler for established developers because the partnership can be used on multiple projects. The investors furnish most of the cash equity needed to complete the deal. For example, in the deal described above between developer and landowner, the developer purchases the land outright from the land seller. The investors put up the cash needed to purchase the land, which was the landowner's equity in the first deal. The developer's arrangement with the investors might closely resemble the deal with the landowner with respect to priorities for cash distribution:

- **Priority 1**—All cash available goes to investors until they have received their total cash investment (*return of equity*).
- **Priority 2**—The next cash available also goes to the investors until they have received, say, an 8 percent cumulative (or noncumulative) return on their investment (*return on equity*).
- **Priority 3**—The next cash available goes to the developer until the agreed fee is reached.

- **Priority 4**—All remaining cash available is divided between the developer and the investors based on the agreed-on terms and conditions. (With institutional investors, multitiered "waterfall" provisions are more common.)

Every term of the deal is negotiable, including the order of priorities and the amount of personal liability on the development loan. A straightforward 50/50 split between the developer and the investors, without any priorities, used to be typical, and some large developers still use that format; but beginners typically must give a larger share to investors to attract their interest. In a 50/50 split with no priorities, developers are able to take out profit as each acre is sold, but such deals are rare today. The risk to investors is that developers may sell off the prime tracts, take the profit, and then fail to sell off the balance of the project, leaving the investors with a loss. Most investors, therefore, insist on receiving all their equity before developers participate in any profit. Until this milestone is achieved, compensation for developers may be structured as a percentage of net proceeds, and reimbursement of professional fees for work performed on the project. It is not uncommon for land developers to earn only the small development fee until the last segment of lots is sold; then they receive the bulk of their profit.

DEVELOPER AND LENDER. Some lenders provide more favorable debt financing for a deal—a higher loan-to-value ratio, for example, or lower initial interest rate—in exchange for some percentage of the profits in the form of a *participating loan*. In this structure, all the deal financing might be structured as debt, but the loan is convertible at various points to a predetermined amount of equity: the "equity kicker." For the developer, this arrangement is the easiest form of joint venture because it involves only one other party. The lender can structure involvement in a variety of ways. The financing can be considered a 100 percent loan, or some portion can be considered equity. The difference between a 100 percent loan and, say, an 80 percent loan with 20 percent equity is that the equity portion usually receives a "preferred return" rather than "interest." The preferred return is paid when cash is available, whereas interest must be paid immediately. Some development loans have accrual provisions that allow interest to be accrued in a fashion similar to that for preferred returns. They allow the project to accrue unpaid interest into future periods until cash is available to pay it. The split with inexperienced developers could be 65/35 or 75/25, with the lender receiving the larger share. Joint ventures with lenders usually allow developers to receive a fee for administrative expenses. Developers may request fees of 5 to 10 percent of construction costs, but 3 to 5 percent is more common.

Construction

The construction phase of land development consists primarily of grading the land and installing drainage systems, streets, and utilities. Land development involves fewer subcontractors than building construction, but the process can be just as complicated, not least because of the role played by the public sector. The facilities built by land developers are usually dedicated to the locality to become part of its urban infrastructure. The locality maintains the streets, and the utility company, which may also be a city agency, maintains water and sewer lines. Consequently, all facilities must be built in strict accordance with utility company standards; city, state, and federal codes; and management practices. Even infrastructure that will remain private may be required to be built to public standards and inspected accordingly.

If possible, the contractor should be part of the development team from the beginning. Even if developers will not select a contractor until after plans and specifications are completed, they should go over preliminary plans with a construction manager who can offer money-saving advice for various aspects of the design layout. The following tips are useful in dealing with general contractors:

- Negotiated-price contracts are usually better than competitively bid contracts. On smaller jobs, developers should negotiate with two or three qualified contractors simultaneously and take the best deal.
- A fixed fee for the contractor of, say, $5,000 to $10,000 for a $100,000 to $200,000 job (costs based on actual dollars spent, verifiable by audit) is recommended. For change orders, developers should pay the contractor the additional cost including project management, but no markup. Equipment should be charged based on direct time and fuel in operation.
- Developers should hire a member of an engineering company whose business currently is slow to be on site to check that everything is installed properly. Developers should not rely solely on the engineer's certification and should ensure that the engineer will spend enough time on site. The engineer of record (responsible for the original drawings) should

certify the work (check progress at least twice per week); the on-site engineer should check that everything is installed properly and should be present for deliveries and for any event that requires quantity surveying to price, such as remedial fill for inadequate subgrade. An engineer should also be present for any visits by inspectors, who should arrange their visits with the engineer.
- The standard 10 percent retention of payment for subcontractors is recommended. Subcontractors should sign lien releases and bills-paid affidavits with every request for a draw. The general contractor must obtain these affidavits and releases from the subcontractors and suppliers before paying them.
- When a contractor does not perform satisfactorily, developers should notify the contractor in writing (by registered mail), citing the specific paragraphs of the contract that are being violated and stating the possible consequences if performance does not improve by a certain date. This step is particularly important for items under regulatory control, such as site stormwater management, because a contractor's negligence can expose owners to fines.
- When hiring a general contractor to construct for-sale housing, developers should include a clause stating that any deceptive trade practice suits that are not warranty items belong to the general contractor, not the developer.

A developer may choose to be its own general contractor, hiring various subcontractors to do the work—for example, an excavation subcontractor to move dirt, a utility subcontractor to install water, storm, and sanitary sewer drains, and so on. One deterrent to subcontracting in this manner is the difficulty in coordinating the work of the separate subcontractors and controlling the condition of the site during the transition from one subcontractor to the next. For example, the paving contractor may complain that the utility contractor left the manholes too high or that more dirt is needed. The developer/general contractor must then choose between paying a late charge to the paving contractor, who must wait until the utility contractor comes back to correct the problem, or paying the paving contractor exorbitant change fees to fix it. If the project is coordinated correctly, the utility contractor is still on site when the paving contractor arrives, allowing any apparent problems to be solved immediately. Another deterrent is that experienced contractors know the minutiae of legal and regulatory requirements, where

Key Points on Contracting

Contracts are necessary for controlling costs, scheduling, and performance of those involved in a project. Everything should be put in writing. Contracts are a commitment. Once signed, backtracking can be difficult, although any good contract will have a process for dealing with acts of God and unforeseeable circumstances.

The Contracting Process
- Bidding
- Assembly of bid package contents
- Prebid meetings
- Bid review and award
- Review of bidding issues and ethics
- Review of other issues

Contract Contents
- Details of commitments
- Behaviors agreed to that benefit and bind future managers
- Firm commitments versus general understandings (These represent a meeting of the minds; words on paper must reflect intention of parties and need involvement of principals.)
- Fee structure: fixed fee, GMAX (guaranteed maximum price, with contractor potentially incentivized by sharing any savings), time and materials (T&M), or hybrid
- Different regimes for portions of work, with well-defined work on a guaranteed maximum and unknowns handled under prearranged T&M (All developers avoid T&M contracts whenever possible.)

Bid Package Contents
- Complete drawings
- Bid submission package terms with instructions
- Payment conditions and terms
- Schedule commitments
- Inspection and progress payments
- Incentives
- Change order provisions
- Retention provisions
- Dispute resolution language
- Basic contract terms
- Right not to award
- Right not to select low bidder (This right may be restricted in projects with public components.)

Prebid Meetings
- Meeting on site
- Including all personnel who will be involved (owner's rep, contractor's rep, engineers, architects)
- Achieving a meeting of the minds: everyone knows the expectations and where to get answers
- Defining who can make decisions for each party
- Conveying full understanding of site conditions
- Getting a sense of who everyone is and how they will work together

Source: H. Pike Oliver, Urbanexus, Seattle, Washington.

---

a lack of attention can be expensive and cause delay. The general contractor is encouraged to withhold 10 percent of the contract price from the utility subcontractor until the city accepts the utilities or at least until the reviewing engineer has issued final approval of the installation.

One problem that developers encounter is deliberate bidding mistakes. Most contracts are bid on price per unit (not as a fixed price) calculated from the engineer's estimate of quantities. If subcontractors see an area in which the quantity of an item was underestimated, they may bid lower on other items so that they get the job. They deliberately bid high on the item for which the quantity was underestimated so that the developer ends up paying more on the total contract after the correct quantity has been determined. Engineers should not be allowed to bid *and* to supervise the site; otherwise, developers will never know whether money was lost. It is better to negotiate a price-per-unit contract and then convert the bid to a fixed-price contract as soon as quantities

can be better determined, perhaps after vegetation and topsoil are cleared, making subgrade visible. The developer may pay a little more to allow for a margin of error in the quantity takeoff, but major overcharges are then limited to truly unknown items, such as unforeseen soil conditions.

During construction, the following steps are important to remember:

- Supervise subcontractors closely. A subcontractor who needs a piece of equipment for another job is likely to remove it unless the developer is watching closely.
- Plan drainage correctly for each lot. The usual five to 10 feet (1.5–3 m) of fall from one side of the property to the other is a sufficient slope. Storm sewers are normally located in the streets, so lots should slope toward the street whenever possible. As many lots as possible should be higher than curb height. Excavating shallow streets may save money at the front end but may cost money in the long run.

- Work closely with the electric utility contractor to determine the location and price of transformers and other required gear. Carefully review designs to know what existing conditions the design requires: common omissions are a concrete pad or a level-graded gravel base. These conditions should be noted as "NIC," not in contract, and the manager should know who is providing them, at what cost.
- Design and execute grading carefully. Grading is cheaper than constructing retaining walls, but a poorly executed grading job can lead to costly repairs, maintenance headaches, back-charges by builders, and even lawsuits from homeowners. Developers should employ an engineer familiar with the rapidly evolving technologies of slope retention. Compost, engineered fabrics, and various techniques may eliminate the need for retaining walls under some conditions.

If FHA financing is planned for homes in the subdivision, the developer should pay especially close attention to grading to ensure that it meets FHA's strict requirements. Although FHA and U.S. Department of Veterans Affairs (VA) financing for homebuyers can greatly aid the sales pace of a subdivision, especially for lower-priced homes, developers must understand not only standards but also the institutional process of scheduling, inspection, and approval.

If possible, all rights for off-site road, drainage, utility, and other easements should be obtained, or at least optioned, before buying the property. The seller should assist the developer in this effort, according to specific terms that should be negotiated in the earnest money contract. The price for obtaining off-site easements can increase dramatically after closing if the neighboring landowner knows that the easement is required for development.

Marketing

Historically, developers are not directly involved in retail sales to the general public, unless they also build homes or are engaged in condominium or recreational developments; this is changing as developers work to differentiate their projects by lifestyle and image. Subdivision marketing begins before the developer closes on the land and continues until the last lot is sold. Various aspects of marketing, including public relations, advertising, staffing, and merchandising, are described in detail in chapter 4. Certain items, however, are unique to land development.

For the land developer, the primary marketing objective is selling lots to builders, but the sale of houses to consumers drives lot sales. Except for large-volume builders, who purchase large blocks of lots, most builders take down a few lots at a time. In most subdivisions, builders handle the sale of their houses themselves or use outside brokers. The developer is not involved directly with house sales but may undertake advertising and public relations for the subdivision as a whole. Increasingly, the developer markets affiliated builders as an extension of the development team, sometimes called a "guild" or "preferred partners."

MARKETING BUDGETS

Marketing budgets are based on the estimated cost of marketing, promotions, and sales strategies. A typical marketing budget is 5 to 7 percent of gross sales for nonrecreational projects and 10 to 12 percent for recreational projects. The budget includes 1 to 2 percent for advertising and the balance for commissions for the sales staff and cooperating brokers.

Large developers generally use their own in-house sales staff to handle direct marketing. Even if they use an outside brokerage firm, however, developers need an in-house marketing director and sufficient staff to represent their interests in day-to-day negotiations. These professionals will require a space to show plans and meet with buyers.

Small development firms should consider using one or more local brokerage firms as sales staff or as a source of sales referrals. In larger markets, some brokerage firms specialize in new homes and have established marketing programs for builders and developers. The great majority of real estate agents have never sold a new home and are not experienced in community marketing.

The sooner a marketing director is hired, the better. Before construction begins, the marketing director can help by getting to know the market area. The marketing director should be skilled at sales techniques and at motivating sales personnel and should have firsthand experience with the types of products being sold. If sales are handled in-house, a minimum of two salespeople should be hired, with one or two more available to help during peak periods.

Some developers argue that salespeople should be paid on commission; others advocate a combination of salary and commission. A few rely on straight-salaried staff, although salaries may need to be quite high to attract top-notch brokers. Prizes, bonuses, and competitions are proven good practices. Higher commission rates may be paid for selling "problem" lots or homes, and bonuses should be awarded if sales personnel exceed monthly or yearly quotas. If experienced sales staff are in short supply, investing in sales training for staff is worthwhile, even for those whose job is primarily administrative. These sales personnel are the first impression your project will make.

MARKETING TO HOMEBUILDERS

Many different methods can be used to market a subdivision. Apartment, retail, or office sites are marketed directly to building developers. Lots in custom home subdivisions may be sold directly to homebuyers, who then hire their own custom builder or select from a list of builders approved by the developer. In some cases, a custom builder is also the developer. In most cases, however, the developer sells lots to builders who, in turn, sell to homebuyers. Developers may operate at a distance from the customers who drive demand for their product. A close, supportive relationship with builders is therefore essential, and marketing is only one part of this relationship.

Market studies should indicate the types of builders for developers to target in marketing the development. Builders with a strong reputation in the market will have an edge in attracting homebuyers. Interviewed for the first edition of this book, Don Mackie of Texas-based Mill Creek Properties gave advice still useful today. Developers should not let first-tier builders control their subdivisions. "They will want 10 to 15 lots at the beginning and a rolling option on the rest. They will build four models and construct six to 10 specs at a time. You need to give them enough lots for models and specs, with a rolling option as they sell the specs.

"In pioneering areas, you convince builders by telling them how much you will spend on promotion: 'Here's what we will spend. If we don't do what we promise, we will take the lots back.' You get better absorption if you can keep traffic moving around in the subdivision. On smaller, 100-lot subdivisions, you must choose between selling all the lots to one major builder or working with small builders who take one or two lots each. Smaller builders will use one of their spec houses as a model and an office."[44]

To obtain commitments from builders, developers should begin contacting potential builders as soon as the land is tied up. Savvy local builders are often experts on the area, and developers should solicit their advice on the target market and its preferred products.

Developers should meet with and examine the completed projects of homebuilders who build the type and price of product market studies recommend. New developers should be able to compete effectively against well-established developers by offering builders a continuing lot inventory, minimum cash up front, and seller financing. Ideally, builders should be required to put up a 10 percent downpayment, but beginning developers may have to settle for any amount that is sufficient to hold builders' interest.

After preliminary contact with prospective builders and as soon as a preliminary plat is available, the developer should prepare a marketing package. This package should include information about the site and the neighborhood (shopping, schools, daycare facilities, churches, and recreation) and data about the site, including the subdivision plan, restrictive covenants, amenities, and the marketing program.

Terms for buying lots vary depending on the market. In softer markets, builders may put down a token amount of, say, $1,000 cash per lot. When the commitments are made before site development, builders are not obligated to take down or close on the stipulated number of lots until the engineer has certified that the lots are ready for building. Before then, builders have the option only to buy the lots at the specified price. The option (or purchase contract) is not a specific performance contract. In other words, if builders fail to close, they lose only their earnest money.

Once the lots are ready for building, builders are usually liable for interest on the lots that are committed but not yet closed. If a rolling option exists, builders are committed to taking down a certain number of lots at a time. Builders may pay cash for the lots, with funds provided by the builder's construction lender, or the developer may finance the lots for builders during the period between closing and start of construction. For example, builders may commit to take down two lots immediately for model houses and have an option to purchase 30 lots every six months, beginning, say, January 1. If the builder exercises the option, the interest meter starts running on January 1 for the portion of the 30 lots not closed on that date. Six months later, if the builder does not exercise the option on the next 30 lots, the lots are released for sale to other builders. Obviously, the method and sequence of financing that is customary in a market must be determined well in advance, during the developer's business plan process, so that adequate capital is available in the foreseeable range of sales pace.

If the developer wants to use the builder's credit to help secure the development loan, rolling options on lots are not sufficient. If possible, beginning developers should have a firm contract of sale for the lots covered by the development loan, either to a creditworthy builder or to a smaller builder with a letter of credit for the unpaid balance of the sales price.

MARKETING LARGER PARCELS

In addition to single-family or townhouse lots, a larger parcel may also include commercial sites for apartments, offices, or other uses

Two main sources of business are outside brokers and online listings. Experienced outside brokers require the payment of a generous commission, but many developers believe they are well worth the investment; the potential market is both shallow and, with chain retail and service business, possibly national, not local.

Typically, the buyer of a $1 million site puts up $25,000 to $50,000 of earnest money, in cash or by way of a letter of credit. Standard closing times range from 60 to 120 days, depending on the market. Buyers almost always want the option to buy or the right of first refusal on adjoining sites. Developers should try to avoid giving these options, which can complicate a future sale, but they may be granted as part of a larger deal. Declining to give options is especially important during the initial project stages when the developer is trying to encourage absorption.

SITE MERCHANDISING

Whereas advertising is intended to reach a wide audience and to persuade people to visit a development, merchandising is designed to stimulate the desire of potential buyers once they come to the site. The developer should encourage all the builders to place their models in the same area. In this way, the builders benefit from the traffic generated. Each builder builds two to four models in separate but interconnected areas. The model home "park" should be large enough to illustrate the effect of the land plan, including common spaces, street furniture, landscape standards, and pedestrian paths. The developer is responsible for the landscaping and common area maintenance of these facilities, which can illustrate to buyers the developer's attention to detail.

The design of the sales office and arrangement of model units are central to the merchandising plan. Sig-nage that is coordinated with other marketing materials should lead visitors directly to the sales office, the model houses, and the major amenities. Smaller subdivisions can generally support only a very modest visitor center, such as a trailer furnished as a sales center, a portion of an amenity building such as the fitness center or club, or an existing home furnished for temporary use.

INTERSTATE MARKETING

In recreational and larger land development properties, the developer may want to market to out-of-state residents. Jo Anne Stubblefield cautions that interstate marketing of land is a legal minefield and that even the establishment of a promotional website can trigger (sometimes costly) legal responsibilities for developers. "By and large, we've found that marketing consultants are clueless regarding the legal issues that surround the marketing of land. Tending toward zealous promotion, they are in a hurry to get to the grand opening and push the process of establishing a website, mailings, and other promotions." Establishing a website to market land is considered the legal equivalent of advertising in a publication with national subscribers. Like a mass mailing, it is interstate marketing. Stubblefield adds that about half the states require registration of a sale, full disclosure, or both. "Many states claim to have 'uniform acts' that are interchangeable with other states' regulations. They are almost never uniform. To market the project in multiple states, developers should not rely on marketing consultants to negotiate this terrain, but should consult a lawyer with a national practice before even starting the marketing of the project."[45] These laws are poorly understood by most developers, but compliant practices are actually well defined for most states, if the sales and management team are educated on the requirements.

Development Maintenance after Completion

Among the developer's most important tasks is the creation of a proper set of mechanisms to handle long-term maintenance after the project is complete. Such mechanisms protect not only the developer's investment but also the investment and living environment of the future residents of the subdivision.

A developer's stewardship of the land may take many forms. First, a developer may make express guarantees or warranties concerning the care of streets, landscaping, and amenities when selling lots to builders. Second, a developer normally creates and records a set of deed restrictions and protective covenants. The covenants enable residents to enforce maintenance and building standards when other residents violate the restrictions. Third, a developer normally creates a homeowners association that sets and modifies rules of community governance, bears the financial and management responsibility for long-term maintenance, has the power to collect and spend money on common areas, and helps build a sense of community. Fourth, unless streets are to be made private, a developer dedicates streets, and sometimes amenities, to the city or county. The city or county then takes responsibility for various public services, such as street cleaning and repair, parkway mowing, and trash removal. Because the types of public services available differ from city to city, a developer must make sure that all public services are provided. Trash and recycling collection, for example, is a municipal service in some jurisdictions but is handled by private contractors in others.

PROTECTIVE COVENANTS

Protective covenants, which embody the agreements between the seller and purchaser covering the use of land, are private-party contracts between the land subdivider and the lot or unit purchasers. Covenants are intended to create and ensure a specific living environment in the subdivision. Purchasers of lots and houses in the subdivision should perceive the covenants as assurance that the developer will proceed to develop the property as planned and that other purchasers will maintain the property as planned. Strict enforcement of suitable covenants gives each lot owner the assurance that no other lot owners can use their property in a way that will alter the character of the neighborhood or create a nuisance. Unnecessarily picky restrictions may turn some buyers away, so language must be tuned to the target audience. Lenders and government agencies, such as FHA and VA, often require covenants as a means of protecting the quality of the neighborhood and the condition of the houses.

Deed restrictions and covenants can augment zoning and other public land use controls by applying additional restrictions to size of lots, building massing, location of structures, setbacks, yard requirements, architectural design, and permitted uses. Affirmative covenants can be used to ensure that certain land remains as open space and that the developer will preserve certain natural features in that space. They may also create a mechanism for assessing homeowners on the maintenance of common facilities, ranging from roads to fiber-optic networks.

If both public and private restrictions apply, the more restrictive condition is operative. Covenants should take the form of blanket provisions that apply to the whole subdivision, and they should be specifically referenced in each deed. These covenants, together with the recorded plat, legally establish a general scheme for the development. They should be made superior to any mortgage liens that may be on record before recording the covenant to ensure that everyone is bound by the restrictions, even someone buying a house through foreclosure.

Although covenants are automatically superior to any future lien, many covenants and restrictions also provide for an automatic lien for payment of homeowners association fees and assessments. The documents must provide that the lien for assessments be automatically subordinated to purchase money liens. Not all covenants are legally enforceable, however. Covenants that seek to exclude any buyer on the basis of race, religion, or ethnic background are both unconstitutional and unenforceable.

Usually, developers do not want to be the enforcers of covenants in established neighborhoods, unless a long-term building project requires them to keep control over an area. Subdividers may retain control over enforcement as long as they are active in the subdivision. Thereafter, however, the covenants should grant enforcement powers to the homeowners association and to individual owners as control of the association's duties transfer. Control usually transfers under conditions outlined in state law, often increasing toward homeowner control as a percentage of lots are sold. Some cities also require a provision that lets the city take over enforcement under certain circumstances.

The covenants should not be recorded until developers have received preliminary subdivision approvals, review of which will often include any proposed covenants and restrictions. Covenants frequently do not have to be recorded until issuance of the first deed. Stubblefield advises, "Don't write yourself into any covenants until you have to."[46]

Further, if developers intend to use FHA, VA, or other sources of federal financing (such as the Government National Mortgage Association [Ginnie Mae] or the Federal National Mortgage Association [Fannie Mae]), they should ensure that the proposed covenants meet with the approval of those agencies. The FHA and VA have jointly developed acceptable model legal documents.

DESIGN CONTROLS. Provisions for design control should reflect the tastes and attitudes of the target market. The types of design controls and degrees of constraint differ, depending on whether the target market is production builders or custom builders. For the developer who is selling finished sites, the best basic mechanism for design control is to include an "approval of plans" clause in the purchase agreements for building sites.

Even though individual designs may be attractive, incongruous styles may detract from the overall appearance of a subdivision. A design review committee should therefore be established to approve proposed designs. Such a committee also shields the developer from accusations of arbitrariness.

Encouraging good design is easier than discouraging bad design. The developer's primary tool is to specify dimensional limitations, such as yard setbacks, building heights, bulk, and signs. But size covenants may backfire. For example, the city of Highland Park, a wealthy Dallas suburb, passed severe lot coverage limitations. Builders of houses that averaged 6,000 to 7,000 square feet (560–650 sq m) responded by building two-story boxes that completely filled the allowable building envelope. Similar boxes have appeared on small lots in other communities such as Beverly Hills, California, where soaring lot prices virtually guarantee that buyers will build houses as large as possible on their lots.

Covenants that are too restrictive may lead to boring uniformity and eventual rebellion among residents, leading many developers to minimize restriction by covenant. Communities have faced lawsuits over paint colors, swing sets, pickup truck bans, and other elements that were too rigidly controlled by covenants. One of the most difficult areas to control is future alterations and additions. Materials are difficult to match or become obsolete. Costs change over time. New fire codes may prohibit the use of certain materials, such as the once-popular cedar shake roofing. New technologies are developed, such as small-scale satellite dishes, and lifestyles change, as with the proliferation of home-based work. Covenants should therefore provide for a procedure to accommodate changes over time—by variance or amendment. The design review committee must consider not just the project under review, but the potential precedent when it approves a variance from the specified restrictions.

Developers walk a fine line between introducing too little and too much restriction. Developers want to maintain the value of the subdivision without overly limiting the market. A potential homebuyer who cannot keep the family boat or camper on the property may look elsewhere for a house.

EFFECTIVE TERM AND REVISION. Although some covenants may include a definite termination date, covenants should generally be designed to renew automatically and *run with the land* indefinitely. Property owners also should be able to revise the covenants with the approval of a stipulated percentage of other property owners. The developer may decide to allow some covenants to be revisable with a simple majority vote, whereas other covenants may require approval by 75 percent or even 90 percent of property owners. The developer may also want to allow homeowners to revise some covenants, such as changes in fencing, after three to five years, whereas others, such as "single-family use only," may be revised only after 25 to 40 years, or with near unanimous approval. Proposed revisions in covenants should be submitted sufficiently ahead of time to allow property owners to review them—three years for major covenants and one year for minor covenants.

ENFORCEMENT. Legally, anyone who is bound by covenants may enforce them against anyone else who is bound by them. Because doing so may set neighbor against neighbor, providing a homeowners association with the power of enforcement is the best solution. Failure to enforce a covenant in a timely fashion may render the covenant void. For example, in a Dallas subdivision, the homeowners did not enforce a covenant that restricted fencing of an open-space easement running along the back of the owners' lots. Several years later, the homeowners association attempted to enforce the covenant against several homeowners who had fenced the open space. The homeowners who had fenced in the open space successfully challenged the association on the grounds that the covenant was void for lack of previous enforcement.

COMMUNITY AND CONDOMINIUM ASSOCIATIONS

The developer must create the association and file the articles of incorporation and bylaws before selling any lots to homebuilders or individual buyers. Any sales that predate the establishment of the association are exempted from the association. Therefore, forming the community association is a critical part of the developer's initial activities.

TYPES. The two most common types of homeowners associations are community associations with automatic membership, and condominium associations.

Community Association with Automatic Membership. In most subdivisions in which fee simple interest in the lots is conveyed to buyers, membership in a community association occurs automatically when a buyer purchases a dwelling or improved lot. The association may hold title to real property such as open space and recreational facilities in the subdivision. It is responsible for preserving and maintaining the property. Members have perpetual access to the common property. They must pay assessments to finance the association's activities and must uphold the covenants.

Condominium Association. This approach resembles the community association, except for the form of ownership. When someone purchases a condominium, the title applies only to the interior space of the particular unit. The structure, lobbies, elevators, and surrounding land belong to all the owners as *tenants in common*. Owners are automatically members of the condominium association and have voting privileges and responsibilities for operating and maintaining the common facilities.

LEGAL FRAMEWORK. An automatic community association includes five major legal elements: a subdivision plat, an enabling declaration, articles of incorporation, bylaws, and individual deeds for each parcel. The subdivision plat is the recorded map showing individual lots, legal descriptions, common spaces, and easements. The plat should indicate areas that will be dedicated to the association, as well as those that will be excluded from dedication, or which may be open for use by the public. Certain parcels may be reserved for the developer, for future development activity. The plat should also reference and be recorded with the enabling declaration, which sets forth the management and ownership of common areas, the lien rights of the association against all lots, the amendment procedures, the enforcement procedures, and the rights of voting members.

The articles of incorporation and bylaws are the formal documents for creating a corporation with the state. The articles of incorporation set forth the initial board of directors, procedures for appointing new directors, membership and voting rights, amendment procedures, dissolution procedures, and the severability of provisions. The bylaws of the association describe the rules by which the association will conduct business. They set forth the composition and duties of

the board and the indemnification of officers of the association and describe the role and composition of subordinate boards, such as the design review board.

Each individual deed conveyed by the developer should reference the declaration of the association. The developer should summarize the formation, responsibilities, and activities of the association in clear disclosures that homebuilders can give to their buyers.

THE DEVELOPER'S ROLE. Homeowners associations, protective covenants, and the common facilities managed by homeowners associations are as important to the overall success of a subdivision as the subdivision's engineering and design. If handled properly, they can serve as a major component of the developer's marketing strategy.

The developer usually donates commonly owned land and facilities to the homeowners association. The costs are covered by lot sales to builders. For the purpose of property taxes, permanently dedicated open space has no real market value and is either not assessed or taxed at all or assessed at a nominal value, with the taxes paid by the homeowners association.

During the course of development, the developer usually maintains the open space and common facilities. These responsibilities are turned over to the association when the development is completed. Control of the association passes from the developer to the residents when the residents elect the officers of the association. The developer should design the accounts and record keeping so that the transition to the association is smooth.

The developer establishes initial assessments for homeowners that must realistically reflect the number of residents of the community at any one time. Because buyers evaluate monthly association assessments the same way they do monthly mortgage payments, the assessments cannot be too high. Although developers would like to place as much of the burden as possible on the association, they should keep the assessment competitive with that of other subdivisions.

Residents appear to be somewhat more tolerant of association dues than they are of general taxes because the results of dues are more directly apparent. The upper limit to place on dues depends on local conditions. In Orange County, California, for example, before Proposition 13 limited property taxes to 1 percent of the house purchase price, homeowners tolerated a combined tax bill (property taxes plus special district assessments) of up to 2 percent of the house value. Homeowners may tolerate as much

GENERAL ADVICE

The senior person on the development team responsible for the project should not serve on the board. Many developers ignore this advice, but they should understand that doing so opens the developer and the association to conflict-of-interest claims.

The developer should not try to do everything alone. The developer should document whatever it or the association does and should never underestimate the role of the association manager. The developer should budget for these tasks, even if they will be done by development staff for the foreseeable future.

Do:

- Observe the required corporate formalities, such as holding regular meetings, keeping a corporate minutes book, and properly authorizing and documenting all board actions.
- Purchase or renew adequate insurance.
- Collect assessments and increase assessments as necessary.
- Enforce architectural control.
- Review the association's budget and produce quarterly and annual reports.
- Always remember to protect members' interests.
- Use due care in hiring personnel, including compliance with nondiscrimination laws.
- File tax returns and other required IRS forms.
- Require the developer to complete and convey the common areas in a timely manner.
- Order an impartial inspection of the common areas by the association.
- Maintain common areas adequately.

Don't:

- Enter into long-term contracts, such as maintenance, against the bylaws of the association. If the contract turns out not to be in the best interest of the association, developers could be liable.
- Enter a dwelling unit without authorization.
- File a lawsuit after the statute of limitations expires.

Source: Wayne Hyatt, *Protecting Your Assets: Strategies for Successful Business Operation in a Litigious Society* (Washington, DC: Urban Land Institute, 1997).

---

as an additional half percentage point per year in association dues in areas where the association owns and operates substantial common open space and recreation facilities.

Conclusion

Beginning developers will find many opportunities in land development. Particularly for individuals with expertise in legal, urban design, engineering, and entitlement issues, the higher risk of land development can be mitigated by thorough knowledge and good management. Although land development may be combined with building development, in general, it should be considered a separate business to be evaluated on its own merits.

Land development is one of the riskier forms of development: it depends on the public sector for approvals and infrastructure support, involves a long investment period with no positive cash flow, and, especially in large projects, requires the ability to change direction to meet changing markets and economic situations. New developers should concentrate on smaller, less complex deals. Problem sites, such as those containing environmentally sensitive areas, can offer attractive opportunities, but developers should be wary of getting bogged down for several years in litigation and entitlement disputes. An exception to this principle is infill sites, where effectively coordinat-

ing the needs of neighbors can result in a development that is more valuable and better-located than might otherwise be available or affordable.

Without a track record, developers will find that obtaining financing without significant cash equity and strong financial statements is almost impossible. A financial partner, or a cooperative landowner, may be required. Nevertheless, land development offers the opportunity to use commitments from builders as collateral for securing financing. Those starting out will find that seller financing and joint ventures with landowners and financial institutions can enable them to build a track record and successfully launch a development career.

Although opportunities are always present, so are pitfalls. Cities are holding land developers responsible for an ever-higher share of the cost of providing public infrastructure and facilities and for solving environmental problems that may be larger than the project at hand. Neighbors can feel possessive about land uses they are accustomed to, and they can be resistant and distrustful of change, often with good reason. The approvals process represents a last chance for conservation advocates, and owners proposing development may, despite their earnest best efforts, find their projects characterized as an irresponsible stewardship of community resources. In many cases, developers are becoming the de facto agents of cities in building arterial streets, libraries, fire stations, and sewer and drainage facilities and in cleaning up toxic waste and restoring environmentally sensitive land. The liability of developers for construction standards, especially streets, utilities, and drainage, extends for many years after developers have sold out of the subdivision.

Cities and land developers have always formed a kind of partnership because land development has been the primary vehicle by which cities grow. As the burdens of responsibility shift more toward developers, developers must come to understand not only how to build financially successful subdivisions but also how to create places of enduring aesthetic value, and to ensure the fiscal, social, and environmental health of their cities.

NOTES

1. Sometimes called "super pads." The buyer is responsible for installing local streets and utilities. Lots are often subject to design guidelines imposed by the master developer.

2. H. James Brown, R. S. Phillips, and N. A. Roberts, "Land Markets at the Urban Fringe," *Journal of the American Planning Association* (April 1981): 131–44.

3. "Smart growth" is defined in different ways, but at its core, it is about accommodating growth in ways that are economically sound and environmentally responsible and that enhance the quality of life.

4. Most communities require public hearings for subdivision approval but not for building plans, which are approved by the building department only. Public hearings are political by definition and involve much more risk—of disapproval, reduction in density, or increase in exaction cost. Building department approvals are essentially administrative: as long as one satisfies the regulations, approval is automatic.

5. Joe Barnes, interview by author, 2021.

6. Specifically, the lender's release price may be a percentage of the projected price or a wholesale value per lot. If the release is defined as a percentage of a projected price, the bank may require the same value, even if it is a higher percentage of the new, lower lot value. If so, the developer has to make up the difference.

7. Harlan Doliner, partner, Nixon Peabody LLP, Boston, Massachusetts, interview by author, 2000.

8. Doliner, interview.

9. Jack Willome, former CEO, Rayco, Ltd., San Antonio, Texas, interview by author, 1987.

10. Don Mackie, partner, Mill Creek Properties, Salado, Texas, interview by author, 1987.

11. Title insurance companies do not survey property and therefore do not insure against encroachments and boundary disputes that would be disclosed by a proper survey. A correct survey, however, corresponds to the description in the deed, and if the description in the deed is wrong, the title insurance company is liable. The company ensures the accuracy of the documents.

12. This paragraph and the next two are based on an interview with Steve MacMillan, chief operating officer, Campbell Estate, Kapolei, Hawaii, in 2002.

13. See Mike Davidson and Fay Dolnick, "A Glossary of Zoning, Development, and Planning Terms," *Planning Advisory Service Report*, no. 491/492 (Chicago: American Planning Association, 1999).

14. Jo Anne Stubblefield, interview by author, 2020.

15. Scott Smith, interview by author, 2000.

16. Al Neely, interview by author, 2000.

17. Tim Edmond, interview by author, 2000.

18. Roger Galatas, president, Roger Galatas Interests, The Woodlands, Texas, interview by author, 2001.

19. *Golden v. Planning Board of the Town of Ramapo*, 285 N.E.2d 291 (N.Y. Ct. App. 1972). This case upheld regulations for timing, phasing, and quotas in development, making development permits contingent on the availability of adequate public facilities.

20. *Construction Industry Association v. City of Petaluma*, 522 F.2d 897 (9th Cir. 1975). The U.S. Supreme Court let Petaluma's residential control system stand after lengthy court battles initiated when the city was sued by homebuilders.

21. Kevin Lynch and Gary Hack, *Site Planning*, 3rd ed. (Cambridge, MA: MIT Press, 1985), p. 124.

22. Galatas, interview.

23. Galatas, interview.

24. Matthew Kiefer, attorney, Goulston & Storrs, Boston, Massachusetts, interview by author, 2010.

25. The city might require the developer to pay for, say, the first one or two lanes of paving, with the city paying the rest. Alternatively, it might require the developer to pay for or install the entire arterial, with subsequent reimbursement by other developers whose subdivisions front the arterial.

26. Kiefer, interview.

27. Although the terms *gross acres* and *net acres* are commonly used and understood, *net usable acres* is far less popular.

28. Richard B. Peiser, "Optimizing Profits from Land Use Planning," *Urban Land,* September 1982, pp. 6–10; and Ehud Mouchly and Richard Peiser, "Optimizing Land Use in Multiuse Projects," *Real Estate Review,* Summer 1993, pp. 79–85.

29. The compound return is $(1 + 0.3)1/3 - 1 = 0.09139$, or 9.139 percent. The general formula is $(1 + r)1/n - 1$, where r equals the total rate of return and n equals the holding period.

30. All return figures presented here are IRRs. They give the annual return on equity per year that should be made on an alternative investment (with annual compounding) to accumulate the same total amount of money by the end of the life of the project.

31. The rate of return on equity is the same as the discount rate used for determining the present value of a stream of future cash flows. It is also the same as the target IRR that an investor would use as the hurdle rate for making an investment.

32. Net operating income and capitalization are defined in detail in chapter 4. NOI is the common measure of project income, minus operating expenses, without considering debt service or taxes.

33. Roger Glover, founder, Cornerstone Homes, Richmond, Virginia, interview by author, 2022.

34. Steve Kellenberg, principal, Kellenberg Studio, Laguna Beach, California, interview by author, 2020.

35. Kurt Culbertson, chairman, Design Workshop, Aspen, Colorado, interview by author, 2021.

36. See Walter Kulash, *Residential Streets*, 3rd ed. (Washington, DC: Urban Land Institute, 2001).

37. Kulash, *Residential Streets.*

38. See Jeanne Christie, "Wetlands Protection after the *SWANCC* Decision," *Planning Advisory Service Memo* (Chicago: American Planning Association, 2002), pp. 1–4.

39. EPA Nonpoint Source Control Branch, *Reducing Stormwater Costs through Low Impact Development (LID) Strategies and Practices,* EPA 841-F-07-006 (Washington, DC: U.S. Environmental Protection Agency, 2007).

40. EPA, *Reducing Stormwater Costs.*

41. EPA, *Reducing Stormwater Costs,* p. 9.

42. EPA, *Reducing Stormwater Costs,* p. 34.

43. EPA Office of Water, *Economic Benefits of Runoff Controls* (Washington, DC: U.S. Environmental Protection Agency, 1995).

44. Donald Mackie, interview by author, 1987.

45. Stubblefield, interview.

46. Stubblefield, interview.

TERRY ALLEN

Chickahominy Falls is a 200-acre (81 ha) residential subdivision in Hanover County, Virginia, which is a rapidly developing exurban area 10 miles (16 km) north of Richmond. Centered on a 10-acre (4 ha) farm, Chickahominy Falls represents a new generation of *agrihoods*—planned communities that replace or supplement traditional amenities like golf with community farm and food programming. This exemplary community offers lessons in stakeholder relations, approvals, design, marketing, and community management.

THE DEVELOPER

In 2001, after a career in commercial real estate, Roger Glover founded Cornerstone Homes, a developer-builder of communities restricted to people age 55 and older. As a developer-builder, Cornerstone builds and incorporates key property management services. The Crescent Group, an integrated land development firm, pursues and develops the communities that Cornerstone builds. The Crescent/Cornerstone partnership has grown to more than 30 staff members and includes land and construction project management and an in-house sales and marketing team—but it remains small enough to quickly pursue a new idea.

CONCEPT AND MARKET

Along with many other homebuilders, Cornerstone identified demographic drivers of a market for "one-story, maintenance-free homes in smaller, more intimate communities" for a growing older population. These buyers were ready for a lifestyle change, but many were not retired. And they wanted proximity to a "real city." Based in Richmond, which has a rapidly growing "meds and eds" sector and a strong industrial job base, Crescent acquired 200 acres of unentitled land north of the city, less than a mile from Interstate 95.

Zoned mostly for agricultural use, the site had a recent history of failed rezonings to high-density residential use, amid a strong real estate market in suburban Richmond. "The first high-density project through had shown the public a bad example," Glover says, "rallying opposition to density here." Two years before Crescent

Chickahominy Falls and other "agrihoods" incorporate agriculture, food, and lifestyle programming in planned communities. A subscription plan offers residents fresh local produce, and the farm is a centerpiece of both marketing and community events.

139

acquired the property, a comprehensive plan update designated a portion of the land for up to four homes per acre. Though this medium density would not make Cornerstone's homebuilding feasible, it was a recognition that the community needed to plan for growth. Still, when Glover first approached the planning director and supervisor, "they were not interested in considering this property again for rezoning anytime soon."

Glover began the project with few connections in the immediate community, but county officials offered a narrow path forward. If Glover could garner the support of potentially impacted neighbors, both for the concept and for his company, the county would reconsider a zoning change. The first concern Glover had to address was the perception that density would "overwhelm the schools." The 55+ concept could be expected to draw few school-age children, so Cornerstone was able to quickly address that concern. The project also included plans to build trails and natural amenities that would connect existing residents to the project, which helped give neighbors a stake in the project.

Even then, a relatively compact development like Chickahominy Falls felt at odds with the area's rural character. Centering the proposed community around a working farm, and connecting with local agriculture, improved the project's "fit" for some potential objectors. Even so, approvals required many one-on-one meetings with neighbors to discuss more individual concerns. County officials' early opposition to the project cited neighbors' opposition, but multiple layers of environmental review and regulation were just as substantial, given the project's location in the Chesapeake Bay watershed. All these factors added time and expense, but ultimately the agrihood concept, with a variety of environmentally sensitive features, was successful. The cohesive identity of the community required that Cornerstone take the lead on vertical building, and the company committed to build 80 percent of the homes, with some specialty types produced by other local builders.

DESIGN

To avoid monotony, and to offer products in various price bands, Chickahominy Falls includes eight distinct neighborhoods. More than 20 unique floor plans are available, ranging from 1,550 to 3,550 square feet (144 to 330 sq m), with two to five bedrooms, and two to 4.5 baths. Duplexes and quads offer "missing middle" type homes that offer choices and a broader price range. Design is varied, and materials used include wood siding, brick, and stone, which convey the character of each street.

Homes at Chickahominy Falls line a system of curved streets that are flanked by woods, which host a winding trail network and a stream and an improved pond that serve as semi-natural amenities. These amenities are colocated with vertical buildings for recreational uses. The plan avoids protected wetlands, and where possible, it makes them visual amenities to the recreation network. The community's jewel, Woodside Farms, is run out of a custom-built barn, which also hosts event and dining spaces and the community's sales and operations offices. Envisioned as a model farm, the operation was endowed with substantial upfront capital to fund best practices in soil management, controlled irrigation, and other approaches to improve quality and efficiency. The farm is the main point of entry for the development. It is walkable and visible from most spots in the neighborhoods, which ensures that the community farm is the first sight that residents see upon arrival, and a constant marker of place.

AMENITIES AND COMMUNITY OPERATION

Although the community farm is the centerpiece, other typical amenities round out the community's "active adult" image and define a second focal point for the community. The clubhouse, pool, fitness centers, fishing pond, miles of walking trails, and outdoor fitness stations have all been designed to contribute to a clean, natural farm aesthetic and a laid-back community feel.

A nod to the movement for local and sustainable food systems, the farm at the center of Chickahominy Falls was established with the aim of profitability, so that it could eventually be taken over by semi-independent owner-operators. Under a community-supported agriculture (CSA) program, residents get five pounds of produce bimonthly for $10 to $20, and a number of resident volunteers work for the CSA. Aside from the low-cost labor, farm work promotes community engagement and reinforces the "active" part of "active adult community." The farm also can host small events and farm stays. Cooking classes, pop-up restaurants, and a meal-kit service are all being pursued as a way to make small-scale agriculture sustainable in a residential neighborhood of this scale.

FINANCING AND DEVELOPMENT

Glover describes Chickahominy Falls' financing as "pretty old school," but with more leverage than most. Equity from private investors accounted for about 25 percent of the land acquisition and horizontal development, with a 75 percent loan-to-cost loan from a large regional bank. Homebuilding is 90 percent financed by a separate revolving construction loan.

The predevelopment process involved about six months for feasibility analyses, two years for entitlements, and one year for planning and engineering. Site development has been phased, with the first phase (12 months) taking slightly longer than the subsequent phases (about nine months on average). Before the COVID-19 pandemic, each home took about four to five months to construct. Since the pandemic, facing supply and labor constraints, it is not uncommon for construction to take six months.

Glover was careful to build out two neighborhoods simultaneously only if there was a substantial difference (approximately $50,000) in the starting price points. Appealing to multiple buyer types helps to ensure that a relatively large development in a niche market area is not outpacing absorption. Otherwise, construction is phased so that each phase is triggered when current work is near sellout.

SALES

With sales beginning in 2019, Chickahominy Falls was more than 50 percent occupied by February 2022, with an additional 10 percent of its homes under contract.

Some of the smaller homes in the development, notably in the Farmstead neighborhood, have a starting price in the high $300,000s. Meanwhile, homes in Little Meadows, a serene corner of the development closer to the Chickahominy River, start in the high $500,000s. Some homes in the Woodside Meadows neighborhood, which is a short walk from the development's fishing pond, have sold for upwards of $650,000. In general, properties that back up to the Chickahominy River command a $40,000 premium.

Although these figures far exceed the area median home price of $280,000 for southern Hanover County, they are broadly in line with the sales prices for newly constructed subdivisions in the suburban areas of Richmond, which have seen growth.

At Chickahominy Falls, most homes are presold as lot-home packages, rather than builder-financed specifications. Most are also semi-customizable, with optional upgrades from the base unit including higher-end kitchens, a screened porch, and other features. Cornerstone has found that most buyers add 10 to15 percent worth of upgrades. Although the homes have sold well, Glover's primary headache has been bringing new lots online because "the approvals on subsequent phases have been really slow."

Supply chain issues and labor shortages in the wake of the COVID-19 pandemic greatly reduced profit margins on homebuilding, revealing a risk in preselling. Glover honored pricing for buyers who committed in 2020, but costs escalated wildly by the time those homes were delivered in 2021. The razor-thin resulting margin was disappointing, but Glover views Cornerstone's long-term reputation (keeping promises) as the more important asset.

Broker fees also cut into Cornerstone Homes' profit margins. According to Glover, broker fees cost Cornerstone as much as $12,000 per home, and this is a major reason that the firm uses in-house marketing. Glover also says that with more people starting the homebuying process online, marketing becomes more about convincing a potential buyer to visit rather than about cultivating a "pipeline" of brokerage firms aware of the project. Glover's long experience in age-restricted communities has taught him that "older buyers typically require four times more touches" in the sales process compared with a conventional subdivision. The agrihood concept requires even more time and attention to tell the story.

LESSONS LEARNED

Agrihoods can be a way of addressing concerns about rural development pressure because they can reconcile the need for new housing with an existing agrarian character. Moreover, a well-integrated farm and food program can be a powerful draw, not only as an amenity, but as a center of community identity and engagement. Developers who adapt this concept must exploit every part of its value: cooking classes, events, CSAs, volunteerism, and education. Execution is key and must remain realistic and flexible. Agriculture beyond the scale of a garden, in a community of less than 1,500 units, requires not only substantial upfront investment but also operating subsidy. Constant attention is required to break even, which many developers assume to be a safe assumption in this concept.

Given the focus of this book, the relative unimportance of environmental, social, and governance (ESG) factors, on either investment or retail transactions, was surprising. With small, private investors, ESG and other screens of institutional money were not relevant. But even among buyers, a very "green" development has found success mostly by marketing lifestyle and authenticity. "We're pretty green, but I can think of very few examples of sales where that was a leading factor," says Glover. In fact, a number of deeper green-building offerings, such as a rooftop solar power system, have not gained traction with buyers.

The past decade has seen a fruitful coincidence: a large aging demographic cohort of potential buyers arriving alongside regulatory concerns about schools and other fiscal realities that can be relieved, in some jurisdictions, by age-restricted developments. Roger Glover foresees that the market for 55+ communities will remain strong in an aging country, but he warns that older adults are "mostly discretionary buyers." In other words, providing amenities that they value may be a more relevant marketing strategy than emphasizing fundamentals. The preferences of older buyers are also becoming just as varied as any other group, with the concept being applied to large-lot subdivisions, high-rise towers, and everything in between. Marketing to "the 55+ cohort" is not a single approach, and it is best clarified as "which 55+ cohort, where, and why?"

Source: Roger Glover, founder, Cornerstone Homes, Richmond, Virginia, interview by author, 2021.

Multifamily Residential Development

4

RICHARD B. PEISER

Overview

This chapter focuses on multifamily residential development, primarily rental income property, but it also covers topics common to all forms of development. The chapter begins with a discussion of income property development and incorporates a detailed discussion of each step of the development process for rental and condominium units. This chapter primarily addresses rental housing. Condominium development (for-sale multifamily housing) is similar in many respects to apartment development (rental multifamily housing) except for the financial analysis. (Several fundamental subject areas for condominiums, such as site acquisition, the regulatory process, site engineering, and financial analysis of for-sale condos, are covered in detail in chapter 3.)

Despite the apparent preference of U.S. households for owning single-family dwellings, multifamily housing continues to be an essential housing type for a broad range of the population. Apartments house the young and old alike, whether they are millennials preferring urban lifestyles, aspiring homeowners, empty nesters, residents who cannot afford to own a home, or renters by choice—those who choose to rent apartments even though they could afford to buy a single-family house. To its residents, multifamily housing offers convenience, affordability, and flexibility.

Like other real estate, multifamily residential development is highly cyclical. Typically, in times of low interest rates, multifamily units are built by the thousands. Conversely, when interest rates are high (relative to the historically low rates below 5 percent seen in the early 2020s), multifamily construction slows considerably. However, low interest rates make for-sale houses more affordable, which reduces demand for rental apartments. And in times following deep recessions, rents are often too low to make new apartments economically viable. In the aftermath of the Great Recession of 2008–2009, the single-family

home rental market took off. It has become a new asset class for private equity funds.[1]

Major demographic trends also exert substantial influence on multifamily construction. As local growth rates influence the overall demand for units, the composition of the population influences the demand for particular types of multifamily housing. The aging of the baby boomer generation continues to play a leading role in the demand for housing, but echo boomers have even larger numbers than their baby boom parents. As many members of the baby boom generation reach 65 years old, demand is increasing for retirement housing, as well as other housing types geared for the active adult market, assisted living, and continuing care. Between 2010 and 2020, the number of echo boomers reversed the decline in younger households of the previous decade and fed demand for apartments.

Runway at Playa Vista is a mixed-use commercial and social center in Playa Vista, California. It was designed to contain a central "main street" with a wide array of retail shops and restaurants totaling nearly 200,000 square feet (18,600 sq m). Above the retail space is 30,000 square feet (2,800 sq m) of creative office space and 220 apartments with large windows, balconies, and articulated walls animating the street.

Even with only modest immigration, minorities are fueling 73 percent of household growth, with Hispanics leading the way at 36 percent of total household growth.[2] Unlike white household growth, the majority of which is single-person households, minority growth adds demand for all housing types, especially family apartments. Studies show that aging baby boomers and generation X (those born from 1961 to 1981) are increasingly interested in urban living. Demand for apartments and condominiums in cities and redeveloping suburbs is increasing, presenting opportunities for infill development, rehabilitation of older structures, and new types of medium- and higher-density housing.

PRODUCT TYPES

Residential building development includes everything from single-family houses to high-rise apartment buildings and condominiums. The market can be segmented in a variety of ways, either by ownership or building type:

- **Rental Products**—Rental apartments, such as garden, low-rise, mid-rise, and high-rise buildings, and rental houses. Tenants in rental apartments are lessees of the landlord. Their interest may range from a verbal agreement with the landlord for a month-to-month lease to a lease term ranging from six months to one year. Leases longer than one year are rare.
- **For-Sale Products**—Condominiums, cooperatives, and timeshares. *Condominiums* are arrangements in which the household has individual ownership of its unit (defined as the space enclosed by the unit's interior walls) plus an undivided ownership interest in the property's common elements. In a *cooperative*, the residents of the building do not own their unit, but own shares in the corporation. The corporation holds the title to the building, and residents lease their units from the corporation. Since the passage of condominium legislation in 1961, cooperative forms of ownership are rare except in New York City, Washington, D.C., Chicago, and parts of Florida. *Timeshare ownership* is the right to use, or the fee simple ownership of, real estate for a specified period each year, usually in one-week increments. Many multifamily buildings in vacation destinations around the world use timeshare ownership.
- **Design**—Number of stories, walkup or elevator, courtyard or open space, amenity spaces, and parking arrangement. Parking requirements often determine the type of residential building constructed.

Residential Product Types

SINGLE-FAMILY PRODUCTS
- Single-family houses (one unit per lot)
- Patio houses (or zero-lot-line)
- Duplexes (two attached units, either side by side or upper and lower floors)
- Townhouses (attached units on separate lots)

MULTIFAMILY PRODUCTS
- Garden apartments (typically one to three stories)
- Low-rise apartments (four to five stories, often on top of one to two stories of parking)
- Mid-rise apartments (seven to nine stories, typically eight stories because of fire code height limits)
- High-rise apartments (more than eight stories, often 18 stories because of economies in construction cost from nine to 18 stories; elevator, structure, and fire safety costs are similar, so developers generally prefer 18 stories to something in the mid-range)

- **Type of Construction**—Wood frame versus concrete or steel. Wood frame is nearly always used for single-family and townhouse construction. It is cheaper than concrete or steel construction. Podium construction, which is a hybrid form of wood frame over a steel- or concrete-framed first floor, is increasingly being used for multifamily buildings up to four or five stories. The lower floors are often used for parking, retail, or offices. Types of construction are defined in the International Building Code and range from Type I (concrete and steel) to Type V (wood frame).[3]

Phil Hughes, president of Hughes Investments, points out that construction costs go up dramatically above 75 feet or eight stories because of the fire codes (firefighter access from the ground). He is experimenting with a six-story concrete tilt-wall construction technique—a two-story panel on top of a four-story panel—with brick veneer that is 5 percent cheaper than normal concrete construction. "The 5 percent goes a long way and will hopefully be offset by a 15 percent premium in rent in new town centers with mixed use and walkability."[4] The new building has a 20-foot ground-level retail floor with five nine-foot-ceiling (10 feet floor-to-floor) apartments above. The floors have identical layouts to allow for stacked plumbing which significantly reduces cost.

Within each general product category, further distinctions can be made based on the segmentation of the target market—by income, family composition, and age. Each market segment demands different floor plans, room sizes, finish details, and amenities.

Product types are often confused with forms of ownership. *Apartment*, for example, is often used as a generic term covering both multifamily rental and for-sale (condominium) products. In China, "apartments" are almost always for-sale. Although the form of ownership greatly influences product design, marketing, and financing, it may refer to any physical product type. Technically, any rental property can be designed for, or converted to, for-sale condominiums. Similarly, any for-sale product can be operated as rental property if condominium covenants permit it. This chapter focuses on multifamily residential development—rental and condominium apartments.

The construction cost for each of these product types determines the rent that must be charged. Lower-density wood-frame garden apartments with surface parking cost less than one-third as much to build (on a per-square-foot basis) as high-rise apartments with elevators, a steel or concrete frame, and structured parking. Underground parking can add another $60,000 to $80,000 or more per parking space.

The 2010s saw a movement by aging baby boomers back to the city, a trend that was enhanced by millennials working in high-tech jobs who enjoyed the 24-hour lifestyle, walkability, and excitement there. According to Randolph Hawthorne of RGH Ventures, "In general, a lot of people who would [have moved] into houses are now renting high-end apartments in the cities, basically for lifestyle and convenience." He continues, "There seems to be a demand in the high end for apartments. People find it almost easier to finance a high-end project because it's not a big increase in rent to add amenities (and in fact the cost of amenities is less than the increase in rent and generates better financial feasibility). That means you can get your development off the ground when financing is not available for other types of apartments."[5] Hawthorne adds that most costs for newly built apartments are inelastic (land cost, financing, architectural and engineering fees, and basic construction) so the marginal extra costs for high-end finishes—for example, stone countertops—are easily recovered by premium rents.[6] In gateway cities such as Boston, New York City, Los Angeles, Washington, D.C., and San Francisco, rents of $4 to $5 per square foot fueled overbuilding of luxury apartments in the late 2010s and early 2020s. The COVID-19 pandemic and more telecommuting seemed to spur an exodus from urban centers, and housing prices and sales accelerated in outer suburban and urban fringe locations. Whether those effects will be sustained remains to be seen.

GETTING STARTED

Developer Edward Zuker states, "No one can start on their own without a track record and relationships. It is essential to develop the knowledge and contacts while working for someone else before starting your own ventures. This can be accomplished by working in a larger corporate setting or starting with smaller deals and working your way up."[7] He adds, "Developers often start as local homebuilders and then use the profits from one project in order to branch out into other property types because they already have

Advice on Getting Started

Don't focus too much on the money. Younger developers may think, "If I can just find the money, I can get this done." In fact, it should be the other way around: Find good deals first and then the money will come. Phil Hughes notes that the fundamentals are always the same: location and amenities.[a]

Think of problems as your biggest friend. They provide the opportunity to see a solution that others haven't seen. Everyone is looking for the shiny perfect deal, but the most value is created when there's a (fixable) problem.

Be flexible. Michael Lander's first project took over five years just to get entitled. By the time the project was ready, the market had already changed.[b]

Be sure to have proper documentation. You need a mutually agreed-on retainer, reliable base map with topography, land dedications or easements, and identifiable unbuildable areas or areas that must be preserved. You also need an American Land Title Association (ALTA) report, a market research study, architectural guidelines (when applicable), full design criteria from the builder client, and a reasonable work schedule.[c]

Remember that development is a multiphase process. The more you understand the potential for disruption in any one of those phases, the better off you will be.[d]

[a]Phil Hughes, interview by author, October 31, 2019.
[b]Michael Lander, founder, The Lander Group, Minneapolis, Minnesota, interview by author, November 11, 2019.
[c]Art Danielian, founder and chairman, Danielian Associates, Irvine, California, interview by author, February 28, 2020.
[d]Tom Montelli, partner, Post Road Residential, Boston, interview by author, February 11, 2020.

an established base and the experience of building. In addition, they have income coming in that can sustain them during downturns and make them more attractive borrowers to lenders."

Methods of construction and issues regarding marketing and design are similar, whether a developer is building single-family or multifamily units. The differences are often ones of scale and whether the units are for rent or for sale.

Most homebuilders (that is, builders of single-family houses) act as their own general contractors, and much of the profit in homebuilding is derived from construction. Profit margins, which typically range from 10 to 15 percent (over hard and soft costs), must cover construction and sales risk.

Many developers of multifamily projects also do their own construction, but others hire third-party general contractors. Unless they already own a construction company, beginning developers should probably start with a third-party general contractor. Once they have developed a track record, they can consider establishing a construction division in-house. The general contractor absorbs the construction risk and earns the construction profit, which typically runs around 8 percent of hard construction costs. The development profit, which typically runs from 8 to 15 percent of total cost, is in addition to the contractor's profit. The development profit represents the difference between the capitalized value—the market value—of the property at stabilized occupancy and the total development cost to reach that point.

In general, developers bring a wide variety of backgrounds, approaches, and concepts to their first projects. The key to success is skillfully executing the steps in the development process and paying attention to every detail. Jerome Rappaport, Jr., at New Boston Fund, states, "The first requirement is for developers to have the skill set to cover all of the tasks necessary to implement the project, either through their own past experience or expertise on their team. Development is a lot more than site control. It also entails construction implementation, financial controls, budget compliance, government relations, neighborhood relations, marketing, and sales."[8] He adds, "Regardless if you have a big or small staff, the name of the game as a developer is to manage and oversee your staff—whether in house, consultants, or contractors. You need to hire quality people who have the different types of expertise you need for the project. There may be a little more control if you have an in-house team, but you still have to do over-sight and management [even] if your team is lean or in-house."[9]

For those starting out, Rappaport advises, "Become an expert in one part of the process (for example, pre-development financing) and then branch out to other phases of development." He stresses the importance of knowing everything about the development process, from top to bottom, for investors, stakeholders, architects, contractors, and future residents to have confidence in you.[10]

Michael Lander cautions that newcomers to a market are often overly optimistic. "It is difficult to do a quick turn deal with refinancing to get your equity out." Upgrades and other improvements take time, even in a cosmetic rehab deal, as do leasing vacant units and raising rents in existing units to increase the net operating income (NOI) and support the refinancing. A common beginner mistake, he adds, is thinking that the cost can be easily lowered (that thinking belies a lack of construction experience). "You need real understanding of project costs before thinking that you know everything about development."[11]

Every project should have a story that the developer can tell to regulatory agencies as well as potential

FIGURE 4-1 Timeline of Events

Ideally, developers do not close on the land until they are ready to start construction. In most cases, however, land sellers will not wait that long.

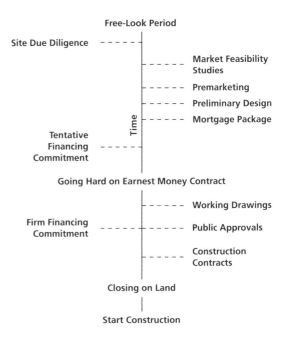

investors and lenders about what makes the project unique. How does it fill a particular niche in the marketplace that is undersupplied? Tom Montelli of Post Road Residential in Boston says, "The investment thesis is something the developer should always be able to articulate to an investor before [the start of] the project."[12] For example, Montelli's "investment thesis" for a market-rate multifamily development is this: If the project is next to transit and the town or city has a growing job base and limited supply of new housing, then all these factors combined will result in high returns and high impact for both the investor and developer.

Project Feasibility

Project feasibility encompasses the full range of analyses that a developer must perform before committing to a given project. As feasibility analysis progresses, the developer must acquire more and more information that will indicate whether it makes sense to proceed further. During the feasibility period, the project may be canceled at any time, usually limiting losses to the costs of the feasibility study plus the cost of tying up the land. Positive information, however, usually justifies making the next incremental expenditure to acquire additional information. Project feasibility includes four major activities:

- market analysis/concept planning;
- site selection/engineering feasibility;
- regulatory approvals; and
- financial feasibility.

In some cases, these activities are performed sequentially; more often, they overlap. Developers must be satisfied, however, that all four activities have been completed before making a final go/no-go decision to purchase the land. Moreover, developers must treat the findings of their research objectively and not become overly enamored with their site or concept.

Ideally, developers do not finalize the acquisition of a site until they are certain that the project will go ahead; in practice, that means all financing commitments are in place for both debt and equity and major public approvals have been received. For beginning developers, most of the steps taken during the feasibility period are aimed at securing financing and ensuring that no surprises show up later during construction or lease-up. Today, regulatory approvals make it very difficult to have everything in place before closing. For example, land sellers are rarely willing to wait for discretionary approvals, such as those by a design review board, planning board, or city council. Developers must

feel very confident that they will be able to secure the necessary approvals and financing to risk closing on the land. No developer wants to be stuck with land that they cannot develop as they intended.

MARKET ANALYSIS

Market analysis occurs both before and after site selection. The choice of sites depends on the market that the developer wants to target. High-quality market information is essential to determine accurately what to build, whom to build for, and how much to build.

No matter how familiar a developer is with the local submarket, an up-to-date market study is indispensable, both to support project financing and to verify current rents and unit types that are most in demand (number of bedrooms, amenities, configurations, and quality, for example). The primary benefit of analyzing the market before selecting a site is that such an analysis will help identify the niches in the market—what is most in demand, where supply is lacking.

The more clearly a developer defines the target market, the more specific the requirements are for a site. For example, when a developer knows who the prospective homebuyers or tenants are—their preferences, their income level, their family situation—then the developer has the facts needed to make careful

Following is a short summary of a market study conducted for ARCOS apartments, a multifamily development in Sarasota, Florida. The full study can be found online at americas.uli.org/PRED.

In 2015, John Burns Real Estate Consulting (JBREC) analyzed the market and development prospects for Framework Group, a development firm based in Tampa, Florida, with an interest in developing a luxury residential community in Sarasota. That same year, the city of Sarasota created a zoning overlay with density bonuses to incentive downtown development, and Framework Group saw that local markets along Florida's Gulf Coast seemed to be heating up. The subject site that Framework Group had in mind was a vacant lot in the Rosemary District in the heart of downtown Sarasota. To understand market trends, Framework Group hired JBREC to conduct a holistic market analysis of Greater Sarasota.

The Sarasota metropolitan statistical area (MSA) is a high-occupancy apartment market area, and in its market analysis, JBREC forecast new market-rate demand for apartments of 2,146 units per year. Using a 12 percent capture rate for the submarket of Sarasota, new demand is forecast to be 258 units (.12 x 2146).[1] As shown in figure A, the new demand is added to estimated turnover (527 units) to yield total estimated annual demand in Sarasota of 785 units per year. JBREC forecast a lease-up rate of 19 units per month, for a one-year absorption of the entire complex of 228 units. This represents a 29 percent capture rate (228/785) of apartment renters in the Sarasota area who can afford rentals of $1,000 per month or more. The calculation seems reasonable given there was minimal existing supply and only one new apartment complex under construction—One Palm with 140 units.

JBREC also illustrated in its market analysis the monthly rental rate and total number of units in Sarasota. With this information, JBREC was able to help Framework Group determine the base rent range for these properties, which helped Framework Group consider the strength of the rental market and begin thinking about unit mix programming. JBREC recommended

that Framework Group develop a total of 228 residential units—ranging in size from 525 square feet to 1,400 square feet—with unit mix programming that consisted of 11 studio units, 80 one-bedroom units, 103 two-bedroom units, and 34 three-bedroom units. JBREC also recommended a $1.81 price per square foot weighted average, broken down as follows: $1.90 price per square foot for studio units, $1.87 price per square foot for one-bedroom units, $1.58 price per square foot for two-bedroom units, and $1.50 price per square foot for three-bedroom units. In consideration of growth, JBREC recommended a 2 to 2.5 percent yearly growth that placed the average net price per square foot at $1.99 by 2018. In addition, based on qualitative information acquired from on-the-ground research at comparable properties, JBREC recommended that Framework Group's development include premium communal building and in-unit amenities to compete with surrounding properties.

The market analysis was integral to Framework Group's recognition that the Rosemary District and Sarasota would absorb new luxury residential units at the time of the project's expected completion in 2018. By applying an analytical lens to Sarasota itself, JBREC was able demonstrate to Framework Group that the local Sarasota market was in fact heating up. As noted by Lesley Deutch, managing principal at JBREC, "It's important to look at who's living in the area, who's moving to the area, what the industries are, and how to create something that's different than the niche. The market study is the essence of real estate. If you get it right, the development process goes a lot better than if you don't."[2]

At the time of ARCOS's opening in 2018, three years after JBREC's market study, the recommended average net price per square foot of $1.99 for all units proved right on: The average net price per square foot upon opening was $2.00. Framework Group also incorporated the recommendation of premium building amenities (library, heated pool, private offices, parking garage) and in-unit amenities (balconies, kitchen appliances, custom built-in closets). The actual unit breakdown varied

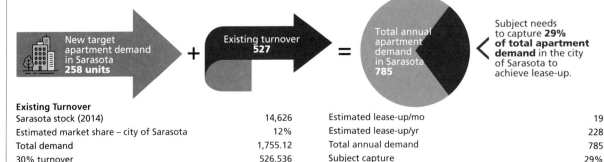

FIGURE A **Apartment Demand in Sarasota**

New target apartment demand in Sarasota **258 units** + Existing turnover **527** = Total annual apartment demand in Sarasota **785**

Subject needs to capture **29% of total apartment demand** in the city of Sarasota to achieve lease-up.

Existing Turnover			
Sarasota stock (2014)	14,626	Estimated lease-up/mo	19
Estimated market share – city of Sarasota	12%	Estimated lease-up/yr	228
Total demand	1,755.12	Total annual demand	785
30% turnover	526.536	Subject capture	29%

slightly from the market analysis with 26 studio units, 95 one-bedroom units, 96 two-bedroom units, and 11 three-bedroom units. The project performed well during the initial lease-up period, and Framework Group decided to incorporate an art gallery on the ground-floor that benefits ARCOS residents, the general Sarasota public, and students at the Ringling College of Art and Design. While Framework Group is generally pleased with its development decisions, one area could be improved: the company would incorporate more one-bedroom units and more balconies as demand has been increasing for those components since opening. Ultimately, the market analysis influenced the project's site planning, unit mix and selection, design and aesthetics, and amenities provided, and Framework Group acknowledges that the success of ARCOS was largely dependent on the JBREC market study (figure B). As stated by Phillip Smith, president of Framework Group,

"We were really trying to set the bar very high and enter new territory. I needed the market study to successfully demonstrate to my lenders that there may not have been an identical market comparison in the area but that the projected goal was a reasonable assumption."[3] Ultimately, JBREC's market study demonstrated that the projected goal was reasonable, and Framework Group attests that a thorough, well-researched, and accurate market study plays an integral role in any successful development project.

[1] The demand computation is shown in figure B. The full market study is on the ULI book website. (See americas.uli.org/PRED.)

[2] Lesley Deutch, managing principal, John Burns Real Estate Consulting, Boca Raton, Florida, interview by author, May 19, 2020.

[3] Phillip Smith, Framework Group, Tampa, Florida, interview by author, May 2020.

Source: Richard Peiser and Julian M. Huertas originally wrote this market study in September 2021 and updated it in March 2022.

FIGURE B **JBREC Market Study**

Annual HH Income	Monthly Rental Rate[a]	Total HH 2014[b]	Total HH 2019[b]	% Rental HH 2014[c]	2014 Calc. Renter HH	% Rental HH 2019[c]	2019 Calc. Renter HH	Annual New Rental HH[d]	% that Rent Apartment Homes	# that Rent Apartment Homes[e]
DEMAND FROM HOUSEHOLD GROWTH			**TOTAL HOUSEHOLDS**		**RENTAL HOUSEHOLDS**					
$0 to $25,000	$0–$700	83,275	75,311	40%	32,898	49%	37,190	858	40%	343
$25,000–$35,000	$700–$1,000	40,305	35,595	38%	15,387	48%	16,986	320	37%	118
$35,000–$50,000	$1,000–$1,400	48,300	53,243	31%	15,043	39%	20,728	1,137	37%	421
$50,000–$75,000	$1,400–$2,100	63,622	78,309	26%	16,331	32%	25,127	1,759	35%	616
$75,000–$100,000	$2,100–$2,900	37,307	52,456	19%	6,903	23%	12,133	1,046	35%	366
$100,000–$150,000	$2,900–$4,300	34,309	44,213	12%	4,167	15%	6,713	509	30%	153
$150,000+	$4,300+	25,649	35,595	11%	2,931	14%	5,085	431	30%	129
Total	**Total**	**332,767**	**374,722**	**28%**	**93,661**	**33%**	**123,962**	**6,060**	**35%**	**2,146**

Monthly Rental Rate	Total Demand		
$0–$700	343	Economy.com projects 12.6% growth in the next five years (2.5% per year) in the Sarasota MSA.	JBREC increased the overall renter rate +/–5% and adjusted rate by income category to account for growth.
$700–$1,000	118		
$1,000–$1,400	421		
$1,400–$2,100	616		
$2,100–$2,900	366		
$2,900–$4,300	153		
$4,300+	129		
Total	**2,146**		
Monthly Rate – Relevant	1,685		

[a] Assumes that in the Sarasota MSA, households pay 34.3% of their annual income toward rent, per the U.S. Census Bureau's American Community Survey (ACS) 2010. While percentage paid by income level may vary, the calculation is intended to establish reasonable rent ranges for perspective. Some households will spend more and some will spend less.

[b] Estimated total existing households and annual household growth between 2014 and 2019. Total HH for 2014 per U.S. Census Bureau. Data are adjusted based on ACS distribution. The growth for 2019 is from Economy.com.

[c] Percentage of area households that are renter occupied by income level, per ACS 2011. For 2019 the overall renter rate is adjusted upward by 5% given the expectation of higher renter ratio trend in coming years. Percentages by income increase given the adjusted household income distribution.

[d] Calculated gain in renter households, 2014 to 2019. Those income categories that show a decrease in households will not show household growth demand.

[e] Percentage of renters by income level that are likely to rent apartments. Data per U.S. Census Bureau. Census reports 35% of all households in the Sarasota MSA who rent, rent in structures that are 5+ units. For purposes of this analysis, JBREC defined these as apartments. JBREC model varies by income level assuming that lower income households are more likely to rent apartments than higher income households (which may tend toward single-family homes).

Source: John Burns Real Estate Consulting calculations of Environmental Systems Research Institute, U.S. Census Bureau, and American Community Survey data.

decisions. Particular market needs imply particular site requirements. If a need for high-end apartments is identified, for example, a developer should be willing to pay more for a superior site with special amenities, such as views, trees, water features, or recreational opportunities.

Bill McLaughlin at AvalonBay Communities advises that "any product requiring a high degree of customization, modification, or specification to the actual physical space will have a limited ability to compete. You can only do it in a location where it makes sense. For example, you probably won't be building a brand new six-bedroom [co-living] suite with one common area in the suburbs as the costs to spec are high, and [you] won't have much flexibility to compete."[13]

John Porta, founder of Covington Development, states, "Don't start telling yourself stories and make up all these reasons like [the favorable market] is going to be like this forever. That's when you'll easily get hurt."[14]

The market study done before buying a property is not as comprehensive as the in-depth analysis done after the site is selected. Market information is not only time-consuming to gather but also expensive to obtain, so a developer should concentrate on specific issues:

- What geographic submarkets have the greatest need for apartments/condominiums?
- What product type is in greatest need?
- What product types are attractive to renters/buyers and why?
- Who is the target market? What are the demographic characteristics (age, income, household size) of potential renters/buyers who have the greatest need for apartments?
- What types of units (number of bedrooms and bathrooms) or unit sizes are expected in this market? What is the appropriate rent/price range?
- What types of features, amenities, and services do renters/buyers expect?

The focus should be on *greatest need* rather than on vacancy rates or hottest areas. While a low vacancy rate suggests need, it does not equate to demand. Need is measured by the relationship between demand (the absorption rate for new units) and supply of units (existing and anticipated) for a particular submarket. The submarket is identified not only by geographic area but also by product type and renter profile.

Developers often confuse existing supply with need. Certainly, historical absorption rates of existing supply are an important factor for predicting future absorp-

tion, but because a particular product type is absent from an area does not necessarily mean that demand exists for that product type. Often a product type is not there because there is no demand for it.

In summary, the goals of the preliminary market analysis before site selection are to

- **identify holes in the market**—look for market niches where demand exceeds supply and locations and circumstances that offer special opportunities to build a project serving a particular market; compare existing apartment stock/population to other comparable cities;
- **define the target market for the project as narrowly as possible**—the number of units needed with particular designs, amenities, unit characteristics (number of rooms, size, and mix of units), and rent range; and
- **develop a market strategy**—whether to compete directly with other projects or to look for market niches with unmet demand.

Once a site is selected, the submarket should be analyzed in much greater detail. By collecting submarket information on rents, unit sizes, types of renters, levels of activity, and vacancies for each unit type for as many comparable projects in the area as possible, a developer will be able to determine how best to position a project. A project-by-project catalog of existing multifamily developments in the submarket should be created and used to decide whether to engage in direct competition with other local properties or to cater to a market niche that shows need and little competition.

The late developer Marvin Finger said once a site is placed under contract, "market analysis goes right to the top of the list of due diligence. In my firm, we send in-house staff people to interview property managers and analyze the current needs of tenants in properties that we consider to be in the same market and price range. Often we follow that up with a professional management company to confirm our findings."[15]

Location, site, and market potential determine the appropriate product to be developed. An urban locale demands a different type of residential development from a suburban one. The typically higher price of urban infill land requires higher densities. Greater automobile dependency in suburban communities necessitates more parking. A historic neighborhood might have specific height and architectural controls that dictate development parameters for a particular site. A costly waterfront site with panoramic views will require higher rents from luxury apartments or condominiums than renters in entry-level housing can afford.

The identified market segment should suggest special types of development. If the research detects strong demand from young families with small children, then the project should be planned with this market segment in mind, and the greatest number of units should be large enough for such households. If the target market is young, first-time renters, a moderately priced project with fewer amenities and maximum unit space for the dollar might fit the bill. An urban site appealing to young professionals may require exercise rooms, pool rooms, common area lounges, and other amenities attractive to millennials. A growing elderly population might suggest a need for a retirement community and elder care facilities. Dan McCoy at BSH Companies focuses on student housing, which has become its own niche. He says, "In student housing, the desire by the tenant is the same for a medical office. Proximity rules the day, so to speak. Proximity to the university is the most important component of student housing development just as doctors want to be as close as they can to hospitals."[16]

Although developing and marketing rental products that have leased well in the past is often easy, a developer may find greater reward—both financially and in terms of serving a public need—in developing a new type of product or location, such as a new town center. However, in times of economic stress, financing innovative product types may be more difficult. Comparable residential projects might not currently exist in the immediate market area; but if the demand analysis shows a need, the analyst should explore the possibilities. In an overbuilt market, less standard types of development may lead to better opportunities, but that consideration will entail looking beyond the immediate market area for examples of successful comparable projects.

Traditionally, the largest multifamily housing markets have been those at both ends of the housing spectrum: young singles and couples, and older empty nesters. In addition to these age-related cohorts, lifestyle niches provide further market potential. They include people in all income and age brackets who traditionally would purchase a single-family home but for any number of reasons choose multifamily living instead. In many instances, they make up target markets for more innovative product types.

DEMAND AND SUPPLY. A formal market analysis increases in importance as developers move farther away from familiar locations and product types. Beginning developers are unlikely to have the firsthand knowledge of local market conditions required to compete successfully. They need to make an extra effort to collect reliable market information before making even basic decisions about site selection.

Market Area. The developer's first task is to define the geographic study area. The study should start with the metropolitan area (data are available for each MSA) and then proceed to the locality where the project is to be located. Ultimately, it will focus on the narrow submarket area where the project will compete directly with other similar projects.

The narrow submarket is defined as the area of generally comparable population characteristics and is usually limited to one or two surrounding neighborhoods. Although the employment center or corridor that the project serves generally defines the broader market, the *primary market area* is usually restricted to a radius of two or three miles (3–5 km) around the project and may be even smaller, especially if freeways, railroads, or other physical barriers exist between neighborhoods. It may be larger if the proposed product is very specialized, or if the market area contains few direct comparables. An understanding of local renters and competitive projects is essential for determining the market area.

A *secondary market area* should also be defined. This area includes apartment projects that may not be directly competitive but offer an alternative to renters who are less sensitive about location.

The importance of defining the correct market area cannot be overemphasized. All too often, beginning developers omit competing projects or include an area so large that absorption rates are overestimated. In addition, many market areas are hard to define because they have no particular identity in the marketplace. This lack of identity poses problems not only for market definition but also for future lease-up and sales because projects perform better in areas that have distinctive identities. Creating a market identity where none exists can be quite a challenge.

Several factors are relevant to delineating the target market area for a proposed development:

- **Travel Time from Major Employment Centers**— Since traffic congestion is a serious problem in most metropolitan areas, housing decisions are usually based on proximity to employment. By identifying major employment centers and making assumptions regarding acceptable commuting time, market analysis defines a target market area.

- **Mass Transportation Facilities and Highway Links**—Commuting patterns and times are based largely on ease of access; thus, the target market's geographic size is influenced by the availability of mass transit, the location of transportation corridors, and the speed at which they operate at peak travel times. Convenience of transportation and availability of public transit are especially important considerations for multifamily development.

- **Existing and Anticipated Patterns of Development**—Most urban settings contain areas of both growth and decline. Growth areas might be distinguished by desirable attributes, such as proximity to employment, availability of affordable housing, physical attractiveness, and/or outstanding community facilities. Declining areas may also offer opportunities, especially for affordable housing or housing for retirees.

- **Socioeconomic Composition**—An area's demographic characteristics—income, age, household characteristics, and others—influence housing choice and location. (Note that it is illegal in the United States to target market segments based on race, religion, or ethnicity.)

- **Physical Barriers**—Natural features such as rivers, bluffs, and parklands, as well as constructed features such as highways or intensive development, can sometimes form a wall through which the market's boundaries do not penetrate.

- **Political Subdivisions**—Municipal boundaries can be especially important when adjoining jurisdictions differ markedly in political climate, tax policies, or status, or hold different attitudes about growth. School district boundaries are important if households with school-age children represent a target market segment. To simplify data collection, it is sometimes necessary to manipulate a target market area to conform to a political jurisdiction, such as a county or planning district in a county or city.

Demand Factors. On the demand side, the market study measures the number of households with particular age, size, and income characteristics. Market research firms employ a variety of statistical techniques to refine their estimates of the number of households, but their basic approach is the same and takes into account the following factors:

- employment growth in *basic* industries (manufacturing and other industries that generate sales outside the city);

- employment growth in *service* industries (retail, local government, real estate, professionals, and others whose activities support the local community);

- percentage of growth expected to occur in employment in the city and submarket;

- socioeconomic characteristics, such as population, age, education, income distribution, and household size and characteristics—families with children, couples without children, singles, divorcees with children, and so on; and

- in- and out-migration.

Each factor must be carefully analyzed so that the developer understands the characteristics of the target population groups. From these statistics and other market surveys, the market analyst estimates the number of new households moving into an area or being created by marriage or divorce from within the area (by income, family composition, and age). From the total and year-over-year change in the number of households, the number of those who will need apartments or condominiums is computed based on historical ratios combined with new information about income and preferences. This estimate of annual demand represents the *absorption* or *take-up* of units in the submarket for the year. *Absorption* is the most important number in the market analysis because it provides the total quantity of units that will likely be rented in the submarket for the year. These aggregate *absorption rates* (units absorbed per year) are then broken down into absorption rates for individual product types and unit types. For example, a study that indicates demand for 500 apartments per year for a given market area is incomplete. It should subdivide that number according to product type: say, 350 adult units, 100 of which are luxury units, and 150 family units, 50 of which are luxury units.

Supply Factors. The supply of housing includes the existing housing stock, the units currently under construction, and the units planned for the future. The vacancy rate is usually considered the most important indicator of market need, but it can be very misleading. For example, vacancies may be 40 percent in older buildings without central air conditioning but as low as 5 percent in newer buildings. Equally important, a 15 percent vacancy rate in a submarket with only 100 total units may be quickly absorbed, especially if a new company is planning to move into the area; elsewhere, however, 15 percent may indicate a very soft market. A more meaningful measure is *total number of months needed to absorb the existing and planned inventory*. This number is based on the estimated demand as measured by the absorption rate expressed in units per month. The computation is illustrated in the next subsection.

Information about the existing housing stock and vacancy rates can best be determined by personal inspection and interviews with managers of surrounding apartment complexes. Even though such information may be proprietary, most managers are willing to cooperate, especially if the developer promises to reciprocate when the project is completed. Neighboring property managers are usually willing to share information because they recognize the value of cooperating with one another about bad tenants, break-ins, and other issues of mutual concern. Other sources of information include local real estate boards, local homeowner and apartment associations, public utility companies, mortgage companies, lending institutions, and the Federal Housing Administration (FHA).

The most common mistake that developers make in estimating supply is to ignore units on the drawing board—that is, projects that have not been announced and do not yet appear in any standard sources, such as city building permits. Often, local brokers, bankers, and architects are the best-informed sources concerning planned units. Of course, many such units will never be built and some planned projects will never get off the ground, but the most likely estimate of the number of units that will be built should be included in the projections of future supply.

Capture Rates. The percentage of total demand in the submarket that a project absorbs (units leased or sold per month) is the *capture rate*. A fundamental principle of market analysis is that, in the long run, a project will capture its pro rata share of total supply. If a project has 200 units and total supply currently available for leasing is 2,000 units, the developer's expected capture rate is 10 percent of the total supply. This capture rate is multiplied by the demand. In the example above, if demand is 100 units per month, the developer's pro rata capture rate would be 10 units per month. At that rate, it should take 20 months to lease-up 200 units.

The most common mistake in market analysis is to assume that one's own project is better than the competition's and will achieve a higher capture rate than that indicated by the pro rata share. While every developer believes his/her project is best-in-class and will out-perform the competition, the truth is that competitors faced with losing market share will eventually cut prices to attract more tenants. In the long run, projects are unlikely to capture more than their

A.O. Flats at Forest Hills, Jamaica Plain, Massachusetts, is a highly sustainable LEED Platinum–certified, transit-oriented, mixed-income community with 78 apartments, 1,600 square feet (150 sq m) of retail space, and 2,500 square feet (230 sq m) of community space to host resident amenities. The development prioritized racial equity and inclusion through its contracting and hiring goals.

pro rata share, no matter how much better they are than the competition because of competitors' willingness to reduce their prices to a level at which they can recapture their share of the market.

Net Market Absorption and Months to Absorb Current and Projected Inventory. The decision concerning whether the market is strong enough to proceed with project development depends on one of the key outputs of the market analysis: the number of months required to absorb the current and projected inventory of units in that submarket. This figure should be broken down according to the different unit types planned for development. For example, the market study may show a short six-month inventory of one-bedroom units but a long 24-month inventory of three-bedroom units. The number of months to absorb the inventory would preferably be 12 or fewer for apartments. Twelve to 18 months is considered soft but not impossible; longer than 18 months should be avoided unless the developer has truly strong reasons to believe that the product will be absorbed significantly faster than that of the competition.

To illustrate, suppose that the market analysis indicates demand for 1,200 middle-income adult apartments per year in the developer's submarket. Suppose further that the current inventory of existing vacant units is 500 apartments with another 500 units under construction and that the developer is aware of 400 units on the drawing board. Suppose the developer estimates that he has learned of only half of all units planned (for a total of 800), but of the planned units, perhaps only 60 percent (480) will likely be built. Thus, the total supply of units is an estimated 1,480, and the estimated absorption period will be 14.8 months:

Vacant units	500
Units under construction	500
Planned units estimated to be built	480
Total estimated supply	1,480
Total estimated annual demand	1,200
Total estimated monthly demand	100

Number of months to absorb projected inventory = Total estimated supply ÷ Total estimated demand =

$$\frac{1,480}{100} = \textbf{14.8 months}$$

In this example, if the developer plans to begin construction immediately and open for occupancy in 12 months, the current and projected supply will be only about three months of inventory when the developer's units come on-stream.

What is a reasonable number of months of absorption of inventory? The lease-up period is derived from the projected number of units absorbed each month by unit type. A soft market is usually one with 18 months or more of projected inventory (including vacant, under-construction, and planned units). The period required to lease up the project is a critical component of the budget since it determines the line item for "interest carry during lease-up." Although no widely accepted guidelines exist, developers customarily include a 12-month leasing reserve plus some cushion in the form of a contingency reserve in case leasing takes 16 to 18 months. Although a larger reserve gives both the developer and the lender additional protection in case the market turns sour, too large a reserve will make the project appear more costly than the competition, which will scare off investors and lenders. Although reserves should be as large as possible, they cannot be too generous or the construction budget will be too high relative to the competition.

MARKET STUDY GUIDELINES. The following guidelines should be observed for the market study to be most useful to lenders, investors, and developers:

1. Give specific directions to the market research firm concerning boundaries of both primary and secondary areas to be researched and the types of products to be researched. The larger the boundaries and the greater the number of product types, the more expensive the study will be.

2. Be aware that general statistical information is by itself inadequate for making market decisions. Critical differences exist between market studies that collect general statistics on the market and those that gather data on specific projects. The latter type is significantly more expensive but is essential unless developers are *certain* that the market is good and the competition is weak. General statistics—housing inventory, vacancies, average rents, average unit sizes, number of housing starts in the past five years, number and dollar volume of permits, number of completions—are a useful starting point, but they must be supplemented with current survey data from projects in the specific market area. Even if the market research firm has a database with project-by-project information, the data should be updated to reflect the latest market conditions.

3. In general, do not rely on vacancy rates alone (vacancy rates may be helpful indicators of market demand in areas where rates are very low). The preferred indicator is the number of months of inventory in the marketplace—the time it will take at projected absorption rates to consume the existing supply of units, units under construction, and units on the drawing board. The number of months of inventory correlates directly with the amount of interest reserve that developers will need.

4. Hire the best firm available to undertake the market study. Firms that specialize in rental apartments and condominiums for particular market areas have information at their fingertips that other firms charge thousands of dollars to replicate. Developers certainly do not want to pay a firm to collect raw data from scratch. They should evaluate firms on the basis of their information sources and track record: How accurate have they been in their projections? Which banks and other financial institutions rely on their studies?

A good market study for multifamily residential development should include the following:

1. Figures for the total yearly demand for the metropolitan area, the city, and the submarket where the project is located. *Demand* refers to the number of multifamily units that will be absorbed during the period in which the project will be under construction and leased. Demand forecasts are based on household growth, age distribution, income, homeownership rates, and proximity to employment centers.

2. Figures for total supply on a project-by-project basis. The data on each project should include

» target market, location, developer, completion date;
» number of units by type (one bedroom, two bedroom, and so on);
» square footage of each unit type;
» rent or sales price for each unit, along with premiums and concessions;
» vacancies (if possible, by unit type);
» amenities of complexes; and
» amenities of individual units (appliances, fireplaces, and so on).

3. An assessment of how many units (for rent or for sale) the market will absorb each month by unit type. As already noted, developers should guard against anticipating unreasonably large capture rates and should run stress tests (scenarios) on cash flows assuming they capture only their pro rata share of the market.

Data from geographic information systems make market analysis today much more sophisticated than it was in the past. Lesley Deutch at JBREC says market analysis starts with "location analysis." "We look at it first [from] a regional perspective. We'll take a look at a much larger scale to understand the regional factors. This is because, for apartment development, residents won't always come from a little five-mile radius, so you really need to understand the region as a whole."[17] After understanding the region, they focus in on the local market to understand what is surrounding the proposed development site, in particular, where services are—grocery stores, schools, big box retailers, and entertainment. "Usually, people who are renting are looking for convenience, so we need to find where those conveniences are."[18] She adds that they then go to even tighter geographies analyzing the surrounding uses—access and egress, schools, school districts, employment proximity, and retail. The firm has a program that puts dots for every business owner and can map 15-minute, 30-minute, and 45-minute radii from employment centers and businesses.

Deutch emphasizes the importance of visiting the competitors. Market researchers will ask questions such as, What are your occupancy rates? What are your lease upgrades? "You can ask the leasing agent at the front desk what the most used amenity is. And if it's the fitness center or the card room, you start to understand what people are using and what types of tenants live there." Deutch notes, "There's all sorts of little nuances we look at to understand what a project will need." She offers several examples:

• "We'll . . . ask leasing agents, 'When people walk in the door, do you usually have more demand for one-, two-, or three-bedroom units?' A lot of the times they'll say, 'We have no three bedrooms, I wish we had more.' Or they'll say, 'The studios went right away.' This allows you to understand where the demand is coming from. So that part of it is huge, and you can't get that from downloading data."

• "[We] also try to find out if there's a premium on the third floor or first floor. For the third floor, there's no one on top of you but you have to walk up. So if there is a premium on the third floor, that usually means that tenants are younger. If there's a premium on the first floor, that usually means tenants are older."

• "If you drive around and see kids' bikes on the balconies, you can understand the types of renters living there."

• "Sometimes you see lots of dog parks and people walking their dogs, so you get a sense who the tenant can be."

• "You can go inside, and if you see lots of dog treats sitting on the counter when you come in, that's info to you that you'll need pet amenities."

• "If you go in the middle of the day and there are no cars around, then a lot of people are commuting to work."

• "Visiting the site in person gives you a sense of who's living there—the leasing agent can't tell you that."

The last analysis the company does is basic employment growth, employment by sector, job growth, construction growth, occupancy rates in the general market, and general demographics. These points go in the back of the report—they provide a template for big-picture thinking. "If we see big job gains in a market, this tells what direction the market is headed. For demographics, we look at both five-mile and 10-mile radii."[19]

Market analysis today relies much more on focus groups and interviews to determine tenants' needs although focus groups are a limited sample and the quality of the input is unknown. Economist G. U. Krueger offers the following advice:

- Once you have examined long-term prospects, look at the local economies in which you are operating. A national developer can look at the MSAs where there will be more growth than others. How well connected is the local economy in which you are operating to the global economy and how well can it serve the global economy? Is it being driven by the manufacturing sector producing goods the rest of the world needs or value-added design (as in Silicon Valley)? Stick with metropolitan areas and their hinterlands that service and are connected to the global economy.
- If an area is not part of the global system, it will be hard for it to achieve any sort of meaningful economic development unless there is massive government investment.
- You cannot rely on demographic research for small-scale projections. One approach is to talk to realtors in the field and visit projects that are similar to your concept. You need to know what you are looking for and get away from the notion that this exercise is to justify the decision to your boss or the lender. Talk to sales agents and try to get a current buyer profile and then look at the demographic models.
- Lenders should scrutinize the content and methodology of market analysis as a major component of their investment decisions.
- Even market research cannot help you if you do not have a strategy to use that information to maximize the asset value.[20]

Market analysis needs to be forward looking. Tim Cornwell at the Concord Group makes several points. Developers need to take into account the time required to build a product (current market trends might no longer hold true by then). The peak population may be 30 years old when the analysis is done, but the developer should look at least five years ahead to account for development time and provide suitable product for the market down the road. Where will renters be in five years? What needs and demands will they have? Cornwell says clients are all talking about millennials (with good reason): the average age of residents in actual projects is 36 to 39 years old. "What about re-urbanizing baby boomers though? They once wanted the suburban school districts and amenities but may no longer need them anymore. What next?"[21]

Cornwell adds that the past does not tell you everything about the future. Job relocation is blurring metro market divisions. Rather than migrating to the suburbs for cheaper housing, people are looking at moving to less expensive cities such as Phoenix and Las Vegas from Southern California, and Boise and Reno from San Francisco.

Phillip Smith at Framework Group recommends caution about market studies. He says, "By the time I would engage in a market study, I've already made some rent assumptions based on my understanding of the area and demographics. Also, I've already done my preliminary underwriting about land costs. I'm making some assumptions about any environmental cleanup and construction costs." He notes that market studies are very helpful when you're trying to raise capital. "It's generally an expectation (not so much a requirement) from investors that you'll get a market study done—unless you have some overwhelming empirical evidence that your project will succeed. It's just good due diligence on an investor's part to ask for a market study and to expect that I'm going to come with another take on that market."[22]

SITE SELECTION

According to a real estate adage, the worst reason for developing a parcel is that you already own it. Although ownership of a plot of land may not by itself be a good reason for developing it, a site should not be eliminated from consideration just because a developer owns it. Land in the path of growth is typically worth holding until higher use and greater density are justified. Almost every site can be developed for some purpose. The developer's challenge is to identify the *highest and best use*—the use that maximizes the property's land value.

During the acquisition process, the ability to buy more time can be crucial. For example, when Peiser Corporation and Jerome Frank Investments purchased a site in Dallas for a 160-unit apartment project, they had what seemed to be a comfortable 120-day period during which to close. However, the project was economically attractive only if the partnership could obtain permission to issue tax-exempt housing revenue bonds available for low- and moderate-income housing, and approval from the city council was needed to issue the bonds. Housing revenue bonds were a new program for Dallas, and the city council postponed the hearing date multiple times while working out the details of the bond program. Fortunately, the partnership had negotiated the right to extend the closing by up to three months at a cost of $5,000 per month, and the extra time allowed the partners to receive the necessary approvals. Options to extend the closing are especially important in hot markets where the seller may receive a higher offer from another buyer.

LOCATION AND NEIGHBORHOOD. The success of a real estate project is often said to depend on three factors: location, location, location. People typically ask some basic questions when looking at property: (1) How far is my child's school? (2) How far is my place of employment? (3) How far is it to get a cup of coffee? (4) How far to get a tank of gas? Location can be categorized by macrolocation factors and microlocation factors.[23] *Macrolocation* refers to a property's proximity to major urban nodes, *microlocation* to a property's immediate environs. A property's long-term value depends not only on its current macrolocation and microlocation but also on how the two are changing over time.

Both macrolocation and microlocation influence multifamily residential development. Macrolocation determines what part of the city offers the best long-term potential to preserve and enhance value—proximity to downtown and suburban employment centers, major growth corridors, medical centers, regional shopping and entertainment, regional parks, and recreation. Microlocation determines how well a site is situated in its immediate neighborhood—access to freeways and arterial roads, quality of schools, parks, shopping, daycare, and health care facilities. Ideally, a site is visible from a major road yet situated to ensure privacy, a sense of security, and a low noise level.

The ability to foresee changes in the urban fabric before others is one of the hallmarks of the most successful developers. Whether their predictions are based on careful research, intuition, luck, or some combination of all three, successful developers understand the dynamics of location well enough to survive over the long term. The key is getting out in front of development—seeing where growth is going before others do. Being in front of the crowd offers the advantage of lower land prices. Once an area has been fully discovered and has many new projects, land prices will reflect everyone's expectations of continued growth, and finding sites at prices where the numbers work will be much harder. For beginning developers, this cuts two ways. Being in a well-established area makes it easier to finance the project. Undiscovered or less popular areas may raise questions for potential investors about the area's future. That said, everyone likes a good deal. Finding land below the radar screen (that is not on the market) is a proven strategy, but finding such opportunities takes time, research, and connections.

An important component of developers' success is the fiscal health of the cities or suburbs where they build. If the level of public services in a city declines, real estate values decline as well. Successful developers understand how much they depend on the physical and financial health of the communities where they build—which is why so many of them are active in community affairs.

It takes a lifetime of practice to fully understand all the dimensions of location that affect real estate value over time. Trends in public investment, private investment, design, demographics, and personal preferences are critical components of location. The rate of change in most American neighborhoods is very slow—often 30 to 50 years from peak to trough. It is much faster in poorly designed or poorly built neighborhoods, however, which often cycle downward within 15 to 20 years after they are built. On the other hand, some neighborhoods seem only to increase in value. The reasons often pertain to not only location but also the availability of shopping, open space, and other amenities—as well as ongoing investment by private owners to renovate and improve their properties.

The character of adjacent areas also affects the use of an undeveloped parcel. If adjoining areas are compatible, they can enhance the desirability of a proposed multifamily project. When they are declining, dangerous, or showing decay such as graffiti, developers should proceed very cautiously.

In recent decades, a common practice has been to locate higher-density multifamily projects closest to commercial and industrial districts. Doing so provides a buffer to single-family areas and allows the multifamily residential areas to benefit from proximity to the higher-capacity streets and more intensive commercial and employment centers that help support higher population densities. In turn, cluster and attached housing is often located as a buffer between multifamily housing and lower-density single-family development.

More recently, however, these planning practices have come into question. Local governments are increasingly willing to view development proposals in terms of integrating rather than separating different uses. This point is illustrated by the increasing flexibility of land use controls through the widespread acceptance of mixed-use zoning and concepts that have long been associated with good planning but popularized by the new urbanists. Such development plans permit the mixing of previously separated uses,

Located in Seattle, Orenda is a community-driven project with a mix of studio and one-, two-, and three-bedroom units affordable to households earning 65 to 120 percent of the area median income. The first two floors are occupied by the Odessa Brown Children's Clinic, which offers health services, and the Tiny Tots Development Center.

provided they are properly designed. The result is often a more varied, efficient, and attractive development. Walkable, mixed-use neighborhoods have fewer cars and more amenities than homogeneous, single-use neighborhoods.

A good site for multifamily development is one that has positive synergy with surrounding land uses. For example, a multifamily site in an established or emerging suburban business core offers residents the convenience of employment and commercial services within easy driving or walking distances. In recent years, market analysts have employed geographic information systems to help identify the best walkable neighborhoods by scoring an area—commonly referred to as "walk" scores—based on easy walkability to stores, transportation, and parks. A site in an area with several other successful apartment projects may also be more desirable than one that stands alone because of amenities, shopping, and mass transit that are attracted to concentrations of apartments. The best locations are naturally costlier than those with detrimental surroundings but are usually worth the additional expense, particularly for high-end development. The desirability of walkable, mixed-use neighborhoods has led to a wave of development of high-quality urban housing in mixed-use districts such as Brooklyn; the Washington, D.C., baseball stadium district; and the Boston Seaport. AvalonBay, one of the most prominent multifamily-focused real estate investment trusts (REITs) in the United States, currently builds twice as many apartments in urban markets as in suburban markets.[24]

In considering compatibility, developers should be aware of potential liabilities that could be incurred from building residential units too close to conflicting uses. For example, proximity to large storage tanks of gas, oil, and other flammable material should be avoided. Noise and pollution from traffic, airplanes, and trucks directly impact rents and vacancy rates. On the other hand, for student housing and micro-units, proximity to self-storage is an asset. Developers need to protect themselves against possible liability by examining the potential conflicting uses near a given site.

SIZE AND SHAPE. The best size for a site varies according to local market conditions, including lease-up rates, acceptable unit densities, and preferred amenity packages. For example, suppose a developer wants to build a project that can be leased within 12 months of its completion. If 15 units can be leased per month (180 units per year) and the product being built has an average density of 24 units per acre (60/ha), then the ideal site would be 7.5 acres (3 ha), that is, 180 divided by 24. The size of a site is also influenced by property management considerations. Although the optimum number of units varies with each project, many developers consider 150 to 200 or more units the minimum number necessary to support a full-time on-site maintenance staff, and they look for sites that are large enough to accommodate that many units. In Los Angeles, where the availability and cost of land make it very difficult to assemble sites large enough for 200 units, developers often build several smaller complexes in a neighborhood that are run as a single project with shared property management and maintenance staffs.

Design options vary with the size of the site. A narrow site may prevent the inclusion of double-loaded parking or back-to-back units (which typically increase efficiency and reduce costs).[25] A deep site may require a loop road or a turnaround for fire trucks. The developer should always draw a preliminary site plan to see how a site can be laid out before going hard on an earnest money contract.

Beginning developers should look for individual tracts that are large enough to accommodate the type of product they want to build. They should avoid tracts that require assembling several parcels under different ownership. The process of land assembly is virtually a development business in itself, with its own risks and rewards. Problems associated with assembling tracts include multiple closings, extra legal costs, multiple lenders, and the possibility that key parcels will not close. Incomplete assembly carries costly penalties for developers, who may have to pay exorbitant prices for outparcels or spend extra money on design and construction to squeeze as many units as possible onto a less-than-ideal site.

ACCESSIBILITY AND VISIBILITY. In evaluating a multifamily site's accessibility, a developer should ask several questions:

- How will prospective tenants approach the property? What will they see as they drive to the site that may make it more or less desirable? (In brochures and advertisements, developers often select the most attractive, although not necessarily the shortest, route to a project from the major roads.)
- How will visitors enter the property? Will they be able to turn left across traffic? Can approval for curb cuts and/or multiple entrances be obtained?
- Will the current roadway network support the additional traffic generated by a new development?
- Will it be difficult for residents to exit the project?
- How long will it take residents to travel to work, schools, shops, and recreational facilities?
- Is the site served by public transportation?
- Is road construction planned? (If so, rentals will be severely impaired during the construction period.)
- Are existing roads adequate for the type of development planned? (In general, high-density development requires collector and/or arterial street access, whereas lower-density development can be undertaken on smaller local streets.)

Visibility is critical for marketing and leasing. Prospective residents must be able to see a project to know that it is there. A developer can enhance a project's visibility in several ways. These include using special design elements, special landscaping features, striking colors, off-site signage, flags, and nighttime lighting, especially of the frontage. The aim should be the creation of an appealing, distinctive project.

SITE CONDITIONS. Apartment and condominium development offers somewhat more latitude with respect to the physical characteristics of a site than do other types of development. A developer of multifamily residential projects is less constrained by slopes and by the size and shape of parcels because residential building pads tend to be smaller and more flexible than pads for office or industrial buildings. Residential building layouts can be manipulated to fit odd-shaped parcels. Nonetheless, a developer must still carefully evaluate every potential aspect of a site, including its slope, geology, soils, vegetation, and hydrology.

Slope and Topography. Developers have always been attracted to hilltops and other places offering views. Moderately sloping sites are preferable to steep or flat land. Slopes create opportunities for more interesting design, such as split-level units and varied rooflines. They also help reduce the amount of excavation needed to provide structured parking in denser developments (densities greater than 35 units per acre [85/ha] usually require some form of parking structure).

Improvement costs, on the other hand, rise sharply on slopes greater than 10 percent. Retaining walls, special piers, and other foundations can add to the time and cost of construction. Further, some cities—San Diego, for example—have adopted hillside development ordinances that restrict development of steeply sloping sites. Allowable densities are reduced on slopes greater than 15 percent, and development is forbidden on slopes greater than 25 percent.[26] Flat land may also create additional expense. Sewers must slope downward to create flow; thus, pumping stations may be required if a site is entirely flat or if part of the site lies below the connection point to the city sewer line.

Geology, Hydrology, and Soils. In earthquake-prone areas, a geologic survey is essential. If a site is crossed by fault lines, it may be unbuildable. The same is true of a site in an area with abandoned subterranean mines. Even though building around the fault line or mine may be possible, obtaining insurance may be impossible. Moreover, proximity to a fault line creates an intractable marketing problem. Fracking has caused states such as Oklahoma and Texas, which rarely had earthquakes, to see minor and even major earthquakes above 4.0 on the Richter scale.[27]

If a site contains, or borders on, a creek or wetlands area, a floodplain study must be conducted. Areas that are wet only part of the year may be considered vernal pools, which may be protected under the North American Wetlands Conservation Act of 1989.[28] Standing water on a site may also indicate the presence of an underground stream, which must be located because some portion of the site will almost certainly be unbuildable. A developer should be able to obtain a rough approximation of how much land lies in the floodplain or wetlands area by hiring a civil engineer and ecologist/biologist who has done work in the area.

Like floodplains, soil conditions are problematic. Even if a site looks clean, a developer should always hire a geologist to take soil samples of a site before purchasing it. Geologists usually take at least one core sample near each corner of a property and one or more in the center to determine what type of soil is present, its viscosity, its plasticity, its bearing capacity, and the depth of the water table and underlying bedrock. Good soil such as sandy loam is moderately pervious to water. Clay soils, however, expand and contract with water, which may cause foundations to crack. Impervious soils cause increased water runoff. If rock is located near the surface of a site, excavation may cost significantly more than for a site with deep soil.

Vegetation. Plant cover provides useful information about soil and weather conditions. Red maple, alder, hemlock, and willow indicate wet ground that is poorly drained, whereas pitch pine and scrub oak are signs of dry land and good drainage.

Efforts should be made to preserve mature trees. Large, healthy trees face several dangers. Construction activity under a tree can compact the soil and may kill the tree. Builders often do not like saving trees because it makes their work more time-consuming and costly. Trees often die during construction because of chemical poisoning. Even if they survive construction, they often die later because their root systems have been disturbed or because the amount of water they receive has been altered. A developer should consult a tree surgeon about saving trees and should clearly mark and place a protective barrier around trees that are to be preserved.

Other forms of vegetation may also require special handling. Grasslands, particularly in coastal areas, are a crucial component of erosion control. Many kinds of grasses, vines, shrubs, and wildflowers provide wildlife habitats or are included on the endangered species lists, and their preservation becomes a legal issue.

Stormwater. In the past, stormwater runoff has been handled by the most convenient method possible: the rapid disposal of surface water through closed, manmade systems. Stormwater runoff has often been mismanaged under this philosophy, aggravating the velocity and volume of runoff problems downstream and increasing the pollution of local streams. Potential legal issues concerning the effects of stormwater management on adjacent properties during and after construction have led many jurisdictions to adopt stormwater management standards restricting the quantity and velocity of runoff after development to no more than predevelopment levels. Many areas also require filtration or treatment of stormwater before its release. Detention and filtration ponds are common in stormwater management systems, the former designed to slow down stormwater runoff and the latter designed to filter stormwater through layers of materials, such as sand and gravel to remove pollutants.

The preparation of a functional and aesthetic stormwater runoff plan requires coordination among the project's architects, engineers, planners, and landscape architects. Much of the runoff can be handled through passive design elements—including proper grading, swales, and landscaping materials—rather than engineering systems. Such considerations need to be part of the early design plan. Recent trends in stormwater management encourage eliminating large stormwater ponds in favor of smaller "rain gardens" located throughout the development. Local stormwater management regulations may vary by state or locality.

Existing Buildings. In most cities, developers must receive approval to demolish any structures on a site. Historic structures are protected, but even nonhistoric buildings usually require demolition permits. Before purchasing a site for major renovation or redevelopment, developers should make certain that they can evict the current tenants. Eviction can take a long time—often four to six months or more—and can be expensive, especially if relocation assistance is required from the developer. In extreme cases, the developer may be required to find or build the tenant a comparable unit.

ENVIRONMENTAL ISSUES. Environmental due diligence is required now for every development site (see chapter 3). A preliminary Phase I environmental site assessment (ESA), performed for $3,000 to $10,000, gives the developer a history of the property and indicates the need for any further investigation. Every potential lender requires at least a Phase I ESA report, so a standard part of purchase contracts is that the offer is subject to the buyer's determination that no significant environmental problems exist.[29]

Phase I scope does not include air quality, lead paint, lead pipes, asbestos, radon, or mold investigations, which may be concerns when buying an existing apartment project, especially an older project. Evidence of water damage may indicate a mold problem. The seller should inform the buyer of any problems past or present, but the buyer is still responsible for taking care of them to obtain financing.

Many urban infill sites have at least one environmental issue. In most cases, no remediation is necessary. But if dirt must be removed or, in the worst case, groundwater is contaminated, cleanup costs can be enormous. If the Phase I ESA indicates a "recognized environmental condition," a Phase II ESA is required. The cost of the Phase II ESA depends on the type of problem but generally costs $15,000 to $30,000.[30] Above-ground tank removal may be relatively minor, but the presence of underground tanks, contaminated soil, or other conditions may require 40 to 50 borings.[31] Phase II includes soil borings, ground-penetrating radar to find underground tanks or dumping, and monitoring wells and test pits. If a condition that requires notification under state law is identified, then a set of phased reports and timelines for completing the documentation, removal, and restoration must be followed.[32]

The seller is responsible for cleanup, but once the sale has closed, the new owner becomes part of the chain of title and may be liable in the future. In any case, the cleanup must be completed before lenders will finance new construction. Because environmental problems are so prevalent, lenders seek environmental insurance policies and guarantees from the buyers to indemnify them from problems. The insurance can be costly, but it has made many sites developable that were not so before.[33]

EASEMENTS AND COVENANTS. An easement conveys one party's right to use the property of another. The land for whose benefit the easement is created is called the *dominant tenement*. The land that is burdened or used is called the *servient tenement*. Generally, unless easements are created with a specific termination date, they survive indefinitely.

Only the beneficiary of the easement—the dominant tenement—can extinguish them. Subsequent owners of property that have existing easements may have to purchase the easement back from the current beneficiaries.

Protective covenants, also called *deed restrictions*, are private restrictions that run with the land; that is, once created, they remain in force for all future buyers or heirs. Deed restrictions may be created by a property owner at any time. Once created, however, they remain in force unless all parties subject to the covenants agree to remove them. Developers usually establish deed restrictions at the time they subdivide, or *plat*, a property. Some covenants expire automatically after a number of years under state statute, as in Texas and Florida, but others never expire. To be enforceable, covenants must usually be filed with the county recorder and thus will appear in a title search.

Developers must carefully review any and all deed restrictions because such restrictions can kill a project even after developers have invested a great deal of time and money. In Dallas, for example, one case involved a subdivision that still had single-family-only restrictions in place despite the presence of many nonresidential uses. A developer placed a contract on property there assuming that the existing nonresidential uses effectively voided the restrictions. Although the developer may have been able to overturn the restrictions in court, he found that no bank would lend him money on a site that had restrictions against the intended use.

UTILITIES. Water, sanitary and storm sewers, electricity, gas, and other services are critical factors in site selection. Before purchasing a site, a developer should always confirm that services not only are nearby but also have available capacity. Even if a major waterline runs adjacent to a property, it may be unavailable to that property because the line's capacity is already committed or because the city is concerned about a loss in water pressure. When verifying that service is available, a developer should never simply take the word of the land seller and should instead visit the appropriate city departments or retain a civil engineer to do so.

Water and sanitary sewer services are the most costly utilities to bring in from off site. When water and sanitary lines must be brought in, the developer should undertake the work rather than wait for the city or utility company to do it to ensure that the work is performed concurrently with the project. Electricity, gas, and telephone services are usually provided by private utility companies. Except for remote sites, those utility companies usually provide service to the site at no cost to the developer since they recover their investment through charges to the end user. Each locality has its own fee structure and method of handling utility services.

A developer should ask several questions about utilities:

- How long will it take to obtain service?
- How much will it cost?
- When is payment due?
- When does one have to apply for service?
- Are public hearings involved (they may cause delays and increase the political risk)?
- Is the provision of service subject to any potential moratoriums?
- Are easements needed from any other property owners before services can be obtained?
- Can it be put underground?
- Is the capacity of the service adequate?

Some municipalities with scarce water have responded by imposing high water hookup fees on residential building permits. Others have imposed strict requirements for conserving water, such as the use of flow-restricting devices on plumbing features, installation of drought-tolerant landscaping, and, in some extreme circumstances, partial or total moratoriums on development until new water supplies are available. Developers should check the availability of water at a site and, if it appears that supplies are limited, understand fully what will be required before water can be hooked up there. Some sites are forced to be annexed to the adjacent city to get water.

Even with commitments for utilities in hand, things can go wrong. Tom Montelli describes having a commitment from National Grid to connect his firm's project, The Pioneer, in Everett, Massachusetts, to the main gas lines in early June 2018. However, the union went on strike during contract negotiations. Pioneer could not get gas. Montelli says the company had two options: (1) "Sit on our hands and wait. If the deal blew up financially, the lender could have come in and taken the keys to the project." Or (2) "Find a solution." The solution was to convert mechanical units in 40 percent of the apartments to propane and get four 500-gallon propane tanks to provide heat while they were leasing up. The strike went on for 13 months, and the project eventually switched back to natural gas. "All in, the 'solution' cost us about

$500k. And that was cost that was unbudgeted for, at a time when we weren't cash flow positive yet in the lease-up. However, the indirect ramifications turned out to be even more significant. The debacle delayed our eventual sale and increased the duration of the investment period. So it had effects on our [internal rate of return], etc. Also, most importantly, we would have sold before COVID-19 hit if it weren't for [National Grid]."[34]

REGULATORY ISSUES. The regulatory process has become increasingly difficult, and the ability to secure the necessary regulatory approvals has become the developer's primary concern in many communities. The increasing complexity of development regulation has created a whole new field of development—developers who bear the risk of obtaining necessary approvals and entitlements (see chapter 3) and then sell the fully entitled land to another developer to build out the property. Developers often receive the highest return on their investment from successfully obtaining entitlements because they incur the highest risk.

Even when land is appropriately zoned, no guarantee exists that developers will be able to build what they want to build. In some jurisdictions, additional hurdles must be overcome, such as approvals from design review boards and neighborhood planning committees. Setback, parking, environmental, air quality, and fire code regulations affect the density that developers can achieve on a parcel, regardless of the density allowed in the zoning.

The regulatory process is described more fully in chapter 3. The following issues arise frequently with multifamily development.

Zoning. Zoning determines the building envelope and the density for a site. Specific issues usually covered in the zoning code include the number of units allowed, parking requirements, height limitations, setback restrictions, floor/area ratios, and unit size requirements. Some zoning codes give actual density constraints, for instance, up to 24 units per acre (60/ha), whereas others stipulate minimum land area per unit, such as 1,500 square feet (140 sq m) of land per unit. The other major zoning constraint for apartments is parking. A common requirement is one parking space per bedroom (up to two spaces for a three-bedroom apartment) plus spaces for visitors. A developer may petition to change the zoning or obtain a variance, but that process is often long and arduous, especially if higher densities are involved.

Many suburbs are hostile to multifamily housing, and NIMBYism (the not-in-my-backyard syndrome) tends to focus more on multifamily development than on any other product type. Developer Jerome Frank, Jr., advises, "For a beginning developer, it's very difficult—unless the land is already zoned—to find and develop a piece of property that needs rezoning. Find land that's already zoned and pay for the zoning."[35] Marvin Finger added, "Even extremely low-density upscale developments represent nothing but evil to the surrounding single-family owners. To overcome this perception, you have to employ the premier professional, who would probably be an attorney, to negotiate your case in that neighborhood. It cannot be done in-house."[36]

Developer Ken Hughes advises beginning developers to avoid landmarks commissions for historic structures: "In Texas, if you go through a landmarks commission review process, there is no opportunity for appeal. It is not territory for the inexperienced developer." He adds, "We do not like to build replicative architecture on infill lots in historic districts. If we are interested in building a more contemporary structure, we can avoid the landmarks commission by going directly to the planning and zoning board."[37]

Mixed-Use and Transit-Oriented Development. Cities tend to be more favorably inclined toward higher-density development in two areas: near transit stations and in close-in neighborhoods where mixed-use development is favored. Many cities have *transit-oriented development (TOD) overlay districts* where they encourage apartments and higher-density development. The California Department of Transportation recommends that communities establish minimum zoning densities in TODs equal to the maximum density the market will support.[38] Projects within TODs typically have lower parking requirements (maximum one per unit) and receive preferential treatment for public approvals. Ken Hughes cautions, however, "Most transit authorities do not know how to acquire land or develop it; therefore, most stations are not amenable to higher-density development. Between 30 and 40 stations will be opening in the Dallas area, but only about five or six of those are appropriate for high-density development." Hughes adds, "People view no change as preferable to better change if they do not know how to define 'better.' The developer must clearly know what makes projects work; people recognize this even if they don't know why they work. The developer is the 'imagineer' who must understand what people respond to emotionally even if they cannot identify it."[39]

Fire Codes. Fire codes have particular importance for residential construction because residential buildings are usually wood frame and therefore especially prone to the risk of fire. Fire codes determine the number of stairways each unit requires as well as the maximum distance each unit can be from a fire hydrant. The codes directly affect the number of units that can be placed on a site as well as the cost of building them.

Many communities encourage developers to install fire sprinklers in apartment projects by imposing stringent requirements on wood-frame construction without sprinkler systems. Beginning developers should consult architects who are familiar with local fire codes and the type of product under consideration to determine the best way to meet fire regulations. Even if fire sprinklers are not required by code, developers are well-advised to install them. The complex will be more competitive when the time comes to sell it, and insurance costs will likely be lower.

As wildfires become more frequent in fire-prone areas, the fire codes can be very restrictive. Fire codes determine building heights based on the highest elevation that firefighters can reach with a ladder from the ground. The codes spell out acceptable building materials (untreated wood cladding and wood shingles are forbidden in many areas) and dictate the width of stairways and passages to ensure firefighters' access around all buildings. They also specify allowable vegetation and turn-around radii for fire trucks.

Rent Control. Developers considering multifamily rental housing projects must consider the degree of rent control prevailing in the area and local politicians' general attitudes about rent control. Rent control ordinances often restrict developers' and investors' ability to obtain the rents required to make the project feasible or to raise rents to keep up with inflation and expenses.

Apart from the obvious economic disadvantages of rent control that restricts rent increases, developers have a harder time obtaining financing for projects in communities with rent control. And once built, such projects require property managers who are experienced with the paperwork. Nonetheless, affordable and workforce housing are in great demand and present opportunities for developers who can navigate the regulations and limitations.

Building Codes. Building codes are legal documents that set minimum requirements for sanitary facilities, electrical work, lighting, ventilation, construction, building materials, fire safety, plumbing, and energy conservation. They are local laws that vary

Hazel SouthPark, a six-story building in Charlotte, North Carolina, with 203 rental apartment units, is an example of a mid-rise apartment building. It includes 14,000 square feet (1,300 sq m) of retail space and a parking garage.

from city to city. The United States has no uniform building code; municipalities generally use one of four separate model codes as the basis for their particular regulations. Although the trend is toward greater uniformity, developers must still deal with a diverse set of codes, which are often applied inconsistently.

A major problem for developers is that governments do not accept responsibility for review of the plans. Although one department may review and stamp a plan "approved," the local government's field inspectors, who exercise considerable control over a project, often interpret the codes differently but do not weigh in before construction begins. To make the process of obtaining permits as smooth as possible, developers should work with local development professionals and consultants. Any questions about interpreting the local building code should be addressed as early as possible in meetings with those in the building department who check plans. During construction, developers are well advised to build a strong working relationship with code enforcement officials—in particular, building inspectors.

Condominium Conversions. Condominium conversions—the conversion of rental units to for-sale units—provide an attractive entry point for beginning developers because seller financing is often available. The development process is shorter and less risky than in projects built from the ground up or projects involving major rehabilitation, and the amount of money developers must raise is also usually smaller. The major risks

stem from construction loan interest for the units during the sales period and renovation expenses for upgrading the units. Condo conversions tend to occur in waves, often associated with hot markets following a recession. These waves typically coincide with significant price increases in new condominium construction and the availability of existing apartment buildings well below replacement cost—often following a building boom when apartments were overbuilt. Beginning developers should be wary of the high number of units available for conversion to condominiums from apartments built during the period leading up to the last recession.

Conversions are subject to special regulations in many communities. Concerns about preserving their rental housing stock have caused cities such as New York and San Francisco to pass laws that limit or complicate condominium conversion. Before entering the conversion business, developers should carefully investigate local procedures, which can be time-consuming and intricate. The advice of a local attorney who specializes in condominium conversion is critical and should be sought before developers commit to a project.

Developers should be wary of litigation over construction defects in condominiums. California experienced a frenzy of such litigation activity in the 1990s, when attorneys organized condominium associations to sue their developers before a 10-year time limit on construction lawsuits expired. The result was a dramatic decrease in new condominium construction. Changes in liability laws combined with tighter construction supervision have restored condominium construction activity somewhat, but concerns about litigation still overshadow the market. Savvy developers employ an inspector to photograph the project in great detail during construction. Not only does this documentation help protect the developer against construction defect litigation; it also makes the contractor more conscientious, knowing that the work will be inspected before it is covered up.

Exactions and Impact Fees. To recover what is perceived as the public cost of new development, local ordinances often require developers to dedicate land, improvements, or fees as a condition of approval. In the past, such dedications were primarily for the basic infrastructure necessary to serve the development site, such as on-site roads and utilities. Now, however, dedications or exactions are often required for off-site improvements above and beyond the immediate infrastructure needed for a development site. These can include improvements to arterial streets, flood-control facilities, sewage treatment plants, schools and parks, fire and police stations, open space, or almost any other public necessity.[40] Despite many alternatives for financing capital improvements (e.g., taxes, general obligation bonds, revenue bonds, tax increment financing, user charges, special assessments, and special districts), the trend has been toward more widespread use of exactions by local governments.[41]

Some local governments have adopted standards for exactions. Others determine exactions project by project, thereby complicating a developer's ability to predetermine a project's feasibility. When no standards exist to measure exactions, developers can use exactions levied on similar developments in the area to estimate exactions for a feasibility analysis.

In small developments, which make up the lion's share of multifamily housing developments, exactions are made through impact fees more often than land and infrastructure improvements. Requiring the dedication of parks, schools, and other public facilities would be too great a burden for a small site. Instead, municipalities combine the fees obtained from multiple small developments to provide the necessary public improvements at some off-site location. A 2019 national survey found that impact fees averaged $8,034 for apartments of 1,000 square feet (93 sq m), compared with $13,627 for a single-family unit of 2,000 square feet (186 sq m). Average apartment impact fees ranged from $21,703 in California to $762 in Missouri. Livermore, California, had the highest fees of $58,941.[42] The largest fees were for roads, water, wastewater, parks, and schools. Other impact fee categories included drainage, library, fire, police, and general government. Interestingly, impact fees for commercial uses are lower (per 1,000 square feet): retail averages $6,760; office is $5,408; industrial is $3,942.[43]

FINANCIAL FEASIBILITY ANALYSIS

The next important step in feasibility analysis is financial feasibility. In essence, this analysis is the one lenders require to ensure that the project will live up to its performance expectations. The process for analyzing the financial feasibility of apartments is similar to the process for all income property. It begins with a simple back-of-the-envelope capitalization and ends with a multiyear discounted cash flow analysis that includes returns to investors or joint venture partners.

Evaluating financial feasibility for all income property development involves several stages of analysis, each more detailed than the previous one, from land purchase to a final go/no-go decision on a property. How much analysis is necessary before purchasing land? Experienced developers working in their own area know from experience what they can spend for land. They know the local market and therefore know when they see a good deal. Beginning developers, however, must overcome several handicaps:

- lack of experience in determining a workable price;
- lack of visibility in the brokerage community, so they hear about deals only after larger players have rejected them; and
- less staying power, so they must be more careful about which deals to pursue.

The main difficulty that developers face in terms of financial feasibility studies is understanding what type of analysis is appropriate at what stage. Too much detail too early is a waste of time and money. Too little detail gives insufficient information on which to base informed decisions. Analysis of any income property involves five stages:

- **Stage 1** (the pro forma statement)—simple capitalization of pro forma NOI based on a stabilized property scenario;
- **Stage 2**—discounted cash flow (DCF) analysis of annual cash flows during the operating period and based on a stabilized property scenario;
- **Stage 3**—combined analysis of the development period and the initial operating period up to the point of stabilization of the property;
- **Stage 4**—monthly cash flow analysis during the development period; and
- **Stage 5**—DCF analysis for investors.

This chapter concentrates on Stages 1, 2, and 3, and a before-tax version of Stage 5.[44] Of all the stages of analysis, Stage 2 is the most important. It is known by various names, including *discounted cash flow analysis*,

The subject of this case study is 28 Austin Street, a transit-oriented, energy-efficient, mixed-income four-story, 68-unit apartment building. The building has 23 affordable apartments (33 percent of the total), 5,000 square feet (465 sq m) of first-floor retail with two stores, 90 underground parking spaces for residents, a 135-kilowatt rooftop solar array, 125 municipal parking spaces at grade, a landscaped public plaza, and a playground. It is located in the village of Newtonville in Newton, Massachusetts, and was developed by Austin Street Partners on a 99-year ground lease under a public/private partnership with the City of Newton.

Austin Street Partners is a joint venture of Oaktree Development, a long-time Boston area residential developer with expertise in modular housing, and Dinosaur Capital Partners, a Boston-based real estate investment, development, and advisory firm. Oaktree's principals are Arthur Klipfel and Gwen Noyes. Dinosaur's principals are Mark Dufton and Scott Oran. Oran, as a long-time Newton resident, became the face of the project's development team.

Newton is a suburban city of 88,000 just west of Boston comprising 13 villages, each with a distinct personality. Known as the Garden City, Newton developed as one of the country's earliest streetcar suburbs with scheduled rail service stopping in the village of Newtonville beginning in 1832. The Boston Marathon's famed Heartbreak Hill is on Newton's Commonwealth Avenue, an Olmsted-designed, winding, landscaped boulevard. With limited development opportunities and a stubbornly antigrowth tilt, median single-family-home prices exceeded $1 million by the end of 2013 and $1.43 million by 2021.

Despite rising single-family-home prices, Newton's villages struggled economically. In 2007, Newton's Comprehensive Plan first suggested that underutilized municipal parking lots in the villages could be an opportunity for redevelopment and village revitalization. Like many other American suburbs, the city had a regional mall and a number of shopping centers that threatened the street retail and vitality of its villages.

Oran was an active volunteer in Newton and from 2007 to 2009 served on the mayor's Citizens Advisory Group (CAG). Faced with rising municipal expenses and revenues capped by Massachusetts' Proposition 2½, the CAG sought to identify "tactics and strategies to improve the City's operational efficiency and effectiveness in future fiscal years."[1]

The CAG cited the Comprehensive Plan and identified a number of underutilized and deteriorating city-owned parking lots in village centers as opportunity sites to enhance the vitality of the city's villages and create new housing opportunities. The group also noted the potential for generating new municipal revenue and real estate taxes through sales to developers.

In 2012, the Newton Board of Aldermen (now Newton City Council) designated Newtonville's Austin Street Municipal Parking lot, with its aging 157 spaces, as surplus property and rezoned the site to allow for a five-story mixed-use development. Its location across the street from a commuter rail station, as well as a supermarket and drugstore and near numerous restaurants and shops made it an ideal transit-oriented development location. A request for proposals (RFP) was issued in 2012. The RFP required developers to make 25 percent of the apartments affordable to households earning no more than 80 percent of area median income.

Recalling the CAG's work and believing in its goals of revitalizing the city's villages, Oran helped form Austin Street Partners with Dinosaur and Oaktree to respond to the RFP. Utilizing Oaktree's expertise, the partnership proposed a sustainable, factory-built modular building that would minimize disruption to Newtonville during construction. In April 2013, five other private and nonprofit developers responded to the RFP as well. An advisory committee was established to vet the proposals and advise Newton's mayor.

In May 2014, Mayor Setti Warren called Oran to say, "We selected you but not your project." Oran says the Austin Street Partners "went on a listening tour for a year, meeting with various neighborhood groups and other stakeholders—both for and against. We mobilized affordable housing advocates, senior advocates, and environmental advocates to show their support for the project. We reduced the number of apartments from 80 to 68 and lowered the height from five stories to four stories, with one underground level of parking, and we added $400,000 in construction mitigation funds for off-site parking, interim bus services, and local business aid." When residents expressed continued concerns about the adequacy of the parking, the city required that the developer reconstruct 125 public parking spaces to replace the crumbling 157-space surface public parking lot, while building the four-story building above and a 90-space parking garage for residents below. In addition, 50 of the at-grade parking spaces had to be available throughout construction.

The land acquisition was structured as a 99-year ground lease from the city with a 99-year renewal option. The amount due at the beginning of construction was $1.05 million, plus $750,000 for municipal infrastructure improvements. Local pundits suggested that Austin Street Partners won the bid not only because the proposal promised the city $1.8 million while minimizing disruption through modular construction but also because Oran was viewed as "the local guy" who was known to and trusted by city officials.

Like all projects larger than 9,999 square feet (929 sq m) in Newton, the mixed-use redevelopment of the Austin Street municipal parking lot required a special permit, which in turn required a two-thirds vote—16 out of 24 city councilors. Thus, despite meeting the RFP requirements, conforming to all the city council's rezoning standards, and undertaking a year-long campaign to redesign the project to win public support, the project still needed the city council's approval. In May 2015, Austin Street Partners applied for a special permit to build the apartments.

28 Austin Street in Newton, Massachusetts, is a transit-oriented, energy-efficient, mixed-income apartment building. Amenities include a fourth-floor outdoor common deck with room for parties. The 350 solar panels installed on the roof provide electricity for all the common areas and reduce the electricity consumption in the units by 50 to 60 percent.

The application turned out to be very controversial. The 28 Austin Street project became the fulcrum of the debate over what kind of city Newton should be. Contentious public hearings dragged on for seven months. Like many suburbs, Newton had been very restrictive on new rental housing. In a city with over 32,000 housing units, only 80 apartments had been approved in the prior 10 years. With little new housing production, the city's stock of affordable housing remained stubbornly below the state's 10 percent minimum. But Newton's residents were getting older and housing more expensive. With median home prices over $1 million, there were few good alternatives for residents wanting to downsize from their large single-family homes or for young people just starting out.

At a December 2015 city council meeting, which ran almost until midnight, Austin Street Partners finally got 17 votes to approve a special permit—but only after agreeing to a last-minute demand to increase the percentage of affordable apartments to 33 percent (23) from the 25 percent (17) required in the city's own zoning and RFP. After three years of work, Austin Street Partners faced certain failure unless they secured the special permit. Oran says, "We decided to throw a Hail Mary pass and agreed to an increase to 33 percent affordable." That meant adding six more affordable dwelling units than budgeted and taking at least $1.2 million out of the project's value. They were no longer sure if the project was

financially feasible or financeable. But, at least, Oran recalls, "We got to live for another day."

Affordable-housing advocates were upset that Austin Street Partners was setting a bad precedent that would lead to fewer apartments in the long term because the higher requirement was uneconomical. Disgruntled opponents of the project—despite winning the concession—challenged the special permit and sued the city. It took until May 2017 to settle the case.

Rob Gifford, former chief executive of AIG Global Real Estate, who also lives in Newton, says "NIMBYs will rarely say they are against affordable housing. But they say we should not let for-profit developers build luxury housing along with the affordable units. However, nonprofit developers have not been getting it built in Newton."[2] Gifford explains that nonprofit developers are building small projects with a few units here or there, but they are not able to assemble enough capital to build larger projects. He states, "There are only two ways to do it—building a market-rate project where you can subsidize 20 percent of the units to be affordable, or assembling enough capital through a mix of federal, state, and local subsidy programs, all of which are in short supply."

In the interim, Austin Street Partners got a lucky break. Massachusetts Governor Charlie Baker had created a Workforce Housing Fund, and they received a commitment for a $1.3 million,

40-year, zero-interest loan. This funding filled the gap created by the city council's last-minute demand for additional affordable units.

Following settlement of the special permit lawsuit in May 2017, Austin Street Partners moved quickly to finish construction drawings, select a general contractor, and finance the project. Construction finally began in early 2018—five years after the firm had responded to the city's RFP.

MODULAR CONSTRUCTION FROM CANADA

To minimize disruption in a busy village center, Austin Street Partners had committed to build a modular project rather than a conventional stick-built project using a factory in Quebec, Canada, that "promised to save time but not construction cost per square foot."[3]

While the modular boxes were being planned and manufactured in Canada, site work began in Newtonville. Because Austin Street Partners had agreed to maintain 50 public parking spaces on site throughout construction, a complex phasing plan was created. First, concrete footings were poured and then paved over to allow for parking on the rear third of the site. Then a massive 90-car garage in a 30,000-square-foot (2,787 sq m) basement was excavated and constructed. Finally, a post-tensioned concrete slab was constructed at the first and second floors that would form a podium for the modular construction.

While on-site construction quality was good, a tight labor market slowed the exacting post-tension concrete work for the foundation and podium, and that work took longer than anticipated. Hence, the erection of the modular boxes was delayed, reducing the expected time-savings advantage.

The modular units are wedding-cake slices through the building—about 65 feet (20 m) long by 14 feet (4 m) wide. Each modular unit might contain a bedroom and bathroom of one apartment, plus a common hallway, and a kitchen, dining room, and living room of another apartment. In the climate-controlled factory the length of a football field, each box moves along an assembly line, starting with a robotic nailer to create a floor and walls and ending with fully finished rooms. When the modular boxes leave the factory, they are fully painted, with finished flooring, complete bathrooms with fixtures, and kitchens with counters and cabinets. Everything is complete except grout for the tile. When erected on site, each modular box—with two sets of structure for walls, floors, and ceiling—is twice as strong as conventional construction. And the double wall and floor construction allow for very little sound transmission.

Transporting 65-foot-long slivers of apartments across international borders, however, is not without challenges. Canadian and U.S. standards differ. The developer viewed 9-foot (2.7 m) ceilings as an important U.S. market requirement. Taller ceilings make smaller apartments feel more spacious and are uniformly provided in luxury buildings. Unfortunately, Canadian modular transport trailers with more sophisticated suspension are a foot taller than American trailers, seemingly making 9-foot ceilings too tall for highway transport in Massachusetts. The developer was forced to survey every highway bridge and hire a consultant to convince the Massachusetts Department of Transportation to change its outdated regulations regarding the maximum height of modular homes permitted on Massachusetts highways. The developer also had to hire separate police details to accompany the trailers through each state. And because the factory, due to manufacturing expediency, does not build the boxes in the same order they must be erected, the developer was forced to rent and improve a one-acre staging area in an adjacent town to accommodate the inventory, storage, and preparation of the modular units prior to their erection on site.

The first two (out of a total 105) units arrived with cracks. The suspension on the trailers was adjusted for a smoother ride over rutted winter roads, and that problem was solved.

The promise of modular construction is that you do the same thing over and over. But if there is a problem, it also gets repeated over and over. With a tight schedule, the factory unfortunately had quality control issues.

The biggest problem was that the heating, ventilation, and air conditioning subcontractor at the factory did not follow the architect's specifications and installed flexible round ducts rather than rigid square ducts. The flexible ducts in several units got crushed or torn during construction, constricting or disrupting the airflow for heating and cooling. When testing in the field revealed insufficient air flow, the finished ceilings in multiple units had to be cut open to identify the problems and fix them; then the ceilings had to be repaired and repainted.

Likewise, the developer asked the architect to replace the originally specified 30- by 60-inch (76 by 152 cm) tubs in the master bedroom bathrooms of two-bedroom apartments with more marketable showers. The shower basins were also nominally 30 by 60 inches, but when finished with wallboard and tile, the clearance was reduced to less than 30 inches. State code requires 30 inches of clearance. While the state's third-party inspector signed off on the change in the Quebec factory (the state hires third parties to inspect the modular boxes in the factory), the local building inspector refused to acknowledge the state approval. The developer sought a variance from the state's plumbing board but lost. The remedy was to spend $60,000 to build wider thresholds for each shower to achieve the required clearance.

Another inspection problem arose when the project's energy efficient European casement windows did not meet Newton's newly adopted fire egress code. The new code requires windows to have a four-inch (10 cm) opening limit so children cannot fall out, but they also must be able to open fully for fire escape. The fix was for the manufacturer to ship overnight and install newly designed quick-release child-proof latches in all bedrooms.

Antonio Tenreiro, project executive with NEI General Contracting, was the general contractor (GC) for the project. This was the firm's sixth modular project. He says, "The customized unit layout increased the complexity of mechanical design and coordination for this project."[4] He notes that the biggest lesson learned from the project has to do with how a contract for the modular units is negotiated: in this case the ownership team negotiated the contract and then passed it to the construction team. He says, "If the developer wants to do a modular contract, you must allow the general contractor to negotiate, or be in the negotiations, so that there are no construction issues that arise later in regard to scope or materials bought." NEI faced a multitude of change orders for items they felt were not 100 percent negotiated.

A second takeaway pertains to the schedule. The average developer for modular systems should expect to budget 6 to 8 months lead time for systems to be delivered after negotiation of the contract. The timing depends on the quality of the drawings and engineering specifications. The GC also needs time with the architects and engineers to work through how everything is going to fit perfectly before the modular systems begin production. Shipping from Canada added numerous complications. The Canadian modular company took delivery of the modular units at a satellite site that the developer procured in a neighboring town and then delivered them to the 28 Austin Street site.

Third, it is worth spending the money to have an on-site quality control person at the factory while the modules are being made. Fourth, the GC's involvement earlier in the design process can help ensure that everything will fit together properly. This project involved two design firms (one for the wood-framed modular units and one for everything outside the modular units) and two engineering firms—which could have been better coordinated. Fifth, modular construction promises to save time but requires much greater coordination compared with more typical panelized construction or a stick-framed building. For example, everything in the modular boxes is predrilled and precut. This level of coordination takes a long time. Everything must go right for modular projects to deliver the time savings. If something goes wrong, one may need to wait for another shipment. NEI has yet to see the promised time savings after six projects.

BUDGET

The original 2013 budget for construction was $17.2 million with an $815,000 owner's contingency. By the time a guaranteed maximum price contract was signed in 2018, the budget had grown to $22.95 million with a $1.65 million contingency. With required change orders, the total came to almost $24.6 million and used the full contingency. The modular unit building cost went from $7.85 million in the 2018 budget to $8.5 million with change

orders (about one-third of the total construction cost or $125,000 per unit). While the $800,000 in change orders to the modular units was the largest use of the contingency, other charges included higher-than-anticipated costs for disposal of contaminated soil, common area upgrades, and unbudgeted retail tenant buildouts.

To reduce costs, the developer decided to eliminate a common landscaped deck over municipal parking on the sunny south side of the building and converted planned balconies to "Juliet-style" balconies on all but four of the most expensive top-floor units.

As a side note, Tenreiro says two of the trades at 28 Austin were union, and the rest were nonunion. "It wasn't a big deal working union and nonunion trades on the same job."

AMENITIES

Amenities include a library, conference room, dining room, living room with big screen television, and a fourth-floor outdoor common deck with room for parties. The 350 solar panels installed on the roof provide electricity for all the common areas and reduce the electricity consumption in the units by 50 to 60 percent.

The package room has a Butterfly security system with keypad controls. Delivery people have passcodes from the property manager to access the room. Cameras record who enters the room in case someone takes the wrong package.

Parking includes 90 secure underground spaces, including 14 electric vehicle chargers for residents' exclusive use, and 125 public spaces at grade.

The southern exposure is more valuable than the northern exposure, and corner units rent for more.

LESSONS LEARNED

Paying for a full-time quality control person in the modular factory is worthwhile. Production took only six weeks so the payback would have more than covered the cost.

Timing for lease-up is critical for success. Leasing in greater Boston is seasonal, with highest demand and rents over the summer and early fall when more than 150,000 students return annually. Rents decrease and lease-up velocity is slower through late fall and winter and only recovers in spring. Leasing slows dramatically from Thanksgiving until March.

[1] City of Newton, "Citizen Advisory Group Named to Study Newton Finances," press release, May 13, 2008, https://www.newtonma.gov/home/showpublisheddocument?id=21685.

[2] Robert Gifford, Newton, Massachusetts, interview by Richard Peiser, October 20, 2019.

[3] Scott Oran, interview by Richard Peiser, October 18, 2019.

[4] Antonio Tenreiro, interview by Julian Huertas, February 12, 2020.

FIGURE 4-2

Typical Development Period and the Operating Period for a Project in Dallas, Texas

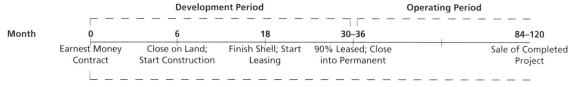

Just as the architect draws many versions of a building before settling on the final design, the developer goes through many iterations of Stage 2 analysis to obtain better information. In the first iteration, rents, expenses, costs, and other assumptions are crude estimates based on cursory evaluation. By the time the developer is ready to commit to the earnest money contract (that is, remove any contingencies that would allow the return of the full purchase deposit on the land), the analysis should have provided the best information possible about the property's expected performance. This information is the basis for computing expected returns to the developer and investors—assuming the property is purchased at the specified price. If the property is to be built, then the total all-in estimated project cost from inception to stabilized occupancy is used instead of the purchase price.

The stages of analysis correspond to major hurdles in the course of financing a project. Stage 1 is the

multiperiod cash flow analysis, and *justified investment price analysis*. Appraisers do a form of Stage 2 analysis when they compute the unleveraged returns on a building for the operating period—from the time of stabilized occupancy to final sale in seven or 10 years.[45]

Distinguishing the development period from the operating period can be helpful (figure 4-2). The development period runs from the time the developer purchases the land through lease-up of the property. The operating period begins when the property is put into service, but appraisers and lenders typically evaluate the property from the time it reaches stabilized occupancy, normally 90 or 95 percent (5-10 percent vacant), to the time of assumed sale, usually seven or 10 years. The permanent mortgage is typically funded during the stabilized occupancy period (although in some cases it may be funded in stages during lease-up). Stage 2 analysis is used to evaluate this operating period. It is the developer's version of the architect's sketch pad.

FIGURE 4-3A

Stage 1a: Rental and Sales Revenue Summary

Apartment Unit Types	No. of Units	Monthly Rent/sq ft	Area/Unit (sq ft)	Total Area (sq ft)	Monthly Rent Per Unit	Annual Rent Total
Market-Rate Apartments	45	$4.25	896	40,320	$3,808	$2,056,320
Affordable Apartments	23	$1.90	896	20,608	$1,702	$469,862
Total Apartment Gross Rental Revenue	**68**	**$3.46**	**896**	**60,928**	**$3,096**	**$2,526,182**
Other Rental Revenue[a]						$27,000
Miscellaneous Revenue[b]						$12,240
Total Property Revenue	**68**	**$3.51**	**896**	**60,928**	**$3,096**	**$2,565,422**

Condominium Retail	No. of Units	Sales/sq ft	Area/Unit (sq ft)	Total Area (sq ft)	Sales Per Unit	Annual Sales Total
Condominium Retail[c]	2	$300.00	2,500	5,000	$750,000	$1,500,000
Total Sales Revenue	**2**	**$300.00**	**2,500**	**5,000**	**$750,000**	**$1,500,000**

[a]Other Rental Revenue includes additional revenue derived from leasing space at the property. Examples of Other Rental Revenue include rent for parking, rooftop telecommunication devices, storage space, and billboards. Specific to this analysis, Other Rental Revenue is based on income generated from 15 of the 90 parking spaces at $150 per space per month.

[b]Miscellaneous Revenue includes additional revenue as a result of conducting daily business activities. Examples of Miscellaneous Revenue include late fees and penalties, forfeiture of deposits, and lost key fees. Specific to this analysis, Miscellaneous Revenue is estimated to equal $25 per unit per month.

[c]Underwriting note: for purposes of demonstration, this analysis assumes that the two retail spaces are presold as condominium units to retail end users.

developer's cursory analysis based on simple pro forma income and cost estimates. Stage 2 justifies the overall value of the investment as an operating real estate venture and is given to mortgage brokers and lenders who will provide permanent financing. Stage 3 gives the developer a picture of the overall development, from inception through final sale. Stage 4 goes to the construction lender to support the estimated construction loan and the size of the interest reserves during construction and lease-up. Stage 5 is given to potential investors in support of the returns they will receive if they invest in the property under a specific deal structure.

STAGE 1—SIMPLE CAPITALIZATION. Figures 4-3 to 4-9 illustrate the stages of analysis for 28 Austin Street, a 68-unit apartment building in Newton, Massachusetts. The project includes 45 market-rate apartments, 23 affordable apartments, 5,000 square feet (464.5 sq m) of first-floor retail, 90 underground parking spaces for residents, rooftop solar, a landscaped public plaza, and 125 at-grade municipal parking spaces. The Stage 1 analysis consists of five subparts beginning with the rental summary, loan computation, and development cost, and ending with the simple return computations.

FIGURE 4-3B — Stage 1b: Pro Forma NOI

	Factor	Annual Revenue/Cost
Gross Potential Revenue[a]		$2,526,182
Less: Vacancy	5.00%	($126,309)
Less: Bad Debt	0.25%	($6,315)
Add: Other Rental Revenue		$27,000
Add: Miscellaneous Revenue		$12,240
Effective Gross Revenue		**$2,432,798**
Operating Expenses[b]		
Property Management	3.00% of Effective Gross Revenue	$72,984
Controllable Costs[c]	$4,379 per unit	$297,800
Real Estate Taxes	1.13% of 75% of cost before int and reserve	$251,600
Insurance	$250 per unit	$17,000
Utilities	$250 per unit	$17,000
Replacement Reserve	$150 per unit	$10,200
Total Operating Expenses	$9,803	$666,584
Net Operating Income		**$1,766,214**

[a]Gross Potential Revenue is provided in more detail by the Rental and Sales Revenue Summary exhibit, excluding Other Rental Revenue and Miscellaneous Revenue. Vacancy and Bad Debt are customary deductions to gross revenue.

[b]Customary operating expense items have been shown. "Per unit" expense items are applied against the number of apartment units. Real Estate Taxes are based on 75 percent of the estimated Total Development Cost before Interest and Reserve, excluding the Condominium Retail. The Tax Rate is a close approximation of the rate stipulated by the municipality.

[c]Controllable costs typically include salaries and administrative, marketing, and maintenance expenses.

> **All spreadsheets in chapter 4 are available online in supplemental materials at americas.uli.org/PRED.**

FIGURE 4-3C — Stage 1c: Maximum Loan Calculation

MAXIMUM LOAN CALCULATION FOR INCOME PROPERTY, APARTMENTS ONLY	
Pro Forma Net Operating Income (NOI) and Value	
Pro Forma NOI[a]	$1,766,214
Capitalization Rate	5.50%
Value of Income Property Only (NOI / Cap Rate)	**$32,112,980**
Loan Terms	
Interest Rate	4.00%
Amortization (years)	30
(i) Loan Based on Loan to Value (LTV)	
Maximum LTV Percentage per Lender[b]	60.00%
Maximum Loan Based on LTV for Income Property	**$19,267,788**
(ii) Loan Based on Debt Coverage Ratio (DCR)	
Monthly NOI	$147,184
Maximum DCR per Lender	1.20
Portion of NOI to cover Debt Service (NOI/DCR/12)	$122,654
Maximum Loan Based on DCR Stipulated NOI	**$25,691,205**
MAXIMUM LOAN CALCULATION FOR TOTAL PROJECT	
Maximum Loan (Lesser of LTV or DCR)[c]	
Maximum Loan for Income Property, lesser of (i) or (ii)	$19,267,788
Add: Loan for Condominium Retail[d]	$975,000
Add: Development Subsidy Loan[e]	$1,300,000
Total Project Loan	**$21,542,788**

[a]The pro forma NOI figure is provided in figure 4-3b and does not include any revenues from the condominiums.

[b]It is also customary for the Maximum Loan based on the LTV percentage to be compared to the project or acquisition cost.

[c]In the typical valuation of pure income properties, the maximum debt calculation ends with selecting the lesser of the two loan values, one based on LTV and the other on DCR.

[d]For purposes of this analysis, the Condominium Retail is assumed to be financed with a loan equal to 65 percent of the total Sales Revenue.

[e]Specific to this development case, the developer was able to secure an additional 40-year, zero-interest loan as a result of providing apartment units affordable to households earning 80 percent of the area median income.

FIGURE 4-3D Stage 1d: Development Costs

	Project Description			Total	Apartments	Retail
1	Project Description			Total	Apartments	Retail
2	Number of Units			70	68	2
3	Site Area			74,480		
4	Square Footage – Net Rentable			65,928	60,928	5,000
5	Square Footage – Common Areas			15,912	15,912	0
6	Square Footage – Parking			60,754	60,754	0
7	Square Footage – Total			142,594	137,594	5,000
8	*Percentage of Total Square Footage*			*100%*	*96%*	*4%*
9	Development Costs[a]					
10	Land	$14.10	per site sq ft	1,050,000	1,013,182	36,818
11	Impact Fees – Off-site Utilities per Municipality			750,000	723,702	26,298
12	Extraction Fees – Municipal Parking, Open Space per Municipality			850,000	820,195	29,805
13	Environmental Remediation	$2.00	per site sq ft	148,960	143,737	5,223
14	Construction Hard Cost	$160	per gross sq ft	22,815,040	22,015,040	800,000
15	Hard Cost Contingency	7.00%	of hard cost	1,597,053	1,541,053	56,000
16	Soft Costs:					
17	Architecture and Engineering	6.00%	of hard cost	1,368,902	1,320,902	48,000
18	Developer Overhead and Fee	5.00%	of hard cost	1,140,752	1,100,752	40,000
19	Legal, Permits, and Other Fees	3.00%	of hard cost	684,451	660,451	24,000
20	General and Administrative/Marketing	1.00%	of hard cost	228,150	220,150	8,000
21	Taxes during Construction, estimate			100,000	96,494	3,506
22	Insurance during Construction, estimate			50,000	48,247	1,753
23	Total Soft Costs			3,572,256	3,446,996	125,260
24	**Total Development Cost before Interest and Operating Reserve**			**$30,783,309**	**$29,703,905**	**$1,079,404**
25	**Estimate of Development Subsidy Loan Interest[b]**					
26	Development Subsidy Loan	$1,300,000		1,300,000	$1,300,000	0
27	Construction Loan Interest Rate	0.00%				
28	Construction Period (months)	12				
29	Average Draw	55.00%				
30	Estimated Construction Loan Interest			0	0	0

Stage 1a—Rental and Sales Revenue Summary. Stage 1 analysis is used to develop the two simple return measures common to all income properties—overall capitalization rates and cash-on-cash returns. To compute these ratios, begin by projecting NOI, project development costs, and leverage (maximum mortgage amount) for the proposed project. Figure 4-3a shows the rental and sales revenue summary. For 28 Austin Street, the 45 market-rate apartments rent for $4.25 per square foot or $3,800 per unit for an 896-square-foot (83 sq m) average-sized unit. Rent on the retail space is $25.00 per square foot ($269/sq m) per year. Based on the rent potential, the two retail spaces were sold as condominium units for $750,000 each, or $300 per square foot ($3,229/sq m).

Stage 1b—Pro Forma NOI. The first step is to create a pro forma statement that estimates rents and expenses for the stabilized project. Inputs include the types and sizes of apartments to be built and market rents for the apartments (see figure 4-3b). The other needed inputs are estimated vacancy rate and operating expenses. Both income and expense estimates should reflect any specific features of the project and local conditions as they will be at the time leasing begins; for example, if the project is expected to require a year to design and build, then rents and expenses should be projected for a year later. For 28 Austin Street, the pro forma indicates total income of $2,432,798 and NOI of $1,766,214 (see figure 4-3b).

Stage 1c—Maximum Debt Calculation. The project's pro forma NOI is the basis for determining the size of the permanent mortgage. Lenders use two common criteria to determine the maximum loan amount: debt coverage ratio (DCR) and loan-to-value

31	**Estimate of Construction Loan Interest**				
32	Construction Loan	$20,242,788	20,242,788	$19,267,788	975,000
33	Construction Loan Interest Rate	4.75%			
34	Construction Period (months)	12			
35	Average Draw	55.00%			
36	Estimated Construction Loan Interest		528,843	503,371	25,472
37	**Total Loan Interest Reserve**		**$528,843**	**$503,371**	**$25,472**
38	**Estimate of Operating Reserve**[c]				
39	i Gross Potential Rent (monthly)	210,515			
40	ii Operating Expense (monthly)	−55,549			
41	iii Construction Interest (monthly)	−80,128			
42	iv Monthly Cash Burn Rate (ii + iii)	−135,676			
43	v Break-even Occupancy [iv / i]	64.4%			
44	vi Lease-up Months until Stabilization	12			
45	vii Monthly Vacancy Absorption Rate [1 / vi]	8.33%			
46	viii Lease-up Months until Break-even [v / vii]	8.00			
47	**Total Operating Reserve[d] [iv * viii / 2]**	542,705	542,705	542,705	0
48	**Total Development Costs**		**$31,854,857**	**$30,749,981**	**$1,104,876**

[a]The following outline of development costs includes customary expenses. For this analysis, the $1.05 million ground lease is simplified as the purchase cost of the land. Also, the development costs are allocated between the Apartments and Condominium Retail by percentage of area.

[b]This is a preliminary estimate of interest costs during the construction phase. A more accurate estimate will be made as part of the Stage 3 analysis and an even more accurate estimate would be appropriate for a Stage 4 analysis (not shown). The Development Subsidy Loan is included only for the sake of integrating the Subsidy Loan into the model; otherwise, it is a zero-interest loan and does not result in additional Interest Reserve needs.

[c]Establishing an Operating Reserve is customary practice in the early Stage 1 analysis and presented here for illustrative purposes. Operating Reserve represents the maximum amount that would be required to cover Operating Expense and Construction Interest before the project reaches Break-even Occupancy. Operating Expenses are given in the pro forma. Construction Interest is calculated based on the assumption that the Construction Loan is fully drawn and the Interest Rate is constant. Break-even Occupancy is the percentage derived by taking the sum of the Operating Expenses and Construction Interest (the Cash Burn Rate) divided by the Gross Potential Rent. Then, the months to reach Break-even (line 46) is derived by performing the following calculations: first, input the number of months required to reach full occupancy, or Lease-up Months until Stabilization (line 44); then calculate the monthly vacancy absorption rate by taking the inverse of the Lease-up Months until Stabilization, that is, 1/12 = 8.33% absorption per month as shown here (line 45); next, calculate the Lease-up Months until Break-even by dividing the Break-even Occupancy by the Monthly Vacancy Absorption Rate, that is, 64.4% / 8.33% = 7.44, rounded up to 8 months (line 46). This is the number of months required to reach Break-even Occupancy. (Note that this method assumes vacancy is absorbed in a straight-line fashion, month-over-month.) Finally, to arrive at the Operating Reserve, take one-half of the product of the Cash Burn Rate and the number of months required to reach Break-even, 50% of (135,676 x 8 months) = 542,705 (line 47).

[d]Operating Reserve is calculated as the product of the Monthly Cash Burn Rate and the Lease-up Months until Break-even.

(LTV) ratio. The maximum loan amount is the lesser of the amounts resulting from the two computations.

The DCR is a tool for measuring the financial risk of an investment. It is calculated by dividing NOI by the debt service for the project. A DCR of 1.0 means that NOI equals the debt service for the project. For income-producing properties, most lenders require a DCR of at least 1.2. The DCR represents the cushion by which the NOI could fall before the property had insufficient cash flow to pay the debt service on the mortgage. The greater the cushion, the less risk of default. Lenders want as much cushion as they can get. Developers prefer more leverage (as large a mortgage as they can get) because it reduces the equity requirement.

The NOI can be divided directly by the DCR to determine the maximum monthly mortgage payment that can be assumed for the loan. Given the lender's requirements for amortization and interest, it is then possible to calculate the maximum loan that could be serviced by the project's income, less the extra coverage. For 28 Austin Street, a DCR of 1.2 would allow monthly payments of $122,654 (monthly NOI divided by 1.2). Assuming an interest rate of 4.00 percent and 30-year amortization, the maximum loan a lender would allow is $25,691,205 (the present value of $122,654 for the given rate of interest and term (months):

$$PV\ (PMT - 122,654,\ i = 4.00/12,\ n = 30 \times 12)$$

To establish the maximum loan available using the LTV ratio, the first step is to determine the project's value, which is calculated by applying a capitalization rate to the pro forma NOI. The capitalization rate is determined by the market and by the recent selling price of similar properties. It reflects the relationship between a property's income and its value. The lender ultimately requires an appraisal to verify the income and assumptions about the capitalization rate used to establish the value. The value is then multiplied by the LTV ratio to determine the maximum loan amount. In this case, a capitalization rate of 5.50 percent yields a value of $32,112,980. With an assumed maximum LTV ratio of 60 percent, the most the lender will lend under the LTV constraint is $19,267,788.

Lenders typically look at both criteria when underwriting a loan and use the more restrictive one. When interest rates are low, LTV tends to be more restrictive; when interest rates are high, DCR tends to be more restrictive. In this example, LTV is more restrictive and the maximum loan on the property would be $19,267,788 for the apartment portion of the project (see figure 4-3c). Moreover, specific to 28 Austin Street, the retail condominium portion of the project is assumed to be financed at 65 percent of the expected condominium sale price, or $975,000. And the developer was able to obtain a zero-interest loan of $1,300,000 for providing 23 apartments at below-market rates, for tenants who earn 80 percent or less of the area median income. Together, the apartment, retail condominium, and subsidized development loans total $21,542,788.

Stage 1d—Development Costs. Development costs are the other part of the equation needed to evaluate a project's feasibility. An overall cost estimate for the project must be calculated. It should include the cost of acquiring the site, construction costs, and soft costs—such as legal and accounting fees, architecture and engineering, and contingencies. In addition, it should include financing costs during construction as well as interest and operating losses until the property reaches stabilized occupancy and the permanent mortgage is funded (taking out the construction loan). Eventually, the developer will have firm cost bids for building the project. The initial financial feasibility analysis, however, relies on the developer's experience from other similar projects and information provided by contractors and consultants.

Phil Hughes notes the risk of paying for completed architecture and engineering drawings to get a firm price when even partially completed drawings can run into $100,000s. Instead, his firm relies heavily on projects done recently, reliable subcontractors, and performance standards. Contractors typically work on the basis of a guaranteed maximum price (GMP); any savings are split (negotiated from 90/10 to 60/40),

with the majority going to the developer since the contractor is already receiving overhead and profit.

The costs should also include the developer's overhead and costs associated with the initial marketing and lease-up of the project. As an initial rough estimate, interest costs can be approximated by assuming an average draw and length of the loan.

The operating reserve during lease-up, yet another development cost, can be approximated by assuming a lease-up period and computing the rent lost from vacancies during that time. Computing the break-even occupancy of the income property is a useful first step. For 28 Austin Street, the monthly operating expenses and construction loan interest expenses sum to $135,676 per month. To cover this monthly cash burn and break even each month, the property would need to collect 64 percent of the gross potential rent. In turn, the 64 percent is the break-even occupancy rate. Next, based on market knowledge and a market study, the developer would determine the number of

FIGURE 4-3E ## Stage 1e: Summary Analysis and Simple Ratios

Net Operating Income (NOI)	1,766,214
Total Development Cost	31,854,857
Less: Development Cost of For-Sale Condominiums	*(1,104,876)*
Total Adjusted Cost for Income Property Only	30,749,981
Overall Return, Overall Cap Rate (NOI/Total Adjusted Cost)	**5.7%**
Net Operating Income	1,766,214
Annual Debt Service of Conventional Mortgage[a]	(1,103,848)
Annual Debt Service of Development Subsidy Loan[a]	(32,500)
Cash Throw-Off (CTO or before-tax cash flow)	629,865
Total Adjusted Cost for Income Property Only	30,749,981
Permanent Mortgage[b]	(19,267,788)
Development Subsidy Loan[b]	(1,300,000)
Equity	10,182,193
Cash-on-Cash Return (CTO/Equity)	**6.2%**
Development Profit for Apartments Only (w/o condominiums)	
Net Operating Income	1,766,214
Overall Cap Rate at Sale	5.50%
Capitalized Value (NOI/Cap Rate)	32,112,980
Less: Total Adjusted Cost	*(30,749,981)*
Development Profit	**1,362,999**

[a]Annual Debt Service reflects the total mortgage principal amount of $19,267,788, interest rate of 4.00%, and amortizing over 30 years as calculated in the Debt Calculation (figure 4-3c). Note that the Development Subsidy Loan, although a zero-interest loan, is amortizing over a 40-year period, resulting in an additional $32,500 in annual debt service expenses.
[b]Permanent Mortgage and the Development Subsidy Loan are presented in figure 4-3c, Maximum Loan Calculation.

months required to reach the break-even occupancy. Finally, assuming a straight-line absorption rate, the operating reserve is calculated by multiplying the number of months to break even and the monthly cash burn, then dividing the product in half.

Figure 4-3d shows total development costs for 28 Austin Street before interest and lease-up of $30,783,309 (line 24). With estimated interest during construction of $528,843 (line 37) and an operating reserve during lease-up of $542,705 (line 47), the total project costs sum to $31,854,857 (line 48).

Stage 1e—Simple Ratios. Stage 1 analysis is sometimes called a "back-of-the-envelope analysis" because the simple ratios, or returns, can literally be computed on the back of an envelope. Still, the overall return, or overall cap rate, (NOI divided by total project cost) and cash-on-cash return (cash flow after debt service divided by equity) are the two measures of return cited most commonly for income property. Historically, for an apartment project, cash-on-cash returns in excess of 10 percent are desirable. Initial cash-on-cash returns are often in the 6 percent range and, as inflation picks up, they may go even lower; developers will look to the future for higher cash flows and profit from sale of the complex. Again, the simple ratios are most appropriate for income producing assets, so it is important to adjust the inputs to isolate the income property from the for-sale condominiums. In the 28 Austin Street example, the cost of the condominiums is deducted to determine the net cost of the rental apartments (see figure 4-3e). Thus, the overall return is 5.7 percent ($1,766,214 ÷ $30,749,981). The cash-on-cash return is 6.2 percent ($629,865 ÷ $10,182,193). Both returns are on the low side, but the combination of the subsidies, additional cash flow from the for-sale condominiums, and the low interest rate environment makes the project more attractive. Figure 4-3e also shows development profit of $1,362,999, which represents the market value of the apartments at stabilized occupancy minus total project costs to reach that point.

In summary:

Total Apartment Project Cost (figure 4-3d)	$30,749,981
Less: Mortgage and Subsidy Loan (figure 4-3c)	$20,567,788
Equity	**$10,182,193**
NOI (figure 4-3b)	$1,766,214
Less: Debt Service of both Conventional and Subsidy Loans (figure 4-3e)	$1,136,348
Cash Flow after Debt Service	**$629,865**

Note: Numbers are rounded to the nearest dollar.

STAGE 2—DISCOUNTED CASH FLOW ANALYSIS.
Discounted cash flow analysis of the operating period is the most important of the five stages. Lenders, appraisers, and investors all use it to project returns of the proposed development. Even if the developer plans to sell the project as soon as it reaches stabilized occupancy, Stage 2 analysis is the most widely used methodology to evaluate an income property investment or development (see figure 4-4a).

To calculate operating cash flows, the pro forma NOI is projected over time, usually seven or 10 years, showing growth in both rents and expenses. In this case, both rents and expenses are assumed to increase at a rate of 3 percent per year. (Note that the numbers presented here were prepared before the startling jump in inflation to more than 8 percent in 2022 resulting from the war in Ukraine, COVID-related supply chain shortages, and the enormous fiscal stimuli from the Trump and Biden administrations).

At the end of Stage 2, three internal rates of return (IRRs) are computed—the unleveraged before-tax IRR, the leveraged before-tax IRR, and the leveraged after-tax IRR. These three IRRs, in addition to the two simple return measures for overall cap-rate and cash-on-cash return, constitute the five most important measures of project performance. Many investors also like to see the equity multiplier—the ratio of total undiscounted cash received divided by the equity.

Appraisers and many institutional investors focus on the unleveraged before-tax returns because those numbers give the "pure" real estate value of the property (without financing or income tax considerations). Pension fund retirement accounts do not pay taxes and often buy properties on an all-cash (unleveraged) basis. Both leveraged and unleveraged analysis can be done on the same spreadsheet simply by changing the assumptions about the mortgage and income taxes.

Developers use Stage 2 analysis to determine whether the proposed project offers an attractive rate of return. The DCF analysis is performed many times as more detailed and accurate information becomes available about design, development costs, and anticipated rents (see figure 4-4a). The initial runs of Stage 2 analysis may focus on the unleveraged returns for the project—the IRR on all-equity financing of total project cost, annual cash flows representing the full NOI (with no mortgage or debt service), and the adjusted sale price at the end of the seven-year holding period. The IRR represents the relationship between the present value of the cash flows from operations and sale, and the capital invested. Technically, it is the

HEATHER MARIE COLLINS

annual rate of return (discount rate) that equates the present value of the future cash flows with the initial investment. This return should range from about 10 to 15 percent, depending on the type of property, its location, and interest and inflation rates. (The higher the inflation rate, the higher the overall return.) The unleveraged rate of return takes into account the NOI for each year of ownership, starting from the time the building is fully occupied and ending with the sale of the project. The unleveraged (before-tax) return for 28 Austin Street is 8.83 percent (line 95), which is lower than the historical unleveraged IRRs for a project yet-to-be developed. Although the IRR is low, the low interest rate environment at the time generated extremely favorable leverage and very attractive cash-on-cash returns. IRR requirements change directly with changes in interest rates and inflation.[46]

Note that in the example, Stage 2 analysis begins *after* the building reaches stabilized occupancy. All the interest subsidies during lease-up are included in the to-tal investment cost. Alternatively, one could assume that Year 0 figures include only development costs through the end of construction—up to the certificate of occu-pancy—and Years 1 and 2 (if needed) are the lease-up years. In that case, the project does not reach stabilized income until Year 2 (see figure 4-5, Stage 3a Analysis). Vacancy rates are one minus the occupancy rates and would be inserted into the Stage 2 analysis for Years 1 and 2. The resulting negative cash flows are included in the Development Costs spreadsheet (see figure 4-3d) under Estimate of Operating Reserve (line 38).

Including lease-up in Stage 2 rather than in the total development costs lowers the apparent IRRs but makes it easier to see how different lease-up rates af-fect the cash flows during the lease-up period and the total development costs.[47] These nuances are incorpo-

Honoring the cultures forming a diverse area of Los Angeles, LA Plaza incorporates interpretive signs, cultural iconography, and traditional building materials in an urban mixed-use village. The development includes 355 multifamily units, of which 20 percent are affordable. The unit mix includes live/work lofts, studios, and one-, two-, and three-bedroom family-focused apartments. Amenities such as a dog park, a pool, a fitness center, a community lounge, and roof decks provide settings for social interaction and recreation.

rated explicitly into the more detailed analysis of Stage 3. In summary, operating reserves can be estimated during lease-up as part of the total development costs (figure 4-3d) or in Years 1 and 2 of the Stage 2 analy-sis through the vacancy rates.

Appraisers calculate the present value of the future cash flow stream at a discount rate determined by the market. The discount rate is used to convert future cash flows to a present value. It also represents the investor's required rate of return. The resulting present value represents the value today of the building once it is fully leased. The difference between the present value of future cash flows and the development cost is the developer's profit, also known as net present value (NPV). Using the NPV method of DCF analysis, a prospective investment must show a positive NPV to justify the investment. The unleveraged NPV of 28 Austin Street is $1,440,558 (figure 4-4a, line 96). This amount is the development profit for the project at time 0 (the present value), assuming that the unlever-aged rate of return in the marketplace is 8 percent. If the discount rate were lower, the development profit would be higher.

Aside from the NPV and IRR, developers are primar-ily interested in their return on equity. The return on equity is also expressed as a leveraged IRR and takes into account the financing (leverage) and personal income taxes of the owner/developer. Stage 2 analysis focuses on the returns on the project as a single, undivided investment with one individual (the owner/developer) putting up all the equity and receiving all the cash flows.

Figure 4-4a shows the leveraged analysis of the project with mortgage financing. Developers focus on the leveraged before-tax and after-tax returns on equity because investment in the project must compete with returns available from other investments, such as stocks and bonds. The Austin Street project's before-tax IRR is 16.39 percent (line 104), and the after-tax IRR is 13.60 percent (line 113). With low-risk money market accounts paying 1 to 3 percent in 2021, 28 Austin Street's return more than adequately compensates for the risk of to-be-developed real estate.

INCLUSION OF FOR-SALE UNITS IN STAGE 2 OF THE INCOME PROPERTY SPREADSHEETS.
Combining for-sale units with income property units significantly complicates the Stage 2 analysis. The combination is included here because such developments are increasingly common. The advantage of including for-sale units is that the sales bring in early cash flows that can significantly raise IRRs. The condominiums appear in several spreadsheets, including Stage 1a Rental and Sales Revenue Summary (figure 4-3a), Stage 1c Maximum Loan Calculation (figure 4-3c), Stage 1d Development Costs (figure 4-3d), Stage 2a Discounted Cash Flow (figure 4-4a), and Stage 2b Condominium Cash Flow (figure 4-4b).

Stage 2 uses the cost allocation from Development Costs for tax purposes. Only the apartment cost is used for the depreciable basis. (Cash flows from the sale of the condominiums are incorporated in the return calculations at the bottom of figure 4-4a). Figures for Sales Revenues, Before-Tax Cash Flow from Condominiums, and After-Tax Cash Flow from Condominiums are taken from figure 4-4b and included in the three IRR calculations. As already noted, 28 Austin Street would not be as good an investment if the for-sale condominiums were omitted.

WHEN TO DO STAGE 2 ANALYSIS.
The DCF analysis of a project should be updated at each of the following points:

1. **Before a developer submits the earnest money contract**—By setting up the DCF model at this stage, subsequent updates will be easy to accomplish. The purpose of the analysis at this stage is to reconfirm that the project is worth the time and investment required to proceed with the feasibility studies

In addition to the information used for Stage 1, the developer will need estimates of soft costs for financing points; interest; and legal, marketing, administrative, architecture, and engineering costs as well as estimates of the time to lease-up the project and vacancy rates for the initial operating years during the lease-up period.

2. **After a developer signs the earnest money contract but before going hard on the contract**—By this time, the developer should have formed a firm concept of the proposed project, including a site plan and a building program that defines the number of units obtainable, the mix of units, and average unit sizes. Equipped with information from market studies, the developer can arrive at detailed projections of rental income based on a breakdown of unit types and more accurate rents per unit.

The decision to go hard on the earnest money contract usually hinges on the findings of consultants' studies, especially those regarding soils, floodplains, utilities, easements, and zoning, which should uncover any factors that may affect what can be built and how much it will cost. This information is critical before the developer's at-risk investment is increased through nonrefundable earnest money.

3. **After a developer goes hard on the land purchase contract but before closing on the land**—The developer wants to accomplish as much as possible before having to close on the land. Ideally, the developer would like to have a tentative financing commitment. To produce both the mortgage brochure and the next iteration of the DCF, the following information is needed:

   » market studies that define unit mix, unit size, amenities, and rent per unit;
   » conceptual design drawings that have sufficient detail to be used to obtain construction cost estimates (often very difficult to produce before land closing without putting considerable dollars at risk); and
   » construction cost estimates from two or three general contractors (unless the developer has an in-house construction staff or a contractor as part of the team). For purposes of comparison, the contractors' bids should follow the 16 categories laid out on the standard form issued by the American Institute of Architects. The developer should be especially careful to specify what the bid will and will not include.

FIGURE 4-4A Stage 2a: Analysis, Discounted Cash Flow

1	Project Costs					Total	Apartments	Condominiums
2	Land Cost					$1,050,000	$1,013,182	$36,818
3	Total Dev Cost before Interest and Optg Reserve					$30,783,309	$29,703,905	$1,079,404
4	Total Construction Interest					$528,843	$503,371	$25,472
5	Total Operating Reserve					$542,705	$542,705	$0
6	Total Development Cost					$31,854,857	$30,749,981	$1,104,876
7	**Financing Assumptions**							
8	Equity					$10,312,069	$10,182,193	$129,876
9	Development Subsidy Loan[a]					$1,300,000	$1,300,000	$0
10	Interest Rate						0.00%	0.00%
11	Amortization						40	40
12	Annual Debt Service					$32,500	$32,500	$0
13	Mortgage Principal[a]					$20,242,788	$19,267,788	$975,000
14	Interest Rate						4.00%	4.00%
15	Amortization						30	30
16	Annual Debt Service					$1,159,706	$1,103,848	$55,858
17	**Depreciation Assumptions**							
18	Building Basis[b]					$30,804,857	$29,736,799	$1,068,058
19	Life (in years)					27.5		
20	Straight Line (calculated)					$1,120,177	$1,081,338	$0
21	**Alternate Project Cost Assumptions If Vacancy Is Overridden[c]**							
22	Total Dev Cost before Optg Reserve					$31,312,152	$30,207,276	$1,104,876
23	Equity					$9,769,364	$9,639,488	$129,876
24	Building Basis					$30,262,152	$29,194,094	$1,068,058
25	Straight Line					$1,061,603	$1,061,603	$0

26	**ANNUAL CASH FLOWS FOR APARTMENTS**		Year 1	Year 2	Year 3	Year 4	Year 5	Year 6	Year 7
27	*Input to override static vacancy[c]*		*0.0%*	*0.0%*					
28	Gross Potential Revenue	3.00% inflation	2,526,182	2,601,968	2,680,027	2,760,428	2,843,241	2,928,538	3,016,394
29	*Less: Vacancy*	5.00% vacancy	(126,309)	(130,098)	(134,001)	(138,021)	(142,162)	(146,427)	(150,820)
30	*Less: Bad Debt*	0.25% bad debt	(6,315)	(6,505)	(6,700)	(6,901)	(7,108)	(7,321)	(7,541)
31	Effective Gross Revenue		2,393,558	2,465,365	2,539,325	2,615,505	2,693,970	2,774,790	2,858,033
32	Total Operating Expenses	3.00% inflation	666,584	686,581	707,179	728,394	750,246	772,753	795,936
33	**Net Operating Income**		**1,726,974**	**1,778,783**	**1,832,147**	**1,887,111**	**1,943,724**	**2,002,036**	**2,062,097**
34	*Less: Annual Debt Service (see below)*		*(1,136,348)*	*(1,136,348)*	*(1,136,348)*	*(1,136,348)*	*(1,136,348)*	*(1,136,348)*	*(1,136,348)*
35	**Cash Flow after Debt / Before-Tax Operating Cash Flow**		**590,625**	**642,435**	**695,798**	**750,763**	**807,376**	**865,688**	**925,749**
36	*Less: Taxes (see below)*		—	—	—	—	*(50,880)*	*(89,900)*	*(118,499)*
37	**After-Tax Operating Cash Flow**		**590,625**	**642,435**	**695,798**	**750,763**	**756,496**	**775,787**	**807,249**
38	**DEVELOPMENT SUBSIDY LOAN CALCULATION**		Year 1	Year 2	Year 3	Year 4	Year 5	Year 6	Year 7
39	Beginning Balance		1,300,000	1,267,500	1,235,000	1,202,500	1,170,000	1,137,500	1,105,000
40	Ending Balance		1,267,500	1,235,000	1,202,500	1,170,000	1,137,500	1,105,000	1,072,500
41	Amortization of Principal		32,500	32,500	32,500	32,500	32,500	32,500	32,500
42	Interest Expense		—	—	—	—	—	—	—
43	**MORTGAGE CALCULATION FOR APARTMENTS**		Year 1	Year 2	Year 3	Year 4	Year 5	Year 6	Year 7
44	Beginning Balance		19,267,788	18,928,475	18,575,338	18,207,814	17,825,316	17,427,235	17,012,935
45	Ending Balance		18,928,475	18,575,338	18,207,814	17,825,316	17,427,235	17,012,935	16,581,756
46	Amortization of Principal		339,313	353,137	367,524	382,498	398,081	414,300	431,179
47	Interest Expense		764,536	750,712	736,324	721,351	705,767	689,549	672,669

48	DEPRECIATION CALCULATION FOR APARTMENTS	Year 1	Year 2	Year 3	Year 4	Year 5	Year 6	Year 7
49	Beginning Balance	29,736,799	28,655,461	27,574,123	26,492,785	25,411,446	24,330,108	23,248,770
50	*Less: Annual Depreciation*	(1,081,338)	(1,081,338)	(1,081,338)	(1,081,338)	(1,081,338)	(1,081,338)	(1,081,338)
51	Ending Balance	28,655,461	27,574,123	26,492,785	25,411,446	24,330,108	23,248,770	22,167,432
52	Cumulative Depreciation Taken	1,081,338	2,162,676	3,244,014	4,325,353	5,406,691	6,488,029	7,569,367
53	Cumulative Replacement/Capital Reserve (see below)	10,200	20,706	31,527	42,673	54,153	65,978	78,157
54	Remaining Book Value[d]	29,678,843	28,608,011	27,537,494	26,467,302	25,397,444	24,327,930	23,258,771
55	**INCOME TAX CALCULATION FOR APARTMENTS**	Year 1	Year 2	Year 3	Year 4	Year 5	Year 6	Year 7
56	Net Operating Income	1,726,974	1,778,783	1,832,147	1,887,111	1,943,724	2,002,036	2,062,097
57	*Add: Replacement/Capital Reserve*	10,200	10,506	10,821	11,146	11,480	11,825	12,179
58	*Deduct: Interest*	(764,536)	(750,712)	(736,324)	(721,351)	(705,767)	(689,549)	(672,669)
59	*Deduct: Depreciation*	(1,081,338)	(1,081,338)	(1,081,338)	(1,081,338)	(1,081,338)	(1,081,338)	(1,081,338)
60	Taxable Income/(Loss)	(108,700)	(42,761)	25,305	95,568	168,099	242,974	320,269
61	*Less: Passive Loss Offset[e]*	—	—	(25,305)	(95,568)	(30,587)	—	—
62	Taxable Income	—	—	—	—	137,512	242,974	320,269
63	*Cumulative Passive Loss Carryforward[e]*	(108,700)	(151,460)	(126,155)	(30,587)	—	—	—
64	*Annual Income Taxes* 37% rate	—	—	—	—	50,880	89,900	118,499

65	**SALE CALCULATION OF APARTMENTS**	Year 7
66	Cash Flow from Sale[f]	
67	Sale Price (cap rate applied to following year NOI) 5.50% cap rate	38,617,456
68	*Less: Commission* 1.50% rate	(579,262)
69	*Adjusted Sales Price*	38,038,194
70	*Less: Development Subsidy Loan*	(1,072,500)
71	*Less: Remaining Mortgage Balance*	(16,581,756)
72	Before-Tax Cash Flow from Sale[g]	20,383,937
73	*Less: Total Tax at Sale (recapture & capital gain, see below)*	(3,318,721)
74	After-Tax Cash Flow from Sale	17,065,216
75	**Tax Calculation of Sale**	
76	Adjusted Sales Price	38,038,194
77	*Less: Remaining Book Value[d]*	(23,258,771)
78	Total Taxable Gain	14,779,422
79	*Less: Passive Loss Carryforward[e]*	—
80	Total Net Taxable Gain	14,779,422
81	Recapture Gain	7,569,367
82	(i) Tax on Recapture 25% rate	1,892,342
83	Total Capital Gain	7,210,055
84	*Deduct: Capital Reserves*	(78,157)
85	Net Capital Gain[g]	7,131,898
86	(ii) Tax on Capital Gain 20% rate	1,426,380
87	Total Tax at Sale (i + ii)	3,318,721

> **All spreadsheets in chapter 4 are available online in supplemental materials at americas.uli.org/PRED.**

179

FIGURE 4-4A Stage 2a: Analysis, Discounted Cash Flow | CONTINUED

	Investment Year 0	Year 1	Year 2	Year 3	Year 4	Year 5	Year 6	Year 7
88 **RETURN MEASURES**								
89 **Unleveraged IRR**								
90 Development Cost	($31,854,857)							
91 For-Sale Revenues[f]		1,455,000						
92 Net Operating Income		1,726,974	1,778,783	1,832,147	1,887,111	1,943,724	2,002,036	2,062,097
93 Adjusted Sales Price								38,038,194
94 Unleveraged Cash Flow	($31,854,857)	$3,181,974	$1,778,783	$1,832,147	$1,887,111	$1,943,724	$2,002,036	$40,100,291
95 **Unleveraged IRR**	8.83%							
96 **Net Present Value @ 8.0%[g]**	$1,440,558							
97 **Equity Multiple**	1.66							
98 **Before-Tax IRR**								
99 Equity	($10,312,069)							
100 Before-Tax Cash Flow from Condominiums[f]		454,528						
101 Before-Tax Operating Cash Flow		590,625	642,435	695,798	750,763	807,376	865,688	925,749
102 Before-Tax Cash Flow from Sale								20,383,937
103 Total Before-Tax Cash Flow	($10,312,069)	$1,045,154	$642,435	$695,798	$750,763	$807,376	$865,688	$21,309,686
104 **Before-Tax IRR**	16.39%							
105 **Net Present Value @ 12.0%**	$2,641,758							
106 **Equity Multiple**	2.53							
107 **After-Tax IRR**								
108 Equity	($10,312,069)							
109 After-Tax Cash Flow from Condominiums[f]		324,982						
110 After-Tax Operating Cash Flow		590,625	642,435	695,798	750,763	756,496	775,787	807,249
111 After-Tax Cash Flow from Sale								17,065,216
112 Total After-Tax Cash Flow	($10,312,069)	$915,608	$642,435	$695,798	$750,763	$756,496	$775,787	$17,872,465
113 **After-Tax IRR**	13.60%							
114 **Net Present Value @ 12.0%**	$896,851							
115 **Equity Multiple**	2.17							
116 **Simple Return Measures**		Year 1	Year 2	Year 3	Year 4	Year 5	Year 6	Year 7
117 NOI/Adjusted Project Cost Excluding For-Sale Condos		5.6%	5.8%	6.0%	6.1%	6.3%	6.5%	6.7%
118 Before-Tax Cash Flow / Equity		5.7%	6.2%	6.7%	7.3%	7.8%	8.4%	9.0%
119 Tax Shelter/Equity		0.0%	0.0%	0.2%	0.9%	0.3%	0.0%	0.0%

[a] The Development Subsidy Loan and Mortgage Principal are presented in figure 4-3c. The condominum mortgage is for the construction loan. From the developer's perspective, the condominium is sold for cash.

[b] The Building Basis is the difference between the total project cost and the land value.

[c] If the user wants to incorporate vacancy rates during lease-up directly into a spreadsheet, the user may do so by entering the vacancy rates in line 27 for year 1 and year 2. If these cells are not zero, then Total Development Cost, Equity, and Building Basis are taken from lines 22–24.

[d] For this analysis, a simplifying assumption has been made that the yearly replacement/capital reserve (shown as being included in the operating expenses in figure 4-3b) are accumulated during the hold period and spent on capital needs immediately before the sale of the property. Consequently, the replacement/capital reserve amount spent on capital needs is not depreciated. The amount is added to the Remaining Book Value at the time of sale, thereby reducing the estimated capital gains from the sale of the property.

[e] Current tax regulations treat real estate investments as a passive activity for non–real estate investors. As a result, tax losses in real estate are considered passive income losses and can only be taken against other passive income (with minor adjustments for small investors). In the event that an investor does not have any passive income, the passive losses are carried forward until they can be used against future passive income. For more information, see William B. Brueggeman and Jeffrey Fisher, *Real Estate Finance and Investments*, 13th ed. (New York: McGraw-Hill, 2010).

[f] Cash flows related to the sales and profit of the For-Sale Condominiums are calculated separately and shown in figure 4-4b. Note that For-Sale Revenues is net of brokerage commissions.

[g] Net Present Value equals the discounted present value of future cash flows, less the initial investment. Note that the Stage 2 analysis assumes all equity is invested at the beginning of the project.

FIGURE 4-4B

Stage 2b: Analysis, For-Sale Condominium Cash Flow

Cash Flow Determination for Condominiums

Sales Revenues	1,500,000
Less: Commissions	*(45,000)*
Less: Condominium Releases to Lender	*(975,000)*
Less: Interest Paid	*(25,472)*
Before-Tax Cash Flow	454,528
Less: Taxes	*(129,546)*
After-Tax Cash Flow	324,982

Mortgage Info for Condominium Retail[a]

Borrowings/Releases	975,000
Interest Owed	25,472

Tax Determination for Condominiums

Sales Revenue	1,500,000
Less: Commissions, 3%	*(45,000)*
Less: Development Costs and Expenses[b]	*(1,104,876)*
Profit	350,124
Tax Rate	37.0%
Tax Liability	129,546

[a]This analysis assumes that the condominiums are effectively presold and the Construction Loan is repaid upon completion. The Interest Owed is calculated in figure 4-4a.

[b]For this analysis, expenses pertaining to the marketing and sales of the condominiums have been accounted for as a development cost.

In today's lengthy approvals environment, accomplishing all the above is increasingly difficult if not impossible before closing on the land.

STAGE 3—COMBINED ANALYSIS OF THE DEVELOPMENT AND OPERATING PERIODS. Before making a firm commitment on the earnest money, the developer should compute a more refined estimate of cash flows during the development period and the operating period. Stage 3 analysis provides measures of return for the entire life of the proposed project and is therefore more accurate than Stage 2. Stage 2 assumes that equity is invested at the time of stabilized occupancy, whereas in fact it must be invested before construction begins. Because the time frame is extended one to two years before Stage 2 analysis and the initial years produce little if any cash flow, the IRRs for Stage 3 are necessarily lower than for Stage 2. Nevertheless, they represent the most accurate picture of how the project will perform.

Stage 3 evaluates cash flows quarterly during the development period, taking into account the anticipated construction schedule and projected monthly lease-up rate. It also shows when equity and debt funds will be needed and how long they will accrue interest before the project's cash flow can support the debt service. In the 28 Austin Street example, costs are projected quarter by quarter.

Stage 3 is the most complicated of the spreadsheets presented here. It has three parts. Figure 4-5 shows the quarterly cash flows during the development period (construction and lease-up). Figure 4-6 shows the sources and uses of cash accumulated by year for the development period. It summarizes project costs and separates the capitalized costs from the first-year operating losses. Both are project costs that need to be funded, but they are treated differently when calculating income taxes: operating losses after the certificate of occupancy is received are deductible, while capital costs are not. Total project cost, total capital cost, depreciable basis, operating reserves, and cash resulting from the permanent loan takeout are inputs to figure 4-7. Figure 4-7 combines the development period cash flows and the operating period cash flows in a single overall spreadsheet. The quarterly figures from figure 4-5 are summed to obtain annual numbers in figure 4-6 and are brought forward to figure 4-7. This analysis resembles Stage 2 analysis except that the construction and lease-up years (1 and 2) are included, whereas Stage 2 analysis assumed that the first year already had stabilized occupancy. Note that the cash flow for Year 1 is zero because all the equity is invested before Year 1 (Time period 0) and all costs are covered by construction draws.

Stage 3 provides a much more refined estimate of construction interest and operating reserves during lease-up than Stages 1 and 2. In Stage 3, the estimate for construction interest is $397,453, compared with $528,843 in Stage 1 (figure 4-3d, Development Costs). Stage 3 shows no operating losses in Year 2 (figure 4-6) compared with $542,705 in the Operating Reserve estimate for Development Costs (figure 4-3d). The resulting total capital cost, including the interest reserve, is $31,180,762 (from Stage 3b, summarized below). This result compares with $31,854,857 in Stage 1d (figure 4-3d).

	Stage 1d (fig. 4-3d)	Stage 3 (fig. 4-6)	Difference
Construction interest	$528,843	$397,453	$131,390
Operating reserve	542,705	0	542,705
Total	1,071,548	397,453	674,095

The construction period interest is lower in the Stage 3 analysis primarily because equity is assumed to be used to pay for initial construction before the

FIGURE 4-5

Stage 3a: Analysis, Cash Flows during Development Period, Including Initial Lease-Up and Sales Activities

		Data	Total	Investment Year 0	Year 1 Total	Year 2 Total	CONSTRUCTION Quarter 1	Quarte
1	**Development Costs**							
2	Land	$1,050,000	1,050,000	1,050,000	0	0		
3	Impact and Extraction Fees	$1,600,000	1,600,000		1,600,000	0	$400,000	$400,0
4	Environmental Remediation	$148,960	148,960	74,480	74,480	0	$74,480	
5	Construction Hard Cost	$22,815,040	22,815,040		22,815,040	0	$5,703,760	$5,703,7
6	Contingency	1,597,053	1,597,053		1,597,053	—	399,263	399,2
7	Soft Costs:							
8	Architecture and Engineering	1,368,902	1,368,902	342,226	1,026,677	0	1,026,677	
9	Developer Overhead and Fee	1,140,752	1,140,752		1,140,752	0	$285,188	$285,1
10	Legal, Permits, and Other Fees	684,451	684,451	342,226	342,226	0	342,226	
11	General and Administrative/Marketing/Lease-up	228,150	228,150		228,150	—	57,038	57,0
12	Taxes during Construction	100,000	100,000		100,000	—	25,000	25,0
13	Insurance during Construction	50,000	50,000		50,000	—	12,500	12,5
14	**(i) Total Development Cost before Int and Optg Reserves – Apts**	**$30,783,309**	**30,783,309**	**$1,808,931**	**$28,974,378**	**$0**	**$8,326,131**	**$6,882,7**
15	**Operating Income/ (Loss) during Lease-up**							
16	Initial Occupancy upon Opening	35%						
17	Months to Reach Stabilized Occupancy	9.00						
18	Apartments Leased per Quarter				0	44		
19	Cumulative Number of Apartments Leased				24	68		
20	Vacancy Due to Lease-up (% of Gross Potential)[a]				100%	24%	100.00%	100.00
21	Stabilized Vacancy (% of Gross Potential)	5%			0%	5%		
22	Overall Vacancy Rate				100%	26%	100.00%	100.00
23	Gross Potential Revenue[b]	3%	631,546	2,526,182			2,526,182		
24	Vacancy Loss[c]			(644,548)			(644,548)		
25	Bad Debt[b]	0.25%		(6,315)			(6,315)		
26	Effective Gross Revenue			1,875,319			1,875,319		
27	Operating Expenses[b]	3%		(666,584)			(666,584)		
28	**(ii) Net Operating Income – Apartments**			**1,208,735**	**0**	**0**	**1,208,735**	**$0**	
29	**Condominium Sales Schedule**			2		1	1		
30	Units Sold					1	2		
31	Cumulative Units Sold			1,500,000		750,000	750,000		
32	Revenue per Unit			1,500,000		750,000	750,000		
33	Condominium Sales Revenue			(45,000)		-22,500	-22,500		
34	Expenses[d]			1,455,000		727,500	727,500		
35	**(iii) Condominium Net Income**								
36	**Net Cash Flow before Debt (ii) + (iii) - (i)**			**(28,119,574)**	**(1,808,931)**	**(28,246,878)**	**1,936,235**	**($8,326,131)**	**($6,882,74**
37	**Cash Flow Activity from Financing (see below)**								
38	Loan Proceeds, Draws, Fundings, and Releases			40,291,529	0	21,069,913	19,221,616	894,541	6,882,7
39	Loan Interest Paid			(938,296)	0	0	(938,296)	0	
40	Loan Amortizations and Paydowns			(19,726,991)	0	0	(19,726,991)	0	
41	**Net Cash Flow after Debt**			**(8,493,332)**	**(1,808,931)**	**(7,176,965)**	**492,564**	**($7,431,590)**	
42	**Initial Equity Contribution Account**								
43	*Total Development Costs before Int and Optg Reserves*	30,783,309						
44	*Maximum Loan Balance[e]*	20,242,788						
45	*Development Subsidy Loan[e]*	1,300,000						
46	Initial Equity	9,240,521	9,240,521	1,808,931	7,431,590	0	7,431,590	
47	Additional Equity[f]		0	0	0	0	0	0	
48	Initial Equity Account Ending Balance			9,240,521	1,808,931	9,240,521	9,240,521	9,240,521	9,240,5

> **All spreadsheets in chapter 4 are available online in supplemental materials at americas.uli.org/PRED.**

Quarter 3	Quarter 4	Quarter 5	Quarter 6	Quarter 7	Quarter 8	Quarter 9	Quarter 10	Quarter 11	Quarter 12	Year 3 Total
										0
$400,000	$400,000									0
										0
5,703,760	$5,703,760									0
399,263	399,263									0
										0
										0
$285,188	$285,188									0
										0
57,038	57,038									0
25,000	25,000									0
12,500	12,500									0
6,882,749	$6,882,749	$0	$0	$0	$0	$0	$0	$0	$0	$0
		15	15	15	0	0	0	0	0	0
	24	39	53	68	68	68	68	68	68	68
100.00%	100.00%	54%	32%	11%	0%	0%	0%	0%	0%	0%
		0%	0%	0%	5%	5%	5%	5%	5%	5%
100.00%	100.00%	54%	32%	11%	5%	5%	5%	5%	5%	5%
		631,546	631,546	631,546	631,546	650,492	650,492	650,492	650,492	2,601,968
		(340,539)	(204,324)	(68,108)	(31,577)	(32,525)	(32,525)	(32,525)	(32,525)	(130,098)
		(1,579)	(1,579)	(1,579)	(1,579)	(1,626)	(1,626)	(1,626)	(1,626)	(6,505)
		289,427	425,643	561,859	598,389	616,341	616,341	616,341	616,341	2,465,365
		(166,646)	(166,646)	(166,646)	(166,646)	(171,645)	(171,645)	(171,645)	(171,645)	(686,581)
$0	$0	$122,781	$258,997	$395,213	$431,743	$444,696	$444,696	$444,696	$444,696	$1,778,783
	1	1	0	0	0	0	0	0	0	0
	1	2	2	2	2	2	2	2	2	2
	$750,000	$750,000	$750,000	$750,000	$750,000	$750,000	$750,000	$750,000	$750,000	$750,000
	750,000	750,000	0	0	0	0	0	0	0	0
	-22,500	-22,500	0	0	0	0	0	0	0	0
	727,500	727,500	0	0	0	0	0	0	0	0
6,882,749	($6,155,249)	$850,281	$258,997	$395,213	$431,743	$444,696	$444,696	$444,696	$444,696	1,778,783
6,882,749	6,409,874	(472,875)	0	0	19,694,491	0	0	0	0	0
0	0	(236,680)	(233,872)	(233,872)	(233,872)	(196,661)	(195,804)	(194,938)	(194,064)	(781,467)
0	0	(8,125)	(8,125)	(8,125)	(19,702,616)	(93,538)	(94,395)	(95,260)	(96,135)	(379,327)
$0	$254,625	$132,602	$17,000	$153,216	$189,746	$154,497	$154,497	$154,497	$154,497	617,989
0	0	0	0	0	0	0	0	0	0	0
0	0	0	0	0	0	0	0	0	0	0
9,240,521	9,240,521	9,240,521	9,240,521	9,240,521	9,240,521	9,240,521	9,240,521	9,240,521	9,240,521	9,240,521

FIGURE 4-5

Stage 3a: Analysis, Cash Flows during Development Period, Including Initial Lease-Up and Sales Activities | CONTINUED

CONSTRUCTION

	Data	Total	Investment Year 0	Year 1 Total	Year 2 Total	Quarter 1	Quarte
49 Development Subsidy Loan Account[g]							
50 Beginning Balance				0	1,300,000	0	
51 Loan Draws, Fundings, and Paydowns:							
52 Loan Funding		1,300,000	0	1,300,000	0	0	
53 Loan Amortization Paid	40	(8,125)	(32,500)	0	0	(32,500)	0
54 *Trial Balance before Interest*		*1,283,750*		*1,300,000*	*1,267,500*	*0*	
55 *Average Trial Balance before Interest*		*960,781*		*650,000*	*1,271,563*	*0*	
56 Loan Interest:							
57 Interest during Construction Period	0.0%	0	0	0	0	0	
58 Interest during Operating Period	0.0%	0	0	0	0	—	
59 Interest Paid from NOI Apartments	Yes	0	0	0	0	0	
60 *Trial Ending Balance*		*1,267,500*		*1,300,000*	*1,267,500*	*0*	
61 Additional Equity Required (to maintain max loan balance)		0	0	0	0	0	
62 Ending Balance			0	1,300,000	1,267,500	0	
63 Construction Loan Account[h]							
64 Beginning Balance				0	20,167,366	0	899,8
65 Loan Draws, Fundings, and Releases:							
66 Construction Draws		20,242,788	0	20,242,788	0	894,541	6,882,7
67 Operating Deficit and Sales Loss Funding		0	0	0	0	0	
68 Loan Releases[i]	65%	(945,750)	0	(472,875)	(472,875)	0	
69 *Trial Balance before Interest*		*19,694,491*		*19,960,673*	*19,694,491*	*894,541*	*7,782,6*
70 *Average Trial Balance before Interest*		*18,550,114*		*17,405,736*	*19,694,491*	*447,271*	*4,341,2*
71 Loan Interest:							
72 Interest during Construction Period	4.75%	397,453		397,453	0	5,311	51,5
73 Interest during Operating and Sales Period	4.75%	938,296		0	938,296	—	
74 Interest Paid from NOI[j]		(816,273)		0	(816,273)	0	
75 Interest Paid from Condominium Sales[j]		(122,023)		0	(122,023)	0	
76 *Trial Ending Balance includes Accrued Interest*		*19,694,491*		*20,167,366*	*19,694,491*	*899,853*	*7,834,1*
77 Additional Equity Required (to maintain max loan balance)		0	0	0	0	0	
78 Payoff of Construction Loan by Permanent Loan (line 87)		(19,694,491)	0	0	(19,694,491)		
79 Ending Balance		0	0	20,167,366	0	899,853	7,834,1
80 Permanent/Takeout Loan Account[k]							
81 Beginning Balance				0	0		
82 Debt Service:	$282,073.54 quarterly	0		0	0		
83 Interest Paid from NOI	4.00%	0		0	0		
84 Principal Amortization Paid from NOI	30	0		0	0		
85 *Trial Ending Balance before Other Loan Activity*		*0*		*0*	*0*		
86 Loan Proceeds and Additional Paydowns:		0		0	0		
87 Loan Proceeds (Takeout Construction Loan)		19,694,491		0	19,694,491		
88 Additional Principal Paydown		0		0	0		
89 Ending Balance		19,694,491		0	19,694,491	0	
90 Total Loan Interest Accrued and Unpaid		397,453	0	397,453	0	5,311	51,5
91 Total Loan Draws and Funding		21,542,788	0	21,542,788	0	894,541	6,882,7

[a]The Vacancy calculation assumes that the units leased in the present quarter are economically realized in the middle of the quarter. Hence, the Vacancy for the quarter is an average of the vacancy from the prior quarter and present quarter.

[b]The following estimates pertaining to the revenue and expenses of the apartments are taken from figure 4-3b, the pro forma. Gross potential Revenue and Operating Expenses are inflated by the percentage shown.

[c]Vacancy Loss is a product of the Overall Vacancy Rate, which was determined by the absorption schedule in the preceding section.

[d]Expenses related to the marketing of condominium units have already been included as part of the development costs. The expenses shown here are simply the sales commissions, 3 percent.

[e]The Maximum Loan Balance and Development Subsidy Loan were previously provided in the Maximum Loan Calculation worksheet, figure 4-3c.

[f]Lenders want to ensure that developers have sufficient equity invested up front. They may require that all the equity be invested first before draws from the construction loan are allowed. In this analysis, all of the scheduled equity is invested up front. Moreover, any positive Net Operating Income is applied to the debt service of the Development Subsidy Loan and then the Construction Loan. However, if the user changes the assumptions on the timing of the development costs, lease-up, or absorption rate, and/or adds additional expenses during the construction period, then the Construction Loan may attempt to assume these additional costs; eventually, though, it capped at the Maximum Loan Balance. A cap could result in additional equity being required to fund any cash flow shortfalls during the development period. The user should check that the maximum Equity Account balance does not exceed the initally scheduled Equity.

CONSTRUCTION		LEASE-UP				FIRST STABILIZED YEAR				
Quarter 3	Quarter 4	Quarter 5	Quarter 6	Quarter 7	Quarter 8	Quarter 9	Quarter 10	Quarter 11	Quarter 12	Year 3 Total
0	0	1,300,000	1,291,875	1,283,750	1,275,625	1,267,500	1,259,375	1,251,250	1,243,125	1,267,500
0	1,300,000	0	0	0	0	0	0	0	0	0
0	0	(8,125)	(8,125)	(8,125)	(8,125)	(8,125)	(8,125)	(8,125)	(8,125)	(32,500)
0	1,300,000	1,291,875	1,283,750	1,275,625	1,267,500	1,259,375	1,251,250	1,243,125	1,235,000	1,235,000
0	650,000	1,295,938	1,287,813	1,279,688	1,271,563	1,263,438	1,255,313	1,247,188	1,239,063	1,239,063
0	0	—	—	—	—	—	—	—	—	0
—	—	0	0	0	0	0	0	0	0	0
0	0	0	0	0	0	0	0	0	0	0
0	1,300,000	1,291,875	1,283,750	1,275,625	1,267,500	1,259,375	1,251,250	1,243,125	1,235,000	1,235,000
0	0	0	0	0	0	0	0	0	0	0
0	1,300,000	1,291,875	1,283,750	1,275,625	1,267,500	1,259,375	1,251,250	1,243,125	1,235,000	1,235,000
7,834,154	14,850,799	20,167,366	19,694,491	19,694,491	19,694,491	0	0	0	0	0
6,882,749	5,582,749	0	0	0	0	0	0	0	0	0
0	0	0	0	0	0	0	0	0	0	0
0	(472,875)	(472,875)	0	0	0	0	0	0	0	0
4,716,902	19,960,673	19,694,491	19,694,491	19,694,491	19,694,491	0	0	0	0	0
1,275,528	17,405,736	19,930,929	19,694,491	19,694,491	19,694,491	0	0	0	0	0
133,897	206,693	—	—	—	—	—	—	—	—	0
—	—	236,680	233,872	233,872	233,872	0	0	0	0	0
0	0	(114,656)	(233,872)	(233,872)	(233,872)	0	0	0	0	0
0	0	(122,023)	0	0	0	0	0	0	0	0
4,850,799	20,167,366	19,694,491	19,694,491	19,694,491	19,694,491	0	0	0	0	0
0	0	0	0	0	(19,694,491)	0	0	0	0	0
4,850,799	20,167,366	19,694,491	19,694,491	19,694,491	0	0	0	0	0	0
						19,694,491	19,609,079	19,522,809	19,435,674	19,694,491
						(196,661)	(195,804)	(194,938)	(194,064)	(781,467)
						(85,413)	(86,270)	(87,135)	(88,010)	(346,827)
						19,609,079	19,522,809	19,435,674	19,347,664	19,347,664
					19,694,491	0	0	0	0	0
					0	0	0	0	0	0
0	0	0	0	0	19,694,491	19,609,079	19,522,809	19,435,674	19,347,664	19,347,664
133,897	206,693	0	0	0	0	0	0	0	0	0
6,882,749	6,882,749	0	0	0	0	0	0	0	0	0

The Development Subsidy Loan is a zero-interest loan that is amortized over 40 years. This analysis, for the sake of simplicity, assumes that any Net Operating Income is first used to pay the debt service of the Development Subsidy Loan before being applied to the Construction Loan. Additionally, it assumes that the Development Subsidy Loan balance is paid in full at the end of the holding period with the sale of the project.

In this analysis, if the Trial Balance of the Construction Loan exceeds the Maximum Loan Balance, it is assumed that there will be a partial paydown of the Loan and Additional Equity Required.

Construction Loan Releases are determined by the sales of the Condominium Retail units. This analysis assumes that Loan Releases are scheduled at 65.0% of the revenues and that both units are sold upon completion.

Note that income during the lease-up period is sufficient to pay for the construction loan interest during the lease-up period. This result is specific to this case due primarily to two factors: (1) the pre-leasing of the apartment units reduced the amount of time to stabilize the unit, and (2) the sales of the condominiums provided additional cash flow and reduced the construction loan balance. Compare these results to the initial assumptions in establishing an Operating Reserve in the Stage 1 analysis.

The Permanent/Takeout Loan account is provided for the benefit of the user who prefers to include the first year of stabilization after lease-up. Upon stabilization, a developer will refinance the existing construction loan with a permanent/takeout loan. In this scenario, the refinancing occurs at the end of Year 2. It is assumed that the takeout loan is equal to the lesser of the initial debt sizing calculation, figure 4-3c, or the ending balance of the construction loan. This assumption is conservative and precludes the model from showing any proceeds from the refinancing. The loan's debt service is calculated as a self-amortizing, fixed-rate loan using the original interest rate from figure 4-3c and a 30-year amortization period.

FIGURE 4-6 Stage 3b: Development Costs Summary

1	USES	Total	Year 0	Year 1	Year 2
2	Total Development Costs	$30,783,309	$1,808,931	$28,974,378	$0
3	Construction Loan: Capitalized Interest[a]	$397,453	0	397,453	0
4	Total Capital Costs	$31,180,762	$1,808,931	$29,371,831	$0
5	**Operating and Sales Loss**				
6	Net Operating Loss from Apartments	0	—	0	0
7	Net Sales Loss from Condominiums	0	—	0	0
8	**Financing Costs during Operations and Sales**				
9	Development Subsidy Loan Interest	0	—	0	0
10	Construction Loan Interest during Lease-up	938,296	—	0	938,296
11	Loan Releases	945,750	—	472,875	472,875
12	Loan Paydowns and Amortizations	32,500	—	0	32,500
13	Construction Loan Balance to Be Refinanced	19,694,491			19,694,491
14	Distributable Cash Flow after Debt	747,189	—	254,625	492,564
15	**TOTAL USES**	**$53,538,989**	**$1,808,931**	**$30,099,331**	**$21,630,726**
16	**SOURCES**				
17	**Loan Fundings and Construction Draws**				
18	Development Subsidy Loan Funding	1,300,000	0	1,300,000	0
19	Development Subsidy Interest Accrued to Loan	0	0	0	0
20	Construction Loan Draws and Funding	20,242,788	0	20,242,788	0
21	Construction Interest Accrued to Loan	397,453	0	397,453	0
22	Permanent Mortgage/Takeout/Refinancing	19,694,491			19,694,491
23	Proceeds from Refinancing				0
24	Operating and Sales Income				
25	Net Operating Income of Apartments	1,208,735	—	0	1,208,735
26	Net Sales Revenue of Condominiums	1,455,000	—	727,500	727,500
27	Equity Fundings				
28	Equity Funded, Year 0	1,808,931	1,808,931	—	—
29	Additional Equity Fundings, Development Period	7,431,590	0	7,431,590	0
30	**TOTAL SOURCES**	**53,538,989**	**1,808,931**	**30,099,331**	**21,630,726**
31	Check				
32	Equity for Capital Investment (equity sources + cash flow from ops – positive cash flow after int)[b]	11,157,067	1,808,931	7,904,465	1,443,671
33	Equity for Capital Investment (Total Capital Costs – Loan Sources)	11,157,067	1,808,931	7,904,465	1,443,671

34	**Capital Costs**	Total	Apartments	Condominium
35	Total Development Costs Excluding Interest	30,783,309	29,703,905	1,079,404
36	Interest Accrued during Construction[c]	397,453	383,517	13,937
37	Total Capital Costs	31,180,762	30,087,422	1,093,341
38	**Depreciable Basis**			
39	Total Capital Costs – Income Property	30,087,422	Annual Depreciation Estimate	
40	Land Cost	1,013,182	27.5	Life Years
41	Depreciable Basis (Capital Cost, minus Land)	29,074,239	$1,057,245	Annual Deprec.
42	**Operating Reserve**			
43	Operating Loss during Lease-up	0		
44	Interest Accrued during Lease-up Period	938,296		
45	*Less: Interest Paid from NOI during Lease-up Period*	-938,296		
46	Total Operating Reserve Funded by Construction Loan	0		

		Total	Apartments	Condominium
47	**Total Net Project Costs**			
48	Total Project Cost (Capital Costs plus Operating Reserve)	31,180,762	29,703,905	1,079,404
49	*Less: Positive Cash Flow after Interest*[d]	*-237,939*	*-237,939*	*0*
50	Total Project Cost after Lease-up	30,942,823	29,465,966	1,079,404
51	**Construction Loan Takeout at Stabilization**			
52	Permanent/Takeout Mortgage, Gross[e]	19,694,491		
53	Construction Loan Ending Balance	-19,694,491		
54	Cash Proceeds from Construction Loan Takeout	0		

[a]Capitalized Interest is the Construction Loan interest that accrued during the development period.

[b]Equity for Capital Investment provides a helpful check for Stage 3. One must be careful not to double-count this equity since it comes not only from new equity but also from positive operating cash flows during lease-up. Lines 32 and 33 should be equal for each year.

[c]For clarity, the accrued interest was allocated pro rata by Project Cost.

[d]The Positive Cash Flow after Interest includes Line 14, the Distributable Cash Flow after Debt, less any cash flow activities resulting from the sale of the condos, Lines 11 and 26. In this way, the amount deducted from the Total Project Cost includes only the positive cash flow after debt from the apartments.

[e]In this analysis, the Permanent/Takeout Mortgage amount is the lesser of the initial debt sizing calculation, figure 4-3c, or the ending balance of the construction loan. This assumption is conservative and precludes the model from showing any proceeds from the refinancing event. The user should take precaution if choosing to relax this assumption in the underwriting. Separately, the Development Subsidy Loan is assumed to stay in place throughout the holding period and is not included in the refinancing.

FIGURE 4-7 Stage 3c: Analysis, Combined Annual Before- and After-Tax Cash Flows during Development and Operating Period

	ANNUAL CASH FLOWS		DEVELOPMENT PERIOD		INVESTMENT PERIOD				
			Year 1	Year 2	Year 3	Year 4	Year 5	Year 6	Year 7
2	**Apartments Operating Income**								
3	Gross Rent	3%	0	2,526,182	2,601,968	2,843,241	2,928,538	3,016,394	3,106,886
4	Vacancy Rate	5%	100.00%	25.51%	5.00%	5.00%	5.00%	5.00%	5.00%
5	*Vacancy ($)*		*0*	*(644,548)*	*(130,098)*	*(142,162)*	*(146,427)*	*(150,820)*	*(155,344)*
6	*Bad Debt*	0.25%	*0*	*(6,315)*	*(6,505)*	*(7,108)*	*(7,321)*	*(7,541)*	*(7,767)*
7	Effective Gross Revenue		0	1,875,319	2,465,365	2,693,970	2,774,790	2,858,033	2,943,774
8	*Operating Expenses*	3.00%	*0*	*(666,584)*	*(686,581)*	*(707,179)*	*(728,394)*	*(750,246)*	*(772,753)*
9	Net Operating Income		0	1,208,735	1,778,783	1,986,792	2,046,395	2,107,787	2,171,021
10	**Condominiums Net Income**								
11	Sales Revenue		750,000	750,000	0				
12	Expenses		(22,500)	(22,500)	0				
13	Condominium Net Income		727,500	727,500	0				
14	*Less: Development Costs (Hard and Soft)*		*(28,974,378)*						
15	*Add: Loan Proceeds, Draws, Fundings during Lease-up*			*21,069,913*	*19,221,616*				
16	*Less: Construction Loan Interest during Lease-up*		*0*	*(938,296)*					
17	*Less: Amortizations and Paydowns during Development*		*0*	*(19,726,991)*					
18	*Less: Annual Debt Service (Subsidy and Permanent Loan) (see below)*					*(1,160,794)*	*(1,160,794)*	*(1,160,794)*	*(1,160,794)*
19	**Cash Flow after Debt/Before-Tax Cash Flow**		(7,176,965)	492,564	617,989	825,997	885,601	946,993	1,010,227
20	*Less: Taxes (see below)*		*(69,485)*	*(69,485)*	*0*	*0*	*0*	*0*	*(119,720)*
21	**After-Tax Cash Flow**		(7,246,450)	423,079	617,989	825,997	885,601	946,993	890,507
22	**Development Subsidy Loan Calculation**[a]		Year 1	Year 2	Year 3	Year 4	Year 5	Year 6	Year 7
23	Beginning Balance	1,300,000	0	1,300,000	1,267,500	1,235,000	1,202,500	1,170,000	1,137,500
24	Ending Balance		1,300,000	1,267,500	1,235,000	1,202,500	1,170,000	1,137,500	1,105,000
25	Amortization of Principal	40 years	0	(32,500)	(32,500)	(32,500)	(32,500)	(32,500)	(32,500)
26	Interest/Annual Payment	0.00%	32,500	0	0	0	0	0	0	0
27	**Mortgage Calculation**[b]		Year 1	Year 2	Year 3	Year 4	Year 5	Year 6	Year 7
28	Beginning Balance	19,694,491	0	0	19,694,491	19,347,664	18,986,707	18,611,043	18,220,075
29	Ending Balance		0	19,694,491	19,347,664	18,986,707	18,611,043	18,220,075	17,813,178
30	Amortization of Principal	30 years	0	0	(346,827)	(360,957)	(375,663)	(390,969)	(406,897)
31	Interest/Annual Payment	4.00%	1,128,294	0	0	(781,467)	(767,337)	(752,631)	(737,326)	(721,397)

32	DEPRECIATION CALCULATION[c]		Year 1	Year 2	Year 3	Year 4	Year 5	Year 6	Year 7
33	Beginning Balance			29,074,239	28,016,994	26,959,749	25,902,504	24,845,259	23,788,014
34	*Less: Annual Depreciation (assume straight line)*			*(1,057,245)*	*(1,057,245)*	*(1,057,245)*	*(1,057,245)*	*(1,057,245)*	*(1,057,245)*
35	*Ending Balance*			*28,016,994*	*26,959,749*	*25,902,504*	*24,845,259*	*23,788,014*	*22,730,769*
36	*Cumulative Depreciation Taken*			*(1,057,245)*	*(2,114,490)*	*(3,171,735)*	*(4,228,980)*	*(5,286,225)*	*(6,343,470)*
37	*Remaining Book Value*			*29,030,177*	*27,972,931*	*26,915,686*	*25,858,441*	*24,801,196*	*23,743,951*
38	**INCOME TAX CALCULATION FOR CONDOMINIUMS**		Year 1	Year 2	Year 3	Year 4	Year 5	Year 6	Year 7
39									
40	Condominium Net Income		727,500	727,500	—				
41	*Deduct: Allocated Share of Development Cost*	*539,702*	*(539,702)*	*(539,702)*	*—*				
42	*Taxable Profit/(Loss)*		*187,798*	*187,798*	*—*	*—*	*—*	*—*	*—*
43	Tax Liability from Condominium Sales	37.00% rate	69,485	69,485	—	—	—	—	—
44	**INCOME TAX CALCULATION FOR APARTMENTS**		Year 1	Year 2	Year 3	Year 4	Year 5	Year 6	Year 7
45	Net Operating Income		—	1,208,735	1,778,783	1,986,792	2,046,395	2,107,787	2,171,021
46	*Add: Replacement/Capital Reserve*			*10,200*	*10,506*	*10,821*	*11,146*	*11,480*	*11,825*
47	*Deduct: Interest*		—	*(938,296)*	*(781,467)*	*(767,337)*	*(752,631)*	*(737,326)*	*(721,397)*
48	*Deduct: Depreciation*		—	*(1,057,245)*	*(1,057,245)*	*(1,057,245)*	*(1,057,245)*	*(1,057,245)*	*(1,057,245)*
49	Taxable Income/(Loss)		—	(776,606)	(49,423)	173,031	247,665	324,697	404,203
50	Passive Loss Offset		—	—	—	(173,031)	(247,665)	(324,697)	(80,636)
51	Taxable Income		—	—	—	—	—	—	323,567
52	Passive Loss Carryforward		—	(776,606)	(826,029)	(652,998)	(405,333)	(80,636)	—
53	Annual Income Taxes	37.00% rate	—	—	—	—	—	—	119,720
54	**SALE CALCULATION OF APARTMENTS (including tax)**		Year 1	Year 2	Year 3	Year 4	Year 5	Year 6	Year 7
55									
56	**Cash Flow from Sale**								
57	Sale Price (cap rate applied to next year NOI)	5.5% cap rate							40,657,297
58	*Less: Commission*	1.50% rate							*(609,859)*
59	Adjusted Sales Price								40,047,438
60	*Less: Development Subsidy Loan*								*(1,105,000)*
61	*Less: Remaining Mortgage Balance*								*(17,813,178)*
62	Before-Tax Cash Flow from Sale								21,129,260
63	*Less: Total Tax at Sale (recapture and capital gain, see below)*								*(3,564,675)*
64	After-Tax Cash Flow from Sale								17,564,585
65	**Tax Calculation at Sale**								
66	Adjusted Sales Price								40,047,438
67	*Less: Remaining Book Value*								*(23,743,951)*
68	Total Taxable Gain								16,303,487
69	*Less: Passive Loss Carryforward*								*—*
70	Total Net Taxable Gain								16,303,487
71	Total Depreciation Taken								6,343,470
72	(i) Tax on Recapture	25.00% rate							1,585,868
73	Capital Gain								9,960,016
74	*Deduct: Capital Reserves[d]*								*(65,978)*
75	Net Capital Gain								9,894,039
76	(ii) Tax on Capital Gain	20.00% rate							1,978,808
77	**Total Tax at Sale (i + ii)**								**3,564,675**

	RETURN MEASURES	Year 0	Year 1	Year 2	Year 3	Year 4	Year 5	Year 6	Year 7
78	**RETURN MEASURES**								
79	**Unleveraged IRR**								
80	Project Cost	($1,808,931)	($28,974,378)	$0					
81	For-Sale Revenues – Condominiums		$727,500	$727,500	$0				
82	Net Operating Income – Apartments		$0	$1,208,735	$1,778,783	$1,986,792	$2,046,395	$2,107,787	$2,171,021
83	Adjusted Sales Price – Apartments								$40,047,438
84	Unleveraged Cash Flow	($1,808,931)	($28,246,878)	$1,936,235	$1,778,783	$1,986,792	$2,046,395	$2,107,787	$42,218,459
85	**Unleveraged IRR**	**10.69%**							
86	**Net Present Value @ 8.0%**	**$3,924,039**							
87	**Equity Multiple**	**1.73**							
88	**Before-Tax IRR**								
89	Initial Equity Required[e]	($1,808,931)							
90	Before-Tax Operating and Sales Cash Flow		($7,176,965)	$492,564	$617,989	$825,997	$885,601	$946,993	$1,010,227
91	Before-Tax Cash Flow from Sale								$21,129,260
92	Total Before-Tax Cash Flow	($1,808,931)	($7,176,965)	$492,564	$617,989	$825,997	$885,601	$946,993	$22,139,487
93	**Before-Tax IRR**	**20.44%**							
94	**Net Present Value @ 12.0%**	**$4,137,612**							
95	**Equity Multiple**	**2.88**							
96	**After-Tax IRR**								
97	Initial Equity Required	($1,808,931)							
98	After-Tax Operating and Sales Cash Flow		(7,246,450)	423,079	617,989	825,997	885,601	946,993	890,507
99	After-Tax Cash Flow from Sale								17,564,585
100	Total After-Tax Cash Flow	($1,808,931)	($7,246,450)	$423,079	$617,989	$825,997	$885,601	$946,993	$18,455,092
101	**After-Tax IRR**	**17.15%**							
102	**Net Present Value @ 12.0%**	**$2,353,545**							
103	**Equity Multiple**	**2.45**							

[a]The Development Subsidy Loan is carried over from the prior figure 4-5 where the Cash Flow after Debt includes the Subsidy Loan debt service. Since this analysis of the combined development and operating periods resumes the Subsidy Loan beginning in Year 3, there are 39 amortizing years remaining of the original 40-year amortization schedule. Also note that the Development Subsidy Loan is a zero-interest loan.

[b]The permanent mortgage balance was determined in figure 4-3c. The permanent mortgage replaces the outstanding construction loan upon stabilization of the project. Note that the construction loan is interest only, whereas the permanent mortgage is amortizing.

[c]The depreciable basis is the total project cost, excluding land costs and operating losses during the lease-up period. The remaining book value includes the land cost. Personal property is included in the depreciable basis here for simplicity. It can be tracked separately. Also, apartment buildings may be brought onstream at different successive months as construction is completed. A separate depreciation spreadsheet may be added to account for these nuances. That level of precision, however, is inappropriate for Stage 3 analysis since other assumptions are, at best, good approximations.

[d] In this analysis, a simplifying assumption has been made that the yearly replacement reserves (shown as being included in the net operating income in figure 4-3b) are accumulated during the holding period and spent on capital needs immediately before the sale of the property. Consequently, the replacement reserve amount spent on capital needs is not depreciated and serves to increase the remaining book value; or, the amount is deducted from the estimated capital gains on the sale of the property.

[e]The Initial Equity Required is calculated on a quarterly basis as shown in figure 4-5, Year 0. For subsequent Years 1 and 2, see the next line, Operating and Sales Cash Flow. Also, in those years where there are quarters with both cash shortfalls and positive cash flows, the amounts have been netted out in this annual DCF presentation.

> All spreadsheets in chapter 4 are available online in supplemental materials at americas.uli.org/PRED.

construction lender starts to fund the construction loan. Lenders usually require that the entire equity be invested before they fund the construction loan. With equity funding the initial phases of construction, the average construction loan balance is usually less than the 60 to 65 percent required by the bank. In this case, Stage 1d assumes an average draw of 55 percent (figure 4-3d, line 35). Less conservative is the assumption that units pay rent from the beginning of the quarter in which they are leased because many of those leases will start in the second or third month of the quarter. Operating losses are nonexistent in Stage 3b because both the quickened pace of absorption by pre-leasing the units and the condominium sales are assumed to offset the operating losses during lease-up. The capital costs from Stage 3d are summarized in figure 4-8. Several numbers are key inputs to the combined annual DCF analysis in Stage 3c, such as the Depreciable Basis and the Total Operating Reserve.

The more precise figures for construction interest and operating reserves in Stage 3 give the developer ammunition to discuss with the construction lender the amount of reserves actually needed. The lender wants to be as conservative as possible, ensuring that sufficient interest reserves are available to protect the developer in the event of construction delays or slower lease-up. The developer must have these resources available but would prefer not to have to set them aside if they are not needed. An estimate that is too conservative raises the total project cost unnecessarily and may make the project uncompetitive.

The IRRs shown in figure 4-7 for Stage 3c analysis indicate that the before-tax IRR is 20.44 percent (line 93) and the after-tax IRR is 17.15 percent (line 101). These figures are more accurate estimates of the project's performance than the Stage 2 analysis—in which the before-tax IRR was 16.39 percent and the after-tax IRR was 13.60 percent—because they take into account quarterly construction draws and projected lease-up. Normally, IRRs for Stage 3 analysis are lower than for Stage 2 because the positive cash flows from stabilized performance occur in Year 3 rather than Year 1. They are higher in this illustration, however, because the more accurate estimates of construction interest and operating reserve during lease-up produce lower overall development costs.

STAGE 4—MONTHLY CASH FLOWS DURING THE DEVELOPMENT PERIOD. Stage 4 analysis is not shown. It focuses on just the development period and refines the cash flow projections to support the

FIGURE 4-8 Summary of Stage 3 Costs			
Capital Costs	**Apartments**	**Condominiums**	**Total**
Total Development Cost Excluding Interest (figure 4-5, line 14)	$29,703,905	$1,079,404	$30,783,309
Interest Accrued during Construction (figure 4-5, lines 57 and 72)	$383,517	$13,937	$397,453
Total Capital Costs	$30,087,422	$1,093,341	$31,180,762
Depreciable Basis			
Total Capital Costs – Income Property			$30,087,422
Land Cost (figure 4-3d, line 10)			$1,013,182
Depreciable Basis (Capital Costs minus Land)[a]			$29,074,239
Operating Reserve			
Operating Loss during Lease-Up (figure 4-5, line 36, if negative)			$0
Interest Accrued during Lease-up Period (figure 4-5, lines 58, 73, 83)			$938,296
Interest Paid from Cash Flow (figure 4-5, lines 59, 74, 75, 83)			($938,296)
Total Operating Reserve Funded by Construction Loan			$0
Total Net Project Costs			
Total Project Cost (Capital Costs plus Operating Reserve)			$31,180,762
Positive Cash Flow after Interest (figure 4-5, lines 28, 53, 58, 73)			($237,939)
Total Project Cost after Lease-up (Year 0 through Year 2)			$30,942,823
Construction Loan Takeout at Stabilization			
Permanent Mortgage for Income Property (figure 4-5, line 87)			$19,694,491
Construction Loan Ending Balance (figure 4-5, line 78)			($19,694,491)
Cash Proceeds from Construction Loan Takeout			$0

[a]Segregating costs for furnishings and tenant improvement (TIs) from the building basis improves the apparent returns to the developer. This will definitely be done for the actual project accounting, but it reduces the conservative estimates desired for feasibility analysis.

request for the construction loan. Stage 4 analysis resembles the quarterly analysis shown in figure 4-5, but the projections are made monthly rather than quarterly. The schedule in figure 4-5 assumes that the project will be built during the first four quarters and leased over the next four quarters. The estimated lease-up time (12 months) is calculated from the anticipated absorption of apartments based on the market study. The project reaches stabilized occupancy after the second year.[48] A primary purpose of the monthly analysis of the development phase is to estimate the amount of the loan that needs to be set aside to cover interest expenses and operating losses during construction and startup. Based on the quarterly cash flow computation in figure 4-5, the total project capital cost is $31,180,762 (also figure 4-6, lines 4 and 37 and figure 4-8). The net project cost after the first year of operations, or lease-up, is $30,942,823.

A monthly Stage 4 analysis would provide an even more accurate estimate of these figures. Developers sometimes do only a Stage 3, presuming that quarterly cash flow analysis will provide a sufficiently accurate picture of their funding needs. But monthly projections are recommended because they give both the developer and the lender the most accurate picture of funding needs and serve as a useful tool for monitoring cash flows once construction begins.

STAGE 5—DISCOUNTED CASH FLOW ANALYSIS FOR INVESTORS: JOINT VENTURE–SYNDICATION ANALYSIS. Stages 1, 2, and 3 examine the real estate project in its entirety. All equity and all subsequent cash flows are assumed to be invested or received by a single owner or developer entity. The final step in the analysis is to divide the cash flows for the whole project into the investor's and developer's shares.

Stage 5 is the joint venture–syndication analysis. It is used to structure the deal between the developer and the equity investors. Developers use Stage 5 analysis to determine the best combination of preferred returns and profit splits to offer investors to attract the required equity for the project. That usually means experimenting with a number of deal combinations before making a final selection. Because different types of equity investors are accustomed to different deal structures, the final structure depends on whom the developer is approaching for equity.

Although the final version of Stage 5 for the offering package is usually prepared by an accountant on an *after-tax* basis, the developer's analysis typically focuses on *before-tax* cash flows and IRRs to the investor. The project's viability hinges on attracting sufficient equity capital, and the investor's IRR is one of the key measures of return.

Stage 5 analysis should be done before the developer makes a firm commitment for the earnest money for the land. If the investor's IRR is below 12 to 15 percent (15 to 18 percent or higher is common), the land price or purchase price is too high to offer investors attractive returns. Alternatively, investors can be given a greater share of the profits; but if too little money is left over for the developer, the deal is not worth doing.

Figure 4-9 shows the before-tax Stage 5 analysis. The cash flows in figure 4-9, line 8, are taken from the Stage 3c combined analysis in figure 4-7, line 92. Note that although the Stage 5 analysis illustrated here uses cash flows from Stage 3, it can just as easily be tied

to Stage 2 analysis. In that case, before-tax cash flows from Stage 2 (figure 4-4a, line 103) would be inserted in Stage 5 (figure 4-9, line 8).

The investor who puts up the equity typically requires a preferred return. The preferred return is most often cumulative—that is, if funds are not sufficient to pay the preferred return, the deferred return is added to the equity balance and accrues interest. In this case, the investor receives a 10 percent cumulative preferred return.

The investor puts up 90 percent of the equity and the developer puts up 10 percent. The investor gets 90 percent of all cash flows until all of the equity and cumulative preferred returns of 10 percent have been received. Then, the remaining cash flow is split 70/30 between the investor and the developer until the investor has earned a 15 percent IRR—the first waterfall or hurdle rate. Thereafter (after paying back all the equity, the cumulative returns of 10 percent, and the first waterfall of 15 percent), any remaining cash flow is split evenly between the investor and developer. The investor's IRR is 17.6 percent; the general partner's (developer's) IRR is 36.9 percent, which is much higher because the developer's equity investment is only 10 percent. Note that in this deal structure, the developer's equity and the investor's equity are "pari passu," treated equally until the initial 10 percent preferred return is met. An alternative structure would subordinate the developer's equity payback to the investor's, in which case the developer would not receive any cash flow until the investor had received back all of his or her equity. No deal structure is "typical." The developer has to devise a structure that will attract the necessary equity. Typical terms change over time as the market changes and depending on whether equity money is plentiful or tight.

When the deal involves a single large investor, the terms are negotiated directly between the developer and the investor. Institutional equity investors typically require 75 to 80 percent of the profits. Developers can often raise money more cheaply from private individuals.

WHAT TO WATCH FOR. Financial analysis is often misused. Experienced developers sometimes scoff at the latest DCF and IRR techniques because the old rules of thumb (e.g., capitalized value should exceed cost by a comfortable margin, say 15 to 20 percent, or cash-on-cash return should be 10 to 11 percent) work just as well when a project is obviously a good investment. Stage 2 analysis can easily be misused to overestimate a project's returns. Beginning developers especially should be aware of the major pitfalls:

FIGURE 4-9 ## Stage 5: Analysis, Investor Return

1	Initial and Additional Equity[a]				$8,985,896				
2	Investor Equity Contribution[b]				90%				
3	Developer/General Partner (GP) Equity Contribution				10%				
4	Preferred Return, Pari Passu				10%				
5	Waterfalls, Hurdles, Tiers				Split to GP		Hurdle Rate		Up to Limit
6	First Waterfall, Hurdle				30%		10%		15%
7	Second Waterfall, Hurdle				50%		15%		100%

			DEVELOPMENT PERIOD		OPERATING PERIOD				
		Investment Year 0	Year 1	Year 2	Year 3	Year 4	Year 5	Year 6	Year 7
8	Before-Tax Cash Flow	($1,808,931)	($7,176,965)	$492,564	$617,989	$825,997	$885,601	$946,993	$22,139,487
9	Distribution of Preferred Return	0	0	(492,564)	(617,989)	(825,997)	(885,601)	(946,993)	(2,342,881)
10	Return of Invested Capital	0	0	0	0	0	0	0	(8,985,896)
11	Cash Flow for 1st Waterfall	0	0	0	0	0	0	0	10,810,710
12	*First Waterfall to Investors*	*0*	*0*	*0*	*0*	*0*	*0*	*0*	*(4,046,125)*
13	*First Waterfall to GP*	*0*	*0*	*0*	*0*	*0*	*0*	*0*	*(1,734,054)*
14	Cash Flow for 2nd Waterfall	0	0	0	0	0	0	0	5,030,531
15	*Second Waterfall to Investors*	*0*	*0*	*0*	*0*	*0*	*0*	*0*	*(2,515,265)*
16	*Second Waterfall to GP*	*0*	*0*	*0*	*0*	*0*	*0*	*0*	*(2,515,265)*
17	**RETURN OF INVESTED CAPITAL AND PREFERRED RETURN, PARI PASSU (INVESTOR AND GP ACCOUNTS)**								
18	**Capital Account**								
19	Beginning Balance		1,808,931	8,985,896	8,985,896	8,985,896	8,985,896	8,985,896	8,985,896
20	Capital Contributions	1,808,931	7,176,965	0	0	0	0	0	0
21	Return of Invested Capital	0	0	0	0	0	0	0	(8,985,896)
22	Ending Balance	1,808,931	8,985,896	8,985,896	8,985,896	8,985,896	8,985,896	8,985,896	0
23	**Capital Account, Investor**								
24	Beginning Balance		1,628,038	8,087,306	8,087,306	8,087,306	8,087,306	8,087,306	8,087,306
25	Capital Contributions	1,628,038	6,459,268	0	0	0	0	0	0
26	Return of Invested Capital	0	0	0	0	0	0	0	(8,087,306)
27	Ending Balance	1,628,038	8,087,306	8,087,306	8,087,306	8,087,306	8,087,306	8,087,306	0
28	**Capital Account, GP**								
29	Beginning Balance		180,893	898,590	898,590	898,590	898,590	898,590	898,590
30	Capital Contributions	180,893	717,696	0	0	0	0	0	0
31	Return of Invested Capital	0	0	0	0	0	0	0	(898,590)
32	Ending Balance	180,893	898,590	898,590	898,590	898,590	898,590	898,590	0
33	**Preferred Return Account[b]**								
34	Beginning Balance		0	180,893	605,008	946,110	1,113,313	1,237,632	1,312,992
35	Preferred Return Earned	0	180,893	916,679	959,090	993,201	1,009,921	1,022,353	1,029,889
36	Distribution of Preferred Return	0	0	(492,564)	(617,989)	(825,997)	(885,601)	(946,993)	(2,342,881)
37	Ending Balance	0	180,893	605,008	946,110	1,113,313	1,237,632	1,312,992	0
38	**1ST WATERFALL**								
39	**Waterfall Return Calculation, Investor**								
40	Beginning Balance		0	244,206	1,050,625	1,865,125	2,614,592	3,422,835	4,297,063
41	Waterfall Return Accrued	0	244,206	1,249,727	1,370,690	1,492,865	1,605,285	1,726,521	1,857,655
42	Distribution of Preferred Return	0	0	(443,308)	(556,190)	(743,398)	(797,041)	(852,294)	(2,108,593)
43	Distribution for Waterfall	0	0	0	0	0	0	0	(4,046,125)
44	Ending Balance	0	244,206	1,050,625	1,865,125	2,614,592	3,422,835	4,297,063	0
45	**Waterfall Return Calculation, GP**								
46	Distribution of Preferred Return	0	0	(49,256)	(61,799)	(82,600)	(88,560)	(94,699)	(234,288)
47	Distribution for Waterfall	0	0	0	0	0	0	0	(1,734,054)

	Investment Year 0	DEVELOPMENT PERIOD		OPERATING PERIOD				
		Year 1	Year 2	Year 3	Year 4	Year 5	Year 6	Year 7
48	**2ND WATERFALL**							
49	**2nd Waterfall Return, Investor**							
50	Beginning Balance		0	1,628,038	10,900,075	29,331,266	66,006,441	139,303,147	285,841,307
51	Waterfall Return Accrued	0	1,628,038	9,715,344	18,987,381	37,418,572	74,093,747	147,390,454	293,928,613
52	Distribution of Preferred Return	0	0	(443,308)	(556,190)	(743,398)	(797,041)	(852,294)	(2,108,593)
53	Distribution of 1st Waterfall	0	0	0	0	0	0	0	(4,046,125)
54	Distribution for 2nd Waterfall	0	0	0	0	0	0	0	(2,515,265)
55	Ending Balance	0	1,628,038	10,900,075	29,331,266	66,006,441	139,303,147	285,841,307	571,099,937
56	**2nd Waterfall Return, GP**							
57	Distribution of Preferred Return	0	0	(49,256)	(61,799)	(82,600)	(88,560)	(94,699)	(234,288)
58	Distribution of 1st Waterfall	0	0	0	0	0	0	0	(1,734,054)
59	Distribution for 2nd Waterfall	0	0	0	0	0	0	0	(2,515,265)
60	**Investor Share of Equity and Cash Flow**							
61	Equity Contributions	(1,628,038)	(6,459,268)	0	0	0	0	0	0
62	Return of Invested Capital	0	0	0	0	0	0	0	8,087,306
63	Distribution of Preferred Returns	0	0	443,308	556,190	743,398	797,041	852,294	2,108,593
64	Distribution of 1st Waterfall	0	0	0	0	0	0	0	4,046,125
65	Distribution of 2nd Waterfall	0	0	0	0	0	0	0	2,515,265
66	Investor Before-Tax Cash Flows	(1,628,038)	(6,459,268)	443,308	556,190	743,398	797,041	852,294	16,757,290
67	**Investor Before-Tax IRR**	**17.6%**							
68	**Net Present Value @ 12.0%**	**2,045,264**							
69	**GP Share of Equity and Cash Flow**							
70	Equity Contributions	(180,893)	(717,696)	0	0	0	0	0	0
71	Return of Invested Capital	0	0	0	0	0	0	0	898,590
72	Distribution of Preferred Returns	0	0	49,256	61,799	82,600	88,560	94,699	234,288
73	Distribution of 1st Waterfall	0	0	0	0	0	0	0	1,734,054
74	Distribution of 2nd Waterfall	0	0	0	0	0	0	0	2,515,265
75	GP Before-Tax Cash Flows	(180,893)	(717,696)	49,256	61,799	82,600	88,560	94,699	5,382,197
76	**GP Before-Tax IRR**	**36.9%**							
77	**Net Present Value @ 12.0%**	**1,649,032**							

^aThis simplified investor return analysis assumes that the equity required, as calculated in the Stage 3 analysis figure 4-7, is offset by cash flows in the same period. Hence, the equity shown here is on a net basis.

^bThis analysis assumes that the investor and the developer have equal priority to the preferred return and that the payback of their respective equity is proportional to their contributed amount. Hence, the preferred return and capital account calculations are performed on an aggregate basis and later individually proportioned according to their proportionate share and waterfall tier.

All spreadsheets in chapter 4 are available online in supplemental materials at americas.uli.org/PRED.

Multifamily Residential Development

- underestimating costs;
- overestimating rents;
- underestimating operating expenses, especially after five years;
- underestimating or omitting a reserve for replacements;
- underestimating or omitting expenses for tenant turnover, such as repainting and replacing carpets, draperies, and appliances;
- overestimating rent escalation;
- assuming a sale-year capitalization rate that is too low (which increases sale value); and
- not allowing a sufficient interest reserve during lease-up or assuming an insufficient lease-up time.

Errors in analysis are compounded by developers' natural optimism. Making one optimistic assumption, such as too short a lease-up period, may not alter the results too much; but when two or three such assumptions are made, the resulting returns may represent a *very* optimistic and unrealistic case. Thus, developers must take care that they use *most likely* values for each assumption and avoid erring on the *optimistic* side.

Another common mistake is going into too much detail too early in the analysis. A basic rule is that the level of detail should be no greater than the accuracy of the information analyzed. Analyzing monthly cash flows when first looking at a project is not appropriate because the data for costs and rents are so crude that the extra detail does not help; such an analysis might even make it harder to see what is going on. Therefore, Stage 4 monthly cash flow analysis is appropriate only after considerable time and money have been spent collecting the best possible information about operations and development costs.

Finally, use common sense. The various measures of return should correlate with standard rules of thumb. Good projects typically meet the following measures of return, although they vary according to the degree of risk and current interest and inflation rates:

Measure of Return	New Development	Stabilized Property
Cash-on-cash return (cash throw-off/equity)	7–10%	6–9%
Overall return (overall cap rate: NOI/total cost)	10–11%	8–10%
Unleveraged IRR	12–15%	9–11%
Before-tax leveraged IRR	20–25%	13–18%
After-tax leveraged IRR	15–20%	9–14%
Investor's before-tax IRR	16–20%	12–16%

These rules of thumb are rough guidelines. Returns may be higher or lower, depending on the risk associated with a particular deal and the general economic environment and geographic location. The returns also vary with inflation and interest rates. The returns listed above have trended downward significantly since the 1990s as a result of the enormous influx of cash into real estate during the economic expansion of the 2000s. The economic crisis of 2008–2009 caused the rates to jump from their low point in 2007. With the historically low interest rates of the early 2020s, investors' required yields remained well below their historical averages.

The status of the property is a critical component in determining which cap rates and rates of return are appropriate. "New development" refers to apartment projects that have already received full entitlements and are ready to start construction. The return expectations include construction and lease-up risk; but if zoning approvals are required, the return expectations would be even higher. "Stabilized property" refers to apartment projects that are fully leased (90 to 95 percent occupancy) and have funded their permanent mortgages. These returns are in line with those that private investors would expect. Institutional returns for investment-grade apartments would be lower—between 1 and 3 percent IRRs. "Investment-grade apartments" are projects that are attractive to institutional investors—typically new projects or well-seasoned projects of 150 or more units in prime locations, or somewhat smaller projects in high-priced cities such as New York, San Francisco, Los Angeles, and Washington, D.C. The size requirement is tied to the number of units necessary to support professional on-site management.

Financial analysis is an iterative process. Stage 2 analysis is performed many times as the developer collects increasingly better information about a project. Fortunately, once the model is set up, entering new information and rerunning the model is a mere 10-minute exercise. The most important point is to double-check that the assumptions and results make sense. Simple measures of cash-on-cash returns and capitalization rates still apply. Developers should avoid the trap of creating so complicated a spreadsheet that key numbers become lost in pages and pages of analysis.

THE GO/NO-GO DECISION. Each stage of project feasibility requires a go/no-go decision. A decision to go forward does not commit the developer to construction but does take the developer to the next level of investment and risk. Each level may involve substantial or very little additional commitment. For example, some projects may have the necessary regulatory approvals already in place, thereby allowing the developer to apply directly for a building permit as soon as construction drawings are done and financing is in place. For various reasons, other projects may require little investment in feasibility studies—the physical aspects of the site are already known, the lender does its own appraisal, the market has been proved through past experience, preliminary engineering is unnecessary, or the architect provides preliminary design drawings on spec.

The importance of holding down front-end costs cannot be overemphasized. That money is purely risk money because the odds are heavily against a project's proceeding. Developers want to avoid purchasing land until they are reasonably certain the project will go ahead. Sometimes they must go hard on the land, which involves a major increase in risk money, even when entitlements or other major risk factors are unresolved. The key to success is knowing what information is required and obtaining it at the lowest cost. A developer must walk that fine line between spending money unnecessarily and doing sufficient investigation to evaluate the property properly.

The two most important decisions—especially for developers with limited resources—involve the purchase of the land and the beginning of construction. Both usually require large financial commitments.

The DCF analysis provides data that influence the go/no-go decision to purchase the site:

- expected dollar profit;
- IRR;
- amount of total money needed;
- amount of equity and debt needed; and
- length of the commitment.

The decision to purchase is not made solely on the basis of the DCF analysis, however. The developer must also weigh other available investment alternatives, the amount of risk involved in the project, and a host of other considerations. The developer should ask the following questions:

- Does the developer have the personnel and capital resources to carry through the project?
- Is this really the project that the developer wants to spend the next three years or so working on?
- Is the project worth the developer's time, effort, and risk?

- Is the project of such a scale that the developer can survive major delays and unforeseen difficulties? If not, is this project worth risking the loss of all the developer's assets?

Design

The developer's design concept should be based entirely on the target market—not personal preferences. The rental apartment and for-sale condominium markets are segmented into many submarkets, with each niche demanding specific elements. Submarkets vary enormously by demographics, level of competition, and preferences related to unit mix, unit finishes, parking arrangements, and amenities. Design standards and preferences vary enormously from one geographic region to another. No matter how good the pro forma for a project might look, if the product does not satisfy the market's needs at a price that customers can afford, the project will not succeed.

Each building type, from suburban garden apartments to downtown high rises, offers a different set of problems and opportunities for design to meet the needs of the submarket. Luxury garden apartments, for example, typically include some or all of the following features: generously sized rooms, kitchens with deluxe appliances and cabinetry, ceramic tile or marble bathrooms, vaulted and/or nine-foot-high (2.7 m) ceilings, fireplaces, balconies, in-unit laundry facilities, and community recreational facilities, such as exercise rooms, swimming pools, and tennis courts. Other features might include extra soundproofing, security systems, elevators, and attached garages with direct access for residents. Property management services might include grocery shopping, pet sitting, dry-cleaning delivery, and trash pickup.

Luxury urban apartments typically include many of the features of the garden apartments mentioned above. They generally have concierge services, security/doorman services, underground or structured parking, modern appliances, high-end kitchen and bathroom finishes, in-unit laundry, fitness and business centers, club rooms, and other community amenities. Luxury urban apartment communities compete with a very high level of resident services and lifestyle advantages. Rents often include floor and view premiums. Special design features, such as loft-style units, also command premiums. Although each of these features and services increases development costs, renters of the highest-end apartments will pay for all of them, and the increased rent should justify

Multifamily Housing Forms

ATELIER

UNION WEST

	ATELIER	UNION WEST
Location	Dallas, Texas	Chicago, Illinois
Typology	High-Rise	High-Rise
Number of units	417	357
Number of stories	41	15
Construction start date	Q2 2018	Q1 2018
Completion date	Q2 2021	Q1 2020
Location of parking (garage, surface, underground)	10 stories above grade (podium setup with units/amenities above) and two levels below grade that are owned by others	One level below grade and two levels above grade (podium setup with units/amenities above)
Hard construction costs only/net rentable sq ft	~$134 million or $290/net rentable sq ft	~$103 million or $392/net rentable sq ft
Average rents/sq ft	~$3,900 or $3.50/sq ft	~$3,000 or $4.00/sq ft
Retail sq ft	~15,000 sq ft	~12,500 sq ft
Website/contact info for the project	https://www.atelierdallas.com/	https://www.unionwestchicago.com/
Regional home price index*	270.53758	176.16789

*S&P/Case-Shiller Home Price Index, St. Louis Federal Reserve, https://fred.stlouisfed.org/series/MIXRSA.

the additional cost. In fact, competition may make it difficult to rent the project if it does not have these features and services.

In comparison, renters of lower-end apartments cannot pay for many such features. Nonetheless, in some areas (Texas, for example), even the lowest-end garden apartments feature club rooms and swimming pools, private balconies, cable television, and high-speed internet.

The developer is responsible for establishing the development program within which the architect will work. The developer should choose an architect experienced with the particular product being planned but should not let the architect dictate unit mix, unit sizes, or amenities; these decisions should be made jointly and on the basis of the market analysis for the geographic subarea where the project is located. Design decisions should take costs and ease of maintenance into consideration. Although the architect's mission is to design the project, the developer must have sufficient design skills to give the architect the required guidance. The developer's ability to mentally visualize the design and floor plans is vital to success. Fortunately, computer-aided design (CAD) helps develop-

ers visualize the drawings through three-dimensional computer renderings. CAD is also helpful for marketing because it allows potential customers to visualize the new development as it is being built. CAD enables viewers to "walk through" a proposed project, looking at every room from any number of viewpoints.

Time spent scrutinizing the plans during design is among the most important tasks of the entire project. The developer should mentally walk through every unit, look out every window, and envisage every view inside and outside the apartment. What does someone see first when opening the apartment's front door? That view will create the first impression for renters or buyers when they open the door of model units. Fixing something with the architect during the design phase is much easier and less expensive than making changes out in the field or, worse, after the building is built. As Phil Hughes puts it, "The eraser is cheaper than the jackhammer!"

Multifamily residential buildings are among the most complex buildings to design. They must accommodate the functional needs of a large number of people at a relatively high density while protecting individuals' privacy. At the same time, the buildings must provide a sense of ownership and a sense of

MAISON BETHESDA

Bethesda, Maryland
Mid-Rise
229
6
Q2 2019
Q1 2022
Two levels below grade

~$60 million or $288/net rentable sq ft

~$3,800 or $4.00/sq ft
0 sq ft
https://www.maizonbethesdamd.com/
290.8298

LAS OLAS WALK

Fort Lauderdale, Florida
Mid-Rise
456
8
Q2 2018
Q1 2021
Eight stories above grade wrapped by units/amenities

~$91 million or $217/net rentable sq ft

~$2,800 or $3.00/sq ft
0 sq ft
https://www.10xlivinglasolaswalk.com/
350.79053

AZOLA SOUTH TAMPA

Tampa, Florida
Garden
214
3 and 4
Q2 2021
Q3 2022 (anticipated)
Surface parking

~$26 million or $132/net rentable sq ft

~$2,000 or $2.15/sq ft
0 sq ft
https://www.azolasouthtampa.com/
330.37833

place and community. Ultimately, multifamily residential design entails a series of compromises between notions of ideal living conditions and the economic realities of higher-density dwelling.

UNIT MIX

The mix of units by size and type should be based on the market study. Unit types most often range from studio apartments to two- and three-bedroom units with two baths; some include extras, such as sunrooms, dens, and lofts. In many markets, apartment developers are seeing increased demand for luxury units for empty nesters who are downsizing. In projects designed for lower-income renters, family-sized units should predominate. If the target market is young singles just starting out, demand will likely be strongest for a mix of two-master-bedroom roommate units and one-bedroom units for singles. In very high-rent urban locales, studio units are popular; but in suburban areas, demand for such small units is almost nonexistent.

Nationally in 2019, the median size of new multi-family units built for rent was 1,057 square feet (98 sq m) and for-sale was 1,350 square feet (125 sq m).

The average—1,203 square feet (111 sq m)—was 93 square feet (8.6 sq m) bigger than the 2010 value of 1,110 square feet (103 sq m). Unit size has increased every decade. In 1990, the median was 955 square feet (90 sq m), up from 882 square feet (80 sq m) in 1985. The percentage of new units constructed with three or more bedrooms fluctuated between 2010 and 2019. The 2010 figure stood at 12.26 percent, rising in 2011 to 18.12 percent, then falling in 2012 to 16.87 percent. By 2019, the percentage had dropped to 11.36 percent. Overall, however, these percentages are up significantly from the 7 percent of new three-bedroom units constructed in 1985.[49] At the same time, studio and micro units have been getting smaller—even less than 300 square feet (28 sq m)—to help bring down skyrocketing rents in gateway cities like New York City.

Certain niche markets play a role in determining unit types. For example, apartments housing students require special floor plans that include three- and four-bedroom units, because most students share units. In other areas, the difficulty in getting approvals because of neighborhood opposition to higher density and increasing land and permitting costs may force developers to pursue higher-income tenants. Architect Art Danielian says, "Trends are changing fast now. There are creative ways to handle the growing market for 'multigenerational' floor plans, better ways to deal with seniors' housing (including assisted living), and multifamily rental housing at various pricing and density levels."[50] Micro units are another trend. The tiny size of the units is offset with building amenities. Small units offer the highest rent per square foot. Success depends on how well the amenities are integrated.[51]

SITE DESIGN

A good site plan respects the natural characteristics of the site and its surroundings. The primary determinants of the site plan are the desired and permitted density, parking layout, and requirements for emergency access. The density of the project in turn is determined by zoning and the market. Generally, one-story apartments or townhouses yield seven to 12 units per acre (17–30/ha); two-story garden apartments with surface parking comfortably yield 12 to 18 units per acre (30–45/ha); and three-story garden apartments with surface parking yield up to 30 units per acre (75/ha). Structured parking, usually accommodated in one or two levels under the apartments or in a separate structure, is required to achieve densities greater than 40 units per acre (100/ha).

Fire codes typically permit a maximum distance of 150 feet (45 m) between a fire road or hydrant and a building. Local fire officials should be consulted early in the design process to determine requirements.

Mass transit is another consideration. Although required minimum density numbers vary by location, a minimum density of 10 to 17 units per acre (4.05 to 6.88 per ha) is generally needed to support a mass public transit system; densities greater than 36 per acre (14.57 per ha) are generally needed to support both bus and rail. Appropriate density ranges by station type are 75+ units per acre (30.35 per ha) for urban core, 25 to 75 units per acre (10.12 to 30.35 per ha) for town center or commuter town center, 15 to 50 units per acre (6.07 to 20.23 per ha) for neighborhood stations, and 15 to 50 units per acre (6.07 to 20.23 per ha) for arterial corridors.[52]

Conflict is inherent between those who want lower apartment densities and the goal of promoting smart growth (i.e., walkable communities that are less dependent on the automobile and will better support mass transit). "The developer's challenge is to sell the lifestyle of the walkable neighborhoods, proximate to transit, to people who might be considering a car-oriented development with larger houses and lots."[53]

PARKING AND ACCESS. Parking—its dimensions, arrangement, and location—is more important than building coverage in the design of a project. One parking space per bedroom is standard, although parking requirements are being greatly reduced, even to zero, near transit and urban nodes. Typically, 1.75 to 1.8 parking spaces per unit is the recommended standard, and two spaces per unit are mandatory with for-sale condominiums in most areas. One-bedroom condominiums generally do not sell as well as two-bedroom condominiums except in dense urban areas. Even where standards are lower, however, the availability of parking may be necessary for units to sell well. In some locations, developers can count on-street parking as part of their requirement, but occupancy may suffer if street parking is hard to find.

If possible, pedestrian circulation should be kept separate from vehicular access, although walking distances between parking and units should be as short as possible.

Concrete parking areas and driveways are cost-effective in the long run. Although they cost more initially, they look better and are cheaper to maintain than asphalt parking. Parking costs vary widely due to regional differences in construction costs, soil conditions, permitting, and codes. Architect and designer Scott Simpson estimates $3,000 to $5,000 per space for surface parking (asphalt on grade). For structured parking framed in steel or precast concrete, he estimates the cost to be $17,500 to $30,000 per space, depending on the economies of scale—the fewer spaces, the higher cost per space. The cost of underground parking can easily skyrocket. The deeper the excavation, the higher the cost. Underground parking can range from $25,000 per space to about $100,000 per space for high-cost structures, such as underground parking on waterfront sites that require significant waterproofing.[54]

Recovering the full cost of parking can be challenging. Using the 1 percent rule for the monthly rent needed to cover each $1 of additional capital cost, an owner would need to receive an added $500 per month in rent to cover the cost of a $50,000 underground parking space.

Underground garages are especially expensive to build because they require fireproofing, waterproofing, air handlers, and drainage or sump pumps. Carports are rarely built today, but they may be cost-effective, especially in areas with intense sun or severe climates. Care should be taken to make them structurally sound because flimsy carports have collapsed in heavy winds, rains, and snow, damaging the cars below. Carport roofs are attractive for solar panels.

The increasing prevalence of electric and autonomous vehicles will affect the parking equation. Electric vehicles will require more charging stations in garages, and autonomous vehicles will change the number of parking spaces needed per unit. Cities will likely be slow to reduce parking requirements, but some developers are already making changes in their parking designs. For example, some are designing parking garages with level floors to facilitate a change in use from parking to office or residential when demand for parking drops to the point that fewer parking garages are needed. The cost is high, however; such changes can add 30 percent to the cost of parking construction.

Ride sharing is also increasing, so pick-up and drop-off areas for passengers and places for vehicles to wait are important. Jerry Rappaport at New Boston Fund says, "It's necessary to think about sense of arrival on site, the types of signage, how to get where. Are there enough utility rooms, and are there adequate spaces for packages to be delivered?" He observes that not having adequate space for package deliveries is a major mistake; his firm learned this lesson, but many developers do not think of it. As the consumption of e-commerce rises, delivery of packages is becoming the norm. Having designated spaces for these packages to be delivered and a secure system for tenants to retrieve them is a necessity.[55]

AMENITIES AND LANDSCAPING. The selection of amenities begins with the market analysis. A good market analysis answers several questions: What are comparable properties in the market area offering? Do projects with certain amenities have an edge in marketing, or do lower-priced projects with fewer amenities attract more residents? And perhaps the most important: Will residents pay for the amenities?

Amenities help sell the product. What some communities consider essential, others view as luxurious. Generally, when amenities are desired and used, residents will pay a reasonable price for them—unless operating costs do not correspond with residents' income levels. Therefore, the developer should design not only what the residents like but also what they can afford.

Swimming pools and outdoor Jacuzzis are standard amenities in many suburban areas, and attractively landscaped pools can add much to the marketability of a complex. In complexes designed for families, a wading pool for children separate from the adult pool should be provided. Complexes targeted toward young singles might feature dog parks and "soft" programming (e.g., social activities).

Los Angeles architect Scott Johnson observes, "Amenities have become more elaborate and are considered big differentiators in the market to compensate for smaller unit sizes as people may spend more time in common areas." He notes several trends in amenities, including the following:

- Luxury apartments usually feature elaborate media/social lounges and libraries.
- Different amenities attract different demographics (e.g., millennials versus baby boomers); some higher end units may even have children's play areas (typically for visiting grandchildren).
- Pet care has become much more common—even on-site grooming.
- Fitness rooms used to provide mostly free weights, benches, and cardio equipment; now they rely more on digital, stream-based content.
- There is growing interest in converting historic buildings and loft buildings to residential units. Features include higher ceilings, exposed ceilings, drywall ceilings, recessed lighting, exposed concrete, and industrial-size windows."[56]

Landscaping should be as maintenance-free as possible. Focal planting areas with seasonal color should be located near the project's entrance, the leasing office, the pool, and courtyards. The design of the landscaping and sprinkler system should be an integral part of the site plan. Detailed plant design may be left until later, but the general plan should be completed before construction begins. Indeed, many local governments require a landscaping plan before they issue a building permit.

Depending on the market niche, a play area for children or even a daycare center may be a valuable amenity to include. Most projects should allow some space for play areas even if the development is geared largely to a singles market, as some of the residents will likely be part-time parents.

Landscaped areas can serve as buffers, are usually visually attractive, add to the project's overall market appeal, and serve as passive recreational areas. A six-foot-wide (1.8 m) walking trail surrounding the property can be used for walking, running, biking, or skating and costs little to construct and maintain.

Hints for Successful Multifamily Residential Design

- Be flexible when targeting a market. If the market for a project turns out to be very different from the developer's initial expectation, the presence of basic features with a broad market appeal will help sales or rentals.
- Ensure that common areas for stairs, elevators, corridors, lobbies, laundries, and so forth do not occupy more than 18 to 20 percent of total heated rentable areas.
- Include property managers in all design review meetings. They can make many useful contributions to the design process.
- Do not put family units on the third floor of walk-up buildings.
- Design units to meet the affordability requirements of the target market. Renters look primarily at total rent, not rent per square foot.
- Make sure that a project will not bring financial ruin if units must be rented rather than sold. Condominiums often end up as rental units because of changing market conditions.

- When possible, enclose a project's open space with buildings, creating courtyards free from cars. Views of cars detract from the courtyard environment and may reduce attainable rents.
- Avoid creating canyon-like areas and barracks-like buildings.
- Avoid placing air-conditioner condensing units in areas where children will play.
- Plan ahead for trash disposal. Make containers easy to reach, easy to clean around, and screened if possible.
- Note that the U.S. Postal Service requires that mailboxes be grouped together. Place mailboxes near the manager's office so that the manager can see tenants as they come and go.
- Provide storage facilities near the pool for outdoor furniture during the winter.
- Ensure that the leasing office is visible from the street, is easy to find, and has reserved parking close by.

Some new developments include community gardens, as well as private outdoor space adjacent to units. Integrating landscaped areas with active recreational facilities, such as pools and children's play areas, yields the most attractive site plan.

Landscape design must consider the climate, terrain, and cultural influences of the region where the project is located. Sustainable landscape designers effectively use hardy indigenous plants that provide interest during all seasons. Xeriscaping, a method of landscaping that relies on proper plant selection and planning to conserve water, minimizes the use of chemicals and reduces the amount of labor-intensive maintenance by carefully considering the site's climate, soil, existing vegetation, and topography. Such methods can be applied to any climate or site. A sustainable landscape will reduce labor inputs, making it less expensive to implement and maintain. Plant selection, implementation, and maintenance build on the design process, each having sustainability as a major consideration.

EXTERIOR DESIGN

The choice of exterior materials and architectural designs should closely relate to the target market's preferences and the character of the local community. The style and materials of a new project should be compatible with existing development in the surrounding area. A project in a newly developing area should aspire to set the tone for future development.

Regional traditions and climate play important roles in the exterior design of apartment buildings. Brick is a common material throughout the South and along the East Coast. Stucco is popular in the Southwest, whereas wood or composite siding is most common in the northern United States.

Economies of scale can be achieved by minimizing and repeating building types. The fewer the number of building types, the greater the potential for minimizing costs. Wall segments and roof trusses can be prefabricated in groups, and labor costs fall when more work can be done by semiskilled workers. At the same time, however, marketability may require considerable variety in appearance. Long, straight walls and rooflines should be avoided. Individual buildings should not extend more than 200 feet (60 m).

Marvin Finger stated that his development company never went to the architect with a generic design. "We go to the neighborhood and select the prominent features of the building elevations of that upscale community and then we take that to the architect to enhance and work into the proposed facade."[57]

The building's exterior should express the individuality of the apartment units within. Balconies are useful as private outdoor space and are often instrumental design elements in denoting individual apartments. Six feet (1.8 m) is usually considered the optimal depth for a usable balcony—anything larger may cause excessive shading of windows below, and anything smaller may be useful only for storage, which is unsightly. Inset balconies are visually more attractive and can be useful in establishing privacy. Such balconies in combination with an L-shaped plan allow two rooms to open onto one balcony.

The roof should help establish a residential character as well as shed rain and snow. The silhouettes of various roof forms can create a friendly, village-like impression. As with the rest of the exterior of the building, roof design is determined partly by regional traditions and styles.

Utility meters, transformers, and trash bins—always potentially unsightly—should not be overlooked during design. A bank of meters, for example, can be quite obtrusive. Utility companies prefer that meters be grouped together and usually have a say in their placement. Submetering also allows for optimal placement of meters away from visible areas.

INTERIOR DESIGN

One objective in designing an apartment interior is to make a relatively small space seem larger than it is. Large windows and angled walls that lead the eye around corners can help in this regard. Windows are important not only for the views they offer but also for the light and ventilation they permit. Natural ventilation of an apartment requires that windows be placed on at least two exposures, not necessarily in the same room and preferably on opposite walls. In any room, natural lighting is improved when light comes from more than one direction. L-shaped units offer greater design opportunities than do square or rectangular units. And higher ceilings can be an effective means of increasing the impression of space. A cost analysis should be done, however, to determine the cost of an increase in the exterior building envelope. The traditional eight-foot (2.4 m) ceiling height has been replaced with nine or even 10 feet (2.7 or 3 m) as the standard, especially in luxury apartments and condominiums.

Most markets today demand laundry facilities in the units and fully equipped kitchens with dishwashers, garbage disposals, wood cabinetry, and built-in microwave ovens. Adequate kitchen and storage areas make apartments more livable. The kitchen for a one-bedroom apartment should provide a minimum of 16 linear feet (5 m) for counters and appliances. Each bedroom should offer a minimum of 12 linear feet (3.6 m) of closet space, and guest and linen closets should provide another four linear feet (1.2 m) of storage. These standards can be met in a floor plan of 700 square feet (65 sq m) in a one-bedroom apartment

and 1,000 square feet (95 sq m) in a two-bedroom apartment. In smaller units, some compromises may be necessary.

In most markets, two-bedroom units should have two baths, with one bathroom for guests' use accessible from the hall, without walking through a bedroom. In higher-priced developments, master baths often include soaking tubs, separate showers, and double vanities. Quality at the lower end has risen correspondingly.

Successful developers worry about every detail. In small apartments, for example, circulation is critical. The design should pay careful attention to how the doors will open so as to minimize conflicts and obstructions. In large developments, full-scale mock-ups of prototypical units are worthwhile. The cost is modest, and the savings can be huge. Computer renderings can simulate the *appearance* of the units very closely but not the actual construction aspects. Mock-ups serve two main purposes: (1) They reveal problems in the design. (2) Subcontractors can use them to familiarize themselves with the plan; make decisions about the placement of wiring, plumbing, and ductwork; and correct potential conflicts between subcontractors. For example, a plumbing pipe may interfere with the best route for an air-conditioning duct. Such conflicts otherwise may not become apparent until the construction stage.

Finish materials in an apartment should be chosen for ease of maintenance and to reflect the tastes of the market. Vinyl tile is commonly used in kitchens, baths, and entries, although ceramic tile or stone may be used in higher-end apartments. Other rooms are typically carpeted, with the quality of the carpet varying with the market. Alternatively, flooring may be hardwood or simulated wood.

Certain optional features can add value to the unit in terms of additional monthly rents. Bookcases, decorative moldings, ceiling fans, and under-cabinet lighting can all increase a unit's sense of quality but are desirable only if they are supported by the market. Fireplaces, for instance, take up space, and many tenants of smaller apartments are reluctant to pay the increased rent charged for such amenities. The appropriateness of amenities such as washer/dryers also depends on the market. To recover amenity costs, the developer should be able to increase an apartment's monthly rent by at least 1 percent of the incremental cost of any amenities. For example, units with a $2,000 fireplace should be able to command rents at least $20 per month higher than those without fireplaces.

Separate heating, ventilating, and air-conditioning (HVAC) systems for each unit are typical for most garden and mid-rise developments. Mechanical systems can be contained in the walls, ceilings, or roof spaces of the unit but require an outside compressor. The compressor can be located on the roof, where it must be screened and integrated with the roof design, or on the ground outside the unit, where its noise is more noticeable and where it may create an obstruction and undesirable play spot for children to jump off. Scott Simpson notes that in high-rise projects, "[variable air volume] is common. However, chilled beams have recently caught on, and raised floors are gaining traction as well. The location, climate, orientation, and local market all play a role in system selection. Also, if the building is slated for LEED [Leadership in Energy and Environmental Design] certification, then heat recovery wheels are often added. Some lower-end apartment buildings use through-wall unit ventilators, so it is definitely not a question of one size fits all."[58]

Up-to-date wiring systems are essential. Units should be prewired for cable television, security systems, internet connections, and multiple telephone lines, with outlets in all rooms. Retrofitting wiring in a completed building is expensive and difficult. More and more developers see the wisdom of building smart buildings, with all systems integrated and controlled by computer. Such technology is essential in luxury apartments and before long will be expected in lower-end projects as well. John Porta in Brentwood, Missouri, buys and upgrades existing apartment buildings. He observes, "Laundry is a critical factor that remodeling can't always easily accommodate. Latino residents require bigger kitchens. Gen-Y residents want a nice-looking kitchen, but it does not have to be particularly functional." He adds that kitchens vary somewhat from market to market, as do amenities and exteriors, but interior layouts are largely consistent. "Parking can be a revenue center in certain cities and in others, it is a standard amenity for which you cannot charge an additional fee."[59]

Wellness is becoming a feature of apartment design. Lou Minicucci obtained a Fitwel Certification for his project in Newburyport, Massachusetts, by including several amenities:

- updated air filtration for ventilation, with each unit independent from the others;
- upgraded MERV (a measure of a filter's efficiency) filters from 7 to 13;

- better air quality in common area with ultraviolet light;
- pumped-in fresh air;
- vending machines with healthier snacks;
- signs encouraging the use of stairs rather than elevators (physical exercise and energy savings);
- room-darkening shades for better sleep quality; and
- a bike sharing program, bike trails, and walking trails.

Minicucci states, "You want to aggregate these small details to make a healthier community, but these components generally are not quantified."[60]

Art Danielian adds that walls and floor systems need to be designed to abate sound and reduce noise transmission. This requires constructing two separate walls between units with one inch separation between the walls. An assemblage of materials in the floor system can also eliminate the kind of noises associated with walking or stomping in an apartment.[61]

Scott Johnson sees a number of trends in interior design:

- higher quality finishes and appliances;
- smaller appliances as units get smaller;
- more gas stoves than electric;
- smaller units, often with no separate dining room but with an open kitchen and dining at an island; and
- ongoing debate over tub versus shower. (Younger generations tend to spend comparatively less time in the bathroom, so a trend toward showers—which take up less space—is likely.)[62]

DESIGN ISSUES

PRIVACY AND SECURITY. The layout of apartment buildings needs to provide privacy for each apartment, regardless of the project's density. Many of the techniques employed in the design of the site, units, and building exteriors are devices for creating visual separation between units. Building codes also provide useful criteria: for example, a code might stipulate that a wall with windows should be separated from a facing wall with windows by at least 30 feet (9 m), that a wall with windows should be separated from a facing wall without windows by at least 20 feet (6 m), and that two outside walls without windows should be separated by a minimum of 10 feet (3 m). Vertical and horizontal projections, such as walls and balconies, should be placed in a way that helps screen views into bedrooms from other apartments or from common spaces.

Security is an important consideration in site design. A plan that minimizes the number of entries to a project provides greater control of traffic and therefore better security. Entries to units should not be hidden from view, and walkways and breezeways should be visible from several points. Exterior lighting can do much to create a feeling of security. At the same time, exterior lighting should be designed so that light does not shine directly into apartment units or adjacent properties or cause glare for passing motorists.

Electronic security systems for individual units as well as project entrances are common in some parts of the country, most notably in California, Florida, and Texas. Gated community entrances are another growing and somewhat controversial trend. Although the gate lends an air of security as well as prestige to some communities, research does not indicate that crime rates are lower in gated communities. Jerome Frank, Jr., notes, "People are very concerned about covered parking or garage parking and related issues of security. People like to see a security gate. They are a maintenance hell and don't provide much security, but [they work] psychologically." He adds, "Many higher-density apartments deal with this issue by putting parking in the middle. How traffic is handled—vehicular and pedestrian—has to be worked out in terms of planning for overall circulation (proximity of parking to housing and the length of walk to one's unit, for example)."[63]

Other changes due to technology include the following:

- integrated smart home systems (e.g., Alexa, Google Home) in higher-end projects;
- residential concierge management software;
- updated mailrooms (e.g., to accommodate packages and fresh deliveries, with some even having refrigeration); and
- electric vehicle charging stations.[64]

Incorporating a separate, secured space for package delivery is important. This did not used to be an important component of design. Due to the rise of e-commerce, residential buildings need a place to store packages until they can be delivered to residents. If a unit owner is at work for most of the day, a package could sit out and easily be stolen or damaged by inclement weather. Designing cameras to be placed in the mailroom provides an extra level of security. "It may also be necessary to have designated drop off zones on [rooftops] if Amazon drone delivery becomes normalized."[65]

Design elements can be used to create a sense of ownership. Studies of successful subsidized housing projects have shown that tenants take better care of their apartments when a "semiprivate" transition area is provided between the outdoor public space and their private apartment. Tenants like to be able to assume ownership of this transition space. This concept can also work well for luxury apartments. The semiprivate space may range from an inset doorway to a fenced-in front patio.

SUSTAINABILITY. Energy efficiency and water use regulations are already very strict in many states. Solar panels are becoming more cost effective and are being required in new homes and apartments in some states.[66] Tom Montelli says, "Designing and building sustainability is a win-win. It's a win for our customers, and it's a win for us in the capital markets. Customers today are environmentally conscious and smart, so they respond positively to these initiatives. And it's also a good way to conduct business, generally being a good steward for the environment. For returns, it is beneficial [and] can be conducive to your long-term operating efficiencies."[67] Examples of green components in Post Road Residential projects are solar arrays, smart thermostats, LED lighting everywhere, occupancy sensors for LED lights (which can turn off lights when no one is in the space), plants in amenity spaces, panelized construction to eliminate waste, electric vehicle charging stations, bike share programs and bike docking stations, and dedicated open space.[68]

Phil Hughes always tries to add flexibility in design to allow for condominium conversion—for example, installing separate gas and electricity meters and building with concrete or steel, which are higher quality. But these components add about 15 percent to the cost that cannot be recovered by 15 percent additional rent. The cost does get recouped when the unit is sold as a condo, but he says few developers will do this because it is too much of a commitment for a build-to-sell type of developer.[69]

RENTAL APARTMENTS VERSUS CONDOMINIUMS. The design of rental housing differs from the design of for-sale (condominium) housing in a number of respects. Security and privacy are even more important issues in condominiums than in apartments. If rental and for-sale units are in the same complex, they should be physically separated because the proximity of rentals hurts the sale of condominiums. Renters do not face the long-term investment of a mortgage and are less likely to be critical of a less desirable location within the complex as a whole. Many condominium complexes forbid investor-owned rental units because owner-occupants do not want to live next to renters.

Some condominium developers recommend higher bedroom counts in the unit mix. In general, a condominium project should have a smaller number but a greater variety of dwelling units per building, compared with a rental project. Kitchens need additional countertop space and cabinets. Baths must have better appointments. Closets and general storage areas must be larger.

One-quarter to one-half more parking spaces per condominium unit is often required, compared with rental units. Moreover, condominium parking spaces should be identified and separated from rental unit spaces. However, assigned spaces can create management problems as a result of the misuse of those spaces.

DESIGNING TO SAVE COSTS. Developers must make many tradeoffs between construction costs and operating costs. For example, the use of exterior wood siding may save construction costs, but because it needs frequent repainting, its use may increase maintenance costs; in contrast, brick is a more costly but permanent material. High-maintenance materials also depress the sale value of a rental project; proper accounting for operating expenses indicates the extent to which replacement reserves and maintenance expenses reduce net operating income.

APPROVALS

Some developers believe that the safest way to deal with local government officials is to tell them very little until documents are submitted for project approval. This policy, however, is not wise. If any public review is required, the developer should meet with an official of the reviewing agency before drawing up preliminary plans. A preapplication conference is a good way to meet the planning staff and learn their interests and concerns. In turn, the planning staff can inform the developer of requirements to consider during the planning stage. The conference also gives the developer the chance to involve the staff in the project, thereby encouraging a sense of cooperation that is likely to make the entire project proceed more smoothly.

Even when the developer can apply directly for a building permit, members of the planning department may be able to provide valuable information before the design plans are drawn up. For example, the fire inspector at one building department informed Peiser Corporation and Jerome Frank Investments of proposed changes that the project architect had not heard of regarding the regulations governing fire walls. The changes made it more economical to use sprinklers than floor-to-rafter fire-rated partitions. Six months later, when they returned for plan approval, the proposed changes had taken effect. Thus, the fire inspector's forewarning saved Peiser and Frank the time and money that would otherwise have been necessary to redraw the plans.

A developer should not spend too much money on preliminary plans in case, as often happens, the project does not proceed. But sufficient care should be taken so that the plans satisfy government agencies and financial backers. Further, the most creative part of the design process often occurs when drawing preliminary plans. The preliminary plan phase can be divided into a rough concept planning phase and a refined schematic phase. Rough concept plans consist of floor plans and elevations that may be prepared for testing the market for financing and for tenants; refined schematic drawings represent the last opportunity for major design decisions. Refined schematic drawings are also used to solicit lenders and tenants. Once the plans are approved, most major features of a project cannot be changed.

A collaborative design process is important for ensuring that the design is as functional and marketable as possible. Regular meetings should be held with property managers, construction superintendents, and leasing managers to obtain their input and to have them critique the latest plans. Beginning developers should ask mentors and other developers to review the plans as well. They may see problems in the design that others do not.

Many communities hold design review hearings that are open to the public. The developer should meet with design review board members (often local architects) as soon as possible to learn about their primary concerns. Neighbors usually have strong opinions about the design, including facades, ingress, egress, parking, materials, landscaping, elevations, open space, and views. Developers should be prepared to answer their criticisms. Meeting with them sooner rather than later in the design process is advisable. The meetings can help establish a rapport if the neighbors feel that their concerns are being addressed. In addition, the neighbors may understand the compromises and tradeoffs better if they are part of the process rather than being asked to react to final plans.

Tips for Working with Architects

- Keep a direct line of communication open with the design architect. Intermediaries are a liability in the initial phases of design.
- Establish team milestones to ensure that the project stays on schedule.
- Use an initial design workshop to streamline the concept design phase.
- Always use a qualified contractor who has experience and legitimate references and involve that person from the very beginning of the design process.
- Consider software options to distribute the latest set of plans to all subcontractors and make all plan revisions and updates accessible. Make sure to date every plan set and revision.
- Pay very careful attention to the circulation of the building and site plan. Sometimes, the investment in a computer simulation helps clarify unresolved issues about circulation.

- Invest in design that creates a particular ambience and sense of identity, but keep cost considerations in mind.
- Identify the norms for the region when choosing amenities and functional systems.
- Always have a furniture plan drawn up for each apartment type proposed by the architect. Sometimes, the design may seem very good, but the configuration and dimensions of the rooms will not allow for even the most typical furniture, such as couches and larger beds, to be positioned well in the unit.

Sources: Jan Van Tilberg, Van Tilberg, Banvard & Soderbergh, Santa Monica, California; and Paige Close, Looney Ricks Kiss Architects, Memphis, Tennessee.

Community outreach is mandatory for public approval in California and some other states because social, economic, and environmental factors must be addressed in a way that community members, planning commissioners, and city council members will understand. They must mutually agree that sustainable and environmental elements have been appropriately included and addressed. This process can take a good amount of time and money.[70]

Final plans and specifications become part of the official contract package used by the contractor and submitted to the lender and the city building department. They include the construction drawings and material specifications required to build the project.

Unless a developer is certain that the project will go ahead, final plans and specifications should not be ordered until all feasibility studies are completed, all predevelopment approvals—such as zoning changes—are in place, and a tentative financing commitment is received. Final plans and specifications, which typically cost three or four times as much as the preliminary plans, represent a major increase in at-risk investment. They must be completed in their entirety before plans can be submitted to the city for a building permit. In some cities, the building permit process is so lengthy that a developer cannot afford to make any major changes to the plans once they have been submitted.

Because the drawings and specifications become contract documents, the more precise they are, the better. At the same time, items such as air-conditioning equipment should not be specified too exactly in case

the contractor can make a cost-saving substitution. Change orders during construction are the single largest source of construction cost overruns. Unfortunately, they are unavoidable, and developers should carry a 5 percent construction contingency for these unexpected events. The fewer changes that are made, the fewer opportunities the contractor or subcontractor has to raise the contract price. If the developer has done his homework properly during preliminary planning, the process of obtaining final drawings should be routine. The contractor should be involved as early as possible in reviewing the drawings to minimize problems in the field and provide cost-to-value assistance to the entire development team.

Financing

Rental apartment projects, like other income property developments, have traditionally relied primarily on three types of financing: construction loans, permanent loans, and equity. For-sale condominium projects, like land development, do not have permanent loans because the buyers of individual units obtain their own permanent loans. Condominium developers require only equity and a construction loan, the latter covering the construction and sales period. In contrast, in rental apartment projects, the developer uses the permanent loan to *take out* the construction loan as soon as the project reaches a specified level of income or occupancy. The amount of the construction loan usually equals that of the permanent loan because the construction lender will lend up to, but no more than, the amount that the permanent lender

URBAN CATALYST DEVELOPMENT

Lancaster Urban Village is a catalytic redevelopment in the historically impoverished southern sector of Dallas. The initial phase involved the assembly and redevelopment of 14 properties that included 193 apartment homes, 14,000 square feet (1,300 sq m) of retail and small office space, a shared parking garage, and an area to accommodate public gatherings and events.

will fund. The construction lender looks to the permanent lender's mortgage to retire or "take out" the construction loan.

Equity makes up the difference between total project cost and the amount of the construction and permanent loans. At one time, construction and permanent loans often covered 100 percent of project costs, and developers were not required to contribute additional equity. After the savings and loan crash of the late 1980s and the Great Recession in 2007–2009, however, rigid loan coverage requirements were put in place which usually demand that equity cover 25 to 40 percent of the project's value at completion. This completion value is the capitalized value of the stabilized NOI after all construction and lease-up risk is over. Because the completed project value usually exceeds the total all-in development cost (the difference is development profit), the permanent lender's LTV ratio as a percentage of completed project value should result in a higher LTV ratio as a percentage of development cost. For example, if the completed capitalized value of a project is $12 million, and total all-in development costs are $10 million, then a 60 percent LTV requirement by the lender will result in a $7.2 million permanent loan, or 72 percent of total development cost.

Equity is the most expensive source of funding because equity investors receive returns only after other lenders have been repaid. Equity investors therefore

have the riskiest position, and they require much higher rates of return than lenders do to compensate for the risk of being in the first-loss position. Construction lenders usually require developers to invest most or all of the needed equity in a project up front, before they begin to fund the construction loan, to ensure that the developer has enough money to complete the project. Even after the construction loan has been retired by the permanent mortgage, equity investors receive cash flow only to the extent that the property produces cash flow over and above the annual mortgage debt service. If a shortfall occurs, developers (or their investors) are responsible for injecting additional equity to cover the shortfall so that the bank always receives its full monthly debt service payment when it is due. Otherwise, the permanent mortgage goes into default, and lenders can begin foreclosure proceedings on the project.

For beginning developers, the task of finding lenders is perhaps the hardest job after finding equity investors (although in a capital-rich environment, great projects will attract eager investors). Lenders look chiefly at track record, credit, and the project itself. By definition, beginning developers lack a track record, and they rarely have the financial net worth of more experienced developers. Thus, the project must be well above average in terms of its market feasibility, design, and economic appeal to capture a lender's interest. Beginning developers can improve their chances of securing loans by undertaking a joint venture with experienced developers and/or wealthy individuals. Beginning developers should also bear in mind that smaller localized lenders are more likely than large banks to consider their requests. Many developers begin as homebuilders, which allows them to build relationships with lenders that carry over to subsequent larger projects. Lenders are just as concerned about the way developers handle their business (meet deadlines, handle draw requests, build within budget, and so forth) as they are about the size of developers' previous projects. Regardless, they must be satisfied that the developer has the competency to complete larger, more complicated projects. (See chapter 2 for a review of the various financial institutions that provide construction and permanent financing for real estate.)

CONSTRUCTION LOANS

Traditionally, developers obtained a permanent loan commitment before obtaining a construction loan commitment, even though construction financing occurs before permanent financing. The construction lender approved the construction loan on the basis of the promise that the loan would be retired by the permanent loan at some specified date. In the early 1980s, however, when interest rates soared, open-ended construction loans without permanent takeouts became common. Floating rate *miniperms*—three- to five-year construction loans that carried over into the operating period—were granted on the expectation that permanent rates would come down.[71] The provision of open-ended loans, however, generally depends on the track records and financial statements of developers.

The construction loan is characterized by its short term, installment draws, variable interest rate, and single repayment when the project is completed and the construction loan is taken out by the permanent loan.[72] The developer files draw requests with the construction lender each month as work progresses on the project. The lender's inspectors check the property each month to confirm that the work was done, and the lender then funds the request by transferring money into the developer's project account. This money is available for the developer to pay the contractor (see figure 4-10). The amount, term, and interest rate of the construction loan are defined by the loan agreement. Interest payments are added to the loan balance at the end of each month so that the developer does not have to make out-of-pocket payments for interest. If the project is not fully leased and the permanent loan is not funded within the stated term limit, the construction lender is technically able to *call the loan*—that is, demand immediate payment from the developer. In practice, however, the construction lender does not want to have to foreclose on a bad construction loan as long as a reasonable likelihood exists that the project can be completed successfully. If the developer has kept the construction lender regularly informed about the project's progress and reasons for delay, the lender will probably be willing to extend the construction loan term by six or 12 months. Such extensions almost always require the payment of an additional one or two points. In times of economic crisis, lenders may be under regulatory pressure to reduce real estate exposure and may be unwilling to extend loans. At such times, the developer stands to lose the project if he or she cannot come up with substantially more equity or bring in a replacement lender.

Construction loans suffer from a high degree of uncertainty because construction projects themselves are subject to delays caused by weather, labor troubles,

and material shortages; cost overruns; bankruptcies by contractors and subcontractors; and leasing risk (lease-up rates and rents that fall below expectations). Consequently, lenders providing construction funding take special precautions to ensure that they are protected.

Moreover, construction lenders have become increasingly suspicious of the viability of permanent commitments. Permanent loans sometimes contain such stringent covenants (which developers must meet before funding is provided) that the takeout loan funding is questionable. In negotiating permanent takeouts, developers must ensure that they have bankable commitments—that is, commitments that construction lenders will lend against.

The lender's security comes from two sources: the project itself and the developer's credit. The developer is typically required to sign personally (accept full personal liability) on the construction loan and must show a net worth at least equal to the loan. During economic downturns, the credit requirements may be even more stringent, and the developer may have to prove a *liquid* net worth (cash, stocks, and bonds) equal to the amount of the loan.

CALCULATING INTEREST FOR A CONSTRUCTION LOAN

Suppose a developer has a $1 million construction loan with two points ($20,000) paid up front (out of loan proceeds). Assuming 10 percent annual interest, interest on the construction loan and the draw schedule are shown in figure 4-10. The bank will accrue interest monthly. The loan must be repaid at the end of the 12th month.

For apartments, the construction loan usually has a term of one to three years, which must cover both the construction and the lease-up periods. Interest rates depend on the developer's credit and typically range from 1 to 3 percent over prime with one or two points up front.[73]

Construction lenders usually require the developer to put the total required equity into the project on the front end, before the developer can draw down the construction loan. Any necessary equity must therefore be raised before construction can begin

Interest is calculated each month on the average daily balance. Developers can make precise calculations of their interest requirements (as illustrated in figure 4-10), but banks have their own method for estimating interest during construction and lease-up. For example, if the total construction loan amount is $10 million with a one-year term at 10 percent interest, the bank may apply a standard factor as high as 0.75 to determine the average loan balance, even though the developer may show the average loan balance to be 0.5 percent of the final amount. This factor is used to determine the interest reserve, or $750,000 in this example ($10,000,000 × 0.75 average balance × 10 percent interest × 1 year).

Construction and permanent lenders require a first lien on the property.[74] Existing loans automatically have a superior position to subsequent loans under the rule of "first in time, first in priority." Thus, any prior loans, such as seller financing or land development loans, must be paid off, releasing the senior liens, at the time of the first construction draw. This rule means that seller financing *must* be subordinated (the seller agrees to accept a second lien position) for a construction or permanent lender to fund the mortgage. Construction loan draws are tied to stages in the construction process, called *percent completion*, based on an appraisal of the work completed to date. The appraisal is conducted by an inspector hired by the lender. If the value as measured by the preagreed formula for percent completion is lower, additional draws will not be permitted, regardless of the dollar amount expended by the developer. The developer makes a detailed line-item budget of off-site expenses, such as street improvements and traffic signals; on-site expenses, such as asphalt and landscaping; and direct construction expenses for the whole project. For example, the developer may tell the lender that 50 percent of the concrete work is done and ask for 50 percent funding of the line item for concrete. The lender's inspector may check and say that only 40 percent of the work has been done. The developer may attempt to convince the inspector that more work has been done, but the inspector's opinion will prevail for monthly construction loan draws. Construction loans have traditionally been made by *institutional* lenders, namely, commercial banks and sometimes insurance companies and pension funds. Institutional lenders are subject to scrutiny by the Federal Reserve, which carefully monitors loan balances and reserves. If a loan is not repaid on time or if interest payments are not made, the loan is placed into a separate category that requires significantly higher *loan reserves* (cash balances held by the bank to offset potential losses).

The Financial Institutions Reform, Recovery, and Enforcement Act (FIRREA) was enacted in 1989. Among other things, it regulates the amount of bank

FIGURE 4-10 Calculating Interest for a Construction Loan

Month	Beginning Balance	Interest Charges	Current Draws	Ending Balance
0			$20,000	$20,000
1	$20,000	$167	40,000	60,167
2	60,167	501	80,000	140,668
3	140,668	1,172	80,000	221,840
4	221,840	1,849	100,000	323,689
5	323,689	2,697	100,000	426,386
6	426,386	3,553	100,000	529,939
7	529,939	4,416	100,000	634,355
8	634,355	5,286	100,000	739,641
9	739,641	6,164	100,000	845,805
10	845,805	7,048	100,000	952,853
11	952,853	7,940	80,000	1,040,793
12	1,040,793	8,673	0	1,049,466
Total		**$49,466**	**$1,000,000**	

Total amount to be repaid to the bank:	$1,049,466
Effective yield to the bank:	14.49%

reserves required to cover high-risk real estate loans. The average equity reserve was raised to 6 percent to minimize defaults. The rates are variable and depend on whether the loan is standard, development, or speculative. Many law firms specialize in compliance with FIRREA.[75]

Banks are eager to avoid any construction loans that involve unnecessary risk, meaning new developers have an especially hard time obtaining financing. That difficulty notwithstanding, community banks are likely to be the most willing construction lenders to beginning developers.

Loan reserves are established internally based on the perceived risk of each particular loan. Banks often hold appraisals to be valid for a year or more depending on the property, stability of tenant, and stability of the market. Under unstable market conditions and periods of declining property values, banks may require appraisal updates more frequently than one per year.

The task of finding a construction lender is much simpler if a developer has a takeout loan commitment for the permanent loan. Jerome Frank, Jr., emphasizes that finding the lowest loan rate is less important than establishing a relationship with a good banker: "A quarter to a half point in interest is not going to make or break the deal. The most important thing for the developer is not going to be the rate but the time—making sure that he negotiates enough time for himself to get it done."[76]

Claudia Piper at Webster Bank in Massachusetts notes that there are three scales of banks: (1) large national banks (e.g., Bank of America, Wells Fargo), (2) middle market regional banks (e.g., Webster Bank), and (3) local banks (e.g., Berkshire Bank). "Typically, large national and regional banks won't directly work with people starting out without a track record unless they already have experience with institutional developers. Banks are more focused about the performance and track record of the sponsor than the attractiveness of the deal itself—even more so after the Great Recession."[77] Lou Minicucci says that for his small-to-medium size development company in Boston, "You need to find banks that have the lending capacity to provide the money you're looking to borrow and have the comfortability to lend that capital." For example, on a recent project in Lynn, Massachusetts, with a $78 million construction loan and a $32 million equity raise, the firm went to a bank it knew had enough size and enough appetite to lend that money.[78]

How much experience do lenders look for to start a relationship? Piper responds that they look for 10 years of solid experience on projects, preferably of similar scale and product type. The hard loan criteria at her bank include the following:

- liquidity at least 10 percent of the loan amount;
- net worth at least equal to the loan amount; and
- for value-add projects, similar but slightly lower requirements.

She points out that these requirements are not just for principal repayment, but more for completion guarantees. "The last thing banks would want to deal with is a half-completed project!"[79]

Does having money in the bank help? For business banking, definitely yes. However, having the property operating account at the bank is less important because banks already have enough deposits and they cannot legally require borrowers to keep the money in the bank.

Before the construction loan can be closed, the bank needs to approve the appraisal, and an environmental inspection needs to take place. Piper says Webster Bank has a third-party engineer review the budget. The normal term of the loan is two to three years for construction plus one year for lease-up and one year for stabilization. Anything longer will add 25 basis points to the interest rate. The lender will stress test the interest rate to make sure the developer can withstand a 100 to 150 basis point increase

in rates (which are tied to LIBOR [London Interbank Offered Rate] or prime rates and are floating).[80] Contingencies are also important. Piper likes to see contingencies of 5 percent for both soft costs and hard costs.

The construction interest reserve for lease-up can be reduced if there are pre-leases (unusual in apartment projects) or phased construction (in which move-ins begin in early buildings—after the developer receives certificates of occupancy—while other buildings are still under construction). These arrangements are often possible in garden apartments which have multiple small buildings, each with four to 24 units. If the bank needs more interest reserve, it may require the developer to wait to receive the developer fee until the project is completed.[81]

Tom Montelli observes that any delays negatively affect the interest reserve. "You have a certain amount of money based on your projected project delivery date to pay the lender for the interest on the loan. If there's any delay, then you're not going to have your economic occupancy, and you'll owe the money for a greater period of time. Interest reserve is a very big risk because it's so sensitive to schedule." He adds that hard costs are another important line item that can have cost overruns. "Hard costs are so important because often [they are] 70 percent of your overall budget, so you better have confidence in your construction number." One way to ensure a construction number is going to be the final construction cost number is to have completed design drawings. "If you start your project earlier than 100 percent construction drawings, there is a risk of seeing change orders from the general contractor, meaning something came up in the design as he started that wasn't on the original plans. The developer is responsible for paying [for] those changes."[82] On the other hand, Phil Hughes believes that having completed construction drawings before getting construction bids requires too much time and money. While his long-standing relationship with contractors and subcontractors mitigates change order risk, he prefers to expedite construction through a guaranteed maximum price contract with a savings clause.[83]

Randolph Hawthorne observes that tension always remains between the construction lender and the permanent lender about who is going to finance the lease-up risk. "People are pretty skilled at building competently without significant time overruns. The real risks are what the demand is and how quickly the property will lease-up initially, which have a huge effect on the pro forma. In times of optimism, you see a lot of open-ended construction loans, the so-called miniperms without a forward commitment for permanent financing. When markets get soft or when people get concerned about regulatory pressures, they do not seek open-ended construction loans but look for forward commitments and permanent financing instead."[84]

Karl Zavitkovsky, formerly at Bank of America in Dallas, says it is important to distinguish between loans provided by small banks and loans provided by big banks. Smaller regional banks originate loans that they plan to keep on their own balance sheets, whereas large banks syndicate the loans to other banks and get them off their books as soon as possible. Large developers such as JPI and Trammell Crow Company depend on banks with high-volume credit facilities—those that deal in $15 million to $20 million and larger syndicated transactions. "Smaller banks tend to underprice the big institutions, because they do not have the portfolio exposure limitations of big banks. Big banks issue loans with flexible pricing language that reserves the right to ratchet up the interest rate, say from LIBOR plus 200 to LIBOR plus 225 to syndicate it. Even with these types of tools, it is almost impossible to syndicate loans on spec buildings because of current attitudes in large financial institutions."[85] Beginning developers who must find a third party to guarantee the loan should look for an experienced developer or investor who knows how to manage the construction loan from start to finish. Someone with deep experience in the industry will give the lender confidence that the loan will be repaid even if problems arise during construction.

PERMANENT FINANCING

Permanent financing—a long-term mortgage on the completed project—is a critical ingredient, especially for projects undertaken by beginning developers who are unlikely to receive construction financing without a permanent loan takeout. Permanent loans come in many forms. In addition to bullet loans and the standard fixed-rate, adjustable-rate, and variable-rate mortgages, lenders make participating loans and convertible loans.[86] Participating loans give lenders a "participation" in cash flows after debt service and sometimes a participation in residual cash flows from sale. These participations, called *kickers*, raise lenders' IRRs above the loan rate by an additional 2 or 3 percent—an amount sufficient for lenders to consider funding 80 to 95 percent of a project's costs.

Conduit loans (so called because the loan originator in effect has a conduit through Wall Street directly to investors) have significantly increased the amount of mortgage money in recent years. Mortgage brokers, banks, and other lenders prenegotiate the sale of a package of mortgages, say $100 million, to a Wall Street underwriter under certain terms. They then proceed to originate the mortgages to borrowers or to buy existing mortgages from other originators. The Wall Street underwriter sells the package of mortgages to investors, using the proceeds to reimburse the originator. Sales of commercial mortgages in the secondary market, of which conduit loans represent one form, are a relatively new phenomenon. They follow years of evolution of single-family residential mortgage sales in the secondary market through quasi-governmental organizations such as Fannie Mae and Ginnie Mae.

In the case of a conduit loan, the original borrower is known as the *sponsor*. Typically, this individual is the owner of a completed project—a large-scale building—and is seeking new sources of capital. The owned building is put up as collateral for the loan. The *originator* is the institution that loans the money against the building at a discounted rate to the sponsor. The *issuer* could be that lending institution or another institution that securitizes and issues a bond against the collateral.

Mezzanine loans are second loans that reduce the amount of equity a developer needs. Because they increase the leverage and therefore the risk of default in a project, primary mortgages typically have covenants that preclude a mezzanine loan without express permission of the primary lender. Mezzanine loan interest rates, which take a senior permanent loan from 60–65 percent LTV to 75 percent, carry rates of 7 to 9 percent in the low interest rate environment of early 2022. Mezzanine loans on construction take a senior construction loan of 65–70 percent LTV up to 80 percent, with interest rates of 10 to 13 percent and one to two points.[87]

The popularity of different types of permanent mortgages changes frequently, sometimes every few months. The basic alternatives for permanent loans, however, remain the same—a fixed-rate or adjustable-rate mortgage for 60 to 75 percent of value, or some form of participating mortgage or mezzanine loan for 75 to 90 percent of value that gives the lender higher returns to cover the additional risk associated with higher leverage.

FINANCING ISSUES

Developers should be aware of a number of issues related to financing.

PERSONAL GUARANTEES AND LOAN FUNDING.

Although standard practices may vary, most developers must personally guarantee their construction loans. On occasion, they may also be required to guarantee some part of their permanent loans (such as the top 25 percent),[88] at least until their projects reach some threshold level of debt coverage or occupancy.

When times are good, lenders have more money available than good projects to lend on, so they ease their requirements in order to compete for business from experienced developers. When times are tough, loan requirements become more restrictive. Loan-to-value ratios are lowered and debt service coverage ratios are raised. Personal guarantees also become much more prevalent. Beginning developers should be prepared to sign personally on their construction and development loans. They should be able to avoid personal liability on standard permanent loans for fully leased properties.

No developer wants to be a perpetual guarantor of the loan. Many developers refuse to agree to unconditional liability and will negotiate for some performance criteria that release them from personal liability. The following are some alternative compromises:

- Lenders cannot call on the guarantor directly in the event of default. They must instead foreclose on the defaulting property and obtain a legal decision against the guarantor. Because judicial foreclosures can be time-consuming and expensive, lenders may prefer to take over the property immediately in return for releasing the developer from some or all of the liability under the guarantee.
- The note limits the amount of any deficiency over time. For example, if the loan is current for three years, then the guarantor's liability reduces to, say, 50 percent of any deficiency.
- The note states that if all the land improvements have been installed within budget and the project has been completed, then the developer's (guarantor's) liability reduces to zero after three years.
- The developer places money in escrow to cover potential losses. Suppose a developer undertakes a project appraised at $12 million but it requires only $10 million in costs. The developer may borrow the full $12 million, leaving $2 million in escrow to eliminate any personal liability. This solution, of course, involves added interest costs, which in turn add to the project's risk.

Personal liability is defined as meaning either the "top half" or "bottom half" of the loan. If a project with a $10 million loan sells for $7 million, a guarantee of the top half means that the developer owes the deficient $3 million. A guarantee of the bottom half means the developer owes nothing unless the project sells for less than $5 million. In some cases, ambiguously worded loan documents that fail to specify whether the developer is guaranteeing the top or the bottom half of a loan have caused the developer and lender to end up in court. The prospect of a long court battle to satisfy the deficiency has motivated some lenders to settle with developers.

Beginning developers have difficulty eliminating personal liability altogether, but they can negotiate to limit it. If they can limit their liability to a specified amount, they may be able to sell pieces of that liability to their investors along with pieces of the transaction. However, raising equity is hard enough without also asking investors to accept liability for potential losses. If they do accept liability, they will expect to receive more equity (a greater share of the upside).

BALANCE SHEET. For construction loans, the developer's balance sheet must be strong enough to satisfy the lender that it will get paid back. Nicolas Lizotte states, "Debt financing is dependent on either government insurance on the loan or an equity partner with a significant balance sheet to back the project. Fannie Mae and Freddie Mac are looking for a balance sheet with assets equal to the amount of the loan and liquid assets equal to the annual debt service. The balance sheet must belong to a key principal in the project for it to fulfill this criterion."[89]

CLOSING. Obtaining the funding for a permanent loan (closing the loan) may involve almost as much work as originally securing the lender's commitment to provide that funding. The loan commitment document specifies the requirements for permanent loan funding. Typical requirements include a certified rent roll showing the property's actual cash flow as well as all signed lease documents. Loan closing can be an exasperating process, and any issues not clearly spelled out in the original commitment can come back to haunt the developer at closing. For example, loan documents may be ambiguous as to whether a project must be 90 percent leased, 90 percent occupied, or 90 percent occupied and paying rent. Lenders usually take the most restrictive interpretation, so developers are well advised to ensure that qualifying standards are described precisely.

Some loan commitments require that a project have attained certain rental objectives, say, 80 percent occupancy for a specified period—one month, six months, or 12 months before the permanent lender will fund the mortgage. The shorter the period for qualification, the better for the developer. Lenders often require that releases, credit reports, or other paperwork be obtained from all tenants. Such procedures should be confirmed at the outset, thereby allowing the property manager to obtain the necessary documentation as tenants sign new leases. One option is to attach an estoppel letter to the lease at signing—one that the permanent lender preapproves. Obtaining such documents later can be much more difficult and costly.

Closing on condominium loans can pose a different set of problems. When markets are soft, sales may not reach targets set by permanent lenders, and developers may be obliged to give investors unsold units in lieu of a cash return. If a developer subsequently decides to consolidate ownership and to convert a project to a rental project, the price of acquiring units sold previously may be very high. The FHA, which insures condominium mortgages, requires that at least 35 percent of the units in a complex be owner-occupied (down from 50 percent). If sales in a new project are going poorly, the developer may not reach the threshold of sales that are required for buyers to obtain mortgages on their units, causing the entire project to fail as a condominium. Even when sales are strong, the number of investor-owned (non-owner-occupied) units may cause funding difficulties.[90]

How difficult loan closings are depends on the local real estate market at the time of closing. When conditions become soft, lenders naturally become more concerned about the safety of their investments and thus more rigorous in the enforcement of the various requirements for closing.

DEALING WITH ADVERSITY. Sooner or later, every developer has to deal with adversity. Adversity comes in many forms—difficulties getting approvals, construction delays and cost overruns, slow lease-up or sales, property management problems, just to name a few things that can go wrong. How developers deal with adversity often determines their ultimate success. For dealings with lenders and investors, the most important principal is to be honest about problems and keep them informed. No one likes surprises, especially about problems that have been going on for some time. Investor Teo Nicholas offers some sage advice for working with lenders:[91]

- Understand that pro formas don't always work. You will get turned down from time to time.
- Consider other solutions for loan guarantees such as cross-collateralization or alternative loan structures.
- Work with your lenders. Talk through ways to fix problems. "Help them help you."
- Don't take loan rejection or lender intransigence personally: their hands are often tied by regulators or other forces beyond their control.
- Don't overlook the fact that your lender may be right! They've seen a lot of deals. They don't like saying "no." They just don't want you to get in trouble. Use it as a learning opportunity.
- Never ever burn a bridge. Poisoning the well even if you direct the anger to a particular person almost always comes back to haunt you.

Nicholas adds that other factors may help the developer obtain loans:

- The appetite for lending changes during different times of the year.
- Look for shifts (good and bad) near year-end and quarter-end.
- Lenders might have benchmarks or quotas for the period.

EQUITY. Raising equity is often the most difficult task for beginning developers because they do not have a track record or stable of investors. Beginning developers usually turn to "friends and family" to provide equity for their first projects. Jerry Rappaport states, "You better do it right the first time because investors are not going to come back again if you do it wrong the first time. Beginning developers need to learn how to pronounce 'risk,' learn how to present risk, learn how to mitigate risk, and learn how to raise money to give the first investor the confidence to invest in you." He adds, "The words 'conservative' and 'transparent' are two words I do not like to hear. I like to hear 'I understand the risk, this is the risk I'm talking about, and this is how I'm going to deal with the risk' rather than 'I am being conservative, so you should accept my numbers.'"[92]

Nate Kline at One Wall Partners says different investors have different timelines in which they can make deals and different amounts of capital to invest. "We soon learned who to go to if we needed $1 million for something versus who to go to if we needed $10 million for something. The investors are rarely one [and] the same."[93] Friends and family investors and family offices typically prefer to invest directly in individual deals through private placement limited partnerships with the developer as the sponsor and general partner. The next step after friends and family investors are institutional investors—insurance companies, pension funds, and endowments. Institutional investors prefer larger deals—usually $30 million to $50 million or more total cost—and require the sponsor to have a significant track record (five years or more experience in developing similar projects and five to 10 or more completed and successful projects).

One Wall has created a co-mingled fund. It learned that a lot of investors (e.g., insurance companies, pension funds, endowments, family offices) want to get exposure to real estate but either (1) don't want to invest on a deal-by-deal basis, or (2) take too long in deciding whether to invest. One Wall found that these types of investors will invest on a fund basis. Opening and operating the fund was possible only because One Wall Partners has a track record. The fund also allows investments in third-party sponsors of projects. "It's a more natural fit for the fund because the fund itself is focused on preferred equity, and there's a lot of demand from other sponsors in preferred equity/gap financing in the deals that they have."[94]

EQUITY: JOINT VENTURES AND SYNDICATIONS. Developers use a variety of joint venture formats to raise equity, provide loan guarantees, and secure financing. This section focuses on joint ventures with equity partners.

Syndications are a form of joint venture in which equity from a number of smaller investors is raised through a private or public offering subject to regulations of the Securities and Exchange Commission. Investors in syndications receive a security interest similar to what they own in stocks or bonds, whereas joint ventures of only a few parties typically, but not necessarily, involve direct real estate interests. Every joint venture deal is different. Nonetheless, certain formats are more common, such as those described by the following three developers.

Harry Mow, the late board chair of Century West Development in Santa Monica, California, recommended keeping things simple. "If you cut too sharp a deal with your investors, you probably won't get them to invest in another deal." Mow, whose company did its own construction, added a 15 percent fee to the hard and soft costs (excluding land and financing costs). The fee paid the superintendent, the project manager, corporate overhead, and the costs of raising equity. If the construction loan was suf-

ficiently large to cover the 15 percent fee, it was paid out in installments during construction. Otherwise, it was left in as a loan to the partnership until the property was sold, when the partners received it out of sale proceeds. Cash flow from operations and sale of the property is typically distributed in the following order:

1. The limited partners receive back their capital.

2. The limited partners receive a 6 percent cumulative return.

3. The limited partners and the general partners split the remainder equally. The developer also receives a 5 or 6 percent management fee and a 6 percent brokerage fee for selling the property.

Richard Gleitman, president of R.J. Investments Associates in Sherman Oaks, California, gives his equity partners—who tended initially to be friends and business associates—50 percent of the profits and an 8 percent noncumulative preferred return. He recovers all cash advances for land, entitlements, or other initial expenses for a project from the equity partners when they make their initial investment. Gleitman creates the joint venture before the close of land escrow, as soon as he has reliable financial projections. Gleitman's firm charges a minimal contractor's fee—2 to 3 percent of hard costs—and a larger management fee—4 to 5 percent—that help cover the cost of using the largest, most-active outside broker in an area to sell a project.

In his first deal, Paul Schultheis, president of Real Property Investment Inc., in Arcadia, California, raised $400,000 in cash, splitting profits 50/50 with investors after they received back their capital. Because he had no previous direct experience, Schultheis brought in a builder and a broker/marketing director as general partners. He and his brother acquired the land, secured planning approvals, and performed the front-end work. The broker received 10 percent of the general partners' share of the deal; the three other partners received 30 percent each.

Jerry Rappaport states, "Private equity firms currently take the position that 2.5 to 10 percent co-investment is insufficient to encourage a joint venture partner to remain diligent through downturns and will either push much harder for higher co-investment or profit participation that happens at a much higher threshold and may represent a development fee rather than complicating the ownership structure. Ten to 40 percent is now expected. The private equity market has evolved such that senior management are co-invested and . . . own more of the company and of the upside, so that senior management decisions are directly aligned with performance."

Rappaport observes that the sponsors of one of the deals in which the New Boston Fund invested—Vincent G. Norton's Schoolhouse at Lower Mills project—"could have taken the construction cost savings achieved and put it toward their equity contribution, or they could have reduced its basis to make it easier to carry. Instead, the developers used the savings to fund upgraded interior finishes and amenities."[95]

In structuring joint ventures with investors, the priorities of payback and cash distributions are even more important than the final split of profits. As indicated in the previous examples, investors commonly receive back their investment before the developer shares in any profit. When both the investor and the developer have money invested in a project, the investor may receive, say, the first $100,000 as a priority payback before the developer receives the next $100,000 of cash flow. Priorities become a way of dealing with risk—the person who bears the most risk receives money back last. Risk is higher because, if a loss occurs, there may be no money left to pay back lower priorities.

Preferred returns are similar to interest on money invested in a savings account. The difference is that they are paid only if cash flow is available—like dividends—whereas interest must be paid currently whether cash flow from a project is available or not (if not, then the general partner must cover the interest from other sources or default on the loan). The basic concept behind preferred returns is that the investors will be paid back as a top priority at least the equivalent interest on their investments that they would earn in an interest-bearing account. Although many deals have no preferred returns, beginning developers are advised to include them because they make raising equity a little easier. Investors like the notion that they will receive back their initial equity plus a preferred return before the developer receives any profit. It is customary for the developer to receive a "development fee"—3 to 5 percent of total costs (sometimes excluding land) during construction to cover overhead. But any significant profit to the developer carries a lower priority than the investor's return of capital and preferred return.

One of the simpler and more common deal structures has four priorities (similar to Harry Mow's structure described above):

1. Investors receive a current preferred return.

2. Investors receive unpaid but accrued preferred returns.

3. Investors receive back their equity.

4. Investors and the developer split the remainder according to a *profit split* ranging from 80/20 (80 percent to the investors) to 50/50.

The payment of preferred returns can be structured as *cumulative* or *noncumulative*. In the case of a cumulative preferred return, any unpaid preferred return in one period is accumulated until funds are available to pay it in a later period. A noncumulative preferred return does not accumulate in this fashion, and if cash flow in a given year is insufficient to cover all or part of the preferred return, the unpaid balance is forgotten and left unpaid.

The *current* preferred return is that amount owed each year, found by multiplying the preferred return rate by the equity. For example, if the preferred return rate is 8 percent and the equity is $1 million, the current preferred return is $80,000. Figure 4-11 (see americas.uli.org/PRED) shows how the cash flows and IRRs would differ for the same deal under the two different preferred return structures. Both deals illustrate a 10 percent preferred return with a 50/50 split of the remaining profits. Note that the cumulative preferred return is accrued in Years 1 and 2, because the cash flows of $5,000 and $8,000 are insufficient to cover the 10 percent preferred return of $10,000. The outstanding sum is finally paid off in Year 5. Because of the accumulation provision, the total cash flow to the investor is $104,000, compared with $100,500 in the noncumulative case. The investor's IRR is 17.02 percent, compared with 16.60 percent. The developer's total cash flow is less in the cumulative case, $54,000 as opposed to $57,500, because the investor receives more from the same total project cash flows.

In some deals involving cumulative preferred returns, the *accrued return balance* earns interest. Many developers, however, prefer not to pay such interest because it further reduces their share of the proceeds without enhancing the marketability of their deals. Another variation gives accrued but unpaid preferred returns a lower priority, and they are paid *after* the investor's equity is paid back. This twist further helps the developer, because current preferred returns are reduced as investors' equity is paid back (from annual cash flows that exceed the current preferred return).

Tips on Joint Ventures and Deal Packaging

- In drawing up the partnership agreement, be very clear as to the rights and duties of each partner. Use arbitration to resolve disputes.
- Beware of "dilution squeeze-down" provisions that allow investors to squeeze the developer out if a project does not generate a given level of current return.
- Consider overborrowing. Some developers recommend overborrowing if possible because it allows them to withdraw money from a project without tax. However, overborrowing increases the risk of default, and few if any lenders will allow it in the post–Great Recession environment.
- Make sure that investors have no right to tell the developer how to run the project.
- If investors commit money to be paid in the future, make sure that the money is available by persuading investors to post letters of credit.

DEVELOPER FEES. One of the most delicate issues in raising equity is when and how much the developer will receive. Both investors and lenders want assurances that their positions are ahead of the developer's—and that they get back their money as well as a reasonable return on their money *before* the developer receives significant profit. They want assurances that the developer has strong incentives to work hard on their behalf throughout the development process.

This situation creates potential conflicts of interest, which are generally resolved in favor of the investors. When Peiser Corporation raised its first equity, a popular refrain (uttered mainly among members of the firm) was "developers have to eat too." Lenders and investors unfortunately like to see very thin developers. They believe that the more money the developer receives on the front end of a deal, the less incentive the developer has to work hard on their behalf. Therefore, they want to see virtually all the developer's compensation, both in fees and profit share, deferred until the end (final sale of the project). The developer, on the other hand, needs to at least cover the out-of-pocket costs for managing the deal and for performing all the functions necessary to complete it properly. As a rule, lenders allow the developer to take out 3 to 5 percent of the construction cost to cover direct overhead costs—in addition to any on-site construction superintendents.

Developers can receive fees from a number of different activities in the course of a deal. The fees fall into two main categories: (1) compensation for specific achievements such as construction management, leasing, and property management; and (2) a share of the upside profits. Even when fees are earned, the timing of payment to the developer is subject to the priorities described previously. The developer, for example, may earn fees totaling 10 percent of the

development cost during construction and lease-up of the project but be allowed to receive (or take out) only half of those fees during the construction and lease-up period. The other 5 percent may be subordinated to the investors' receiving back all their equity plus any preferred return.

The developer's share of upside profits is, by definition, paid on the back end of a deal, usually when it is sold. Most joint venture agreements also allow the developer to take out cash if a project is refinanced, although even in that case, the cash is often subordinated to return of capital and preferred return to the investors. Refinancing often occurs when a project achieves certain rental objectives, such as major lease rollovers at higher rents. If, for example, the developer refinances a project for $5 million that previously had a $4 million mortgage, $1 million in cash is left over after paying off the old mortgage. This cash from refinancing is especially attractive because it does not create any immediate tax consequences and therefore is available in its entirety for distribution. The joint venture agreement specifies how the money is to be distributed. It may call for splitting the entire proceeds of refinancing 50/50 between the developer and the investors, or the developer may receive a share of the refinancing only after the investors receive, say, $500,000, or only after the investors receive back all their equity.

An infinite number of deal structures are possible. Joint ventures with institutional investors (firms that invest money on behalf of their own clients, such as pension fund advisers) are described in detail in chapter 6.

Beginning developers cannot usually attract institutional investors. The advantage of starting with smaller deals is the greater ease of raising $100,000 or $200,000 in equity compared with $1 million or more. The developer usually raises money from family or friends, who will want a fair deal, and the developer must decide what to offer them. Because of a beginning developer's inexperience, the investors, however supportive personally, will want the developer to defer as much compensation as possible.

Simple deal structures are recommended, primarily because they are easier to explain to potential investors. For tax reasons, it is advantageous to set fees that can be expensed immediately rather than being amortized over five years or, in some cases, never expensed at all. An experienced real estate tax accountant is an essential member of the developer's team, even before the process of raising equity begins.[96] In addition to the developer's fee, other common fees include those shown in the box "Front-End Fees."

INVESTORS' PRIMARY CONCERNS. Investors are most concerned with the following five aspects of joint venture deals:

1. **Preferred Return Yields**—These yields tend to approximate the interest rate on money market accounts plus 1 to 3 percent. In 2010 and 2011, for example, preferred returns typically ranged from 6 to 10 percent multiplied by the equity account balance at the beginning of each year. In 2022, the preferred returns range from 6 to 8 percent.

2. **Share of Residual Profits** (also called "carried interest" or "promote")—In deals sold privately and in joint ventures with financial institutions or large investors, profit splits range from 80/20 (80 percent to investors) to 50/50. In public syndications, the profit split is usually 80/20 or at best 70/30. The percentage to investors is higher because stockbrokers and financial planners who sell the deals claim that investors are reluctant to buy into projects that offer lower profit shares.

3. **Downside Liabilities**—Most syndications and joint ventures are structured as limited partnerships that restrict investors' downside liabilities. Unless investors sign notes for more than their direct equity investment, their downside risk is limited to the loss of their equity.

4. **Cash Calls**—Cash calls occur when a partnership requires additional equity from the investors to meet its obligations. Sophisticated investors tend to be more concerned about the handling of cash calls. Most partnership agreements have provisions

that penalize partners for not making cash calls that dilute their interest. For example, consider a partner, Smith, who has invested $50,000 out of total equity of $100,000 for a 50 percent interest. Suppose each partner makes a $10,000 cash call. Smith fails to come up with his $10,000, so the other partner, Jones, must come up with $20,000. In a prorated dilution arrangement, Jones would have invested $70,000 out of $120,000, reducing Smith's interest to $50,000 out of $120,000, or 41.67 percent. A penalty clause might reduce Smith's ownership by, say, 1 percent for each $1,000 he fails to produce, giving him a 31.67 percent interest. In the extreme, although not uncommon, case, Smith could lose his entire interest.

5. **Developer Fees**—The treatment of front-end fees differs considerably between private offerings and public syndications (including Regulation D private offerings to 35 or fewer "nonqualified" investors).[97] Stockbrokers and financial planners selling public syndications and Regulation D private offerings

focus on the ratio of front-end fees to total equity raised and frequently will not offer a deal where front-end fees account for more than 25 percent of total equity. By comparison, in private joint ventures, front-end fees often exceed 25 percent of total equity, especially for new apartment projects in which the developer is also the contractor. The construction fee alone may exceed 25 percent of the equity, as it is based on total construction costs. For example, an 8 percent construction fee on a $1 million construction cost is $80,000. If $200,000 in equity were needed, this fee alone would be 40 percent of the equity raised.

THE ADVANTAGES OF PRIVATE OFFERINGS.

Public offerings and Regulation D syndications may appear to be better deals for the investor, but they tend not to be, for three reasons. First, developers dislike giving away more profits than necessary and so prefer to engage in private ventures. The deals sold by outside brokers are therefore often those for which a developer could not raise private money and may consequently be a lower preference for the developer. Second, Regulation D offerings and public offerings involve much greater expense for legal work, due diligence, and broker commissions. Third, developers must make a certain level of profit or they will not stay in business. If they must take lower front-end fees and a lower share of residual profits, they usually compensate by "selling" the project to the syndication at a higher price.

For example, Harry Mow's company, Century West, packaged deals in which the front-end load on a $1 million deal with 80 percent financing was 45 percent of the equity rather than the 25 percent syndicators prefer. However, the price to the partnership was his actual direct cost. A public syndication offering has a lower ratio of fees to equity but a higher total project price to the partnership, and therefore higher risks to the investors.

In addition to the higher front-end load in private offerings, Century West received 50 percent of the residual profits after the investor received a 6 percent preferred return. Despite the seemingly higher fees, Century West's deals were very well received by investors who appreciated the opportunity to buy into projects at cost rather than at a higher price that included development profit.[98]

Economically, the ratio of front-end fees to total equity raised is much less important than the investor's expected returns. Unfortunately, brokers, financial planners, and others who sell real estate securities focus on such ratios rather than on the likelihood that investors will achieve certain levels of return. For public offerings through securities brokers and financial planners, developers must conform their deals to syndication standards in the marketplace at the time. Jerry Rappaport points out, "There is an ever-growing pool of high-net-worth individuals focused on retirement with burgeoning amounts of money for whom real estate will be an important part of their portfolios." He says, "Two strategies for securing private equity funding are (1) sell the team's track record and capacity to a local private equity real estate fund, or one that is known to have funded private developers, and understand its underwriting criteria as you identify, seed, and execute predevelopment activities; or (2) go to the Urban Land Institute annual conference to learn the rules, tie up the project, and then hire a consultant to help you source the private equity so that you will create a small sense of competition."[99]

Developers will find that private syndications to small groups of investors remain a mainstay for raising equity. Developers must always be careful to observe legal requirements for private syndications, such as registering the offerings in each state where they plan to solicit investors.

GOVERNMENT PROGRAMS AND WORKING WITH NONPROFIT ORGANIZATIONS

Government programs are no longer as fruitful a source of financing for subsidized housing as they once were, but they still can provide helpful financing to new developers. Over the years, numerous government programs have been created to generate low- and moderate-income housing, and housing support programs remain available from federal, state, and local sources.

Housing revenue bonds are issued to finance construction of housing in which a specified proportion of the units will be rented to low-income households. These securities may provide financing either directly or through a loans-to-lenders program and may be secured in whole or in part by federal agency guarantees or subsidies. To qualify for issuing tax-exempt bonds, developers must set aside 20 percent of the units to renters with incomes below 50 percent of the area median income, or, alternatively, 40 percent of the units may be rented to individuals with incomes below 60 percent of the area median income.

Tax credits are currently the primary source of funding for low-income housing. Created by the

How the Bascom Group Raises Apartment Equity

Derek M.D. Chen, Jerome A. Fink, and David S. Kim formed the Bascom Group in 1996 to purchase value-added real estate in Southern California. Bascom's primary objectives were to (1) capitalize on the recovering Southern California economy by investing in multifamily rental properties with a three- to five-year turnaround, (2) diversify its portfolio in Southern California by location and industry, and (3) provide investors with attractive current *cash-on-cash yields* and total investment returns.

Bascom seeks "the worst property on the best block." The firm targets multifamily properties located in infill areas with high barriers to entry that offer value-added opportunities. Targeted properties need renovation or suffer from poor resident profiles relative to the competing trade area, below-market rents, high expenses, high vacancies, poor management and marketing, and undercapitalization.

Bascom creates single-purpose limited liability companies (LLCs) to own and operate each property to protect its entire portfolio in the event that any single property defaults or has issues that could affect other properties in the portfolio. These LLCs are capitalized from several sources, including (1) private and institutional investors contributing pari passu (equally) or preferred equity and subordinated debt (for example, second mortgage loans and mezzanine financing), and (2) traditional institutional lenders funding senior mortgage debt (for example, a primary mortgage loan). A typical structure requires 5 to 10 percent Bascom-sponsored equity, 10 to 20 percent institutional co–venture partner equity or mezzanine financing, and 70 to 80 percent senior mortgage debt.

The equity typically requires a minimum preferred return of 9 to 12 percent and allows for Bascom to participate in the profits after the preferred returns are paid currently. This equity structure aligns Bascom's interest with that of the passive investor by creating an incentive for Bascom to maximize the total return to the investor. The senior mortgage debt is typically a three- to five-year year bridge loan based on total cost (property plus renovation cost) with a LIBOR-based interest rate, which is similar to a construction loan. The lender retains funds for renovation (lender holdback) and releases it to the sponsor as work is completed, allowing Bascom to purchase and renovate the property with much less equity.

During the Great Recession, the firm benefited from the fact that it did not cross collateralize its equity (pledge one project as a guarantee for other projects). Bascom's longtime equity partner, Chenco Holdings based in Taipei, raised equity in relatively small increments of $10 million per fund from a handful of related investors. Each fund had a duration of three to five years compared with a more common eight to 10 years. Chenco deployed capital quickly so that in the end, it lost money only in its 11th fund. Chenco provides its funds "sponsor" capital—Bascom's share required by its institutional partners, such as GE Capital, Lehman Brothers, Warburg Pincus, and Rockwood. Bascom's deal with the institutional funds at the peak of the market in the mid-2000s was a 90/10 equity split (90 percent institution and 10 percent Bascom) with a 10 percent preference and a 50/50 profit split over 10 percent. When Bascom first started doing institutional deals and was unproven, the investment split was 80/20 with a 60/40 profit split after a 14 percent preference to the investors.

Kim observes, "The environment in 2022 is that aging baby boomers who represent one-third of the population need

---

Tax Reform Act of 1986, tax credits are granted to each state on a per-capita basis and are administered competitively through the states' housing agencies. Developers may use the credits for new construction, rehabilitation, or acquisition of residential properties that meet the following minimum requirements:

- Twenty percent or more of the residential units in the project are both rent restricted and occupied by individuals whose income is 50 percent or less of the area median gross income, *or* 40 percent or more of the residential units in the project are both rent restricted and occupied by individuals whose income is 60 percent or less of area median gross income.
- Properties receiving tax credits must stay eligible for 15 years.

Developers who receive the credits typically sell them to investors to raise equity for their projects. In low-cost areas, tax credits will likely cover all of the equity needed. But in high-cost areas such as Boston and Los Angeles, additional subsidies from various grant programs will be needed to cover the full equity requirements.

Building under government programs can be time-consuming and frustrating. Government financing programs involve more paperwork and other hurdles than private financing. The programs often contain vague guidelines that cause differences in interpretation. Associated legal costs can also be onerous.

Beginning developers who are interested in low- and moderate-income housing development should investigate the financing programs available by contacting local housing departments, redevelopment agencies, predictable income for their retirement. We are in an environment with significant deficits for pension funds. They face tensions between income and growth. The more underfunded they are, the more private equity (PE) they need to invest in order to generate higher returns. This makes it easier for us to raise money now. Major city pension funds are the 'have-nots.' They are more desperate to get 8 percent returns instead of 6 percent. Consequently, PE will get more allocation.

"After the Great Recession a typical deal would provide a 10.5 cap at stabilization with midteens (14 percent) pretax leveraged returns. We offered an 8 percent preferred return to the investors with a 90/10 equity contribution (90 percent from investors and 10 percent from Bascom). Distributions are pari passu up to 8 percent and then a 70/30 upside split (70 percent to investors and 30 percent to Bascom) after 8 percent. Bascom receives a 1.5 percent acquisition fee on the total basis and a 1 percent annual asset management fee. The firm uses third-party property management and receives no other fees for construction, refinancing, leasing, or disposition. Our deal structure is the same today. There is too much capital, so operators like us have leverage.

"If I'm going to invest in a startup developer, they have to have been doing similar development previously for someone else. They must be passionate and have learned patience for delays, dealing with government and NIMBYS and opposition. The fundamental economics must be in place. We look for a 30 percent premium in the cost of replacement over their purchase price. It can take six to seven years to realize value in a development deal. Beginning developers need a general partner with a balance sheet like ours. If they need a guaran-

tor, the developer will need to give up 25 to 30 percent of the deal. The bigger the scale of potential cost overruns, the larger share they will need to give up.

"When we provide capital for new developers, Bascom puts up all the pursuit and sponsor capital and debt capacity in exchange for 50 percent of the company. If the management team puts up 20 percent of the pursuit and sponsor capital, we receive a 40 percent interest; if they put up 40 percent of the capital, we receive a 30 percent interest."

Bascom's value-added deals involve a certain amount of risk. At each step in the process—from purchasing to renovating to operating to disposition—Bascom's principals have learned that surprises will happen and risk cannot be totally eliminated. The tenant profile may be worse than anticipated and higher-than-expected turnover may result. The cost of renovation may increase because of labor shortages or increases in materials' costs or simply because of conditions discovered after work begins. Although the use of high leverage can magnify a deal's potential total returns, it can also hurt cash flow if interest rates rise more than expected. Clear roles, goals, and expectations for investors, lenders, property managers, and even residents are paramount to ensure that each investment meets the mutually agreed-on pro forma. Most important, it is clear that frequent reporting and the open disclosure of any issue or surprise are critical to maintaining a trustworthy relationship between investors and lenders.

Source: David S. Kim, managing director, the Bascom Group, Irvine, California, interviews by author, September 2002, June 2010, and January 2022.

state housing finance agencies, the U.S. Department of Housing and Urban Development, and Fannie Mae. A number of low-income housing programs, including the Low-Income Housing Tax Credit (LIHTC), give nonprofit organizations an advantage in obtaining money, the result of government policies to encourage the growth of community-based nonprofits.

The nonprofits often lack development expertise and are eager to form joint ventures with private developers to build housing. Although financing for low-income housing limits the amount of profit a developer can earn, the limits are high enough to make such housing development attractive. The financing programs provide beginning developers a source of money that may be easier to qualify for than private banking sources. Moreover, tax credits, once obtained, are easily sold to investors (because of the virtually

guaranteed tax write-offs) and effectively take care of equity requirements, the hardest money for beginning developers to raise. Although nonprofit partnerships offer special opportunities for financing, they also bring much greater complexity, paperwork, time, and the need to apply for multiple loans. Experienced nonprofit organizations can greatly assist beginning developers in the process, while inexperienced nonprofits may make their lives impossible. As with any partnership, success depends on the personalities of the people involved.

Randy Hawthorne observes, "Demand for LIHTC units is pretty constant. There is a limited amount of upfront profit you can generate, so you generally need some soft money. The tax credit business became robust enough that it is just a matter of pricing. The business model is viable."[100] The amount of the tax credit is based on the percentage of units reserved for low-income tenants and the cost of purchase and rehabilitation, excluding land. For example, suppose a project costs $100,000 for the land, $400,000 for an existing building, and $1,000,000 for rehabilitation. Suppose also that 80 percent of the units are low income, that there are no tax-exempt bonds, and that the state agency awarded $70,000 per year of credits. The credits are computed as follows: The building purchase credit is $400,000 × 80% × 3.5%, or $11,200; the rehabilitation credit is $1,000,000 × 80% × 9%, or $72,000. The total maximum credit is $83,200, but that is more than the award by the state, so the deduction is limited to $70,000 per year. If the market value of the credits was $0.85, then the developer could sell them for $70,000 × 10 years × 85%, or $595,000. With total costs of $1.5 million, this amount of equity would give a 39.6 percent equity-to-cost ratio, which should be large enough to cover the developer's entire equity requirement.

Tax credits for historic rehabilitation may be attractive vehicles for beginning developers. To qualify for the 20 percent rehabilitation credits, a building must be a "certified historic structure," that is, listed individually in the National Register of Historic Places or located in a registered historic district and certified by the secretary of the interior as being of historical significance to the district. To illustrate how these credits work, suppose that a historic building costs $1 million to acquire and requires rehabilitation work that costs $500,000 plus architecture fees of $50,000. The allowable deduction would be $550,000 × 20%, or $110,000. State historic tax credit deductions of a similar amount may also be available, bringing the total to $220,000. The deduction can be taken in full the year the building is placed in service. Any unused write-off can be carried forward 15 years or back three years.

Randolph Hawthorne states, "The very best historic preservation opportunities were seized years ago. . . . Most of the properties that would still qualify for historic preservation tax credits will be more marginal locations, will be difficult projects, and will involve more complex construction issues. Developers of rehabilitation projects typically have availed themselves of both LIHTCs and historic preservation tax credits to fill the equity gap." He adds, "You will occasionally still see historic preservation deals being done and there is a developed market for those tax credits. There are funds available for that purpose as well."[101]

A third tax credit opportunity is the New Markets Tax Credit Program for investments in designated Community Development Entities (CDEs) to stimulate private investment and facilitate economic and community development in low-income communities. CDEs must be certified by the Community Development Financial Institutions Fund of the U.S. Department of the Treasury. The credit allows investors to receive tax credits equal to 39 percent of the cost of the investment. The credit is taken over a seven-year period: 5 percent for each of the first three years and 6 percent for each of the last four years.[102]

Construction

General contracting is distinct from development (see chapter 2 for a general discussion of construction contractors). Many general contractors engage in development, and many developers, especially of residential products, engage in construction; nonetheless, they are two different businesses, each with its own set of risks and rewards. In general, if a project makes economic sense only if the developer can earn a contractor's profit, then it is not worth pursuing. Many projects undertaken by developers to keep their contracting arms busy have led those developers into bankruptcy.

Most major difficulties faced by developers who perform their own construction arise from the need to run another business—a labor- and detail-intensive business—that leaves them insufficient time to pay adequate attention to their development activities. Most of the major benefits of an in-house construction company stem from the developer's ability to take care of construction problems rapidly and to exercise control over costs of change orders. Construction does offer a relatively easy entry into development, and many homebuilders draw effectively on their construction background to make the transition into apartment development.

Residential construction differs from nonresidential construction in many ways. Typically, residential construction involves smaller subcontractors, a smaller scale of construction, and a less skilled, nonunion workforce. The architect's role is also more limited in residential than in nonresidential development. Usually, the architect is not involved in the residential bidding process and does not manage subcontractors' work for compliance with plans and specifications. Any time that the architect does spend is usually priced on an hourly basis instead of a fixed-fee basis, thus raising costs for developers who keep changing their minds.

John Porta, owner of MLP Investments in St. Louis, has never looked at his property management or construction arms as revenue centers. "We focus solely on managing our own assets in order to protect our interests. The same is true for our construction entity." He adds, "A typical general contractor, who is not accustomed to doing wood-frame construction, cannot function as efficiently as our own in-house arm." MLP sources many fixtures from overseas. The firm also favors panelized apartment construction since it replicates the same model in each market.[103]

Post Road Residential likes to use the lump-sum-agreement type of construction contract. "This is the purest form of the guaranteed maximum price contract because the price is guaranteed." This type of contract enables the contractor to manage all the subcontractors. Post Road never deals with subcontractors. This puts the responsibility on the general contractor (GC). The lump-sum contract has three main line items: total construction costs, overhead, and fee. A typical guaranteed maximum price (GMP) contract has a fourth line item for contingencies that is controlled by the GC. By removing contingencies from the GC's contract in a lump-sum agreement, the developer retains more control over the construction budget. Instead of allowing the contractor to tap into the contingency at will, Post Road Residential puts the hard cost contingency outside of the GC's budget and into the total development budget.[104]

If a GC has a good buyout for framing under a lump-sum contract relative to the budget specified in the construction contract with the developer, the GC keeps any cost savings. However, if a GC has a bad buyout for framing, the developer does not see any change order or cost increase to the construction budget. Most important, the GC cannot tap into a contingency line item to cover up an expensive buyout. This allows the developer to spend contingency money in a responsible way that has a return on investment in the future, such as improving amenity packages or upgrading unit finishes. "Therefore, assuming the lump-sum construction budget that Post Road Residential receives from a GC is competitive to the market, we'll always prefer this contract type because it reduces cost risk once the drawings are complete and the project is underway."[105]

Art Danielian offers the following advice to reduce construction cost overruns:

1. Have predetermined and regularly scheduled meetings with the contractor to identify future problems. "Look ahead at their schedules and materials to see if there is something that will cost more than what was budgeted. Any change order down the line can result in additional cost. If additional services are not requested in a timely manner when the changes occur, this can lead to even more additional costs."

2. Be aware that cost overruns during construction can result from
   » inadequate construction documents;
   » not having early preliminary construction cost estimates during the design process;
   » accepting inexperienced and low-bid subcontractors who tend to nickel and dime the builder;
   » lack of strong leadership in construction management; and
   » poor scheduling and an inadequate contingency budget.

3. Conduct "value engineering" meetings with the builder and selected key subcontractors to reduce costs without sacrificing design. If needed, develop an alternative design solution to circumnavigate a problematic detail or condition. To reduce the cost of construction altogether,
   » keep designs simple to build;
   » reduce skilled labor costs; and
   » increase speed of building by having some components built modularly in the factory.

4. Take advantage of modularization when possible. Modularization is important for dealing with the industry's increasing problem of the availability of skilled field labor. "Skilled labor is getting $45 to $80 per hour in the California marketplace right now, whereas construction factory workers make $15 per hour and can be more efficient because they're working in an automated factory system." The factory environment can produce a superior product using less expensive labor and delivering a home in less time. Modular and panelized construction is quicker, costs less money, requires less labor, and the quality can be just as high.[106]

MANAGING AND SCHEDULING THE JOB

In construction, one quickly learns that delays are the norm rather than the exception. Most problems occur around scheduling different subcontractors or material deliveries—hence, the importance of employing a good construction manager who can monitor the work of subcontractors as well as deal with architects, engineers, and city inspectors. A job superintendent—ideally, one with at least five years of experience on comparable projects—should always be on site to monitor subcontractors. This person handles the purchases from major suppliers and manages the contracts with all subcontractors who do the labor, giving the developer full control of construction while minimizing the number of direct employees.

One benefit of developing multifamily residential projects containing several buildings rather than one large building is that, with proper scheduling, the first units can be occupied and producing income well before the last units are completed. The contractor can facilitate early completions by paying subcontractors on the basis of buildings completed rather than on percentage of contract completed. The subcontractors, on the other hand, may prefer to run their crews from building to building. For example, a framing contractor may prefer to frame the first story of all buildings before starting the second story. Therefore, the developer may need to negotiate a rolling completion schedule as part of the subcontractor's contract.

One way to ensure cooperation between the construction and property management teams is to have both belong to the same entity and under one roof rather than hiring them on a fee basis. The developer's job superintendent should maintain a good line of communication with city inspectors. And the developer should have a business relationship with building department officials.

The developer should be personally involved in negotiating contracts and working with each subcontractor. At preconstruction meetings, the job superintendent talks directly to the people who head the different trades—both bosses and the foremen who will actually be on the job. These meetings allow people to meet and get to know one another, leading to a smoother operation. While construction is in progress, the developer should convey orders through the superintendent.

Building mock-ups of each of the major unit types may save time and money during construction. Bringing all the subcontractors together to review the mock-ups helps them identify potential sources of conflict during construction. For example, the air-conditioning subcontractor may find joists that need to be cut to run ventilation ducts or pipes or wires. By identifying these problems in advance, the subcontractors can find solutions before they have replicated the same problem in 50 units. When such problems arise, even though the subcontractors are responsible for fixing them, the developer almost always ends up having to pay more money.

The biggest source of cost overruns is change orders. A contractor almost always finds discrepancies in the plans and specifications that he can claim were not part of his original bid. The question of who should bear unanticipated costs is a constant source of conflict between the developer and the contractor—or, if the developer is acting as general contractor, between the GC and the subcontractor. For example, when Peiser Corporation and Frank Construction were building August Park Apartments in Dallas, they discovered that a pony wall (half-height) in one of the units had mistakenly been built to the ceiling. It blocked the view across the apartment when one entered the unit, making the apartment seem smaller and less inviting. The developers had every right to require the subcontractor to bear the expense of tearing down the wall and rebuilding it in the 20 units that had already been framed. Recognizing that if they did so, the subcontractor would find other ways to get back the cost of rebuilding the wall, they decided to live with the problem in the units that were already framed as long as the rest of the units were done correctly. This decision paid off later when the subcontractor did not charge extra for a change order that was not on the plan. In small construction projects, the give-and-take between the developer and the subcontractors is constant. Rigidly enforcing every construction plan detail usually come backs to haunt the developer.[107] One way for the developer to anticipate issues that might lead to cost overruns is to set up regularly scheduled meetings with the GC and job superintendent to monitor progress.

With regard to the architect's role, Jerome Frank, Jr., says, "Make sure that the architect conducts 'construction observation' but not 'inspection.' This is an important legal point. If you're inspecting, that means that you're also able to stand behind what you're saying."[108] Architects generally do not provide authorized direction for building in the field. Architects make observations and point them out to the client or contractor, then the client or contractor decides what action to take based on the observations.

INSPECTIONS

Construction involves numerous inspections, all of which must be correctly performed if the developer/contractor is to guard against liability. In addition to city building inspectors, the construction lender usually requires an outside inspector to verify that work is completed in conformance with plans and specifications. Most lenders will cooperate with a developer to find a mutually agreeable inspector. The developer should ask the lender for recommendations for an inspector and then consult with other builders on that inspector's reputation.

Developers should hire an outside inspector on any project above $2 million, even if the bank does not require it. Inspectors not only protect developers and the bank from lawsuits by independently verifying that work is correctly performed but also help ensure that subcontractors' work conforms to plans. Moreover, developers should undertake several inspections to protect themselves, including an independent engineering inspection of all foundations (to check that they are level and correctly located and elevated and to test the strength of cable tendons and concrete) and a verification that soil has been properly compacted. On government-funded projects, a government inspector may work on the site. When changes or additional requirements are made in the middle of a job, work should not proceed without a change order approved by the proper authorities to ensure that it is paid for. Dan Kassel, copresident of Granite Homes in Irvine, California, hires an inspector to videotape homes during construction. This record of the quality of work underneath the wallboard is available in case the firm later gets sued for construction defects. The inspector also helps ensure that the work—especially the work that is eventually covered up—is performed properly. The developer's liability, as well as the contractor's, can extend for 10 years or more after the completion of a building, so this documentation can be invaluable.

SUBCONTRACTORS AND DRAWS

Typically, apartment subcontractors are smaller than nonresidential subcontractors and are not bonded. To be competitive, most builders rely on nonunion subcontractors but also appreciate that they will sometimes go out of business or fail to complete a job. Developers should not automatically avoid working with a financially weak subcontractor. They should, however, check on the subcontractor's clients, suppliers, banks, and record and make sure that the subcontractor pays social security taxes. "Just be careful," cautions Jerome Frank, Jr. "Check his insurance coverage. If he doesn't have liability insurance, then you arrange for him to get it and charge him for it."[109]

Every time a subcontractor makes a draw, the developer/contractor should have the subcontractor sign a *lien waiver* and an affidavit showing that suppliers, taxes, insurance, and other bills have been paid and then attach the lien waiver to the check stub and file it in the job's folder. The purpose of the lien waiver is to prevent subcontractors from subsequently claiming nonpayment or one of their suppliers from filing a lien. Liens, even completely unwarranted, can delay loan closings and sales. If a lien is filed, a developer can post a bond for the amount of the lien or leave money in escrow to cover the potential liability.

One of the most difficult problems in construction is removing a subcontractor whose work is substandard. To reduce the associated delays, some developers require subcontractors to sign a stringent subcontract that provides for their removal for slow work or nonperformance.

INSURANCE

A good insurance agent who specializes in construction is invaluable to a contractor. Developers/contractors must be familiar with many different types of insurance: workers' compensation insurance, subcontractor's general liability insurance, builder's risk insurance, completed operations insurance, and contractor's equipment floater. Like the general contractor, subcontractors must each have their own builder's risk insurance that covers, say, the theft of material from a site. The job superintendent should get a copy of each subcontractor's insurance and check that they have workers' compensation, general liability, and builder's risk insurance before they begin work. Taking out completed operations insurance is also advisable; it protects builders from claims for injury or damage caused by building collapse or structure failure after completion. It does not, however, cover faulty workmanship.

Marketing

Marketing begins while a project is still on the drawing board and does not end until a project is sold. In the residential development business, developers cannot create a market where one does not already exist. On the contrary, their foremost objective is to identify the specific market segment for which more housing is needed and design the best possible product to serve that need. Marketing is the process of finding the renters or buyers and attracting them to the property at a time when they are in a position to make a decision. Marketing serves a number of objectives:

- analyzing what market to pursue and what product to build;
- persuading buyers and renters—through careful presentation—that the product meets their specific needs;

- packaging the product and offering assistance to enable those people to buy or rent it; and
- ensuring afterward that the product meets their expectations.

Insufficient predevelopment market research can result in a product that has been built for a certain market but does not appeal to that market. In such cases, developers must determine which market the product does appeal to and then repackage it to attract that market. Although almost any product will sell or rent at a low enough price, its developer is unlikely to turn a profit if prices must be discounted.

Jerome Frank, Jr., says developers can do two things for marketing and public relations: "You can market your company's history—for example, if you are Lincoln Properties or a similarly large company, you talk about the 'Lincoln style.' But what you're really selling is the company's management style." Alternatively, developers can sell the personality of the property, promoting the uniqueness of the development. "Find something in every development that you like and get excited about, for example, beveled mirrors over the fireplace or an abundance of closets, so that your manager gets really excited about it also. Some developers spend a lot of money on club rooms and swimming pools and in many ways waste money, especially in markets where low- to moderate-income tenants are targeted. Potential residents might be attracted to these amenities at first but find that interior features in the units are more important in the long run. In luxury markets, however, it is the sense of community that residents find in an apartment complex that attracts and holds tenants. Luxury apartment complexes feature their clubhouses, exercise rooms, game rooms, and paneled gathering places near the main entrance. The integrity of the management company is very important for dealing with clients. The developer has to exhibit a continued commitment to constantly train the property's managers."[110]

Market analysis is vital not only for predevelopment feasibility studies but also throughout the life of a project. Ongoing market analysis assesses the accuracy of the original analysis of the target market and identifies any important changes in market projections, rents, prices, and even the target market itself. Typically, 12 to 24 months elapse from completion of the first market study to the leasing of a project, and, in the interim, major changes may have occurred in the market. The developer must constantly monitor the market, especially by watching neighboring projects,

to remain up to date on current rental activity, pricing, concessions, and preferred physical characteristics and amenities. Changing market strategy in midstream can substantially increase construction and operating costs, but failing to respond to market changes can be fatal.

Bill McLaughlin says, "Customers have much better access to information and knowledge than before. Say, if I wanted to move to Nashville, instead of having to set up a physical tour or picking up the rental listing, now I can just spend half an hour online, have a comprehensive understanding of the market, and do a virtual tour of every asset—without ever leaving my desk. Whereas before you would just rely on ads in classifieds or vacancy signs on the street. Customers are enormously empowered these days. You can't keep stamping out the same widget and expect to have the same success."[111]

Tom Montelli hires a branding and marketing firm to help create a sense of community for projects. According to Montelli, "The more you brand the community successfully, the better the community itself is. Customers care about the sense of the community." Post Road Residential creates organic community through better amenity design, better building design, and more curated marketing and branding. Montelli notes, "Community building is the integration of our design and the project's brand. Sometimes we develop sites that have history. And we often incorporate that into the building design, and then we build a brand around that."[112]

DEVELOPING A MARKET STRATEGY

A market strategy is the philosophy the team supports and consistently follows throughout the life of the project. The strategy focuses on what is to be done, why, and the projected outcome. The cornerstone of any market strategy is its target submarket. Once that target has been identified through market analysis, every aspect of development—from design through property management—should reinforce the appeal of the project to that submarket.

After the development program and marketing strategy are established, preparation of project objectives can help the marketing team understand the strategy as well as the basic facts about the product and the market. The property's advantages should be clearly defined. What makes the property different, better, or more marketable than its competitors? In short, what makes it special from a marketing point of view? A project's distinctiveness may be its affordability, location, aesthetics, units, lifestyle, or other characteristics that make it outshine the competition.

The marketing plan ties into the established marketing strategy and can be thought of as a blueprint for the advertising campaign, public relations efforts, and leasing activities, including hiring and managing the leasing staff and preparing budgets and schedules for each component.

The plan also specifies the design of all elements to create a coordinated image for the project. Based on the target market's profile and the project's distinctive selling points, it defines an overall theme to be carried out in all community design elements. These include the name, logo, signage, sales displays, interior design, brochures, and other print and media materials.

THE MARKETING AND LEASING BUDGET

The marketing and leasing budget should cover all aspects of marketing. That includes appropriate amounts for exterior and interior marketing-related features, pre-leasing activities, general marketing, and promotional materials and events. A typical marketing budget includes the following:

- **Exterior Marketing**—Directional signs, identification signs, banners, and flags;
- **Interior Marketing**—Model apartments, sales displays;
- **Pre-leasing**—A website, flyers, voicemail setup, staff, signs for construction and leasing, advertisements in appropriate websites and publications;
- **Recognition Marketing**—Advertising campaign, staff, promotional materials, public relations, press releases and other print media, community involvement in charitable events, memberships in community organizations; and
- **Other**—Nominations for awards, move-in gifts, goodwill gestures to outside leasing agents and contractors.

Kevin Thompson, who was a marketing manager for multifamily projects for many years, estimates the firm's marketing budget for different types of apartments as follows:

- **Suburban Garden Apartments**—$1,000 per unit;
- **Urban Mid-Rise**—$1,000 to $1,500 per unit; and
- **Urban High-Rise**—$2,000 to $3,000 per unit (leasing is done by floor, rental prices are higher than other types of apartments, and conversion rates [from leads to leases] are lower).

While 10 years ago, 60 to 70 percent of the total marketing budget went to digital marketing, today that number is 95 percent. Very little is done in newspapers, television, or radio (1 percent). The remainder goes to temporary signage, banners, and outdoor signage—for example, on subway platforms and billboards (one billboard can cost $2,500 to $5,000). These figures pertain to the period of active lease-up. When the property is stabilized, marketing costs decline substantially, to just a fraction of the lease-up numbers.

Artificial intelligence is becoming a very important part of marketing. Individuals can engage with a bot (short for "robot," a computer program that acts as an agent for a user) to ask specific question such as, What is your pet policy? Where is the nearest school? Bots are like virtual leasing agents. They are 75 percent more likely to convert a visitor to a website than other means.[113]

LEASING AND SELLING. Prospective residents are sophisticated home shoppers, and the leasing staff should be chosen accordingly. Staff should be well-trained professional sales personnel, experienced in dealing with clients.

The old rule of one leasing agent for every 100 units in a new project is considered inadequate today. With staffing at that level, agents do not have time to give prospective residents the service and attention they need. If the leasing center is understaffed, sales are lost. Hiring additional personnel is cost-effective when compared with the cost of losing leases.

Even the best leasing team can convert only a percentage of leads to leases. The purpose of advertising is to generate the prospects. AvalonBay, a multifamily REIT with properties nationwide, converts 25 to 30 percent of its appointments—prospects who visit online or walk in the door—to leases. The firm experiences a 30 to 35 percent no-show rate. Its conversion rate of leads to appointments is 8 percent for email and 35 to 40 percent for telephone. Therefore, each lease requires 67 email leads and 14 phone leads.

Because apartments turn over regularly, marketing is a continuous and long-term effort. Therefore, a well-trained, professional sales staff contributes a great deal to the project's marketability. Some developers use in-house teams of leasing and sales agents, which gives the developers greater control over the leasing and sales process but also entails greater management responsibilities. An alternative is to use leasing companies that specialize in grand openings and initial lease-up. Because such firms are rewarded according to the number of leases signed rather than the long-term performance of the project, the developer should monitor tenants' creditworthiness very carefully. Another solution is to engage the services of an outside agency to take ongoing responsibility for marketing and leasing the project.

PRICING. Pricing, the most important tool for influencing leasing in the short run, cannot be based on pro forma projections. Rents must reflect current market conditions at the time the property is being leased, especially the prices charged by neighboring projects. Pricing should be monitored weekly, or even daily. Conditions change quickly, and a vacant unit costs a developer much more than a slight reduction in rent. Many companies use dynamic pricing algorithms to adjust pricing almost daily.

Funding requirements for permanent mortgages usually specify a target NOI that must be met for the mortgage to be fully funded. This target implies an average rent level. In declining markets, the developer may be obliged to obtain rents that are above market rate.[114] In such cases, the developer must find other incentives to bring the *effective* rental rate (including all concessions) in line with the current market. To make a project more competitive in a soft market, a developer can

- give concessions, such as a half to a full month's free rent;
- reduce the amount of the deposit required;
- offer accruing deposits, whereby tenants make little or no initial deposit and earn deposit credits at the rate of $20 or $30 per month, which they receive at the end of six months or so (this incentive also helps improve the punctuality of payments);
- provide free cable television or other services that normally carry a monthly charge;
- install additional appliances, such as microwave ovens, ceiling fans, and washer/dryers (such appliances represent a permanent capital improvement to the unit);
- offer decorating allowances for carpet, wallpaper, window coverings, or light fixtures;
- offer privileges at health or other clubs; or
- offer giveaways, such as televisions, vacations, or iPhones (this strategy may work for new hot items, but prospects and residents up for renewal prefer cash in hand).

Point-of-sale incentives are also invaluable tools for selling condominiums. The amount and type of sales incentives depend largely on local market conditions.

Kevin Thompson, formerly of AvalonBay, says the company tries to maintain occupancy at the 96–97 percent level at all times. "During the 2008–2009 recession, rental rates dropped 5 to 10 percent below previous peak levels, and we used pricing and other concessions to attract prospects."[115]

PUBLIC RELATIONS

The purpose of public relations is to create a favorable public image. The result of good public relations is free advertising. Proactive public relations include housekeeping functions (i.e., day-to-day communications with residents and the public) and crisis communications and management (to address on-site incidents that necessitate notifying residents and that might generate negative media coverage).

Public relations play an important role on site and off site. Developers who enjoy good off-site public relations are active in their communities with civic groups, the local chamber of commerce, churches, and other organizations. Developers who promote on-site public relations ensure that visitors to their sites receive a positive general impression—a neat and orderly site and sales office and polite staff, among other things.

Public relations experts are particularly useful to developers by virtue of their relations with local news media. Through their contacts, they should be able to obtain coverage for announcements and news releases about a new property. Potentially newsworthy events include purchasing the land, obtaining financing, closing loans, the ground breaking, the grand opening, the first families to move in, attaining certain lease hurdles, human interest stories about tenants (especially stories that highlight a special feature of the project, such as units for the handicapped), and special events. Other stories may be crafted about the product itself, featuring such elements as the design of the interior or exterior.

Public relations firms may also stage special events for a developer. Useful events include press parties, previews of a complex for community leaders and media representatives, and sponsored community events aimed at fundraising. Award competitions are another fruitful source of favorable publicity and provide third-party endorsement for a project.

Newsletters are a particularly effective public relations tool. Their frequency depends on the size of and the level of activity in an individual project. Newsletters, through email and occasionally by direct mail, should be sent to residents, area employers, brokers, prospects, neighborhood stores, and community facilities. They are helpful for attracting prospective buyers and tenants and for informing current residents about what is going on in the community. Most important, newsletters suggest to residents that the management cares about them. Usually, an advertising agency designs the newsletter and a public relations firm writes the copy, though many public relations firms handle the whole process.

A public relations campaign waged by a large development firm should target different groups with different messages:

- **Land Sellers**—Building faith in the developer's ability to perform;
- **Lenders**—Building faith in the developer's capacity to deliver what was promised and to repay loans;
- **Government**—Announcing that the company takes care of consumer complaints and is a good citizen in its dealings with the public sector;
- **Future Employees**—Creating the impression that the company is a fun and profitable place to work;
- **Competitors**—Conveying a sense of mutual respect and a shared readiness to work together in industry and civic organizations to address common problems;
- **Customers**—Establishing the developer's preoccupation with satisfying the demands of customers; and
- **Media**—Conveying respect and a willingness to share information.

ADVERTISING

The primary purpose of advertising is to motivate potential tenants and buyers to visit a project. Advertising is vital but can be very expensive. Discussions with other local developers, property managers, and advertising agencies can help identify the best media for advertising the project. Advertising agencies typically recommend that the advertising budget equal about 1 percent of the developer's hard costs. This amount is variable, however, depending on market conditions and the property's size, nature, and visibility.

The most prestigious advertising agency may not necessarily be the best for a beginning developer who requires considerable personal attention. A developer should interview at least three firms, obtain recommendations from their clients, and then select a firm that is genuinely interested in the developer's account. Advertising agencies provide various services, including developing a long-range advertising strategy, planning individual programs, selecting the best media for

presentation, preparing copy and design layouts, and monitoring the performance of their efforts.

Advertising for a project typically employs a common logo, theme, and style. A well-crafted logo can be used in advertising, on signage, brochures, and stationery, and even as a design motif. A project's name likewise plays an important role in creating an image for a project. New developers should promote a project's name first, with the developer's name of secondary importance. Names should be descriptive, not misleading. A complex should not be named "Forest Hills" if it sits on a Kansas-like prairie.

The most cost-effective media for advertising vary by project and location.

WEBSITES. The internet is the dominant marketing tool to reach potential renters and buyers, so a good website is essential to advertise a property. Smaller developers may wish to have their properties linked to websites and internet apartment rental services that provide information on a variety of properties. In this way, individual properties that might not be able to attract attention on their own can piggyback on the larger service to gain visibility in the internet marketplace. Websites dedicated to one property or a group of related properties involve much more than making an initial investment and waiting for customers to access the information. They make it possible to customize information and provide details for prospects, such as floor plans, photographs, virtual tours, and neighborhood amenities. Websites require ongoing maintenance to ensure that information is up-to-date and accurate.

CALL CENTERS. Call centers are an important extension of the advertising industry, but they are more expensive and less effective because they are competing against bots. The trend is toward more self-service and virtual leasing. Still, the ability to respond to phone calls and emails 24/7 is important.

BROCHURES. Developers should ensure that work on advertising brochures begins at least two months before they will be needed. The brochures should be ready for mailing to local employers, brokers, community leaders, and apartment locators during construction as part of premarketing. Despite the need for early preparation, brochures should not tie developers to specific figures; therefore, they should not contain prices (which change continually) or bound floor plans (people always want the floor plan that has already

Digital Marketing

Digital marketing has evolved and now plays a key role in generating leads. Social media was mostly an afterthought 10 years ago, but now it is a crucial part of not only building a brand but also driving real leads. This is especially true for the younger "digital native" generation that grew up using social media.[a] Kelley Shannon, vice president of marketing at the Bozzuto Group, states that the goal of advertising on social media is to generate awareness. Her firm posts images of properties showing amenity spaces, events, and "meet the team" and other activities that create buzz for a property or the company's brand. (Bozzuto uses very little conventional advertising because it is expensive and not very targeted, although the firm does use a lot of banners and signs.) Shannon and her team summarize their approach to digital marketing as follows:

1. Your website is the digital "front door" of the building. Make sure that the message is consistent with the actual building and any other online presence (social media, etc.). People spend time across all these channels, so they need to line up.

2. Paid searches and search engine optimization are important. Make sure that the property pops up in search results when the target audience types relevant words into the search bar (e.g., "apartments in Cambridge, MA"). These tools will make your marketing budget more efficient and improve the conversion rate (into actual leads and value creation). Paid searches are often charged on a pay-per-click basis, meaning the company pays the search engine each time someone clicks on the advertisement.

3. Internet listing services (i.e., online platforms such as Zillow, Apartments.com, and others) are another way to engage potential customers. Their payment structures vary; sometimes you pay per listing, sometimes per contact, and so on.

4. Social media may not always look like it is driving direct leads, but it does drive a lot of activity. "People turn to social media, just like they turn to the review ratings . . . to see what people are saying about a community, what that community is up to; to determine whether they're going to feel comfortable living there, whether they're going to find their place, find their fit, find their tribe." Make sure that it is continually monitored, especially during the lease-up periods when the leasing team may be more focused on leasing. Somebody needs to be focused on the social media presence.

5. Geofencing is a virtual geographic perimeter that helps target marketing messages to people within a certain radius of a property. This is a form of advertising on mobile devices: ads pop up on the target demographics' social media or search feeds. Anyone who comes within, say, a mile radius of a project can be served display ads if they are on networks or search engines where the firm has purchased ads.[b]

Best Practices and Takeaways

- Have a presence on as many channels as possible.
- Rely on the "rule of seven": consumers look at least seven times before they make a decision, and social media is definitely one of the critical places that they look.
- Use lead generation and lead nurturing to build brand and asset awareness. How do people find out about your property? Typically, 6 to 8 percent of leads turn into actual leases. Some hotter assets may see 14 percent lead conversion. Stabilized buildings may have lower conversion (4 percent) because of low availability—a good problem to have.
- Work backward from lead conversion and renewal rate to target how many leads the team needs to bring in (e.g., 8 percent conversion, 50 percent renewal). Then figure out how many leads a month are needed to lease all the units. Monitor the conversion numbers consistently and adjust strategy as needed.
- Maintain dashboards for marketing effectiveness (e.g., marketing cost per lead and cost per lease, by property, by source, by month, by quarter).
- Track your customers' "journey" to understand where they are looking in their search. There is a lot of back and forth between social media, property websites, and so on. Even after the decision to rent, before moving in, people will continue to review these channels and begin to root themselves into the community.
- Use technology not only for marketing but also to improve the customer experience. Being digital-first even before the COVID pandemic helped Bozzuto weather the turbulence. In 2020, Bozzuto surpassed its lead goal by 6 percent (the goal was set before COVID). The cost per lead and per lease decreased by 15 percent and 13 percent, respectively.

[a] Kelley Shannon, senior vice president of marketing and customer engagement; Noel Carson, vice president of marketing and creative director; and Chintimini Meadow Keith, vice president of corporate communications, The Bozzuto Group, interviews by author, 2021 and 2022.

[b] The Bozzuto Group contracts with Brainlabs to handle the technical side of its digital media. They pay for search terms such as "apartments that allow pets."

been rented or sold out). Prices should be listed on a separate page that can be easily changed. The square footage of a unit should be omitted from a floor plan unless its inclusion is a very competitive advantage. Special features and amenities, however, should be emphasized.

Many developers opt for a folder with a high-quality printed cover and pockets inside for inserts. The jacket is the major printing expense; inserts can be changed and updated as needed. Brochures can be all shapes and colors. When people are shopping for apartments, they pick up a number of materials and are more likely to notice distinctive brochures. Brochures that fold into the shape of, say, a door key or a house may cost extra to print but are more memorable. According to Kevin Thompson, "Professional high-quality photography is the key to success for both brochures and websites." Nowadays, beyond a printed brochure, video photography, 360-degree virtual tours, and drone footage can enhance the developer's presentation. High resolution is very important, so investing extra money to get a beautiful result is worthwhile. The photographs should emphasize lifestyle, with people actively enjoying the amenities in a project. "Be cognizant of fair housing. Photos should feature people of every shape, color, size, and disability."[116]

NEWSPAPER, RADIO, AND TV ADVERTISING. Advertising in newspapers, radio, and television is less prevalent than in years past. It is relatively expensive and cannot target or track the market as effectively as digital marketing. However, developers should consider the profiles of subscribers/listeners/viewers and compare them with the target market for the project. These forms of advertising may have a place in the project's marketing plan, particularly if the target market includes boomers/seniors who may continue to use these forms of media. AvalonBay, for example, may occasionally run an ad to announce a major new property in Boston or New York City. However, it spends less than 1 percent of its advertising budget on newspaper ads and no longer pursues the classified sections of newspapers' websites.

SIGNS. Billboards help establish name identity and may be useful as directional signs near a project. Transit advertising—such as bus banners, bus benches, and commuter station posters—can also be an effective way of keeping the developer's name in the public eye. Directional signs are probably the most effective signs of all. Removable "bootleg" signs are an inex-

pensive and efficient means of bringing people to the project from major arterials within a two-mile (3.2 km) radius for special events.

MERCHANDISING. Most advertising aims to tell people about a project and entice them to visit it. Merchandising is different: it involves on-site displays and practices. Visitors' first impressions are critical to a project's success, so particular attention should be paid to the condition of entrances, signs, landscaping, and buildings. A pleasant environment should be created as soon as possible, even while construction is still in progress. A well-designed and carefully located entrance not only helps merchandising but also bolsters a project's future identification in the neighborhood. Entrance signs and nameplates should be modest, designed to blend with the character of the community. Generous landscaping may be expensive, but it is also cost-effective—as a visit to any successful project demonstrates. Restrictive signs (prohibiting, say, walking on the grass) should be pleasant and inoffensive and designed, when possible, to relate to other merchandising features.

SALES OR LEASING OFFICE. The sales or leasing office should be easy to find and should open to attractive views of interior courtyards or other features of the project. Colors and furnishings should be consistent with the project's theme and chosen with the target market in mind. In the sales office, brochures, models, and maps should be placed so that visitors can view them at their leisure. Drawings of the apartment site plan and unit plans make attractive and informative wall hangings. Graphics give visitors an impression of what an uncompleted project will eventually look like. Perspective drawings are important. Visualizing a project from two-dimensional plans is difficult for most people. Small models of the project, although expensive, make attractive focal points and can help renters and buyers see how their apartments are located with respect to major amenities, access, security, and views. Aerial photographs also help show a project's relationship to off-site facilities, such as schools, churches, libraries, daycare centers, shops, and parks.

MODEL UNITS. Model units play an important part in selling and leasing by giving customers a sense of what the unit will look like and what they can do to personalize it. Model units should be close to the sales office, offer pleasant views of either the project or the surrounding area, and benefit from afternoon sunlight (afternoon is the most popular time for visitors).

Although decorating a sample of every unit type is unnecessary, those units that are decorated are likely to lease or sell more quickly. Decor for the models should be selected to appeal to the target market and should make the units look as large and bright as possible. Doors may be removed to add to a sense of spaciousness. Nonstandard built-ins should be avoided because they may mislead customers and because the model units may be moved to different locations in the complex once the project is leased. Background music, colors, and lighting can all be used to enhance the presentation. AvalonBay increasingly relies on virtual models, which are much easier to manage and much less costly (about half of the traditional model budget).[117]

CONDOMINIUM SALES. Marketing for condominiums is similar to that for single-family houses. Despite their desire to sell units during construction, developers have found that few buyers will commit themselves before they have seen the completed lobbies and amenities.

For smaller projects, an in-house sales staff is often uneconomical, and many developers use outside brokers, who are paid on commission. Developers who own other apartment houses or condominiums find that word-of-mouth advertising can be very effective. Some developers send out announcements to tenants or owners at their previous projects every time they open a new project. Paying a referral fee of, say, $100 to tenants or owners in other projects often helps generate sales, although in some states this practice violates real estate license laws.

John Math in Lake Worth, Florida, recommends that to sell 50 to 100 condominium units, a developer should hire a sales manager plus one salesperson. For projects of 100 to 200 units, two salespeople should be hired. Their total compensation should amount to 1.5 to 3 percent of gross sales. Many successful salespeople prefer to work totally on commission. If a developer expects them to be in the office during certain hours of the day, they should receive a salary plus commission or a draw against commission.[118]

Many condominium developers and lenders restrict non-owner-occupied units. The concern is that absentee owners take less care of their property and thereby depress sales to owner-occupants, who will pay the highest prices. At the same time, developers need to be flexible and prepared to respond to changing market conditions. When condominium sales are slow, some companies choose to operate the projects as rental units. Paul Schultheis, a developer in Arcadia, California, undertook a condominium project during a downturn in the market: "We set up an intensive marketing budget with an all-out push for 90 days. Only three of the 16 units were sold. We decided to change direction and set the building up as apartments. Now we own a deluxe-deluxe apartment house."[119] In many cases, however, projects conceived as condominiums do not work financially as apartments and subsequently lose money or go through foreclosure.

Operations and Management

No matter how well it is designed and built, an apartment project will be profitable only if it is well managed. Furthermore, management must be competent at many levels for a project to succeed:

- initially marketing and leasing up the project (often assigned to an outside source);
- marketing and leasing on an ongoing basis;
- collecting rents, handling accounts, and keeping records;
- making ongoing reports to owners;
- maintaining and repairing units, readying them for new tenants;
- maintaining and repairing building systems and common areas;
- maintaining landscaping and building exteriors;
- hiring and training new staff;
- keeping residents informed about apartment policies and operating activities of interest to them;
- initiating services for residents;
- dealing with residents' complaints;
- maintaining good relations with brokers, community organizations, and local government;
- maintaining good relations with managers of neighboring apartments to share information and work together on security and other common problems; and
- developing budgets and operating plans.

The nature of the relationship between the developer and the property manager depends, in part, on the property's size, the extent of the developer's property portfolio, and the nature and structure of the businesses. The manager can be the developer, the developer's employee, a subsidiary or in-house department of the development/property company, or an individual or third-party management company under contract. Most large apartment property companies, including REITs, manage their own properties through an in-house department or owned subsidiary company.

For most apartment projects, the decision on whether to use an outside property manager is based on the developer's willingness to invest time in the project. Properly addressing residents' needs and maintaining the property are extremely time-consuming. Most smaller developers prefer to delegate these responsibilities to a qualified property manager.

Even though most developers would prefer not to be in the management business, many feel that only by managing their own projects can they get the service they need. Beginning developers usually do not have an organization in place, however, and must therefore rely on outside managers. Greg Vilkin, a California developer, notes that property management fees have dropped as larger management companies compete for business. "You are not going to make money if you do management, as you can hire someone at a 3 percent fee." Vilkin considers 3 to 3.5 percent of gross rent to be the cost of outside property management.[120]

In selecting outside managers, beginning developers should look for companies with a good reputation for managing a particular type of property in terms of size, design, and tenant characteristics. It is also useful to investigate on-site procedures for accounting and collecting rents. An audit should be performed at least twice a year, preferably quarterly. The auditor, who should appear unannounced, reviews collection reports, rent rolls, and individual leases and inspects vacant units to ensure that no "skimming" is occurring.

The management company should prepare monthly reports that show gross potential income, actual income, and line-by-line expenses. The reports should also detail which units are vacant and which are not producing revenue. Cash receipts should be deposited daily. Monthly cash collection reports should be reviewed and approved by off-site staff.

The larger the property and its operating budget, the more likely it can accommodate specialists on staff, such as equipment engineers, gardeners, painters, or security guards. Many developers consider 150 or 200 units the minimum number necessary to support a full-time maintenance staff consisting of a property manager, assistant manager, maintenance worker, and porter. Smaller properties may begin by employing a resident manager, which may be less expensive in the short run but is usually inadequate in today's markets. In many urban areas, however, assembling a site that will support 150 units is very difficult, so developers have learned how to cope with smaller complexes. Harry Mow's strategy in Santa Monica, California, was to build a number of small complexes—typically 18 units on up-zoned single-family lots—to support shared management and maintenance staff across several nearby complexes.

The developer should endeavor to have as much good information as possible on future operations and maintenance (including but not limited to costs) to make informed design decisions. Property managers can make many useful contributions to the design process and should be included in all design review meetings. The increasing importance of residents' personal and property security can be addressed in part by improving design. Property managers' perspectives, based on experience with defensible space, can be valuable in this effort.

Note that although the operation and management of condominiums are the responsibility of unit owners through their condominium association, the developer must establish the legal framework for the condominium association (see chapter 3).

HIRING STAFF

Property management is one of the fastest-growing specializations in the real estate profession, "emerging as a managerial science. Today, property managers must have at their fingertips the knowledge, communication skills, and technical expertise needed to be dynamic decision makers. They also must be versatile, because they may be called on to act as market analysts, advertising executives, salespeople, accountants, diplomats, or even maintenance engineers. Interpersonal skills are needed to deal effectively with owners, prospects, tenants, employees, outside contractors, and others in the real estate business."[121]

Developer Jim Perley in Los Angeles summarizes his property management strategy this way: "Empower property managers as small business managers. Allow them to respond to market conditions by offering concessions to maintain occupancy. We want our managers to be comfortable enough with the owners to propose solutions. Owners should function as coaching staff: it is critical that they listen to input from personnel in the field. . . . Managers like having a relationship with the owner." He notes that delegation helps the manager feel good and helps the owner by freeing up time and energy to focus on business development.[122] Perley adds that a property manager should be able to handle technological software that comes with running a property. However, most important, the property manager should be streetwise and have good rapport with tenants. "Because two-thirds of our properties are affordable, the property manager can encounter some rough customers. For this reason, the best property manager is tough, affirmative, and respected while having a customer-service outlook. Hire a property management team that wants community and cares about the building and residents."[123]

Beyond hiring and training, a third component of effective customer service is feedback and reward. Leading apartment management companies tend to stress the bottom-up "culture of service" in their organizations, based on closely monitoring residents' satisfaction and compensation schemes that reward employees for keeping residents satisfied. Perley states, "Change the playbook for every property. No property is the same. Adjust to your property manager's leadership style. You're still the leader and in charge of the property, but you need to let the property manager use his/her own style to manage the property. Remember, you're in it for the long term with the residents, not the short term. The community is their home. There's an emotional attachment with a 'home' that is very different from commercial space. You should run the property in the most safe, efficient, and community-oriented way as possible."[124]

TURNOVER

The most volatile element in net operating income is usually the turnover rate. Although turnover sometimes offers a good opportunity to raise rents for units renting near the market rate, turnover can be costly in terms of rent lost during vacancies and of the renovations and cleanup required to prepare an apartment to rent again. In general, after a property has reached stabilized occupancy, the focus turns to keeping the property stable.

"It's good to raise rents, but the more important key number you should watch is turnover. Reward your management for renewing leases of existing tenants. Make sure that there is not a lot of turnover. That's a key thing to watch; stabilization, during the long run, keeps turnover and maintenance costs down."[125] Every turnover entails a minimum loss of two weeks of rent plus up to $500 for cleaning and carpet shampooing. In garden apartments, for example, turnover rates average 55 percent per year and can reach as high as 70 percent. In soft markets, turnover can exceed 100 percent.

Turnover occurs for many reasons, some of which—a tenant changing jobs, for example—lie outside the developer's control. But the developer can reduce turnover that is due to poor construction, design,

maintenance, or management. Residents become disenchanted if their refrigerator leaks, if their unit is too noisy, or if they cannot find parking.

Property management experts stress the importance of communication to reduce turnover. Owners should communicate often and regularly with managers and staff so that all parties understand their goals and concerns. On-site managers should communicate regularly with residents, answering questions and reducing uncertainty among tenants. For example, if a swimming pool must be emptied to make repairs, tenants should know when they will be able to use it again.

Problem tenants can create difficulties for an entire complex. Controlling noise and other irritants among neighboring tenants is critical for maintaining low turnover. The property manager can set the stage from the beginning by going over a written list of rules and regulations for the property with tenants before they move in, then asking tenants to sign the rules signifying that they understand them. When problems arise between tenants, the manager should first try to reach an amicable solution with both parties. Moving a tenant to a different unit sometimes solves the problem. If one party is at fault and an amicable solution does not work, the lease should be used to enforce the rules of the property, up to and including eviction. Timely response and firm enforcement of rules are vital for maintaining good tenant relations.

Jim Mattingly at LumaCorp in Dallas emphasizes property maintenance and customer service. "We believe that you have to have a good, solid product. Even if it is older, it has to be attractive." On-site personnel training emphasizes people skills. To stimulate a culture of customer service, LumaCorp concentrates on improving ratings on online apartment rating services. This real-time feedback helps staff focus on customer service. He adds that the relationship between property managers and residents is the key to success. Mattingly advises spending more money on marketing, resident functions, and communication.[126]

Online community engagement platforms enhance resident satisfaction and retention. Ben Pleat, founder and chief executive of Cobu, says, "Living in apartment buildings can be an isolating experience. Cobu makes it easy for residents to connect with their neighbors and neighborhood, turning apartments into homes."[127] Cobu helps create a strong sense of community by encouraging building managers to listen to residents and to set up a virtual platform for residents to meet and interact with one another. Each property

Blossom Plaza in Los Angeles's Chinatown District is a transit-oriented mixed-use development. Along with 20,000 square feet of ground-level retail and restaurant tenants, the development has 237 urban apartments located above the mixed-use podium, with 20 percent reserved as affordable units. A wide range of environmental building, site, and construction strategies target the project for LEED Gold certification.

has a curator who not only manages community and resident dialog but also creates events for residents to get to know one another. In addition, the virtual platform allows residents to set up their own clubs and social activities as well as arrange for dog walking and picking up groceries for elderly neighbors. The more engaged residents are with their neighbors and the community, the lower the turnover rate.

The COVID-19 pandemic dramatically changed the way leasing and move-ins are done. Everything that needed to be done at the leasing office can now be done remotely and 24/7.[128] Property owners are now able to monetize things that were not worth the administrative burden previously. For example, they can charge for parking that used to be free. They can even do surge parking price increases. Teo Nicolais says the gulf between mom-and-pop services and pros is growing. "Failure to acquire the tech will put you behind."

Nicolais asks, "Should one consider self-managing? Most entrepreneurs will self-manage initially. It acquaints you with the job, and you will eventually hire someone else to do the work for you. It saves cash flow in the short term, but you cannot afford to donate your labor. You should charge a market-rate management fee and charge it to the property. If your property cannot afford a professional property manager, you have a major problem. It probably was a bad deal to start with!" Even very large companies

like Vanke in China do not make much money from property management, but it is their primary source of contact with customers and tenants and helps them ensure that properties are well maintained. This is especially important in large multibuilding properties where dissatisfaction among existing tenants can severely hurt rental and sales to new customers. Bad online reviews can be devastating.

REFINANCING AND SELLING THE PROPERTY

One of the great advantages of owning property is the ability to refinance it and take out the additional financing proceeds tax free. As the NOI increases over time, savvy owners will refinance their properties regularly to take advantage of the tax-free cash they receive by obtaining larger mortgages. Jim Mattingly advises beginning developers to design flexibility into their financing. For LumaCorp, this flexibility has meant looking for longer, open-ended payment periods so the company is not obligated to refinance a property in any given year. Mattingly recommends that developers try to negotiate a window of two years or more in which to refinance so they can choose the year.[129]

The life cycle of property management has three stages: leasing up the property, stabilizing income, and positioning the property for sale. The third stage usually involves a different management approach from the first two.

When the time comes to sell a project, on-site staff should be informed about the developer's goals and should be given some financial incentive to motivate them to help put the property in the best possible physical and financial condition for sale. This period can be intense, as rents are raised and vacancies are filled. Experienced developers recommend that residents not be informed of a pending sale, but each tenant should receive a letter immediately *after* the sale. In Texas, for example, the law requires that tenants be notified within 48 hours of a sale about the status of their security deposits, which are transferred with the asset.

Cash flow is generally the most important consideration for buyers. Some steps will increase short-term cash flow at the expense of long-term profitability. For example, some developers become less selective about tenants to increase their occupancy and the rent roll when they get ready to sell a property. Other owners cut back on operating expenses and capital expenditures. Sophisticated buyers will use their own experience with respect to operating costs so that sellers' attempts to artificially reduce costs or raise occupancy will have little effect on the sales price. Short-term efforts to raise cash flows are not advisable, but many sellers do it. If a sale does not go through, the owner will have to deal with the consequences of the short-term strategy, such as getting rid of unreliable or troublesome tenants.

Conclusion

Beginning developers will find multifamily residential development one of the easier points of entry into the development industry, especially if they have some background in homebuilding. Like other types of development, multifamily housing is rapidly evolving. The process begins and ends with market analysis. Correctly identifying the depth, characteristics, and preferences of the target market is essential. Otherwise, delivering a product that best serves the market's needs will be impossible.

Jim Perley notes that a beginning developer has to adapt to new situations and try to predict the flow of situations. "You are trying not only to make money but also to develop a good product. It is . . . important to build equity and develop a good staff to make a difference."[130] Marvin Finger also emphasized the people side of the business. "The three components of multifamily development are location, product, and management. If you don't have the location, the product and the management will not make a difference and you'll never be successful. If you have the location, you can miss on the product somewhat if it is reasonably designed. But you must have the people if the product is to be sold." During the COVID-19 pandemic, many leases were finalized strictly through online websites and documents. But most people still sign their

Advice on Property Management

Stable occupancy with low turnover and high-quality tenants who pay market rate rents punctually is every property manager's goal. The following advice will help achieve it:

- If you make promises, deliver.
- Check the credit and criminal history of new tenants through credit agencies, applicant-screening services, and web-based services.
- Make vacant units ready for occupancy quickly; ready units lease more quickly and reduce vacancy loss. The manager's challenge is to balance the need to respond promptly to current residents' requests for service with the need to prepare newly vacated units for occupancy. If a large number of units must be prepared or a large number of service requests are pending, outside contractors may need to be called in.
- Minimize the chances of a large number of move-outs in any one month by carefully monitoring lease expiration dates and staggering expiration dates for new leases accordingly.
- Collect the first month's rent plus a security deposit from new tenants to guard against their leaving without giving notice.
- Work hard to hold on to current tenants in a slow market. For lease renewals, meet with tenants 45 days before their lease is due to expire.
- Deal with problems quickly and efficiently; unresolved problems will only grow.
- Remember that fewer callbacks by tenants on maintenance and repairs mean greater tenant satisfaction and fewer turnovers.
- Even when cash flow is low, try to minimize cutbacks on maintenance, repairs, and replacements, because they can lead to a lower standard of maintenance.

lease in person, creating a bond with that individual in the office. "It's very important not to have turnover in the office. You must groom and build an organization that is somewhat permanent, because people create relationships. When these relationships are not in place anymore, tenants will take their business elsewhere. People are key in the management business."[131]

To obtain financing today, new projects must demonstrate solid cash flows and produce real economic returns. This trend should offer long-term benefits to developers who face less tax-motivated competition. REITs and pension funds have helped generate more money for apartment development by buying new and existing properties and making forward commitments to buy projects under development. In the wake of the financial crisis of 2008–2009, apartments became the favored product type, and that remained the case through the teens and into the early 2020s. Institutional buyers prefer markets that are hard to build in, where future competition is less likely to increase dramatically. Apartments saw historically low capitalization rates—below 4 percent in some markets—in the late teens, and surprisingly they have been as strong or stronger during the COVID-19 pandemic. Many forces—baby boomers selling their homes to enjoy city living, millennials joining the workforce, the displacement of people during the pandemic, and general inflation in 2022—have combined to increase demand for apartments, putting pressure on rents to rise more quickly. Developers are finding opportunities to build apartments for new niches. One example is people in upscale communities who no longer want to own and maintain a large suburban home but want to stay in the same community and rent.

Many factors are raising the cost of apartment construction: more stringent fire codes; energy, sustainability, and parking requirements; density restrictions; and standards for amenities. At the same time, the scarcity of land, neighborhood opposition to development, stricter environmental regulations, and growing difficulties with public approvals are raising the price of land. Rents are rising as well—more sharply than in the past (historically, rents have lagged behind inflation in the general economy)—which makes apartments more financially attractive to the developer but likely increases the pressure for rent control in many communities. Although new apartment construction on suburban greenfield sites remains the easiest way for beginning developers to start, smaller urban infill projects, conversions of older industrial and office buildings to apartments, and affordable housing programs (such as tax credits) offer appealing opportunities for beginning developers. Their most important goal should be to build a track record of successful projects in which tenants, investors, and lenders are pleased with their performance. There are advantages to working on smaller, simpler projects rather than larger complicated ones. Completing three smaller projects over three to four years will take a beginning developer further than completing one large project over the same period.

NOTES

1. Wall Street investors such as Blackrock, Blackstone, Colony, and Goldman Sachs have established private equity funds to buy single-family homes for rent. Invitation Homes has more than 80,000 homes; Front Yard Residential Corporation, now called Pretium, owns 55,000 homes for rent; Mynd, owned by Investor, has 20,000 homes. (June 2021 data, found on companies' websites.)

2. Joint Center for Housing Studies of Harvard University, *The State of the Nation's Housing, 2009* (Cambridge, MA: Harvard University, 2009).

3. International Code Council, "Types of Construction," chap. 6 in *2015 International Building Code*, October 2015, https://codes.iccsafe.org/content/IBC2015/chapter-6-types-of-construction.

4. Phil Hughes, president, Hughes Investments Inc., Greenville, South Carolina, interview by author, October 31, 2019.

5. Randolph Hawthorne, RGH Ventures, Brookline, Massachusetts, interview by author, 2021.

6. Hawthorne, interview, 2021.

7. Edward Zuker, Chestnut Hill Realty, Chestnut Hill, Massachusetts, interview by author, September 2009.

8. Jerome L. Rappaport, Jr., founder and owner, New Boston Fund, Boston, interview by author, November 2009.

9. Jerome L. Rappaport, Jr., founder and owner, New Boston Fund, Boston, interview by author, November 5, 2019.

10. Rappaport, interview, 2019.

11. Michael Lander, founder, The Lander Group, Minneapolis, Minnesota, interview by author, November 11, 2019.

12. Tom Montelli, partner, Post Road Residential, Boston, interview by author, February 11, 2020.

13. William McLaughlin, executive vice president of development, AvalonBay Communities, Boston, interview by author, October 9, 2019.

14. John Porta, partner, Covington Development LLC, and owner, MLP Investments LLC, St. Louis, Missouri, interview by author, October 31, 2019.

15. Marvin Finger, The Finger Companies, Houston, Texas, interview by author, 2000.

16. Dan McCoy, founder and managing partner, BSH Companies, Atlanta, Georgia, interview by author, 2010.

17. Lesley Deutch, managing principal, John Burns Real Estate Consulting, Boca Raton, Florida, interview by author, May 19, 2020.

18. Deutch, interview.

19. Deutch, interview.

20. Gerd-Ulf Krueger, founder, Krueger Economics, interview by author, 2009.

21. Tim Cornwell, principal, The Concord Group, San Francisco, interview by author, November 11, 2019.

22. Phillip Smith, Framework Group, Tampa, Florida, interview by author, May 2020.

23. See Richard B. Peiser, "The Determinants of Nonresidential Urban Land Values," *Journal of Urban Economics* 22 (1987): 340–60.

24. McLaughlin, interview.

25. *Double-loaded parking* has parking stalls on both sides of the driveway. *Back-to-back apartment* units adjoin along the rear wall. This shared wall can accommodate plumbing for both units and reduces the total amount of outside wall per unit, thereby saving money.

26. The San Diego general plan requires at least 1 acre (0.4 ha) for lots with an average slope of 15 percent or less, 2 acres (0.8 ha) for an average slope of 15 to 25 percent, and four acres (1.6 ha) for an average slope greater than 25 percent. Neal LaMontagne, County of San Diego Department of Planning and Land Use, interview by author, 2000.

27. Oklahoma's 5.6 earthquake in 2011 is not blamed on fracking. But fracking and large amounts of fluid disposed into the ground may lubricate already stressed faults, making it easier for them to slip and cause an earthquake. See Charles Choi, "Did Fracking Cause Oklahoma's Largest Recorded Earthquake?," *Scientific American*, November 14, 2011, www.scientificamerican.com/article/did-fracking-cause-oklahomas-largest-recorded-earthquake.

28. The act contains no specific definition of vernal pools. Instead, it relies on the U.S. Fish and Wildlife Service's *Classification of Wetlands and Deepwater Habitats of the United States* (report no. FWS/OBS-79/3, December 1979) for defining types of wetlands. Typically, a vernal pool is a shallow, intermittently flooded wet meadow, generally dry for most of the summer and fall. David Buie, U.S. Fish and Wildlife Service, interview by author, 2000.

29. Ned Abelson, director, Goulston & Storrs, Boston, interview by author, March 2, 2021. Also, Phil Hughes recommends asking the engineer to include a sentence in the summary report: "No further action necessary" (unless, of course, further action *is* necessary). Phil Hughes, interview.

30. Ambrose Donovan, principal, McPhail Associates, Cambridge, Massachusetts, interview by author, March 3, 2021.

31. Abelson, interview.

32. Donovan, interview. Costs are for Massachusetts. Other states may be less expensive, but the requirements are the same for environmental assessments and the costs may not vary as much as land and other costs do.

33. Greg Vilkin, president, Forest City Development, Los Angeles, interview by author, 2000.

34. Montelli, interview. He adds, "We still did very well on the sale, but COVID (and the buyer's inability to project rent growth in underwriting for the first few years) took a lot of money off the table."

35. Jerome J. Frank, Jr., Jerome Frank Investments, Dallas, Texas, interview by author, 2000.

36. Finger, interview.

37. Kenneth Hughes, president, Hughes Development, LP, Dallas, Texas, interview by author, August 2009.

38. California Department of Transportation, *Transit-Oriented Development Compendium*, June 2005, https://rosap.ntl.bts.gov/view/dot/27614.

39. Kenneth Hughes, interview.

40. For an excellent discussion of exactions, see Julian C. Juergensmeyer, Thomas E. Roberts, Patricia E. Salkin, and Ryan M. Rowberry, *Land Use Planning and Development Regulation Law* (St. Paul, MN: West Academic Publishing, 2018); Steven Eagle, *Regulatory Takings* (Washington, DC: LexisNexus, 2020); Cecily Talbert Barclay, David L. Callies, and Julie A. Tappendorf, *Development by Agreement: A Tool Kit for Land Developers and Local Governments* (Washington, DC: American Bar Association Book Publishing, 2012); Arthur C. Nelson, James C. Nicholas, and Julian C. Juergensmeyer, *Impact Fees: Principles and Practice of Proportionate-Share Development Fees* (New York: Routledge, 2017); Barry Cullingworth and Roger W. Caves, *Planning in the USA: Policies, Issues, and Processes* (New York: Routledge, 2014); and Alan Altshuler and Jose Gomez-Ibanez, *Regulation for Revenue: The Political Economy of Land Use Exactions* (Washington, DC, and Cambridge, MA: Brookings Institution and Lincoln Institute of Land Policy, 1993).

41. For a good overview of alternatives for financing infrastructure improvements, see Robert W. Burchell and David Listokin et al., *Development Impact Assessment Handbook* (Washington, DC: Urban Land Institute, 1994).

42. Clancy Mullen et al., *National Impact Fee Survey: 2019* (Austin, TX: Duncan Associates, 2019), www.impactfees.com/publications%20pdf/2019survey.pdf#:~:text=NATIONAL%20IMPACT%20FEE%20SURVEY:%202019%201%20This%20report,to%20compare%20fees%20charged%20by%20different%20jurisdictions.%2.

43. Mullen et al., *Impact Fee Survey*.

44. An illustration of Stage 4 analysis and the full after-tax Stage 5 analysis is available at americas.uli.org/PRED.

45. Stage 2 analysis is standard throughout the real estate industry and is taught in most real estate graduate schools and executive training courses. Most real estate finance textbooks describe DCF analysis in detail; see, for example, William B. Brueggeman and Jeffrey Fisher, *Real Estate Finance and Investments*, 13th ed. (New York: McGraw-Hill, 2010); and Charles Long, *Finance for Real Estate Development* (Washington, DC: Urban Land Institute, 2011).

46. When interest rates are well below overall capitalization rates, cash-on-cash returns on equity skyrocket as leverage (debt/total project costs) increases. Because inflation is a component of the IRR (along with risk and real return rates), the IRRs required by investors are also lower.

47. To avoid double-counting, remember to use the total development costs *before* lease-up in the Stage 2 analysis.

48. Time period zero is typically considered to be the point at which the developer closes on the land. When closing occurs long before construction starts, the simpler method is to assign time period zero to the start of construction and to include land carrying, design, and other earlier costs as "costs to date."

49. U.S. Census Bureau, "Characteristics of New Housing," https://www.census.gov/construction/chars/.

50. Art Danielian, founder and chairman, Danielian Associates, Irvine, California, interview by author, February 28, 2020.

51. Teo Nicolais, president, Nicolais LLC, Denver, Colorado, interview by George Zhang, April 28, 2020.

52. Tom Hopper, *Research Brief: Transit-Oriented Development Explorer (TODEX)*, Massachusetts Housing Partnership, December 17, 2019, https://www.mhp.net/news/2019/todex-research-brief. See also Robert Cervero and Erick Guerra, *Urban Densities and Transit: A Multi-Dimensional Perspective*, UC Berkeley Center for Future Urban Transport Working Paper no. UCB-ITS-VWP-2011-6, September 2011, www.reconnectingamerica.org/assets/Uploads/201109DensityUCBITSVWP.pdf.

53. Colette Santasieri, *Planning for Transit-Supportive Development: A Practitioner's Guide*, FTA Research Report no. 0057, June 2014, https://www.transit.dot.gov/sites/fta.dot.gov/files/FTA_Report_No._0057.pdf.

54. Scott Simpson, senior director, KlingStubbins, Cambridge, Massachusetts, interview by author, September 2011, and 2022. Costs updated in 2022.

55. Rappaport, interview, 2019.

56. Scott Johnson, design partner, Johnson Fain, Los Angeles, interview by author, November 31, 2019.

57. Finger, interview.

58. Simpson, interview, 2011.

59. John Porta, owner, MLP Investments LLC, St. Louis, Missouri, interview by author, July 2009.

60. Louis Minicucci, president, MINCO Development, North Andover, Massachusetts, interview by author, February 4, 2021.

61. Danielian, interview.

62. Johnson, interview.

63. Frank, interview, 2000.

64. Johnson, interview.

65. Danielian, interview.

66. California became the first state to require solar panels in most new homes and apartments although there is discussion on whether it is a mandate. Sammy Roth, "California Might Not Require Solar Panels on New Homes, after All," *Los Angeles Times,* November 11, 2019, www.latimes.com/environment/story/2019-11-11/california-might-not-require-solar-panels-on-new-homes.

67. Montelli, interview.

68. Montelli, interview.

69. Phil Hughes, interview. Many apartment developers sell their projects when they reach stabilized occupancy. Developers who plan to convert their rental apartments to condo ownership must have strong staying power to hold out for the time when the market for condo conversion becomes attractive.

70. Danielian, interview.

71. Phil Hughes notes that many lenders seemed to raise their interest rate much higher for a forward commitment after 2008. Volatility increases with interest rate uncertainty. The fear of interest rate increases was affecting mortgage and construction loan rates in early 2022, just before interest rates jumped dramatically as inflation skyrocketed.

72. Both construction and permanent loans are called *mortgages* because they are backed by the collateral of the property.

73. A *point* represents a front-end fee equal to 1 percent of the loan amount. Points are usually paid out of the loan proceeds. On a $1 million loan with two points, the lender receives $20,000 in fees, and the developer receives the net amount of $980,000. Points are a normal part of the developer's financing costs and should be included in soft costs.

74. Hard-money lenders may accept a second lien position, but their interest rate will be much higher than a regular lender.

75. Richard Klein, senior vice president of corporate development, Environmental Industries Inc., Calabasas, California, interview by author, 2000.

76. Frank, interview, 2000.

77. Claudia Piper, senior vice president, Webster Bank, Winchester, Massachusetts, interview by author, March 23, 2020.

78. Minicucci, interview.

79. Piper, interview.

80. LIBOR is the interest rate offered by a specific group of London banks for U.S. dollar deposits of a stated maturity. LIBOR is used as a base index for setting rates of some adjustable-rate financial instruments.

81. Piper, interview.

82. Montelli, interview.

83. Phil Hughes, interview.

84. Randolph Hawthorne, RGH Ventures, Brookline, Massachusetts, interview by author, 2000.

85. Karl Zavitkovsky, managing director, Bank of America, Dallas, Texas, interview by author, 2001.

86. See Brueggeman and Fisher, *Real Estate Finance,* chapters 4 and 5, for how to calculate a mortgage.

87. Steve Bram, president, George Smith Partners, interview by author, January 2022.

88. "Top 25 percent" means that the developer guarantees the first 25 percent of loss. For example, if the loan is for $1 million and the lender loses $300,000, the developer is responsible for the first $250,000 of the loss.

89. Nicholas Lizotte, Sagamore Residential, Port Chester, New York, interview by author, October 2009.

90. Brenda Richards, "New FHA Guidelines Expand Access to Condo Mortgages," *Forbes*, August 15, 2019, www.forbes.com/sites/brendarichardson/2019/08/15/new-fha-guidelines-expand-access-to-condo-mortgages/?sh=38b6f75a323b.

91. Nicolais, interview.

92. Rappaport, interview, 2019.

93. Nate Kline, chief investment officer and principal, One Wall Partners, New York, interview by author, May 8, 2020.

94. Kline, interview.

95. Rappaport, interview, 2009.

96. Real estate tax accounting is a highly specialized area. Although all accountants are familiar with depreciation rules, the categorization of upfront fees requires a specialist with experience in the technical aspects of real estate partnership tax and law.

97. Regulation D private offerings are not subject to the intense review by public agencies that public offerings receive. Public offerings must be offered to no more than 35 "nonqualified" investors, who are defined as investors with a personal net worth of less than $1 million or income of less than $200,000 per year. A Regulation D private offering may be offered to an unlimited number of "qualified" investors.

98. Harry Mow, president, Century West, Santa Monica, California, interviews by Richard Peiser, 1989, 1991.

99. Rappaport, interview, 2009. "Sidecar" investors are large national funds that will coinvest equity in projects along with the local owner-operator syndicator/fund. The syndicator/fund's deal with the sidecar investor may provide several different forms of fees—a management fee of up to 150 basis points, or no fee and an override, or no fee or override but annual property management fees.

100. Randolph Hawthorne, RGH Ventures, Brookline, Massachusetts, interview by Kristen Hunter, August 2009.

101. Hawthorne, interview, 2009.

102. *Federal Register*, vol. 75, no. 67, April 8, 2010, Notices, p. 18017.

103. Porta, interview, 2009.

104. Montelli, interview.

105. Montelli, interview.

106. Danielian, interview, 2020.

107. Frank, interview, 2000.

108. Frank, interview, 2000; and Jerome J. Frank, Jr., Jerome Frank Investments, Dallas, Texas, interview by George Zhang, September 20, 2021.

109. Frank, interview, 2000.

110. Frank, interview, 2000.

111. McLaughlin, interview.

112. Montelli, interview.

113. Kevin Thompson, director of relationships, Primary, interview by Richard Peiser, February 2022.

114. Permanent lenders have been stung by artificially inflated rental rates and usually require full disclosure of all rental concessions.

115. Kevin Thompson, corporate vice president of marketing, AvalonBay Communities, Arlington, Virginia, interview by Richard Peiser, June 2010.

116. Thompson, interviews, 2010 and 2022.

117. Kevin Thompson, corporate vice president of marketing, AvalonBay Communities, Arlington, Virginia, interview by author, August 2011.

118. John Math, president, Associated Property Management, Lake Worth, Florida, interview by author, October 2001.

119. Paul Schultheis, interview by author, 2001.

120. Vilkin, interview.

121. Floyd M. Baird, Marie S. Spodek, and Robert C. Kyle, *Property Management*, 6th ed. (Chicago: Dearborn Real Estate Education, 2004), p. 1.

122. Jim Perley, president, Western America Properties, Los Angeles, interview by Kristen Hunter, June 2009.

123. Jim Perley, president, Western America Properties, Los Angeles, interview by Julian Huertas, October 2019.

124. Perley, interview, 2019.

125. Frank, interview.

126. James Mattingly, president, LumaCorp Inc., Dallas, Texas, interview by author, June 2009.

127. Ben Pleat, founder and chief executive, Cobu, Boston, interview by George Zhang, February, 2021.

128. Nicolais, interview.

129. Mattingly, interview.

130. Jim Perley, president, Western America Properties, Los Angeles, interview by author, 2000.

131. Finger, interview.

5 Office Development

SOFIA DERMISI

Overview

Office buildings are being affected profoundly by a multidimensional disruptive perfect storm, which is triggering significant leaps in the development, perception, and use of office buildings.

The key disruptors include (1) the COVID-19 pandemic and the unprecedented worldwide closure of office buildings that prompted the normalization of remote work; (2) structural and technological innovations, including the use of sustainable materials, the adoption of architectural elements that promote occupants' physical and mental well-being, and spatial internet of things and computing (using sensors that produce real-time data, which when combined with spatial computing produce 3-D models that expedite information sharing and decisions[1]); and (3) workplace evolving needs, such as a major generational shift in the workforce, the great resignation wave, less growth of the labor force, and office space based on liquid workforce needs (working from home, working from anywhere, working from the office [WFH/WFA/WFO], need-based space, etc.).

Developers are adopting structural, sustainable, and technological innovations that can significantly propel the marketability of office buildings upon completion. This chapter focuses on office buildings built or retrofitted by beginning developers—costing under or around $50 million and ranging from 50,000 to 100,000 square feet (4,645–9,300 sq m).

CATEGORIZING OFFICE DEVELOPMENT

Office developments are categorized by class, building type and height, use and ownership, types of office space, and location.

CLASS. Office class is linked with space quality, which is determined by several factors, including age, location, finishes, materials, amenities, and tenant profile (see figure 5-1). Office space is generally divided into three major classifications:

1. **Class A**—New, highly efficient properties in prime locations with first-rate amenities and services, as well as older upgraded buildings with prestigious or landmark status. Some might be defined as trophy buildings based on the prominence of the architect or other features.[2] They achieve the highest possible rents and sales prices in the market (top 30 to 40 percent of the market).

2. **Class B**—Older, somewhat deteriorated buildings in good locations with finishes, amenities, and services that are lower than class A. Newer properties might also be designated as class B if they offer lesser services and amenities. They achieve lower rents and sales prices compared with class A properties.

3. **Class C**—Facilities with inferior mechanical and building systems, below-average maintenance, and very limited services compared with class B. Rents and sales prices are the lowest in the market and are often in less-attractive locations than class A or B buildings.

The Eight in Bellevue, Washington.

FIGURE 5-1 Characteristics Determining Office Classification

				CLASSIFICATION OF BUILDING CHARACTERISTICS			
Class	Location	Recognition/age	Floor layouts/ amenities	Rents	Systems	Finishes	Services
A	Best location (e.g., mass transit, etc.)	Prestigious (e.g., landmark), sustainability certifications, mainly new buildings; premier tenants	Innovative layouts, significant amenities, connection with nature and community, building apps for active community	Asking gross rents are at the top 30–40%	Most modern mechanical, elevator, HVAC, and utility systems	High-quality design and materials	Professionally managed; above-average maintenance, management, and upkeep; on-site personnel; sufficient parking
B	Average to good	Prestigious (e.g., landmark), sutainability certifications, few new buildings; some premier tenants	Average layouts and amenities	Asking gross rents between A and C	Adequate mechanical, elevator, HVAC, and utility systems	Average-to-good quality design and materials	Professionally managed; average-to-good maintenance, management, and upkeep; may include on-site personnel
C	Less desirable	Limited possibility of prestigious buildings	Some inefficient layouts, minimal to no amenities	Asking gross rents are at the bottom 10–20%	Mechanical, elevator, HVAC, and utility systems are less adequate and have not been upgraded	Finishes need updating	Below-average maintenance, management might not be on site, and minimal upkeep
D							
E							

Sources: Buy Team, "A Report Card for Commercial Building Construction," CoreLogic, March 31, 2017 (https://www.corelogic.com/intelligence/a-report-card-for-commercial-building-construction/); BOMA/International, "Building Class Definitions" (https://www.boma.org/BOMA/Research-Resources/Industry_Resources/BuildingClassDefinitions.aspx); BOMA/Quebec, "Office Building Classification Guide" (https://bomacanada.ca/wp-content/uploads/2016/09/building_classification14ang.pdf).

[a]Ratings used for cost and other valuation purposes of commercial buildings.

There are also five classifications of construction indicators, with the first three aligning with quality classifications of buildings (see figure 5-1).

BUILDING TYPE. Seven major office building types are widely used for categorizing purposes:

- **Typical Office**—single structure with office use being the main revenue stream; possibly a minor retail component;
- **Office Condo**[3]—floors or sections can be sold;
- **Medical Office Building (MOB)**[4]—at least 75 percent of the structure includes tenants associated with the medical field;
- **Mixed-Use Development (MXD)**—one or more structures combining at least two significant revenue streams (e.g., retail, office, residential); suburban MXDs cover more than 15 to 20 acres (6 to 8 ha) with buildings of various heights;

- **Garden Office**—low-rise structures clustered together in office parks with extensive landscaped areas;
- **Flex Space**—one- or two-story buildings usually located in business parks that facilitate an office component combined with space for light industrial or warehouse use; and
- **Secured (or Sensitive) Compartmental Information Facility (SCIF)**[5]—these facilities have multiple feeds, security, and ventilation systems.

BUILDING HEIGHT. Buildings are categorized by height as follows:

- **High-Rise**—typically higher than 12 stories;
- **Mid-Rise**—four or five to 12 stories; and
- **Low-Rise**—one to three or four stories.

The Council of Tall Buildings and Urban Habitat suggests that better indicators of building height designation are (1) height relative to context (comparison with other structures in the area and local zoning codes), (2) proportion (slenderness of the building against low

rame	Floor	Roof	Walls
tructural steel columns and eams, fireproofed with masonry, oncrete, plaster, or other oncombustible material	Concrete or concrete on steel deck, fireproofed	Formed concrete, precast slabs, concrete, or gypsum on steel deck, fireproofed	Nonbearing curtain walls, masonry, concrete, metal and glass panels, stone, steel studs and masonry, tile or stucco, etc.
Reinforced concrete columns and eams; fire-resistant construction	Concrete or concrete on steel deck, fire-resistant construction	Formed concrete, precast slabs, concrete, or gypsum on steel deck, fireproofed	Nonbearing curtain walls, masonry, concrete, metal and glass panels, stone, steel studs and masonry, tile or stucco, etc.
Masonry or concrete load-bearing walls with or without pilasters; masonry, concrete, or curtain walls with full or partial open steel, wood, or concrete frame	Wood or concrete plank on wood or steel floor joists, or concrete slab on grade	Wood or steel joists with wood or steel deck; concrete plank	Brick, concrete block, or tile masonry, tilt-up, formed concrete, nonbearing curtain walls
Wood or steel studs in bearing wall, full or partial open wood or steel frame, primarily combustible onstruction	Wood or steel floor joists or concrete slab on grade	Wood or steel joists with wood or steel deck	Almost any material except bearing or curtain walls of solid masonry or concrete; generally combustible construction
Metal bents, columns, girders, purlins, and grits without fireproofing, incombustible onstruction	Wood or steel deck on steel floor joists, or concrete slab on grade	Steel or wood deck on steel joists	Metal skin or sandwich panels; generally incombustible

urban backgrounds), and (3) tall building technologies (for example, vertical transport technologies).

USE AND OWNERSHIP. Office buildings can be classified by their users and owners. Buildings can be single- or multiple-tenant structures. A building designed and constructed for a particular tenant that occupies most or all the space is called a *build-to-suit* development. A building designed and developed without a commitment from a tenant is considered a *speculative* building. Another possibility might be an adaptive use/conversion of a building, which focuses on changing a building's use through major renovation.

TYPES OF OFFICE SPACE. Buildings offer their occupants significant space differentiation—a postpandemic report from JLL[6] emphasizes the importance of this differentiation and the need for spaces that boost human experience through social spaces (cafés, lounges), a connection with nature (outdoor spaces,

plants), focus work (concentration pods, focus rooms), learning and development (training rooms, virtual reality cafés), creativity (brainstorming, fab/innovation labs), and project and collaboration.

Even before the pandemic, office space was evolving beyond the conventional layout and included

- **executive suites**—larger enclosed offices with access to additional amenities and assistants;
- **creative space**—entertainment area with games, advertisements, and pods;
- **coworking space**—ranging from hoteling, dedicated space, and a shared kitchen;
- **accelerator**—typically for startups, with space for mentoring, networking, etc.;
- **incubator**—combination of office/lab space, with some financial assistance made available; and
- **innovation center/district**—areas with entrepreneurial activities.

Office Development

LOCATION/DESIGNATION. Before the COVID-19 pandemic, in most urban areas, distinct types of office nodes existed that were distinguished by their location. Innovations in technology and computer science (e.g., artificial intelligence), combined with the COVID-19 pandemic and physical-distancing restrictions, are redefining the workplace—from the traditional office building to the WFH/WFA model. The COVID-19 pandemic raised various questions regarding the future needs of the workforce and the office elements needed to retain talent and competitiveness:

1. **Central Business District (CBD)**—High land costs in CBDs encouraged increased densities in the form of mid- and high-rise structures. Typical tenants include headquarters/main hubs of Fortune 500 companies, law firms, insurance companies, financial institutions, government, and other services requiring high-quality prestigious space.[7] In a postpandemic world, quality space and amenities are critical for in-person workplaces to remain competitive.

2. **Beyond the CBD**—In a postpandemic world, the importance of office buildings beyond the CBD or downtowns is increasing as they allow employees flexibility by offering WFA satellite and coworking options that are closer to employees' homes, and, therefore, businesses have access to an employee talent pool in more remote areas.

   » **Suburban Locations**—Lower land costs and availability offer greater options outside CBDs. Suburban nodes of large and small office buildings are often found in business districts, in clusters near freeway intersections, or in major suburban shopping centers. Rents are traditionally lower than the CBD and tenants include regional headquarters, high-technology and engineering firms, smaller companies, and service organizations.

   » **Neighborhood Offices**—Small office buildings are frequently located away from the major nodes, where they serve the needs of local residents by providing space for service and professional businesses. Neighborhood offices can be integral parts of neighborhood shopping centers or freestanding buildings and their remote locations can offer an additional option for short-term rental for group projects.

   » **Business Parks**—Business parks include several buildings accommodating a range of uses from light industrial to office. These developments vary from several acres to several hundred acres. Flex-space office buildings, with capabilities for laboratory space and limited warehouse space, are typically located in business parks.

Technological innovations and the COVID-19 pandemic triggered the evolution of a virtual office location by way of the metaverse.[8] Although in its infancy, digital real estate in the metaverse is a reality, with absolute ownership and the ability to virtually develop, lease, and sell office buildings,[9] and office workers interacting with each other through their virtual avatars and mixed-reality capabilities. For example, in January 2022, TerraZero Technologies provided the first mortgage for a virtual real estate purchase in the metaverse. JPMorgan Chase opened a lounge, and HSBC purchased digital real estate to develop a stadium.[10] There are multiple metaverses, with real estate being transacted with cryptocurrencies in blockchain environments.[11] The lot or property sale is recorded in a unique non-fungible token (NFT) coded in the public domain.

TRENDS IN OFFICE BUILDING DEVELOPMENT

Office market conditions are highly cyclical and susceptible to both internal and external shocks. Developers use innovative scorecards or dashboards for simulated performance pre-construction, during construction, and post-construction to provide a holistic assessment of cost, embodied carbon, schedule, supply chain transparency, human health, and regional availability. According to Bill Pollard[12] of Talon Private Capital, additional trends in office development include:

- **Sustainability**—Some city building codes are reaching LEED Silver certification. New construction is required to be all-electric in some cities; buildings are installing electric vehicle charging stations and microgrids. And, more buildings are pursuing multiple sustainability certifications (e.g., LEED, Fitwel, WELL).
- **Technology**—Introduction of smart-building technologies is a must for performance monitoring and attracting tenants. Demand is focused on buildings with cutting-edge technology such as touchless entry, mobile connectivity, and sought-after amenities such as high-quality HVAC, health and wellness, energy efficiency, and appealing common areas.[13]

- **General needs**—Future office buildings will need to be designed for a range of modalities (normal, pandemic, climate crisis, multihazard, etc.) to ensure resiliency[14] and to accommodate on average 150 to 175 square feet (14 to 16 sq m) of space per worker, although studies[15] on optimal workplace design promote densities of 75 (tech space) to 150 square feet (7 to 14 sq m).

MARKET TRENDS. In the 1980s, significant increases in liquidity combined with investor and developer optimism led to overbuilding, causing substantial vacancies—around 20 percent—in the early 1990s (worst modern commercial real estate cycle). It required a decade of economic expansion to decrease those vacancies to 10 percent—when 8 percent is considered normal. The 2001 recession triggered employee layoffs and corporate cost cutting, leading to short-term higher vacancies and lower rents. The Great Recession of 2008 led to a financially frozen market (lack of debt and equity) and lingering effects through 2012, with vacancies hovering around 16 percent and new developments facing challenges. During the COVID-19 pandemic, office building owners were sheltered due to corporate tenants, long leases, and renegotiation of short-term extensions of expiring leases. However, as the hybrid workforce model is broadly adopted and the office footprint is adjusted accordingly, some are estimating a demand drop of 15 percent.[16] Other major concerns are the expiration of 11 percent of the U.S.-leased office stock in 2022, when the national office vacancy is 12.2 percent; market uncertainty of big tech (major technology companies); the increasing number of office building loan-securities, which are already on watch lists or special services (21.2 percent as of February 2022); and the $320 billion in loans backed by office buildings that are maturing in 2022–2023, when interest rates are increasing.[17]

The Eight, a 25-story office building in Bellevue, Washington, is targeting to be the first building in Bellevue certified LEED Platinum v4. The building's design incorporates significant health and wellness innovations and provides community-building amenities. The Eight's lobby provides ample seating for work/play and relaxation, and opens to a landscaped plaza with native plants and pedestrian walkways. The ground floor includes 11,000 square feet of retail space and a 1,853-square-foot mass timber standalone retail pavilion. The Eight also offers seven alternating indoor/outdoor balconies throughout the building with stunning views, native landscaping, and multiple areas for seating.

FROM SUSTAINABLE TO ESG OFFICE BUILDING DEVELOPMENT

Developers, owners, and tenants are expanding their sustainability objectives from an Energy Star rating and LEED certification to comprehensive environmental, social, and governance (ESG) strategies. It is difficult to monetize cost savings from sustainability designations (possibly 5 to 10 percent) because cost includes both implementation and maintenance, according to Jeff Jochums, executive vice president at CBRE.[18] In a post-pandemic world in which WFH/WFA/WFO is a reality, adopting ESG strategies offers a competitive advantage for an office building. Environmental strategies can be assessed based on certifications, with carbon footprint becoming increasingly critical. Social strategies can include worker well-being, satisfaction, and equity. Governance strategies focus on establishing benchmarks and transparency among stakeholders and enhancing transparency through a diversity, equity, and inclusion lens. A recent survey by PwC and ULI[19] shows that 80 percent of respondents consider ESG when making operational or investment decisions, with larger companies starting to assess climate-risk analytics. In addition, major credit rating agencies (S&P, Moody's, Fitch Group, and DBRS Morningstar) are incorporating ESG in their credit ratings. Gensler Research is conceptualizing/implementing the "Morphable Office" with four critical elements: experience supercharger, connection to outdoors, community catalyst, and impact investments (e.g., operable windows, open stairways).[20] Murphy McCullough of Skanska notes The Eight, a 25-story office tower in Bellevue, Washington, has incorporated similar features, with indoor/outdoor space, seven private tenant decks on the sides of the buildings, and a rooftop deck, targeting LEED BD + C Platinum certification (see p. 243).[21] Sakriti Vishwakarma, an analyst at CBRE, emphasizes that technology companies focus on innovative office space while increasing their sustainability goals through multiple certifications and ESG.[22] For example, Microsoft's inviting campuses (e.g., activity-based plazas) reflect the company's increasing focus on ESG.

ENVIRONMENTAL STRATEGIES AND SUSTAINABILITY CERTIFICATION. Buildings and construction sectors account for 36 percent of the global final energy consumption (two-thirds from operations and one-third from construction) and 37 percent of energy-related carbon emissions.[23] Developers, owners, and tenants are increasingly incorporating sustainability statements in their missions and even though sustainability certifications can be costly, their importance is overriding that consideration. Several sustainability certifications lead some developers to establish their own minimum requirements; however, the needs or requirements of area tenants and investors are the determining factors for the pursuit of certification.[24] Fortune 500 and big-tech (e.g., Facebook, Apple, Amazon) tenants include sustainability in their mission, pushing for various certifications.[25] The most prominent types of sustainability certifications adopted among new and existing office buildings are Energy Star (energy consumption benchmarking); LEED (overall property sustainability and most recognized corporate and institutional investor certification, according to Gregg Johnson[26] of the Wright Runstad Company); Fitwel (health); WELL Building Standard (health and well-being); ILFI zero carbon certification; and Salmon Safe (linking site development/management practices with the protection of agricultural and urban watersheds).

In determining which sustainability certification to pursue for a new office building, the building development team considers core values and goals as well as the associated costs of building a sustainable structure because sustainable structures will be more expensive to build than nonsustainable structures. The development team also considers the differentiations among the various certification levels; for example, Johnson of Wright Runstad, Chris Hellstern of Miller-Hull, and

David Yuan of NBBJ note that efficient insulation, higher-quality glass, and higher levels of HVAC controls are required for LEED Platinum certification.[27]

The building development team should place emphasis in one or more of the following areas in determining the certification(s) to pursue:

- **Energy savings**—Typical certifications are Energy Star and LEED. Some developers consider the Energy Star label more effective as it emphasizes energy efficiency with a greater impact on the operating budget. LEED requires upfront capital that may take more than three years to recapture, and therefore, often exceeds a merchant builder-developer's holding period. Building codes in some areas are at the LEED level, however, a higher level of certification with long-lasting savings will require additional building systems controls, such as heat exchangers, displacement air systems, double-wall systems, and active shading systems, which have upfront cost premiums. By adopting multilayered energy systems, the building can circulate air more effectively while synchronizing electric lighting with daylight using lighting controls. Pollard notes even LEED Silver certification could reduce utility bills by more than 25 percent, however, it requires a highly integrated design process; deep commissioning to ensure alignment of operation with design intent; facilities and occupant education; and ongoing maintenance planning, compliance, and eventual upgrades.[28] Finally, additional energy savings can be achieved with fully electric buildings in areas where electricity is produced through hydropower.
- **Carbon footprint**—Typical certification is ILFI. There are several factors determining a building's carbon footprint, such as the type of structural system (e.g., steel, concrete, cross-laminated timber); the transportation distance of the utilized material especially if the material is not locally sourced; the amount of new material versus recycled/repurposed; and the type of energy use. Some cities have decarbonization pathway requirements.
- **Office worker well-being**—Typical certification is Fitwel. Developers use sustainable material, energy systems, and functionality beneficial for occupants' health. Other elements include operable windows, air exchanges, filtering (a minimum MERV-13 filtration[29]), HVAC, and avoidance of the Living Building Challenge red-list materials, which pose serious health risks for building occupants.

ENVIRONMENTAL STRATEGIES AND ENERGY INNOVATIONS AND EFFICIENCY. Since 2015, investments in energy efficiency have increased by 40 percent.[30] The use of detailed energy models allows architects to optimize a building's energy use beyond the reduction of energy demand through proper building massing, orientation, skin materials, window design, types of mechanical equipment, energy control systems, and envelope performance.[31] Developers can reduce energy costs by investing up front in continuous building envelopes that do not provide thermal bridges. The energy efficiency of the exterior facade can be improved with active and passive shading systems and other thermal technologies, while harvesting rainwater and daylight. For example, a rain-screen wall is a pressure-equalized system with minimum operational maintenance cost, although there is an upfront cost. As office occupants' interest in accommodating electric vehicles increases, especially among technology tenants, developers should review the various renewable-energy and energy efficiency incentives offered through DSIRE (database of state incentives for renewables and efficiency).[32]

In interviews, Pollard, McCullough, Johnson, and Yuan[33] describe common systems of energy demand-reduction including

- **chilled beams**—water transports energy 10 times more effectively than air, making this more efficient for larger buildings;
- **geothermal wells** (more difficult in dense areas as large footprint is needed);
- **geoexchange** mechanical systems (lesser depth than geothermal);
- **daylight controls and smart view glass** that automatically dims glass, decreasing the HVAC loads;
- **dedicated outdoor air systems (DOAS)** to decouple ventilation from heating and cooling;
- **heat recovery wheels/heat pumps** and reduced air infiltration in the facade;
- **microgrids and on-site generation with photovoltaics,** including some new window panels;
- **solar glazing** with canopy structure on the roof, which allows light penetration; and
- **daylight harvesting**, which reduces the use of artificial light, linking operable windows with HVAC systems, which are increasingly preferred with building management systems to allow for occupant notification and automatic operation to suit weather conditions and building operations.

The most energy-efficient buildings tend to be smaller in size (e.g., 50,000 square feet [4,645 sq m]) as sun harvesting with photovoltaic technology is becoming increasingly efficient and the price of the technology is continuously decreasing; geothermal also is an option.[34] If the energy demand cannot be satisfied with on-site renewables, off-site is an option such as off-site photovoltaics or wind turbines that are within the same utility grid region.[35]

New systems allow property managers to continuously monitor energy consumption, benchmark, and monitor and/or address malfunctions, and as a result, they can inform tenants how their behavior affects both energy and water use.[36] In addition, larger tenants can map internally the number of sick days per year of their employees in various buildings because a link between mechanical/HVAC systems and sick days has been established.[37]

Energy efficiency can be measured by the *U-value*, which measures the rate of heat loss expressed in Btus per hour per square foot per degree difference between the interior and exterior temperatures. The U-value is the reciprocal of the total resistance of construction multiplied by a temperature or solar factor. As a rule, U-values should be a minimum of 0.09 for insulated exterior walls and 0.05 for insulated roofs. The architect and mechanical engineer can provide recommendations for insulation.

Glass reflection plays an important role in determining energy use and is measured as the *shading coefficient*, which equals the amount of solar energy passing through glass divided by the total amount of solar rays hitting the glass. The lower the coefficient (more expensive to achieve), the larger the amount of heat reflected away from the building's interior.

ENVIRONMENTAL STRATEGIES AND CARBON FOOTPRINT—STRUCTURAL FRAMES. Buildings and construction account for 37 percent of energy-related carbon emissions.[38] Reduction in structure-embodied energy can be achieved with a low-cost premium[39] by optimizing the concrete mix (14 to 33 percent reduction), using high-recycled content rebar (4 to 10 percent reduction), and using low- or non-embodied carbon insulation and finish materials (16 and 5 percent reduction, respectively) (see figure 5-2). However, selecting low- or non-embodied carbon glazing products requires a 10 percent cost premium and offers a 3 percent reduction. Two open-source tools that support low-embodied carbon design and construction strategies are the Athena

Impact Estimator for Buildings, which offers users an assessment of a building's comprehensive life cycle; and the Embodied Carbon in Construction Calculator (EC3), which is used to determine the embodied carbon impacts of different building materials. In addition, the UpStream forestry and carbon life-cycle assessment (LCA) tool is an open software that assesses the carbon storage and greenhouse gas (GHG) emissions associated with wood products that have environmental product declarations (EPDs),[40] and Tally provides an assessment of a building's life cycle at each phase of design, both tracking and reducing the global-warming potential of the design.[41]

Some architects begin with an embodied carbon consideration of the different structural systems, comparing their global warming potential along with their efficiencies (see p. 247). The toxicity and embodied carbon of the materials used for those structural systems, and the location of raw materials needed, are then factored along with cost and erection times before a recommendation is made.

The biggest decision regarding the structural frame is whether to use carbon-sequestering materials like cross-laminated timber (CLT) or other engineered wood products.[42] According to Julianna Plant of Lase Crutcher Lewis[43] and others,[44] choosing a structural frame depends on several factors:

- **Zoning**—If there is a height constraint, concrete is a better option as it has a lower floor-to-floor requirement versus steel, which requires 11 feet or 13 feet. However, concrete needs to be formed and poured and may take 25 to 40 percent longer to construct versus steel.

- **Tenant flexibility**—Steel buildings are more flexible than concrete, especially for technology tenants who require telecommunications. Steel requires fireproofing in contrast to concrete, which does not; concrete's finishes are much cleaner.

- **Type of structure/schedule/carbon footprint**—If the structure is a high-rise, steel takes more structural depth and needs higher floor-to-floor height than concrete but construction is faster when using steel than when using concrete. If it is a low- or mid-rise, using CLT can be explored as it has the lowest carbon footprint. In early 2019, the International Code Council approved 14 changes to the International Building Code (IBC), including the introduction of three new construction types and the ability to build up to 18 stories of mass timber,[45] although mass production of tall CLT structures has not begun.

- **Other**—Other factors that influence the decision are supply chain issues, local construction practices, owners' values, and project opportunities.

ENVIRONMENTAL AND SOCIAL STRATEGIES—WORKERS' WELL-BEING. Investors and tenants are increasingly interested in workers' well-being and resiliency as productivity increases, sick days are reduced, and talent is more likely to be attracted to and retained in healthy buildings.[46] The WELL Building Standard and Fitwel certification system focus on occupant well-being through the enhancement of buildings, which can include providing COVID-19 response toolkits for projects, facility cleaning protocols, increased ventilation solutions, and humidity controls.

FIGURE 5-2 Embodied Energy by Material

	Cement and concrete	Steel	Timber
Background	Building requires concrete (contains cement)	Emissions have dropped by 60% since 1990s due to technological improvements and recycling.	Introduction of cross-laminated timber becoming viable for low- to mid-rise structures due to technology and cost
Where do emissions come from	60% from chemical reactions from clinker production and 40% from burning of fossil fuels to produce clinker	Steel production methods	Timber harvesting and manufacturing
Ways to improve	Concrete ready mix can be cost effective and can lower the embodied carbon of concrete.	Using relatively low-emissions (or zero-emissions) energy sources such as hydroelectric, renewable hydrogen, solar, or wind for steel production	Improvements in cultivation method, harvest, and end-of-life use; timber is considered a lower-carbon alternative to steel and concrete when used as structural material.
Nonresidential market share (2017)	34%	46%	10%

Source: Rebecca Esau, Matt Jungclaus, Victor Olgyay, and Audrey Rempher, *Reducing Embodied Carbon in Buildings: Low-Cost, High-Value Opportunities*, RMI, 2021.

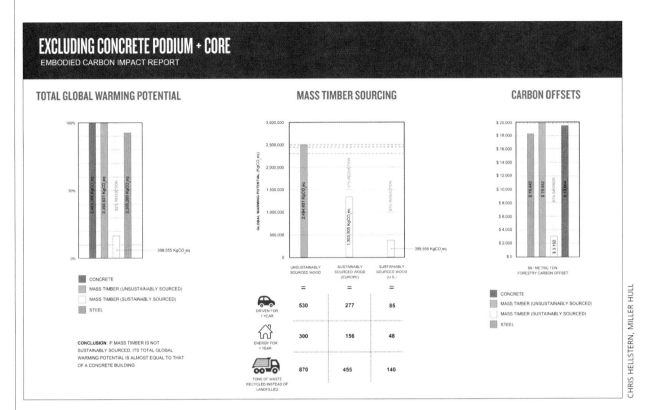

EXCLUDING CONCRETE PODIUM + CORE
EMBODIED CARBON IMPACT REPORT

TOTAL GLOBAL WARMING POTENTIAL

CONCRETE
MASS TIMBER (UNSUSTAINABLY SOURCED)
MASS TIMBER (SUSTAINABLY SOURCED)
STEEL

CONCLUSION: IF MASS TIMBER IS NOT SUSTAINABLY SOURCED, ITS TOTAL GLOBAL WARMING POTENTIAL IS ALMOST EQUAL TO THAT OF A CONCRETE BUILDING.

MASS TIMBER SOURCING

CARBON OFFSETS

CONCRETE
MASS TIMBER (UNSUSTAINABLY SOURCED)
MASS TIMBER (SUSTAINABLY SOURCED)
STEEL

CHRIS HELLSTERN, MILLER HULL

According to several executives,[47] the following architectural design elements can significantly affect the health and wellness of occupants:

- **Natural light**—Daylighting (passive strategy), active shading systems (which reduce glare), and circadian light systems are increasingly used to improve the building environment, especially among companies with employees traveling worldwide to help them reset their biorhythms. In addition, some buildings have side cores and higher floor-to-floor height that allow for significant light penetration (see p. 248).
- **Ventilation**—Natural ventilation (passive strategy) and biophilic design allow occupants to be better connected with the natural environment. Some structures have 100 percent fresh air HVAC systems—avoiding air recycling.
- **Connectivity**—Design promotes movement horizontally and vertically within spaces using "irresistible stairs" while reducing convergence points; diverse programming with pockets offering prospect and refuge; branded environments; and technology. Outdoor and indoor spaces are connected via operable windows and/or terraces.
- **Indoor air quality and assessment**—Avoiding chemicals of concern in the building; using air quality sensors and bipolar ionization technology such as needlepoint bipolar ionization (NPBI) technology.

Architectural companies undertake an embodied carbon analysis at several phases of design. An example of the output of such analysis is provided here.

EVOLVING TRENDS/NEEDS IN THE WORKPLACE. The workplace had begun transforming (by increasing open and shared space) to accommodate the generational shift underway in the workforce and the changing expectations of that workforce—the COVID-19 pandemic has prompted further workplace considerations.

Generation Shift. In 2022, the workforce consists of five generations: traditionalists (born 1925–1945) make up 2 percent of the workforce; baby boomers (born 1946–1964) make up 25 percent; generation X (born 1965–1980) make up 33 percent; millennials/generation Y (born 1981–2000) make up 35 percent; and generation Z (born 2001–2020) make up 5 percent.[48] For the first time, both gen X and millennials outnumber baby boomers in the workforce. A survey by the Gensler Research Institute found that all generations of office workers agree on the primary office purpose of team collaboration, however, generational differences for how generations prefer to work are present.[49]

A report from Pew Research Center suggests teleworking has a strong following even among those

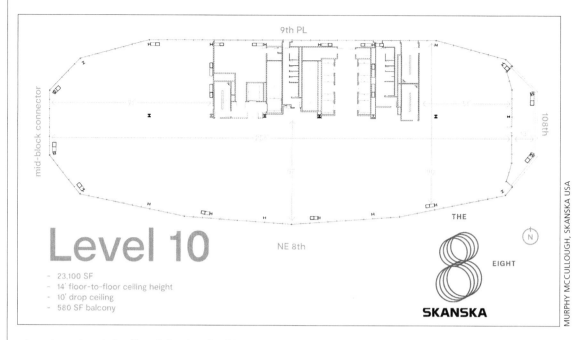

Level 10

- 23,100 SF
- 14' floor-to-floor ceiling height
- 10' drop ceiling
- 580 SF balcony

9th PL

mid-block connector

108th

NE 8th

THE **8** EIGHT

N

SKANSKA

who returned to their offices following the COVID-19 pandemic as it was easier to achieve work/life balance while remote.[50] In cases where home and office are in proximity, workers were more inclined to return to their office, with the only consistent downside of teleworking being the reduced coworker connection.

According to a Cushman & Wakefield report on the office of the future that compares millennial/gen Z employees with all employees, the former prefer to be in the office three to four days per week whereas c-suite employees prefer to be in the office one to two days per week.[51] However, a PwC and ULI survey of millennials and gen Zers showcases a major interest in work/life balance.[52] Overall, space demand is expected to be lower than before the pandemic, with experts anticipating, however, a "flight to quality"—something developers should consider.

The Great Resignation. The COVID-19 pandemic triggered a wave of global resignations that Associate Professor Anthony Klotz of Texas A&M University coined the "Great Resignation."[53] Klotz expects resignation rates to remain higher than usual for some time because turnover is contagious and organizations that are trying to remain flexible and deploy new tactics will attract new workers but also lose existing workers. A global analysis of 4,000 companies found that resignation rates are highest among mid-career employees, especially in technology and health care.[54] In November 2021, the United States reached a 20-year high in resignations, with the top underlying reasons being low pay, lack of advancement opportu-

The unique design elements of The Eight in Bellevue, Washington, include a side core and floor heights of 14 feet, which offer maximum light penetration.

nities, and feeling disrespected, according to a survey conducted by the Pew Research Center.[55] Another survey showed that burnout is a critical cause of resignation, while remote work and flexibility are key elements employees look for when changing jobs.[56]

Shift in Employee Office Space Expectations Postpandemic. With the pandemic accelerating the demand for workplace flexibility, companies are using surveys to assess employees' perception of office space and other priorities.[57] Microsoft[58] and Cushman & Wakefield,[59] among others, suggest major departures from prepandemic expectations, with the most relevant to developers being the following:

- Extreme flexibility (encompassing policy, physical space, and technology)—Employers who focus on building an empathetic and collaborative culture tend to also see value in emphasizing work/life balance and individual autonomy, as these traits help people feel empowered, valued, and understood. As one-half of hybrid employees expect to shift to remote, and gen Zers are feeling more isolated, office hubs could offer the support needed. Allowing employees the choice of work location (WFH/WFA/WFO) is critical in retaining and attracting talent, with recovery achieved by balancing[60]

» efficiency (financial priority: enabling efficient use of space);

» effectiveness (business performance priority: ensure effective and equitable collaboration; certain companies are moving from a hybrid model [a mix of WFO/WFA] to a flexible model based on what employees need,[61] allowing for in-person core collaborative group meetings, as well as asynchronous remote work or one-on-one meetings); and

» engagement (people priority: facilitate engagement with culture and knowledge and reinvent the office to be worth the commute, both due to the type of work, and the quality of space).

• Physical and digital worlds need to be bridged with space and technology, as hybrid work has led organizations to retool their offices to be collaborative spaces with equitable experiences for in-person and remote employees.

• Rebuilding social capital and culture, with the expectation that eventually the fear of missing out (FOMO), in combination with the right amenities, will lead to more WFO.

OFFICE SPACE TRANSFORMATIONS

Aging infrastructure—more than one-quarter of U.S. office building stock (more than 4 billion square feet [371,600 sq m])[62] is at least 60 years old—cost-prohibitive renovations and flight from CBDs to more affordable high-growth markets have triggered the obsolescence of office space. This reality, along with the transition to a liquid versus static workforce and a "worker-centric" workplace, requires the availability of boundless agile workplace options. Social and technological evolutions are taking place during geopolitical and economic uncertainties,[63] providing insights on the evolution of office space from the prepandemic model:

• **Prepandemic**—50 percent dedicated workspace, 25 percent shared, and 25 percent amenities/services.

• **Postpandemic**—The role of the office has changed, with culture, collaboration, and innovation driving the office's purpose.[64] Companies want their employees back in the office but they are expected to make it an attractive and healthy space and to increase the amenities offered.[65] Yuan advises that the tension that office tenants are experiencing is caused by the unresolved issue regarding six-foot distancing requirements, which means lower density, however, hybrid work means less space.[66] A tenant with a high percentage of

WFH needs less space; however, if the tenant's adopted model is hybrid (WFH/WFO) and employees WFO on certain days, more space is needed unless a non-overlapping schedule is created. Models such as hoteling could work (e.g., some employees Monday/Wednesday/Friday and others Tuesday/Thursday). An analysis of 4,000 companies suggests workers are uncomfortable with density, and reducing it is to cut WFO without cutting square feet; most employees want to work from home Monday/Friday, however this limits space minimization because for the remaining days of the week all employees WFO; and employers are reshaping office space to become more inviting social spaces for face-to-face collaborations and creativity.[67]

As the real estate industry acknowledges hybrid work is here to stay,[68] companies are considering the following questions: Where can work take place? What requires in-person collaboration? Who benefits from spending time in the office? How can workspaces advance company objectives, collaboration, and culture?

To address these questions, the future workplace will need to have the following key elements:[69]

1. Limiting uncertainty by recruiting talent where they live, remaining flexible, and allowing workplace choice (WFH/WFA/WFO) on the basis of tasks and type of employee (full-time, part-time, or freelancer).

2. Workplace policy needs a reset as the physical office will include three types of employees:

   2.1. Primarily office-based: The office is the primary location and it is critical for company culture. Big tech is planning on expanding/modernizing buildings with more collaborative spaces. Smaller technology companies will need to partner with their building to make renovations financially feasible. If the tenant (i.e., technology company) space is mainly open, break rooms and meeting rooms will be needed.[70] At the same time, architects are receiving requests for desk layouts incorporating the six-foot rule (of social distancing).[71]

   2.2. Distributed workforce (blended/hybrid): Employee flexibility (both in-office and remote) could be split-week or designated week-by-week. The office will become a vibrant hub with a mix of touchdown space, hot-desking, and collaboration zones, alongside easy-to-reserve private conference rooms and other quiet areas for heads-down work, which will allow employees to learn/socialize/innovate and to better understand the company's culture. A Gensler U.S. workplace survey[72] shows that postpandemic, the hybrid model is preferred by respondents followed by full-time remote, while less than 20 percent prefer a return to a full-time office workplace model. At the same time, architects are receiving requests for ratios of permanent workstations to hoteling to determine the right balance.[73]

2.3. Primarily remote: WFH/WFA options are becoming vital in retaining and attracting employees. JLL research found that 54 percent of employees work from home at least five days a month and 33.6 percent of employees work regularly at cafés and coworking spaces.[74] Collaboration enablers include services such as Skype, DropBox, Jabber, and Hadoop.

3. Cross-pollinate human resource, workplace, and technology goals: This element allows for synergies and effective communication and placement of workers with the same experience regardless of work location.

4. Workplace footprint assessment: Reviews the current footprint in light of a company's strategy on WFH/WFA/WFO and reimagines the new space on the basis of safety, wellness, productivity, and engagement:

    4.1. Identification of office space needs and strategies to balance space/occupancy needs to include:

    – 4.1.1. Assessment of current space/occupancy, which could lead to two possibilities:[75]

    a) Space realignment (same footprint) with the business goal of effectiveness through improved space utilization, team/business performance, and employee engagement by equally increasing the shared and amenity/service spaces.

    b) Ecosystem of work environments (decrease footprint) with the business goal of optimization through space efficiency, decreasing commuting, business resilience, and employee experience, while assessing productivity/output as well as employee satisfaction. Under this model, "dedicated space" is redefined beyond the workplace to include WFH and satellite office space, "shared space" is redefined to include on-demand space, and amenities/services include a virtual element.

    – 4.1.2. Determination of additional space needs

720 Olive Way (8th + Olive) in Seattle, Washington, is an example of an older structure that underwent a major repositioning. Massive system and lobby upgrades included modern finishes and the addition of casual and working (coworking or meeting) areas.

4.2. Decentralized office strategies

4.3. Building/workplace requirements/amenities:

– 4.3.1. As we move to a new "human-centric" workplace model, the focus/priority shifts to well-being, flexible work, and self-care:[76]

4.3.1.1. Elevating building amenities: Lobbies become a place to work, socialize, and connect. Outdoor gardens and landscaped balconies allow a connection with nature. Incorporating biophilic design principals and amenity spaces for health and wellness are proven to boost occupant wellness, which consequently improves productivity and supports monetary gains for businesses. In addition, creative spaces allow brainstorming while pods and focus rooms are dedicated to focus work. Splurging on prime office space with great amenities and creating an inviting community are critical for companies that need to lure people back to the office.[77]

4.3.1.2. Creating communities: Examples of communities include wellness spaces, tenant apps, partnerships, art shows, lobby events, clubs, retailer activations, and more. The communities are activated via daily small-scale events, monthly programs/activities, and annual major events.

4.3.1.3. Providing flexibility: Flex space and flexible buildings are likely to be more appealing as tenants can more easily transform their space and expand or contract that space as needed.

– 4.3.2. The workplace can take many forms[78] including dedicated seats, on-demand open access, targeted mobility (hybrid dedicated and shared seats), hotdesking (majority is unassigned with reservation availability), re-mote work (WFH), and coworking (communal, suites/dedicated desks, etc.). Floorplans for the various hybrid work models can differ:[79]

4.3.2.1. Activity-based work: Time is split between WFH/WFO.

4.3.2.2. Team-based work: Time is split between WFH/WFO, however the office is used for team task collaboration. Technology companies such as Microsoft are moving from cubicles to "neighborhoods" (an intelligent workplace program) for 25 to 30 employees that include focus rooms, meeting rooms, and amenities (e.g., kitchens, cafés, phone booths, and space to relax—game rooms, areas of privacy, and areas to connect with nature). This type of team-based space achieves a holistic experience that is not only work-related.[80]

4.3.2.3. Event-based work: Most work is done from home but meetings and events are office-based.

TRANSFORMATION OF TECHNOLOGY OFFICE SPACE. Developer-owners offer high-quality spaces to try to attract technology companies as tenants because those properties can achieve higher rent and increased investor interest. Experts interviewed[81] note that postpandemic, technology companies value the following office space features:

- **Larger floor plates** (e.g., 40,000 square feet)—Keep employees on the same floor rather than vertically stacked. Open stairwells can be used as an active space if staking cannot be avoided.
- **Personal space evolution**—Individual (desk) space per person is less, with increases in touchdown or hoteling workstations. Reservable seating is offered even for a day as opposed to assigned with the focus being on collaborative/team-based space (e.g., Microsoft's "neighborhoods").[82] Within these spaces, which are typically occupied by 25 to 30 people, amenities are offered to aid in collaboration, as well as focus and meeting rooms; these spaces are separated by glass or fabric to preserve privacy. In addition, enclosed offices are moved to the interior to provide people in the cub/hoteling areas with more views and light.
- **Amenities**—The assortment of amenity spaces (e.g., food, movie theaters, game and sports facilities), including rooftop decks in smaller buildings, is increasingly important in helping create culture. The preference for lounge spaces is more aligned

Hybrid Work Will Require a Hybrid Workplace

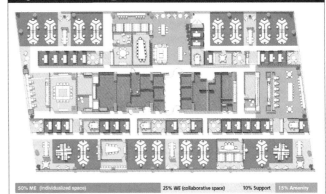

50% ME (individualized space)   25% WE (collaborative space)   10% Support   15% Amenity

ACTIVITY-BASED WORK
Employees split time between home and office and engage in both individual and collaborative activities. They report to a neighborhood shared with their function (or related functions).

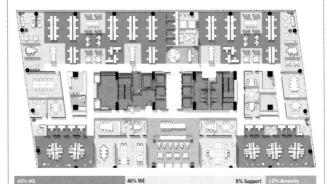

40% ME   40% WE   8% Support   12% Amenity

TEAM-BASED WORK
Employees split time between home and office but come to the office primarily to collaborate with their team on a specific task or project. They report to a "camp site" that is shared with their project team, with additional collaborative and social venues nearby.

15% ME   55% WE   10% Support   20% Amenity

EVENT-BASED WORK
Employees conduct most of their individual work at home and come to the office primarily for scheduled meetings and events. Space is provided for collaboration and engagement.

Source: CBRE.

with what one might see in a boutique hotel, with flexibility and choice being common themes in programming. Because employees can WFH/WFA, the office is becoming part of recruiting employees, by emphasizing differentiations both in culture and facilities. Although smaller tech tenants might not have the capital for significant amenities (e.g., a commercial kitchen or game room), for the first time, landlords and tenants are partnering to offer such amenities, and tenants are willing to pay the small rental premium because those amenities can help tenants recruit top talent. In addition, in dense urban areas, parking is critical and electric vehicle parking is a must.

INFLUENCE OF TECHNOLOGY

Technology is the driving force behind increased efficiency and long-term cost savings. The hybrid workplace requires constant flexibility and responsiveness. These can be facilitated with the use of apps that integrate a building's smart infrastructure, allowing users to check and reserve available desks, access facilities/elevators, conduct surveys, assess the health of the environment, receive notifications/announcements, find colleagues, and report issues.[83]

CONSTRUCTION FACILITATION USING TECHNOLOGY. Technologies such as Building Information Modeling (BIM) are standard for the design and construction of large-scale projects; these technologies can also be applied to smaller projects because they are instrumental in minimizing change orders, postconstruction sustainability benchmarking, and system monitoring.[84]

Another platform being adopted by developers is Microsoft's Azure Digital Twins, in which a digital replica is created that provides live representation and simulations for the property/portfolio assessing various scenarios as well as operation management—although it will take time to utilize among smaller developments.[85] Technologies such as digital twins and BIM are used in building automation systems (BAS), which allow building managers to monitor and create efficiencies in major building systems, such as heat exchangers, automatic dimmers, and OLEDs (organic light-emitting diodes), creating "smart" buildings with single—rather than multiple—network systems communicating through Internet protocol. In some complex projects, augmented reality (AR) and virtual reality (VR) are used for maneuverability purposes as well as for 3-D picture capture for site tours and prog-

ress updates.[86] A developer's budget, market conditions, and the type of tenant pursued will determine the most balanced approach regarding the applied technology innovations and the rent premium tenants will be willing to pay.

SMART BUILDINGS/MONITORING/DATA ANALYTICS TEAMS. Buildings can now be certified based on their digital connectivity, redundancy, and smart technology with WiredScore.[87] Smart-building technologies are enabling centralized command of network/sensor infrastructure, power monitoring, load management, building apps (communication, amenity reservations), battery energy storage, and demand response.[88] They disrupt the traditional building operation roles because a data analytics team[89] must be formed that includes a facilities manager, the information technology department, and office managers. In addition, training employees on cybersecurity is critical to maintain firewalls, notes Laura Ford with CBRE.[90] Other features installed are multiple multifiber building intakes and digital amplification (DA) devices, which prevent or limit telecommunication signal loss, even in basement areas.

The adoption/evolution of the internet of things (IoT) and artificial intelligence (AI) among smart buildings allows[91]

- automated room reservation, building access, campus connectivity, and public safety;
- whole-life carbon footprint reduction through efficient operations;
- reduction of facilities and operations costs due to optimized system performance;
- identification of issues and performance control;
- building benchmarking with market or portfolio; and
- reporting (cities across the United States have energy reporting requirements and smart building monitoring can facilitate this process).[92]

Experts[93] suggest monitoring systems and innovations offered by smart buildings should be implemented in the following areas:

- **HVAC**—Initially, property technology focused on property management technologies (HVAC, air ventilation, and air filtration systems), with automation and monitoring in those areas being the furthest ahead especially regarding temperature and humidity.
- **Energy/water use**—Energy monitoring systems are becoming common through submetering, allowing the owner to track energy consumption

and building energy demand. The data from these systems can be detailed, helping owners to find a single device that may be malfunctioning and to watch energy use trends over time. For buildings with water catchment or treatment systems, a range of devices can be used to track water usage and quality. These systems are essential to help ensure that buildings operate at the high level of performance they have been designed for, and to report to tenants, emphasizing how behavioral changes can affect efficiencies.

- **Monitoring/occupancy**—Innovations in this area include touchless access (turnstiles, parking), touch-sensitive step pads under the carpet, computer vision cameras tracking people and objects, and automated elevator calls and proximity readers.

TECHNOLOGY NEEDED/USED BY TENANTS. Tenants have different needs, with technology tenants being the most advanced. Most tenants require only conduits, power, and multisource fiber cabling.[94]

The shift to WFH/WFA has increased interest in telework-capable systems, with automated tracking cameras and projector screen walls a standard request.[95] Employee productivity can be facilitated and maintained more effectively if employees have access to a fluid digital workspace enhanced with adaptability, scalability, and connected environments that use various existing and emerging technologies such as:[96]

- blockchain/cloud capabilities (data storage is implemented on a wider scale, securing classified documents, etc.);
- AI (60 percent of c-suite executives view AI as critical in developing workplace policies, reviewing CVs, and removing biases, etc.);
- IoT (improve employee safety standards, e.g., voice-recognition elevator systems, hardware, office furniture allocations, and various technologies); and
- mixed and augmented reality (collaborations and problems can be addressed by overlaying digital over a physical entity while providing real-time contextual data). Technology companies, such as Amazon, are focused on AR and experimenting with full-size screens, allowing a mix of in-person and full-scale avatar for interactions. The constraints are bandwidth and processing in an open line.[97] Similarly, Microsoft is experimenting with VR and AR in new buildings using Microsoft Mesh,[98] which allows a mix of reality with a holographic experience with in-person collaboration around the world.[99]

Project Feasibility

As developers assess potential sites, they are mindful of the possible development and disposition timeframe, which depends on serval internal and external factors. Figure 5-3 provides an overview of typical development timeframes for high-rise and mid-rise developments.

MARKET ANALYSIS

A market analysis allows developers to assess the financial feasibility of a project and to demonstrate it to investors and lenders by answering the following questions (see figure 5-4):

- Is there a market (demand) for your type of office development (e.g., style, construction pipeline, amenities, etc.)?
- Are there available sites and potential challenges (e.g., infill, demolition, rezoning, etc.)?
- What are the area rents (tenant base)/vacancies/prices and absorption rate?

The market analysis focuses on demand and supply, which ultimately determines vacancy, rents, cap rates, and property values. Understanding the demands for space quality and characteristics among the existing employers and industries is critical as well as the type of facilities needed (headquarters, regional, or branch offices). The type of tenant to be targeted will affect the design with respect to office depths, parking, amenities, and level of finish. Depending on project scale, if developers do not have access to the CoStar Group database or to CBRE econometric advisers, which provide detailed market condition insights, they will need assistance from market research or brokerage companies.

Tenants typically seek new space for various reasons, such as accommodating additional employees

FIGURE 5-3 Office Development Timeline

	High-rise Office (months)	Mid-rise Office (months)
Acquisition	3	3
Design/Entitlements	24	12
Construction	30	20
TI Buildout	6	6
Stabilization	12	12
Divestment	3	3
Total Time (months)	78	56
Total Time (years)	6.5	4.7

Source: Murphy McCullough, executive vice president, Skanska USA, interview by author, January 2022.

Note: TI = tenant improvement.

and/or a new subsidiary, expanding, improving the quality of their space, consolidating dispersed activities, and improving their corporate image.

DEMAND. Defining the area of competition in the submarkets and region is a critical first step. For regional employment, a step-down approach can be used to allocate employment growth from the region to the local market. Office buildings compete most closely with other buildings in the immediate vicinity. Rents and amenities can vary considerably among submarkets, though regional conditions affect all submarkets. The analysis of the metropolitan economic base involves studying existing office employers and industries and their growth potential.

Projected employment growth is the key driver of office space demand. It includes new and expanding firms in the area, broken down by industry, ultimately yielding office-based employment growth projections for the local economy. Local employment projections are available from commercial brokerage companies as well as local governments and chambers of commerce. Because we are moving toward a model of WFH/WFA and WFO, we must determine demand based on those who WFO and carefully assess the needs of those who WFA, as they might be hybrid. When an area's projected office employment is available, the following equation can be used to estimate the total square footage demanded:

Projected office space demand =
Number of projected office employees
× Gross space per employee

If area employment projections are not available, the following formula can be applied to determine the annual demand in square feet (see figure 5-5):

Office employment demand of industry i =
Change in employment of industry i in the last two years ×
Office share of industry i

Annual office demand in square feet for industry i =
Office employment demand of industry i
× Area's gross space per employee

where i represents a specific industry that
drives office demand.

Tenant space requirements affect the design and type of facility, including average floor area and number of entrances. The bay depth—the distance between the glass line and the building core—is particularly important. Large users frequently desire large

FIGURE 5-4 ## Market Analysis Data and Sources

Data Input	Source
SPACE TRENDS	
Existing, under construction: planned square footage, occupancy, vacancy, absorption, rents, tenant information (square feet leased, lease length, etc.)	CoStar Group; and reports from CBRE, JLL, Cushman & Wakefield, etc.
Competitive development	CoStar Group; FW Dodge; local building, planning, and zoning departments; architects, and brokers/developers
FINANCIAL FEASIBILITY	
Land costs	Key person interviews, recent transactions
Construction costs	Dodge construction reports by McGraw-Hill
Operating expenses	Property managers and reports: Institute of Real Estate Management or Building Owners & Managers Association International *Experience Exchange Report*
EASY TO DO BUSINESS WITH	
Zoning and ease of local permitting	City/county planning department, state environmental protection agency
ATTRACTIVE TAX POSITION	
Area tax structure and incentives	City, county, and state departments of revenue, assessor, and economic development; media
NONTAX INCENTIVES	
Various types of new construction or adaptive use incentives	City, county, and state departments of economic development; business retention, etc.
WORKFORCE DEMOGRAPHICS/TRANSPORTATION	
Public	U.S. Census, Bureau of Labor Statistics/Bureau of Economic Analysis; local and regional economic development and planning agencies
Private	CoStar Group
Transportation infrastructure (access)	Local transportation agencies

Source: Jon DeVries and Sofia Dermisi.

FIGURE 5-5 **Annual Office Space Demand by Industry**

	Change in an Area's Employment	Office Share	Office Employment	Square Footage/ Employee[a]	Annual Office Demand (sq ft)
Construction	−5,000	5%	−250		−50,000
FIRE (finance, insurance, and real estate)	2,000	80%	1600		320,000
Services	5,000	10%	500	200	100,000
Government	3,000	5%	150		30,000
Total		**100%**			**400,000**

Source: Jon DeVries.

[a]The average was estimated to be 200 to 225 square feet per worker, however, technology companies require much less (Microsoft at 175 square feet per worker; Expedia at 125 square feet per worker) (Jochums interview, 2022).

bay depths, but small users require smaller bay depths to increase the proportion of window offices.

The demand for space is affected by multiple factors (e.g., industry trends, location, rents, etc.), however, total office square feet per worker is continuously decreasing and with the WFH/WFA models it is expected to decrease even more. For 2020, JLL reported an average of 196 square feet (18 sq m) per worker;[100] for 2022, the average was estimated to be 200 to 225 square feet (18.5–21 sq m) per worker, with the tech industry average being much lower at 100 to 125 square feet (9–12 sq m) per worker, and office cubicles being 60 to 90 square feet (5.5–8 sq m) per worker.[101] Office cubicles can range from 6 by 6 feet (1.8 by 1.8 m), to 8 by 8 feet (2.4 by 2.4 m), while the physical office room space in most offices is 10 by 12 feet (3 by 3.6 m) or 10 by 15 feet (3 by 4.5 m).

SUPPLY. Office supply is the basis for estimating rents, concessions, design features, desired amenities, and finishes. The key elements of the supply analysis are an inventory of existing competitive buildings within the market area and projects under construction and in planning stages (pipeline). An inventory of competitive buildings should include the following information:

- location;
- gross and net building area;
- scheduled rent per square foot per month;
- lease terms;
- tenant finish allowances;
- building services;
- amount of parking provided, electric vehicle chargers, and parking charges (if applicable);
- building and surrounding area amenities (restaurants, conference facilities, health clubs, and so forth); and
- list of tenants and contact people.

This information provides the basis for estimating rents, concessions, design features, and desired amenities. The submarket definition—areas that include the primary competitors for the subject project—is especially important. All competitive buildings in this area should be carefully documented and the total existing supply plus the future supply of office space needs to be determined. By subtracting the expected supply from the demand for office space, the deficit or surplus of office space for a particular period can be determined. Therefore, the market conditions can be estimated when the proposed building comes online. Vacancy levels are an important part of the supply calculation and vacancy trends can indicate changes in demand. If demand is increasing faster than supply, vacancy rates should be falling, creating a more favorable market for the developer. Alternatively, if supply is increasing faster than demand, vacancy rates should be increasing. The vacancy rate resulting from turnover, sometimes referred to as the *natural* or *stabilized* vacancy, is inevitable.

The absorption time, in months, of all the vacant space can be calculated as

$$(\text{vacant space})_t = (\text{vacant space})_{t-1} \\ + (\text{net construction})_t - (\text{net absorption})_t$$

$$AT = \frac{(\text{vacant space} + \text{new construction})}{\text{net absorption}/12}$$

where t represents the quarter or year the estimate takes place and t-1 the previous period.[102]

For an application of the AT equation, assume that the area of interest has 600,000 square feet (55,700 sq m) under construction, with a vacancy of 1.5 million square feet (139,000 sq m) and a net absorption of 1 million square feet (93,000 sq m), and will require a 25-month absorption period. The AT equation assumes that the rate of new demand growth continues as indicated by the net absorption rate and that there is no new construction in the market other than what has already been started. No firm guidelines exist for determining what constitutes a soft market, although a market with fewer than 12 months of inventory is considered a strong market, 12 to 24 months a normal market, and more than 24 months (18 months in slower-growing areas) a soft market.

A common mistake is to assume that a proposed project will capture an unrealistically large share of the entire market. Developers should have sufficient cash available to cover situations in which leasing takes longer than expected, which can be influenced by timing of the project delivery, amenities, rent levels, and disruptive market conditions (e.g., a pandemic).

SUBLEASED AND SHADOW SPACE. It is important to recognize sublease space in assessing supply because, although technically leased, it is often available, formally or informally, and is thus part of the market competition. In markets with low vacancy, if unanticipated subleased space and new product come online simultaneously, vacancy rates can soar. As companies are adjusting to WFH/WFA, sublease space can be seen as an opportunity for a remote location.

Shadow space, which is defined as the difference between the vacant and available space,[103] is still paid by the tenant, however, it is vacant or not fully occupied and it is not yet available for sublease. It is a potential threat to a building's rental stability during a down cycle because an increase indicates tenant contraction, which can eventually increase vacancy. The presence of shadow space is not optimal for a landlord because it cannot be considered stable income and the space could be offered on the market with a better return.

EFFECTIVE RENTAL RATES. An important distinction in office market analysis is the difference between quoted (*face*) rents and *effective* rents (figure 5-6). Property owners sometimes use incentives to maintain the appearance of certain rent levels while effectively reducing rent for certain times or tenants. Typically, lenders determine a specific rent and pre-leasing threshold as a condition of funding or for releasing the developers' personal guarantee on the construction loan. To meet these conditions in a soft market, developers may offer tenants concessions in the form of free rent for a specified period, such as three to five months for a five-year lease; an extra allowance for tenant improvements (TIs); or moving expenses,

FIGURE 5-6 Calculation of Effective Office Rent

Suppose a developer has an office space of 1,000 sq ft (93/sq m) with a nominal rent of $24/sq ft ($258/sq m) for five years. Concessions include six months of free rent and $3/sq ft ($32/sq m) in extra tenant improvements. The developer's discount rate is 12 percent. To find the effective rent, the developer must convert the lease and the free rent to present value, which can be computed per square foot.

ASSUMPTIONS	
Office space leased (sq ft)	1,000
Rent/sq ft	$24
n (years)	5
Concessions (free rent – months)	6
TIs	$25
Discount rate	12%

SOLUTION	
	Values
PV of lease	$1,078.92
PV of free rent	$139.09
Extra TIs (already started as PV)	$25
PV of effective rent	$914.83
Effective rent – month (PMT)/sq ft	$20.35
Effective rent – annual (PMT)/sq ft	$244.20

Note: PV = present value; PMT = payment.

as long as the rent meets the lender's requirements. The extent of the TIs is always market driven, with tenants pressuring landlords for more during periods of increased construction costs. The TIs depend on tenants' needs, layout, furniture, and finishes.[104] The national average for first generation buildouts is $107 per square foot and for second generation buildouts it is about $85 per square foot.

Rental concessions are harder for market analysts to identify because brokers tend to understate concessions due to the negative influence on their commission. Factors influencing the number and amount of concessions include tenant size, lease term, and tenant credit worthiness. Concessions remain common practice across markets, especially during economic down cycles, and lenders generally use effective rents in their analyses before funding a loan. As markets are currently soft, owners are trying to hold the values and not reduce rents while offering larger consensus packages. In strong markets, building owners do not offer free rent, except perhaps during an initial period when tenant improvements are being completed. Scheduled rental rate increases change the effective rent.

SITE SELECTION

Site selection is a crucial step in the project feasibility analysis because it directly affects the rent, occupancy levels, and sales price. Developers should compare location, access, physical attributes, zoning, and development potential, as well as rents and occupancy of comparable buildings and sites to identify potential opportunities and obstacles. High prices should not deter developers as they are a sign of site desirability.

Office buildings are less flexible in size and shape than are most other development types. Floor plates (area per floor) are a key factor in a building's suitability for a tenant. Those deviating significantly from 25,000 square feet (2,322 sq m) require more than one core due to the travel distance required of individuals. A second core substantially increases building costs because it requires additional stairwells, restrooms, and elevators.[105] Small office users prefer buildings with floor sizes ranging from 16,000 to 20,000 square feet (1,500–1,860 sq m), although smaller floor plates are not uncommon. The most efficient buildings are 100 by 200 feet (30 by 60 m). Such a shape allows a core of about 20 by 100 feet (6 by 30 m) and a typical depth of around 40 feet (12 m) between the core and the exterior wall. Such plain rectangular boxes might be the most cost-effective, but prospective tenants may respond negatively depending on their type of business. For example, major law firms seek buildings that make a statement with their exterior facade and interior amenities, while call centers do not.

When land values are high, the cost of parking structures is often warranted, even though underground cost/stall is significantly higher. Structured parking modules with efficient layouts should be designed in bays that are 60 to 65 feet (18–20 m) wide, with a minimum of two bays; therefore, a parking structure needs to be at least 180 feet (16.5 m) long to efficiently accommodate internal ramps. Full-sized parking spaces range from 8.5 by 16 feet (2.5 by 4.9 m) to 10 by 18 feet (3 by 5.5 m). Two-way aisles for perpendicular parking vary from 24 to 27 feet (7.3–8.2 m) wide. A double-loaded parking module requires a 60- to 63-foot (18.3–19.2m) cross section for two parking places and an aisle, plus the space required for the structure itself. The simplest design requires a minimum of two modules with continuously ramped floors that provide circulation between levels. With circulation and parking along the ends of the structure, the minimum dimension for the entire structure is about 130 by 190 feet (36.5 by 57.9 m).

Topography can play an important role in site selection. Hilly sites may require extensive grading, which will increase construction costs, but they may also provide excellent opportunities for tuck-under parking that requires less excavation than a flat site.

Access is a primary consideration in site selection. Sites should have convenient access to the regional transportation system. Public transit options are important in urban locations. Developers should check the site's highway and transit access with transportation authorities before proceeding, as well as the need for a traffic study.

REGULATORY ISSUES AND ZONING

Office developers need to comply with local zoning and building codes. In addition to the typical zoning restrictions on building setbacks, massing, height, site coverage, solar shadows, and parking requirements, the floor/area ratio (FAR) is critical as some cities award bonuses to developers who provide public amenities in high-density commercial districts. In addition, some government agencies regulate the types of materials, architecture styles, locations of entries, and various other design aspects of office projects. Developers must recognize and work within these restrictions to determine the maximum envelope that their buildings can occupy.

One special regulatory device is transferable development rights (TDRs). TDRs allow for the sale of development rights on a property from one owner to another. Once sold, however, the original owner cannot build any additional square footage than that for which zoning rights were retained. TDRs work well with historic landmark buildings because they might not take the fullest advantage of a site's development potential. In addition, designation of older buildings as historic landmarks can complicate and even prevent major changes to their structure and exterior facade.

Parking requirements vary by location and building type, but they typically stipulate a minimum of four spaces per 1,000 square feet (95 sq m) of rentable floor area. Communities wishing to encourage use of mass transit may however restrict the amount of parking. One concept that can satisfy local government's desire to limit parking while providing the ability to meet tenants' future needs is *deferred parking*. Deferred parking is shown on the approved development plan but need not be built until demand for parking is proved.

TRANSPORTATION. Large footprint office developments are required to provide a traffic impact study during the approval process. Traffic mitigation measures can range from widening the streets in front of a building to adding a traffic signal or widening streets and intersections surrounding a site. Satisfying off-site infrastructure requirements can be extremely costly and time-consuming, not least because of the need to work with public agencies and other property owners.

An office developer may be required to undertake any of the following actions:

- restripe existing streets;
- add deceleration and acceleration lanes to a project;
- construct a median to control access;
- install signals at entrances to a project or at intersections affected by the project;
- widen streets in front of a project or between a project and major highways or freeways;
- build a new street between a project and a major highway; or
- contribute to construction of highway or freeway interchanges.

Instead of requiring certain improvements through exactions, some areas have created impact fee programs (assessed per peak trip generated or a fee per square foot) to cover traffic improvements. The number of expected peak trips generated by the project becomes a critical factor in the cost of the project because fees can be as high as several thousand dollars per peak trip generated. Peak traffic trips can be reduced by adding a minor retail component to a project (a major retail component can possibly increase the traffic impact), providing residential facilities on or adjacent to the site, and providing links with public transportation systems.

Transportation demand management (TDM) programs (or *transportation system management*) have become a popular mechanism for reducing traffic. Several cities require large projects to implement ride-sharing programs, such as car- or vanpools; to include reduced-price passes for public transit; and to provide preferential parking spaces for individuals who carpool. The developer is often responsible for ensuring the implementation of TDMs because they are often a condition of approval. Commuting by bicycle or foot is another strategy some cities encourage. In Boulder, Colorado, for instance, bicycle storage and showers for employees are a requirement for any office development.

FINANCIAL FEASIBILITY

The financial feasibility assessment requires the development of a financial pro forma utilizing market information, various alternatives, and costs. Developers should consult local mortgage brokers and lenders to determine current appraisal and underwriting criteria before considering a project. Christopher Kurz of Linden Associates emphasizes the use of return on cost (ROC) as the returns need to be higher versus other assets.[106] The high interest rate environment is also pushing them to require 10 percent or higher in this market.

Two useful sources for estimating local office buildings' operating costs are the *Experience Exchange Report* published by BOMA International and the *Income/Expense Analysis for Office Buildings* published by IREM. Both reports are published annually with a detailed breakdown of operating costs for different types and sizes of office buildings across the United States. The key to accurately estimating revenues for office projects is to make *realistic* projections regarding lease-up time, vacancy rates, and achievable rents. Developers can apply the SFFS (simple financial feasibility analysis) methodology outlined by Geltner and colleagues as an assessment tool for their go/no-go decision.[107] *Financing for Real Estate Development* is also a good reference on financial feasibility.[108]

Capitalization rates (net operating income/property value) are key in underwriting because a project's debt capacity is a function of its value. Cap rates reflect variable market conditions over time. Developers should always be prepared for possible cap rate increases during construction as the property value then decreases and the lender can request the value difference from the developer, which can be substantial depending on the equity structure. If the developer cannot infuse equity or negotiate a deal, the lender can foreclose (worst case scenario). Refinancing an asset in a period of increasing cap rates is difficult because of the additional equity infusion required by lenders.

Design and Construction

Among the major design decisions are the building shape, design modules, bay depths, type of exterior, and lobby design, all of which create the image and identity for the structure. The market analysis and the local building and fire codes provide the design parameters for the project, which need to be adaptable and flexible to meet the shifting demands of tenants well into the future. Total project costs can be broken down into the percentages shown in figure 5-7.

The percentages shown in figure 5-7 differ depending on the project location (region, downtown versus suburbs), building purpose/type (e.g., medical versus conventional, headquarters versus other), construction methods, features, material, labor costs, and special fees required by local government bodies.[109] In high-rent districts, land is likely to represent a larger portion of the costs.

SHAPE. A square is the most cost-efficient building shape because it provides the most interior space for each foot of perimeter wall. But it often generates the lowest average revenue per square foot because tenants pay for floor area and windows. Rectangular and elongated shapes tend to offer higher rents per square foot but cost more to build because they provide more perimeter window space and shallower bays. Developers prefer rectangular buildings for multitenant speculative space because the interior and perimeter spaces can be more balanced. Nonrectangular shapes often create more interesting office shapes, and higher rents. Beyond the developer's and architect's vision, building shape is influenced by market conditions, environment, land uses, and zoning.

DESIGN MODULES AND BAY DEPTHS. Office buildings are designed using multiple modules, which allow for the repetition of structural and exterior skin materials. Although the design module is most visible on the exterior of the building, it should evolve from the types of interior spaces planned. The market study should suggest the types of interior design (for example, open-plan or executive offices) that are in the greatest demand in the target market.

The most common design module is the structural bay. Defined by the placement of the building's structural columns, the structural bay is generally subdivided into modules of 4 to 5 feet (1.2–1.5 m) with the most common in the United States being 4.5 to 5 feet (1.3–1.5 m), which provide a grid for coordinating interior partitions and window panels for the exterior curtain wall.[110] In Europe and Asia, 3.8 feet (1.2 m) and 5 feet (1.5 m) are the most common.[111] The structural bay determines the spacing of windows, which in turn determines the possible locations of office partitions, ascertaining whether interior space can be easily partitioned into offices of 8 to 12 feet, or 15 feet (2.4–3.6, or 4.6 m) (figure 5-8). Typically, offices are 10 to 14 feet (3–4.3 m) deep, and hallways are 5 to 6 feet (1.5–1.8 m) wide. For example, private office space in Chicago is 10 to 15 feet (3–4.6 m) wide, whereas in Atlanta it is only 8 to 12 feet (2.4–3.6 m).[112]

The bay depth is typically 40 to 45 feet (12–13.7 m),[113] with multitenant buildings with many small

FIGURE 5-7 Office Development Budget Overview

	HIGH-RISE OFFICE	
	$/RSF	Share of overall budget (%)
Land	60.00	7.0
Construction	575.00	67.0
Tenant improvement allowance	110.00	12.8
Design and engineering	55.00	6.4
Project management	7.00	0.8
Property taxes	2.50	0.3
Permits	10.00	1.2
Marketing and leasing commissions	22.00	2.6
Legal	2.00	0.2
Interest	15.00	1.7
Total	**858.50**	**100**

Source: Murphy McCullough interview, 2022.
Note: RSF = rentable square feet.

FIGURE 5-8 Relationship of Module to Interior Office Size

Module Size	Interior Office Width
3-foot	9, 12, and 15 feet
4-foot	8, 12, and 16 feet
5-foot	10 and 15 feet
5½-foot	11 and 16½ feet

Examples of Structural Bay Modules

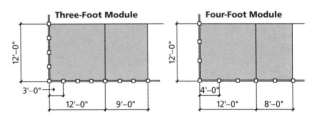

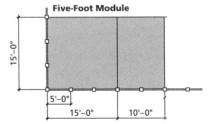

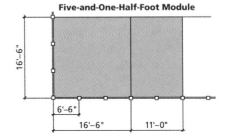

Note: Multiples of the module size determine where interior walls are joined to the exterior window wall system.

tenants embracing smaller bay depths—36 feet (11 m)—because they offer a larger number of window offices. In contrast, institutional users prefer 40- to 50-foot (12–15 m) bay depths, for construction and cost efficiency as well as larger open-space plans.

Developers should also keep in mind that at least 12 percent of the floor plate will be occupied by mechanical equipment, and in older buildings this allocation could be 20 percent.[114]

CEILING HEIGHTS. Floor-to-floor heights are typically between 11 and 14 feet (3.6–4.2 m). In areas where the height of the building is not constrained by zoning or other codes, class A properties' floor-to-floor heights may be 14.5 feet (4.4 m). In Asia, the most common heights are between 13 and 13.6 feet (3.9–4.1 m), while smaller concrete buildings—especially in Europe—are 12.4 feet (3.7 m).[115]

SITE PLANNING

A building should enjoy maximum exposure to major streets, with visible signage. Good site planning provides a logical progression from the street to the building's entrance.

PARKING. In theory, an office building in which each employee occupies an average of 200 to 225 square feet (18.5–20.9 sq m) needs three to four parking spaces per 1,000 square feet (93 sq m), assuming all employees drive separate cars (or use mass transit). The typical area required for each car is 300 square feet (27.8 sq m) for surface parking (which includes parking space and driveway) and up to 400 square feet (37 sq m) for structured parking to include allowances for ramps.[116]

Lenders prefer at least four parking spaces per 1,000 square feet (93 sq m) of rentable space, even though local zoning may require less. However, many developers reduce the parking ratio as a project increases in size.[117] For example, developers commonly provide four parking spaces per 1,000 square feet for the first 250,000 square feet (23,235 sq m), followed with only two spaces for each additional 1,000 square feet (93 sq m). Experienced developers cite inadequate parking as one of the most common flaws in attracting and retaining tenants.

The cost of below-grade parking depends on the number of below-grade levels, water table elevation, and foundations for adjacent structures. According to fixr.com, the current cost for surface parking can range from $1,500 to $10,000, while underground

the cost increases to $25,000 to $50,000.[118] However, the cost doubles for each level below the first underground level.[119]

LANDSCAPING. Landscaping is critical to a project's overall appearance, occupant well-being, and value. It includes vegetation—trees, shrubbery, ground covers, and seasonal color—and might be used to control soil erosion (e.g., retaining walls), mitigate sound, remove air pollutants, control glare and reflection, and serve as a wind barrier.

Landscape costs must be assessed with the landscape architect during design. A reasonable landscape budget accounts for 1 to 2.5 percent of total project costs, however, ESG adoption tends to increase it.

EXTERIOR DESIGN

Exterior design is an invaluable marketing tool and includes exterior building materials, signs, and lighting.

BUILDING MATERIALS. The building materials used are generally part of two distinct systems: the *structural* and the *skin system*. The structural system supports the building and the skin system protects the interior space from the weather. An office building can be built using one of seven structural systems:

- **Metal stud frame**—Generally used for one- to five-story buildings.
- **Concrete tilt-up**—Generally used for one- to three-story buildings and typically employed in flex buildings.
- **Steel frame with precast concrete** (hollow-core planks)—Typically used for low-rise buildings.
- **Reinforced concrete**—Used for both low- and high-rise buildings.
- **Steel**—Used for both low- and high-rise buildings.
- **Composite structures** (steel gravity framing with concrete core)—Used in high-rises and superstructures.[120]
- **CLT**—Used for small to mid-rise structures.

The exterior of an office building can be covered with any number of materials:

- **exterior insulation finish system** (synthetic stucco formed in many shapes);
- **precast concrete** (usually cast off site and shipped to the site and usually not part of the structural system);
- **tilt-up concrete panels** (cast on site and used as part of the structural system, limited to three stories; common in the suburbs, although panels have very limited utility in office buildings due to glazing limitations);

FIGURE 5-9 Exterior Skin Materials and Construction Costs

	2–4 office story (20,000 sq ft) (cost per square foot)		2–4 office story (50,000 sq ft) (cost per square foot)		5–10 office story (80,000 sq ft) (cost per square foot)		Characteristics/ comments	Aesthetics	Long-term maintenance	Energy efficiency
	Conv.	Sust.	Conv.	Sust.	Conv.	Sust.				
EXTERIOR WALL										
Stone veneer (granite and marble)	$188.9		$169.0		$174.4		Used to give building a sense of elegance and permanence. Minimum long-term maintenance.	Excellent	Excellent	Fair, depending on thickness
EIFS (exterior insulation and finish systems)	$177.6		$163.1		$154.8		Used to add architectural details at minimal cost. Fails under certain conditions; water penetration has led to lawsuits.	Very good	Very poor	Good
Precast concrete	$213.9		$186.4			$207.1	Heavier than GFRC but can achieve same detail.	Very good	Excellent	Good
Brick veneer	$209.1	$189.2	$183.9	$172.2	$215.9		Combines structure and skin. Substantial variety to achieve various looks. Height limitations.	Very good, depending on design	Excellent	Good
Curtain wall (including glass)		$240.4		$215.1	$175.2		Used for large expanses of glass in combination with various mullion systems and glass colors. Interesting geometry can be achieved.	Good to excellent, depending on design of glass mullion geometry	Excellent	Depends on glass: high-performance glass excellent; tinted or clear glass poor
Face brick and concrete block		$220.6	$190.7			$192.3	Used for for any building size allowing for a variety of colors, shapes, and textures	Very good	Excellent	Good
Wood clapboard		$184.0	$169.0				Used for smaller buildings. Although durable it requires more upkeeping	Very good	Poor	Good
Metal panel				$174.9	$174.9		Used for high-tech, precise look. Can be finished in wide range of standard or custom finishes.	Excellent	Good (may corrode)	Poor if installed without foam backing
AVERAGE STRUCTURE COSTS										
Substructure	$5.7	$7.3			$1.8	$3.3				
Shell (superstructure, exterior enclosure, and roofing)	$46.2	$48.4			$43.2	$58.3				
Interiors	$25.4	$32.9			$24.4	$26.2				
Service systems (conveying, plumbing, HVAC, fire protection, and electrical)	$63.9	$76.0			$62.2	$68.4				
Subtotal	**$141.2**	**$164.6**			**$131.6**	**$156.2**				
Contractor and architect fees	$47.6	55.66			$42.8	$50.8				
Total building cost	**$188.9**	**$220.3**			**$174.4**	**$207.0**				

Sources: RS Means, "Square Foot Costs with RSMeans Data 2020," 4th edition, 2019; and Scott Peterson, Turner Construction.
Note: Conv. = conventional; Sust. = sustainable; GFRC = glass fiber–reinforced concrete.

- **glass curtain wall system** (a combination of vision and spandrel glass hung in front of the building frame—always used on class A properties);
- **storefront system** (two-story height limit);
- **metal panels** (aluminum or steel finished in a factory);
- **stone** (granite, marble, or slate in large panels or small tiles); and
- **residential materials** (including stucco and brick, used as exterior cladding materials and not as a wall system).

Each structural system can be combined with another to produce economical hybrids, such as a masonry building with metal trusses or prestressed concrete floor units. Concrete tilt-up construction offers an advantage in that the concrete panels serve as both the structural system and the skin (see figure 5-9). Exterior materials can also be combined; for example, a tilt-up building might incorporate a storefront system or precast elements for architectural variety.

SIGNAGE. Signs identify a building and its tenants while creating an overall impression for visitors. Although tenants will negotiate sign privileges, developers should retain sign approval as a condition in their leases. Restrictions should stipulate the size, shape, color, height, materials, content, number, and location of all signs.

The developer's architect should work with graphic and interior designers to create a signage program for individual tenants and for interior and exterior common areas. The best approach is to develop a comprehensive signage program that includes designs, materials, and color schemes for the following purposes:

- building identification;
- directory of major occupants;
- directional signs for vehicular and pedestrian traffic;
- building location directories; and
- interior building service signs.

EXTERIOR LIGHTING. Exterior lighting can enhance the security of building entrances and parking lots and highlight architectural and landscaping features. Inadequately illuminated areas may pose a liability problem. The developer should work with an electrical engineer and architect to design exterior lighting that will accomplish the desired effects while being energy efficient and easy to maintain. Mercury- or sodium-vapor, quartz, LED (light-emitting diode), and fluorescent lights are energy efficient and may be used in exterior lighting fixtures. Many jurisdictions are

concerned about light pollution, requiring the use of high-cutoff lights and limiting the use of architectural illumination lighting the sky.

Lighting standards for parking lots should be placed around the perimeter of the lot or on the centerline of double rows of car stalls. The Illumination Engineering Society recommends a minimum illumination level of two footcandles for outdoor parking areas and five footcandles for structured parking.

INTERIOR DESIGN

The interior design must accommodate various systems—elevators; plumbing; heating, ventilation, and air conditioning (HVAC); lighting; wiring; and life safety—and provide a flexible core and shell, which are very important in attracting tenants. The use of modular systems (flexible walls or partitions) is increasing because of their flexibility to meet tenants' changing needs.

MEASURING SPACE. Multiple national measurement standards exist (gross, rentable, and usable square feet), with BOMA International standards being widely used. There are three key measurements:

- **Gross area** is measured from the exterior walls of the building without any exclusion (basements, mechanical equipment floors, and penthouses).
- **Rentable area** is measured from the inside finish of the permanent outer walls of a building except vertical penetrations (elevators, stairs, equipment, shafts, and atriums). According to local definitions, it may also include elevator lobbies, restroom areas, and janitorial and equipment rooms.
- **Usable area** is measured from the inside finish of the outer walls to the inside finished surface of the office side of the public corridor. Usable area for full-floor tenants is measured to the building core and includes corridor space. An individual tenant's usable area is measured to the center of partitions separating the tenant's office from adjoining offices. Usable area excludes public hallways, elevator lobbies, and restroom facilities that open onto public hallways.

Tenant's rentable area is derived by multiplying the usable area by the rentable/usable ratio (R/U ratio). The R/U ratio is the percentage of space that is not usable plus a pro rata share of the common area. For example, if a tenant rents 1,000 square feet (93 sq m) of usable space in a building with a 1.15 R/U ratio, the tenant pays rent for 1,150 square feet (107 sq m).

Tenants are very sensitive to the R/U ratio, often referred to as the building *efficiency ratio*, *core factor*, or *load factor*. The average R/U ratio for high-rise space is about 1.15 and 1.12 for low-rise space. Developers should be careful to calculate their pro forma project rental income on the actual rentable area and not on the gross building area, which is more appropriately used to estimate construction costs.

SPACE PLANNING. Effective space planning involves five basic components: the space itself, the users, their activities, future uses, and energy efficiency.

The amount of space and its functionality are controlled by a building's exterior walls, floors, ceiling heights, column spacing and size, and the building core.

In a single-tenant or a floor-tenant building, the tenant is responsible for improving the lobby and interior hallways. In a multitenant building, however, the developer improves the lobby, restrooms, and hallways that serve each suite, and individual tenants are responsible for their own suites.

Many modern office layouts use the open-space planning approach, which helps reduce the cost of initial construction and design changes. Partitions in open-space plans are movable, and a variety of furniture and wall systems are available that are attractive and use space efficiently.

An inviting lobby with an identity is critical in attracting prospective tenants even if it comes with a premium for the developer.

ELEVATORS. Tenants' and visitors' initial impressions are shaped by a building's lobby, the type of access (automated/proximity readers), and quality of the interior finish of elevator cabs. Finish materials used in the lobby—such as carpet, granite, marble, brass, and steel—can also be used effectively inside the elevator.

Elevator capacity depends on the types of tenants. Buildings with larger companies tend to need high-capacity elevators to accommodate peak-hour demand, while buildings with smaller companies tend to have lower peak-period demand. Waiting time for elevators should average no more than 20 to 30 seconds; longer waits can affect a tenant's lease renewal decision. The developer will need to decide if they will install standard, destination, or limited-use elevators. The following can be useful for gauging elevator need and capacity:

- The Americans with Disabilities Act (ADA) requires an elevator if the building has three or more stories or each floor exceeds 3,000 square feet (279 sq m).

- One elevator is needed for every 200 to 250 building occupants (for three-story buildings the demand will be lower).[121]
- Buildings with three to five floors require two elevators.
- Ten-story buildings need four elevators and 20-story buildings need two banks of four elevators.
- Thirty-story buildings need two banks of eight elevators.

Many elevator control innovations are being used in high-rises, such as kiosks where riders indicate the floor of preference and the system directs them to the faster elevator (grouping riders to various floors), significantly increasing the speed and capacity of the system.

INTERIOR LIGHTING. Lighting plays a critical role in how users and visitors perceive the building. Owners of existing buildings or developers retrofitting a property can benefit from the energy-efficient commercial buildings tax deduction, which can also be used to write off the indoor lighting retrofit cost.

Several types of artificial light are available for interior applications:

- **Fluorescent**—Fluorescent fixtures are expensive but have the advantage of long bulb life (18,000 to 20,000 hours) and reduced energy consumption.
- **Light-Emitting Diode**—LED fixtures are the most used as they have a long life (25,000-100,000 hours) and vastly reduced energy consumption.
- **High-Intensity Discharge**—High-intensity discharge lighting includes mercury-vapor (frequently used outdoors), metal-halide, and high- and low-pressure sodium lamps. Although they are excellent for illuminating outdoor spaces and are very energy efficient, high-intensity discharge lights offer poor color-rendering properties.
- **High-Intensity Quartz**—Sometimes called *precise lighting*, high-intensity quartz lighting is a new product that is often used in upscale environments. Multifaceted, mirrored backs reflect the light onto specific objects or areas, making high-intensity quartz fixtures appropriate for task-oriented lighting.

Office buildings use mainly direct lighting. Installed in a grid pattern across a dropped ceiling, this solution offers equal levels of illumination across large spaces. Direct lighting is available in integrated ceiling packages, including lighting, sprinklers, sound masking, and air distribution. Indirect lighting uses walls, ceilings, and room furnishings to reflect light from other surfaces. In recent years, indirect lighting has become common for general office lighting to reduce glare on computer monitors. In general, indirect lighting requires higher ceilings to reduce "hot spots" on ceilings and to improve the overall efficiency of the lighting layout.

The electrical engineer, interior designer, and architect all play important roles in designing the lighting system to suit each tenant's needs.

HEATING, VENTILATION, AND AIR CONDITIONING. A building's HVAC system is one of the major line items in its construction and operation budget. Several different types of HVAC systems are available:

- **Package Forced-Air Systems**—These electrical heat pumps, usually located on the roof, heat and cool the air in the package unit, then deliver it through ducts to the appropriate areas of the building. The units are inexpensive to install and work well on one- and two-story buildings.
- **Variable Air Volume Systems**—A large unit on the roof cools the air and delivers it through large supply ducts to individual floors. Mixing units control the distribution of the air in each zone. This system offers great flexibility as many mixing units can be installed to create zones as small as an office, but it is more expensive to install than forced-air systems. The system allows for balance loads and automatically adjusts airflow. Rooms are heated by a heating element in the mixing units or by radiant heater panels in the ceiling.
- **Hot- and Cold-Water Systems**—A combination chiller and water heater is centrally located to provide hot and cold water to the various mixing units in the building. The air is heated or cooled in these mixing units and delivered to the local areas.

The architect and mechanical engineer will provide guidance in the selection of the HVAC system. For a development of about 100,000 square feet (9,300 sq m)—four to five stories of 25,000 square feet (2,300 sq m) of floor plate—the most economical system is a rooftop variable air volume system, but in some markets heat-up systems are more common. The capacity of the system will be determined by several factors, including climate, building design, and types of tenants.

The American Society of Heating, Refrigerating and Air-Conditioning Engineers (ASHRAE) publishes standards on the minimum ventilation rate for different occupancy and building types, relative humidity,

and maximum allowable air velocity. Poor humidity control and leaks in a building can cause sick building syndrome, which exposes building owners to possible lawsuits. ASHRAE's *Humidity Control Design Guide for Commercial and Institutional Buildings* provides guidance on humidity control to the entire building team.[122] The final authority on building ventilation is the local code authority, which may or may not have adopted ASHRAE standards. Standards for air movement and air conditioning depend on building design, climate, glazing, lighting, and building orientation.

A building's HVAC system is typically monitored using local computers and possibly cloud services, which store continuous performance and reporting for medium-sized or large buildings. A well-designed HVAC system divides the building into zones, each controlled by a thermostat. These zones should cover areas with similar characteristics, such as orientation to the sun, types of uses, and intensity of uses. A standard rule of thumb is one thermostat zone per 1,200 square feet (110 sq m). Usually, each zone has one mixing damper that controls temperature by mixing hot and cold air.

SECURITY AND LIFE SAFETY. Life safety and security are important for certain tenants in the design and marketing of an office building. Protecting the building, its occupants, and its contents requires multiple security layers. Depending on the size and type of tenants the building wants to attract, the most secure buildings enforce seven rings of defense:

- site perimeter;
- building standoff;
- building exterior;
- inner perimeter;
- building systems;
- screening and access control zones; and
- safe interior areas for valuable assets or personnel safe havens.[123]

The ability to control access in and out of a building is essential and can be accomplished by several methods, depending on such factors as the building's location and setting, potential threats, tenant requirements, and so forth. During construction, developers need to consider the following:

- perimeter security measures;
- lobby security controls, including electronic monitors and security guards;
- access control card readers on parking and lobby entrances and elevators;
- an intercom system to a 24-hour remote operator;

- surveillance cameras in parking lots and in all egress and ingress points; and
- a lobby entrance for parking users, which might require installation of separate elevators.[124]

Life safety features include sprinkler systems, smoke detectors, fire hoses and extinguishers, and automatic shutoffs for the HVAC and public address systems. Developers should keep in mind that adoption of various life safety systems (mandated or not by area building codes) can lower fire insurance rates.

TENANT LEASEHOLD IMPROVEMENTS

As part of the lease, developers usually provide a set allowance for tenant improvements covering the interior buildout. The allowance provides some level of improvements, with the tenant financing the remaining. Because leases typically do not require the tenant to pay rent during the improvement phase, the developer needs to ensure that work is done on schedule. TIs depend on lease length, tenant's needs, layout, furniture, and finishes, with the national average for first generation buildouts at $107 per square foot and for second generation around $85 per square foot.[125] Pre-COVID, a strong TI for second generation was $40 to $50 per square foot; now it can be $85 per square foot for a five-year lease.[126] For new construction, buildout costs vary widely; new technology/creative space in Seattle averages $130 to $150 per square foot not including furniture, fixtures, and equipment (FF&E). The costs are split—the landlord typically provides an allowance of $75 to $100 per square foot on a new lease and the tenant pays the balance. Prepandemic, it was $100 to $105 per square foot depending on lease term.

TENANT IMPROVEMENT PROCESS. Steps in completing TIs in a small office building parallel the steps involved in constructing the building itself: budgeting; preliminary planning, including design and construction drawings; approvals and permits; contractor selection and bidding; and construction.

- **Step 1: Establish a Budget**—The budget is based on the tenant's needs and the resources available.
- **Step 2: Prepare a Space Plan and Design for the Improvements**—The space planner/interior designer may be under contract with the developer or tenant. If the designer is under contract to the developer, the developer maintains greater control but will be liable for all costs if the tenant backs out of the lease. The design firm is usually selected in one of two ways: (1) the developer selects a design firm and then recommends it to all tenants, or (2) the developer approves three or four firms and then allows tenants to select from the approved list.
- **Step 3: Plan Approval**—Plans are submitted to the local building department for approval and permits. Whenever improvements involve safety or require electrical work or partitions, building permits are required.
- **Step 4: Select a Contractor**—The developer typically selects a single contractor to do all the TIs in the building, but some developers approve three or four contractors and then submit the drawings to each for bids.

WORK LETTERS. A work letter serves as the formal agreement between the developer and the tenant concerning the cost, timeline, and quality of improvements the landlord will complete before the lease commences. Building standard installation (the *building standard*) includes the list of items installed in every tenant suite: partitions; doors and hardware; size and pattern of acoustical ceiling tiles; floor coverings; size, shape, and location of lighting fixtures; electrical receptacles; switches; telephone and data outlets; plumbing connections; HVAC; painting and wall coverings; and window coverings or venetian blinds. If the tenant wants items above the building standard, the work letter also specifies them, their cost, and method of payment.

A standard tenant improvement work letter is created for improvements throughout the building. This document lays out the minimum improvements that will be constructed in every tenant space.

LEVEL OF TENANT IMPROVEMENTS. Typical items specified in a tenant improvement work letter include the following:

- size and type of ceiling tiles used;
- number of linear feet (meters) of wall and doors for every 100 square feet (10 sq m) of rentable space;
- type of wall coverings and color of standard paint;
- quality and type of floor covering;
- number of HVAC registers, mixing units, and thermostats per 100 square feet (10 sq m) of rentable space;
- specifications for the telephone system, including the installation of conduit and boxes and the provision of equipment rooms (this item is negotiable, and many businesses have their own systems and installers); and
- type and extent of computer wiring and of alarm and security systems.

The following are some common upgrades in tenant spaces:

- kitchen bar consisting of a microwave, small refrigerator, and sink;
- full kitchen and lunchroom with a sink, disposal, microwave, refrigerator, and dishwasher;
- executive bar in office with a refrigerator and sink;
- executive bathroom containing a sink, vanity, toilet, and sometimes a shower;
- climate-controlled computer room;
- fireproof safes or fireproof file rooms; and
- built-in fixtures, such as shelves, cabinets, worktables, bookshelves, counters, and other cabinetry.

Financing

Office development requires significant capital. For beginning developers, the lack of track record and experience may present challenges. Typically, beginning developers solicit wealthy individuals as co-investors and pursue crowdfunding; after a sufficiently large portion of the total equity has been accumulated, they approach a local bank for a construction loan. At the same time, the developer would secure long-term permanent financing that would be funded after the building is completed and fully leased. For developers with some experience, the local equity investment partnerships are overshadowed by commercial mortgage–backed securities (CMBSs), national and global real estate investment trusts (REITs), pension funds, foreign investors, municipal bonds, and property trust companies.

The Great Recession caused several changes in lender practices:

- higher equity requirements—the equity required for acquisitions is 30 to 45 percent loan-to-value [LTV] ratio is 55 to 70 percent) and even higher due to credit or other risk;
- recourse—depending on the strength of the guarantor and leasing, the project can have less than 100 percent recourse;
- stricter loan covenants;
- constraint of future TIs and commission funding; importance of tenant credit even for landlords (landlords focus on a tenant's operation in their building and evaluate the possibility of dismantling if a tenant has multiple branches); as well as who guarantees the lease;
- significant pre-leasing (depending on a developer's track record, recourse, and equity in the building); and

- developer's overall profile (banks are now looking at both the proposal for new construction and the financial health of the other projects the developer is involved in).

During market contraction with increased vacancies and lower rental rates, lenders will require[127]

- additional pre-leasing, which can reach 60 percent because that is the threshold when the debt service (DS) is going to be covered when the loan is drawn, or even 100 percent for new developers;
- higher fees and possibly a higher completion guarantee;
- additional equity from the developer, which could be attained through equity investors or crowdfunding for small-scale projects; and
- strict budget controls, with cost overruns being immediately reviewed by the lender with the possibility of a lender-imposed funding pause and a request for the developer to bridge the gap through additional equity.

CONSTRUCTION LOANS

Construction lenders are concerned with leasing, and they require higher pre-leasing from inexperienced developers (40 to 50 percent in normal markets, 50 to 70 percent in soft markets, and more than 70 percent in high-risk cases). The due diligence performed for construction loans is detailed and lenders require concrete proof of rent expectation. The equity requirement can increase from 25 to 50 percent, or greater, depending on factors such as pre-leasing and a developer's experience.[128]

The terms of construction loans range from six months to four years with higher floating interest rates than permanent loans due to increased risk. Construction loan rates are transitioning from LIBOR to SOFR, while smaller community banks offer rates based on prime rate. The final construction rate depends on market conditions and the bank's assessment of the credit risk posed by the project and developer. Upfront loan fees (*points*) are common on most construction loans. Most construction loan agreements call for interest to accrue through the construction period. When construction is complete and the building is leased up, the developer obtains a permanent loan or sells the project and pays off the total loan amount, which includes the accrued interest and the principal balance. Problems that may be encountered by developers include

- failure to leave enough cushion for cost overruns and slower-than-expected leasing;

- constant oversight/monitoring/approval of both construction activity and leases;
- lack of understanding of the covenants in the loan documents that may allow the lender to increase reserve requirements and adjust the terms accordingly; and
- an exit strategy; will there be buyers for the asset if the developer does not want to hold it after construction?

Some pitfalls can occur between the construction and permanent loans:

- **Debt Coverage Ratio (DCR)**—Typically, the construction loan has a three- to four-year initial term and a one- to two-year renewal option.
- **Valuation**—In soft markets, cap rates can increase, which triggers lenders' request for additional equity infusion to renew the loan.
- **Recourse**—After the Great Recession, an increasing number of loans have been recourse ranging from 25 to 100 percent depending on the developer's track record.

PERMANENT LOANS

The permanent mortgage is funded once the building reaches a negotiated level of occupancy—usually, about 70 to 80 percent, a level sufficient to cover debt service on the mortgage. When the loan commitment provides for funding the mortgage before the building is fully leased, usually the developer must post a letter of credit for the difference between the amount that the leases will carry and the full loan amount. Alternatively, the permanent lender may fund the mortgage in stages as the building is leased. Lenders will focus on the effective rather than the market rent, using the lower of the two to underwrite the permanent loan, and they may deduct amounts from the cash flow to cover capital costs and leasing reserves (in case of tenant defaults).

Some office buildings constructed before the Great Recession, during periods of low cap rates, faced financial challenges with both the loan covenants and the LTV ratio because the exit assumptions did not materialize. For example, a building's LTV ratios were 65 to 70 percent, however, cap rates increased, causing property values to decrease 20 percent. Therefore, a shortfall was created for developers and their lenders could request them to cover the difference. If developers cannot infuse equity or a deal is not reached with the lenders, there is expectation of dispositions driven either by banks or by landlords who are trying to reduce the erosion in their equity.

LEASE REQUIREMENTS. Developers must execute leases that satisfy the construction and permanent lenders' requirements with experienced attorneys while avoiding standard lease forms. Specifically, lenders must (1) require proper building maintenance and tenant services to protect their investment; (2) require assignable leases allowing them to collect rents in the event of default; and (3) try to avoid "force majeure" clauses that require tenants to pay rent even if the building is destroyed from a natural/other disaster, although sophisticated tenants will avoid such clauses, even though insurance is available to cover rent when calamities occur. In the event of a calamity, lenders want to receive condemnation and insurance awards first and only then pay the developer. Owners, on the other hand, usually want the insurance money to restore the building.

Lenders tend to dislike rental rates being offset against increases in pass-through expenses. For example, most leases require tenants to pay increases in operating costs over some base figure. Lenders also object to exclusions for increases in management fees and similar items because they reduce the ability of owners to cover these increased costs.

MORTGAGE OPTIONS

Bullet loans (standard 30-year self-amortizing mortgages with a 10- to 15-year call) are a common form of permanent financing for office projects. Interest rates are usually lower for short-term mortgages because of the lower interest-rate risk to the lender over time. Occasionally, when inflation and long-term interest rates are expected to fall, interest rates are higher for shorter-term mortgages than for longer-term ones. Other common forms of financing are participating mortgages, convertible mortgages, and sale-leasebacks, all of which are forms of joint ventures with lenders.

STANDBY AND FORWARD COMMITMENTS

Although experienced developers can obtain open-ended construction financing without a permanent takeout, beginning developers usually cannot. Standby commitments are one alternative. They represent permanent loan commitments from credit companies and REITs that are sufficient to secure construction financing but are very expensive if they are used. Standby loans may run three or more points above prime, thus increasing the default risk during recessions. Ideally, the standby commitment is never funded because it is replaced by a bullet loan or another type of mortgage.

FIGURE 5-10 **Purchase Price Calculation**

	Rate	Square feet (sq ft)	$/sq ft	Rents ($28/sq ft) and vacancy (5%)	Rents ($28/sq ft) and vacancy (50%)	Rents ($26/sq ft) and vacancy (0%)
Gross rent ($28/sq ft)		100,000	$28	$2,800,000	$2,800,000	
Gross rent ($26/sq ft)		45,000	$26			$1,170,000
Vacancy (5%)	5%			$140,000		
Vacancy (50%)	50%				$1,400,000	
Effective Gross Income (Gross Rent minus Vacancy)				**$2,660,000**	**$1,400,000**	**$1,170,000**
Operating Expenses			$5	$500,000	$500,000	$500,000
NOI (EGI minus Operating Expenses)				**$2,160,000**	**$900,000**	**$670,000**
Value = (NOI/cap rate)	8.50%			$25,411,764.71		
Value = (EGI/cap rate) at rents ($28/sq ft) and vacancy (5%)	10.47%			$25,411,746.72		
Value = (EGI/cap rate) at rents ($28/sq ft) and vacancy (50%)	10.47%				$13,374,603.54	
Value = (EGI/cap rate) at rents ($26/sq ft) and vacancy (0%)	10.47%					$11,177,347.24

Another alternative to a permanent mortgage is a presale or forward commitment by a purchaser with the developer borrowing against proceeds from the sale for the construction loan. The presale price is determined based on the market capitalization rate. A forward commitment often includes an earnout provision whereby the developer is paid part of the purchase price and the balance is paid as the leasing is completed.

For example, the purchase price of a 100,000-square-foot (9,290 sq m) building with a $28 per square foot rent and expenses of $5 can be determined by capitalizing the gross rent from executed leases on 95 percent of the building's rentable area at 10.47 percent, which equates to approximately an 8.5 percent cap-rate on the net operating income (NOI). Therefore, if 50 percent of the building is leased, the purchaser would pay $13,375,000 at closing. The balance would be paid as the developer leases the rest of the building (see figure 5-10).

EQUITY

Lenders normally require 20 to 30 percent of the development cost to be funded by equity sources, although it could be higher depending on multiple factors (e.g., development's experience, difference between the project cost and return, market strength, pre-leasing, and lender liquidity).

Joint ventures with lenders and tenants offer one of the easiest methods for covering a developer's equity requirement. Lenders have preferred participating loans, which give them a share of the cash flows during operations and profits from sale while shielding them from liability and downside risk.

LOAN WORKOUTS. All mortgages include lender-imposed loan covenants. One of the major covenants is a predetermined DCR requirement (currently 1.3 to 1.4). Some banks also require a debt yield ratio (DYR) (NOI divided by the loan amount), which does not account for the interest rate.

The loan covenants will outline the following:

- DCR and DYR testing frequency—usually once or twice a year;
- completion benchmarks and repercussions in case of cost overruns or other noncompliance—for example, if the building is expected to be completed in 12 months the lender provides a cushion of up to four months with monitored checkpoints on the schedule and budget; if the building is not completed after the cushion period, the lender can call for a loan default although all options will first be exhausted to avoid foreclosing on properties under construction as long as the developer is truthful and honest; and
- the time frame in which the loan will be repaid.

A developer facing monetary default must take the following steps:[129]

- Contact his attorney, who is qualified to review the legal documentation.
- Prepare a solution for the lender. The developer should analyze the causes of the cash flow shortfall and offer short- and longer-term solutions. For an interest-rate problem, refinancing with a lower rate and a comprehensive exit strategy might be the solution. Another possibility can be a request for interest-only payments, reducing payments for a while on a negatively amortized loan.

- Contact the lender and present a solution before receiving the default letter. Developer honesty is critical in resolving any type of problem.

It is important to understand the type of lender the developer is using and what that lender's guidelines allow. For example, a CMBS lender has fewer flexible guidelines on additional funding and fewer time extensions than other types of lenders. With a regular lender, such as a bank, the developer should know if the bank is healthy as the response can dictate possible outcomes. Assuming the lender is a healthy bank, the next issue for a developer is the types of commitments the bank cannot service.

The strategy for resolving the problem will depend on the type of issue (equity, developer's financial strength, property status, etc.) the developer faces. Whether the loan is recourse or nonrecourse is very important. If the loan is nonrecourse, the developer is in a stronger negotiating position, with the only exception being a "bad-boy" guarantee where the loan automatically becomes full recourse if the developer engages in certain actions (not paying taxes, fraud, intentional illegal action, and so forth). In a nonrecourse loan, the developer can return the keys to the lender and negotiate a minimal cost exit (in a minimum equity situation) in lieu of foreclosure. If, however, there are intervening liens (such as mechanical liens), a no-cost transfer to the lender will be impossible. But a friendly foreclosure through bankruptcy can save money, as long as the developer agrees and has not committed fraud.

Another option might be for the developer to buy back the loan from the bank, for example, if the property is now worth less than the original loan. If the developer wants to salvage the property, avoiding default status is essential because the loan becomes classified and the bank has to report it differently to its examiners. Even if the developer makes regular payments later, the bank might need to treat the loan differently due to its default status.

Marketing and Leasing

Marketing an office building begins in the initial planning phases and continues through construction, occupancy, and asset disposition. The crux of a marketing plan is to identify the target market segment and to convince that segment of the building's desirability. A successful marketing campaign focuses on the criteria that are important to the target market. Important features include:

- exceptional location and access (e.g., mass transit, expressway);
- competitive rental rates;
- efficient floor configuration;
- amenities and services (conference and fitness centers, restaurants);
- distinctive design;
- landlord stability;
- a high standard of tenant improvements;
- an ESG focus, with multiple sustainability certifications, electric vehicle parking; and
- a building app that focuses on features and well-being.

MARKETING STRATEGY

Guided by the market analysis and controlled by a strategic marketing plan and budget, the developer should undertake a variety of initiatives to attract and satisfy the needs of prospective tenants with a systematic approach.

The marketing strategy provides a basic plan for publicizing the project and defines the roles of marketing team members. It should include a project description, target market, ESG features, an analysis of the position in the marketplace, a statement of the developer's financial goals and investment strategy, and exit strategies. A leasing plan with guidelines for rental rates and potential concessions is also essential.

Developers usually start marketing space when the building is in the design phase due to lender requirements, although tenants are reluctant to lease preconstruction space, especially among larger buildings with longer deliveries. A good location often attracts a build-to-suit tenant; however, developers must be willing to adapt the building to the tenant's distinctive requirements, which may later pose problems if the building must be leased to another tenant.

ADVERTISING. Advertising must be well conceived and designed to convey the appropriate image of the project, with a unified theme and style. A name, logo, and identity design—to be used in all materials—can be developed early during the project's conceptual planning phases to ensure continuity in image from design to marketing.

Property advertising has changed by virtue of technology and client needs in recent years. Beyond listing the property information on brokerage websites, a property website can be set up and maintained easily, and include drone videos. Features should include a project overview, building data, typical floor plans, a summary of technical specifications, and a location map. Depending on the project size, scale models can be used for financing and public approvals as well as for virtual reality tours. Photos illustrating construction progress and leasing updates can also help sell the project to prospective tenants before its completion. Emails and progress newsletters are other effective advertising techniques for brokers.

On-site signboards should announce the amount of available space, a contact person, and a telephone number. Signs should be perpendicular to the road, and the letters should be large enough to be read easily by passengers inside a vehicle driving by the site.

BROKERS

Brokers are used in nearly all office-leasing transactions. Existing tenants, however, are increasingly approaching their landlords directly for renewals and extensions to benefit from the lack of the brokerage commission. Leasing can be done by an in-house team or outside brokers. An in-house team allows the developer greater control, but the cost may be prohibitive for a small or beginner developer. Arrangements with brokerage firms can provide market experience and access to a professional sales force, but it does mean that the developer has less control over marketing and leasing.

WORKING WITH OUTSIDE BROKERS. A brokerage firm can bring in-depth knowledge of major competitors and tenants looking for space. In hiring outside brokers, developers should consider the size and competence of the broker's leasing staff, and the number of competitive buildings the broker is working on. Brokers with many clients may not be able to devote sufficient time or interest to a new developer's project. A younger or smaller agency with fewer clients may offer better service but may have fewer contacts.

Brokers may have a contract with the developer that ensures them the exclusive right to negotiate all deals. Alternatively, the developer may opt for an *open listing*, which allows any broker to act as the primary broker on a deal. Developers should keep brokers informed about their project through presentations and monthly news releases. Traditionally, a broker brings a prospective tenant to the developer and assists in negotiating the terms of the lease. In some situations, developers may prefer to negotiate the lease themselves or with the use of legal counsel.

Commission rates for brokers are typically a percentage of rental income determined by market conditions. As a rough guide, a beginning developer could expect a broker to request a 6 percent commission in

FIGURE 5-11 Typical Breakdown of Gross Rent for Office Space[a]

Budget item	$/sq ft
Base rent	**$29.7**
OPERATING EXPENSES	
Payroll	$2.2
Cleaning	$0.2
Cleaning supplies	$0.2
Cleaning contract	$1.3
Repairs and maintenance	$1.0
Utilities	$1.6
Security	$0.7
Administrative	$0.5
Management fee	$0.7
Real estate taxes[b]	$2.6
Insurance	$0.3
Total operating expenses	**$11.2**
Total gross rent	**$40.9**

Source: Bill Pollard, founding principal, Talon Private Capital, interview, 2022.

[a]Typical breakdown of gross rent for a class A office building in the Puget Sound, Washington, area.

[b]Real estate taxes vary considerably.

the first year of the lease with a declining percentage for the later years. The typical payment schedule for brokers' commissions is one-half upon lease signing and one-half upon occupancy or at the time rental payments begin. In cases in which a substantial period of free rent is offered at the beginning of a lease, it is common for a developer to pay one-third of the commission at the signing of the lease, one-third at occupancy, and one-third at the commencement of rent.

USING IN-HOUSE BROKERS. Some developers prefer to employ an in-house staff of leasing agents. Although salaries are costly, an in-house staff can substantially reduce the cost of leasing space because of their lower commissions (typically 3 to 4 percent of the full value of the lease).

TYPES OF LEASES. Three types of leases are used in office projects: gross leases, net leases, and expense stop leases. Each has its advantages and disadvantages.

Gross Leases. The landlord pays all operating expenses, absorbing the risk of rising expenses. A typical rent breakdown is shown in figure 5-11.

Net Leases. Three variations of net leases are common:

- **net lease**—tenant pays a base rent plus its share of certain building operating expenses, such as utilities;
- **net-net lease**—tenant pays everything under a net lease plus ordinary repairs and maintenance; and
- **triple-net lease**—tenant pays all the building's ongoing operating expenses, including capital improvements.

Ultimately, the lease itself, which is a product of negotiation between owner and tenants, defines which expenses fall under the responsibility of the tenant and the owner.

Expense Stop Leases. Expense stop leases involve sharing expenses between the tenant and the landlord. The landlord pays a stated dollar amount for expenses, and the tenant pays any expenses above that amount. Normally, the expense "stop" is determined by an estimate of expenses for the first operating year. Thus, the tenant pays any increases in expenses above the stop over the term of the lease after the second year of the lease term. An expense stop shifts the responsibility for increased expenses to the tenant in much the same way a net lease does. A lease may also be structured so that the tenant is responsible for the increase in utility costs but no other expenses.

LEASE RATES AND TERMS

The lease document provides the terms and conditions under which the tenant's rights to use the space are granted. Developers and corporate tenants have their own leasing forms, and the initial negotiations determine which form will be used as the starting point. Lease negotiations focus on four major issues: rent, term, tenant improvements, and concessions, such as free rent or moving expenses. Anchor tenants (those occupying a significant portion of the building) have lease terms running five to 10 years, with rent escalations every year. The rest of the tenants usually have three- to five-year leases; the shorter term allows the landlord to renegotiate the terms of the lease to match inflation and gives tenants greater flexibility.

The base rent depends on market conditions. If local vacancy rates exceed 15 percent, tenants enjoy a strong bargaining position, and the base rent could be lowered accordingly. Provisions such as *dollar stop* or *full stop* clauses are created to allow for rent adjustments for long-term leases. An estimated dollar amount (the *dollar stop*) for real estate taxes and another amount for other operating expenses and insurance are determined at the beginning of the

lease. Under consumer price index (CPI) clauses, rent is adjusted annually based on the CPI or the wholesale price index, which is tied to the cost of living in the United States. During inflationary periods, developers tend to prefer CPI leases. In softer markets, CPI leases are harder to negotiate. In periods of low inflation, fixed increases may be more common. Tenants are often willing to accept 3 percent annual increases, which in recent years provided larger rent increases than a straight CPI adjustment.

The key to successful lease negotiations is being able to respond to the tenant's needs while negotiating for everything. Does a tenant require free rent for certain periods, low initial rent with later escalations, or above-standard TIs? Generally, smaller tenants prefer higher TI allowances because they often lack the liquidity for improvements in advance; larger tenants often prefer free rent for certain periods.

Every lease should specify the following information:

- location of the space in the building;
- size and method of measuring the space;
- options for expansion, if any;
- duration of lease term, renewal options, and termination privileges;
- rent per square foot (per sq m);
- services included in the lease and costs associated with those services;
- interior work to be performed by the developer under the base rent;
- operating hours of the building;
- the landlord's obligations for maintenance and services;
- the tenant's obligations for maintenance and services;
- escalation provisions during the lease term;
- number of parking spaces, their location, and terms of their use (for example, whether designated or undesignated);
- allowable use of the leased space permitted by local zoning ordinances and building rules;
- date of possession and date that rental payments are due; and
- sublease and assignment privileges, if any.

Operations and Management

Office building management requires regular maintenance, efficient operation, and enhancement of the property's value. Larger buildings have property managers on site, while smaller buildings may share a property manager. The agreement between the developer and the property manager should identify the duties and responsibilities of each party, including the authority to sign leases and other documents, incur expenses, advertise, and arrange bank/trust agreements. Also included are provisions on record keeping, insurance, indemnification, and management fees. Most management fees are quoted as a percentage of effective gross income. Smaller developers might manage their buildings for the fees they generate and to maintain close ties with tenants.

The functions of a property manager affect the property value as they include: maintaining the building, developing and maintaining good tenant relations, collecting rent, establishing an operating plan, creating a budget with monthly updates of income and expenditures, maintaining accounting and operating records, hiring contractors or vendors servicing the building, paying bills, overseeing leasing, developing and managing maintenance schedules, supervising building personnel, providing security, addressing issues related to risk management, coordinating insurance requirements, and generally preserving and attempting to increase the building's value.

The three major operating expenses are taxes, utilities, and cleaning, with the management staff having better control over the latter two. Several strategies can be applied to reduce operating expenses, such as renegotiating service contracts, making staffing changes (on-site personnel can be decreased if the facility has smart systems that allow remote supervision), reducing energy usage, setting back temperature controls, and minimizing downtime and landscaping. Operating expenses of portfolio properties can decrease if electricity is bought in bulk and the same cleaning staff is used for the entire portfolio.

Key issues toward ensuring tenant satisfaction are the coordination of tenant improvements and property maintenance. Many developers have an in-house project manager for construction oversight while maintenance is routine—preventative and corrective on the building's mechanical and structural systems.

One of the most important management tools is the lease agreement. Developers should ensure that leases contain clauses stipulating that

- tenants must not alter the building without the landlord's consent;
- tenants must not do anything that might increase the costs of fire insurance or create noise or nuisance;
- tenants must not use the building for immoral or illegal purposes; and

- if tenants remove floor, wall, or ceiling coverings, they must restore the surfaces to the condition that existed when they first took possession of the space.

The management team needs to provide high-level service to the tenants and build a relationship through scheduled meetings and independent surveys. The team members should also make sure they satisfy the tenant decision-makers, not only the employees.[130] Some companies offer tenant portals that include announcements, forms, life/safety training videos, and so forth.

SELLING THE COMPLETED PROJECT

The decision to sell depends on the needs of the equity partners, the term of the construction or permanent loan, market conditions, and the developer's analysis of alternative investment opportunities.

Office buildings are commonly sold at (1) stabilized occupancy, (2) after the first full year of occupancy (when the first CPI or fixed adjustments occur), or (3) after the leases are renewed. Usually, the highest internal rate of return is achieved if the building is sold as soon as it reaches stabilized occupancy. In competitive markets, however, most developers prefer to wait until just after the leases first roll over or until the first rent escalations have occurred. However, some developers hold buildings for at least seven years.

Developers can take several actions to position a building for sale:

BILYANA DIMITROVA

Postpandemic, some companies have adopted a hybrid policy in which employees work from home part of the week and the office part of the week. A large event space is used for employee gatherings to enhance socialization and the WFO experience.

- Hire a building inspection team to inspect a building's mechanical and other systems and to prepare a report that can be shown to prospective buyers.
- Prepare summaries of a project's income/expenses and ensure that accounting records are in order.
- Make sure that a building is clean and has a well-landscaped and well-maintained appearance.
- Prepare a summary of all outstanding leases on a building.
- Create a website that describes a project's noteworthy qualities—its tenants, management, location, and position in the market.

Conclusion

Development requires vision, resiliency, innovation, and an understanding of constraints, market conditions, and regulations. As building codes evolve by embracing sustainable and resilient practices, and market dynamics adjust to evolving realities, developers must constantly seek the features that will attract and retain tenants and give their new construction a competitive edge. The development firm ARUP emphasizes the need for operations and systems to be designed for multiple scenarios (normal, pandemic, climate crisis, and multihazard) to allow for a quick pivot.[131]

The COVID-19 pandemic, which struck during a generational shift, caused an unprecedented disruption in office buildings. Although it will take time for the determination of the many features that will need to be adopted by a competitive developer in the postpandemic era, some trends are evolving. The McKinsey Global Institute highlights that COVID-19 accelerated: remote work (20 to 25 percent of workers in advanced economies could work remotely three plus days a week on a long-term basis), digitalization (growth in e-commerce, as a surge in digital platforms is underway), and automation (e.g., an uptick in robotics use, process automation, and AI).[132]

In addition, WFH and WFA models are expected to continue after the pandemic because these models are a cost saving for companies—although some tasks are more effective in person. Therefore, the workplace will include three types of employees (primarily WFO, blended/hybrid, and remote [WFH/WFA]). Office developers should focus on creating a "human-centric" destination/experience for their building occupants to draw them to WFO by offering tenants amenities that enhance socialization, team building, (physical and mental) well-being, and problem solving. Even though building codes are in some cases comparable to

sustainability certifications, embracing the overall ESG strategies will further enhance occupant experience and therefore build desirability. Developing specialized hubs and adopting technological infrastructure innovations, which could facilitate mixed-reality capabilities (e.g., Microsoft Mesh), could attract technology tenants and investors even at the remote areas to which they relocated during the pandemic. Many of those that relocated continue to WFH/WFA and companies postpandemic will need to provide remote office capabilities to avoid losing them during the great resignation shift, which is continuing. This environment provides unique opportunities for developers to create marketable hubs even in remote areas. Rents are dependent on location and on tenants willing to pay a premium for it. However, the right location can help attract and retain key employees. In prime locations, office space can generate higher land values than any other use.

This chapter concludes with three cases studies. The first, Fremont Crossing, includes a site with a historic building requiring restoration in addition to a newly constructed building. The second, 8th + Olive, details the acquisition, upgrade/repositioning, and disposition of a property. The third case study, the Commons at Ballard, is a mixed-use, LEED Platinum certified property that participates in the Multifamily Tax Exemption (MFTE) program.

NOTES

1. Cathy Hackl, "Combining Spatial Computing & IoT Can Unleash Data's Full Potential," *Forbes*, August 2, 2020.
2. Maria Sicola, *Commercial Real Estate Terms and Definitions* (Herndon, VA: NAIOP Research Foundation, 2017).
3. Ibid.
4. Ibid.
5. Ibid.
6. Flore Pradère and Marie Puybaraud, *Shaping Human Experience: A Focus on Hybrid Work and Four Emerging Worker Profiles*, JLL Research Report, February 21, 2021.
7. Cathy Stephenson, senior vice president, national director of operations, Grubb & Ellis, Chicago, Illinois, interview by author, summer 2009.
8. Ashutosh Gupta, "What Is the Metaverse?", Garner, January 28, 2022. According to Gupta, the Metaverse "is a collective virtual space, created by the convergence of virtually enhanced physical and digital reality." It includes diverse technology capabilities, internet of things, 5G, artificial intelligence, spatial technologies, and virtual economy (digital currencies and non-fungible tokens).
9. Robert R. Koonin, Jamy Klotzbach, Kinnon McDonald, and Karoline Nunez, "Real Estate in the Metaverse: What Is Digital Real Estate? Why Does It Matter?" *National Law Review* XII, no. 122 (May 2022).
10. Ibid.
11. Ibid.
12. Bill Pollard, founding principal, Talon Private Capital, interview with author, January 2022.

13. PwC and Urban Land Institute, *Emerging Trends in Real Estate: United States and Canada 2022* (Washington, DC: PwC and Urban Land Institute, 2021).

14. ARUP, "Future of Offices in a Post-pandemic World," 2020, https://www.arup.com/perspectives/publications/research/section/future-of-offices-in-a-post-pandemic-world.

15. Tim Kay and Jessica Urbin, "How Will Employee Workspace Needs Change Post-Coronavirus? Determining the Right Number of Employees to Welcome Back at a Time," *Views*, JLL, June 19, 2020.

16. Konrad Putzier and Peter Grant, "Record High Office Lease Expirations Pose New Threat to Landlords and Banks," *Wall Street Journal*, April 12, 2022.

17. Ibid.

18. Jeff Jochums, executive vice president, CBRE, interview with author, January 2022.

19. PwC and Urban Land Institute, *Emerging Trends in Real Estate*.

20. Darrel Fullbright, Duncan Lyons, and Jim Stanislaski, "The Morphable Office: Envisioning the Future of the Office through an ESG Lens," Gensler Research & Insight, October 29, 2022; Ben Tranel and Darrel Fullbright, "The New Shape of Building Design," *Dialogue*, issue 34, 2022.

21. Murphy McCullough, executive vice president, Skanska USA, interview with author, January 2022.

22. Sakriti Vishwakarma, transaction and strategy analyst, CBRE, interview with author, January 2022.

23. UN Environment Programme, *2020 Global Status Report for Buildings and Construction: Towards a Zeroemission, Efficient and Resilient Buildings and Construction Sector* (Nairobi: UN Environment Programme, 2021).

24. McCullough, interview; Gregg Johnson, CEO, Wright Runstad & Company, interview with author, January 2022; Laura Ford, senior vice president, CBRE, interview with author, January 2022.

25. Lisa Stewart, managing director, JLL, interview with author, January 2022.

26. Johnson, interview.

27. Johnson, interview; and interview with Chris Hellstern, AIA, LFA, associate, Living Building Challenge Services Director, Miller Hull, January 2022; and interview with David Yuan, AIA, LEED AP, partner, NBBJ, January 2022.

28. Pollard, interview.

29. EPA, "What Is a MERV Rating?" revised July 1, 2022, https://www.epa.gov/indoor-air-quality-iaq/what-merv-rating.

30. UN Environment Programme, *2020 Global Status Report for Buildings and Construction*.

31. Hellstern, interview.

32. Pollard, interview; Vishwakarma, interview.

33. Pollard, interview; McCullough, interview; Johnson, interview; Yuan, interview.

34. Hellstern, interview; Yuan, interview.

35. Hellstern, interview.

36. Hellstern, interview; Yuan, interview.

37. Yuan, interview.

38. Rebecca Esau, Matt Jungclaus, Victor Olgyay, and Audrey Rempher, *Reducing Embodied Carbon in Buildings: Low-Cost, High-Value Opportunities,* RMI, 2021.

39. Esau, Jungclaus, Olgyay, and Rempher, *Reducing Embodied Carbon in Buildings: Low-Cost, High-Value Opportunities*.

40. Pollard, interview.

41. Hellstern, interview.

42. Pollard, interview.

43. Julianna Plant, senior project manager, Lase Crutcher Lewis, interview with author, January 2022.

44. Pollard, interview; McCullough, interview; Yuan, interview.

45. Think Wood Research, "Mass Timber Stands Tall: Rigorous Testing Drives 2021 Tall Wood Building Code Changes," Research Brief, August 2020.

46. Pollard, interview.

47. Pollard, interview; Johnson, interview; Ford, interview; Stewart, interview; Tranel and Fullbright, "The New Shape of Building Design."

48. Purdue Global University, "Generational Differences in the Workplace," https://www.purdueglobal.edu/education-partnerships/generational-workforce-differences-infographic/.

49. Gensler Research Institute, U.S. Workplace Survey Summer 2021 Report.

50. Kim Parker, Juliana Menasce Horowitz, and Rachel Minkin, *Covid-19 Pandemic Continues to Reshape Work in America* (Washington, DC: Pew Research Center, 2022).

51. Despina Katsikakis, David Smith, Nicola Gillen, Antonia Cardone, Carol Wong, Bryan Berthold, Taylor Van Dam, and Rachel Casanova, *Office of the Future Revisited + Three New Realities Shaping Hybrid Workplace Strategies* (Atlanta and London: Cushman & Wakefield, 2022).

52. PwC and Urban Land Institute, *Emerging Trends in Real Estate*.

53. Ann Kellett, "The Texas A&M Professor Who Predicted 'the Great Resignation,'" *Texas A&M Today*, February 11, 2022.

54. Ian Cook, "Who Is Driving the Great Resignation?" *Harvard Business Review*, September 15, 2021.

55. Kim Parker and Juliana Horowitz, "Majority of Workers Who Quit a Job in 2021 Cite Low Pay, No Opportunities for Advancement, Feeling Disrespected," Pew Research Center, March 9, 2022.

56. Jennie Overton, "The Great Resignation Update: Limeade Employee Care Report," Limeade, 2021, https://www.limeade.com/resources/resource-center/limeade-employee-care-report-the-great-resignation-update/.

57. Ryan Bryant, "Want to Slow the Great Resignation? Try Empathy," CBRE, February 18, 2022.

58. Jared Spataro, "Hybrid Work Is Here. Are You Ready?" *Microsoft 365*, March 2, 2021; Microsoft, *2021 Work Trend Index: Annual Report: The Next Great Disruption Is Hybrid Work—Are We Ready?* March 22, 2021; Microsoft WorkLab, "Great Expectations: Making Hybrid Work," Work Trends Index 2022, March 16, 2022.

59. Despina Katsikakis, David Smith, Rebecca Rockey, Michael Rodriguez, Christopher Leinberger, and David Bitner, "Workplace Ecosystems of the Future," Cushman & Wakefield and George Washington University Center for Real Estate and Urban Analysis, 2020.

60. Despina Katsikakis, Antonia Cardone, and Rachel Casanova, *Leading an Active Recovery to Build the Best Workplace Experience*, Cushman & Wakefield, June 10, 2021.

61. Todd Bishop, "How Zillow's Flexible Work Strategy Is Going, Nearly Two Years Later," *Geek Wire*, February 23, 2022, https://www.geekwire.com/2022/how-zillows-flexible-work-strategy-is-going-nearly-two-years-later/.

62. PwC and Urban Land Institute, *Emerging Trends in Real Estate*.

63. "Accommodating a Liquid Workforce – How to Create the Right Workspace for the Blend of Freelance and Full-time Employees," *Views*, JLL, 2022; Kevin Thorpe, David Hutchings, and Despina Katsikakis, "Global Recovery Journey," Cushman & Wakefield, June 28, 2021; Despina Katsikakis, David Smith, Michael Rodriguez, and Christopher Leinberger, "Purpose of Place History and Future of the Office," Cushman & Wakefield and George Washington University Center for Real Estate and Urban Analysis, 2020.

64. Katsikakis et al., *Office of the Future Revisited + Three New Realities Shaping Hybrid Workplace Strategies*.

65. McCullough, interview.

66. Yuan, interview.

67. Jose Maria Barrero, Nicholas Bloom, and Steven J. Davis, "Why Companies Aren't Cutting Back on Office Space," *Harvard Business Review*, January 25, 2022.

68. CBRE, *The Next Normal – How Hybrid Work Is Transforming Commercial Real Estate Report*, August 16, 2021.

69. Julie Whelan, Karen Ellzey, Lenny Beaudoin, Christelle Bron, Travis Deese, Brennan McReynolds, and Mike Nelson, "Real Estate Strategy Reset - 8 Core Truths Guiding the Future of Work," CBRE, 2021; Brodie Boland, Aaron De Smet, Rob Palter, and Aditya Sanghvi, "Reimagining the Office and Work Life after COVID-19," McKinsey & Company, June 2020; Steve Todd, "Five Types of Hybrid Work Models (And How to Implement)," Open Sourced Workplace, 2022; JLL/Technologies, *The 2022 Corporate Real Estate Guide to a Better Hybrid Workplace*, February 24, 2022.

70. McCullough, interview.

71. Hellstern, interview.

72. Gensler Research Institute, U.S. Workplace Survey Winter 2021.

73. Hellerstern, interview.

74. JLL/Technologies, *The 2022 Corporate Real Estate Guide to a Better Hybrid Workplace*.

75. Katsikakis et al., *Office of the Future Revisited + Three New Realities Shaping Hybrid Workplace Strategies*.

76. Rakshit Ghura, "Why Do Businesses Need to Transition to a Human-Centered Workplace?" *Next-Gen Enterprise*, HCL, October 22, 2021; Cushman & Wakefield, *CATCH'22 Asia Pacific Commercial Real Estate Outlook 2022*, Cushman & Wakefield, December 2, 2021.

77. Kellen Browning, "Big Tech Makes a Big Bet: Offices Are Still the Future," *New York Times*, February 22, 2022; Flore Pradere and Marie Puybaraud, "Shaping Human Experience – A Focus on Hybrid Work and Four Emerging Worker Profiles," JLL, Global Research, February 21, 2022.

78. Holly Dutton, "Amid Office Changes, Workplace Strategies Are Evolving," Commercial Property Executive, October 27, 2020.

79. CBRE, *The Next Normal – How Hybrid Work Is Transforming Commercial Real Estate Report*.

80. Vishwakarma, interview.

81. Pollard, interview; Vishwakarma, interview; Johnson, interview; Ford, interview; Jochums, interview; and Hellstern, interview.

82. Vishwakarma, interview.

83. Siemens, "How Smart Office Technology Supports Hybrid Work," 2022 (https://new.siemens.com/us/en/markets/cre/smart-office.html).

84. Vishwakarma, interview; Johnson, interview.

85. McCullough interview; Vishwakarma, interview.

86. Plant, interview.

87. Andrew Phipps, "What Are Smart Buildings?", Cushman & Wakefield, September 2, 2022.

88. Pollard, interview.

89. PwC and Urban Land Institute, *Emerging Trends in Real Estate*.

90. Ford, interview.

91. Bert Van Hoof, "Data-Driven Workspaces IoT and AI Expand the Promise of Smart Buildings," Harvard Business Review Analytic Services, 2018.

92. Plant, interview.

93. Jochums, interview; McCullough, interview; and Johnson, interview.

94. Johnson, interview.

95. Hellstern, interview.

96. Rakshit Ghura, "Watch Out for These Five Technologies Transforming the Workplace," *Next-Gen Enterprise*, HCL, October 22, 2021; Kevin Mcgee and Anuj Tewari, *Preparing for the New Era of Work: The Fluid Workplace*, HCL, 2020.

97. Yuan, interview.

98. Qian Wen and Jim Walker, "Microsoft Mesh (Preview)," Microsoft, March 22, 2022.

99. Vishwakarma, interview.

100. Kay and Urbin, "How Will Employee Workspace Needs Change Post-Coronavirus?

101. Jochums, interview; Johnson, interview.

102. Jon DeVries, director, Strategic Development Planning, URS Corporation, Chicago, interview with author, 2010.

103. Jared Foster, "What Is Shadow Space and What Does It Indicate," Colliers, November 30, 2020.

104. David Smith, Brian Ungles, and Sandy Romero, *Office Tenant Improvement Cost Guide North America*, Cushman & Wakefield, 2021.

105. Interview with Gabe Reisner, president and CEO, WMA Consulting Engineers, Chicago, Illinois, summer 2010.

106. Christopher Kurz, president and CEO, Linden Associates, correspondence with author, August 3, 2022.

107. David M. Geltner, Norman G. Miller, Jim Clayton, and Piet Eichholtz, *Commercial Real Estate: Analysis and Investment*, 3rd ed. (MBition, 2014).

108. Charles Long, *Finance for Real Estate Development* (Washington, DC: Urban Land Institute, 2011).

109. Jeff Gerardi, "Office Building Construction Costs Per Square Foot," ProEst, February 22, 2021.

110. Avi Lothan, principal, DeStafano Partners, Chicago, interview with author, 2010; and David Eckmann, principal, Magnusson Klemencic Associates, Chicago, interview with author, 2010.

111. Paul Katz, "The Office Building Type: A Pragmatic Approach," in *Building Type Basics for Office Buildings*, by A. Eugene Kohn and Paul Katz (New York: John Wiley, 2002).

112. Gabe Reisner, president and CEO, WMA Consulting Engineers, Chicago, interview with author, summer 2010.

113. Avi Lothan, interview; and Michael Sullivan, principal, Cannon Design, Chicago, interview with author, 2010.

114. Katz, "The Office Building Type."

115. Ibid.

116. Ibid.

117. John Thomas, Ware Malcomb Architects, Irvine, California, interview with author, 2010.

118. Fixr, "How Much Does It Cost to Build a Parking Garage?" fixr.com, updated February 28, 2022.

119. Sullivan, interview.

120. Eckmann, interview.

121. John Van Deusen, "Vertical Transportation," in *Building Type Basics for Office Buildings*, by A. Eugene Kohn and Paul Katz (New York: John Wiley, 2002).

122. Lew Harriman, Geoff Brundrett, and Reinhold Kittler, *Humidity Control Design Guide for Commercial and Institutional Buildings* (Atlanta, GA: American Society of Heating, Refrigerating and Air-Conditioning Engineers, 2001).

123. David V. Thompson and Bill McCarthy, "Security Master Planning," in *Building Security Handbook for Architectural Planning and Design*, by Barbara A. Nadel (New York: McGraw-Hill, 2004), 2.1-2.30.

124. Carlos Villarreal, senior vice president, Whelan Security, Chicago, Illinois, interview with author, 2010.

125. Smith, Ungles, and Romero, *Office Tenant Improvement Cost Guide North America*.

126. Jochums, interview.

127. Johnson, interview.

128. Interviews with Bill Rolander, the John Buck Company, Chicago, 2009; Dennis Harder, Joseph Freed & Associates, Chicago, 2009; and Rafael Carreira, the John Buck Company, Chicago, 2009.

129. Greg Van Schaak, Hines, Chicago, interview with author, 2009; Carreira, interview; Eric Sorensen, the John Buck Company, Chicago, interview with author, 2009; Rolander, interview; Harder, interview; and Anthony Frink, partner, Holland & Knight, Chicago, interview with author, 2010.

130. Karen Krackov, executive managing director-GEMS, Grubb & Ellis, Chicago, interview with author, 2009.

131. ARUP, "Future of Offices in a Post-pandemic World."

132. McKinsey Global Institute, *The Postpandemic Economy: The Future of Work after COVID-19*, February 2021.

Fremont Crossing is an open-air "micro-hub" campus.[1] It includes (1) the restoration and adaptive office use of the Bleitz Funeral Home, which was designated a historic Seattle landmark; and (2) the development of a new four-story office building adjacent to the historic structure, connecting both with one of two open-air courtyards. The project's developer, Pastakia + Associates, is a women-owned/led firm focusing on historic preservation and mixed-use urban infill. The firm's managing principal, Tajal Pastakia, is originally from Mumbai, India, and established the firm in 2007.

Fremont Crossing is located at 310/316 Florentia Street in Seattle, four miles north of downtown, at the southeast corner of Seattle's Fremont bridge, overlooking the ship canal, and near Queen Anne Hill. Downtown Fremont is across the bridge. The general area has attracted many tech firms (e.g., Google, Adobe, Tableau) and life science companies (e.g., Lumen Biosciences) as it features protected bike paths and walkways on both sides of the canal, walkability to Seattle's Gas Works Public Park, and proximity to mass transit and the University of Washington.

BACKGROUND AND SITE

Fremont Crossing includes the Bleitz Funeral Home, which is a Seattle historical landmark registered under Ordinance No.126017 and Chapter 25.12 of the Seattle Municipal Code. The Bleitz Funeral Home was nominated for improvements, and those improvements were approved by the Landmarks Preservation Board on March 1, 2017; the landmark designation was then approved on April 19, 2017. In mid-July 2019, the board and owner agreed on features and characteristics of the designated landmark, which included the site and exterior (except for 1989 and 1991 additions); the city council's decision was filed in mid-December 2019.

The Bleitz Funeral Home is a rectangular-shaped, stucco-clad, concrete- and wood-frame structure with Tudor and Spanish Revival elements. Cross-gable dormers open into the attic. The entry portico has a slightly pointed arch, and the main entrance is in the south-facing two-story anteroom section; the anteroom has a one-story Tudor-style arched porch.[2] The historic home is located on the southeast corner of a 27,720-square-foot (2,575 sq m) lot containing five rectangular lots. Originally built for $16,492 in 1921, the structure's footprint was 38 feet by 80 feet (11.5 m by 24.4 m), with shorter dimensions south and north. In 1962, a three-car garage was added, and in 1988–1991, a 5,000-square-foot (464.5 sq m) single-story expansion was built along the west side of the structure. In 1993 a basement and a first-floor addition were constructed, and in 2014 the first and second floors were renovated.

The property was owned through 1990 by the Bleitz Funeral Home Inc., then sold to University Corp for $1.36 million. In 2016, Warm Springs Investors LLC bought it for $4.2 million. Pastakia + Associates (under Fremont Crossing LLC), in partnership with Pacific Capital Investments and BNBuilders, acquired the property in November 2018 from Warm Spring Investors for $8 million.

FREMONTCROSSINGSEATTLE.COM

Panoramic view of Fremont Crossing in Seattle, Washington.

Tajal Pastakia's interest and expertise in historic preservation and infill development were key drivers for the acquisition and the design of the new office building, which celebrates the area's maritime history along the Lake Washington Ship Canal, while wrapping around the historic Bleitz Funeral Home through a curved, street-level courtyard with wonderful views of the area.

APPROVALS

When the Bleitz Funeral Home received landmark status in 2017, the previous zoning (C2, commercial) was maintained; in 2019 the height restriction was increased from 40 feet (12 m) to 55 feet (16.7 m) under C2-55. Warm Springs Investors acquired the site without entitlements and sold it for a premium to Fremont Crossing LLC, with entitlements for a new office development and adaptive use of the Bleitz Funeral Home. In addition to including a historic landmark, the site is partially designated as a shoreline habitat zone and archeological buffer area. There is also a 40 percent slope (steep slope area), requiring confined development, although the historic building stands in a flat area with just a gradual slope, approximately five feet down from south to north. As it is also in a Frequent Transit Zone, reduced parking was allowed.

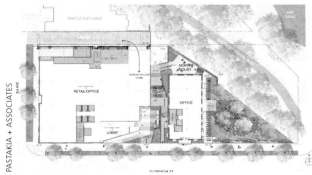

PASTAKIA + ASSOCIATES

Site plan for Fremont Crossing.

Buildings at Fremont Crossing, including the historic Bleitz Funeral Home and new structure.

Fremont Crossing LLC restored the exterior of the Bleitz Funeral Home (which is unreinforced brick), retrofitted the interior to cater to class A office tenants, repaired the windows, and restored the stain glass door. The triangular shape of the southern corner of the site was left open rather than fenced, creating an urban public courtyard. The facade of the newly constructed four-story office building on the northwest portion of the site captures the light-industrial and maritime character of the area along the ship canal. The structural grid is balanced with floor-to-ceiling windows offering unobstructed views of the Fremont Bridge, Lake Union, and the Gas Works Public Park.

The second and third floors of the new building feature a glazed prow—"the treehouse." Its floor-to-ceiling windows on the north side serve as a visual connection between the new and the historic buildings, and the extension over a courtyard provides covered outdoor space on the first floor.

DESIGN AND CONSTRUCTION

Construction on Fremont Crossing began in spring 2019 and was completed in 2020. The class A office space has just over 58,521 rentable square feet (RSF) (5,667 sq m) and close to 12,000 square feet (1,114.8 sq m) of courtyard and rooftop deck social gathering spaces (figure A). The new building additionally includes 34 underground secure parking stalls, storage area for 34 bikes, and showers/locker rooms. Even though the project was completed

before the COVID-19 pandemic began, it includes multiple features that promote social distancing and support safe return to offices:

- The new four-story structure benefits from two internal stairs, which could be programmed as one-way up and the other-way down, promoting less elevator use.
- The floor plates are transformable/fluid, allowing for social distancing and a variety of configurations.
- Multiple, small-amenity spaces and outdoor areas minimize bottlenecks in amenity use.
- HVAC protocols provide fresh air flushing every 1.25 hours, and the windows in the Bleitz Funeral Home are operable.
- The site provides immediate access to the canal trail and is across the bridge from the Burke Gilman Trail.

FIGURE A Office Rentable Square Foot Distribution

Floor	New Building (rentable sq ft)	Bleitz Funeral Home – Historic Adaptive Use (rentable sq ft)
1st	12,414	2,733
2nd	17,817	2,733
3rd	17,133	2,734
4th	2,957	
Total (sq ft)	**50,321**	**8,200**

Source: Pastakia + Associates.

277

MARKETING AND TENANTS

Fremont Crossing was a speculative development focused on attracting area tech tenants. However, the completion of construction just before the pandemic created significant leasing challenges. As part of the stabilized budget, reserve lease-up funds were allocated to give the developer some flexibility in a difficult leasing market. With office buildings slowly being reoccupied since March 2022, the developer is confident that the project's post-COVID-era features will attract more tenants. North Face, for example, has leased both office and showroom space at the Bleitz Funeral Home.

FIGURE B Project Cost Summary

	Total	Per square foot	% of total
Land Acquisition Costs	**$7,000,000**	**$120**	**17.05%**
Tenant Improvements	$6,144,705	$105	14.96%
Project Contingency	$751,115	$13	1.83%
Hard/Development Costs	**$27,113,981**	**$463**	**66.03%**
Architecture and Engineering	$1,256,000	$21	3.06%
Permits and Fees	$426,261	$7	1.04%
Land Use/Permit Consultants	$2,497,086	$7	6.08%
Leasing Commission and Costs	$998,792	$17	2.43%
Soft Costs	**$5,178,139**	**$88**	**12.61%**
Construction Loan Fees and Costs	$364,602	$6	0.89%
Construction Loan Interest	$1,405,433	$24	3.42%
Financing Costs	**$1,770,035**	**$30**	**4.31%**
Total	$41,062,155	$702	

FIGURE C Operation Pro Forma

	Square Feet	RSF/ Year	Total
Historic Building	8,200	$48	$393,600
New Building	50,321	$48	$2,415,408
Gross Rent	**$58,521**		**$2,809,008**
	Spots	Per sq ft	
Parking Revenue	34	$2	$117,000
Expense Reimbursement Revenue			$737,365
Additional Income	**Rate**		**$854,365**
Historic Building	3.0%		($11,808)
New Building	3.0%		($72,462)
Vacancy			**($84,270)**
Effective Gross Income (EGI)			**$3,579,103**
Expenses	**Per sq ft**		
Operating Expenses	$8.50		$497,429
Real Estate Taxes	$5.50		$321,866
Total Expenses			$819,295
Net Operating Income (NOI)			**$2,759,808**
Estimated Costs	$702		$41,081,742
Return on Costs			6.72%
Cap Rate	**3%**		**5%**
Valuation	$91,993,600		$55,196,160
Value per sq ft	$1,571.98		$943.19

FINANCING

HAL Real Estate and Pacifica Capital Investments are Pastakia + Associates capital partners on the project, and City National Bank provided construction financing. The construction loan was $25.6 million, with the total project cost reaching $41 million (**figures B, C, and D**).

FINANCIAL PROJECTIONS

The financial feasibility was developed using the simple capitalization approach as this was a speculative project. The development offers unique accessibility; it is almost adjacent to the expressway and close to the University of Washington, amenities, and tech companies. Even so, the pandemic created leasing challenges. The hope is those will be addressed soon, as employees are returning to their offices.

EXPERIENCE GAINED

The site offered unique opportunities and challenges for the project team. Opportunities included the showcasing and upgrading of a historic structure while bridging it with a new high-tech innovative structure. The retrofitting of a historic structure presented challenges as it needed to be brought up to code and upgraded to make this adaptive use competitive in the digital age. In addition, the new structure required a creative design that embraced the historic building. The developer/architect selected an L-shaped design, which allowed for a mini penthouse on the fourth floor and extra square footage in the treehouse on the second and third floors. Other challenges included the canal water intrusion to the site, which required mitigation, the need to adhere to the shoreline habitat zone, and the need for seismic proofing.

Sources: Tajal Pastakia, developer of Fremont Crossing; and public records. 1. The property was owned through 1990 by the Bleitz Funeral Home Inc. 2. BOLA Architecture + Planning, "Bleitz Funeral Home Landmark Nomination," City of Seattle Documents, January 4, 2016; and City of Seattle—Historical Sites, "Summary for 316 Florentia ST/Parcel ID 197320-0006/Inv # QA004," 2019.

FIGURE D Project Data Overview

Project Data	New	Historic
Developer	Fremont Crossing/Pastakia + Associates	
Architect	SKB Architects	
Contractor	Foushee	
Site Area	0.64 acres (27,720 sq ft)	
Gross Building Area (sq ft)	59,293	8,643
Gross Leasable Area (sq ft)	50,321	8,200
Parking	34 spaces	None
Building Height (ft)	54	22
Construction Cost	$17,374,635	
Total Development Cost	**$41,062,155**	

This case study describes an acquisition/repositioning/disposition case rather than new construction. Nonetheless, it offers useful strategies for using capital investments to elevate a property's profile in a short period of time at the appropriate market timing.

8th + Olive is a 20-story, class A, multitenant office building at 720 Olive Way, in the Denny Triangle neighborhood at the north edge of Seattle's central business district. Talon Private Capital purchased the property under 720 Olive Way Venture LLC in April 2014 for $335.90 per square foot for repositioning. Talon sold the property in November 2017 for $618.40 per square foot.

BACKGROUND

The property was built in 1981 with a rentable area of 300,710 square feet (27,937 sq m) and a 0.7/1,000-square-foot (93 sq m) parking ratio. It features a contemporary brick facade; expansive window line with views of South Lake Union, downtown, and Elliot Bay; and several on-site amenities. At the time of acquisition, it was 84 percent leased but lacked significant upgrades; tenants were paying below-market rents as a "value rate" option for downtown office space. Notable upsides included

- efficient floor plates;
- on-site parking;
- unparalleled amenity base;
- first-rate design and construction;
- excellent access to transportation (two blocks from Westlake light rail station and direct access to I5 expressway); and
- major expansion among high-valued tenants in the area.

In 2013, Seattle-based companies such as Amazon, Boeing, and the Gates Foundation were expanding aggressively in the area. The property was literally well positioned where the city's financial services combined with the largest concentrations of technology and life science companies. Talon saw the opportunity to leverage the property's premier location by making significant upgrades to the building to compete with the area's high-quality class A buildings.

REPOSITIONING PLAN

Talon's plan included dramatic upgrades to the lobby, common areas, and tenant spaces; the addition of state-of-the-art conference and workout facilities; and a rebranding of the building as a modern, creative hub that caters to small and medium-sized technology tenants. These upgrades, as well as positive market conditions and proximity to Amazon in an area with strong demand (93 percent occupancy within a three-block area), led Talon to believe occupancy would increase. Talon made the following specific capital investments:

Interior of 8th + Olive.

TALON PRIVATE CAPITAL

Interior of 8th + Olive.

- **Lobby**—The space was fully remodeled, creating a dramatic two-story glass entrance, bringing a modern finish to the space, and adding casual meeting space valued by tenants.
- **Elevator Lobbies and Restrooms**—Selective upgrades were made, focusing on floors where Talon could monetize the investment through leasing vacant or expiring space.
- **Tenant Spaces**—Investments were made in vacant space, updating ceiling and lighting and creating open work areas valued by tenants.
- **Amenities**—New additions included a state-of-the-art fitness center and conference space, which were increasingly becoming the standard in leading buildings in the Seattle market.
- **Building Infrastructure**—Though not immediately noticeable, investments were made in "back-of-house" building infrastruc-

ture, including modernization of the elevator system to promote the image of a modern building suitable for dynamic tenants.
- **Reserve Capital for Tenant Improvements (TIs)**—Top market tenants would receive additional TIs.

Talon had repositioned a building a block away (1800 Ninth street) with a similar strategy, and that experience provided valuable market and construction insights. However, the primary risk was the effective transformation of the building, and achieving higher rents and occupancy would be key for this repositioning.

FINANCING

The property was acquired in 2014 for $101 million with debt by Eastdil Secured. A loan for $63.5 million (64 percent loan-to-value ratio) with a floating rate was provided by Wells Fargo, providing

---

FIGURE A Acquisition/Disposition Overview

Summary – Acquisition	Pro Forma (estimate)	Actual
Purchase Price	$101,000,000	$101,000,000
Capital Investment	$44,200,000	$44,200,000
Loan Amount	$64,500,000	$63,500,000
Debt Cost	2.40%	2.40%
Net Operating Income, Yr. 1 (NOIy1)	$5,388,711	$5,567,571

Summary – Disposition	Pro Forma (estimate)	Actual
Sales Price	$135,253,000	$186,000,000
Price per sq ft	$450/sq ft	$619/sq ft
Exit Cap Rate	5.50%	4.91%
Length of Hold (years)	3	3
Project Level Internal Rate of Return (IRR)	15.50%	26.70%
Investor Equity Multiple	1.54x	2.02x

FIGURE B Experience Gained

	Acquisition Assumptions	Reality
WHAT WE MISSED		
Building Capital Improvements	$6 million	$11.5 million
Tenant Improvements	$11 million	$17 million
Market Rental Rate	$37.50/sq ft	$43.50/sq ft
Leasing Strategy	Small/med-sized tenants	Large tenants
Exit Price (per sq ft)	$450/sq ft	$575/sq ft
Exit Cap Rate	5.50%	4.50%
WHAT WE GOT RIGHT		
Location	B to A location	Validated assumption
Retail as an Amenity	Important	Critical
Renovation Design	Atrium opportunity; lobby orientation	Airbnb in atrium; thriving lobby

an opportunity to draw additional funds for capital improvements. The equity was a joint venture made up of 80 percent Prudential and 20 percent Talon's private investment partners. The repositioning required significant coordination to properly deploy the capital while marketing outreach was underway to identify new, interesting tenants who matched the upgraded building profile. After modernizing the lobby, the owners were able to attract a new restaurant on the ground floor, and three leading tech tenants (Avvo, Coupang, and Airbnb) signed leases. Talon decided to sell when the building reached 96 percent occupancy. The final sale price of $186 million, or $619 per square foot, well exceeded the pro forma and set the new standard for repositioned office assets in downtown Seattle (figures A and C).

EXPERIENCE GAINED

The first lesson was how critical activating a building's lobby is. The creation of a truly stimulating and energetic lobby allowed Talon to charge higher rents in the building and attract better quality tenants than comparable properties. Even though more money was spent on the restaurant space, those losses were made up through higher office rents. However, a harsh reality for this project as well as others is how long construction takes and how much it costs. Talon budgeted $6 million for building capital improvements, however, it spent $11.5 million, and the project took several months longer than anticipated (figure B). Lastly, hiring an effective and efficient leasing team is pivotal to the project's success.

FIGURE C Discounted Cash Flow Analysis during Holding Period

Year Ending:	Year $/sq ft – Yr 1	June 2015 Year 1	June 2016 Year 2	June 2017 Year 3
Base Rents	$30.27	$9,102	$9,659	$10,426
Abatements	($0.41)	(124)	(548)	(1,861)
Recoveries	$1.91	575	464	341
Other Income	$2.13	640	710	771
Absorption/Turnover	($4.81)	(1,445)	(2,265)	(231)
General Vacancy	$0.00	0	0	(242)
Effective Revenue	$29.09	$8,748	$8,020	$9,204
Operating Expenses	($11.44)	($3,439)	($3,568)	($3,823)
Net Operating Income (NOI)	$17.65	$5,308	$4,452	$5,381
TOTAL CAPITAL AND FEES	($35.09)	($10,552)	($3,224)	($4,091)
NET CASH FLOW (NCF)	($17.44)	($5,243)	$1,227	$1,290
Interest Payments	($3.80)	(1,143)	(1,143)	(1,143)
Principal Payments	$0.00	0	0	0
Loan Draws	$0.00	0	0	0
Equity Capital Holdback	$21.62	6,500	0	0
Proceeds from Refinance	$0.00	0	0	0
Total Debt Service	$17.81	$5,357	($1,143)	($1,143)
Coverage Ratio (NOI)		(0.99)	3.89	4.71
Coverage Ratio (NCF)		0.98	1.07	1.13
Total Distributable Cash Flow	$0.38	$114	$84	$147
Return on Equity (ROE)		0.3%	0.2%	0.3%

HOLDING PERIOD SENSITIVITY			
	Year 1	Year 2	Year 3
Unleveraged IRR	-32.3%	-8.1%	5.5%
Leveraged IRR	-67.3%	-16.9%	13.8%
Residual Sale Price (5.50% Resid. Cap Rate)	$80,942	$97,840	$134,230
Residual Sale Price per sq ft	$269	$325	$446
In Today's Dollars per sq ft Discounted at: 3%		$306.69	$408.50
Effective Annual Appreciation		-5.1%	7.3%
Equity Multiple		0.69	1.47

CAPITALIZATION (ALL-IN)		
	Total (000)s	Per sq ft
Loan	$63,500	$211.17
Equity Before Fees	$45,153	$150.16
Equity Including Fees	$45,153	$150.16
Acquisition Cost	$108,653	$361.32
Purchase Price	$101,000	$335.87
Acquisition Fee	$0	$0.00
Closing Costs	$1,153	$3.84
Capital Reserves	$6,500	$21.62
All-in Cost	$108,653	$361.32

Source: Bill Pollard, founding principal, Talon Private Capital.
Note: IRR = internal rate of return.

The Commons at Ballard is a mixed-use campus/hub with two—connected—buildings, one five-stories and the other six-stories. The complex has 80 apartments, four two-bedroom townhouses, a two-story office space (21,794 square feet or 2,025 sq m) and retail space (19,076 square feet or 1,772 sq m).[1] The design was based on the "commitment to contemporary high-end design, environmental stewardship, and community building through shared spaces."[2] The project has a LEED BD+C: Core and Shell Platinum certification (under v2009) from the U.S. Green Building Council (USGBC) and was the first multifamily project in Seattle to achieve the designation under this version of LEED.

The Commons is located at 5621 22nd Ave NW in Seattle, six miles north of downtown, across from the Ballard Commons Park and the Ballard Branch of the Seattle Public Library. The project opened in December 2016, in an area which has seen significant development growth in recent years. In 2017, the development received the Mixed-Use Development of the Year award by NAIOP and the Multi Family Executive Green Building of the Year award, recognizing the value of truly integrating the live/work/play elements in one site. Additionally, the project received the 2018 Associated General Contractors of Washington award for private buildings in the $20–$50 million category.

BACKGROUND AND SITE

The development is in the civic core of Ballard, at the corner of 57th St NW and 22nd Ave NW, across from the Ballard Commons Park. Due to the location and the mixed-use property type, the developer needed to adhere to the following design guidelines: (1) storefronts on the north and east side of the lot should be active; (2) a consistent two-story wall is required above the north-face of the lot; (3) a set back above the two-story-wall is required, to improve sun exposure/park view; (4) entrances and private open spaces with visual and physical or visual connections to the park are also required; and (5) landscaping should be well integrated.[3]

Several site improvements were needed: for example, the overhead power and communication lines were moved underground, and low-impact stormwater infrastructure and a rainwater harvesting system were installed, as the project was pursuing the highest level of LEED certification.[4] In addition, the rights-of-way were improved with the installation of new curbs, sidewalks, and bioretention planters for stormwater treatment. The work also involved narrowing the streets and ensuring the landscaping was complementary to and aligned with the surroundings.

Because it was a corner lot (30,000 square feet or 2,787 sq m), the developer—Henbart LLC—tried to capture the area's character by building two structures connected with a podium, to create a smaller but an integrated community. This design improved connectivity among the uses, with multiple shared amenities among the residential and commercial tenants, while also allowing for the differentiation of structural systems.

The property was owned by the Katherine C. Vaught Trust, which had held it since 1996. The trustees sold the property to 5601 22nd LLC, owned by Henbart LLC, for $3.4 million in 2011.

DESIGN AND CONSTRUCTION

When acquired by 5601 22nd LLC, the lot had a one-story building and a surface parking lot, which were demolished in 2015. The new construction was completed in 2016, with both towers built of concrete and wood. The exterior facade is a mixture of wood-patterned aluminum, which balanced aesthetics, durability, and life-cycle cost.[5] The unique design has a central lobby and allows complete acoustic separation between uses, while also introducing multiple shared spaces indoors and outdoors for social interaction among all building occupants.[6] The north tower is taller and required a separate structural system to accommodate a large retailer, the two flexible office floors, townhouses, apartments, and rooftop amenities.[7] The office space can serve a single or multiple tenants, with all the office space located in one of the towers.[8]

HENBART LLC

The Commons at Ballard in Seattle, Washington.

The Commons at Ballard has a unique design that considers tenants' needs and includes roof decks that incorporate sustainability features.

The apartments' slab-to-slab height is 10 feet (3 m), office height is 12 feet (3.7 m), and retail height is 20 feet (6 m).

The following are some other building characteristics offered:[9,10]

- 115 underground parking spots;
- air conditioning for all apartments (which is uncommon for the area);
- bike lockers for residents and office tenants on every floor, adjacent to the elevator;
- outdoor lounges at both towers, with the south tower including a galley kitchen and multiple roof decks, and the north tower including a 3,200-square-foot (297 sq m) sky lounge with kitchen, bar, banquette-style seating, and an outdoor space with a fire pit and grills;
- a cantilevered roof over the sky lounge, allowing for year-round use;
- an additional pet area available for all building occupants; and
- a media room for private events.

The residential portion of the project includes five 425-square-foot (39 sq m) studios; 21 open one-bedroom and 26 one-bedroom units, ranging in size from 520 square feet to 700 square feet (48 sq m to 65 sq m); and 32 two-bedroom units (four of which are townhouses), ranging from 850 square feet (79 sq m) to 1,180 square feet (109.6 sq m).

SUSTAINABILITY DESIGNATION/FEATURES

USGBC awarded the Commons at Ballard the LEED BD+C: Core and Shell (v2009) Platinum certification in May 2017. Achieving Platinum certification requires at least 80 points. The points awarded to this project are outlined in figure A.

Several innovative sustainability features led to the Commons achieving the highest certification level:[11]

- high-efficiency windows, which optimize natural daylight throughout all units;
- reverse-cycle chiller to heat hot water;
- LED lighting and rooftop solar photovoltaic panels that reduce energy use 35 percent;
- low-flow plumbing fixtures that reduce water use 42 percent;
- restoration of 27 percent of the site with vegetation and water-saving native plants;
- rooftop bioretention and a rainwater harvesting system, which funnels rainwater into a 20,000-gallon cistern that supplies all landscaping irrigation;
- green roofs wherever possible;

FIGURE A LEED Platinum BD+C: Core and Shell (v2009) – Commons at Ballard

Credit Category	Awarded/Max Points
Sustainable Sites	22/28
Water Efficiency	8/10
Energy and Atmosphere	31/37
Material and Resources	5/13
Indoor Environmental Quality	6/12
Innovation	6/6
Regional Priority Credits	2/4
Total	**80/110**

Source: USGBC, The Commons at Ballard, 2017, https://www.usgbc.org/projects/commons-ballard?view=scorecard.

- electric vehicle charging stations and bicycle storage on each floor;
- Energy Star appliances;
- recycling and composting systems; and
- low-emitting materials and green cleaning products/practices for common areas.

MARKETING AND TENANTS

The Commons at Ballard opened in December 2016 with great success: the office space was fully leased, followed by retail at 85 percent and residential at 55 percent (due to the timing of opening at the end of the year).[12] In contrast to typical mid-rise structures, the developer in this case focused on high-quality finishes, appliances, and amenities. These include quartz counter-tops, Bosch stainless-steel appliances, ample in-unit storage space (including California closets), gas fireplaces for the two-bedroom units, maximized unit balconies, and illuminating bathroom mirrors.[13] Some of the smaller studios were also equipped with a Murphy bed with a desk. As the anchor retail tenant, Bartell Drugs received close to $3 million in tenant improvements. The anchor office tenant, Gravity Payments Inc., came in 2017 and occupies close to 11,000 square feet (1,022 sq m). The property also has four smaller tenants.

FINANCING

First Republic Bank loaned 5601 22nd LLC $33 million in March 2015; the total project cost was almost $47 million (figure B). As pre-leasing was required, the owner secured Bartell Drugs as an anchor tenant, which occupied 14,290 square feet (1,327.6 sq m) beginning in October 2014. Because the area has limited housing affordability options, 17 of the property's units are available under Seattle's Multifamily Tax Exemption (MFTE) program until 2028. The 17 units are five studios for households with 65 percent of area median income (AMI), five one-bedroom units (75 percent

FIGURE B Project Cost Summary

	Total	Per square foot	% of total
Land Acquisition Costs	**$3,400,000**	**$32.57**	**7.25%**
Tenant Improvements	$2,639,488	$25.29	5.63%
Project Contingency	$1,249,104	$11.97	2.66%
Hard/Development Costs	**$36,910,355**	**$353.63**	**78.73%**
Architecture and Engineering	$1,544,968	$14.80	3.30%
Permits and Fees	$586,488	$5.62	1.25%
Land Use/Permit Consultants	$260,638	$2.50	0.56%
Leasing Commission and Costs	$353,785	$3.39	0.75%
Soft Costs	**$4,927,873**	**$47.21**	**10.51%**
Construction Loan Fees and Costs	$420,168	$4.03	0.90%
Construction Loan Interest	$1,103,343	$10.57	2.35%
Financing Costs	**$1,641,262**	**$15.72**	**3.50%**
Total	**$46,879,490**	**$449.14**	

FIGURE C Project Data Overview

Project Data	Apartments	Office	Retail
Developer	5601 22nd LLC/Henbart LLC		
Architect	Studio Meng Strazzara		
Contractor	W.G. Clark Construction Co.		
Site Area	0.69 acres (30,000 sq ft)		
Gross Leasable Area (sq ft)	63,505	21,794	19,076
Parking	137 spaces		
Building Height (feet)	60		
Construction Cost	$33,216,453		
Total Development Cost	$46,879,490		

of AMI), and seven two-bedroom units (85 percent of AMI). In addition to improving the area's housing affordability, the MFTE program has made the property tax exempt since 2016 after the initial reduction of 17 percent (figures C and D).

FINANCIAL PROJECTIONS

The financial feasibility was developed using the simple capitalization approach. The project has been very successful from the beginning as it offered a unique product for the market. Although figure D shows a projected vacancy for office and retail space of 5 percent, it currently has none in those categories; the vacancy exists only for the housing portion of the project (5.9 percent).

EXPERIENCE GAINED

The Commons at Ballard offered unique opportunities and challenges for the project team. This was the first mixed-use, mid-rise, ultra-sustainable, integrated community with high-end finishes marketed in the area—at both market-rate and affordable-housing levels. The challenges came mainly at the beginning of construction, as utilities had to be moved underground and an easement had to be secured due to the proximity of the adjacent property. Another challenge was determining what unit-type mix was financially feasible as part of the MFTE program. The vision from the beginning was that one lobby for the residential and commercial uses would enhance the interaction among the building occupants, which has been very successful.

Sources: Mark Craig, president, Henbart LLC, developer of the Commons at Ballard; public records; and consultants' websites.

1. Mark Craig, president, Henbart LLC, developer of the Commons at Ballard, interview by author.

2. "Henbart LLC Opens the Commons at Ballard with Great Success," The Registry—Pacific Northwest Real Estate, December 20, 2016, https://news.theregistryps.com/henbart-llc-opens-commons-ballard-great-success/.

3. Seattle Office of Planning & Community Development, "Ballard Neighborhood Design Guidelines," 2019, https://www.seattle.gov/Documents/Departments/SDCI/About/BallardDG2019.pdf.

4. Blueline, "Projects: The Commons at Ballard," https://www.thebluelinegroup.com/projects/project-six/.

Type	Studio	1-Bed	2-Bed	Total Units	Square Feet	RSF/Year	Total	Total with MFTE
# Apartment Units	5	47	32	84	63,505	$33.03	2,097,834	$1,992,858
Office					21,794	$38.42	$837,221	$837,221
Retail					19,076	$46.24	$858,877	$858,877
Gross Rent (Residential and Commercial)					104,375		**$3,793,932**	**$3,688,956**
Additional Income					Spots or Units	Income/ Month		
Parking Revenue – Residential					74	$150.00	$133,200	$133,200
Parking Revenue – Commercial					41	$150.00	$73,800	$73,800
Utility Income					84	$65	$65,520	$65,520
Other (forfeited deposits, misc.)							$52,080	$52,080
Total Income							**4,118,532**	**$4,013,556**
Vacancy								
# Apartment Units	5.9%						($124,152)	($118,903)
Office/Retail	5%						($88,495)	($88,495)
EGI (Residential and Commercial)							**$3,905,885**	**$3,806,158**
Apartment Expenses	**$/Sq Ft**				Square Feet			
Real Estate Taxes	$4.48				63,505		$284,220	$48,973
Operating Expenses	$6.73						$427,105	$427,105
Total Apartment Operating Expenses							$711,325	$476,078
Office/Retail								
Operating Expenses	$8.25						$374,456	$374,456
Total Expenses (Residential and Commercial)							**$1,085,781**	**$850,534**
NOI-Residential							1,513,157	1,648,677
NOI-Commercial							1,306,947	1,306,947
Total NOI							**$2,820,104**	**$2,955,624**
Estimated Construction Costs						$449.14	$46,879,490	
Return on Costs							6.02%	

	Total		Total with MFTE	
Cap Rate – Apartments	7%	8%	7%	8%
Cap Rate – Office	3%	5%		
Valuation – Apartments	$23,279,338	$18,914,463	$25,364,262	$20,608,463
Valuation – Office	$43,564,900	$26,138,940		
Value per sq ft – Apartments	$366.57	$297.84	$399.41	$324.52
Value per sq ft – Office	$1,065.94	$639.56		

5. Studio Meng Strazzara, "Commons at Ballard Named Mixed-Use Development of the Year," November 22, 2017, https://studioms.com/news/2017/11/21/commons-at-ballard-named-mixed-use-development-of-the-year.

6. Archinect, "Firms, Studio Meng Strazzara: Commons at Ballard," https://archinect.com/studioms/project/commons-at-ballard.

7. Seattle Daily Journal of Commerce, "The Commons at Ballard," AGC 2018 Build Washington Awards, May 31, 2018, https://henbart.com/wp-content/uploads/2020/01/AGC-2018-Award_Private-Building.pdf.

8. NAIOP, "2017 Night of the Stars Nominations Gallery, Winner: The Commons at Ballard," https://naiop-wa.secure-platform.com/a/gallery/rounds/6/details/3296.

9. The Commons at Ballard, https://commonsatballard.com/.

10. Jenni Moreno, "The Commons at Ballard," Urban Ash, May 26, 2015, https://urbanash.com/blog/commons-at-ballard/.

11. W. G. Clark Construction Co., "The Commons, Seattle, WA," http://www.wgclark.com/work/multi-unit/the-commons/.

12. "Henbart LLC Opens the Commons at Ballard with Great Success," The Registry—Pacific Northwest Real Estate, December 20, 2016, https://news.theregistryps.com/henbart-llc-opens-commons-ballard-great-success/.

13. Robin Chell and Scott Surdyke, "Mid-Rise Apartments Go Upscale to Take on High-Rises," Seattle Daily Journal of Commerce, Real Estate Marketplace Northwest, February 23, 2017, https://henbart.com/wp-content/uploads/2018/06/djc-mid-rise-apts-go-upscale-to-take-on-high-rises.pdf.

6 Industrial Development

SUZANNE LANYI CHARLES

Industrial facilities are the backbone of commerce in the United States and around the world. They are the buildings that support the efficient and effective flow of goods and materials. They facilitate the fabrication, storage, and distribution of goods. The importance of industrial real estate is reflected in the growth and profitability of the industrial real estate asset class in recent years. The COVID-19 pandemic profoundly altered the industrial real estate landscape, which was further propelled by the forces of urbanization, digitalization, and demographic change. Consequently, exciting innovations are on the horizon that will affect the design and operation of industrial real estate and will offer opportunities for savvy real estate developers.

E-commerce has led to a rapidly increasing demand for development of fulfillment center, last-mile, and cold storage facilities, among others. Emerging technologies—such as advanced data analytics, automated storage and retrieval systems, and autonomous distribution—are altering how industrial facilities are used. Innovative new forms of industrial real estate, including urban infill and multistory facilities near population centers, are being developed in response to shifting consumer preferences. And as older industrial facilities become obsolete, some are gaining new life as office and light manufacturing spaces. Moreover, climate change and social inequality are ever more urgent concerns, and companies' environmental, social, and governance (ESG) programs include the development and operation of their industrial facilities. Those trends, which had evolved over several decades, accelerated during the COVID-19 pandemic and are likely to remain important going forward.

Beginning developers may start out by finding land on which to construct a facility or by locating an existing building to redevelop or reposition. A *build-to-suit* development is constructed specifically for a particular tenant to occupy, while a *speculative* development is initiated without a tenant commitment. Build-to-suit developments allow a developer to negotiate with

the tenant to determine the precise specifications to which the facility will be built. Amid robust demand for industrial real estate, truly speculative buildings are rare. In the fourth quarter of 2021, 80 percent of construction completions were under lease contract before the building was completed. Thus, speculative industrial development is not very relevant when the supply/demand balance is heavily weighted in the developer's favor, says John Morris, executive managing director and the Americas industrial and logistics leader at CBRE.[1] A more likely scenario is *spec-to-suit*, in which a developer starts a project and then a broker and its occupier tenant come along and start negotiating.

Developers of industrial properties—also called *operating partners* or *sponsors*—fall into two broad categories: (1) firms that build and then sell the properties, also known as *merchant developers*, and (2) firms that build and then continue to own and operate the properties, holding them on their balance sheets for the long term. Each requires a different skill set.

Booth Hansen Architects designed the 339,000-square-foot (31,500 sq m) build-to-suit industrial manufacturing facility on Goose Island in Chicago, Illinois. The property was subsequently acquired by Prologis in 2021 and serves as a multitenant warehouse and distribution facility.

Merchant developers must be adept at finding suitable sites, gaining regulatory approvals, and managing construction. Developers that follow a long-term ownership and operation strategy must also address leasing, maintenance, and operations management.

The business of industrial development is highly regionally and locally focused. According to Howard Freeman, senior vice president and investment officer at Prologis Inc., to be successful as a developer of industrial real estate requires specific local market knowledge.[2] Thus, beginning developers must strategically choose the market in which they work based on their local knowledge or join forces with a more seasoned partner.

Product Types

An *industrial building* is defined by the NAIOP Research Foundation as "a structure used primarily for manufacturing, research and development, production, maintenance, and storage or distribution of goods or both."[3]

CATEGORIES OF INDUSTRIAL BUILDINGS

The three primary categories of industrial buildings are manufacturing, warehouse, and flex. Within those categories are several subcategories that have distinctive physical characteristics to accommodate specialized functions. Such buildings may be stand-alone structures, or they may be located in industrial areas or in master-planned business parks. The building characteristics of industrial building types are shown in figure 6-1.

MANUFACTURING. Manufacturing buildings accommodate the fabrication or assembly of raw materials into goods or products. There are two types of manufacturing buildings: heavy and light. *Heavy manufacturing* buildings accommodate the production and assembly of heavy-duty goods. They are often large facilities with hundreds of thousands of square feet of space and contain specialized, heavy-duty equipment. When a tenant vacates a heavy manufacturing building, the structure often requires substantial renovations to make

---

FIGURE 6-1 Typical Industrial Building Characteristics

| PRIMARY TYPE | MANUFACTURING | WAREHOUSE | | | | FLEX | |
	GENERAL PURPOSE	GENERAL PURPOSE WAREHOUSE	GENERAL PURPOSE DISTRIBUTION	FULFILLMENT CENTER	TRUCK TERMINAL	GENERAL PURPOSE FLEX	SERVICE CENTER OR SHOWROOM
Primary use	Manufacturing	Storage	Distribution	Distribution	Truck trans-shipment	R&D, office, lab, light manufacturing	Retail showroom
Subsets	Heavy, light manufacturing	Bulk warehouse, cold or refrigerator storage, freezer storage, high cubic volume	Overnight delivery services, air cargo	Direct delivery to consumer	Heavy, light manufacturing		
Size (sq ft)	Any	Any	Any	100,000–1,000,000+	Any	Any	Any
Clear height (ft)	10+	16+	16+	32+	12 to 16+	10 to 24	Any
Loading docks/doors	Yes	Yes	Yes	Yes	Cross-dock	Yes	Yes
Door-to-square-foot ratio	Varies	1:5K–15K	1:3K–1K	Varies	1:50K–5K	1:15K+	1:10K
Office percentage	< 20%	< 15%	< 20%	< 20%	< 10%	30–100%	30%+
Vehicle parking ratio	Varies	Low	Low	Very high	Varies	High	High
Truck yard width (ft)	130	130	120–130	130	130	110	110

Source: Maria Sicola, *Commercial Real Estate Terms and Definitions* (Herndon, VA: NAIOP Research Foundation, 2017), p. 26.

it suitable for another occupant. *Light manufacturing* buildings are smaller, accommodate less capital-intensive activities, and have less of an environmental impact than do those that accommodate heavy manufacturing. Light manufacturing buildings may include a warehouse component where raw materials and assembled goods are stored before they are shipped. Those sites are often easier to adapt to new tenants than are heavy manufacturing buildings.

Traditional industrial buildings frequently cover 25 to 45 percent of a site. Building ceiling heights vary considerably, ranging from 10 to 60 feet (3 to 18.3 m). Dock-height or drive-in doors, or both, for large trucks as well as ample exterior space for such trucks to maneuver are usually necessary. Parking ratios also vary, depending on the planned number of employees.

The development of heavy manufacturing facilities has slowed considerably since the mid-20th century, their place taken over by facilities suited to cleaner light manufacturing industries. Because light industrial uses often focus on technology-based activities, those industries typically produce fewer of the undesirable side effects that limited the location of older heavy industries.

WAREHOUSE. Warehouse buildings are primarily used for the storage and distribution of goods and merchandise. Within the general warehouse category are four major subtypes of facilities: *general purpose warehouse*, *general purpose distribution facility*, *fulfillment center*, and *truck terminal*. Size, ceiling heights, and loading requirements vary among the different types but, in general, they require large, flat sites with space for maneuvering trucks and access to transportation networks.

General-purpose warehouses are buildings in which goods are stored, whereas *general-purpose distribution facilities* are buildings used to facilitate the shipment of goods. *Fulfillment centers* are facilities for goods that are transported from a warehouse and delivered directly to a consumer. *Truck terminals* are facilities that serve as intermediate transfer points where goods are moved from one truck to another.

As demand for logistics facilities has grown, so too have conflicts as developers seek sites for industrial development, particularly when the sites are near residential areas. Some communities oppose the development of warehouse, distribution, fulfillment, and truck terminal facilities because the facilities bring tractor-trailer traffic and increase the wear and tear on local roads. They also create corresponding noise, pollution, and safety concerns and potentially diminish open space and agricultural land uses. To accommodate communities' concerns, negotiating entitlements for a development project may entail community benefits agreements and other changes to initial development plans.

General Purpose Warehouse and Distribution. Over the past decade, e-commerce has caused an enormous shift in how warehouse and distribution centers are used. Previously, trucks would deliver merchandise from factories and that merchandise would then be shipped to retail stores. Although that approach still occurs, the process has had to evolve to respond to customers' online shopping habits; now trucks also deliver merchandise to facilities where it is repackaged for delivery directly to individual customers. Merchandise is moved as pallet loads, but it is also moved as individual items. This type of storage and picking requires sophisticated equipment. Consequently, some facilities have shifted from simple shipping and receiving facilities to technologically more sophisticated and highly automated processing centers.

Warehouse and distribution buildings must be designed to maximize the efficient operations of their users. Fluid truck circulation throughout the site, as well as properly sized and configured truck yards and truck docks, is critically important for the effective movement of goods and materials into and out of the facility. The truck yard dimensions should allow for a single swing of a tractor-trailer rig onto and away from a dock door and for parking of trailers. Precise guidance for site planning appears in the Design and Construction subsection of this chapter.

The employee-to-area ratio for warehouse and distribution centers varies greatly. Traditional warehouses might employ few people. Modern distribution and fulfillment centers that serve e-commerce picking and packing, however, may require a substantial number of employees. As a result, requirements for automobile parking can vary widely. Most warehouses have a minimal amount of office space. Typically, each building has an attractive corner or front elevation with windows for the entry lobby and office portion of the building. The remaining space, which is the majority of the building, is constructed in a straightforward, cost-efficient manner.

In recent years, the minimum clear height of warehouse buildings has increased substantially. To accommodate tall racking systems, ceiling heights of at least 36 feet (11 m) are now common for new class A, institutional-grade warehouse and distribution facilities. Moreover, the square footage of warehouse and distribution facilities has increased substantially in line with the growth of large online retailers and the emergence of large *third-party logistics* companies (3PLs) that handle significant amounts of e-commerce activity. Many other tenants, however, do not use tall racking systems and can efficiently use smaller warehouses with lower clear heights; *shallow-bay* warehouse and distribution facilities typically have bay depths of 120 to 190 feet (36.6 to 57.9 m) and clear heights between 18 and 24 feet (5.5 to 7.3 m).[4]

A *big-box,* or bulk industrial facility—not to be confused with a big-box retailer—is a warehouse and distribution facility that is generally defined as larger than 200,000 square feet (18,600 sq m) with a bay depth greater than 190 feet (58 m) and a clear height greater than 28 feet (8.5 m).[5] (The case study presented at the end of this chapter is an example of a big-box warehouse and distribution facility in the Atlanta area.) The big-box share of the industrial market has been growing substantially. By midyear 2021, occupancy gains in the big-box industrial market hit an all-time high.[6] Amazon is the largest occupier of big-box space in the United States. But demand from traditional retailers and large 3PLs has increased substantially as well.

As demand for expansive logistics space has grown, so has demand for smaller, *last-mile* warehouse and distribution buildings (less than 120,000 square feet [11,100 sq m]) near dense population centers. This trend began before the COVID-19 pandemic but has accelerated significantly, with indications that the trend will continue.[7]

Fulfillment Centers. Fulfillment centers were added as a subset of NAIOP's warehouse category of industrial buildings in 2017 (figure 6-1), reflecting the impact of the growth of e-commerce activity and the increasing demand for buildings to accommodate it.[8] At fulfillment centers, items arrive on tractor-trailers and are stowed, then picked and packed for shipping directly to consumers. Large e-commerce companies, as well as traditional retailers with e-commerce components, may operate their own fulfillment centers. Other e-commerce companies have outsourced warehousing and distribution to 3PL companies, which manage inventory, warehousing, fulfillment, and distribution. Thus, 3PLs have become a significant factor in logistics real estate. As of 2021, 3PLs account for 31 percent of the bulk industrial space market.[9] (See figure 6-2.)

Fulfillment centers may contain a mix of warehouse, distribution, and fulfillment functions as they employ sophisticated stowing, picking, and conveying

system technology. The facilities are often large—it is not uncommon for buildings to be 800,000 square feet (74,300 sq m) to more than 1 million square feet (93,000 sq m). They have many of the same features as warehouse and distribution facilities, including dock doors to accommodate the loading and unloading of goods from trailers, but they may also contain stacked mezzanines of robotic storage platforms. Although the facilities are highly automated, they

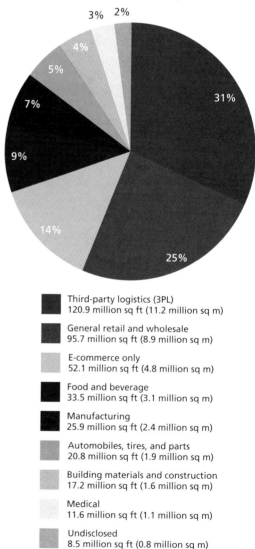

FIGURE 6-2 **Bulk Warehouse Lease Transactions, 2021**

- Third-party logistics (3PL)
  120.9 million sq ft (11.2 million sq m)
- General retail and wholesale
  95.7 million sq ft (8.9 million sq m)
- E-commerce only
  52.1 million sq ft (4.8 million sq m)
- Food and beverage
  33.5 million sq ft (3.1 million sq m)
- Manufacturing
  25.9 million sq ft (2.4 million sq m)
- Automobiles, tires, and parts
  20.8 million sq ft (1.9 million sq m)
- Building materials and construction
  17.2 million sq ft (1.6 million sq m)
- Medical
  11.6 million sq ft (1.1 million sq m)
- Undisclosed
  8.5 million sq ft (0.8 million sq m)

Source: CBRE Research, "U.S. MarketFlash: Rising Transportation Costs Help Fuel Record Warehouse Leasing Pace," CRBE, September 13, 2021.

Note: Bulk warehouse = 100,000 sq ft (9,300 sq m).

require substantially more employees than do traditional warehouses. Consequently, the site coverage for fulfillment centers may be less than 40 percent of the overall site and include about three parking spaces per 1,000 square feet (92.9 sq m). For example, a recently built 857,000-square-foot (79,600 sq m) fulfillment center occupied by Amazon in Orlando, Florida, occupies 36.6 percent of the site and includes about 2,500 parking spaces for cars.[10]

Truck Terminals. Truck terminals, or *transload buildings*, serve as intermediate transfer points where goods are redirected or consolidated from one truck to another or from shipping containers to trucks. They are designed for short-term staging of goods and contain very little to no space used for long-term inventory storage. They are often organized as cross-dock facilities to speed *throughput*—unloading and loading of trailers—and have minimal office space and automobile parking. *Less than truckload* (LTL) shippers are a type of user of truck terminal facilities. LTLs transport lightweight freight and consolidate it into trailers for transportation between major cities or ports.

Transload buildings are typically smaller than are other types of industrial buildings, often less than 50,000 square feet (4,600 sq m) but frequently with extra land for trailer parking and maneuvering.[11] Small transload buildings had the highest rental rate growth of all industrial properties in 2021.[12] Clear heights tend to be lower than in other types of warehouse and distribution facilities because the short-term transfer of goods does not entail the use of the tall racking systems used in other types of warehouse buildings. Clear heights are typically between 20 and 24 feet (6.1 and 7.3 m). Transload facilities follow many of the same design specifications for tractor-trailer circulation and docking as do general-purpose warehouse and distribution facilities.

The role of truck terminals in decontainerizing cargo is important to supply chain efficiency. Consequently, the greatest demand for truck terminals is in markets with the most cargo movement, such as the Inland Empire of Southern California that serves cargo from the Port of Los Angeles.

SPECIALIZED FACILITIES. Within the categories of warehouse and distribution facilities are specialty subtypes. Four subtypes—last mile, cold storage, data centers, and self-storage—have seen demand grow substantially in recent years, fueled by changes associated with the COVID-19 pandemic as well as by broader shifts in U.S. society.

Last-Mile. A relatively new type of industrial distribution facility has emerged in response to consumer demand for next-day and same-day delivery of online purchases. *Last-mile* e-commerce fulfillment centers are located near dense population centers, often on urban infill sites. Kris Bjorson, executive managing director for JLL Industrial, says industrial real estate development has recently focused on last-mile facilities—50,000- to 150,000-square-foot (4,600 to 13,900 sq m) buildings on sites larger than five acres (2 ha) with not only storage, but also delivery vehicle parking.[13]

In pursuit of urban infill locations, companies are willing to forgo some attributes of traditional institutional-grade distribution facilities. A property can have some physical imperfections, but it must have certain characteristics to be suitable for use as a last-mile e-commerce fulfillment center, such as sufficient space for trucks to maneuver and enough employee parking.[14] Breaking with the traditional single-story form of distribution centers, last-mile centers are increasingly going vertical. The development of multistory industrial buildings makes sense in places with high population density, strong e-commerce penetration, and tight market conditions.[15]

Industrial developers must be creative in their sourcing of land and the adaptive use of existing buildings as last-mile fulfillment centers. Examples include obsolete big-box retail and department stores, office space, and—in the case of a mini-delivery hub in New York City—a former automobile dealership. However, changes in use may pose significant legal and zoning challenges that

A 66,000-square-foot (6,100 sq m) former automobile dealership in New York City has been converted into a last-mile e-commerce fulfillment center.

DUSTIN JONES

Industrial Development

take time to resolve. Challenges—such as site control provisions in leases and reciprocal easement agreements (REAs), zoning codes, and loan covenants in place with existing lenders—need to be managed and overcome to successfully transition existing retail spaces to nontraditional retail uses, such as distribution and fulfillment (including last-mile) centers.[16]

Cold Storage. Cold storage industrial facilities provide freezer, cooler, and ambient storage space for perishable goods. Cold storage warehouses hold goods that are in transit not only to supermarkets, retailers, and restaurants, but also directly to consumers. The emergence of grocery delivery services during the COVID-19 pandemic accelerated the growth of this segment of e-commerce, which is projected to continue. Most cold storage facilities are build-to-suit developments, which allow the building specifications to be tailored to the particular needs of the user. Clear heights in cold storage facilities are often higher than in other warehouse types: up to 50 feet (15.2 m).[17]

Data Centers Data centers contain computing equipment, including servers and networking equipment to process and store data. Demand for data centers is growing, coming from technology firms as well as from financial institutions and health care companies. The location of data centers is particularly important; they must be located as close as possible to fiber optic trunk lines.[18] Data centers have particularly robust requirements for highly reliable electrical systems and are ideally served by dual independent feeds from the power grid as well as by redundant chillers and generators.[19] Several real estate investment trusts (REITs) focus exclusively on owning and operating data centers.

Self-Storage. Self-storage properties provide small warehouse spaces to households and businesses that need additional storage space. Individual storage spaces range in size from 100-cubic-foot (2.8 cubic m) lockers to 250-square-foot (23.2 sq m) storage spaces. Factors associated with the COVID-19 pandemic contributed to increased demand for self-storage units and the corresponding record-low vacancy rates in 2021 despite substantial new construction.[20] As with other subtypes of industrial real estate, several REITs focus exclusively on self-storage facilities.

FLEX. Flex buildings are designed to accommodate a variety of uses, including service centers, showrooms, offices, and warehouses. The flex category is further broken down into general purpose flex and service centers or showrooms. Flex buildings are typically one- or two-story structures ranging from 20,000 to 100,000 square feet (1,900 to 9,300 sq m), but size and configuration vary depending on the user's needs. External designs are generally simple, rectangular building shapes with an abundance of glass on the front facade. Developers must understand the market and the users' specific needs to determine the best configuration.

Highpoint Cold is a 227,000-square-foot (21,100 sq m) class A speculative single- or multitenant cold-storage facility developed by Hyde Development and Mortenson Construction and located in Aurora, Colorado. The building is part of Highpoint Industrial Elevated, a planned mixed-use industrial and logistics park. The building has a 34-degree F (1.1 degree C) refrigerated speed bay. The warehouse portion is a –20 to +70 degree F (–28.9 to 21.1 degree C) freezer/cooler with a 50-foot (15.2 m) clear height.

Georgetown Crossroads, Seattle, Washington

Increased customer demand for fast e-commerce deliveries, including same-day delivery, has necessitated locating distribution and fulfillment centers close to population centers. However, a lack of available large parcels of land and building restrictions in urban areas has limited the construction of industrial buildings in locations best situated for last-mile logistics operations.

One solution for accommodating large amounts of square footage on relatively small parcels of urban infill land is to build multistory warehouse and distribution facilities. Multistory industrial buildings can be found in densely populated Asian cities but are not yet common in the United States. The added construction expenses and vehicle access limitations have prohibited their development. But users opting for centrally located urban locations are increasingly looking to multistory facilities. Georgetown Crossroads in Seattle, Washington, developed by Prologis, is one such facility.

Georgetown Crossroads is a three-level, 589,600-square-foot (54,800 sq m) building located five miles (8 km) south of downtown Seattle. The first two floors serve as fulfillment and warehouse space. Level one (239,000 square feet [22,200 sq m]) provides up to 62 dock-height doors and two drive-in doors, with a 28-foot (8.5 m) clear height. Level two (180,300 square feet [16,800 sq m]) is accessed via truck ramps and freight elevators. It has up to 38 dock-height doors and two drive-in doors, with a 24-foot (7.3 m) interior clear height. Level three is offered as build-to-suit space for light manufacturing, laboratory, and office activities with a clear height of 16 feet (4.9 m). Similar to traditional, institutional-grade, single-story warehouse facilities, the building has 50-foot by 45-foot (15.2 by 13.7 m) column spacing, a 60-foot-deep (18.3 m) speed bay, an early suppression, fast response (ESFR) sprinkler system, and a set of 130-foot-deep (39.6 m) truck yards on the first and second levels. An adjacent parking structure can accommodate 635 cars and delivery vans.[a]

Prologis's Georgetown Crossing is one of the first institutional-grade multistory industrial developments to be built in the United States. Because multistory facilities are more expensive

PROLOGIS

Georgetown Crossroads, developed by Prologis, is a multistory industrial facility in Seattle, Washington.

to build, this type of development is best suited for larger cities where developable land is scarce and expensive and where customers demand same- or next-day e-commerce deliveries. For example, industrial buildings taller than three stories often require increased fire-resistant construction, which significantly raises costs. Moreover, the additional vertical circulation (elevators and stairs) required decreases the ratio of leasable-to-gross space. According to Prologis, at most only 75 percent of the gross floor area of a multistory industrial building is leasable.[b] Multistory industrial facilities are limited to a few large densely populated U.S. cities, but as on-demand delivery becomes more popular, other cities may soon follow.

[a]Prologis Inc. and Washington Real Estate Advisors, "Prologis Georgetown Crossroads," marketing brochure (Seattle, WA: Prologis Inc.), http://prologisgeorgetown.com/wp-content/uploads/Prologis-Georgetown-Crossroads-2019.pdf.

[b]Ben O'Neil, *The Future Is Multistory*, Prologis Inc., July 13, 2021, https://www.prologis.com/blog/future-multistory.

R&D flex buildings fall into two categories. One category includes facilities in which research is the primary or only activity. Design of the interior spaces is frequently unique to the specific research. The other type of R&D building is intended to serve multiple uses. It may have one or two stories, and it often has office and administrative functions in the front part of the building and R&D or other uses in the rear. Life science R&D flex buildings are a growing segment of industrial flex space.

Offices in R&D buildings typically have open floor plans to foster collaboration and to facilitate easy rearrangement of spaces and furniture for changing work groups. Many tenants are small startup companies; others are subsidiaries of major corporations. The design of tenant improvements is more important for R&D uses than for other industrial uses and is usually tailored to the needs of specific tenants. The percentage of space allocated to laboratories, research offices, service areas, assembly, and storage

The FACQ flex industrial facility near Ghent, Belgium, combines a 32,000-square-foot (3,000 sq m) showroom and service center, 27,000 square feet (2,500 sq m) of office space, and a 161,000-square-foot (15,000 sq m) warehouse and distribution facility for FACQ, a plumbing and heating equipment company. An eye-catching semitransparent glass-and-steel facade on the office and showroom portion of the building faces the busy nearby highway and serves as an advertisement for the company. The warehouse and distribution portion of the building is of a more traditional warehouse design, located on the back of the building, where tractor-trailers access loading docks.

SUZANNE LANYI CHARLES

varies widely. Hard-to-rent space in the center of large buildings is well suited for laboratories and computer rooms where environmental control is critical and windows are less important.

Multitenant buildings cater to customer-oriented smaller tenants, such as office, showroom, and service businesses. The buildings are generally one story, with parking in the front and dock doors in the rear for truck loading. They provide parking for employees and visitors as well as truck yards large enough for small trucks. Leased spaces are strategically designed so that they can be divided into smaller modules for individual tenants. Frequently, 25 to 50 percent of the interior is improved, leaving the balance of the building as light manufacturing, assembly, or warehouse space.

BUSINESS PARKS

Business parks are multibuilding developments that may accommodate a range of uses, from light industrial to office space, in an integrated setting and may include supporting uses and amenities for the people who work there. Business parks can range in size from several acres to hundreds of acres. They may offer a mix of warehouse, flex, and office space. The primary categories of business parks include the following:

- **Warehouse/Distribution Parks**—Warehouse and distribution parks contain large, primarily single-story warehouse and distribution buildings with ample provisions for tractor-trailer circulation, loading, and trailer parking.
- **Logistics Parks**—Logistics parks focus on the value-added services of logistics and processing goods rather than on warehousing and storage. As centers for wholesale activity, they may also provide showrooms and demonstration areas to highlight products assembled or distributed there.
- **Industrial Parks**—Modern industrial parks contain large-scale manufacturing and warehouse facilities and a limited amount of office space.

- **Research and Development Parks**—R&D parks are designed to take advantage of a relationship with a university or government agency to foster innovation and the transfer and commercialization of technology. Facilities are typically multifunctional, with a combination of laboratories, offices, and light manufacturing buildings.
- **Technology Parks**—Technology parks cater to high-tech companies that require a setting conducive to innovation. They rely on proximity to similar or related companies to create a synergistic atmosphere for business development.
- **Incubator Parks**—Incubator parks or designated incubator sections of research or technology parks meet the needs of small startup businesses. Often supported by municipalities through their economic development agencies or by universities, incubator parks provide flexibly configured and economically priced space for shared services and business counseling.
- **Corporate Parks**—Corporate parks are the latest iteration in the evolution of business parks. Often located at high-profile sites, they may look like office parks, but they often house activities and uses that go beyond traditional office space, including research labs and even light manufacturing.

Rehabilitation and Adaptive Use

Older industrial districts and business parks, especially underused buildings suitable for rehabilitation and small infill sites, offer opportunities to beginning developers. Given fierce competition for well-located, suitable sites for traditional greenfield industrial development, Barry DiRaimondo, chief executive officer of SteelWave, suggests that a particularly promising opportunity for beginning developers is to acquire existing, obsolete industrial properties and then to undertake a light-touch redevelopment of the property as light industrial and creative office space.[21]

The Press is an adaptive use of a former printing press and distribution facility for the *Los Angeles Times* in Costa Mesa, California. The building was originally conceived to include 381,000 square feet (35.4 sq m) of office space and a 51,000-square-foot (4,700 sq m) food hall. The second phase of the project included the construction of a new 190,000-square-foot (17,700 sq m) building on the site. The project was developed by SteelWave in a joint venture with Invesco Real Estate. The two firms invested $150 million in capital improvements in the renovation, which is about $235 per square foot. The development is an example of how aging, obsolete industrial buildings can be reinvigorated with new life and new uses.

SteelWave acquired the 21-acre (8.5 ha) site with an existing 249,000-square-foot (23,100 sq m) warehouse and office structures comprising 112,000 square feet (10,400 sq m) in 2017. The architects, Ehrlich Yanai Rhee Chaney Architects, called for the demolition of parts of the original complex's roof and concrete walls to expose portions of the building's steel structure in a manner they call "selectively subtractive."[a] The retention of remnants of the original buildings—including a portion of an imprint of the original building's signage—evokes the history and unique character of the formerly industrial space while accommodating the demands of office tenants. The 50-foot-high (15.2 m) clear heights of the former printing press room were retained to form a daylit atrium and expansive office space. The former loading docks were transformed into "back porches" that serve as indoor-outdoor space for the office tenants and take advantage of the temperate Southern California weather. The landscape design unites the buildings and connects the redevelopment to nearby properties.

A single tenant signed a long-term lease for the entire development, including the new building. To serve the tenant's specific needs, the food hall idea was abandoned and that area is instead used as office space. The development was completed in 2022.

[a]"The Press," Ehrlich Yanai Rhee Chaney Architects, Culver City, CA, January 10, 2022, https://www.eyrc.com/work/the-press.

MATTHEW MILMAN

MATTHEW MILMAN

The Press, developed by SteelWave, is the redevelopment of a printing press, distribution facility, and newsroom for the *Los Angeles Times* in Costa Mesa, California, into a creative office and light industrial campus.

Some municipalities have established programs to encourage redevelopment of older industrial areas. Redevelopment agencies and economic development agencies may offer incentives such as tax abatements and financing to developers who build in designated redevelopment areas.

Developers have the following rehabilitation and adaptive use opportunities:

- Redevelop obsolete suburban industrial space for creative office and light industrial uses.
- Adapt vacant urban warehouse and retail spaces to last-mile distribution facilities.
- Upgrade low-tech, light industrial buildings to be competitive with newer facilities.
- Rehabilitate major plants, such as outmoded automobile plants, into multitenant warehouses and office or technology buildings.
- Remove heavy industrial facilities, and reuse the land for business parks.
- Adapt obsolete urban warehouses for commercial, office, and residential uses.

Some potential issues surrounding the rehabilitation of older buildings include cost overruns, title problems, building code issues, poor street and utility infrastructure, and unforeseen construction problems. Redeveloping obsolete retail spaces as distribution facilities is difficult in practice because municipalities may be loath to change zoning for retail sites to industrial, because industrial uses provide less lucrative tax revenues.[22] And as David Rabinowitz, director at Goulston & Storrs, points out, developers need to gauge the local political landscape for amenability to zoning changes because changing the zoning of properties near residential areas to include distribution and fulfillment (including last-mile), warehouse, and industrial uses is likely to draw objections.[23]

A major concern that must be addressed is the cleanup of environmental contamination of former industrial sites. By their very nature as the former location of industry, environmental contamination is highly likely. Thus, proper due diligence to fully understand preexisting soil and groundwater contamination is paramount in any redevelopment of a site with a history of industrial uses.

Reengineering older industrial buildings can be particularly challenging. New roofing and insulation, new energy-efficient windows, repair and cleaning of exterior wall surfaces, and painting and other cosmetic improvements are common exterior alterations. A significant portion of the budget may be required to bring a building up to current building codes: providing adequate egress; adding sprinklers and fire alarm systems; installing or upgrading wiring and plumbing; and upgrading or installing the heating, ventilating, and air-conditioning systems.

Environmental, Social, and Governance

Buildings—including building operations and building materials and construction—generate 38 percent of the total annual emissions of global, energy-related carbon dioxide (CO_2).[24] To meet global climate goals that limit warming to 1.5°C, the building and construction sector must reduce energy demand, decarbonize the power sector, and reduce life-cycle carbon emissions.[25] Spurred by recognition of climate- and pandemic-related disruptions and by growing acknowledgment of social inequity, the developers, investors, and users of industrial properties are taking ESG concerns more seriously now than in previous years.

Acknowledging the impacts of companies' entire climate footprint—including Scope 3 emissions— companies are beginning to extend their sustainability goals to their entire supply chain, including their distribution partners. *Scope 3* emissions are "the result of activities from assets not owned or controlled by the reporting organization, but that the organization directly impacts in its value chain."[26]

Rooftop Solar

With large expanses of available space, rooftop solar arrays on industrial buildings appear to be a logical fit. Rooftop solar has the potential to generate clean power that could offset tenants' reliance on fossil fuels to power their operations and help companies, which face pressure from shareholders and the public, achieve their ESG goals. However, several challenges particular to industrial real estate stand in the way of mass deployment of solar arrays on the roofs of industrial buildings.

Although rooftop solar has potential benefits for industrial building developers, owners, and tenants, to date it has yet to be deployed on a large scale in the United States. Three crucial factors affect rooftop solar development. First, the site must receive sufficient sunshine. Second, the site must be located in a place with a favorable regulatory environment such as a jurisdiction in which third-party ownership structures—for example, power purchase agreements (PPAs)—are legal. PPAs are agreements between electricity producers and electricity users (tenants who pay for utilities according to triple-net [NNN] leases). Third, the property should be in a location that has high utility rates, which make rooftop solar an economical alternative.[a]

Despite the advantages, several factors have limited the widespread inclusion of solar power generation on industrial roofs. Developers are often reluctant to encumber a property in a way that might restrict future leasing, sale, or redevelopment. This factor is particularly evident with speculative developments that must remain flexible to attract initially unidentified tenants. Developers express concern that rooftop solar arrays may limit future flexibility, for example, restricting the future placement of rooftop equipment. Single-tenant buildings—particularly build-to-suit facilities—offer more favorable conditions. Some large users of distribution facilities have immense power requirements for charging electric material handling equipment and delivery vehicles, for example. In those cases, the developer may negotiate an agreement for the tenants to buy the power generated on site, an arrangement packaged in the lease.[b]

[a]Adam Knoff, "Industrial Development Is Actually Not All the Same: Cutting-Edge Features Breaking New Ground" (presentation, ULI Spring Meeting 2021, Denver, CO (virtual), 2021).
[b]Knoff, "Industrial Development."

Scope 3 emissions often account for the majority of a company's total greenhouse gas emissions. Reducing the environmental impact of Scope 3 emissions associated with transportation and the industrial real estate within their overall supply chains could have a substantial impact. And for the developers of industrial facilities, buildings that meet reduced emission requirements will therefore have a competitive advantage in attracting future tenants.

An estimated 40 percent of all emissions in global supply chains could be reduced with readily available and low-cost means, such as energy efficiency and renewable power.[27] For warehouse and storage buildings in the United States, lighting accounts for 30 percent of total electricity consumption.[28]

Reducing the carbon emissions associated with lighting in warehouse and distribution facilities is rather low-hanging fruit. Skylights and clerestory windows allow natural light into the space, reducing the need for artificial lighting. Low-energy LED lighting, combined with motion sensor and photocell controls, is a simple way to reduce energy usage. LED lighting reduces tenants' operational costs, and it is becoming standard in institutional-grade logistics facilities. In addition, renewable energy sources, such as solar panel arrays on the roofs of industrial buildings, can reduce dependence on the power grid as well as costs for building tenants. Renewable power is becoming more important for future reduction of greenhouse gas emission as logistics facilities become more automated and as power demands increase to accommodate electrical vehicle and equipment charging.

Project Feasibility

MARKET ANALYSIS BEFORE SITE SELECTION

The market analysis that precedes site selection for industrial development serves three purposes: to identify the types of users that will be served, to identify the type of facility to be built and thus the parameters of the site to be purchased, and to identify where the facility should be located. The developer must be knowledgeable about the regional and particularly local economies and real estate markets. The following factors should be examined:

- national, regional, and local economic trends;
- growth in employment and changes in the number of people engaged in job categories (as measured by Standardized Industrial Classification codes);

- socioeconomic characteristics of the metropolitan area, including rates of population growth and employment patterns;
- local growth policies and attitudes toward industrial development;
- forecasted demand for various types of office and industrial facilities;
- current inventory by industrial subtype;
- historic absorption trends and current leasing activity; and
- historic vacancy rates and current space available.

This information is available from a host of sources, including government and commercial websites, market analysts, data service firms, chambers of commerce, and real estate brokerage firms. Companies such as Colliers, Jones Lang LaSalle, Cushman & Wakefield, CBRE, and others offer quarterly and annual industrial market and submarket reports. In addition to evaluating quantitative data, the developer should consult local brokers, tenants, and other developers to verify the accuracy of the information obtained.

Few market data sources segment industrial space beyond the major categories, making it difficult to assess the performance of individual subtypes. One method of obtaining a rough idea of the various property types when the information is not broken down is to segment properties by size categories. Some firms provide market data broken down by size—big-box industrial buildings, for example.

Before searching for specific sites, a developer must become thoroughly familiar with industrial development patterns throughout the metropolitan area. During that investigation, the developer should learn as much as possible about what the local market conditions are and which types of industrial tenants are expanding or contracting. A developer looking for a site should be concerned with a number of issues:

- availability and cost of land;
- transportation infrastructure, including highway access;
- labor availability and costs;
- tax structure and tax incentives;
- utilities and waste disposal;
- energy rates; and
- comparative transportation rates.

Market preferences, land costs, labor costs, utility costs, and transportation costs can differ dramatically within the same region. The developer's market analysis before site selection should assess the market's preferences regarding factors such as access to transportation and location.

LOCAL LINKS. Local links are critical to many companies. Firms that have frequent contacts with suppliers, distributors, customers, consultants, or government agencies consider the accessibility to firms with which they do regular business as well as the number of trips to be made to and from the business inside the metropolitan area. The firms also assess traffic congestion in and around the site; commuting time for employees and available public transportation; and vehicle cost, including taxes, maintenance, and fuel per mile traveled.

LABOR. Attracting and retaining labor is a top concern for the users of industrial real estate. Although the use of automation and technology is growing in warehouse and distribution facilities, human labor remains essential. E-commerce facilities require more workers than do traditional facilities.[29] Moreover, labor turnover is about four times greater than that of other uses.[30] Labor is in great demand; thus, the location of industrial facilities near and easily accessed from population centers is crucial not only to serve customers but also to attract people who will work at the facility.

CLUSTERING AND AGGLOMERATION. A number of industries—food distribution, garment manufacturing, printing, wholesale flower marts, machinery parts and repair, and commercial groceries and kitchen supplies, for example—tend to cluster together. The clustering, known as *agglomeration*, often relates to time-sensitive products or to the interdependency of firms in a particular industry. High-tech firms tend to congregate in research parks near major universities, where they can take advantage of resources such as laboratories and libraries as well as faculty members, students, and alumni and large pools of highly educated and skilled workers. Venture capital is also attracted to universities because of the commercially valuable discoveries they generate.

ACCESS. Access to transportation is fundamental to all types of industrial properties, although requirements vary by type. Transportation costs typically make up between 45 and 70 percent of users' logistical expenses, compared to only 3 to 6 percent spent on facility fixed costs.[31] Therefore, location and efficient access to transportation networks are critically important for tenants of industrial facilities.

All industrial uses depend on trucking to varying extents, so connections to transportation infrastructure—particularly proximity to interstate highways—are paramount. In the case of regional warehouse and distribution facilities, efficient truck access to highways that provide efficient movement of goods throughout a region is a primary consideration when companies choose spaces to lease. However, in the case of last-mile facilities in densely populated urban areas, a company may compromise on highway accessibility and truck access to be near customers.

Airports exert a strong attraction for industrial users. In many cases, businesses locating near an airport use cargo and passenger services regularly. In other instances, this locational choice is the result of good highway access, available land, and favorable zoning. In addition, container ports, such as the ports of Los Angeles, Long Beach, New York and New Jersey, and Savannah, create demand for nearby industrial space to accommodate imports and exports. The expansion of the Panama Canal to accommodate megaships has increased demand in recent years for industrial space near East Coast ports.[32]

Rail service remains an important factor for some select manufacturing and industrial processes. Generally, companies that deal with heavy goods and materials (paper, beverages, plastics, etc.) are most interested in rail access.[33] Rail access could be an important attribute for some users, but it will not be used by the majority of warehouse tenants. Providing rail access is most advantageous when provided for a build-to-suit tenant that is specifically interested in using rail service. When provided for in a speculative development, rail access may be an expensive and time-consuming feature that is unappreciated by the eventual tenant.

FOREIGN TRADE ZONES. A foreign trade zone is a site in the United States located in or near a U.S. Customs port of entry where foreign and domestic merchandise is generally considered to be in international commerce. Firms located in foreign trade zones can bring in, store, and assemble parts from abroad and export the finished product without paying customs duties until the goods leave the zone. Many foreign manufacturing firms transport their products to a warehouse in the trade zone, store the products until they are ordered by a customer or distributor, and pay the import duties when the product leaves the warehouse. Thus, the firms can have readily available stock without having to pay the associated import fees until the product is actually needed. Being located in a foreign trade zone may be advantageous for some tenants, but it depends on their particular business operations.

SITE SELECTION

Selecting the correct site is crucial to the success of an industrial development, and it is important to ensure that as many criteria as possible are satisfied. Location directly influences a development's marketability, along with the rate at which space can be absorbed during leasing, the rents that can be achieved, and the eventual exit strategy.

EVALUATING SPECIFIC LAND PARCELS. Beginning developers should consider avoiding land that is not ready for immediate development. Obtaining zoning changes, installing major off-site infrastructure improvements, or waiting for the completion of planned transportation improvements tends to require more time and capital than most beginning developers can afford.

Especially important for sites slated for industrial use is that utilities—including water, gas, electricity, internet, and sewer services with appropriate capacities—be available at competitive rates. The site should be flat to accommodate the large pads that are needed for industrial buildings and should have minimal ledge rock, groundwater, or expansive soils. The presence of oil wells, contaminated soils, high water tables, or tanks and pipes can cause major problems and should be carefully studied to determine present and potential dangers.

FINDING AND ACQUIRING THE SITE. Finding the land on which to build an industrial facility is the first and, in a highly competitive real estate market, perhaps the most difficult step. Real estate brokers specializing in industrial properties are a crucial source of information about potential development sites. Building and nurturing relationships with brokers is vital. Developers should first narrow down their target area and then work with brokers familiar with the area to obtain information about sites that may not currently be on the market. Public agencies, such as local planning departments, redevelopment agencies, and economic development agencies, possess considerable information that is useful to developers searching for potential sites. Most municipalities have comprehensive plans that indicate the areas favored for industrial development.

Remaining sites in business parks that are approaching buildout should also be considered as potential development sites. Extra land around existing industrial buildings, often used for storage, may also present opportunities to expand a building for current tenants or to build another facility. Owners of such properties may be interested in becoming a partner for the addition or may prefer to sell the land outright.

Infill sites offer developers the advantages of readily available streets, sewer, water, and other public services. But existing streets may be too narrow and space may be too constricted to conform with the high standards that tenants now expect of business parks. The developer should consult with local neighborhood groups and property managers of neighboring industrial and other properties to learn about potential problems in advance.

Site acquisition for industrial property follows the same four steps as for other forms of development: the investigation before an offer is made, the offer, due diligence, and closing (see chapters 3 and 4).

During the due diligence phase, developers should pay attention to environmental contamination, especially if existing industrial uses are present nearby. Waste spilled locally may be spread by the water table to an otherwise clean site: a small amount of solvent or oil can show up as hazardous waste years after it was spilled. State-licensed civil engineers should perform water and soil tests; if necessary, developers should ensure that enough time is allowed to verify that no contamination is present by paying for an extension to the option.

Most developers face a standard dilemma during site acquisition. They need time to execute thorough due diligence, while the seller wants to close as quickly as possible. Both desires are perfectly reasonable, but protracted periods before closing are usually not met well by an eager seller and can kill a deal, particularly in a highly competitive market. At the same time, rushing into a purchase only to find out later that the site requires major environmental cleanup or going ahead without having financing fully in place may be too high a price to pay to win the property.

As described in detail in chapter 3, site acquisition generally has three stages: a free-look period, a period during which earnest money is forfeitable, and the closing. The agreed-upon terms depend on market conditions. In a hot market, acquisition can be difficult for most developers and nearly impossible for those with financing contingencies.

ENGINEERING FEASIBILITY. Preliminary engineering investigations are a critically important part of the due diligence process. A civil engineer usually leads the site investigation under the developer's direction.

Chapter 3 provides a comprehensive review of the site evaluation process for all types of development. For industrial development, the most significant aspects of this process are the availability of utilities and environmental issues.

Utilities. Many manufacturing and some R&D facilities use enormous amounts of water and electricity. Because most water is discharged into the sewer system eventually, both water and sewage services are affected. A developer's ability to accommodate such customers can be a good draw, especially in areas where the availability of water is limited.

A developer should meet with the local water company as early as possible to discuss plans and to learn about the utility company's current capabilities and limitations. The developer's engineer can obtain preliminary information about flow and pressure from the utility company. Fire departments usually require that the water system and fire hydrants be installed and activated before construction can start on individual buildings.

Some local agencies require the installation of lines to reclaim water for irrigation and industrial purposes. Some localities require that two parallel systems, domestic and reclaimed, be installed. The developer should meet with the sewer company to determine the following:

- the capacity of sewage treatment facilities;
- the capacity of sewer mains;
- whether gravity flow for sewage and drainage is sufficient, or if pumps are necessary;
- the party responsible for paying for off-site sewer extensions;
- the due date for payments and impact fees;
- the quality restrictions imposed on sewage effluent: some sewage treatment plants impose restrictions on the type and quantity of chemicals that firms can discharge into the general sewage system;
- the discharge capacity for sewage effluent;
- the flow standards; and
- the periodic service charges: although the rate structure for service charges does not directly affect the developer, it will influence prospective purchasers of property, especially heavy users such as bottling plants.

Some municipalities use water consumption as the basis for sewer system service charges. Thus, projects that consume large quantities to irrigate landscaping will incur increased charges. In such cases, the developer may attempt to negotiate treatment costs that are based on anticipated discharge rather than on water consumption.

Industrial land developers must usually pay the upfront costs for water and sewage lines and for treatment plants and then recover those costs as part of the sale price or rental income. Costs may also be reimbursed by developers of other subdivisions and by owners of other properties that subsequently tie into those water and sewage mains. Most cities that provide for reimbursement by subsequent developers, however, do not permit the original developer to recover carrying costs. Because of the unpredictable timing of such reimbursements, developers cannot rely on them to help meet cash flow requirements.

For business parks with multiple buildings, developers should provide the local utility companies with information about the types and sizes of buildings in their plans so that they can estimate future demand from the project. Electricity can be a big issue, especially for fulfillment center, manufacturing, and R&D users. The projected demand is used to design the local distribution system as well as the systems that will feed the local systems.

The frequency of power outages and gas curtailments should be investigated because those factors can deter potential tenants and buyers. Frequent outages may influence the developer's choice of target market or may change the decision to purchase the site altogether.

Environmental Regulations. Many federal environmental statutes can affect industrial development:

- The National Environmental Policy Act requires projects that use federal funds to produce an environmental impact statement for approval.
- The Clean Air Act requires the provision of information on anticipated traffic flow and indirect vehicle use.
- The Clean Water Act restricts discharge of any pollutant into navigable and certain nonnavigable waters.
- The Occupational Safety and Health Act requires employers to provide safe working conditions for employees.
- The National Flood Insurance Act limits development in flood-prone areas and requires developers who build in flood-prone areas to meet standards concerning height, slope, and interference with water flow. A project may not impede the water flow speed and volume that exist before development in any floodway traversed by the project.

- The Comprehensive Environmental Response, Compensation, and Liability Act, which is also known as the Superfund law, addresses issues concerning toxic waste.

Individual states and local municipalities may have their own environmental laws that affect industrial development.

Concerns about power and water supply, sewage treatment constraints, and development impacts on sensitive environmental areas require developers to perform very careful site investigations before closing on a development site. Although laws in most states give developers some recourse against prior owners in the chain of title for problems such as environmental contamination, such protections are of little use if developers cannot proceed with their plans.

States continue to work to ease developers' liability when they engage in projects that come with environmental wildcards and potentially massive costs. This trend began in Massachusetts in the 1990s, when the attorney general's office successfully negotiated a number of covenants not to sue developers reclaiming brownfields. The covenants protect developers from financial responsibility for cleanups when they have taken ownership of a parcel but then had to pull out of the project.

Urban adaptive use and the conversion of industrial properties to residential or live/work spaces generate additional concerns for industrial developers. Those conversions can cause incompatible uses in a single zone. Consequently, developers must create environmental impact reports to show, among other things, the traffic and noise effects on adjacent properties. The gradual infiltration of residential uses into industrial zones, as well as industrial uses into residential areas, is increasing the sensitivity of environmental requirements in such newly created mixed-use areas.

MARKET ANALYSIS AFTER SITE SELECTION

Once a site has been secured with a signed earnest money contract, the second and more detailed phase of the market analysis begins. The purpose at this stage is to investigate the immediate market area for information about rental rates, occupancy, new supply, and features of competing projects.

To focus the research and determine which other properties constitute potential competition, the first step at this stage of market analysis is to define the property type or types most likely to be developed at the site. This often-overlooked step can help narrow the research and reduce unnecessary effort.

SUPPLY ANALYSIS. The first task in identifying future supply is to identify properties that are currently under development or construction. A drive through the submarket and follow-up calls to brokers and active developers can yield information about project sizes, completion dates, costs, and rents. Information about proposed projects that have not yet broken ground can be obtained from local planning and building departments, as well as from companies such as CBRE, Cushman & Wakefield, Jones Lang LaSalle, Colliers, and others.

Estimating the amount of space to be added to the industrial supply beyond two or three years is difficult. Industrial buildings take a relatively short time to build, and when vacancy rates are low, the amount of construction can increase quickly. It is useful for developers to examine factors such as the amount of land available for industrial development in the submarket and to estimate the number of years before the available land supply is absorbed, given the likely pace of development. Some market analysts and data providers use econometric models to forecast new construction. Those numbers may not be entirely accurate, but they provide an approximation of future conditions.

Developers should keep in mind that the public sector may influence future supply. Cities and redevelopment agencies offer incentives to industrial tenants. If developers are not offered the same benefits as those available to others, they are at a competitive disadvantage.

An analysis of potential competitors can assess the strengths of the proposed project compared with its competition. A good place to start to collect detailed data is from real estate brokers or management companies involved in marketing industrial developments; they may be willing to provide plans or brochures and marketing materials about individual properties.

The developer should collect information about the following aspects of competing projects:

- overall site area and size of individual lots and buildings if it is a multibuilding development;
- schedule, including date when marketing was initiated;
- occupancy levels at the date of the survey (acres sold, total square feet leased for each type of facility, percentage of space occupied);
- estimated annual land absorption;
- estimated annual space absorption by property type;
- initial and current sales prices and lease rates per square foot (land and buildings);

This sample market study focuses on a proposed big-box warehouse and distribution facility development in the Atlanta area similar to the case study of the Conyers Logistics Center featured at the end of this chapter.

The Atlanta industrial market consists of nine submarkets. The subject site is located in the Snapfinger/I-20 East industrial submarket, which extends eastward from downtown Atlanta along interstate I-20. The South Atlanta and Northeast Atlanta submarkets together make up well over half of the total warehouse space in the region. The Snapfinger/I-20 East submarket is smaller, containing about 6 percent of the total warehouse inventory in the region (see figure A). However, as demand for warehouse space has outpaced supply in the larger submarkets, tenants have increasingly sought space in smaller submarkets like Northwest Atlanta and Snapfinger/I-20 East.[a]

Demand for warehouse and distribution facilities is generally driven by corporate logistics and freight volumes and, increasingly, by proximity to e-commerce customers. An analysis of historical net absorption—the change in occupied space over a given period of time—is one approach to estimating demand. Annual net absorption of warehouse space in the Atlanta region reached 37.8 million square feet (3.5 million sq m) in 2021, a historic high; 1.7 million square feet (157,900 sq m) of that absorption occurred in the Snapfinger/I-20 East submarket[b] (figure B). A substantial amount of the occupancy gains came from tenants occupying big-box space. Absorption of big-box space reached 17 million square feet (1.6 million sq m) in 2020 in the Atlanta region; as of mid-year 2021, net absorption had already reached 15.8 million square feet (1.5 million sq m)[c] (figure C).

Leasing activity has been at historically high levels as well, surpassing that of 2020. The warehouse vacancy rate in the Atlanta region was 3.4 percent at the end of 2021, a year-over-year decline of 310 basis points (3.1 percent). The vacancy rate in the Snapfinger/I-20 East submarket decreased by 80 basis points (0.8 percent) in one year to finish 2021 at 4.0 percent.[d] As a result of the strong demand in the market and record-low vacancy rate, warehouse rents in the Atlanta region increased for a 10th straight year, rising 8.6 percent in 2021. The average warehouse rent reached $5.05 per square foot at the end of 2021. Average rent in the Snapfinger/I-20 East submarket increased to $4.99 in 2021[e] (figure B). Characterization of specific submarket rents and lease terms, as well as physical characteristics, was obtained through a review of comparable properties (figure D).

Record demand was accompanied by record additions to supply. At the end of 2021, 37.8 million square feet (3.5 million sq m) of warehouse space was under construction in the Atlanta region.[f] In the Snapfinger/I-20 East submarket, four buildings totaling 1.4 million square feet (130,100 sq m) were delivered in 2021, and more than 779,000 square feet (72,400 sq m) of industrial space was under construction at the end of the year.[g] Notably, the submarket has maintained consistently low vacancy rates over the past four years, despite the substantial amount of deliveries in that time frame.[h]

The amount of investment activity in industrial real estate in the Atlanta region was substantial in 2021. Nearly $5.5 billion was invested in industrial real estate, surpassing the previous record by more than 100 percent.[i] Big-box industrial facilities in the Atlanta region transacted at just under $90 per square foot on average in 2021.[j]

Overall, the Atlanta region has averaged slightly more than 28 million square feet (2.6 million sq m) of annual absorption over the past two-and-a-half years. Colliers Research anticipates that lease rates will continue to escalate; however, increases will begin to lessen as new supply enters the market.[k] The firm contends that the same market forces that drove the Atlanta industrial market in 2021 will continue into 2022, though not at the record levels of 2021.

[a]Spencer Papciak, correspondence with author, February 25, 2022.

[b]Colliers, *Atlanta Industrial Report 19Q3, 19Q4* (Atlanta, GA: Colliers, 2019); Colliers, *Atlanta Industrial Report 20Q1, 20Q2, 20Q3, 20Q4* (Atlanta, GA: Colliers, 2020); Colliers, *Atlanta Industrial Report 21Q1, 21Q2, 21Q3, 21Q4* (Atlanta, GA: Colliers, 2021).

[c]Amanda Ortiz, Pete Quinn, and Jack Rosenberg, *Big-Box Market Report: North America—2021 Midyear Review & Outlook* (Toronto: Colliers, 2021).

[d]Colliers, *Atlanta Industrial Reports [19Q3, 19Q4, 20Q1, 20Q2, 20Q3, 20Q4, 21Q1, 21Q2, 21Q3, 21Q4].*

[e]Colliers, *Atlanta Industrial Reports [19Q3, 19Q4, 20Q1, 20Q2, 20Q3, 20Q4, 21Q1, 21Q2, 21Q3, 21Q4].*

[f]Colliers, *Atlanta Industrial Report 21Q4.*

[g]Lincoln Property Company Southeast, *Atlanta Industrial Report: Snapfinger/I-20 East Industrial Submarket Q4 2021* (Atlanta, GA: Lincoln Property Company, 2022).

[h]Papciak, correspondence.

[i]Colliers, *Atlanta Industrial Report 21Q4.*

[j]Colliers, *Atlanta Industrial Report 21Q4.*

[k]Colliers, *Atlanta Industrial Report 21Q4.*

Warehouse Space Inventory in the Atlanta Region by Submarket, 2021

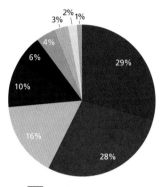

- South Atlanta
- Northeast Atlanta
- I-20 West/Fulton
- Northwest Atlanta
- Snapfinger/I-20 East
- Stone Mountain
- North Central Atlanta
- Chattahoochee
- Central Atlanta

Source: Colliers, *Atlanta Industrial Report 21Q4* (Atlanta, GA: Colliers, 2021).

FIGURE B Warehouse Space Inventory for the Atlanta Market and the Snapfinger/I-20 East Submarket

	SNAPFINGER/I-20 EAST INDUSTRIAL SUBMARKET				ATLANTA INDUSTRIAL MARKET			
Period	Inventory (million sq ft)	Net absorp. (million sq ft)	Vacancy rate	Avg. NNN rent	Inventory (million sq ft)	Net absorp. (million sq ft)	Vacancy rate	Avg. NNN rent
2019 Q3	36.2	0.034	3.9%	$4.09	608.1	6.186	7.0%	$4.42
2019 Q4	36.3	0.152	3.4%	$4.28	612.6	4.197	7.1%	$4.42
2020 Q1	36.7	0.127	3.6%	$4.62	619.8	0.640	7.8%	$4.51
2020 Q2	36.7	0.309	2.7%	$4.70	627.7	4.744	7.6%	$4.56
2020 Q3	37.2	0.060	4.0%	$4.68	633.9	8.427	6.9%	$4.57
2020 Q4	37.5	(0.098)	4.8%	$4.69	641.2	8.306	6.5%	$4.65
2021 Q1	37.5	0.323	3.8%	$4.86	647.1	10.622	5.6%	$4.74
2021 Q2	37.5	0.117	3.3%	$4.90	649.9	6.957	4.9%	$4.90
2021 Q3	37.6	0.381	2.7%	$4.92	653.8	5.561	4.5%	$4.99
2021 Q4	39.3	0.886	4.0%	$4.99	662.1	14.631	3.4%	$5.05

Sources: Colliers, *Atlanta Industrial Report, 19Q3, 19Q4* (Atlanta, GA: Colliers, 2019); Colliers, *Atlanta Industrial Report, 20Q1, 20Q2, 20Q3, 20Q4* (Atlanta, GA: Colliers, 2020); Colliers, *Atlanta Industrial Report, 21Q1, 21Q2, 21Q3, 21Q4* (Atlanta, GA: Colliers, 2021).

Note: NNN = triple-net.

FIGURE C Big-Box Warehouse Absorption, Completions, and Vacancy Rate in the Atlanta Region, 2011 to Midyear 2021

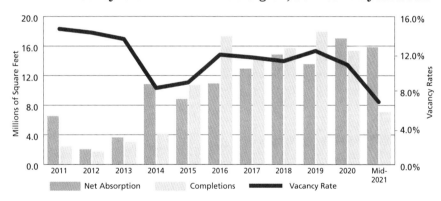

FIGURE D Comparable Properties, Snapfinger/I-20 East Submarket

Property		Area (sq ft)	Year built	Clear height (ft)	Bay size (ft)	Number of dock doors	Asking/ leased rent (NNN, per sq ft)
COMPARABLE PROPERTIES (SELECTED)							
11300 Hazelbrand Road	Covington, GA	322,560	2022	32 - 36	52 x 56	57	$4.08–$4.98
East Atlanta Logistics, Hwy 142	Covington, GA	200,880	2022	32	50 x 50	38	$3.93–$4.77
2420 Old Covington	Conyers, GA	288,477	2021	32	54 x 50	60	$4.19–$5.12
2082 East Park Drive	Conyers, GA	216,000	2020	32	54 x 50	24	$4.95
2430 Dogwood Drive	Conyers, GA	185,000	2019	30	52 x 50	58	$4.23–$5.17
1940 Twin Creeks Parkway	Conyers, GA	240,000	2018	32	48 x 50	44	$4.23–$5.16
1990 Twin Creeks Parkway	Conyers, GA	240,000	2018	32	48 x 50	44	$4.23–$5.16
800 Sigman Road	Conyers, GA	175,000	2016	28	48 x 52	39	$4.95
700 Sigman Road	Conyers, GA	149,760	2008	28	48 x 52	32	$4.50

Sources: Lincoln Property Company, CoStar.

Note: NNN = triple-net.

- lease terms and concessions;
- tenant improvement allowances to finish interior space;
- building characteristics and quality of architectural and landscape design, level of finish, quality of materials, signage, and maintenance;
- development cost per acre;
- major highway access, rail availability, and utilities;
- amenities such as retail services, restaurants, open space, recreation, child care, and health and conference facilities; and
- developer or current owner.

DEMAND ANALYSIS. Unlike demand for office properties, demand for industrial space is generated by changes in corporate logistics, not by job growth. Developers should review measures of metropolitan growth, such as gross metropolitan product, freight volumes, and changes in total population or households. Growth in gross metropolitan product is a good indicator of absorption of warehouse and distribution space, because it is a measure of the output of a local economy. Another indicator is manufacturing output as measured by the Federal Reserve Board's Index of Manufacturing Output. Sometimes demand is tied to growth in another nearby city. For example, warehouse space along the U.S. border in southern California is correlated with the growth of warehouse space in nearby Mexican cities.

After space demand is calculated for a metropolitan area, a final step is to estimate what share of the area's absorption will be captured by the submarket where the property is located. Often, the concept of *fair share* is used. For example, if a submarket accounts for 6 percent of a metropolitan area's industrial space inventory, then its fair share is 6 percent. Another method is to examine the historical share of net absorption in the submarket in relation to the metropolitan area's net absorption over time. That information should provide an overview of how well the area stacks up against other locations. If a submarket is overbuilt, a developer may choose to hold the land for some period of time before beginning construction.

Industrial development provides a back door into both office and retail development, and market analysts sometimes mistakenly include absorption figures for office and retail users in their estimates of demand. The distinction between product types can be made primarily by the amount of tenant improvements. Care must be taken to isolate the percentage of nonindustrial users.

REGULATORY ISSUES

If the developer is building within the existing zoning and subdivision restrictions, the approval process is similar to that for commercial and office buildings. If variances or changes in zoning are needed, however, the approval process may be lengthy and expensive. Planning commissions and city councils tend to be especially concerned about truck traffic as well as noise, pollution, and other negative effects of the planned industrial development. Some communities may be eager to attract the employment opportunities that industrial development may generate, while many others are more concerned about environmental issues and about preserving the character of residential neighborhoods and business districts.

The approval process for business parks is similar to that described in chapter 3. Although the basic procedures for platting industrial subdivisions depend on the local area, most communities begin with some form of tentative approval, such as the tentative tract map in California. After appropriate review by the public, the developer is eligible to obtain a final tract map, also called the subdivision plat. The final tract map indicates the lot lines, setback requirements, allowable floor/area ratios (FARs), and other restrictions that determine the developer's buildable site and its density.

ZONING LAWS. Zoning laws dictate where and in what form various land uses, such as residential, commercial, and industrial, can be built. Traditional "Euclidian" zoning laws aim to separate incompatible land uses. That aim is particularly relevant for industrial land uses because noise, dust, odor, traffic safety, and congestion are paramount, and zoning is designed to establish areas where industrial uses can occur while protecting residents and businesses. Some municipalities use zoning to attract desired industrial development—and the economic benefits it may bring—to designated areas.

Specific zoning categories vary substantially among jurisdictions. The requirements for an industrial zone in one municipality may be very different from those in another. Furthermore, industrial districts may be broken down into categories where certain types of uses are and are not allowed. A developer must consult a municipality's zoning code for specific requirements for development on a particular parcel. A zoning analysis begins by consulting the zoning map to determine the zoning district within which the property is located and then the zoning ordinance; zoning maps are often accessible online.

Several basic types of zoning districts are commonly used for industrial and business park development. Most common are use-by-right districts, planned unit developments (PUDs) or planned developments (PDs), and special purpose districts.

- *Use by right* refers to land uses specifically permitted in a zoning district and therefore not subject to special review or approval, provided they meet all requirements of the district set forth in the zoning ordinance. A developer must obtain a zoning permit, but approval of uses by right is not subject to further approvals.
- *PUD and PD districts*, also called overlay zoning districts, allow flexibility in the design of development projects in specially designed areas. Under PUD or PD zoning, a property is developed in accordance with an approved development plan instead of the standard zoning code.
- Special purpose districts are zoning districts created by jurisdictions to achieve specific planning objectives, tailored to unique characteristics of an area.

Zoning restrictions determine the use, size, bulk, and location of the structures that can be built on a given parcel of land. Typical zoning regulations for industrial buildings include minimum lot area; minimum and maximum floor area; maximum FAR and gross area; maximum building height; minimum lot width; maximum impervious surface area; minimum open space; access; and minimum front, side, and rear yard setbacks. Restrictions also cover parking, landscape buffer, streetscape, and building design requirements.

Although Euclidian-based zoning ordinances have traditionally separated land uses from one another and limited the mix of uses, greater commingling of different land uses has occurred in recent years. The recognition that business parks often end up as sterile work settings without basic services or amenities for employees has led some communities to allow plans that include shopping facilities, restaurants, hotels, and even residential uses.

Industrial developers also pursue rezoning of land that, for example, would shift it from agricultural to industrial uses. Although rezoning land can be highly profitable, it can be a long, difficult, and expensive process—with no guarantee of success.

COVENANTS, CONDITIONS, AND RESTRICTIONS.
Covenants, conditions, and restrictions (CC&Rs) are private land use controls and standards commonly used for business parks. CC&Rs take the form of a legally enforceable instrument filed with the plat or deed of individual buildings. They supplement municipal regulations, such as zoning and subdivision controls, and apply to many aspects of a business park's development, including site coverage, architectural design, building materials, parking requirements, signage, and landscaping.

Design guidelines can be included as part of the CC&Rs or as a separate document. They establish very specific uniform guidelines and criteria regarding bulk, height, types of materials, fenestration, and overall design of the building. Subdivision restrictions sometimes require facilities for employees, such as outdoor lunch areas, recreation areas, and open space.

PUBLIC/PRIVATE NEGOTIATIONS.
Developers frequently must negotiate agreements with local municipalities to secure approval for proposed industrial developments. Those agreements are especially helpful in volatile political climates in which shifting pressures to limit growth may cause local governments to change development entitlements unexpectedly. Public/private negotiations are also required when a developer seeks to work with a public agency on publicly owned land or in redevelopment areas.

In California, for example, public/private contracts take the form of development agreements that usually require considerable time to negotiate. The agreements protect developers from later changes in zoning or other regulations that affect development entitlements and lend an air of certainty to the regulatory process by delineating most rights, requirements, and procedures in advance. Once adopted, no surprises related to approval should occur. Most agencies, however, require something in return, such as special amenities or fees.

The use of public/private negotiations to shape the form of industrial developments is widespread, though not routine. In high-growth areas, public displeasure with the negative impacts of development has led to direct public involvement in negotiations with developers over specific projects. Many municipalities and counties have realized that well-planned industrial facilities can provide significant revenues to the municipalities in the form of property taxes. Some communities have therefore established redevelopment agencies to supervise negotiations with private developers and to represent the community's interests as development proceeds. The public sector's role can include

- sharing risks with the developer through land price write-downs and participation in cash flows;
- creating utility districts and contributing toward off-site infrastructure;
- participating in loan commitments and mortgages;
- sharing operating and capital costs;
- reducing administrative red tape; and
- providing favorable tax treatment.

The role that private developers play is also expanding. Their functions may include paying for major off-site infrastructure and building highway interchanges.

DEVELOPMENT AND IMPACT FEES. Some stages of the regulatory process require public hearings, and many require some form of fee. The developer should understand the full range and scope of charges before closing on a parcel of land for development. Some of the more common fees assessed on industrial development projects include the following:

- **Approval and variance fees**—either a lump sum or a charge for the actual time spent by government personnel on processing an application
- **Plan check fees**—generally, a percentage of valuation
- **Building permit fees**—generally, a percentage of valuation
- **Water system fees**—possibly based on amount of water used, meter size, frontage on water lines, or a combination
- **Sewer system fees**—usually based on expected discharge
- **Storm drainage fees**—usually based on runoff generated or on acreage
- **Transportation fees**—based on trips generated or on square footage (some areas have highway fees, county fees, and local transportation improvement fees)
- **School fees**—charged per square foot in some areas
- **Fire and police fees**—usually based on square footage
- **Library, child care, and various other fees**

The types and amounts of fees vary from one jurisdiction to another. The developer must learn each municipality's and each agency's particular system of imposing fees. Because the fees can be imposed by a multitude of agencies, the developer should check with every agency that could possibly set fees. In many jurisdictions, the building department handles a majority of the fees and can be a good source of preliminary information.

STATE AND LOCAL INCENTIVES. State and local governments have developed a variety of incentive mechanisms to encourage industrial development:

- State and local loans and grants. State and local governments offer commercial loans, loan and development bond guarantees, infrastructure projects that aid particular industries, and even venture capital funds.
- Tax increment financing. TIF districts are geographically designated areas within which the difference between new taxes generated by development and the original taxes is reserved for infrastructure improvements for the designated area.
- Enterprise zones. Enterprise zones are geographically designated areas that offer incentives to companies that locate in the zones. Incentives include property tax abatements, industrial development bonds, exemptions from income and sales taxes, low-interest venture capital, infrastructure improvements, and special public services.
- Opportunity zones. Opportunity zones were created through the Tax Cuts and Jobs Act of 2017 to spur economic and job creation in distressed communities. A Qualified Opportunity Zone is a geographically defined area in which capital investments may be eligible for preferential tax treatment.
- Incubator parks. Publicly owned business incubator parks are designed to accommodate small startup companies. New York State Certified Business Incubators is an example of one such program. Located throughout the state of New York, the facilities provide support for early-stage companies.

Financial Feasibility

As with other product types, financial analysis for industrial development is performed several times during the feasibility period. At the very least, it should be updated three times before closing on the land: (1) before submitting the earnest money contract, (2) before approaching lenders, and (3) before going hard on the land purchase.

At each stage of development, the information gains greater certainty and accuracy. Data from the market study, design information, and cost estimates are incorporated into the financial pro forma as the information becomes available. Developers should not wait until such studies are done, however, before performing financial analysis; cruder information based on secondary sources may be used at earlier stages. For example, as soon as the size of the structure to be built is estimated, the construction cost can be estimated from average costs per square foot for similar projects. Construction cost information is available from companies such as RSMeans, and contractors and other developers may share cost information.

The method of analysis for business park development is different from that for industrial building development. Business park development is a form of land development and follows the approach for analyzing for-sale property described in chapter 3. The stages of analysis for industrial building development are similar to the five stages of discounted cash flow analysis for income-producing property described in chapter 4.

Return expectations vary geographically. But for new industrial development on unentitled land in primary U.S. markets, developers generally target internal rates of return (IRR) on total project cost in the high single digits to low double digits for an all-equity (unleveraged) development project.[34] That amounts to a leveraged IRR in the low teens. The developer should use the financial pro forma to perform sensitivity analysis to test the impact that assumptions with respect to rental rates and concessions, construction costs, financing costs, interest rates, and inflation assumptions, as well as leasing schedules, have on the IRR. For business park development, the developer should also test what effect lowering land prices to sell the land faster has on the IRR.

Design and Construction

Industrial buildings must be designed to maximize the efficient movement of goods and to support the operational functions of their occupants. Functionality, construction costs, and long-term maintenance are the most crucial concerns in the design and construction of industrial facilities. The length of the construction period for a class A warehouse development, like the one outlined in this section, is seven to nine months. Depending on the area of the country in which the site is located, attention must be paid to the timing of the start of construction because of the potential impacts of seasonal weather effects.

The following section presents the major design and construction parameters that a developer should be aware of when planning a speculative, class A warehouse and distribution facility. The elements are embodied in the design of the Conyers Logistics Center, presented at the end of this chapter.

SITE DESIGN

The design of warehouse facilities must include the site and the building in tandem as an integrated whole. The site design is a critical component of the functionality of the facility. The site design orchestrates the efficient movement of goods and materials, primarily via tractor-trailer, into and out of the facility. Site design and civil engineering are the biggest challenges in industrial development; according to Barry DiRaimondo, CEO of SteelWave, "If it isn't done right, the rest of the project will be a mess."[35]

Generally, industrial facilities require large tracts of flat land. Traditional warehouses and distribution centers, as well as truck terminals, require large open floor space, all on one level, to accommodate the users' efficient business operations. Changes in floor level that are across the length of a building and that might be incorporated into other types of commercial buildings are not easily accommodated in a large, single-story industrial building. A grade change of just 1 percent across the length of a 950-foot-long (290 m) building, such as in the case study building presented at the end of this chapter, would result in 9.5-foot (2.9 m) change in elevation. Excavation or fill to address grade changes, even seemingly minor ones, can be very expensive and time-consuming. Therefore, identifying a flat site on which to construct an industrial facility has important consequences for construction costs and time.

The site design of an industrial project should maximize the site coverage while accommodating efficient truck circulation, docking, and parking. Zoning ordinances will dictate required front, side, and rear setback requirements, designating the area of the site where the building may be constructed. Even though warehouse and distribution buildings have gotten substantially larger in recent years, the site coverage of warehouse buildings has decreased, meaning sites are becoming even larger to accommodate the demand for more loading and trailer parking. Deviations from the ideal site configuration can be tolerated, especially if the location is particularly advantageous to the user. But sites with dimensions below a certain threshold will be unsuitable for certain types of industrial development. Conversely, sites that are too large may be too expensive to financially support industrial development.

Each stage of the site design process involves the collection and analysis of information about the site and the identification and evaluation of alternatives. Throughout the process, the developer and design

The site design of the Conyers Logistics Center in Conyers, Georgia, includes two 185-foot-deep (56 m) truck yards flanking the building, each of which accommodates a row of tractor-trailers parked at dock doors and a row of trailer parking.

team should maintain a meaningful dialogue with relevant public agency representatives because they can assist in compliance and in facilitating public support.

VEHICULAR CIRCULATION. Trucks are the dominant mode for the transportation of goods in the United States, accounting for 61 percent of goods by value in 2018.[36] Thus, the site design of industrial facilities must allow for trucks to turn off local roads and be checked into the facility, to circulate through the site to a designated dock, to back up to a dock door, and then to pull away from the building and exit the property.

Understanding the dimensions of a typical tractor-trailer rig in the United States is important when undertaking site planning for a warehouse facility. Trailer lengths vary from 40 feet (12.2 m)—the standard length of a shipping container frame—to the length of single trailers being towed by a truck or truck tractor, 48 and 53 feet (14.6 and 16.2 m). The particular configurations of tractor-trailers affect their maneuverability. The WB-67 configuration—a 53-foot (16.2 m) trailer with an overnight cab—has an overall length of about 73 feet (22.3 m) and a width of 8.5 feet (2.6 m). The WB-67 rig is the longest tractor-trailer rig in most states and the scenario for which institutional-grade logistics facilities should be planned.

In countries where vehicles drive on the right side of the road, the driver is seated on the left side of the truck cab. In this situation, the counterclockwise circu-

lation of trucks through the property is ideal because it allows drivers to look over their left shoulder while backing up to a dock door.[37] Planning for counterclockwise truck circulation may then dictate the building orientation and the location of the property's vehicular entrances and exits.

To accommodate single-swing turns of a WB-67 tractor-trailer, all driveways should be at least 40 feet (12.2 m) wide with a minimum 40-foot (12.2 m) inside curb radius.[38] The design of the site must also take into account space for trucks to queue so that they can be checked into and out of the facility. The amount of truck queuing space varies by building size, local market, and tenant preference.

Because truck traffic—along with the commensurate wear and tear on local roads as well as safety and pollution—is a chief concern of most communities, developers must understand the impact that their proposed developments will have on local roads. For purposes of design, developers should estimate the percentage and directional distribution of truck traffic.

TRUCK DOCKS AND YARDS. The building and site should be designed in tandem to allow for a tractor-trailer rig to back up to a dock door while the two adjacent dock doors are occupied by full rigs. The minimum truck yard depth required depends on the spacing of the dock doors. Assuming dock doors are spaced 13 feet (4 m) on center, truck yards for large warehouse and distribution facilities should be a minimum of 130 feet (39.6 m) deep.[39]

Space devoted to trailer parking is an important site planning consideration as well. Trailers may be parked at dock doors, but they are often also parked in a row opposite the dock doors. A 185-foot-deep (56.4 m) truck yard accommodates tractor-trailer movement as well as a row of parked trailers.

Trailers, when not connected to trucks, have landing legs to support the front portion. The landing legs will damage asphalt pavement over time, as will the rear wheels of trucks as they pull away from the dock. A concrete apron (more durable than asphalt) should be provided where trailers are parked at a suggested depth of 60 feet (18.3 m) extending from the face of the building. Concrete aprons should also be provided for the row of trailer parking adjacent, 40 to 60 feet (12.2 to 18.3 m) from the back of the stall. Alternatively, concrete could be used for the entire yard, but it is more expensive than asphalt.

RAIL ACCESS. Most tenants do not require access to rail. If access is contemplated, however, railroad officials should be contacted early in the design process to determine design requirements, and the approval time is likely to be long. As a rule of thumb, rail door spacing should be 70 feet (21.3 m) on center, and the minimum rail spur radius should be 500 feet (152.4 m).[40]

PARKING. Parking requirements vary considerably for logistics facilities. Traditional warehouses require few parking spaces, while fulfillment centers may require on the order of three spaces per 1,000 square feet (92.9 sq m). The site design must accommodate the minimum number of parking spaces required by the zoning code; however, depending on the number of people working in a facility at any one time and the number of visitors, parking needs may be substantially greater. Adequate employee parking may be seen as an amenity to attract workers in tight labor markets. Parking for automobiles is best kept separate from truck traffic and located near the entrance to the facility.

LANDSCAPING. The design of the landscape surrounding an industrial facility can serve to conceal elements of the building while accentuating others and may be required by local zoning codes. Earthen berms and strategically placed trees can visually screen dock and trailer parking areas, which is particularly desirable when the facility abuts residential areas. But care should be taken not to block drivers' sightlines. Landscaping near pedestrian and automobile entrances can draw attention to building signage, and landscaped outdoor patios can be an employee amenity. The landscaping should ideally include native plants and be low maintenance, hearty, and drought tolerant.

BUILDING DESIGN AND CONSTRUCTION

In tandem with the design of the site, the design of a warehouse and distribution facility must combine functionality with economy of construction and maintenance. Warehouse design should maximize tenants' efficient use of *the cube*—the cubic volume of a warehouse space.

Beginning developers should study the design and construction of other buildings that serve the same local market. Those developers should speak to tenants to learn about the equipment they use, their workflow, and building features they require and to contractors about ways to build economically. And such developers should choose an architect who specializes in the industrial building type that they are planning, as well as speaking to contractors and other developers who have previously worked with that architect.

As with other product types, a team approach to design and construction is most effective. Ideally, the contractor and the leasing agent should be part of the design team beginning in the early stages of the design process and should work with the architect to obtain a design that is both functional and marketable. Local conditions can dramatically affect the design of elements, such as the footings and foundations. Thus, using past construction cost data for a new project is ill advised until more is known about the parameters of the building and site.[41]

Warehouse and distribution buildings can be enormously large structures, but their design is largely based on the simple and ubiquitous wooden pallet. In the United States, warehousing and distribution involves *pallet loads*, the most common way of moving and storing packaged freight. Pallets (about 42 by 48 inches [107 by 122 cm]) are platforms that consolidate goods so that they can be lifted onto and

ASHLEY CAPITAL

off trailers and storage racks using forklifts. Pallet *unit loads* then can be broken down into *sales units*, the smallest unit that a consumer can buy from a retailer. The building and design information presented in the following paragraphs refers to the warehousing of palletized loads. Particular forms of e-commerce fulfillment facilities that enable direct delivery to consumers necessitate the picking and packaging of sales units and will vary in their physical requirements.

CLEAR HEIGHT. The *clear height* is measured as the minimum distance between the finished floor and the lowest structural member of the roof. It indicates the vertical, racked storage capacity of the building. The clear height of a warehouse is an important metric for prospective tenants.

Usable clear heights in warehouse and distribution facilities are governed by limits of the material handling equipment and ESFR sprinkler systems. Until very recently, ESFR sprinklers limited warehouse building ceiling heights to 45 feet (13.7 m), with a maximum storage height of 40 feet (12.2 m). Recently, ESFR systems have been approved for ceiling and deck heights of up to 55 feet (16.8 m), with a maximum storage height of 50 feet (15.2 m), under certain configurations.[42] Those limits are likely to change, however, as new ESFR configurations are approved for use in taller buildings.

RACK SYSTEMS. Pallet rack systems are a primary component of warehouse and distribution facilities. Standardized pallets, as described earlier, are picked up with material handling equipment (forklifts) and placed on rack systems. Racks are typically 48 inches deep (1.2 m) and are spaced back-to-back with a six-inch (15 cm) flue space—required by fire codes—in between. Aisle widths vary depending on the type of material handling equipment used.

A standard 60-foot (18.3 m) speed bay at the Conyers Logistics Center facilitates the staging of goods and materials as they are moved onto and off trailers.

There are three major types of material handling equipment, distinguished by aisle width requirements and height limitations: *standard aisle* (SA), *narrow aisle* (NA), and *very narrow aisle* (VNA). NA reach forklifts are the most common type of material handling equipment in most logistics facilities. They can operate in buildings with 28- to 32-foot (8.5 to 9.8 m) clear heights and up to 40-foot (12.2 m) clear heights with aisles 102 and 118 inches (2.6 and 3.0 m) wide, respectively. VNA equipment can take advantage of clear heights of 36 to 40 feet (11.0 to 12.2 m) with racks spaced as narrowly as 54 inches (1.4 m) apart—often semiautomated at higher speeds—but it comes at a higher cost.[43] VNA equipment is rarely used in buildings with clear heights less than 36 feet (11 m), because less expensive reach forklifts can operate at lower heights. These critical measurements set the dimensions of the structural grid so that columns fall between the racks and within the flue space. Rack systems and NA forklift equipment that fits within a 36-foot (11 m) clear height building are most commonly used.

COLUMN GRID. Speculative warehouse buildings are usually designed as single-story, rectangular buildings with a large interior open area that can accommodate a variety of user operations. Interior columns are a necessary part of the building structure, and their placement has important consequences for the use of the space. Column-free interior space might be desirable, but as the distance between columns increases, so does the cost of the roof structure. Thus, the spacing of the columns must balance function and cost and must accommodate standard rack systems (discussed earlier).

Warehouse facilities are usually configured with the dock doors on the long side of the building (or two parallel sides in the case of a cross-dock facility). The first interior bay adjacent to the dock doors—called the *speed bay*—is where goods are staged for loading and off-loading from trailers. The racking system is usually oriented with the racks perpendicular to the speed bay. Material handling equipment then moves along the speed bay and takes a 90-degree turn into the aisles to access the racks. Therefore, the spacing of the column grid running parallel to the dock doors is dictated by required aisle widths of the material handling equipment used.

For warehouse facilities that have a clear height of less than 32 feet (9.8 m) and that use NA racking equipment, the industry-standard column spacing is 52 feet (15.8 m), to fit three aisles within a column bay. For facilities with clear heights of 32 to 40 feet (11.0 to 12.8 m), the recommended column spacing is 56 feet (17.1 m). For buildings with clear heights of 42 feet (12.8 m) and higher, the recommended column spacing is 58 feet (17.7 m) because of the specialized forklifts and consequent wider aisle spacing required.[44] The accommodation of VNA equipment—designed for buildings with the highest clear heights—is less common in speculative buildings. Planning for NA material handling equipment (reach forklifts) is most common for speculative and spec-to-suit warehouse buildings. The depth of the speed bay is often 60 feet (18.3 m), the longest cost-efficient steel joist span. In e-commerce fulfillment centers, a 56-foot (17.1 m) by 60-foot (18.3 m) column grid accommodates the order picking equipment that is commonly used.

The column spacing in the direction perpendicular to the dock doors is independent from racking system requirements; however, the location of ESFR sprinkler lines and heads plays an important role. ESFR sprinklers are standard in institutional-grade logistics facilities to provide fire protection that meets code requirements for *high-piled storage*. They disperse a higher volume of larger droplets of water than do traditional sprinkler systems and are designed to fully suppress a fire. ESFR sprinklers avoid the need for in-rack sprinklers, but girders and joists, lighting, ductwork, and skylights can affect the position and spacing of ESFR sprinkler heads. The location of ESFR sprinkler lines and heads is optimized when the column grid perpendicular to the dock doors (in line with the rack system aisles) is in 10-foot (3 m) increments. Therefore, 50-foot (15.2 m) and 60-foot (18.3 m) bays are most cost-effective.[45]

The case study of the Conyers Logistics Center presented at the end of this chapter is an exemplar of those design considerations. The big-box distribution building has a 36-foot (11 m) clear height. Organized as a cross-dock facility, its speed bays are 60 feet (18.3 m) deep, and the column bays perpendicular to the dock doors are 50 feet (15.2 m) deep, which accommodates the ESFR sprinkler system. The columns running parallel to the dock doors and speed bay are spaced 56 feet (17.1 m) apart, which allows for the 118-inch (3 m) aisle required for material handling equipment to reach a 36-foot (11 m) height.

DOCK DOORS. Dock-height doors facilitate the loading and unloading of trailers. The number of dock doors and whether they are in a cross-dock configuration affect the efficient use of the cube—the throughput. Dock doors may be provided initially, or knock-out panels can be installed, allowing for additional dock doors should a future tenant require them.

Truck docks are typically nine feet (2.7 m) wide and 10 feet (3 m) high. They are positioned flush with the interior finished floor of the building, at an elevation about 48 inches (1.2 m) off the truck yard surface. Dock levelers adjust for variations in the bed heights of trailers. Pit levelers—mechanical, hydraulic, and air-pressure types—can typically accommodate truck bed heights 12 inches (30 cm) below and 12 inches (30 cm) above the finished floor. They require a recessed pit at the dock door in which the leveler mechanism is installed.

Drive-in doors allow smaller trucks, vans, and forklifts to enter the facility directly. They are often located on the same side of the building and adjacent to the dock-height doors; the earth is sloped upward to allow a smooth transition from the elevation of the truck yard to that of the finished floor of the building. Drive-in doors are typically 13 feet (4 m) wide by 14 feet (4.3 m) high.

The spacing of dock doors affects (and is affected by) the building design (the structural grid), site planning (truck yard depths), and building construction materials (tilt-up concrete panel design). The industry standard spacing of dock doors is 13 feet (4 m) on center, a distance that strikes a balance between maximizing the number of dock doors on the one hand and minimizing the cost of the building structure and wall cladding on the other.

FLOORS. The floor of a warehouse and distribution building is usually a concrete slab resting on a prepared subgrade. A qualified geotechnical engineer must investigate the soil under the proposed building and create a detailed geotechnical site condition report. The report will document the soil type and composition and the elevation of the water table, as well as any soil contamination. The engineer then recommends the specific composition and preparation of the subgrade. The subgrade usually involves several layers of recompacted soil, rock, gravel, and sand. The concrete slab may include steel reinforcement in the form of a mesh of steel reinforcement bars, particularly if the site contains expansive soils—soils that are prone to large changes in volume related to changes in water content. A plastic sheet vapor retarder between the subgrade and the slab may be added to minimize the transmission of water upward through the slab.[46]

The required concrete slab thickness is generally related to the building's clear height. Buildings with clear heights up to 32 feet (9.8 m) generally have six-inch-thick (15.2 cm) slabs; those with 32- to 40-foot (9.8 to 12.2 m) clear heights should have seven- to eight-inch-thick (17.8 to 20.3 cm) slabs; and those with clear heights greater than 40 feet (12.2 m) should have nine- to 10-inch-thick (22.9 to 25.4 cm) slabs.[47] To mitigate naturally developing cracks in the concrete and their effects on the functioning of material handling equipment, saw-cut control joints are located at regular intervals throughout the slab.

Warehouse and distribution buildings generally require floors designated by the American Concrete Institute (ACI) as class 5 with a hard steel-troweled finish, designed for 3,500 psi minimum. Certain high clear height warehouses may require ACI class 9 superflat floors, which must have special hardeners and application procedures.[48] "Superflat" in this context should not be confused with the measure of flatness—the degree to which a surface approaches a geometric plane—and levelness, which are measured in F-numbers. Speculative warehouse facilities usually have a minimum FF (flatness) of 50 and a minimum FL (levelness) of 35.[49]

ROOFS. Roofs are generally constructed in the most cost-effective manner appropriate for the part of the country in which the development is located. Roof systems vary across the United States, but they generally include steel joist girders and joists topped with corrugated steel or oriented strand board decking. The deeper joist girders span from column to column, generally parallel to the speed bay. The smaller joists span from girder to girder, spaced eight to 10 feet on

center. In buildings with concrete tilt-up panels forming the exterior walls (described shortly), the joists spanning the speed bay are supported by the exterior walls. Rigid insulation can be placed on top of the roof decking. Expansion joints, also called slip joints, should be installed to accommodate horizontal movement in large buildings using steel decking.

On top of the roof structure and insulation is the roof membrane, which does the all-important work of keeping water out of the building. The most common type of roof for warehouse and distribution buildings is a thermoplastic polyolefin (TPO) roof. TPO roofing is a single-ply membrane—rolled sheets of material that are ballasted, mechanically fastened, or adhered to insulation to cover flat roofs. TPO membranes have a reflective surface and high albedo, decreasing the solar heat retained and thereby decreasing the energy used to cool the building. A so-called flat roof is actually sloped to allow water to drain, but that slope is limited to the requirements for the ESFR sprinkler system.

Skylights have many benefits in warehouse and distribution buildings. They allow natural light deep into the center of large-footprint buildings, reduce the need for artificial lighting and therefore may reduce energy costs, satisfy energy-code daylight requirements, and potentially provide ventilation. Skylights require a penetration in the roof, however, and if not properly constructed may increase the risk of roof leaks.

EXTERIOR WALLS. The walls of warehouse and distribution buildings are commonly constructed of tilt-up concrete panels. The concrete panels are poured on site as horizontal slabs. Then they are tilted vertically into position by a crane and set on foundations to create the wall structure. The panels are initially supported by temporary bracing; the joists and joist girders are then attached to embedded steel plates to tie the entire structure together.

Tilt-up concrete panels can take on myriad textures and colors. The panels are load bearing, so any openings in the panel (e.g., dock door openings, doors, and windows) must allow for the panel to support itself. Thus, every opening must be flanked with concrete of sufficient width. Because tilt-up concrete panels do not have to be shipped to the site by truck, highway transportation limits do not constrain their size.

An advantage of tilt-up construction is that the building can be erected quickly and economically. The concrete panels take a few days to cure on site, but tilting them into place is quicker and less labor-intensive than are other construction methods. Much of the work is repetitive and done at ground level. Moreover, the construction materials—ready-mix concrete and rebar—can often be sourced locally. The resulting walls are durable and require little long-term maintenance.

BUILDING SYSTEMS. Power requirements have grown substantially for all industrial uses. Logistics facilities are becoming more automated. Conveying systems, robotics, and computer systems have substantial power requirements, as does the charging of electric delivery vehicles, forklifts, and other equipment. Thus, the demand for electrical power has grown substantially in only a few years. Some tenants are demanding 8,000 or 10,000 amps of power.[50] For speculative buildings, however, 2,400 to 3,000 amps service is common.

Warehouses and distribution centers are often climate-controlled to create a comfortable environment for the people who work there and to protect the goods stored. According to Amazon, all of its U.S. fulfillment centers are now air-conditioned.[51]

BUILDING AMENITIES. Logistics facilities are function- and construction-cost-driven developments. However, people work in the buildings, and their quality of life should be considered. Warehouse and distribution facility operators are facing difficulties recruiting and retaining workers. Comfortable, safe, and well-equipped facilities help to create an attractive place to work. Amenities include equipped lounge areas for employees and sufficient employee parking. In areas of the country at risk of severe weather, adequate emergency shelters must be provided so that employees can shelter safely.

Financing

The considerations for financing industrial development are essentially the same as those for financing other income property (see chapter 4). Equity—from the developer or from others—is invested; interim construction money is borrowed until the project is completed and leased. When the project reaches stabilized occupancy as defined in the permanent mortgage agreement, the permanent mortgage "takes out" (replaces) the construction mortgage. For that last step, industrial property may have an advantage over other income property: some mortgage lenders generally believe that industrial development is a more stable investment because its market is less volatile than other markets.

A tilt-up concrete panel is lifted into place to form the exterior walls of the Trade II building of the JAG Logistics Center in Denver, Colorado.

Beginning developers may face challenges financing projects. Dennis Williams, managing director at NorthMarq Capital, advises beginning developers not to get caught up in issues of sponsor strength. They should prepare a package (net worth, liquidity, backers, sources of capital), anticipate questions the lender may have, and have answers ready. Even if their answer is not ideal, having one that addresses the lender's concern gives them a leg up over others.[52]

The structure of financing for business parks is likely to be more complex than that for individual buildings, especially if the developer plans to develop both the park and some or all of the buildings in it. Land development frequently involves more than one interim loan. Separate loans for land acquisition, land development, and building construction may be required. The development of a single facility, by contrast, usually relies solely on a construction loan that also covers part of the land acquisition cost. Equity is required to pay for all predevelopment costs that occur before closing on the property because construction lenders will not fund construction loans before that event. After closing, equity is still required because loans cover only a portion of the project's development costs.

CONSTRUCTION LOANS

Commercial banks and debt funds are the primary sources of construction funding. In the wake of the global financial crisis, banks became very conservative in their lending practices and have largely remained so. If there is any product type with which banks will be more aggressive, it is industrial. But relative to the time before the crisis, construction lenders are still much more conservative than they once were.

Gayle Starr, former managing director of capital markets at Prologis, says that when evaluating a development project, construction lenders look at the project budget and determine if it is realistic. Those lenders examine the projected construction cost estimates, lease-up periods, and tenant improvement allowances and determine whether the budget is robust enough to ensure completion. Construction lenders also look at the condition of the land and any environmental issues. Lenders are concerned with whether they will incur costs associated with environmental issues or be impaired from selling the property if they take the building back in the case of a default. Sophisticated lenders will also look at the details of the building itself to assess whether it is a functional industrial building. They will evaluate the clear heights, column grid dimensions, and number of dock doors, as well as whether it is divisible to leasable sizes, among other concerns.[53]

Construction financing is usually non-amortizing—interest only—with a variable interest rate. Funds are drawn monthly to cover current project costs, including interest on the current loan balance. The developer submits draw requests to the construction lender on the basis of construction completed to date. The lender's inspector verifies that the work has been done; then the lender transfers the money into the developer's project account. The construction loan agreement specifies a deadline for repayment of the principal, typically 24 to 36 months for individual industrial buildings.

A construction loan from a commercial bank may finance up to 65 percent of the cost of the project (loan-to-cost). Smaller banks tend to be a little more lenient in their underwriting, while larger banks are more conservative. Construction loan rates from commercial banks are about 300 basis points over the Secured Overnight Financing Rate (SOFR).

Another source of construction financing is debt funds. Generally, rather than raise capital from the public through their core business as a bank or insurance company does, debt funds raise capital from investors. The cost of capital to the developer is higher, however. The rate on a construction loan from a debt fund could be 500 basis points over SOFR. A construction loan from a debt fund may be preferable to one from a bank because it may be nonrecourse and may fund a higher loan-to-cost, possibly 70 to 75 percent.

PERMANENT LOANS

Once construction of the development is complete and the facility is leased up and producing a set amount of net operating income (NOI), the developer secures a permanent—or *takeout*—loan. The proceeds of the permanent loan are used to refinance the balance of the construction loan.

Permanent lenders are different entities than construction lenders—often life insurance companies or commercial mortgage-backed securities (CMBS) lenders. Permanent lenders have different concerns from those of construction lenders when underwriting a loan. They examine existing leases on the property, including lease rates, types of leases, and terms and provisions of the leases. They also assess the financial capabilities and history of tenants. They are interested in the general health of the industrial rental market and how the leases compare with others in the market. If leases are above market rates, tenants may leave; if they are below market rates, the property will have to be held for a certain amount of time until the leases expire or rise to market levels.

Forward commitments—securing a permanent loan at the start of the development project—are currently not popular. A borrower must pay an interest rate premium for a forward. Generally, the first 90 days are free, followed by three to four basis points per month in rate premium. A forward can be attractive when rates are low; however, borrowers have gotten accustomed to rates staying low, which makes locking in a forward rate less attractive.

Life insurance companies offer traditional, high-quality, takeout loans with low costs and good service. A permanent loan from a life insurance company may finance up to 65 to 70 percent of the value of a development (loan-to-value). The development must usually be at least 85 to 90 percent leased to secure attractive permanent financing. Interest rates on permanent loans are typically 3 to 4 percent. When interest rates are low, lenders often use *debt yield*—NOI divided by the total loan amount—rather than debt coverage ratio as an underwriting metric. The minimum debt yield required by life insurance company lenders is typically 7 to 8 percent.[54]

CMBS lenders will finance up to 75 percent loan-to-value. Pricing can be attractive; however, loan servicing can be more difficult than with a life insurance company. Servicing is decoupled from the origination of the loan; therefore, the master and special servicers are different entities from the originator. When a developer gets into a tough situation (e.g., the global financial crisis or the COVID-19-related crisis) and needs to talk to someone, CMBS lenders can be difficult to reach. For this reason, some borrowers avoid the CMBS route when other alternatives are possible.

Unlike construction loans, which are based on the cost to build the project (loan-to-cost), the permanent loan is based on the capitalized value of the project once completed, leased, and stabilized (loan-to-value). In a development project, ideally the value of the project is substantially higher than are the costs of the project. If the permanent loan is financed too early, the valuation—and consequently the loan amount—may be lower. Getting as disassociated from costs as possible is most advantageous.[55]

It is also important to strategically determine the term of the permanent loan to most beneficially coincide with the expiration of leases and the potential re-leasing of the facility. For example, if the facility is occupied by tenants with five-year leases, a seven-year fixed-rate loan, with some prepayment flexibility in the last two years of the loan, may be most beneficial. That arrangement would allow the developer to benefit from an increase in NOI, and the consequent higher capitalized value, after the building is re-leased. It does not make sense to sell the facility with two years left on the leases; instead, the developer should wait for the bump that comes from re-letting the facility and then sell or refinance the property.

For business parks that combine land development with building development, funding of the permanent mortgage can occur after sufficient time has elapsed for lenders to evaluate a project's track record. When a business park is partially occupied, the developer may use the cash flow from existing tenants to develop the remaining land, thus reducing the need for loans. When a building is sufficiently leased to support the debt service, the permanent lender will fund the long-term mortgage.

EQUITY STRUCTURE

Equity is often the most difficult piece of the development finance puzzle, particularly for beginning developers. Developers often must use their own cash equity to fund predevelopment costs, due diligence, and other initial expenses. Beginning developers often look to personal contacts to raise equity for their initial projects.

Some institutional equity investors will write smaller equity checks—under $5 million. With the help of a broker, a beginning developer who can demonstrate some expertise and success, even if it was while working for another firm, and can accept some potentially unfavorable terms may be able to secure debt equity financing for a small project. Investors are generally looking for unleveraged returns in the low- to mid-teens.

Future tenants can also become partners in a project, an arrangement that provides equity, strength on the financial statement, and pre-leasing activity. Owners of private companies often prefer to own the property where their company operates. They may become joint venture partners, and their companies may become building tenants. Developers who already have a tenant in place or already own a phenomenal piece of property may have to put up only 5 percent and then get a tenant to form a joint venture. A developer in that situation might also be able to presell and get a developer fee and perhaps a promote (explained in the next section). But for a purely speculative building, such terms can be difficult to come by. Once a developer establishes a track record, institutional investors become a more viable source of equity.

JOINT VENTURES

Institutional investors include pension funds, insurance companies, REITs, private equity firms, and other entities that represent large pools of capital. Institutional investors most often act as fiduciaries for individuals, corporations, and other investors who place their money with the institutions to invest on their behalf. Or, as in the case of insurance companies, they have funds to invest from policyholders or depositors representing many different accounts. Fund managers are likely to raise money directly or indirectly through Wall Street in public and private securities offerings.

Industrial developments often use a *waterfall* deal structure. A waterfall deal structure describes in what order the cash flows from a development are distributed to investors. As in the geographic feature, a cascade flows into one pool; when that pool is full, it overflows into the next, and so on until nothing is left. A typical real estate waterfall deal structure prioritizes the cash flow distribution: (1) the return of capital, (2) a preferred return, (3) a lookback return to the capital partner, (4) an equivalent return to the sponsor, and (5) a split of the remaining profit. IRRs, or in some cases equity multiples, are used to denote *return hurdles*, the rates at which returns flow to the next tier and the distribution of cash flows is adjusted.

Tiered hurdle rates are structured to incentivize the sponsor to manage the project profitably. The sponsor stands to earn a greater proportional share of the cash flows if the project's IRR is higher. For an example, refer to the deal structure provided in this chapter. In this case, below a hurdle rate of 15 percent, profits are split 80/20 (investor to sponsor); when the IRR is between 15 and 20 percent, profits are split 70/30;

Deal Structure Illustrated

Figure A illustrates a waterfall deal structure with a three-tier hurdle rate of return.[a] The investor receives its money back and a 10 percent cumulative preferred return on all unreturned equity out of the development cash flows. After the investor receives the preferred return (because it is cumulative, it is accrued if cash is unavailable in the current year to pay it), profits are split 80/20 (the investor receives 80 percent) up to a 15 percent IRR on all cash invested. For undistributed cash above a 15 percent IRR and less than a 20 percent IRR to the investor, the profit split is 70/30. After the investor receives a 20 percent IRR, the remaining profit is split 50/50.

Figure B shows the calculation of the cash flows for the deal. The overall IRR for the project is 38.8 percent on the initial $1,000,000 investment. Positive cash flows total $2,900,000, for a net total of $1,900,000. The investor receives the preferred return of $110,000 in year 2 and $71,000 in year 3 (line 8). The investor is repaid $390,000 of the equity from the year 2 cash flows; the remaining $710,000 is paid in year 3 (line 9). After the equity preferred return is paid, a cash flow of $1,619,000 is available for distribution—$119,000 in year 3 and $1,500,000 in year 4 (line 12). As shown in line 14, the tier 1 distribution allocates 80 percent of the cash flow to the investor, up to a 15 percent IRR, which is $175,330 ($95,200 in year 3 and $80,130 in year 4). The sponsor receives $23,800 in year 3 and $20,033 in year 4 (line 15).

The total cash available for the tier 2 distribution is $1,399,838 (line 18). The cash flows required to give the investor the tier 2 hurdle of 20 percent IRR are shown on line 19. Because the totals for years 1, 2, and 3 consume all the available cash, the total to the investor for those years does not change. To achieve a 20 percent IRR, considering the payouts in earlier years, a payoff of $302,160 is required in year 4. The investor has already been allocated $80,130 from tier 1, leaving a balance of $222,030.

After paying the investor $302,160 and the sponsor $115,189 for tiers 1 and 2 combined in year 4, a balance of $1,082,652 remains available for distribution in tier 3 (line 24). Because the deal structure gives the operating partner 50 percent of the profit above 20 percent IRR, the $1,082,652 is divided 50/50.

The overall IRR for the investor's $1,000,000 investment, considering the return of equity, the 10 percent preferred return, and all three tiers of cash flow, is 29.6 percent (line 35) on total cash flows of $1,219,686. The sponsor's IRR is infinite—it receives a total of $680,314 without contributing any cash to the deal. (The total cash flow of $1,900,000 [line 2] minus the investor's share of $1,219,686 [line 35] equals $680,314.)

FIGURE A Three-Tier Hurdle Rate of Return

Investor's equity investment	$1,000,000
Investor's preferred return	10% cumulative
TIER 1: PROFIT SHARING UNTIL INVESTOR RECEIVES A 15% IRR	
Investor	80%
Sponsor	20%
TIER 2: PROFIT SHARING UNTIL INVESTOR RECEIVES A 20% IRR	
Investor	70%
Sponsor	30%
TIER 3: PROFIT SHARING AFTER INVESTOR RECEIVES A 20% IRR	
Investor	50%
Sponsor	50%

Note: IRR = internal rate of return.

In this illustration, the sponsor receives its profit share concurrently with the capital partner—a pari passu arrangement in which the sponsor's equity is treated exactly like the capital partner's equity. They receive the same hurdle rates of return and priority to distribution of cash flow. In a non–pari passu arrangement, the lookback return gives the investors all the profit until they receive the hurdle IRR for that tier. After that occurrence, the sponsor receives its share of the profit for that tier. That arrangement places the financial partner ahead of the sponsor in receiving any share of the profit.

[a] Put simply, the investor contributes all of the equity—$1,000,000. If the sponsor contributes a portion of the equity, the total cash flow for each tier would not change, assuming that total equity remains $1,000,000. The cash flows to the investor would simply be divided between the capital partner and the developer in proportion to their share of the $1,000,000 total equity.

Lookback Return with Sliding Profit Split

	Cash flows to investor and sponsor	Input	IRR	Total	Year 0	Year 1	Year 2	Year 3	Year 4
1	Cash flows to investor and sponsor	Input	IRR	Total	Year 0	Year 1	Year 2	Year 3	Year 4
2	Development cash flows		38.8%	1,900,000	(1,000,000)	0	500,000	900,000	1,500,000
3	**Preferred return**								
4	Beginning balance				0	1,000,000	1,100,000	710,000	0
5	Equity investment			1,000,000	1,000,000	0	0	0	0
6	Preferred return (cumulative)	10.0%		281,000	0	100,000	110,000	71,000	0
7	Subtotal				1,000,000	1,100,000	1,210,000	781,000	0
8	Preferred return paid to investor			181,000	0	0	110,000	71,000	0
9	Equity repayment to investor			1,100,000	0	0	390,000	710,000	0
10	Ending balance				1,000,000	1,100,000	710,000	0	0
11	**Tier 1: Profit sharing until investor receives a 15% IRR**								
12	**Cash available for tier 1 distribution**			**1,619,000**	**0**	**0**	**0**	**119,000**	**1,500,000**
13	Tier 1 cash flows for investor to achieve 15% return		15.0%	456,330	(1,000,000)	0	500,000	876,200	80,130
14	Tier 1 profit share to investor	80.0%		175,330	0	0	0	95,200	80,130
15	Tier 1 profit share to sponsor	20.0%		43,833	0	0	0	23,800	20,033
16	Tier 1 total profit shares	100.0%		219,163	0	0	0	119,000	100,163
17	**Tier 2: Profit sharing until investor receives a 20% IRR**								
18	**Cash available for tier 2 distribution**			**1,399,838**	**0**	**0**	**0**	**0**	**1,399,838**
19	Tier 2 cash flows for investor to achieve 20% return		20.0%	678,360	(1,000,000)	0	500,000	876,200	302,160
20	Tier 2 profit share to investor	70.0%		222,030	0	0	0	0	222,030
21	Tier 2 profit share to sponsor	30.0%		95,156	0	0	0	0	95,156
22	Tier 2 total profit shares	100.0%		317,186	0	0	0	0	317,186
23	**Tier 3: Profit sharing after investor receives a 20% IRR**								
24	**Cash available for tier 3 distribution**			**1,082,652**	**0**	**0**	**0**	**0**	**1,082,652**
25	Tier 3 profit share to investor	50.0%		541,326	0	0	0	0	541,326
26	Tier 3 profit share to sponsor	50.0%		541,326	0	0	0	0	541,326
27	Tier 3 total profit shares	100.0%		1,082,652	0	0	0	0	1,082,652
28	**Investor summary**								
29	Investor's equity investment			(1,000,000)	(1,000,000)	0	0	0	0
30	Preferred return to investor			181,000	0	0	110,000	71,000	0
31	Equity repayment to investor			1,100,000	0	0	390,000	710,000	0
32	Tier 1 profit share to investor			175,330	0	0	0	95,200	80,130
33	Tier 2 profit share to investor			222,030	0	0	0	0	222,030
34	Tier 3 profit share to investor			541,326	0	0	0	0	541,326
35	**Investor total**		29.6%	**1,219,686**	**(1,000,000)**	**0**	**500,000**	**876,200**	**843,486**
36	**Sponsor summary**								
37	Sponsor's equity investment			0	0	0	0	0	0
38	Preferred return to sponsor			0	0	0	0	0	0
39	Equity repayment to sponsor			0	0	0	0	0	0
40	Tier 1 profit share to sponsor			43,833	0	0	0	23,800	20,033
41	Tier 2 profit share to sponsor			95,156	0	0	0	0	95,156
42	Tier 3 profit share to sponsor			541,326	0	0	0	0	541,326
43	**Sponsor total**			**680,314**	**0**	**0**	**0**	**23,800**	**656,514**

Note: IRR = internal rate of return.

and once the IRR reaches 20 percent, profits are split 50/50. Thus, the structure aligns the investor's and the sponsor's interests in achieving the highest rate of return on investment.

The *preferred return* is the annualized rate of return that the development must attain before the sponsor receives promoted interest or returns. It is the rate of interest on the money invested and can be current or cumulative. In the case of a cumulative (or accrued) preferred return, investors receive a predetermined return on the capital invested whether or not there is sufficient cash flow in any one period. If not, the return is carried over to the next period and interest accrues. After the preferred return hurdle is met (and the initial investment is repaid), excess cash flow is distributed according to the terms of the deal.

Pension fund advisers such as AEW Capital Management and Heitman introduced the concept of *lookback returns* in the 1980s as a means of protecting the rate of return they earned as the capital partner in joint ventures with developers. In their capacity as advisers, they act as investment managers on behalf of pension funds, endowments, and other institutional investors. The lookback return is another tool to ensure that the sponsor properly manages and maintains the property, because the great majority of its profit is not paid until the property is sold.

Promotes entered the developer's lexicon in the early 1990s when Wall Street became a major source of capital. A *promote* is the difference between the sponsor's capital contribution and its share of the profit. For example, if the sponsor puts up 10 percent of the capital in a 50/50 deal, then its equity is promoted by 40 percent. The equity is promoted to receive a disproportionate share of the returns. The promote is, in essence, compensation for the sponsor's nonfinancial contributions to the development—putting the deal together and managing it.

The term *pari passu* describes an arrangement that gives the sponsor's equity the same status as the capital partner's equity. For example, if the sponsor is required to invest 10 percent of the total equity required, that equity is treated the same as the capital partner's equity for the return of capital and the preferred return.

The major points in joint ventures with capital partners can be boiled down to nine main issues: (1) the sponsor's cash equity, (2) the preferred return, (3) the profit share, (4) the lookback return, (5) the pari passu equity payback, (6) the guarantees, (7) the management control, (8) the fees to the sponsor, and (9) the fees to the capital partner. Tradeoffs are possible among the different deal points, and the best choice for the sponsor depends on its needs and priorities. To focus solely on the sponsor's share of the profit, however, would be a mistake: the sponsor's actual return depends more on the investor's preferences and lookback returns and the priorities of payback than on the profit split. The only way to calculate the partners' expected returns is to model the deal and to compute the sponsor's return and capital partner's return under different cash flow scenarios.

NEGOTIATING RISK

The negotiation over major deal points primarily concerns the allocation of risk among deal partners. The capital partner tries to shift as much risk as possible to the sponsor and vice versa. Developers should be aware of the elements of real estate deal agreements described in the following paragraphs.

RECOURSE OR NONRECOURSE. Whether or not a loan is *recourse* or *nonrecourse* is an important concern for developers. A recourse loan holds the borrower personally responsible for repayment of the loan. Loans from smaller banks are likely to be full recourse, while nonrecourse loans may be available from debt funds. To be clear, there is no such thing as a purely nonrecourse loan. Such loans always include carve-outs for fraud, misrepresentation, and bankruptcy, for example.

REPAYMENT GUARANTEE. Lenders are likely to require a repayment guarantee when the loan-to-cost is high, the borrower is less experienced, the location is less than ideal, or there is no pre-leasing. But most often this decision comes down to experience level and leverage. If the construction is financed at less than 50 percent loan-to-cost, a developer is likely to be able to get a nonrecourse construction loan from a bank. If it is financed at less than 65 percent loan-to-cost, the same nonrecourse loan likely comes from a debt fund.

COMPLETION GUARANTEE. Most lenders will require a completion guarantee unless the developer has an institutional partner or a financially strong partner willing to backstop. However, completion guarantees can be relatively low risk in that industrial buildings are simple structures to build, especially if the developer is working with an experienced general contractor.

PREPAYMENT PENALTIES. Prepayment—or lockout—restrictions prevent a borrower from paying off a loan within a given period. Lenders have return obligations to their investors, particularly CMBS lenders; therefore they have an interest in receiving the anticipated yield of the loan. *Yield maintenance* is a type of prepayment penalty that provides the lender with the same yield it would otherwise have earned had the loan not been prepaid. For permanent loans, long-term, fixed-rate financing likely comes with prepayment penalties. Thus, developers should be strategic about the loan term as it relates to the terms of leases and consider when they really need prepayment flexibility. Generally, it is not too expensive to negotiate prepayment flexibility in the last third of the loan, but prepayment earlier in the loan can be prohibitively expensive.

CLAWBACK. A *clawback* in a real estate waterfall structure allows an investor to reclaim promoted interest paid out to the sponsor during the project if, at the end of the deal, the preferred return over the life of the deal is not met. Clawbacks are used to incentivize the sponsor to properly manage the development and maximize returns throughout the deal.

CONTROL. Among the major deal points, control is perhaps the most important. Financial partners have learned that the hardest part of correcting a problem property is often getting control of the asset. The *buy/sell clause* is intended to deal with that risk. The sponsor is naturally concerned about events that would allow the financial partner to take control and wants to avoid a situation in which the financial partner would take over.

CROSS-COLLATERALIZATION. Lenders like to cross-collateralize properties; sponsors do not. If a lender is not getting paid on one property, it can foreclose on other cross-collateralized properties to satisfy any deficit—which puts the sponsor's other properties at risk. Because institutional investors hold an equity position with the sponsor in their deals, they often do not like to see cross-collateralization on permanent loans.

DEAD DEAL COSTS. *Dead deal costs* are monies spent in the due diligence phase of a development project that does not proceed to completion. In addition to the time and effort expended, costs may include third-party legal, environmental assessment, and appraisal fees, among others. Investors prefer to shift the responsibility for such costs to the sponsor and often require that the sponsor pay the majority of dead deal costs.

Marketing

Marketing an industrial project is a multistep process that revolves around (1) creating an identity or niche for the development, (2) identifying target users, (3) convincing them that the space meets their needs, and (4) negotiating the terms of the lease or sale.

Industrial developers should start approaching potential tenants as soon as they option a site or consider developing a site already in inventory. A directed approach that takes advantage of informal contacts often works best. Targeted firms may range from major national companies to regional firms to local firms to any combination of the three. Developers usually begin the marketing campaign by exploiting their existing contacts, but they should also contact key brokers for leads on possible seed tenants. When a project is still in the conceptual stage, the developers will have to persuade tenants that the future building will suit their needs.

As development progresses, other aspects of the marketing program should advance. Those steps include creating a marketing plan, establishing a marketing budget, preparing marketing materials, and creating a leasing program through in-house resources or with external real estate brokers. The strategy and the tone set in marketing materials must reflect the goals of the developers and target the types of tenants indicated by the market analysis. Care must be taken to avoid excessive and unnecessary costs for advertising and promotion.

Local brokers are often the best source of market information because they know who specific tenants are likely to be. Prospective tenants seeking more space or different space may come from adjacent properties. Local chambers of commerce also may provide leads or find potential tenants for a project.

Beginning developers can sometimes turn their lack of experience into an advantage for marketing purposes. Small developers can claim more hands-on involvement and give more personal attention to tenants. Their costs tend to be lower because they have lower overhead than large, established development firms have.

MARKETING STRATEGY

A successful marketing program requires a clear strategy that addresses what the developer is seeking in terms of types and sizes of tenants, rental rates, lease terms and conditions, and length of the lease-up period. Marketing goals should be grounded in the realities of the marketplace as determined by market analysis and any subsequent changes in supply, demand, and the competition. They must also reflect the business objectives of the owners and investors. For example, depending on the exit strategy, some investors might prefer to emphasize short-term value and thus rapid lease-up, whereas others might prefer to hold out for longer leases or institutional-quality tenants that can add prestige and value when the project is sold.

Although the major elements of a marketing program for an industrial development are fairly straightforward, a firm estimate of its costs can be difficult to determine early in the development process. A rough estimate can be made by compiling a comprehensive list of possible marketing activities and preparing a reasonable cost estimate for each item. The compensation scheme for marketing agents and the degree of reliance on outside brokers are important variables in marketing costs, even though fees for agents and brokers are typically separate line items in the budget.

MARKETING MATERIALS

Two elements are essential to a successful marketing program: a technical services package and a sales brochure (property website and flyer).

TECHNICAL SERVICES PACKAGE. The technical services package consists of data describing the project's target market and includes information relating to population growth and other demographic statistics, statutory taxes, real estate taxes, sales taxes, interstate commerce trucking zones and rates, and public services. The package should include information about utilities such as typical water and sewer dimensions, capacity, static pressure, and design flows, as well as information about fire protection services and requirements, electrical capacity, and name and frequency of the rail carrier, if any. The developer gives the technical services package to brokers.

WEBSITE AND SALES BROCHURE. The website and sales brochure describe the ownership, location, and distinctive features of the project. Often prepared with the help of a marketing firm, materials may feature professional photography, videos, animations, and other rich media in addition to standard information about the project. Information should be clearly presented. A professionally designed version of the information provided on the website should be available for download. The sales material should include the following information:

- the developer's or owner's and manager's track record, with information about previous projects;
- a list of anchor tenants, if available;
- the overall development plan that identifies the preliminary parcel configuration and proposed road network;
- technical building information;
- relevant site data, including information about utilities and infrastructure;
- a location map showing the relationship of the project to the region, immediate community, and road and rail networks;
- a detailed map showing access to the site and the immediate neighborhood; and
- a summary of community characteristics drawn from market studies and other sources.

BROKERS

Industrial real estate brokers' commissions are typically calculated as a percentage of rental income, with commissions payable on net rent (most common for industrial), rent plus expenses, or rent plus a portion or all of the fully amortized tenant improvements (unusual). In some markets, the commission structure calls for a declining percentage on the income for the later years of a lease term or a cap on the number of years on which the commission is calculated. Most often, a portion of the commission is paid when the lease is signed, and the balance is paid when the tenant moves in.[56]

Most developers of industrial properties sign an exclusive representation listing with a brokerage firm to market their properties, especially for large projects trying to attract regional or national credit distribution or manufacturing tenants. Once a brokerage representation agreement is made, the brokerage company uses its resources to market the property (websites, videos, tours, open houses, etc.). The exclusive listing agreement specifies commission percentages paid to the landlord brokers and tenant brokers.[57]

Leads for prospects can come from a number of sources. Developers should hold regular meetings with the brokerage community to keep brokers informed of new developments, pricing, and current sales or leases. Moreover, they should offer regular tours. Developers should send information to clients, industry contacts, and brokers known to them in other communities in the region. And they should maintain close contact with local and state economic development agencies, public departments in the community, utilities and railroads, planning commissions, and redevelopment agencies.

LEASING

Prospective industrial tenants focus on three major concerns: location, building function, and effective rent.

Developers should have a guiding principle regarding their own expectations on yield and ask themselves: What do I want to get out of the investment? What do my investors want to get out of the investment? A developer who wants to have a secure cash flow and to reduce risk might take a deal that does not optimize rental rates but stabilizes the asset. Another developer may want to sign a shorter lease with the expectation that rental rates will increase, and a new lease may be signed for a higher rate in the future.

Tenants ultimately focus on effective rent (costs per square foot after all concessions have been taken into account) while looking to secure the lowest cost possible. Leases for single-tenant buildings are typically triple net (NNN). For NNN leases, the tenant is responsible for real estate taxes, insurance, and maintenance.

Lease lengths for industrial facilities vary, depending on the type of facility and the type of tenant. According to CBRE, in 2021 the average length of leases for big-box industrial facilities was slightly longer than 9 years; the overall average lease term for all sizes was 5.5 years.[58] As referenced earlier in this chapter, 3PLs occupy a substantial share of the bulk warehouse market (warehouses over 100,000 square feet [9,300 sq m]). 3PLs typically sign shorter-term leases that match the term of the contract with the shipper they are servicing. Thus, the shorter-term 3PL leases skew the overall average downward. By contrast, a large e-commerce occupier may sign a 10- to 15-year lease for a large fulfillment center facility.

A developer of a speculative building must determine the appropriate level of finish that the market will accept. Tenant improvement (TI) allowances for industrial facilities vary from market to market. The market tenant allowance is a stated amount per square foot. The tenant is responsible for any TI dollars above that allowance. Some tenants may want out-of-market specifications. For example, they may need $20 in TI for building automation when the market tenant TI allowance is $5. An option is to amortize the TI, giving the tenant the market allowance and amortizing the difference over the life of the lease. A developer must also weigh the asking rent and the TI. The higher the TI, the more rent the developer can demand. This dynamic should be kept in mind when looking at comparable rents. The developer must consider the rent per square foot in combination with any free rent and the TI allowance when comparing facilities.

Property Management

Industrial developers have become much more proactive in the management of their buildings and business parks in recent years. This attention is in response to the increasingly complex operation of industrial real estate and greater concern about long-term value.

Management of industrial properties involves three stages: development, lease-up, and stabilized operations. Priorities change during each stage.

STAGE 1: DEVELOPMENT

During the development phase, the developer's major tasks are to coordinate the installation of infrastructure and to attract tenants, particularly seed tenants in industrial parks. Often, the local community is concerned about environmental issues, and the developer must respond to those concerns.

Because of noise, dust, and truck traffic during the development phase, the developer must be a good neighbor. Failure to respond to the community's concerns can result in time-consuming delays in approvals and inspections. On-site management is a necessity. In the case of industrial parks, timely completion of infrastructure is critically important to the seed tenant—the one that establishes an overall identity for the project. If seed tenants encounter delays in occupancy because of poor management, they may convey their dissatisfaction to potential tenants.

STAGE 2: LEASE-UP

Management during the lease-up stage emphasizes the selection of tenants, tenant relations, enforcement of standards, and maintenance of the project's public image. In the case of business parks, although the preliminary parceling of the property is the basis for marketing individual sites, the developer should still maintain flexibility. The principal concerns of the developer during this stage revolve around the compatibility of potential tenants, their locational relationships, and parceling.

Site planning and the design of individual buildings are critical elements in maintaining the project's marketing appeal. For business park development, the developer must enforce restrictions on architecture, outdoor storage, loading, and parking to ensure the project's continuing marketability. Standards should be enforced equally and impartially. Close supervision of standards facilitates the financing of the project during its mature stages.

Shell buildings and multitenant spaces in partially occupied buildings can remain empty for months.

Such buildings need to be properly cared for (e.g., construction debris removed, landscaping maintained) so they do not become unsightly nuisances that lower the value of neighboring property and give the impression of poor management. Developers who lease or sell land to other builders can avoid the problem of unsightly vacant buildings by requiring builders to post a performance bond to ensure conformity to CC&Rs and design controls within a specified period. The bond should specify that exterior walls are finished and the installation of windows and doors is completed; all driveways, walks, parking lots, and truck-loading areas are paved; all construction debris is removed; and the landscaping, including the planting of trees and shrubs in specified locations and installation of sod, is completed and irrigation systems are provided.

STAGE 3: STABILIZED OPERATIONS

The major objective during the third stage is to maximize long-term profitability. Revenues, infrastructure costs, and operating expense projections should be updated quarterly, or at least annually. Financial management tasks include cost accounting, pricing, and tracking of new leasing and sales information, which should cover details about prospects, broker contacts, telephone inquiries, rental rates and available space of competitive projects, and current tenants' lease renewal dates.

The mature stage of a project occurs after it has been completely leased or sold. Management of the completed development and enforcement of restrictive covenants are turned over to an occupants' association, similar to a homeowners association. If the association is voluntary, it can be created as the developer phases out of the project. If it is a mandatory association, it must be established at the beginning of the development so that all tenants and purchasers are bound by its provisions.

The main source of concern for business park developers during this stage is *residuals*—the future proceeds from the sale of buildings developed and any remaining unsold parcels. The developer plays the same role in the association as other owners: if it owns buildings with NNN leases, it should inspect the property at least semiannually. Those inspections are important for determining how well the building is maintained and whether it has any problems of functional obsolescence. Inspections should also bring to light the existence of any restricted activities (e.g., the storage or manufacture of items outside buildings), potential problems, or liabilities resulting from

environmental contamination. In addition, inspections help the owner to assess the health and well-being of the businesses on site.

Various other concerns also bedevil the owners of industrial properties. For instance, in earthquake-prone areas, masonry property built before 1934 must be reinforced. Dealing with tax reappraisals on existing property and working out errors on tax bills can consume enormous amounts of an owner's time. Leaking oil tanks on properties several hundred yards away can contaminate groundwater, making it difficult to refinance nearby properties. Defense contractors often insist on escape clauses from leases because they do not know whether their contracts with the federal government will be extended. All such concerns demand developers' ongoing attention during the operating phase of a project.

Property management for an industrial development varies considerably depending on the building type and whether it is a single-tenant or multitenant building. Covenants play an important role in maintaining a high-quality appearance. Rules with respect to on-site storage, parking, and truck parking and loading areas are just as important as landscape maintenance and trash pickup. Truck parking in older industrial areas can create serious problems, especially if residences are nearby and the trucks impede traffic flow.

Many single-tenant buildings have NNN leases with no provision for an on-site property manager. Even though a lease provides for cleaning up the property and properly disposing of hazardous waste and other sources of contamination, the owner should inspect the property regularly to ensure clean and safe storage practices.

SELLING THE PROJECT

The disposition of industrial properties follows a procedure similar to that for office and retail buildings. The developer can emphasize a number of features to potential buyers such as

- the building's functionality;
- the building's adaptability;
- the site's locational attributes;
- tenants' financial strength;
- the project's financial characteristics; and
- the project's prospects.

In some competitive markets, industrial buildings may not become profitable until after the first increase in rents. Although sales brokers ask for the scheduled commission, commissions are usually negotiable.

Smaller developers will probably have to pay higher commissions to obtain the same amount of attention from brokers as that given to larger developers who can offer more business.

Mounting concerns over environmental contamination make the sale of industrial projects potentially difficult. If the project has any kind of maintenance or fueling facility where petroleum products or chemicals collect, that area will probably have to be cleaned up before the project can be sold. Although everyone in the chain of title is liable for cleanup, the owner is ultimately responsible and should ensure that cleanup happens expeditiously (the owner may be able to recover cleanup costs from the tenant).

Conclusion

Industrial real estate forms the physical supply chain infrastructure that underpins global economies. Rapidly increasing e-commerce activity and supply chain disruptions that accompanied the COVID-19 pandemic in the United States have drawn attention to the need for resilient supply chains and modern industrial facilities. Demand for warehouse, distribution, and fulfillment space has drawn capital to the industrial real estate sector. As economies began to reopen in 2021, structural and cyclical trends converged to propel the industrial real estate sector. Robust demand and a lack of supply, accompanied by rising replacement costs, resulted in record-setting rents and historically low vacancy rates. And the demand for industrial real estate is projected to continue.

Several trends that began in recent years will continue to influence industrial development in the coming years.

- **Supply Chain Resilience**—Users of industrial space are increasingly concerned about the resilience of their supply chains. The shift from *just-in-time* to *just-in-case* began before the pandemic but became even more urgent amid pandemic-related supply chain disruptions.[59] The focus on building more resilient supply chains may lead to higher inventory-to-sales ratios—and thus demand for more warehouse and distribution space—to protect vulnerable supply chains from future disruptions.
- **Automation**—The automation of warehouse and distribution facilities is expected to continue. Automated storage and retrieval systems and autonomous vehicle distribution (long-haul self-driving trucks, drones, and robots) are expected to make supply chains more efficient and industrial facili-

ties more productive.[60] Developers must anticipate and accommodate the changing space and power requirements that those shifts entail.
- **Data Analytics**—Sophisticated data collection and analysis (of both supply chains and operations within buildings) will increasingly inform operators' locational and operational decisions.[61] Operators can identify with great precision the particular parts of metropolitan areas where they must locate to meet their customers' same-day and next-day delivery demands. The specificity puts pressure on developers to secure valuable, often expensive, land for development.
- **New Building Forms**—Growing online shopping and consumer demand for same-day and next-day delivery is driving the development of new forms of industrial warehouse and distribution space near dense population centers, thereby fostering the growth of multistory and last-mile facilities. The new building forms, currently limited to large cities in the United States, are expected to spread to smaller cities as well.
- **Barriers to Supply**—Government regulation is cited as a substantial risk to the industrial real estate sector.[62] In places where new facilities are most needed to service e-commerce demands, increased competition from other land uses, decreased availability of industrial-zoned land, and increased NIMBY (not in my backyard) resistance are limiting development.
- **Climate and Environmental Concerns**—Real estate investors have been slow to factor climate-related environmental risk into underwriting for industrial development. As the risks of climate-change-related property damage become more apparent, that attitude is changing. ESG initiatives are expected to become more urgent concerns as shareholders and the public at large demand more environmentally sustainable and socially just operations throughout companies' supply chains.
- **Long-Term Growth**—Consumption-oriented uses have dramatically increased as a proportion of industrial demand during the COVID-19 pandemic. And given the "stickiness" of consumer habits and expectations, those changes are expected to endure over the long term.[63]

The soaring demand for industrial real estate has driven considerable investment in the asset class in recent years. But, as Matt Mitchell, vice president of Westfield Company Inc., says, currently the "land prices are higher than they've ever been, and land is more difficult to acquire than ever before; entitlements are more difficult than they've ever been before."[64] Beginning developers must choose their projects carefully. More experienced developers and well-capitalized institutional investors may outcompete beginning developers vying for large, well-located parcels. But exciting new forms of industrial real estate and the adaptive use of older, obsolete industrial facilities offer opportunities for those with creative ideas.

NOTES

1. John Morris, interview by author, January 25, 2022.

2. Howard Freeman, interview by Katherine Selch, March 19, 2021.

3. Maria Sicola, *Commercial Real Estate Terms and Definitions* (Herndon, VA: NAIOP Research Foundation, 2017), p. 23.

4. Colliers, *Atlanta Year-End 2020: Industrial* (Atlanta: Colliers, 2021).

5. Colliers, *Atlanta Year-End 2020: Industrial.*

6. Amanda Ortiz, Pete Quinn, Jack Rosenberg, *Big-Box Market Report: North America—2021 Midyear Review & Outlook* (Toronto: Colliers, 2021).

7. Jennifer Smith, "E-Commerce Driving Bigger Demand for Smaller Warehouses, CBRE Says," *Wall Street Journal,* October 10, 2019.

8. Sicola, *Commercial Real Estate Terms and Definitions,* p. 26.

9. CBRE Research, "U.S. MarketFlash: Rising Transportation Costs Help Fuel Record Warehouse Leasing Pace," CBRE, September 13, 2021.

10. Denise Hicks, "Amazon's Prime Location: Here's a Look at Lake Nona's Fulfillment Center's Design," *Orlando Business Journal,* January 22, 2018.

11. Morris, interview.

12. Morris, interview.

13. Kris Bjorson, correspondence with author, March 4, 2022.

14. Patrick J. Kigler, "Fulfillment Centers Spur Competition for Industrial Real Estate," *Urban Land,* October 26, 2017.

15. CBRE Research, "U.S. MarketFlash: Going Up: Vertical Solutions in Industrial & Logistics," CBRE, October 11, 2018.

16. David Rabinowitz, correspondence with author, March 6, 2022.

17. Paul Hyde, "Industrial Development Is Actually Not All the Same: Cutting-Edge Features Breaking New Ground" (presentation, ULI Spring Meeting 2021, Denver, CO (virtual), 2021).

18. Kerry Hawkins and Michael Restivo, "Data Centers: Expensive to Build, But Worth Every Penny," *Views,* JLL, 2021.

19. Hawkins and Restivo, "Data Centers."

20. Urban Land Institute and PwC, *Emerging Trends in Real Estate: United States and Canada 2022* (Washington, DC: Urban Land Institute, 2021).

21. Barry DiRaimondo, interview by author, October 8, 2020.

22. Kigler, "Fulfillment Centers Spur Competition."

23. Rabinowitz, correspondence.

24. Global Alliance for Buildings and Construction, *The 2020 Global Status Report for Buildings and Construction* (Nairobi, Kenya: United Nations Environment Programme, 2020).

25. Global Alliance for Buildings and Construction, *2020 Global Status Report.*

26. EPA Center for Corporate Climate Leadership, *Scope 3 Inventory Guidance* (Washington, DC: U.S. Environmental Protection Agency, 2022), p. 3.

27. World Economic Forum and Boston Consulting Group, *Net-Zero Challenge: The Supply Chain Opportunity* (Geneva, Switzerland: World Economic Forum, January 2021).

28. U.S. Energy Information Administration, "2012 CBECS Survey Data," Table E5, *Commercial Buildings Energy Consumption Survey* (Washington, DC: U.S. Energy Information Administration, May 2016), https://www.eia.gov/consumption/commercial/data/2012/c&e/cfm/e5.php.

29. Bendix Anderson, "Planning for a Next-Generation Industrial Space Near Columbus, Ohio," *Urban Land,* March 17, 2020.

30. Urban Land Institute and PwC, *Emerging Trends in Real Estate.*

31. CBRE Research, "MarketFlash: Rising Transportation Costs."

32. Eric Messer, *Expanding Port Activity Is Driving the Value of Adjacent Industrial Real Estate* (New York: Newmark Knight Frank, 2018).

33. Freeman, interview.

34. Somy Mukherjee, correspondence with author, February 17, 2022.

35. DiRaimondo, interview.

36. Bureau of Transportation Statistics, *Transportation Statistics Annual Report 2020* (Washington, DC: U.S. Department of Transportation, 2020).

37. HPA Inc., *Rules of Thumb for Distribution/Warehouse Facilities Design* (Herndon, VA: NAIOP, 2020), p. 9.

38. HPA Inc., p. 19.

39. HPA Inc., p. 7.

40. HPA Inc., p. 17.

41. HPA Inc., p. 20.

42. HPA Inc., p. 28.

43. HPA Inc., p. 23.

44. HPA Inc., p. 33.

45. HPA Inc., p. 33.

46. American Concrete Institute, *Guide to Concrete Floor and Slab Construction* (Farmington Hills, MI: American Concrete Institute, 2015).

47. HPA Inc., p. 46.

48. American Concrete Institute, *Guide to Concrete.*

49. HPA Inc., p. 41.

50. Mike Sheridan, "Needs for More Power, Flexibility Driving Markets for Industrial Property," *Urban Land,* May 3, 2018.

51. Amazon, "Amazon Virtual Fulfillment Center Tour," YouTube, July 25, 2021, https://www.youtube.com/watch?v=s6OusrTxwxA.

52. Dennis Williams, interview by author, February 8, 2022.

53. Gayle Starr, interview by author, January 27, 2022.

54. Williams, interview.

55. Starr, interview.

56. Howard Freeman, correspondence with author, February 17, 2022.

57. Jessica Ostermick, correspondence with author, March 12, 2022.

58. Morris, interview.

59. Urban Land Institute and PwC, *Emerging Trends in Real Estate.*

60. Steve Weikal and James Robert Scott, *The Evolution of the Warehouse: Trends in Technology, Design, Development and Delivery* (Herndon, VA: NAIOP Research Foundation, October 2020).

61. Weikal and Scott, *Evolution of the Warehouse.*

62. Urban Land Institute and PwC, *Emerging Trends in Real Estate.*

63. Urban Land Institute and PwC, *Emerging Trends in Real Estate.*

64. Matt Mitchell, "Industrial Development Is Actually Not All the Same: Cutting-Edge Features Breaking New Ground" (presentation, ULI Spring Meeting 2021, Denver, CO (virtual), 2021).

| # Conyers Logistics Center, Conyers, Georgia

The Conyers Logistics Center in Conyers, Georgia, is a speculative big-box warehouse and distribution facility developed by Ashley Capital and completed in 2020. Ashley Capital is a privately held real estate investment company cofounded by Paul Rubacha and Richard Morton in 1984. The company focuses on value-added industrial and office properties located in the eastern, southeastern, and midwestern United States. Ashley Capital acquires existing facilities as well as land for speculative and build-to-suit greenfield and brownfield development.

In 2005, Ashley Capital acquired 200 acres (80.9 ha) of land in Rockdale County, Georgia, for the phased development of a class A business park. On the site, it first developed the 150,000-square-foot (13,900 sq m) Twin Creeks Business Center 1 (Twin 1) in 2008, which leased quickly. Then, in 2014, the company developed a 500,000-square-foot (46,500 sq m) build-to-suit facility for Hill Phoenix. The Hill Phoenix facility was sold to an institutional investor that same year. In 2016, Ashley Capital built the 175,000-square-foot (16,300 sq m) Twin 2, which is occupied by a single user, and in 2018 the development was completed with an additional 480,000 square feet (44,600 sq m) in the multitenant buildings known as Twins 3 and 4. Ashley Capital constructed the 448,899-square-foot (41,700 sq m)—447,440-square-foot (41,600 sq m) gross leasable area—Conyers Logistics Center on the remaining 47 acres (19 ha).

LOCATION

Conyers is an industrial hub about 24 miles (39 km) southeast of downtown Atlanta. The site is in the Snapfinger/I-20 East industrial submarket, about one mile (1.6 km) from the nearest access to I-20. I-20 connects Atlanta to Columbia, South Carolina, and points beyond. The development site is about 240 miles (390 km) northwest of the Port of Savannah. See the market study example in chapter 6 for a discussion of the market for warehouse industrial facilities in the Snapfinger/I-20 East submarket.

The site is in Rockdale County, a tier 2 job tax credit county. The Georgia Job Tax Credit Program provides tax credits to businesses engaged in warehousing and distribution, among other operations, that locate in designated counties. A tax credit of $3,500 is provided for each new job created in the five-year period after completion. Ashley Capital estimated 80 jobs would be created by the development.

ENTITLEMENT

The Conyers Logistics Center development is in an I-D (industrial/distribution) zoning district. A warehouse and distribution facility is an as-of-right use. Thus, the development did not require a zoning variance and the development could proceed without delays related to entitlement. According to the Conyers municipal zoning ordinance, I-D districts are intended to establish industrial-use areas along arterial highways, where noise, dust, odor, and truck traffic will not affect established residential areas.[1] This

ASHLEY CAPITAL

The Conyers Logistics Center is a big-box warehouse and distribution facility in Conyers, Georgia, developed by Ashley Capital.

strategic siting of industrial uses is in accordance with the city's comprehensive plan (updated in 2018), and is designed to foster economic competitiveness and job growth, particularly within planned industrial parks and in areas with access to I-20.[2]

The parking requirement for warehouse, transfer, and storage facilities in I-D districts is one parking space per 1,000 square feet (93 sq m) of storage area and one parking space per 200 square feet (19 sq m) of sales or office area. The Conyers Logistics Center contains 20,000 square feet (1,900 sq m) of office space, and the remainder, 427,440 square feet (39,700 sq m), is classified as storage. Therefore, 527.4 parking spaces are required by the zoning code. The facility satisfies this requirement by providing a total of 552 spaces: 323 automobile parking spaces, 125 truck parking spaces in a separate parking lot, and 104 truck parking spaces in the truck yards.

The zoning ordinance also dictates design requirements for industrial buildings within I-D districts. It specifies that the finish material on all exterior building elevations visible from the public way be selected from a list of acceptable materials. The code allows tilt-up concrete panels but forbids material such as concrete masonry units, corrugated steel, and prefabricated steel panels. The code also requires building elevations in industrial districts to be architecturally modulated every 100 lineal feet (30 m) where visible from a public way. Ashley Capital satisfied the city's requirement by adding an alternating paint scheme to visually break down the long south facade visible from the adjacent road.

In addition, the zoning code specifically requires all loading areas to be in the rear and side yards. Loading areas must be screened from view if visible from a public way or off-street parking areas. Ashley Capital added an earthen berm to visually obscure the view of the loading docks from the public road. The company provided the municipality with line-of-sight diagrams to demonstrate the efficacy of the solution in adequately concealing the loading dock facade.

Tractor-trailer traffic associated with industrial development is a perennial concern for municipalities, and tractor-trailer movement into and around the site is a critically important concern for building tenants. As part of the land development process, Ashley Capital conducted a traffic study. To mitigate the city's concerns about truck traffic congestion, the developer agreed to right-in-right-out (RIRO) access to the facility. A RIRO is a type of intersection where only right turns are permitted. RIROs facilitate a more fluid flow of traffic in that trucks entering and leaving the facility are not idling and creating pollution or blocking traffic while waiting to make a left turn across oncoming traffic. The circulation pattern satisfies city requirements and prevents the need for an expensive, $750,000 intersection upgrade and traffic signal installation. However, to construct the necessary internal circulation around the northwest side of the building, the developer had to negotiate an access easement with Georgia Power, the owner of the adjacent property. When developing a speculative logistics facility, Ashley Capital's philosophy is to provide the maximum amount of circulation and accommodations for guard shacks and security. But ultimately, the efficiency of operations is dependent on the tenant's particular use of the facility.

Conyers intends to reconfigure an intersection of two city roads just outside the development to allow for tractor-trailers to more easily negotiate turns. The city requires a portion of Ashley Capital's land to accomplish the new, larger intersection design. Ashley Capital donated 1.17 acres (0.47 ha) of its land to the municipality for this purpose.

DESIGN AND CONSTRUCTION

The Conyers Logistics Center is an exemplar of a class A, institutional-grade warehouse and distribution facility. Ultimately, the entire facility was leased to a large national retailer. However, the facility was developed as a speculative warehouse and distribution facility, so it was initially designed to be flexible enough to accommodate multiple tenants (of at least 100,000 square feet [9,300 sq m]) as well as full-building tenants and to appeal to a range of possible future tenants.

The Conyers Logistics Center was built through a design/build process. Ashley Capital began working with the general contractor, Pattillo Construction, who then chose Pieper O'Brien Herr Architects to design and produce the construction documents for the project. The rectangular-shaped building is 952 feet (290 m) long by 470 feet (143 m) wide, and it is located on the southwest portion of the 47-acre (19 ha) irregularly shaped site. The facility is built upon the remaining undeveloped portion of a 200-acre (80.9 ha) multiphase development. Some of the northern portion of the site is in a floodplain and otherwise undesirable for industrial development. Thus, the overall acreage of the site is larger (and the 22 percent floor/area ratio is smaller) than is typical for a warehouse and distribution facility of this size.

An existing AT&T fiber optic main line ran through a portion of the site. The line had to be relocated to grade and pave the rear truck yard. The relocation process took more than two years from start to finish and cost $40,000. Similar to the AT&T relocation, a sanitary sewer line had to be lowered to allow for the proper grading of the site at a cost of $164,000.

The design of the site facilitates RIRO tractor-trailer access and movement around the building. Dock doors are located on the long sides of the building in a cross-dock configuration that allows for the subdivision of the space, accommodating up to four tenants with each having access to efficient loading and storage, or allows for a full-building tenant to maximize throughput. The long sides of the building are flanked by 185-foot-deep (56 m) truck yards, a depth that accommodates the single swing of a WB-67 tractor-trailer backing up to a dock door as well as a row of trailers parked adjacently. The automobile parking lots are located next to the short sides of the building, and they are a relatively short distance from the pedestrian entrances to the building. Trailer parking is accommodated in the truck yards and in a separate area on the southeastern portion of the site.

The minimum clear height of the building is 36 feet (11 m), which is the standard for new class A warehouse and distribution buildings. An important point: buildings with a 36-foot (11 m) clear height can accommodate typical metal rack systems accessed by narrow aisle material handling equipment (reach forklifts). This height facilitates efficient use of floor area as well as the entire volume of the space—the cube.

The rack system dimensions set the width of the column grid in the building's long, 952-foot dimension. Assuming a 36-foot-high (11 m) racking system and narrow aisle reach forklifts, each 56-foot (17.1 m) bay can very efficiently accommodate three aisles,

FIGURE A | Project Details

Building size	448,899 sq ft
Site size	46.57 ac
Walls	Tilt-up concrete panels
Floor slab	7-in concrete slab
Roof	TPO
Clear heights	36 ft minimum
Column spacing	56 ft x 50 ft
Speed bay	60 ft
Electrical power	2,400 amps
Fire protection	ESFR
Lighting	LED with motion sensors
Dock-height doors	90—9 x 10 ft
Drive-in doors	4—13 x 14 ft
Truck yards	2—185 ft deep
Automobile parking spaces	323
Tractor-trailer parking spaces	229

Note: TPO = thermoplastic polyolefin; ESFR = early suppression, fast response.

with the columns concealed within the flue space between racks. Running the length of the building are 17 column bays, where the dock-height and drive-in doors are located. Dock-height doors are typically spaced about 13 feet (4 m) on center. This spacing allows for nine-foot-wide (2.7 m) doors and the necessary concrete flanking each door to support the load-bearing, concrete tilt-up panels. Forty-five dock-height doors and two drive-in doors are located on each side of the building. A concrete apron extends 60 feet (18.3 m) from the face of the building, and a concrete strip is provided where trailers are parked. Both the concrete apron and strip protect the asphalt paving from wear and tear.

In the short dimension of the building, the two column bays immediately adjacent to the dock doors—the speed bays—are 60 feet (18.3 m) wide. This more generous column spacing, standard in class A warehouse buildings, allows for space for the staging of goods as they are immediately unloaded and loaded onto trailers. The seven interior column bays are each 50 feet (15.2 m) wide. This dimension accommodates a cost-effective installation of an early suppression, fast response (ESFR) fire protection (sprinkler) system, which is standard in class A buildings.

The building also includes energy-efficient LED lighting with motion sensors for interior lighting and photocells for exterior lighting. Clerestory windows—located on the long sides of the building—allow natural light into the building, as do vision panels in the dock doors. The building has a thermoplastic polyolefin (TPO) roof. The white, high-albedo roof decreases solar heat gain and the energy used to cool the building. Project details are listed in figure A.

FINANCING

The total project costs for the Conyers Logistics Center amount to $23 million ($51.40 per square foot). The cost of the land was $1.2 million, far less than current market value. Ashley Capital acquired the land in 2005 as part of a planned multiphase development. The current market value of a similar parcel is estimated to be in the range of $85,000 to $95,000 per acre, which would result in a land cost of $4 million to $4.5 million. The fact that Ashley Capital already owned the land is particularly fortuitous because well-located land, zoned as-of-right for industrial development was difficult to find and expensive to acquire in the supercharged industrial real estate market of 2020.

Building and site construction costs were $16.4 million; additional costs were $650,000; financing costs were $1.03 million; leasing and commissions were $3.1 million; and the project contingency was $660,000. A tenant improvement allowance of about $2.2 million ($5 per square foot) was included in the construction budget (figure B). Construction was financed by a $16 million,

FIGURE B Project Budget

ACQUISITION	
Land acquisition	$1,200,000
Total acquisition	**$1,200,000**
CONSTRUCTION	
Construction cost	15,000,000
Land grading	1,200,000
Additional hard costs	210,000
Total construction cost	$16,410,000
ADDITIONAL COSTS	
Developer fee	215,000
Engineering	45,000
Builder's risk insurance	20,000
Property taxes	15,000
Permits and fees	180,000
Carrying cost	175,000
Total additional costs	**$650,000**
FINANCING	
Lender fee	80,000
Interest reserve	800,000
Title and recording	45,000
Appraisal	10,000
Environmental	10,000
Bank inspection	15,000
Survey	10,000
Legal	60,000
Total financing	**$1,030,000**
LEASING	
Tenant improvements	2,200,000
Leasing commissions	850,000
Total leasing and commissions	**$3,050,000**
Project contingency	660,000
Total project cost	**$23,000,000**

FIGURE C Project Financing

CONSTRUCTION LOAN	
Project cost	$23,000,000
Cost per square foot	$51.40
Construction loan amount	$16,000,000
Construction loan (per sq ft)	$35.76
Loan-to-cost	70%
Interest rate	5.00%
Interest-only (IO) term	3 years
Annual IO debt service	$800,000
PERMANENT LOAN	
Stabilized (year 2) NOI	$1,905,000
Stabilized capitalization rate	6.25%
Property value	$30,500,000
Value per square foot	$68.17
Loan-to-value	52%
Interest rate	6.00%
Term	25 years
Annual debt service	$1,237,059
Debt service coverage ratio	1.54
Debt yield	12%

Note: NOI = net operating income.

interest-only loan through a commercial bank. The construction loan was 70 percent loan-to-cost over a three-year term, at an interest rate of 5 percent. The debt yield—used by lenders when underwriting a construction loan—was 11.9 percent (figure C).

Ashley Capital projected the base rent at $4.50 per square foot, escalating at 2.5 percent annually for five years. The projected stabilized effective gross revenue totals $2.4 million and operat-

ing expenses total $512,000, resulting in a projected net operating income in the first stabilized year (year 2) of $1.9 million (figure D). A capitalization rate of 6.25 percent results in an estimated property value of $30.5 million—a valuation that supports the takeout of the construction loan at a loan-to-value of 52 percent.

The marketing was managed by LaVista Associates, a local broker. It was listed on CoStar and circulated via email blasts through

FIGURE D **Pro Forma**

Year	1	2	3	4	5	6	7	8	9	10
For the year ending	2020	2021	2022	2023	2024	2025	2026	2027	2028	2029
RENTAL REVENUE										
Potential base rent	2,083,393	2,032,356	2,083,165	2,135,244	2,188,626	2,251,610	2,317,302	2,362,341	2,421,399	2,481,934
Absorption and turnover vacancy	(1,328,338)	0	0	0	0	(195,546)	(199,457)	0	0	0
Scheduled base rent	755,055	2,032,356	2,083,165	2,135,244	2,188,626	2,056,065	2,117,846	2,362,341	2,421,399	2,481,934
Total rental revenue	755,055	2,032,356	2,083,165	2,135,244	2,188,626	2,056,065	2,117,846	2,362,341	2,421,399	2,481,934
OTHER RENTAL REVENUE										
Total expense recoveries	144,292	512,277	522,523	532,973	543,633	492,447	502,296	576,908	588,446	600,215
Total other rental revenue	144,292	512,277	522,523	532,973	543,633	492,447	502,296	576,908	588,446	600,215
Potential gross revenue	899,347	2,544,634	2,605,688	2,668,218	2,732,258	2,548,512	2,620,142	2,939,248	3,009,845	3,082,149
VACANCY AND CREDIT LOSS										
Vacancy allowance	0	(127,232)	(130,284)	(133,411)	(136,613)	(115,927)	(119,195)	(146,962)	(150,492)	(154,107)
Total vacancy and credit loss	0	(127,232)	(130,284)	(133,411)	(136,613)	(115,927)	(119,195)	(146,962)	(150,492)	(154,107)
Effective gross revenue	899,347	2,417,402	2,475,404	2,534,807	2,595,645	2,432,585	2,500,947	2,792,286	2,859,353	2,928,041
OPERATING EXPENSES										
Fire protection	17,898	18,256	18,621	18,993	19,373	19,760	20,156	20,559	20,970	21,389
Common area maintenance	46,981	127,789	130,345	132,952	135,611	126,796	129,332	143,911	146,789	149,725
Water and sewer	22,372	22,819	23,276	23,741	24,216	24,700	25,195	25,698	26,212	26,737
Management fee	23,491	63,894	65,172	66,476	67,805	63,398	64,666	71,956	73,395	74,863
Insurance	17,898	18,256	18,621	18,993	19,373	19,760	20,156	20,559	20,970	21,389
Real estate taxes	255,041	260,142	265,344	270,651	276,064	281,586	287,217	292,962	298,821	304,797
Security	1,100	1,122	1,144	1,167	1,191	1,214	1,239	1,264	1,289	1,315
Total operating expenses	384,781	512,277	522,523	532,973	543,633	537,215	547,960	576,908	588,446	600,215
Net operating income (NOI)	514,568	1,905,125	1,952,881	2,001,834	2,052,013	1,895,370	1,952,987	2,215,378	2,270,907	2,327,827
LEASING COSTS										
Tenant improvements	1,118,600	1,118,600	0	0	0	216,129	220,452	0	0	0
Leasing commissions	423,340	423,340	0	0	0	300,511	302,053	0	0	0
Total leasing costs	1,541,940	1,541,940	0	0	0	516,641	522,505	0	0	0
Cash flow before debt service	($1,027,373)	$363,184	$1,952,881	$2,001,834	$2,052,013	$1,378,729	$1,430,482	$2,215,378	$2,270,907	$2,327,827

the local board of Realtors. The facility was eventually leased to a single tenant, a large national retailer, to be its main distribution center for the Atlanta area. The facility was initially designed as a speculative development. The eventual tenant came on board about three-quarters of the way through the development process. The initial design of the facility was flexible enough to accommodate the tenant with a standard tenant improvement package for a speculative building: dock levelers, LED lighting, 20,000 square feet (1,900 sq m) of office space, and a separate trailer staging lot.

The development reached stabilized occupancy in 2021 (year 2). At that point, the construction loan was refinanced through a permanent loan with a life insurance company. Cap rate compression in the interim resulted in a higher property value than initially projected. The actual $28 million, 15-year permanent loan closed in July 2021.

EXPERIENCE GAINED

The Conyers Logistics Center was designed in accordance with the standards set forth in chapter 6. However, even an experienced industrial developer like Ashley Capital faces development challenges and learns from them.

Once the full-building tenant occupied the Conyers Logistics Center, through diligent property management, Ashley Capital noted that the tenant was using the automobile parking areas for tractor-trailer staging. This use was a concern because the asphalt automobile parking lots were not designed to handle tractor-trailer loads. Upon review of the standard lease language, Ashley Capital discovered that the issue was not specifically addressed. The developer subsequently updated the standard lease contract language to restrict the staging of tractor-trailers to the lots specifically designed for that use.

Several challenges faced in the Conyers Logistics Center project relate to the civil engineering work, which presents perennial site-specific challenges to industrial developments. Ashley Capital learned to design oversize stormwater systems and strategically located stormwater retention ponds to accommodate future expansion. The company found that it is simpler to regrade land to reroute stormwater into an existing, properly sized retention pond than to build a new retention pond. Ashley Capital also cautions not to assume that the civil engineer has thoroughly coordinated the construction of the building and various utilities. It found that it is best to double-check for conflicts, such as utility lines crossing one another. Last, to quicken the construction process, Ashley Capital suggests having the design of the soil-cement mixture—used to improve the strength and/or permeability of soils—ready and approved before the earthwork begins. The design process involves collecting samples, mixing cylinders, seven days of curing, break tests, and then mix recommendations, all of which contribute to a two-week period before work can continue.

SUMMARY

The Conyers Logistics Center is an example of a highly successful class A, institutional-grade warehouse and distribution center development. Demand for modern logistics facilities has boomed in recent years to accommodate robust e-commerce sales. This demand is particularly evident in the Atlanta metropolitan area. In 2021, Atlanta recorded its strongest year for warehouse and distribution leasing activity on record for the second straight year. Annual absorption for big-box industrial facilities set records in 2021. The vacancy rate for warehouse industrial facilities in the Snapfinger/I-20 East submarket was 4 percent.[3] And in the summer of 2021, the Port of Savannah had its second-busiest month on record.[4]

Although construction levels increased to record levels as well, so far, demand has outpaced new supply. A lack of land that is both well located and zoned for industrial development challenges the delivery of new facilities to satiate demand. However, Ashley Capital was well positioned. It has owned the site where the Conyers Logistics Center was built since 2005, when it was acquired for far less than current market value. The site is near access to I-20, which connects it to the large and growing population of the Atlanta metropolitan area. And an important point: the land was already zoned as-of-right for industrial and distribution uses, eliminating the need for a potentially lengthy entitlement process. The facility was designed and constructed in accordance with class A institutional-grade standards. Ashley Capital was thus able to bring the Conyers Logistics Center online at precisely the time that tenants were seeking modern, big-box warehouse and distribution space in a supply-scarce industrial real estate market.

"The Conyers Logistics Center is the culmination of a 15-year process that confirms when you buy land in a good location with a supportive municipality, good developments will result," says Paul Rubacha, partner and cofounder of Ashley Capital. "We are proud to have found the right mixture of buildings that provided excellent places for our tenants to conduct business, were an important addition to the industrial inventory of the community, and were a commercial success."[5]

Research assistance by Katherine Selch.

1. Code of Ordinances, Title 8 Planning and Development (Conyers, GA: Municipal Code Corporation and City of Conyers, 2022).
2. *The City of Conyers, Georgia Comprehensive Plan Update 2018,* Atlanta Regional Commission, City of Conyers (Conyers, GA, 2018).
3. Colliers, *Atlanta Industrial Report 21Q4* (Atlanta, GA: Colliers, 2021).
4. Georgia Ports Authority, "10 Consecutive Months of Positive Year-over-Year Growth in Savannah," press release, June 16, 2021.
5. Paul Rubacha, correspondence with author, February 22, 2022.

7 Retail Development

NICK EGELANIAN

Overview

Since this chapter was last revised in 2012, the retail and shopping center industries have matured, resulting in far less new construction annually than at any time in the past 50 years. These industries have evolved in significant ways over time, and at the heart of every major evolution have been fundamental changes in how retail goods and services are delivered to consumers. The most important evolution occurred in the 1970s and 1980s as day-to-day shopping shifted to more convenient open-air retail formats and the once dominant "full-line" department store model was literally deconstructed, department by department, wreaking havoc on most regional malls that these stores had historically anchored.

The shopping center industry, now mature from a growth perspective, remains vibrant and full of opportunity as retail sales grow annually at a 3 to 4.5 percent rate year after year. Nevertheless, with open-air centers now essentially completely built out, retail development has slowed to about 25 percent of peak historic levels. Although this slowdown has occurred as the role of e-commerce has grown, the two trends have little—if any—causal relationship. In fact, by January 2020, the U.S. Census Bureau reported that e-commerce had grown to only 10.9 percent of U.S. retail sales.

The rise in online shopping has led many people to overstate the role of the internet in shaping the future of the shopping center industry. Even when COVID-19 mandates forced some retail facilities to close for months at a time, brick-and-mortar retail facilities still accounted for about 85 percent of every retail dollar spent in the United States—both during the pandemic and after it had eased. Thus, despite declines in U.S. regional mall viability and in U.S. retail and shopping center construction, retail is and will remain one of the most essential, dynamic, and fundamentally misunderstood categories in the real estate industry.

RETAIL AND RETAIL SALES GROWTH

For those who may never have asked—or have simply forgotten—"retail" is usually defined by two simple activities: buying goods at wholesale and selling those goods at retail. In addition to these two imperatives, to be considered a retailer, the retailer must own what it sells—that is, it must take title to the goods it sells. Retailers absorb the cost and risk of inventory ownership as a primary element of their business. Those who do not own the goods may fill many important roles related to retail—shipper, consigner, fulfillment company, transfer agent, and so on—but they are not retailers.

Another unwritten rule of retail is that once the retailer places a product on its store floor, its job is all but finished. The customer is expected to provide the bulk of the labor from that point forward: selecting a cart, making his or her purchase selections, increasingly playing the role of checkout clerk at automated self-check stations, and loading goods into the car. This concept may seem elementary; however, it is not

Tempe Marketplace, Tempe, Arizona.

well understood. Many people assume that the costs to retailers of in-store assembly and curbside delivery (or even more so, home delivery) are minimal. In fact, the costs are enormous, and except in rare cases, when retailers "mess with" that part of the formula, they inevitably eliminate their ability to earn a reasonable profit on such sales.

THE RETAIL ECONOMY. Retail is a nearly $6 trillion annual industry in the United States, with sales historically growing by 3 to 4 percent annually, and it accounts for almost 25 percent of U.S. gross domestic product (GDP). When we add in the manufacture and marketing of retail goods as well as shopping center development, maintenance, and operations, we see an industry responsible—directly and indirectly—for consumer spending that accounts for 65 percent of the country's GDP. The only time that retail sales have fallen for a sustained period since this book was first published in 1992 was during the Great Recession: retail sales fell sharply in 2009 and did not recover fully for several years.

THE VITAL ROLE OF THE SHOPPING CENTER INDUSTRY. The shopping center industry is responsible for housing essential elements of the five world industries that must operate with minimal interruption every day for the modern globalized world to function:

- food and clothing distribution;
- banking industry functionality;
- global energy distribution;
- global communication availability; and
- essential medical service availability.

Each of these industries relies on retail outlets and shopping centers for all or a portion of its product delivery.

E-COMMERCE AND AMAZON. As a speaker, lecturer, and professor in the University of Maryland's graduate real estate development program, the author of this chapter often has the opportunity to poll audiences on their estimates of e-commerce market share. Answers typically range from 40 to 80 percent, with most respondents also believing that the e-commerce giant Amazon is responsible for 75 percent or more of all e-commerce sales volume. In reality, as discussed earlier, e-commerce accounted for only about 11 percent of nationwide retail sales before the beginning of the COVID-19 pandemic in February 2020 (see figure 7-1); that amount is about equal to catalogs' share of nationwide retail

FIGURE 7-1 **Estimated Annual U.S. E-Commerce Sales**

	RETAIL TRADE (MILLIONS OF DOLLARS)		
	Total	E-Commerce	Percent
2020	5,570,393	815,447	14.64%
2019	5,402,272	571,229	10.57%
2018	5,255,425	507,628	9.66%
2017	5,040,214	444,350	8.82%
2016	4,848,096	384,438	7.93%
2015	4,726,111	338,638	7.17%
2014	4,640,651	298,286	6.43%
2013	4,459,238	261,778	5.87%
2012	4,302,229	232,347	5.40%
2011	4,102,952	200,449	4.89%
2010	3,818,048	169,921	4.45%

Sources: U.S. Census Bureau, *Annual Retail Trade Survey*, 2020; and U.S. Census Bureau, *Economic Census*, 2017.

Notes: E-commerce sales are sales of goods and services in which the buyer places an order, or the price and terms of the sale are negotiated, using the internet, extranet, electronic mail, a mobile device (m-commerce), Electronic Data Interchange (EDI) network, or other comparable online system. Payment may or may not be made online. Estimates are based on data from the *Annual Retail Trade Survey*. Estimates have been adjusted using final results of the 2017 *Economic Census*.

sales in 1994. When provided with this information, audiences often simply deny the accuracy of Census Bureau numbers. They are generally even more skeptical when told that Amazon is responsible for only around 1 to 2 percent of annual U.S. retail sales and that, overall, Amazon's retail operations have not been profitable to date.[1]

What accounts for this disconnect between perception and reality? The United States has about 8.5 billion square feet (790 million sq m) of brick-and-mortar retail space, or about 24.5 square feet (2.3 sq m) per capita, as a result of 60 years of continuous construction growth at rates much higher than the rate of population growth. That growth started with the building of regional malls and accelerated with the building of open-air shopping centers in even greater numbers. With the multidecade conversion to open-air retailing formats all but complete, we have now entered a new era of shopping center maturity. As malls, once thought indestructible, fail and more convenient strip center retailers pick up market share, casual observers are tempted to conflate slowing mall sales with increasing e-commerce sales—but this is simply not the case.

While analysts and journalists are quick to connect the two as cause and effect, the reality is more complex. As this edition goes to press, more than two years after the start of the COVID-19 pandemic, brick-and-mortar retail sales account for about 85 percent of U.S. retail sales (as already noted). That is largely because brick-and-mortar shopping center space continues to be the single most efficient retail delivery system for most retail goods and services. Unlike brick-and-mortar sales, internet sales are burdened by the hidden costs of shipping, returns, last-mile-delivery logistics, and other factors that ensure that almost no internet company, including Amazon, makes a profit. In fact, Amazon's cost of fulfillment more than doubled from around 16 percent of sales in 2011 to a whopping 32.3 percent of sales by 2021. Shipping and handling costs add up to tens of billions of dollars annually, and are mostly absorbed by sellers. Likewise, few brick-and-mortar stores turn a profit on "click and collect" or curbside-pickup orders. In that case the culprit is high in-store labor costs.

So why do they do it? There are many reasons sellers sell at a loss. For now, it is sufficient to understand that, while technology is likely to continue to drive change, brick-and-mortar retail construction will remain vital—even if it no longer grows at the lightning pace of the past.

SHOPPING CENTER BASICS. Shopping centers form a unique subset of real property within the commercial real estate sector. Unlike other forms of real estate, shopping centers are characterized by their primary purpose: the delivery of goods and services to end users (i.e., consumers). The underlying value of shopping center and retail real estate derives primarily from the total value of transactions that occur in these buildings. Not surprisingly then, the function, positioning, and valuation of shopping centers is governed by a set of rules and practices largely different from any other type of real estate.

Although shopping centers have taken many forms over the last century, this definition, first proposed by the Urban Land Institute in 1947, remains relevant:

> A shopping center is a group of operationally unified commercial establishments built on a site that is planned, developed, owned, and managed as an operating unit related in its location, size, and type of shops to the trade area that it serves.

The ultimate goal of every shopping center is to generate sales by creating a compelling environment for the delivery of goods and services to consumers. Retail, including shopping center real estate, is the only type of real property for which the fundamental value of the real estate is determined by the level of sales generated in the buildings themselves. Hence the age-old mantra "location, location, location."

In the past, shopping centers were most often classified by their size, location, or physical characteristics, with retail uses and the types of products sold playing only a small role. Today, retailers and retailing have evolved and stratified, as has the shopping center industry. The types of goods and services offered now better define two broad classes of shopping centers and the principles governing them: Shopping centers act as the end of the distribution pipeline for either "commodity" goods and services or "specialty" goods and services (in simpler terms, purchases primarily for household daily needs versus purchases involving expenditure of discretionary time and funds for nonessential purposes). The gap between the size, function, and need for each of the two types of retail is wider than ever, with "commodity" retail accounting for an estimated 80 to 85 percent of all retail sales and the more glamorous "specialty" retail accounting for only 15 to 20 percent of total retail sales.

The fundamental mechanics of building shopping centers have changed little since this book was first published in 1992. Yet the way retail buildings are arrayed by developers and used by retailers has changed dramatically. Now more than ever, shopping center developers, both seasoned and new to the business, must carefully plan to either efficiently deliver commodity retail goods and services or creatively stimulate expenditures of discretionary time and income by delivering unique and appealing specialty retail places and product mixes.

Thus, understanding the mechanics of creating and building shopping centers remains essential. But even more important is understanding the primary market segment—commodity or specialty—a center will serve. Where will the shopping center operate? What are the size and characteristics of the trade area it will serve? What is the competitive environment in which it will operate? And what are the fundamental development principles by which it will deliver on its potential.

100 Years of Shopping Center Evolution

To best discern retail development opportunities, developers need to understand not only the commodity and specialty retail paradigms, but also the underlying design and development principles fundamental to each. By placing each in its proper historical perspective, developers will be better able to understand how shopping centers function and resist the temptation to follow obsolete shopping center definitions that have been a staple in the industry for decades.

The purpose here is not to provide a shopping center history lesson but rather to point out that development templates for commodity and specialty retail shopping centers are fundamentally different. Only by understanding how and why shopping centers function the way they do today, along with the historical evolution of shopping center formats, can shopping center developers maximize sales and investment returns by optimally merchandising and positioning future developments to provide consumers and retailers with the shopping centers they most need and prefer.

GENERAL MERCHANDISE STORES— FROM GENERAL STORES TO FULL-LINE DEPARTMENT STORES

GENERAL STORES. General stores are widely considered the predecessors of what later became known as full-line department stores. By most accounts, general stores were originally conceived as stores that carried "general lines of merchandise," catering to a wide variety of needs. The stores stocked routinely used items and functioned as the main shopping depots for the communities they served. In time, these stores evolved into "chains," such as Kresge, W.T. Grant, and the Golden Rule Store, the Wyoming-based predecessor of JCPenney.

FULL-LINE DEPARTMENT STORES. Full-line department stores became the urban successors to the general store format, eventually developing into large retail establishments with an extensive assortment of goods organized by category into separate "departments." Bennett's of Irongate in Derby, England, is considered the oldest department store in the world, founded in 1734 and still trading in its original location.

Department stores were first introduced in the United States by Rowland Macy, with his Macy's dry goods store, and Benjamin Altman, founder of Lord & Taylor, in New York. These pioneering stores were later followed by Abraham & Straus in Brooklyn, Marshall Field & Company in Chicago, and others throughout the country. Two popular catalog retailers—Sears, Roebuck & Co. and Montgomery Ward & Co.—also opened storefront locations to sell their products.

With schools, churches, theaters, parks, and other public facilities located nearby, city centers formed the core of communities, large and small, and retail was tightly intertwined in the day-to-day fabric of society. Department stores were vital to these "downtown shopping" districts, and by the mid-1900s, most major cities and many smaller ones throughout the United States boasted their own homegrown versions. From Macy's and Gimbels in New York to Hudson's in Detroit, Frederick & Nelson in Seattle, and the venerable Bullocks in Los Angeles, early department stores sold most anything a modern household would need. Full-line department stores provided consumers with a variety of product choices ranging from housewares to jewelry, furniture, clothing, stationery, and electronics. Eventually, these full-line departments stores came to sell virtually every category of consumer goods, including sporting goods, toys, electronics, and automotive supplies. This model of retail shopping dominated U.S. retailing well into the 20th century.

SHOPPING CENTER "DRIVERS"

ROADS AND MOBILITY. Without roads, there are no shopping centers. There is retail, of course, but not modern shopping centers. The massive shopping center industry of today grew from a few connected buildings in the mid-20th century to about 8.5 billion square feet (790 million sq m) of retail and shopping center real estate in the United States today.

As rudimentary as it may seem, before mass production of automobiles, most Americans, lacking the mobility we take for granted today, lived in or near city centers and looked there to satisfy virtually all their household goods and service needs. Urban centers in the United States were modeled after well-established and centuries-old European counterparts. Most often, they featured an integrated mass transportation system and functioned not only as the center of commerce, but also as the social, cultural, and political center of the community. General merchandise stores were the backbone of retailing.

By the late 1940s, assembly-line automobile manufacturing had taken hold, and the automobile quickly became the standard of U.S. transportation. With the Great Depression and World War II behind it, the country entered an era of prosperity, made possible by the automobile, inexpensive gasoline, and a newfound sense of personal mobility. Construction of the Interstate Highway System and secondary road networks became national priorities and set the stage for unprecedented population migration from cities to abundant

and inexpensive suburban housing. That rapid growth, in what were once inaccessible rural areas, spawned the era of suburban growth and urban sprawl.

This era of increased individual mobility meant horizontal expansion for most American cities. The result was less dramatic for existing large cities like New York and San Francisco with existing infrastructure modeled after European cities. But in emerging cities—such as Atlanta, Los Angeles, and Dallas—the road systems became the primary means of mobility.

THE ROAD FROM DOWNTOWN SHOPPING TO REGIONAL MALLS

Over the past century, fundamental changes in transportation systems and retail distribution systems have dramatically altered the organization and function of shopping centers and the shopping center industry as a whole. Each generational change in transportation systems and retailing formats has led to major "revolutions" in shopping center design, often in fits and starts with experimental successes and failures along the way. Nothing is more fundamental in retailing and shopping center design than the way consumers move from place to place and transport goods from retail stores to their homes and businesses. Likewise, the way retailers choose to display and distribute goods is fundamental to understanding the shopping center infrastructure they require.

As suburbs rapidly expanded, so did the need for convenient new shopping infrastructure to support these growing populations. New road systems, characterized by hub-and-spoke arteries and "beltway" rings, tied suburbs to cities, and suburb to suburb, and made possible a period of unprecedented shopping center growth. Regional department stores and expanding national chains followed population growth to the suburbs. Lacking established commercial districts in which to locate their suburban

Galleria Dallas in Dallas, Texas, is an example of a regional shopping mall.

units, retailers, in collaboration with shopping center developers, experimented with new shopping center formats, eventually settling on the "city under a roof" regional mall format. Ultimately, they created nearly 3,000 regional malls nationwide.

Although regional malls were not the only form of shopping center developed during this period, they did form the centerpiece of the new retail delivery system. Anchored by full-line department stores, they became the primary means by which consumers obtained a wide array of goods and services for the next 30 years. This development model, influenced almost entirely by the personal mobility afforded by automobiles, revolutionized the retail industry and ushered in an extended period of decline of downtown shopping districts. Further, because most relatively new suburban communities lacked well-developed social and cultural centers, American malls became de facto social gathering places—even if poorly conceived for this purpose.

U.S. SUPREME COURT DECISION: *UNITED STATES V. PARKE, DAVIS AND CO.* Less understood than the impact of highway construction is the impact of the U.S. Supreme Court's decision in the 1960 landmark case *United States v. Parke, Davis and Co.*[2] Before the *Parke Davis* decision, manufacturers of products sold at retail routinely enforced the fair-trade price at which their goods were sold by retailers. Such arrangements permitted manufacturers to enforce minimum retail pricing by refusing to sell to retailers who sold below the suggested price, essentially preventing retailers from competing on price in the sale of most consumer goods.

The *Parke Davis* case, decided in a 5–4 ruling written by Justice William Brennan, determined that retail pricing established and enforced by manufacturers amounted to an illegal restraint of trade under the Sherman Antitrust Act, citing Parke Davis's conduct as an illegal restraint of trade via a "vertical price fixing" scheme. While the decision has been weakened somewhat by one recent case, the basic principle that retailers may sell products at self-determined discount prices was established, thereby ushering in an era of discounting by so-called big-box and category-killer retailers. Without *Parke Davis*, there likely would be no Walmart. And unfortunately for full-line department stores, with the *Parke Davis* case opening the door to what eventually would become an avalanche of discount retail chains setting up shop, one retail category at a time, these more expensive and less convenient full-line department stores and the malls they anchored were doomed.

COMMODITY RETAILING AND THE DEMISE OF REGIONAL MALLS

The regional mall business model reached maturity in the mid-1980s, however, even before that point, the model began to develop cracks. The seeds of its undoing were planted by the earliest innovations in distribution and merchandising, which later took hold and eventually decentralized the department store model, changing the way Americans shop forever.

Discount stores—long dominated by Kmart and regional chains such as Caldor, Ames, Zayre, Gemco, Jamesway, Korvettes, S. Klein, and others—began to gain market share and slow the growth prospects for full-line department stores This effect was particularly evident in consumables, where discounters had a decided cost advantage. In the 1980s and 1990s, discount chains Walmart and Target developed even better distribution logistics, which—along with offshore production—dramatically reduced operating costs. The cumulative effect on full-line departments stores was devastating.

With widening assortments and low everyday pricing, these retailers came to dominate commodity retailing. During this period, department store giant Dayton Hudson, recognizing this realignment, made the strategic decision to abandon its full-line department stores in favor of its Target stores division. Target's discount store format was outperforming its well-regarded namesake—a true harbinger of the changing fortunes in both industries.

The introduction of new big-box or category-killer retail stores did the most damage to the full-line department store industry and regional malls. One

by one, new, more efficient single-category retailers were introduced, each offering merchandise assortments once exclusive to department stores and malls, in more convenient formats and locations, and almost always at lower prices. These developments eventually "killed" those categories in department stores. From appliances and home furnishings to automotive services and electronics, new large-format big-box retailers (e.g., Best Buy, PetSmart, Marshalls, Michaels, and Jiffy Lube) slowly became the preferred distribution model for these goods and services.

Beginning in 1992 with 280 Metro Center, located in Daly City, California, and developed by San Francisco–based Terranomics, "power centers" featuring big-box retailers capitalized on the trend by clustering these retailers in large open-air centers. The centers featured building and operating costs dramatically lower than regional malls and offered consumers convenient locations, everyday low pricing, and greater selection than full-line department stores. No surprise: thousands of these centers were built nationwide in the ensuing decades and largely supplanted development of new department stores. American consumers quickly transitioned from buying commodity goods in department stores and regional malls to buying most of these goods in discount and big-box stores.

The rise of the discount shopping model enabled by the *Park Davis* ruling permanently damaged the viability of that shopping format, and the industry that built and operated regional malls—once 3,000 strong and thought invincible—rapidly contracted. More than half the remaining malls lost their anchor stores and became functionally obsolete between 1980 to 2000. During the same period, as with any industry experiencing contraction, department store and regional mall ownership began extended periods of consolidation. During this time, Macy's and Simon Property Group became the leaders in their respective industries by absorbing failing department stores and smaller regional mall owners. Consequently, these companies came to own top-performing assets in their industries but also were left holding hundreds of underperforming department stores and regional malls.

The nation's best national department store chains also suffered precipitous declines, facing competition not only from Walmart, Target, and other big-box retailers, but also from nimbler and better-located department stores like Kohl's, which largely abandoned regional malls in favor of decentralized locations. Montgomery Ward failed and was liquidated; Sears, although not immediately driven out of business, was largely marginalized and is in the last stages of liquidation today. JCPenney, which began an extended period of decline soon after it relocated from New York to Dallas in 1992, now operates only as a thinly capitalized arm of Simon Property Group, the county's largest mall owner.

Following its shopping spree buying other declining department store brands, Macy's, once a coastal powerhouse with fewer than 250 highly productive stores, grew to more than 1,200 stores. That number is now down by about half, and many analysts believe that to survive long term, Macy's will need to jettison its barely sustainable store base in the Midwest and South. It would be better served by developing a specialty retail service and merchandising model suitable for the higher-end specialty retail malls and open-air centers in the country, mostly along the East and West Coasts and in a few larger and more affluent inland cities like Chicago, Houston, Dallas, Denver, and Phoenix. Those who once thought Macy's would be lucky to end up at half its largest size now wonder if it can adapt quickly enough to sustain a 150-store base long term.

REGIONAL MALLS AND LIFESTYLE CENTERS

The demise of the original department store and regional mall models forced mall owners to either accept steadily declining sales (and rents) or offer a more exclusive and specialized shopping experience to retain and build customer interest.

THE NORDSTROM EFFECT DIES OUT. Nowhere was this more evident than in the ensuing competition for Seattle-based Nordstrom, which at the time was rapidly expanding. Nordstrom, a department store in name only, offered a uniquely crafted mix of apparel, shoes, jewelry, and cosmetics, with few of the other traditional full-line department stores categories. By combining this product mix with an aesthetically appealing shopping environment, including live piano performances, an appealing café, and legendary customer service, Nordstrom became synonymous with specialty retailing by the early 1990s.

During this period, the form of ownership (either private or real estate investment trusts), access to capital, underlying market demographics, and competitive market forces all played crucial roles in determining the future of virtually every regional mall.

With most malls in decline, competition for new Nordstrom stores became fierce. The cost to "secure" a Nordstrom store soared, and the cost of failing to

secure a store was, in most cases, even higher. A small number of regional malls thrived by converting to specialty retail merchandising, usually with Nordstrom in tow; many more, unable to make the transition, failed. Between 1980 and 2005, fewer than 100 new Nordstrom stores opened, while nearly 2,000 malls failed and/or were converted to alternative uses.

Still, by the end of the second decade of the 21st century, the Nordstrom effect had lost altitude as increased reliance on low-cost, fast-fashion, soft-goods giants like H&M and Zara, along with changing demographics, ate into Nordstrom sales. Nordstrom also aggressively expanded its Nordstrom Rack discount concept, often close to flagship stores, further eating into sales. In a final blow to its flagship stores, the chain began to reduce inventory and increasingly rely on internet sales. The net effect of these strategic and tactical changes was waning sales at flagship stores. Ironically, as Nordstrom opened its last two namesake stores in New York City and Norwalk, Connecticut, in 2019, it was only months away from announcing its largest round of store closings in company history. Today, the piano players entertaining shoppers in stores are gone, as are the tales of extraordinary service. Many industry observers speculate as to whether the company will be able to sustain a smaller flagship store base at all over the long term.

THE ERA OF OPEN-AIR LIFESTYLE CENTERS FADES. Most smaller specialty retailers (e.g., Chico's, Talbots, Williams-Sonoma, Coach, and Banana Republic) expanded rapidly from 1990 to 2008, and a relatively small number of regional malls successfully transitioned to specialty retail merchandising. That left the shopping center industry to face a shortage of quality specialty retail space at the same moment that regional malls were failing at an accelerating rate: The dominant commodity retail shopping center formats had left small-store specialty retailers with few reliable anchors. Developers, with no clearly defined specialty retail shopping center template to replicate, spawned the ill-defined and somewhat chaotic "lifestyle center" industry.

With commodity retailing reduced to a simple convenience/price formula, consumers, more than ever, demanded "better" specialty retail shopping venues. Power centers, discount stores, and the new commodity retailing paradigm (i.e., centers with retailers offering goods primarily for household daily needs) had not only permanently weakened the merchandising model employed successfully for decades by department stores and regional malls; they had also exposed a key weakness in most malls—their failure to function as places conducive to social interaction, cultural exchange, and connection.

Lifestyle centers—including University Village in Seattle; Bethesda Row, in suburban Washington, D.C.; and Rice Village in Houston—successfully fused better, more aspirational retail shops with appealing architecture and outdoor lifestyle settings. This was the birth of the lifestyle center industry. More recent examples include a revived Hyde Park in Tampa, Florida, and Pike and Rose, in Montgomery County, Maryland; each one added its own take on lifestyle center retailing with formats ranging from urban street grids to suburban mixed-use centers emerging from converted "strip" centers.

The lifestyle center development industry celebrated many early successes, but the shopping center development community and specialty retailers could not agree on a replicable development formula. This left a legacy of confused, often disappointed retailers and consumers and, most important, uneven sales results and lagging investment returns. Many lesser versions of these centers relied on discount commodity retail stores as anchors and thus failed to deliver on the core promise to elevate lifestyle. Today, fewer and fewer such centers are being developed.

Classifying Shopping Centers: Commodity versus Specialty Retail

TRADITIONAL SHOPPING CENTER CLASSIFICATIONS

Shopping centers have traditionally been characterized according to markets served, general tenant characteristics, and center size. Common classifications include the following:

- **Convenience Centers**—Typically anchored by personal/convenience stores, such as a minimarket, convenience centers typically range up to only 30,000 square feet (2,800 sq m).
- **Neighborhood Centers**—Built around supermarkets, neighborhood centers typically range from 60,000 to 100,000 square feet (5,600 to 9,300 sq m).
- **Community Centers**—These centers generally provide many of the convenience goods and personal services offered by neighborhood centers with a wider range of soft-good lines (e.g., apparel) and hard lines (e.g., hardware and appliances). These centers, range up to 250,000 square feet (23,200 sq m).
- **Regional Malls**—Regional malls include one or two full-line department stores and provide a variety of additional shops, as well as a range of services and recreational facilities, in formats typically ranging

Easton Town Center

Perhaps the most ambitious of all lifestyle center undertakings is Easton Town Center in Columbus, Ohio. This mixed-use development successfully integrated 90 acres (36 ha) of shopping, hotels, and office uses at the center of a 1,300-acre (526 ha) master-planned community. Ambitious in both concept and scope, the shopping center achieved a well-crafted balance of "place" and "product" with carefully selected retailers, restaurants, shops, and attractions in a setting unequaled in the market. Today the center features more than 45 restaurants, including one on the top floor of the flagship Restoration Hardware store, which anchors the newest phase of the center.

STEINER + ASSOCIATES

The expansion of the Easton Town Center in Columbus, Ohio, continues the evolutionary path of the previous phases from a traditional Main Street retail project into a true mixed-use environment by introducing more open space, office space, specialty retail, boutique hospitality, and housing. At its center, the Yard is anchored by a large media screen, performance stage, and canopy structure that can transform to accommodate a variety of community events.

from 250,000 square feet (23,200 sq m) to more than 900,000 square feet (83,600 sq m).

- **Super-Regional Malls**—These malls offer an extensive variety of shops, as well as services and recreational facilities. They are typically designed around three or more full-line department stores and range up to 1.5 million square feet (140,000 sq m) or larger.
- **Specialty Centers**—Specialty centers comprise a multitude of variations of these basic categories and can include a broad set of atypical center types, such as entertainment, fashion, off-price, outlet, megamall, home improvement, and historic and lifestyle centers.
- **Power Centers**—Power centers are a type of super community center that contain at least four category-specific off-price anchors, including category-killer retailers, big-box stores of 20,000 square feet (1,900 sq m) or more, price-oriented warehouse clubs, and discount department stores.

NEW RETAIL AND SHOPPING CENTER PARADIGMS

The shopping center definitions above, which unfortunately are still employed in the shopping center industry today, long ago became inadequate for properly classifying today's commodity and specialty shopping centers. In fact, they are often misleading. In most cases, however, there are no widely accepted industry definitions for classifications such as community, entertainment, off-price, and super-regional center. The developer is left to interpret the terms. In the meantime, the terms have been used to loosely

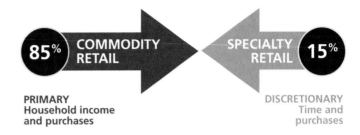

FIGURE 7-2 21st-Century Retail Alignment: Two Distinct Shopping Center Industries

85% COMMODITY RETAIL

SPECIALTY RETAIL 15%

PRIMARY
Household income
and purchases

DISCRETIONARY
Time and
purchases

refer to groupings of shopping centers having certain dominant size or merchandise orientations.

Virtually all directional change in shopping center use and classification can be traced to the introduction of big-box or category-killer commodity retail formats. Aside from diminishing the role of full-line department stores, these retailers have changed the underlying way in which commodity retail goods and services are presented and sold to the public. The removal of virtually all commodity retail products from the best-performing regional malls has completely revamped the underpinnings of today's thriving malls.

Consumers now make very different choices when selecting preferred commodity and specialty retail shopping venues (each of which is defined more fully below). In fact, consumers are motivated by completely different considerations in selecting preferred retail venues in each case. Most often, they purchase commodity and specialty retail products on separate shopping trips; and even when making purchases on combined trips,

FIGURE 7-3 Commodity Retail: Price versus Convenience Equation

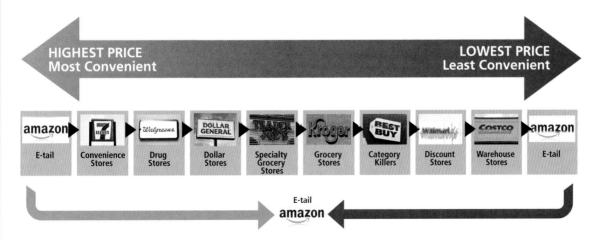

HIGHEST PRICE
Most Convenient

LOWEST PRICE
Least Convenient

| amazon E-tail | 7-ELEVEN Convenience Stores | Walgreens Drug Stores | DOLLAR GENERAL Dollar Stores | TRADER JOE'S Specialty Grocery Stores | Kroger Grocery Stores | BEST BUY Category Killers | Walmart Discount Stores | COSTCO Warehouse Stores | amazon E-tail |

E-tail
amazon

Price versus Convenience

As illustrated below, the local CVS drug store, a nearby Safeway grocery store, the nearest Target store, and a more remotely located Costco warehouse store, all sell Bounty paper towels, a commodity retail item used in many U.S. households. By design, there is an inverse relationship between convenience and price in the price/convenience equation offered by each of these retailers. Of course, other factors (e.g., the quantity to be purchased, packaging formats, and sales promotions) all influence the price at which each retailer is able to sell to the consumer. But in virtually all cases, convenience equates to higher price, and conversely, lower price equates to less convenience.

Case Study—Retail choices for the purchase of one "giant" size roll of Bounty paper towels in Annapolis, Maryland (assuming the consumer resides in central Annapolis)

Choice	Retailer	Location	Price	Price Equation
1	CVS Pharmacy	Four city blocks from the customer	$3.13 (single roll)	Most Convenient – Highest Price
2	Safeway Grocery Store	1.5 miles from the customer	$2.99 (single roll)	Somewhat Convenient – Moderately High Priced
3	Target Store	5.5 miles from the customer	$2.29 (multipack)	Less Convenient – Lower Price
4	Costco	14.5 miles from the customer	$1.79 (bulk package)	Least Convenient – Lowest Price

shoppers are motivated differently in their shopping choices within each group. Most important to shopping center developers, the factors that motivate consumers' preferences in commodity retail shopping centers are almost always opposite to the factors that motivate selection of specialty retail shopping venues.

Today's commodity and specialty retail shopping center paradigms are clearly differentiated as follows (see figure 7-2).

COMMODITY RETAILING: THE PRICE/CONVENIENCE EQUATION.
Webster's Dictionary defines "commodity" as a "good or service whose wide availability typically leads to smaller profit margins and diminishes the importance of factors other than price; one that is subject to ready exchange . . . within a market." Operating essentially as functional distribution points, commodity retailers are the final stop in the transmission of goods from factory to consumer. Consumers rarely have an emotional attachment to these kinds of goods and services, so these centers, and the retailers that occupy them, are designed simply to deliver a combination of low operating costs (which translate to lower prices) and a range of convenience. Thus, you have the key variables to remember in commodity retailing: *price* and *convenience*. As a rule, the *more* convenient the commodity retailer's location, the higher the price of its goods will be—by design. Conversely, the *less* convenient the commodity retailer's location, the lower the price of its goods will be. (See figure 7-3.) Commodity shopping centers can range from stand-alone drug stores built on small parcels of land to a large grouping of big-box or category-killer

retailers presented in the large (power) center format.

Successful commodity retailers, having carefully selected the mix of price and convenience they wish to offer, endeavor to build the consumer's trust in their price/convenience equation. Likewise, in choosing between competing commodity shopping centers, consumers consciously or unconsciously select the mix of price and convenience that suits them—all the time or at least on the shopping trip in question.

SPECIALTY RETAILING: THE PRODUCT/PLACE EQUATION.
Webster's Dictionary defines a "specialty" product as "a special object or class of objects; a product of a special kind or of special excellence," that by its nature requires "discretionary income" and/or "discretionary time" to use or acquire.

Whereas trust in the price/convenience equation motivates choice in most commodity retail transactions, a far different equation motivates the choices consumers make in where to spend their *discretionary time* and *discretionary income*. These choices are not about speed and efficiency; consumers here are motivated by their perception of the aesthetic appeal and stimulation of the experience offered by the shopping environment (place) and the quality and mix of retailers (product). Unlike the relatively emotionless commodity retail shopping decision, specialty retail shoppers judge the quality of the overall experience based on how they feel emotionally about their use of limited discretionary time and dollars (see figure 7-4). The true test of the specialty retail decision is whether it brings happiness or pleasure versus the logic of the commodity retail decision.

With most day-to-day needs efficiently satisfied with little attention to the experience, consumers are left to choose where to spend their extra, or discretionary, time and income outside the home. Although some regional malls have successfully transitioned from all-encompassing "suburban downtowns" to the new specialty retail paradigm, most have not.

Unlike the well-understood "city under one roof" model behind the original regional mall format or the "drive-up warehouse" principle behind most commodity retail, development of specialty retail centers requires mastering a more complex set of disciplines. The new generation of successful specialty retail centers did not follow a replicable physical plant format. Instead, developers followed replicable principles, delivering a mix of product (retailers) and place (buildings, open spaces, finishes, amenities, and attractions) unique and appropriate to the markets they serve. Because individual markets vary greatly in market spending potential, tastes, and existing competition, the mix of product and place that's right for one market can rarely be successfully replicated in another. And though there are successful specialty retail venues that emphasize primarily one or the other, *most* specialty retail development requires a unique and compelling mix of both product and place to succeed.

Specialty shopping centers include a collection of retail shops appealing primarily to the consumer's discretionary time and income, regardless of physical format (see figure 7-5). Examples include

- mixed-use centers featuring bookstores, theatres, restaurants, women's boutiques, and other specialty retailers;

Keys to Specialty Center Development

- **Measure Specialty Market Trade Area**—Conduct a professional assessment of the level of discretionary income available for specialty retail demand in the market and the level of existing competition.
- **Develop a Compelling Product/Place Mix**—Create a compelling mix of product and place appropriate to the trade area and existing market conditions.

The high number of failed lifestyle center developments can be traced in most cases to a failure in one or both of these key areas.

- lifestyle centers designed in an open-air format, presenting upscale national retailers (e.g., Chico's, Talbots, Williams-Sonoma, Crate and Barrel, and Coach);
- regional malls, often anchored by upscale fashion department stores (e.g., Nordstrom, Nieman Marcus, and Bloomingdale's);
- high streets featuring best-in-class luxury retailers, boutiques, and service offerings;
- factory outlet centers; and
- theme parks with theme park retail.

Each of these retail venues competes for the same consumer discretionary time and income.

SLOWING SHOPPING CENTER CONSTRUCTION AND INDUSTRY MATURITY

Despite overall brick-and-mortar retail industry strength, after nearly 60 years of industry growth, construction of new shopping centers has slowed considerably. The industry has already replaced most obsolete malls with more modern centers of all types, and there is now no need for further replacement.

FIGURE 7-4 Specialty Retail: Derive Pleasure/Emotional Engagement

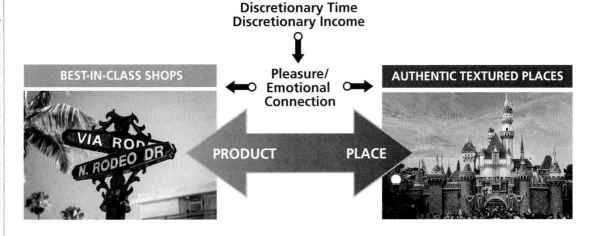

Discretionary Time
Discretionary Income

BEST-IN-CLASS SHOPS ← Pleasure/ Emotional Connection → AUTHENTIC TEXTURED PLACES

PRODUCT   PLACE

Retail Development

FIGURE 7-5 Specialty Retail Formats

TRADITIONAL MALLS

OUTLET CENTERS

THEMED CENTERS AND ATTRACTIONS

MIXED-USE AND OPEN-AIR CENTERS

HIGH STREETS

While a casual observer may be tempted to view this as a sign of industry weakness in the face of internet retail growth, the two have little to do with each other. Internet retail sales and growth have had little, if any, impact on the shopping center industry. Instead, after years of building out a new industry, supply has simply caught up to demand. In the years ahead, growth will occur in two primary areas: in urban infill areas having the lowest supply and in suburban growth areas where population growth requires the addition of new facilities.

E-COMMERCE

One of the most common questions shopping center developers ask is, "What impact is the internet having on shopping centers and development opportunities?" Inevitably, the question is followed by a comment relating to Amazon's dominance and the likelihood that more and more shopping will be done online.

Certainly, any discussion of retail and shopping center development in the years ahead must take into account the influence of online retail options. Given long-term trends, the percentage of online purchases will likely continue to increase, albeit at a slower and slower pace, as time passes. Still, there is little empirical evidence that online sales have had a significant

impact on shopping center development. As noted above, by 2020, e-commerce had succeeded only in replacing catalog sales, which had peaked at just shy of 11 percent of retail sales in 1994. Certain product lines (e.g., books) have been disproportionately affected by changes in technology that eliminated the need for physical retail packaging for many software and media products.

In the case of the book retailing industry, the evidence suggests that internet purchasing options, pioneered by Amazon more than 15 years ago, did not result in the closure of a single store; store closures began when book and media products became available electronically. Similar scenarios have played out in photo processing and DVD rental, areas in which basic changes in technology, not e-commerce, fundamentally altered the need for brick-and-mortar stores.

Successful retailers today almost always have multichannel distribution strategies (e.g., brick-and-mortar, online, wholesale, and other options) and encourage customers to use multiple channels when making the final buying decision. The interplay of consumer behavior within multiple distribution channels is well beyond the scope of this publication. However, evidence suggests that, while retailers will continue to integrate technological options into the buying experience, developers' primary role will continue to be delivery of shopping center facilities that meet the needs of retailers and consumers.

In the case of specialty centers, evidence again suggests that to date, technology has had little effect on consumer preferences regarding where to spend discretionary time and income.

After more than 25 years of aggressive promotion, the last 10 with aggressive infrastructure growth, Amazon, the largest e-commerce company operating in the United States, has not generated any meaningful profit from internet retail. As of this writing, Amazon is closing physical stores and cutting investment in new warehouse space. The problem stems from a subscription model that promises customers near instant shipping (along with other goodies like Prime Video), but hemorrhages shipping and handling costs. While volumes predictably rose during the pandemic when many brick-and-mortar stores were forced to close, Amazon's shipping and logistics costs rose faster than income, increasing from 15.6 percent of retail sales in 2009 to nearly 33 percent of retail sales in 2021, a simply unsustainable burden.[3] Even in grocery distribution, Amazon has not generated a profit and has seen market share fall after spending $13 billion in 2017 to purchase Whole Foods.

Of course, none of these data suggest that Amazon is not a major force in the market or that e-commerce is not a significant factor in retail. They simply demonstrate that there are limits to the effect e-commerce will have on the shopping center industry long term, and that the industry will remain the backbone of retail distribution in the hyper-competitive retail marketplace.

Development Opportunities in the New Shopping Center Paradigms

COMMODITY RETAIL

Contrary to some conventional thinking, the commodity retail sector is quite healthy in the United States, having mostly completed nearly 35 years of building new shopping centers at a growth rate much greater than the rate of population growth over the same period. With commodity retail successfully deployed throughout the country, development opportunities within this segment of the shopping center industry are now more limited. Still, ample development opportunities exist in the following areas:

- **Redevelopment of Underperforming Centers**—Underperforming centers can be redeveloped with value-added merchandising in high-demand areas.
- **High-Growth Retail Categories**—High-growth commodity retail segments include dollar stores and discount grocery chains such as Lidl and Aldi. The dollar store industry alone is expected to add more than 20,000 stores over the next 10 years.
- **High-Visibility Pad Buildings and Small-Format Centers**—These retail buildings range from single-tenant banks and fast-casual restaurants to 5,000- to 10,000-square-foot (465–929 sq m) buildings for use as fast casual restaurants, mobile phone stores, coffee shops, and so on.

Four Approaches to Product and Place Mixes

A review of the best specialty retail venues serving the Orlando, Florida, market illustrates the range of specialty retail choices available to consumers today. Four distinct approaches to a mix of product and place present consumers with different, but successful, specialty retail venues operating adjacent to a short five-mile stretch of Interstate 4:

- **Park Avenue**—A legacy retail street located in the upscale north-central Winter Park community offers a unique collection of eclectic shops, boutiques, restaurants, cafés, and national retailers, presented in a quaint, walkable, village-like setting.
- **Mall at Millenia**—Forbes Cohen's Nordstrom-anchored center was developed in the traditional regional mall format; located near Universal Studios, it blends beautiful finishes with unique-to-market high-end retail shops and restaurants.

- **Orlando Premium Outlets**—This Simon-owned outlet center offers extraordinary product in the form of best-in-class couture and luxury brands arrayed in an outlet format—in an otherwise physically unremarkable place.
- **Disney World**—One of the world's best-known brands, Disney World offers multiple best-in-class venues, creating extraordinary places with what is generally perceived to be moderate-to-low quality retail and restaurant products.

Each of these specialty retail shopping centers offers a unique combination of place and product, and they all perform well above industry standards. In Orlando, the unique combination of resident population, convention guests, and visitors to the city's many attractions will likely draw additional specialty retail shopping venues to the retail mix in coming years—despite the competition from Disney World.

- **Grocery Stores and Power Centers in Areas Experiencing Population Growth**—In most parts of Texas, for example, population has grown at an average rate of over 2.5 percent annually since 1990, with the Dallas/Fort Worth market alone adding over 1 million people in each of the last two census periods.
- **Densely Populated Urban Areas**—In most urban areas, high costs and barriers to entry have limited commodity retail shopping center development. However, retailers such as Target, Trader Joe's, Wegmans, TJX brands, and others are increasingly entering these markets as part of mixed-use developments. These areas represent the largest segment of the U.S. retail market not yet fully served by commodity retailers.

SPECIALTY RETAIL

With full-line department stores and regional malls in the final phases of their decline and consolidation, significant development opportunities will emerge in the future as supply and demand imbalances develop within the specialty retail sector.

HYBRID SHOPPING CENTERS. Some developers have succeeded in mixing commodity and specialty retail concepts in so-called hybrid shopping centers. These centers seek to satisfy all the customer's needs with one-stop-shopping by delivering both commodity retail and specialty retail goods and services in a single shopping center.

No doubt, examples of successful hybrid shopping centers exist in the United States and around the world, particularly in complex urban and mixed-use environments with constrained real estate options and/or high barriers to entry. However, their development involves inherent merchandising, placemaking, and development conflicts. Thus, we recommend against building these centers and have not included them as development options for entry level or even experienced shopping center developers.

Hybrid centers are generally a risky development format due to inherent conflicts between the elements of price and convenience that underlie optimal commodity retail shopping center development and the elements of better product and placemaking essential to well-executed specialty retail centers. The same is true in reverse: the higher costs and placemaking design principles central to specialty retail degrade the price/convenience equation essential to commodity retail and shopping centers.

In practical terms, while these two shopping options might coexist adjacent to one another, the cross-merchandising of both commodity and specialty retail within one shopping center will rarely, if ever, maximize the sales opportunity of either one.

CROSSOVER TENANTS. Some retailers can function effectively in both commodity and specialty retail environments. There is no science behind or clear definition of the types of retailers that can cross over, market to market, but some have succeeded in multiple formats. They include Costco, Whole Foods, Trader Joe's, Bed Bath & Beyond, Bass Pro Shops, Ulta Beauty, Old Navy, Books & Co., Panera Bread, and Starbucks. In most cases, the primary orientation of these retailers depends on how consumers in each individual market use and perceive them.

That list is not intended to be exhaustive, but it does demonstrate the possibility of influencing tenant mix by merchandising crossover tenants creatively. Crossover tenants most often deliver a hybrid offering in one of two ways:

- They deliver select upscale or specialty products within an otherwise commodity product environment (e.g., Costco, largely a discount operation, offers $300 bottles of wine and $1,000 cameras side-by-side with Kraft Macaroni and Cheese and gallon-size dairy products).
- They supply a product line featuring commodity versions of the line along with upscale or luxury options within the same product line (e.g., Bed Bath & Beyond offers everyday wine glasses along with options ranging up to Waterford and Riedel crystal wine glasses).

Site, market, and shopping center research will help identify and validate opportunities to experiment with alternate merchandising strategies using crossover tenants. We caution, however, that merchandising these tenants in one format or the other, without adequate consideration, can significantly influence consumer perception and acceptance of the shopping center in question.

NEW URBANISM AND FORM-BASED CODES. Urban planners and architecture schools throughout the country are almost universally advancing the idea of new urbanism. The concept is defined by the Congress for New Urbanism as a planning and development approach based on the principles of how cities and towns had been built for the last several centuries: walkable blocks and streets, housing and shopping in close proximity, and accessible public spaces. In other words: New Urbanism focuses on human-scaled urban design.

We do not take a position on the overall soundness of this planning approach. However, when New Urbanist planning principles are applied to large-format commodity retail shopping centers and to ground-floor space in residential buildings, the result is often underperforming retail space that is incompatible with sound design principles associated with most commodity retailers in suburban or nonurban environments. As such, New Urbanist design principles, applied indiscriminately in the form of form-based codes or geometric codes, may lead to planning and cost redundancy, poorly designed retail space, and persistent underuse and/or vacancy.

By applying sound principles of commodity and specialty retail design, massing, and functionality, many of the unintended negative consequences of indiscriminately applied new urbanism can be avoided, resulting in overall improvement to the built environment.

Fundamental Predevelopment Analysis

The feasibility of every shopping center development should be viewed through several analytical filters, each of which forms a primary basis of support for the shopping center under consideration. The four predevelopment filters are

- market assessment;
- physical site considerations;
- public approvals and handling opposition; and
- financial analysis.

The analytical, or filtering, process for assessing both commodity and specialty retail shopping centers is identical; however, the metrics applicable to each site analysis vary, depending on the type of development planned. As such, the descriptions of the underlying analytical processes will generally not differentiate between commodity and specialty development in this portion of the chapter.

The four analytical filters are presented in the general order in which they occur in practice. To some degree, however, all four usually occur somewhat simultaneously, providing checks and balances in the

predevelopment process. In day-to-day practice, the developer is often introduced to a site before conducting any market analysis. In such situations, developers should resist the temptation to "justify" a predetermined market conclusion rather than conduct an unbiased market study. Some of the greatest mistakes in shopping center development have occurred in large part because of errors of this type.

MARKET ASSESSMENT—TRADE AREA AND SALES POTENTIAL ANALYSIS

While some of the market and trade (i.e., geographical) area data available to retailers and developers has changed in recent years, the basic process behind trade area analysis remains largely unchanged. At its heart, every evaluation of a retail location is an assessment of the demand for retail goods and services contrasted with the supply of retail facilities in the market that cater to this demand. A key goal is to identify the delta between demand for goods and services and the available supply of retail filling those needs in a particular trade area.

The practice of engaging in sophisticated retail location analysis became more and more important in the post–World War II era, as the U.S. economy grew rapidly. Fueled largely by affordable housing and widely available automobiles, undeveloped areas outside central cities—suburbs—became the primary focus for new housing and corresponding population growth. The need for new shopping center infrastructure followed.

The emergence of large clusters of suburban populations presented challenges for retailers who had operated primarily in city centers to that point. Where should new stores be located, and what types of stores should be included in new shopping centers? Larry Smith, Richard Lawrence Nelson, and others started consulting firms in the 1950s specifically to address such questions. The new firms developed the basic techniques and methodologies of retail locational analysis which are still in use today in a variety of modified forms.

Analysts evaluating new retail projects today define trade areas by evaluating a range of external factors, including strength of competing shopping centers; quality of access to the competing centers (expressed in time and distance); and the presence of physical (e.g., rivers, expressways), cultural, or socioeconomic barriers that may affect the trade area. Owners of existing retail projects being evaluated for expansion or repositioning can also draw upon the results of customer intercept surveys, along with detailed in-house retailer customer data (if available) within an operating center.

The sections that follow further describe each of the analytical approaches employed today by developers and retailers.

TRADE AREA DEFINITION. Trade areas are established by assessing key external factors, as outlined below.

Time and Distance Analysis. Particularly for commodity goods, shoppers will go to the largest collection of retail facilities of a given type that fits the price/convenience equation most desirable to them. For example, a site that competes with a strong retail shopping center, easily accessible by a high-speed arterial, will have a constrained trade area in the direction of that strong retail center. Conversely, the absence of a competing retail center and equally good arterial access will ordinarily allow a more expansive trade area in that direction; the only limitation will be travel time.

Trade Area Barriers. Trade area barriers impede the flow of potential customers and, as such, significantly influence the size and draw of a trade area. Barriers exist in two broadly defined forms: physical and cultural/socioeconomic.

- Geographical or physical barriers, including rivers and mountains, reduce customer draw and sales potential even when bridges or roadways penetrate them. Physical barriers also may include man-made impediments, such as expressways, railroads, and large public facilities like airports.
- Socioeconomic and/or cultural variations in population makeup and neighborhoods can function as barriers, either when socioeconomic identification restricts movement between population groups, or when the population in one area consumes differently than another because of differences in income, tastes, and/or needs.

STRENGTH OF COMPETITION. The character and extent of retail competition in the area surrounding a site is a key factor in determining trade area boundaries. Where there is little competition, the trade area can extend a great distance, limited only by the time and distance a shopper is willing to spend in travel (discussed above). Where competition does exist, it must be carefully evaluated to determine not only its makeup and character, but also its effectiveness in generating sales.

A retail location with high-identity tenants that have good market acceptance and perform well will have a great impact on the competitive effectiveness of a new location. The trade area boundary will have to be limited to account for this type of existing shopping center. However, if an existing shopping center is missing one or more key retailers, it can be vulnerable to a new retail development at a well-situated location.

Intercepting Locations. With the passage of time, population growth can occur in areas less conveniently served by existing shopping centers, and construction of new arterials can dramatically alter traffic flow. A competing location that is well situated at a key arterial interchange or intersection in a newly emerging area can negatively affect an existing, competitive facility, perhaps even resulting in the departure of one or more anchor stores in favor of the new location. In such cases, the trade areas of both the new center and the existing shopping center will be altered, and the trade areas for the proposed center and the existing competition may actually overlap.

Daytime and Other Population Measures. In addition to evaluating the size and character of the trade area's resident population, in some cases it is equally, or more, important to assess the size and character of the daytime worker and tourist populations contributing to, or in some cases driving, a trade area. Information on the resident population is primarily derived from Census Bureau tabulations and U.S. Postal Service postal route data. Information on daytime populations comes primarily from Bureau of Labor Statistics business and employee counts by zip code area. And tourist information can be obtained from data compiled by local and state convention and visitor agencies.

Alternative Data Sources. As noted above, owners of retail properties may survey customers in existing shopping centers. This information affords perspective about where customers live, their socioeconomic makeup, the number of stores shopped, the amount spent, and so on. Such surveys do not, however, account for shoppers who may not patronize the shopping center at all—information that is most critical when repositioning an existing property. In these cases, small consumer discussion groups (focus groups) are commonly used to help develop the data. Telephone surveys, used frequently in the past to obtain shopping behavior information, have become less reliable because intercepting consumers by phone has become increasingly difficult.

Advanced Analytics: Geofencing. Geofencing is one of the most powerful new tools in the arsenals of retailers and shopping center developers. A geofence is a virtual perimeter around a designated area; geofencing captures data within that perimeter. It provides the shopping center industry with real-time data, harvested from cellphone users to determine usage patterns and practices in shopping centers.

In its most basic form, geofencing can be used to ascertain consumer behavior in and around a retailer or shopping center or within an entire trade area. In more sophisticated applications, the data can be combined with other data to triangulate and pinpoint consumer behavior. With this information, shopping center owners can see the exact impact of adding or losing shopping center retailers and understand where they are winning and losing the battle for sales. While an exhaustive review of geofencing is not possible here, developers should note that failure to use this technology in the modern age of shopping center research would be tantamount to malpractice in the legal field.

TRADE AREA SUBDIVISIONS. Any trade area may be divided into two or more zones reflecting differing socioeconomic characteristics of the customer base and levels of competition. In general, the primary trade area is defined so as to account for 70 to 85 percent of total sales, depending on the regionality of the given location. That primary area may, however, include multiple subdivisions that together represent the complete drawing potential of the location in question.

TRADE AREA DEMOGRAPHICS.

Core Demographic Data. Shopping center analysts use demographic data on trade area population to support locational decisions. Such data typically include measures of density, median household income, educational attainment, ethnic composition, and occupational classifications. Research professionals have found over time that certain levels of population density within specific demographic subgroups are necessary to adequately support sales for a range of retail uses. For example, minimum population requirements can range from 5,000 to 10,000 to support a drug store location, to over 200,000 for a large regional-scale discount store. Income and other characteristics are used to further refine these measures.

Psychographics. Psychographic analysis uses a system of lifestyle clusters that represent an aggregation of different demographic, income, and consumption characteristics. The clusters are named to provide a visual image of the population group, such as Blue Blood Estates, Kids n Cul-de-Sacs, Blue Chip Blues, and Bohemian Mix. Some retailers have identified certain lifestyle cluster groups as important targeting criteria. Ideally the lifestyle cluster system should be used in conjunction with standard demographic and income information to afford the greatest screening perspective to the researcher.

SALES OPPORTUNITY AND SUPPORTABLE SQUARE FOOTAGE. The final step in qualifying a retail location is calculating sales opportunity and supportable square footage for the proposed shopping center. These measures are calculated in a three-part process designed to assess the level of unmet spending potential in the trade area and the square footage of retail, if any, needed to satisfy that potential.

Spending Potential. The first step is to calculate the total "spending potential" available within the trade area. This potential is defined as the product of per capita or per household expenditure for specific merchandise classes (e.g., groceries, apparel and accessories, furniture and floor coverings) and the trade area population in a given year. Spending potentials are calculated for a number of years in a defined study period and expressed in constant dollar terms to negate the effect of inflation over the study period. Whether purchased from a private vendor or estimated by the researcher, per capita and per household spending potential for various goods are based on a combination of U.S. census tabulations of retail trade and U.S. Bureau of Labor Statistics long-term studies of consumer expenditures by household type.

Spending Potential Capture/Leakage. A corollary to the first step is to determine how well existing shopping centers and retailers in the trade area are serving the market, as evidenced by their capture of the available spending potential. This measure is established by comparing spending potential with actual retail sales in a given year. The U.S. census of retail trade is specific enough to develop a retail sales projection, but this information should be supplemented with sales information derived from today's more sophisticated modeling techniques. Historically, if spending potential exceeded actual sales in the trade area, a condition described as sales "leakage" existed, indicating that a significant gap existed between spending potential and actual sales in the trade area. That finding would indicate a need for additional retail and shopping center supply to fill the sales gap in the area measured. This technique does not inherently differentiate commodity and specialty retail, and if not applied correctly to actual market conditions, it can result in faulty conclusions.

Market Share. Forecasting the future sales opportunity of a new or redeveloped shopping center within a given trade area is the fundamental next step in this process. The forecast is usually based on more than one form of analysis, to establish a likely market share range. The typical starting point is to identify a group of more and less successful centers that can function as analogs to a spectrum of operating environments and relative sales performance. This approach uses proprietary owner information and can take the form of a multivariable predictive model that scores the locational and core customer identification factors (described above). Regardless of how comprehensively detailed the model is, most experienced researchers find that the model's conclusions need to be refined based on experience and field review, to appropriately account for the population and competitive characteristics of the geographical area under study.

Other approaches to market share estimation are based on a pro rata share of a given type of retail space operating within the trade area or affecting it from outside. Judgments are also made regarding the volume of sales that can be drawn by reversing spending outflows and by taking market share from existing shopping centers that may be less affected by planned new development.

Overall, the work of developing market share analogs must be done with a high degree of care, as such information is fundamental to arriving at an accurate sales forecast for the location under study.

Supportable Square Footage. The third step in calculating sales opportunity is to contrast the market share identified for the study site with the spending potential over the study period. Other non–trade area factors—such as the spending of daytime populations near the site, visitors to the trade area, and persons living in an area too diffuse to be studied geographically—are then added to arrive at the ultimate sales opportunity. These additional factors typically account for 15 to 30 percent of total sales, depending on the type of location and retail development under study. For major urban retail streets and resort markets with heavy tourist influence, the non–trade area sales contribution can account for up to 100 percent of forecasted sales.

MEASURING RETAILER SALES POTENTIAL. Individual retailers employ a methodology similar to that described earlier to come up with sales estimates for new stores under consideration. Retailers are, however, also privy to a wealth of additional proprietary information related to core shopper groups at their other stores, levels of market capture under different competitive circumstances, and sales by zip code area and/or census tract—all of which facilitates even more accurate sales forecasting. This proprietary information allows retailers to establish a range of detailed store analogs against which to measure proposed new store performance. In addition, geofencing is leading to even greater levels of sales forecasting.

Given the availability and depth of this information, retailers can readily build a trade area definition and quickly determine the likely market share of the available spending potential and sales opportunity with core shopper groups. From this market share estimate they can then develop a projection and test store viability at various sales volumes by plugging in a rent number and backing into the needed level of sales to support that rent estimate.

GLEANING ADDITIONAL PERSPECTIVE FROM RETAILER SALES FORECASTS. In addition to performing the trade area and sales potential analyses, shopping center developers will also benefit from evaluating the sales opportunity for specific target retailers (as the retailers themselves do). In the case of single-tenant development, this exercise is critical to successfully underwriting project feasibility.

PHYSICAL SITE CONDITIONS

Selecting an appropriate site for shopping center development first requires defining the general location and project size necessary to satisfy market demand and thoroughly vetting specific opportunities and constraints unique to the site(s) under consideration. Factors including access, topography, site shape and size, and availability of utilities must all be considered. And sites intended for a specific commodity retail use must fit the basic "convenience" parameters required for that use. Other fundamentals, described below, must be closely assessed.

Although all types of real estate development share commonalities, shopping center development differs significantly in many respects, requiring distinct terminology and performance measurements. Perhaps most important for the shopping center developer is recognition that retail real estate is the only type of property in which fundamental measures of property value are directly related to the volume of transactions taking place on the site. As such, success in shopping center development depends almost entirely on the success of the retail tenants in the project, as measured by sales per square foot and profitability.

SIZES AND DIMENSIONS OF SITES. Shopping centers can be developed at a range of densities, but the most common configuration for small suburban centers is a one-story building covering 25 percent of the site, or a floor/area ratio (FAR) of 0.25. For this configuration, the site area needs to be approximately four times more than the gross building area of the project. A rule of thumb is to build approximately 9,000 square feet per acre (828 sq m/ha). Urban infill projects, however, might allow 100 percent site coverage and include no on-site parking requirement. Large-scale power centers and other commodity retail offerings are proportionate in impact. Specialty centers, however, often include multiple uses, dedicated open spaces, and public facilities—which puts them beyond the scope of this discussion.

In suburban areas, where land availability is less constrained, the ideal shopping center site should be a regular and unified shape, undivided by highways or dedicated streets. Although the term "strip center" connotes a long narrow site, a square site with an L-shaped center that wraps around a parking lot is often preferable. Triangular sites may also work, especially if they are surrounded by major arterial streets and provide good access from numerous directions. The best use of the odd portions of a triangular or irregularly shaped site may be to develop freestanding facilities. In select, urban-infill locations, ideal sites are often not available, requiring innovative design and retailer flexibility.

SITE VISIBILITY AND ACCESS. Site visibility and unimpeded vehicular access are critical in retail site selection. Shopping center sites should be accessible from multiple points, and generally, the larger the market to be served, the more points of access will be required. Traffic counts on roads serving the site are a key measure of the potential drive-by market. The volume of customers who actually pass the site and proximity to major intersections is a major advantage for any site. Likewise, a site's orientation to the principal roads serving it or to other adjacent uses that may generate customers is critical. One caveat: even though traffic flow attracts retail business, a site that fronts on a thoroughfare with many competing distractions (including other retail stores and signs) can be less desirable than a site on a less heavily traveled arterial with fewer distractions, provided the other

components of access and trade area are positive.

For retailers whose peak business is defined by the time of day, a location on a specific side of the road can be crucial. For example, doughnut or bagel shops prefer locations on the drive-to-work side, while gas stations prefer to be on the drive-home side.

PHYSICAL SITE CHARACTERISTICS. Because most shopping centers are horizontal (rather than vertical) in nature and have a large footprint, a flat or gently sloping site is usually preferable. More steeply sloping sites can be adapted, but that process may entail higher site improvement costs and lower operational efficiency and may present a number of design, visibility, and access challenges.

Sites in floodplains, on solid rock, or with a high-water table should be avoided if possible. When considered, such sites require considerable supplemental analysis to quantify and mitigate risk. If the area has known subsoil problems (e.g., rock, sand, high density/low moisture, low-permeability clay), the extent of those characteristics and potential cost implications should be thoroughly assessed.

Even with careful analysis, a small refuse dump, unrecorded oil or gasoline storage tank(s), well head(s), septic tank(s), or agricultural drainage fields in the middle of a grid might be missed. Retaining a local soil investigation company with a history of work in the area is generally advisable, as local professionals are more likely to be aware of the history of the site and latent site conditions that may impede development.

Buyers should also be alert for environmental issues other than wetlands. These can include illegal dumping; groundwater contamination; floodplain encroachment; and contamination from asbestos, pesticides, or PCBs (polychlorinated biphenyl). The presence of endangered species, historic structures, or archeological remains on the site can significantly delay or, in the worst case, prevent development. All these factors can lead to costly remediation and/or significant project delays, with attendant cost overruns.

SITE ACQUISITION. After a site with desirable physical characteristics has been identified, the developer should follow the general site acquisition steps outlined in chapters 3 and 4 of this publication. One site acquisition scenario that is especially pertinent to retail development involves acquisition of an existing center needing renovation or expansion or the consolidation of several adjacent smaller obsolete buildings into a single parcel. The key factors to look for in acquiring centers for renovation are an outdated appearance and local market or demographic changes that suggest potential for bringing in new tenants or repositioning the shopping center.

SITE ENGINEERING. Design requirements for most shopping centers dictate that the development site be relatively level. Slope and other unusual features of a site's topography should be planned to achieve maximum compatibility between the shopping center and the site's natural characteristics. Regardless, an engineering firm with local experience should be retained to assess on-site soils and to identify any other special site problems.

Site Slope. In very limited circumstances, if the best available site has significant slope, and the slope corresponds to the grades of surrounding roads, an opportunity may exist for a two-level arrangement of buildings and parking. For example, a sloping site with trees that must be preserved can be reshaped to accommodate a stepped, but still essentially single-level, center. Vehicles use a sloped access road, and pedestrians use wide steps (or an adjacent ramp) to move from level to level. A front-to-back design is also possible, but that configuration isolates upper and lower tenants from each other. It may be a satisfactory solution if the tenant mix can be logically divided or if the less attractive level can be leased to nonretail residential or office uses.

The ideal slope for a parking lot is 3 percent, which allows for sufficient drainage but helps to prevent runaway shopping carts and difficulties with hard-to-open, heavy car doors. A slope of 7 to 8 percent is allowable in limited areas, such as entry drives. (In areas with substantial ice and snow, a maximum slope of 5 percent is typical.) If the site has areas of steeper slope, the parking lot can be divided into terraced pads separated by landscaped strips.

Stormwater Management. Stormwater runoff is a major issue in shopping center design due to the large amounts of land covered by buildings and pavement in a typical retail project. Reducing or delaying runoff may involve significant cost. Most communities have limited storm system capacity and often require methods to control stormwater runoff. These can include rooftop ponding, temporary detention basins or bioswales (e.g., in portions of the parking lot), detention or retention ponds, or other mechanisms for reducing the runoff rate and total runoff from a developed site. Stormwater management systems take into account both water storage and visual appearance and should be an integral part of the overall project design. Most

municipal environmental regulations will require stormwater management and mitigation measures as part of standard approvals processes.

PUBLIC APPROVALS AND HANDLING OPPOSITION

ZONING AND SITE PLAN APPROVALS. The zoning provisions and public approvals required to develop a retail site must be studied carefully before a site is purchased. Early on, the developer should carefully explore the attitudes of local residents, zoning staff, and the approving body—generally and specifically—toward the proposed shopping center. In cases where a rezoning may be necessary, the developer should initiate informal discussions with local zoning officials and retain respected local zoning counsel to assist in the process. Some provisions may be open to interpretation, or perhaps amendment, ranging from FARs, building height, and parking requirements to lot coverage, setbacks, and permitted uses.

Shopping center developments carry with them several special regulatory concerns including the probable traffic impacts, compatibility with surrounding uses, environmental effects, stormwater runoff, and, in some cases, impacts on existing retailing. Developers have often found that specific standards included in commercial zoning ordinances are either incompatible with retailers' needs or simply too difficult or impossible to satisfy without variances or special exceptions.

In many jurisdictions, political considerations have resulted in policies, ordinances, and directives containing strict design and use guidelines. These may be part of the comprehensive plan or part of adopted policy statements. In some cases, they are unofficial "policies" that guide the evaluations done by planning staff. In addition, developers often encounter biases and barriers in the local planning and approval processes that apply to any retail proposal for rezoning or for site plan and architectural approval for a building permit. In some communities, zoning to a planned use development (PUD) district may be possible; however, while site-specific zoning may allow greater regulatory flexibility, it will likely trigger a much more thorough review of the project overall.

ENVIRONMENTAL CONSIDERATIONS. A range of environmental issues, such as potential wetlands and habitats for endangered species, may affect the viability of a proposed site. Obtaining as much information as possible about the present and past uses of the site is critical. And it is always better to discover impediments to development sooner—in the site review process—than later.

The presence of hazardous subsurface materials or farming contaminants may also render a site unsuitable without costly cleanup efforts, so the site should be thoroughly vetted by qualified environmental firms. (For more detail, see chapter 3).

Still, "in densely populated areas where land is scarce, redeveloping industrial sites and previous retail venues into new shopping centers is often the only opportunity for growth. In such cases, wetland preservation concerns are less likely to arise than issues relating to the problem of latent residual contamination."[4]

FINANCIAL ANALYSIS

The financial feasibility of a shopping center can be determined only after a specific development program has been defined for a specific site. At that point, the developer can properly estimate development costs, operating revenues, financing options, and expected levels of investment return. This process can be very dynamic and commonly involves significant back-and-forth discussion as development programs are decided, budgets are prepared, income projections are made, and pro formas are prepared and refined. Plans and information will inevitably fluctuate in the planning process as costs, tenant types, amenities, and design features are added and adjusted.

Generic aspects of the financial analysis process are discussed in greater depth in chapter 4. The discussion here focuses on financial issues unique to shopping centers and, in particular, the more predictable subset of commodity shopping centers. Specialty shopping centers, while analyzed through the same process, are far more complex in planning and execution and are beyond the scope of this publication.

CAPITAL COSTS. The feature box on p. 352 highlights capital costs unique to shopping center development. Those costs, although different from costs for other commercial real estate projects, play no greater or lesser role in determining project feasibility than the costs discussed in chapter 4. Note that one of the capital costs unique to shopping centers is the tenant buildout allowance, which can vary widely from tenant to tenant.

INCOME PROJECTIONS. The initial analysis and subsequent refinements of rents and tenant reimbursements are a critical step in determining the feasibility of any shopping center development project. Shopping center income projections must be based on a leasing plan that represents the developer's estimate of square footage to be leased to specific types of tenants. As such, the allocation of space to various classes of tenants is a critical component of the financial feasibility analysis. Although the preliminary income side projections are based on well-considered assumptions, such assumptions must be validated in the market in the form of signed leases.

The process of estimating shopping center revenues is unlike estimating revenues for other income-producing properties. All shopping center rental rates are directly and indirectly related to sales productivity. Rental rates vary substantially, depending on the type of shopping center, target tenants, and market conditions. Commodity retail shopping centers, for example, tend to have more predictable rental ranges and lower operating costs. Rental rates for specialty retail shopping centers vary widely, as do the operating costs, primarily because placemaking strategies, shopping center amenities, and construction costs vary widely.

Design and Construction

The most important consideration in selecting a shopping center architect is identification of the type of shopping center to be built: commodity or specialty. The utilitarian principals underpinning the design of most commodity retail buildings differ fundamentally from the placemaking principles applicable to specialty retail shopping center design. The formulaic design approaches that create efficiency and predictability in neighborhood and power center design are not well suited to specialty centers: placemaking architecture values aesthetics over efficiency.

For example, in the case of typical grocery-anchored or power centers, the particular design aesthetic, although important for public approvals and general perception, is not usually critical for the shopping center's success. In contrast, when creating specialty centers, every case involves some element of placemaking—and in some cases, the "place" that is created is far more important to the shopping center's success than any other aspect.

As with financing (discussed earlier), the design principles applicable to specialty center development are far more varied and complex than those applicable to commodity centers and beyond the scope of this publication. Again, the discussion here focuses on the basic principles applicable to commodity centers.

The initial design consideration for every shopping center is the creation of a preliminary site plan and

Capital Costs for Shopping Centers

LAND AND LAND IMPROVEMENTS

Land or Leasehold Acquisition
- Cost of land
- Good-faith deposit
- Broker's fee
- Escrow
- Title guarantee policy
- Standby fee
- Chattel search
- Legal fee
- Recording fee

Off-Site and On-Site Land Improvements
- Off-site streets and sidewalks
- Off-site sewers, utilities, and lights
- Relocation of power lines
- Traffic controls
- Surveys and test borings
- Utilities
  - » Water connection to central system or on-site supply
  - » Storm sewers
  - » Sanitary sewer connection to system or on-site disposal
  - » Gas distribution connection to central system
  - » Primary electrical distribution
  - » Telephone distribution
- Parking areas
  - » Curbs and gutters
  - » Paving and striping
  - » Pedestrian walkways
  - » Traffic controls and signs
  - » Lighting
  - » Service area screens and fences
- Landscaping
  - » Grading
  - » Plants

BUILDINGS AND EQUIPMENT

Shell and Mall Building
- Layout
- Excavation
- Footings and foundations
- Structural frame
- Exterior walls
- Roofing and insulation
- Subfloor
- Sidewalk canopy
- Sidewalks and mall paving
- Loading docks and service courts
- Truck and service tunnels
- Equipment rooms, transformer vaults, cooling towers
- Heating and cooling—central plants or units
- Incinerator
- Community meeting rooms
- Offices for center management and merchants association
- Electric wiring, roughed in
- Plumbing, roughed in
- Fire sprinkler system
- Public toilets
- Elevators, escalators, stairways
- Contractor's overhead and profit
- Pylons
- Shopping center signs
- Mall furniture, fountains, etc.
- Maintenance equipment and tools
- Office furniture and equipment

Tenant Improvements
(if paid for by developer)
- Tenant finish allowance
- Storefronts
- Window backs and fronts
- Finished ceiling and acoustical tile
- Finished walls
- Interior painting
- Floor coverings
- Interior partitioning
- Lighting fixtures
- Plumbing fixtures
- Doors, frames, and hardware
- Storefront signs
- Store fixtures

OVERHEAD AND DEVELOPMENT

Architecture and Engineering
- Site planning
- Buildings and improvements

Internal and Financing
- Interest during construction
- Construction and permanent loan fees
- Loan settlement costs
- Appraisal costs
- Legal fees for financing

Administrative Overhead and Construction Supervision
- Construction supervision
- Field office expense
- Bookkeeping
- Home office expense
- Travel and entertainment
- Salaries and overhead of staff
- Printing and stationery

Leasing Costs and Legal Fees
- Leasing fees paid to brokers
- Salaries and overhead of staff
- Scale model, brochures, etc.
- Legal fees—leasing
- Legal fees—general

Other Overhead and Development
- Market and traffic surveys
- Zoning and subdivision approvals
- Outside accounting and auditing
- Real estate taxes
- Other taxes
- Insurance
- Advertising and promotion of opening
- Landlord's share of formation and assessments of merchants associations
- Miscellaneous administrative costs

Source: Michael D. Beyard and W. Paul O'Mara et al., *Shopping Center Development Handbook*, 3rd ed. (Washington, DC: Urban Land Institute, 1999), p. 57.

Note: Items in this list are for all types of shopping centers, including enclosed regional malls.

building configuration plan. Shopping centers by their nature involve the efficient movement of customers on and off the property and in and out of retail stores. As a result, shopping centers—more than any other type of real estate—must be designed to accommodate a large volume of customers flowing through multiple points of access throughout the facility. The placement of buildings and parking lots, as well as the creation of efficient pedestrian and vehicular circulation patterns, must optimize the appeal and accessibility of every store in the center, while creating functional delivery systems for tenants.

SHOPPING CENTER CONFIGURATION

A variety of retail layout schemes have evolved as basic shopping center land use concepts over many years with varying degrees of success. Once the underlying retail use of the shopping center has been determined, the first design consideration is identifying the most suitable configuration for the site. For small centers the primary design focus is on ease of access, adequate parking, and visibility from the primary roadway system. In urban locations, effective pedestrian connections and access to streets and transit may be far more important than access to parking, which may or may not be located on site.

COMMODITY CENTERS. Ideally, commodity shopping centers are laid out with good sight lines for all storefronts, and modest variations in setbacks and elevation to provide contrasting design elements for individual tenants. Bay depths, widths, and column spacing should be designed to provide maximum flexibility for tenants of various shapes and sizes.

The configuration of smaller neighborhood or community shopping centers depends largely on three factors: the shape of the site, the nature and intensity of surrounding roadways, and the space requirements of the intended tenants. Other important considerations include site utilization/efficiency, parking constraints, length and depth of buildings, and visibility of tenants. The most common configurations for these types of centers are variations on three general shapes: linear, L-shaped, or U-shaped. These basic layouts can vary with the use of setbacks, curves, and multiple independent buildings.

A linear arrangement is still the most common configuration for smaller, unanchored strip centers and grocery-anchored neighborhood centers. The linear layout is basically a straight line of stores sharing common architectural elements, often tied together by a coordinated canopy system. In neighborhood centers, this configuration usually places two major retailers, most often a supermarket and another mid-size anchor tenant, in the most prominent locations in the center, with adjacent spaces programmed for smaller tenants. A linear center (and its variations) is generally the least expensive structure to build and is easily adapted to most site conditions. Linear centers typically range from 500 to 1,000 feet (152.5 to 305 m) in length, including anchor tenants. When a center's length exceeds about 300 feet (90 m), building setbacks and architectural features should be visually distinguished.

Parking is usually placed at the front of small shopping centers to allow for easy access, though some centers use different configurations. Truck parking and deliveries should occur at the rear of the shopping center, where employee parking is also most optimally located.

Sites in urban areas invariably present different challenges affecting site plan and building configuration. Most often these sites are constrained by a variety of factors. These include limited size, close architectural and pedestrian relationships to adjacent buildings, historic preservation and neighborhood consensus, transit access, and limitations on automobile traffic generated and/or provision of adequate parking.

The following are among the concerns uniquely applicable to urban retail sites:

- **Streetscape**—Public policy and urban design considerations often favor or require the placement of buildings along the street with limited setback to enhance the city's streetscape.
- **Parking**—The placement and availability of parking may become a critical issue, driving the creation of new public and/or parking resources.
- **Loading and Deliveries**—Truck delivery traffic and customer parking may have to be intermixed, necessitating deliveries before or after operating hours.
- **Multistory Retail Stores and Restaurants**—Although street-level retail is the most accessible and desirable design, tight urban sites may require a multilevel solution to produce enough square footage for financial feasibility. In some instances, this requirement results in two-level stores that have traditionally been one level. McDonald's among fast-food restaurants, Harris Teeter among supermarkets, and Target among general merchandise stores all operate multilevel stores.

SPECIALTY CENTER SITES. Specialty retail shopping centers are, by design, intended to influence the expenditure of discretionary time and income. Sites selected for these centers must be sufficient in size, location, and orientation to create the kind of places appropriate to both the market and the intended retail tenants. As such, the layouts of these facilities should be designed to respond both to the interests of the target market and to the expectations and demands of the specialty retailers who will occupy the center. Although specialty centers may be developed as a variation of a linear configuration, there are few design constants constraining site selection. A unique site configuration may even contribute to the creation of place that is essential to most specialty centers.

INGRESS AND EGRESS

Efficient ingress and egress are critical to shopping center success. Road improvements are often required in the site planning process to provide for efficient location and number of curb cuts. The use of entrance deceleration and exit acceleration lanes must also be taken into account, as should the need for stop lights to allow turns and to control traffic flow. All these issues should be fully addressed during the feasibility study period.

PARKING AND CIRCULATION

Parking and on-site circulation plans are required by zoning codes and created as part of the site planning process; retailers will also be interested in these plans, and many will stipulate specific requirements. In designing these aspects of any shopping center, the objective should be not just to meet the letter of the law, but to design facilities that best meet the day-to-day needs of customers and retailers alike.

THE ROLE OF PARKING. Parking availability, access, and ease of use form the customer's first impression of the shopping center, particularly commodity centers. The goal is for parking to be generally available and accessible with minimum thought and effort by the customer. Customers who have trouble finding easily accessible parking at a shopping center will inevitably disfavor that center.

In commodity retail centers, the location and availability of parking is perhaps the single most important element of the customer experience, and inadequate or poorly located parking can by itself defeat the primary goal of delivering a convenient retail experience. Each individual commodity retail use has developed specific needs—from convenience stores all the way through to warehouse retail outlets. Specialty

retail parking tends to be more densely massed and more often includes more costly parking structures and underground parking facilities. Paid parking is not common in retail; when it is used, detailed plans,

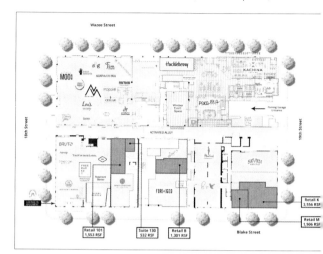

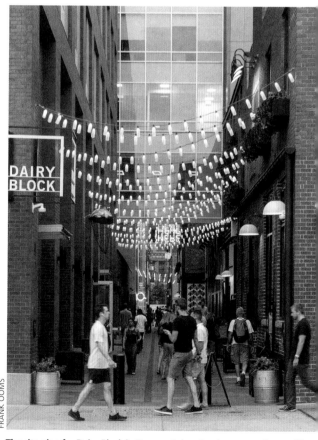

The site plan for Dairy Block in Denver, Colorado, showcases the retail/restaurant layout that consumes 73,000 square feet (6,782 sq m) along the entire city block. The blue area represents the activated Alley area where guests and tenants mix and mingle.

FRANK OOMS

including parking systems and validation standards, become essential.

Parking is generally treated as a land cost in retail development; that includes the costs of decks and underground parking facilities, where applicable. Likewise, when paid parking is used, parking revenue is considered a form of income, like rent. In more complex parking arrangements involving public financing of parking facilities, revenue may be shared.

Local building and zoning codes generally set the standards for shopping center parking. Sometimes, providing parking above those standards can be just as important to a shopping center's operational and financial success as meeting the code-mandated minimums.

PARKING REQUIREMENTS. Typical parking requirements for shopping centers range from three to five parking spaces per 1,000 square feet (93 sq m) of the center's gross leasable area (GLA), depending on location and uses. For centers with higher percentages of restaurant, entertainment, and/or cinema uses, parking requirements are higher. Early studies by the Urban Land Institute and the International Council of Shopping Centers recommended a standard parking requirement of five spaces per 1,000 square feet of GLA, but this standard evolved as centers were built in increasingly urban and mixed-use environments. Numerous factors can affect the amount of parking required, including the availability and proximity of mass transit, the amount of walk-in versus destination trade, and individual tenant requirements. Today—particularly in densely populated and urban areas—more and more attention and planning are devoted to availability of short-term parking for delivery services, for flexible parking for customers using services like Uber, and in anticipation of autonomous vehicles sometime in the future.

PARKING DESIGN. The layout of surface parking may be perpendicular or diagonal. Perpendicular (90-degree) parking economizes space; facilitates circulation; and allows two-way traffic through the aisle, the safety of better sight lines, greater parking capacity, and shorter cruising distances for drivers seeking a space. Diagonal (angular) parking, with 45-degree or 60-degree angles, provides one-way circulation, is easier for drivers to enter and exit, and involves fewer conflicts between adjacent vehicles when occupants open car doors. Diagonal layouts also provide greater maneuverability for sport utility vehicles and minivans. Ideally, aisles should be aligned perpendicular to store-fronts to allow shoppers to walk directly from their cars to the front of stores. The aisles themselves may be curved or angled to meet physical requirements of the site or the design. Parking aisles that run parallel with storefronts should be avoided because customers must then cut between cars, which can be hazardous.

For smaller, unanchored commodity centers, however, perpendicular parking is often best placed along the storefronts. This design accommodates quick visits to the stores and fast turnover of prime spaces. It does, however, create a somewhat more hazardous situation, as shoppers can step out into moving traffic from between cars.

AMERICANS WITH DISABILITIES ACT. Since 1992, the Americans with Disabilities Act (ADA) has mandated the number and location of parking spaces accessible to handicapped individuals in public places, including shopping centers. ADA guidelines clearly state, "First priority should be given to measures that will enable individuals with disabilities to get in the front door." For shopping centers with multiple front doors, this guideline can be a significant challenge in both interpretation and implementation.

For example, a shopping center with 100,000 square feet (9,290 sq m) of GLA and requiring 400 parking spaces, would need eight handicapped-accessible spaces under ADA guidelines. These spaces need to be located next to curb ramps to walkways along the storefronts. In addition, they need to be positioned in front of or near the anchor tenants and then occasionally along the remaining storefronts. Additionally, at least one handicapped-accessible space should be in front of a convenience store. Thus, while eight dedicated handicapped-accessible spaces may be sufficient to meet the ADA requirement in this example, a number greater than the minimum may be needed to best serve anticipated customer volume.

Although not required by the ADA, the provision of designated reserved spaces for expectant mothers, military veterans, curb-side delivery, prescription pickup, and even "star employees" has become increasingly common today. These allocations are generally negotiated by individual retailers, particularly commodity retailers, motivated to provide convenient solutions for specific needs.

LIGHTING AND LANDSCAPING

Lighting and landscaping provide safety and stormwater runoff protection, respectively. Both are essential elements of the site plan approval process for all shopping centers. They not only play important roles in creating appealing aesthetics in shopping centers of all types; they play an even more central role in specialty retail shopping centers, where lighting and enhanced landscaping are key elements in placemaking and the creation of higher-level aesthetic appeal. A discussion of the dedicated open spaces and public facilities that are often included in large-scale specialty centers is beyond the scope of this publication. A discussion of the basics follows.

LANDSCAPING BASICS. Attractive landscape features at shopping center entrances contribute to creating a positive first impression and should be coordinated with the location and design of shopping center signage. In general, landscaping for a parking area generally should be confined to trees and massed plantings in wells or clearly delineated areas. Plantings should be located where they will not interfere with maintenance of the parking area or with snow removal and storage and will vary significantly depending on climate conditions. Minimum landscaping requirements are set by local code and enforced as part of the site planning process.

Landscaping on the perimeter of a shopping center can effectively mask parking areas from the street and buffer the center from nearby residential areas. Regardless of the technique used, landscaping should not hide the center from public view. Retailers will want to ensure this is not the case, as well. Hardy ground covers, shrubs, and bushes concentrated at appropriate places in the buffers and trees that can be pruned to provide a high canopy are good solutions.

In commodity centers, small planting areas in the pedestrian zones, next to and between buildings, and in conjunction with architectural features and furniture can provide buffers from large parking areas and an attractive pedestrian environment. In specialty centers, fountains, water features, and seasonal plants are used extensively to create a pleasant atmosphere and offer pleasing vistas to visitors and tenants.

LIGHTING BASICS. The primary objective of shopping center lighting is to provide the customer with both real and, just as important, the perception of safety and security. Lighting on buildings is also sometimes used to illuminate storefronts at night, particularly when the architecture is distinctive. Under-canopy lighting enhances pedestrians' vision, and accent lighting can be used to enhance the center's appearance. Frequently, under-canopy signage lights and lights from inside

stores are sufficient if display windows are well lit.

Exterior lighting is both an essential safety feature and a potential design feature used to create an image and character for shopping centers. Providing a higher level of light attracts more attention to the center at night and enhances the sense of security. However, that intensive lighting is often viewed negatively by adjacent residents.

An effective lighting system requires consideration of a variety of factors, including mounting height, spacing, light control, and light sources. The latter should be evaluated based on efficiency, durability, color of light, and light output. Lighting in parking areas should be placed on poles located in islands at the ends of parking bays or on the dividing line between bays when the bays are longer than the spread of the selected light fixture. The lighting scheme should usually provide a minimum of about one and one-half foot-candles at the pavement surface.

BUILDING STRUCTURE AND SHELL

Standards vary widely for retail building design and construction depending on use and function. This section provides only general guidelines for basic commodity retail structures and should be used only as a general reference guide.

BUILDING STRUCTURE. Small shopping centers are usually constructed of a lightweight steel roof-framing structure and tilt-up concrete walls or concrete masonry units. The design of foundations for shopping center buildings varies from region to region and from

STEINER + ASSOCIATES

The expansion of the Easton Town Center connects to the customer through a vibrant mix of art and architecture, united by public plazas and creative programming.

site to site, depending on subsurface conditions. Generally, however, caissons or spread footings are used to support columns and bearing walls, and a four- or five-inch-thick (10–13 cm) concrete slab is allowed to "float" within the storefront. Tolerances of movement for the floor slab are set by most major tenants and generally should not exceed three-fourths inch (2 cm).

FLOORS. Variations in flatness are a concern. Finishing techniques using a laser screed can significantly reduce variations, but the underlying soil may require treatment with lime or cement to reduce shrink and swell and maintain level floor slabs over time. Alternatively, on-site soils can be replaced with fill materials of higher quality to achieve the same objective.

When floor slabs are poured in the normal sequence of building shell construction, allowances must be made for plumbing lines to serve future restrooms. Water and sanitary sewer lines should be placed parallel to and three feet (0.9 m) away from the rear wall of the building. The rearmost five feet (1.5 m) of slab should not be poured until tenants decide where to locate restrooms.

Any location designated for restaurant use should be constructed *without* a slab during initial construction because of the heavy utility needs of restaurants and the varied nature of their layouts. In such cases, the slab should not be poured, if possible, until the space is leased and the tenant has designed a layout for utilities.

SHELL COMPONENTS. Like other key building components, exterior facing materials used in shopping center construction contribute to a shopping center's image and consumers' overall perception of it. Using more than one material can create an attractive and well-conceived exterior appearance and a distinctive identity, particularly in specialty centers.

Except when side and rear-facing walls are readily visible to adjacent property owners, or when upgrades are required as part of the site plan approval process, the choice of method for enclosing the side and rear walls is driven almost exclusively by cost. Tilt-up concrete wall panels are often favored, primarily due to their low overall cost. Tilt-up walls designed for a 15- to 20-foot (4.6–6.1 m) height are only five and one-half to seven inches (14–18 cm) thick and may serve as load-bearing structural walls. An alternative is to use load-bearing concrete masonry units, eight or 12 inches (20 or 30 cm) thick. Both these wall materials can be painted, plastered, or bricked.

Most insulation of retail building shells is installed

as tenant finish items; nevertheless, insulation should be installed by the developer at perimeter walls and above ceilings. Another design practice that will affect the location of insulation is the trend toward higher vertical spaces achieved by eliminating a ceiling and leaving ductwork and piping exposed. The only place for insulation in this approach is on top of the roof decking or directly on its underside.

Special consideration must be given when renovating older structures, as stripping the building down to the shell frame may expose residual contaminants such as asbestos and lead paint. Cement asbestos tile and sprayed asbestos insulation were common in the 1950s. Removal of these products follow prescribed remediation practices that may prove costly and will likely negatively affect the economic feasibility of a rehabilitation project.

FRONT ELEVATIONS. Creating highly functional and attractive storefronts and building facades is critically important. The object of every shopping center is to encourage consumers to voluntarily enter the buildings to purchase goods within the facility. Appealing entrances are fundamental. Developers should allow tenants to create their own identities and use their individual company design standards whenever possible. This is true for both commodity and specialty retailers and centers, but it can be particularly important in specialty centers where consumer expectations are heightened considerably.

A shopping center's exterior facing materials contribute to its image and the perception of quality. Using more than one material can create an attractive exterior and a distinctive image. Materials should be capable of being speedily assembled and erected, durable and easily maintained, and, ideally, available locally.

A variety of facing materials are used in designing and constructing typical shopping center facades: for example, masonry, metal panels, wood, tile, and stucco-like synthetic finish systems (i.e., exterior insulation finishing systems, or EIFS). Of these choices, EIFS has become a standard building material in commodity shopping centers of all types due to its cost and flexibility. Masonry is the most durable and offers great flexibility in treatment. It's very durability, however, makes it more difficult and expensive to alter once installed.

The choice of material also depends on the character of the community, the region of the country, and local weather conditions. For example, in the Midwest and East, masonry is one of the most common standards of quality, while in the West, tile, wood, adobe brick, and stucco are more commonly used.

Any of these materials may be used to build a colonnaded walk or arcade, the traditional means of sheltering customers and protecting storefronts from the weather. Canopies may be cantilevered from the building elevation or supported by freestanding columns. Their size is determined by the chosen architectural style; 10 to 15 feet (3–4.5 m) is an ample width for a walkway.

CEILING HEIGHTS. Although most stores require 11- to 12-foot (3.3 m) finished or open ceilings, some small stores find ceilings as low as nine feet (2.7 m) acceptable. Most big-box tenants, as well as supermarkets and general merchandise stores, require finished ceilings heights of 13 feet (4 m) or higher.

The space between the finished ceiling and the roof usually contains air-conditioning ducts, electrical wires, plumbing lines, and other utility hardware; such equipment may require as much as two to three feet (0.6–0.9 m) of space between the finished ceiling and the structure. When open-web steel joists are used, much of the ductwork and other lines can be threaded between the webs. Thus, the clear distance from the floor slab to the underside of the roof varies with the structural design.

ROOF SYSTEMS. Shopping center roofs are often one of the most costly and difficult aspects of construction and operation for shopping center developers, and roof leaks are one of the most common complaints of shopping center tenants. A typical shopping center roof should last 12 to 15 years, but correctly installed and proactively maintained, it can last 20 years or more. As a rule of thumb, roofs should slope to ensure good drainage. The future installation of rooftop-mounted heating, ventilation, and air conditioning (HVAC) units and/or photovoltaic (solar) panels should be anticipated when designing the roof, with allowances made for their weight and prefabricated roof curbs provided to minimize random penetrations of the roof.

Three principal types of roofing are used for shopping centers: built-up, single-ply membrane, and modified bitumen. Since 2000, single-ply roofs have become most common, used now in more than 50 percent of new construction. The elastomeric properties of these rubber-type membranes allow them to stretch and move with the roof deck, helping to prevent tears. Within this subset of roofing materials,

the three dominant categories of membranes used are ethylene propylene diene monomer (EPDM), polyvinyl chloride (PVC), and thermoplastic polyolefin (TPO). EPDM is essentially a rubber membrane, PVC is a plastic, and TPO, the newest entry, combines the properties of both EPDM and TPO membranes.

Additionally, white membrane roofing has been developed in response to concerns about energy efficiency and the environment. Although white membranes may cost twice as much as black membranes, the cost savings in energy expenses over the life of the roof can offset the additional expense and may even generate significant savings, depending on location.

UTILITIES. To allow for flexibility in operations, structural elements such as plumbing and heating stacks, air-conditioning ducts, toilets, and stairways should be placed on end walls or on the walls least likely to be removed if the store is enlarged or the space redivided. Keeping all utilities, including water lines, overhead should be seriously considered. An overhead leak may cause some damage but can be more easily located and repaired. Leaks under the slab are much more damaging and expensive to repair and disrupt use of the space. If overhead water lines are used, measures must be taken to ensure that the lines are not exposed to freezing temperatures.

Plumbing. For tenants such as supermarkets, restaurants, and dry cleaners (i.e., any tenants that require large plumbing installations), installation of the floor slab usually should be deferred until these tenant spaces are leased. Formulation of these tenants' under-floor requirements is likely to extend past the developer's shell construction schedule.

Electricity. Generally, a primary source of electricity provided by the developer is located at the rear of the building and individually metered. Each tenant is then required to provide the secondary electrical service from the meter, subject to the landlord's review and approval.

HVAC. Individual HVAC units typically are provided for each tenant in commodity centers. Once delivered, tenants are usually assigned responsibility for their individual units under their lease terms. Because energy costs and energy conservation are important considerations, a mechanical engineer should be retained to select the most appropriate HVAC system. That individual (or firm) will be familiar with the alternative gas and electric systems available; will be able to evaluate initial, operating, and maintenance costs; and can recommend the best system.

TENANT SPACES

STORE SIZES. Store widths and depths vary for different types of tenants. Chain stores typically have specific prototype store dimensions and, in general, seek to avoid significant deviation. For most new shopping centers, however, the design of the shell usually requires wide spans between structural columns so that stores can be inserted into modules with minimal conflicts with columns. When conflict does occur, columns can be disguised as part of the fixtures and often can be used as part of a store's decorative features.

In general, shallow depths (to a point) are better and can accommodate a greater breadth of tenants. For neighborhood and community centers, store depths can range between 40 and 120 feet (12–37 m). A key principle in determining store depths is to rely on the proposed mix of tenants and the store frontage they are likely to require. To accommodate varying depths, building(s) should be designed with offsets at the front and rear to vary the depth. Some tenants will be satisfied with and may even welcome an L-shaped space that wraps around a small, shallow boutique space.

INTERIOR FINISHES. Space leased by a tenant typically contains designated frontage, unfinished party walls separating the space from retail neighbors, an unfinished floor, and exposed joists for roof support. The rear door and utility stubs are generally located in plans for the shell but can be repositioned as part of the lease deal.

Most developers use an allowance for finishing tenant space beyond a designated "shell" delivery condition. In most commodity retail shopping centers, the industry standard delivery condition is referred to as a "vanilla shell." Subject to small variations, a vanilla shell delivery typically includes the following building features:

- building shell complete (with walls taped and spackled, ready for tenant's wall treatment);
- storefront installed;
- rear door installed;
- bathroom(s) installed to code;
- standard two-by-four florescent lighting installed to code;
- utilities delivered to premises;
- floors installed, level and ready for tenant floor treatment;
- base building insulation installed;
- HVAC installed (not distributed); and
- water-tight roof installed.

Note, however, that depending on shopping center type and market conditions, the delivery condition may vary from a raw shell to a turn-key buildout. Additionally, allowances (usually expressed as dollar amounts per square foot) are provided by developers and used by tenants to pay for any upgrades to these delivery standards.

TENANT SIGNAGE. Signs for shopping center tenants are, first and foremost, critical to creating tenant identity and visibility. They are also an important source of a project's image, vitality, and atmosphere and should be an integral part of building design. Options for tenant signage are numerous and include

- specially shaped box signs;
- individual internally illuminated letters with Plexiglas faces;
- open-face letters with exposed neon;
- reverse-channel letters with halo-effect lighting;
- bare neon, with or without special backgrounds;
- individual letters mounted on a common raceway, with or without a "receiver" channel;
- internally illuminated sign bands; and
- graphics screened onto canvas or "Panaflex" awnings.

Tenants almost always pay for and install their own signs. However, shopping center developers should always exercise control over what tenants can display through a declaration of permitted and prohibited signage and should provide specific signage type and quality standards, also known as design guidelines. Developers may wish to be even more specific about details of the signage program and limit some aspects of what is permissible under the sign ordinance, such as temporary signs.

Historically, some developers insisted on uniform scale, size, and placement of retail store signs. This practice, while easier to administer, has been largely discredited because it creates a monotone sign standard that defeats the purpose of maximizing individual tenant recognition. The practice restricts tenant identity and is believed to reduce sales of heavily promoted national tenants which rely on display of their individual "trade dress" to attract customers.

In general, individual tenant signage is governed by each community's sign ordinance. In some communities, a developer may be able to submit a signage program that deviates from the standard and obtain approvals tied specifically to the center for which it is proposed.

Merchandising and Leasing Shopping Centers

The most desirable tenant mix for a proposed shopping center is determined by a variety of factors, including the development concept, the size and type of center, competition in the area, the target market, and trends in consumer preferences. Here again the discussion will concentrate on commodity centers; the degree of complexity and variation in specialty centers requires a detailed discussion, which is beyond the scope of this publication.

A shopping center's composition is ultimately determined by the developer's ability to attract and negotiate acceptable leases with desired prospective tenants. The tenant mix should be based on the market analysis (discussed earlier), but meeting the goals of the initial leasing plan entirely may not be possible; tenants' preferences and varied requirements will inevitably result in ongoing revisions to the original leasing concept.

The tenant mix for any commodity shopping center will depend almost entirely on the type of center under consideration. For most developments, a balanced tenant mix that includes both strong credit-rated national firms and strong local merchants is considered ideal.

In all types of centers, the developer must be flexible in selecting tenants and negotiating leases with them. Interior arrangements and tenant leases will be adjusted numerous times as negotiations proceed. A plan that includes at least two tenant types targeted for each space provides flexibility in leasing.

A critical factor to keep in mind when selecting tenants is that the resulting mix should provide balanced interplay among the stores. The success of a shopping center's tenant mix lies not in including or excluding a specific type of tenant, but in selecting and combining a group of mutually reinforcing tenants that will serve the needs of the particular market.

SHOPPING CENTER LEASING

Leasing a shopping center is more complex and demanding than leasing any other type of development. It involves creating an effective leasing plan, obtaining commitments from anchor tenants early in the process, and then leasing the smaller spaces according to the leasing plan. The leasing plan represents the center's investment potential and is fundamental to the planning process. Every leasing plan should include a space-by-space analysis with alternate proposed tenants and a complete tenant-mix strategy.

Prepared early in the development process, the leasing plan addresses the best tenant mix, the placement of tenants within the center, rent schedules, the pricing of store spaces, and lease specifications. The leasing plan is a living document that should be modified frequently, as the project evolves from concept to completion.

ORGANIZING A LEASING PROGRAM. Most developers choose to employ a third-party brokerage company with extensive contacts and experience to lease their center. Agreements with third-party leasing agents should address such issues as exclusive versus open listings, full commission structure, participation of in-house leasing staff, and leasing incentives. The leasing agent should be on the development team from start to finish and should provide guidance in the subtleties of tenant selection.

The developer must be actively involved in all stages of leasing, especially in the procurement of anchor tenants and in setting the merchandising strategy for the balance of the shopping center. Leasing is much more selective in shopping center projects than in office projects; the objective must not be simply to lease space but to lease the right space to the right tenant and understand how one tenant may affect another. Thus, setting priorities for the leasing staff and maintaining those priorities are imperative.

Generally, development of a small shopping center cannot move forward without commitments from anchor tenants. Thus, marketing to likely anchor tenants must begin very early in the process. Key tenants—such as a supermarket, discount store, or drugstore—should be tied in closely with the development team in planning the project. These tenants will want to influence the developer's decisions on building treatment and architectural style, parking, signage, and landscaping.

In evaluating potential tenants, the developer should consider numerous factors, including

- principal use;
- merchandise sold;
- size and dimensions;
- lease economics;
- lease term and buildout requirements;
- use-clause and exclusive restrictions;
- compatibility with other tenants;
- credit rating and references;
- special lease considerations;
- housekeeping practices; and
- use of hazardous materials.

ANCHOR LEASING. Identification and procurement of anchor tenants is one of the first steps in a leasing program. Developers must consider the pros and cons of the various types of tenants. For example, superstore centers can make the search for local tenants difficult because the wide-ranging services of superstores can eliminate as many as 10 types of tenants. Convenience stores are growing in popularity as anchor tenants in small centers and as attractive volume stores for larger strip centers, but they also may cause problems in leasing to other retailers: convenience stores sell a wide variety of goods and may insist on the exclusive right to sell certain items such as beer, milk, and bread. Other items sold at convenience stores—liquor, fast food, and ice cream, for example—can also cause clashes with other tenants that sell those items. Supermarkets, drugstores, and even gas stations usually do not want to be located in a center with a convenience store.

The expansion plans of anchor-type tenants often serve as the driving force behind center development. For example, larger discount stores such as Target, Walmart, and Kohls are often cited as promoters of the resurgence of strip centers. New food retailers like Aldi and Lidl entering a market are also highly sought after.

LOCATING TENANTS. The placement of tenants within a shopping center is complex and critically important. Tenants may have strong and sometimes apparently arbitrary views about their desired position. A location that is advantageous for one type of business may be entirely wrong for another. Placement also depends on the size and depth of the space the tenant desires. In deciding locations, developers should consider the following points:

- suitability of the tenant for the location, including the tenant's financial resources;
- compatible and complementary relationship with adjoining or nearby stores;
- compatibility of the tenant's merchandising practice with that of adjoining stores;
- parking needs generated by the tenant; and
- customer convenience.

SETTING BASE RENTAL RATES. Rental rates for any given space depend on local market conditions and shopping center costs. Rent schedules should indicate clearly the tenant's classification, square footage allocation, minimum rent, and rate of percentage rent.

PERCENTAGE RENT. Percentage rent is a payment structure by which the tenant pays a percentage of sales in addition to a minimum base. As already noted, shopping centers are a unique subset of commercial real estate, where the inherent value of the real estate is determined by the volume of transactions taking place within the facility. Taking this point one step further, shopping center owners developed this method of tying some portion of rent to sales performance or to specific productivity hurdles. Percentage rents are negotiable on a case-by-case basis for most large tenants and can range from 1 to 3 percent. For smaller in-line stores, percentage rent can vary widely or not be applicable at all.

THE SHOPPING CENTER LEASE

The center's leases function as an important management tool. Besides establishing obligations, responsibilities, and leasehold arrangements, the leases incorporate the means of preserving, over a long period of time, the shopping center's character and appearance as a merchandising complex. In effect, they establish a permanent partnership between the management and the tenants. A developer without significant retail development experience should retain an attorney with experience in retail leases. The novice developer also needs to have a standard lease form to use as a starting point and to make sure that all important lease elements are addressed.

The way a shopping center is leased in large measure determines the center's customer appeal and degree of financial success. In the retail field, the percentage lease has become the most popular rental contract for both tenant and landlord. In its simplest form, it establishes minimum tenant lease payments and provides upside to the landlord for exceptional sales performance. In such leases, the tenant agrees to pay a rent equal to a stipulated percentage of the gross dollar volume of the tenant's sales. In shopping centers, the most common type of percentage lease is one in which the tenant agrees to pay a specified minimum rent plus a percentage of gross sales over a certain amount.

The percentage lease balances tenants' and the landlord's interests. It means, for example, that the landlord can agree to a lower base rent for a tenant that may not be able to pay a higher rent until its sales have grown sufficiently to afford a higher rent. For the tenant, it means that if the landlord benefits from higher sales, then the landlord has an incentive to market the center to help generate those overages and to provide maintenance, management, and security that keep the center fully operating and attractive to customers.

THE LEASE. Whether or not the shopping center lease includes a percentage rent clause, the preferred lease format is triple net: in addition to a base rent (plus overages if included), the tenant pays its prorated share of real estate taxes, insurance, and maintenance. Many variations of lease terms are possible, including stepped base rent, free rent to achieve the desired base rent, lower base rent combined with a higher percentage so that the landlord takes a greater risk but has a greater gain if the tenant succeeds. This arrangement is often used for desirable first-time tenants who provide a needed special character for a center.

EXCLUSIVES. The exclusive rights to sell a particular category of merchandise within a shopping center are routinely given to anchor tenants, particularly in commodity centers.

USE CLAUSES. Retail leases must set out specifically permitted uses within a leased space. A retailer's permitted uses should be limited to those agreed upon when it signed the lease to take space in the shopping center. This clause prevents a tenant from converting its store to another use or adding new merchandise lines that may conflict with those of other tenants. At a bare minimum, a chain store tenant can agree to operate its store as all the other stores in its chain. In supermarkets, for example, such businesses as pharmacies, bakeries, flower shops, coffee shops, branch banks, and laundry/dry cleaning pickup are but a few examples of new features that, if unanticipated, can affect the viability of other tenants. As another example, a restaurant lease should incorporate an attached menu that can be changed from time to time but sets an expected standard for the food style offered.

PASS-THROUGH COSTS. From management's perspective, establishing the sharing of certain costs in the lease is very important. Lease terms must include a provision for the sharing of real estate taxes, insurance, common area maintenance (CAM), and operating expenses. CAM includes the cost of such routine activities as cleaning and maintaining the parking lot and other common areas, snow removal when needed, security, landscaping, lighting, trash removal, and utilities. Operating expenses include the general repair and maintenance of buildings and roofs, seasonal promotional activities, general administrative

and management costs, and the depreciation of machinery and equipment used to maintain the premises and reasonable replacement reserves.

In recent years, the practice of setting "fixed CAM" rates has increased, with lease terms often stipulating fixed or maximum rates of increase. With rising inflation, these practices are receiving increased scrutiny from all parties involved.

Shopping Center Construction

Numerous factors dictate the correct time to begin construction. Most important, the developer should make certain it does not begin prematurely because that would likely lead to problems and higher construction costs. For example, if shell construction begins before anchor tenants are committed and their space requirements known, costly change orders may be necessary. Some communities issue building permits for foundations before approval of complete building plans. Here again, an early can lead to cost increases if final building design approvals are delayed or if approvals result in unanticipated subsurface requirements.

Shopping center construction involves three principal areas of concern: preparation of the site, construction of the building shell, and completion of tenant finishes. The first two—arrangements for the site and shell—do not differ significantly by property type (see the discussion in chapter 2.) The third is particular to retail development and is discussed below.

TENANT FINISHES

Retail tenant finishes present numerous challenges peculiar to retail development. Most important, because this stage occurs after tenant leases are signed, the developer should establish and maintain close communication with every tenant. Successful coordination involves

- a clear understanding of the lease deal and each party's responsibilities;
- agreement on specifications, plans, and procedures;
- ongoing communication so that exigencies are held to a minimum; and
- effective follow-through, enabling both parties to monitor progress.

The responsibilities of each party and the specifications for construction are included in the tenant improvement schedule, usually an exhibit to the tenant's lease.

The construction of tenant finishes usually involves variations on two methods: shell and allowance and build to suit. Each method has its own advantages and disadvantages. The most common approach is shell and allowance, in which the developer constructs the building shell and allows the tenant a specified sum to complete all other permanent improvements to the store (and to contribute its own funds if the budget exceeds the landlord allowance). Tenant allowances vary widely depending on overall lease terms and economics. The amount of the tenant allowance depends on the type and size of the shopping center, the size of the tenant, the importance of the tenant to the merchandising of the shopping center, the tenant's credit worthiness, and other requirements of individual tenants.

In the build-to-suit approach, the developer agrees to complete the tenant finish work and the cost is divided based on the negotiated terms of the deal. This method allows the developer to control the quality and consistency of construction and provides a valuable service for small and less-experienced tenants. It is less likely to be acceptable to an anchor or national chain tenant, which often demands more control over store construction.

A third option is for the developer to simply supply the shell; in that case, the tenant must bear the full cost of buildout beyond that standard. Whatever basis is used, the developer must be sensitive to the tenant's needs if construction is to proceed smoothly. Supplying pertinent information and guidance will help the developer and the tenant coordinate. To that end, the developer should maintain a data book that provides the retailer and the architect/engineer with answers to standard questions. Among other things, the data book should contain

- an index of all the developer's architectural and engineering plans, specifications, and details;
- sections through, and details of, the leased wall construction and any other elements of construction that may affect the tenant's planning;
- definitions of symbols used for walls, partitions, ceilings, doors, various types of electrical outlets and switches, and panel boards; riser diagrams; and door and roof finish schedules;
- definitions of standard mechanical symbols and connections;
- local design factors or criteria available to the tenant's engineer;
- excerpts of unusual building code requirements that will be helpful to the tenant's out-of-town architect/engineer; and
- work rules.

In addition, the developer may provide an outline of the steps and procedures a tenant should follow to have plans and applications approved by government agencies and to file for a certificate of occupancy. The developer also should inform the tenant about any unusual jurisdictional situations and whether union labor is required.

Financing

Shopping center financing differs in many respects from other commercial real estate financing. (See chapter 4 for a complete discussion of the various sources and methods of financing for income property.)

Commodity shopping centers—including neighborhood, grocery, community, and power centers—are generally viewed by lenders as more stable investments than other types of income property. That is because commodity shopping centers tend to be oriented toward the sale of nondurable consumer goods and services, or those items bought regardless of changes in the economy. Supermarkets and drugstores generally can maintain relatively stable sales at all times because they sell products that are needed regularly. In contrast, specialty centers are more subject to fluctuations in the economy and are considered riskier investments. Thus, they are inherently more difficult to finance.

CONVENTIONAL FINANCING

The fundamental rules applicable to shopping center finance have changed frequently over the life of the industry, based on periodic changes in lending practices, economic conditions, and trends within different segments of the shopping center industry. As such, the discussion below is directional only and subject to frequent change.

As a general rule of thumb, to obtain the best financing for a shopping center, the project must be at least 75 to 80 percent pre-leased with long-term creditworthy tenants. Preferred financing terms are available to shopping centers with lease terms of 20 years or more for approximately 50 percent of the space and initial 10- or 15-year leases with creditworthy tenants for the balance of the space.

CONSTRUCTION FINANCING. Construction financing is generally provided by commercial banks during a defined construction period. Lending rates for such financing are generally variable and tied to known indexes, and personal guarantees are almost always required.

PERMANENT FINANCING. Permanent financing is generally provided by institutional lenders and for larger projects in the commercial mortgage–backed securities (CMBS) market. Permanent financing generally is provided on a nonrecourse basis at fixed rates for periods up to 10 years.

PUBLIC FINANCING

In some cases, public financing may be available for all or part of new shopping centers, especially in inner-city areas or in communities actively promoting economic development.

LAND SALES

One means of raising equity financing for shopping center development is to sell parcels to anchor tenants or outparcels to fast-food restaurants, banks, and similar businesses after the center plan has taken shape. The value of these outparcels should increase, often dramatically, as entitlements are finalized for the proposed shopping center, allowing the developer to not only recapture (or offset) equity capital required for the project, but also potentially realize a substantial profit.

Marketing

Most shopping centers benefit from some type of marketing program. Commodity centers should promote key attributes of price and convenience, while the objective of specialty centers should be to promote more broadly the unique environment, retail tenant offerings, and experience associated with the center.

Whether the center is oriented toward commodity retail or specialty retail, the concept of positioning lies at the foundation of a successful marketing plan. Positioning means more than creating a favorable image of a center; it entails a careful analysis of a center's strengths and weaknesses and a close examination of the competition.

The developer should follow these traditional guidelines for setting up a successful promotional program:

- Financial participation in the center's promotional activities should be mandatory for all tenants, and a clause to this effect should be included in the lease.
- The center and its stores should be promoted as a single, cohesive unit. All advertising, including printed materials and radio and television spots, should seek to reinforce this perception.

- The center should be involved in community affairs to build goodwill and increase traffic to the center. For example, the center might financially support major community endeavors or plan and participate in civic events.
- The center's promotional unit and the merchants should always communicate with each other.

For smaller retail shopping centers, with a smaller budget, the marketing program must target a select market and reach it through a precisely targeted approach. An effective marketing plan extends beyond advertising, sales promotion, and special events; it seeks to maximize a center's potential volume through a series of deliberate actions.

Effective marketing should capitalize on the baseline created by anchor promotion and seek to extend the reach and visibility of small tenants as well. Although participation should generally be required as indicated above, national anchor tenants, such as large grocery stores and drugstore chains, often have their own advertising and promotion campaigns and may refuse to participate in center-wide efforts. This is not uncommon and should be evaluated and considered on a case-by-case basis.

PREOPENING MARKETING

New shopping centers need to change consumer patterns to be successful, so creating awareness of the new center well before any grand opening is critical. The following steps can be taken before opening any new shopping center. In the case of large specialty centers, preopening marketing may extend well beyond these entry-level steps:

- At least six months before the center opens (or reopens in the case of renovation or expansion), an aggressive publicity program should be instituted.
- At least three to six months before opening, a merchant's association or a steering committee of merchants should be convened, and a marketing fund should begin operating (subject, of course, to successful pre-leasing).
- When an anchor tenant is in place, joint promotion with the owner and other merchants should begin; this joint effort can stimulate substantial interest in the center.

ONGOING MARKETING

The type and size of the center determines the extent to which ongoing marketing activities should be pursued; once established, small commodity centers may find little need for ongoing marketing. At the opposite extreme, specialty centers should consider multichannel marketing programs to reach a wide variety of potential customers and to establish and reinforce the unique environment offered at the center.

When a merchant's association is used in promotion, it acts as a clearinghouse for suggestions and ideas and is responsible for the programming of promotional events. Lease agreements should stipulate that an association will be formed, that the tenants will pay a specified rate per square foot to the association, and that the developer will pay a certain percentage of the annual costs. The developer/owner must organize and participate in the association and will also often be its guide and catalyst.

If a marketing fund, a technique begun in the 1970s and now widely used, will be created, tenants are still required to provide funds to promote the center, but the fund is totally controlled and administered by the developer/owner. The key advantage of using a marketing fund is that it allows the marketing director to concentrate on marketing and promotion rather than on details of the association.

Property Management and Operation

Changes in consumer preferences, improvements in retail distribution technology and formats, and changes in the very products we buy occur more and more rapidly today, and retailers perpetually evolve to stay fresh, relevant, and competitive. As a result, careful ongoing management, merchandising, and promotion of shopping centers, especially specialty shopping centers, is essential to maintain and maximize long-term value. Unlike most other types of real estate, where change is far less frequent, it is unusual to find shopping centers of any size or type that remain unchanged over even short periods of time. Shopping centers that are not actively managed and merchandised risk being rendered functionally obsolete by failures in these key disciplines.

Shopping center owners provide shopping center maintenance and management in one of three ways: supervising directly, employing a manager to supervise the process, or engaging a third-party management firm. Property management fees typically run from two to five percent of annual center rental income, with three percent representing the industry norm. Fee variation typically relates to the complexity and needs of the particular center, with large specialty centers generally having greater day-to-day needs.

By acting directly as manager, the developer/owner maintains close control of the property and can influence more immediately the quality of the operation. By using an outside management firm, however, the developer may derive certain economies of scale and depth of expertise. Managers who work for a fee generally get a percentage of rental income, usually 2 to 6 percent, depending on the size of the center and the scope of responsibility.

Effective management of shopping centers requires establishing a management approach and plan, executing day-to-day shopping center management duties, and maintaining accurate financial records. The objective is to provide day-to-day operational support for the shopping center, while minimizing operating costs as a percentage of revenue, both with an eye toward the property's long-term value. Perhaps the most important responsibility of the shopping center's management is to stimulate merchants to operate their stores at the highest level of professionalism. This objective can be best achieved by maintaining regular and clear communication with tenants.

Property managers should be highly visible and should conduct at least a weekly review of each store in the shopping center. Senior management should check stores during periodic site visits with each tenant, and when problems arise, management should address the issues openly and directly with the respective tenant(s). In those cases where lease terms have been violated, management should initiate principal-to-principal contact; and in those cases of uncured lease defaults, management should engage counsel to enforce the terms of the lease.

FINANCIAL RECORDS AND CONTROL

Shopping center owners must establish acceptable financial accounting and reporting procedures to collect rents, account for revenues and expenses, conduct annual audits, adjust expenses and percentage rent escrows, and evaluate performance.

Unlike other commercial real estate projects (where tenants pay rent monthly and perhaps contribute toward expenses), rental calculations for a shopping center are more complicated; tenants must furnish sales records and financial reports. Data produced in record keeping—such as monthly information on sales figures, category performance, and productivity per square foot—are critical in determining percentage rents.

General practice calls for payment of the percentage overage annually in accordance with a sales report certified by an outside auditor or a responsible officer of the tenant company. Recently, leases typically provide for *un*certified overage payments on a quarterly, sometimes monthly, basis with an annual reconciliation based on an audited statement provided by the tenant. Such an arrangement levels the flow of income while keeping a tight rein on less financially responsible tenants.

Conclusion

As this book goes to press in 2022, the retail and shopping center industries find themselves at the threshold of what may turn out to be the most consequential period of change in the history of the industry. Unlike in prior generations, when fundamental changes to brick-and-mortar delivery systems shaped change, this time around, changes will most likely center around four primary themes:

- accelerating commodity retail bifurcation between retail concepts serving affluent and less affluent portions of the population;
- increasing market penetration of e-commerce, particularly in affluent and urban population centers;
- dramatic advances in technology used in retail, including advanced geofencing, powerful fifth-generation cellular transmission, extensive use of sophisticated data mining techniques, targeted service and selection algorithms, and decision-influencing artificial intelligence; and
- increased retail and shopping center ownership concentration as the industries continue to mature and consolidate.

In the 10 years between now and publication of the next edition of this book, the power of the smartphone/super computer in the consumer's pocket will increase exponentially. Like Amazon, some retailers will make more profit from mining consumer data than actually selling goods and services. Others will embed themselves into every move their captive consumers make. Still others will distinguish themselves by offering the exact opposite for consumers overwhelmed by the new paradigms or simply wanting a break from the power and influence of information and automation. Regardless, consumers will interact less frequently with other human beings in completing retail transactions and in some cases will not interact with others at all. Already today, companies like McDonalds have invested billions into automated app-based ordering systems that all but eliminate human contact.

Will the increased power and influence of giant retail "information companies" spark more loyalty to trusted brands or will it spark a revolt by consumers? Retail companies are making enormous bets in both directions and consumers will decide.

Beyond retail itself, technology, energy availability, and environmental concerns will inevitably bring about massive changes in how we move about and interact with the physical world. Today's brick-and-mortar retail facilities are geared to mobile consumers driving individual automobiles, but there is no guarantee this paradigm will continue uninterrupted. Changes in individual mobility will undoubtedly influence our interaction with the stores we frequent daily, weekly, and periodically. A single change from individually owned self-driven automobiles to fleets of autonomously directed vehicles, even if initially implemented in only a small part of the transportation grid, will bring profound changes to the consumer's world. That change alone could eliminate the need for a wide array of retailers and perhaps eliminate the need for everything from drivers' licenses to the costly reality of moving violations and parking tickets.

Decisions being made by both businesses and local, state, and national governments will define the next generation of personal mobility—and with it the very underpinning of the brick-and-mortar shopping center industry. Developers of tomorrow will not only be making bets on the strength and viability of retailers; they will be placing huge bets on the very way consumers will interact with the physical world around them, including how they obtain the goods and services they consume. Owners and developers of facilities of all types that provide these goods and services will have to be smarter and more attuned to the world around them than ever before in the generation of brick-and-mortar retail headed our way.

NOTES

1. This information is derived from U.S. Census Bureau reports (which measure and report U.S. retail sales by category on a monthly, annual, and long-term basis) as well as from Amazon earnings reports. See, e.g., U.S. Census Bureau, "Quarterly Retail E-Commerce Sales, 4th Quarter 2019," U.S. Census Bureau News, February 19, 2020, https://www2.census.gov/retail/releases/historical/ecomm/19q4.pdf; and Amazon, Investor Relations: Quarterly Results, https://ir.aboutamazon.com/quarterly-results/default.aspx.
2. 362 U.S. 29 (1960).
3. See Daniela Coppola, "Amazon's Shipping Costs from 2011 to 2021," Statista, February 14, 2022; and Felix Richter, "Amazon's Escalating Logistics Costs," Statista, July 26, 2022.
4. Connie Robbins Gentry, "Economy and Ecology Merge," *Chain Store Age*, January 2001, p. 158.

Easton Town Center is an integrated mixed-use environment that includes retail, open space, art installations, boutiques, and office and residential offerings. Located in Columbus, Ohio, the initial plan for the Easton Town Center expansion was to create a cohesive experience, aligned with the existing center's uses.

Designed to complement the award-wining and established earlier phases of Easton Town Center, the expansion leveraged a creative merchandising approach, along with activated open spaces and engaging art installations to enhance visitor engagement and, ultimately, extend the length of stay for each visit. The expansion has a distinct center—the Yard—anchored by a large media screen, performance stage, and canopy structure (positioned on a rail system so the lawn can be transformed for a variety of events); public swings further reinforce interactive engagement with visitors and animate the community space.

The developer, Steiner + Associates, is based in Columbus and has been building new phases of Easton Town Center for more than 21 years.

PROJECT HISTORY AND MARKET CONTEXT

The first phase of Easton Town Center was completed in June 1999. It was envisioned and developed by a first-of-its-kind partnership between L Brands (formerly Limited Brands), the Georgetown Company, and Steiner + Associates. The partnership set out to create an innovative retail development, dramatically different from the typical enclosed mall.

The partners hoped to build the most upscale, aspirational shopping destination in Columbus, with a diverse mix of best-in-class retailers in an open-air, pedestrian-friendly setting. The initial concept was an urban environment that combined nostalgic charm with a strong "sense of place." The ultimate goal was to create an integrated, mixed-use destination unlike the region had seen before.

With over 1.7 million square feet (6 ha) of mixed-use space (99 percent leased), Easton Town Center has become one of the country's leading urban retail centers. It draws more than 20 million visitors annually and hosts four hotels, with a combined 727 rooms. The project has attracted nearly 200 retailers to central Ohio, including Nordstrom, Macy's, Coach, Apple, Crate & Barrel, Barnes & Noble, Tiffany & Co., Louis Vuitton, and Victoria's Secret. In addition, it offers multiple dining options, including True Food Kitchen, The Cheesecake Factory, RH Rooftop Restaurant, and Smith & Wollensky. A mix of indoor and outdoor activities are available year-round, including free concerts, an outdoor movie series, free fitness classes during the summer, and kids events.

The primary trade area extends more than 50 miles (80 km) and comprises approximately 1.3 million people; a secondary trade area exceeds 5 million people and extends well beyond the state of Ohio. It consistently attracts annual visitors from every

STEINER + ASSOCIATES

The Yard, in the center of the expansion, includes public swings, reinforcing interactive engagement with visitors and animating the community space.

major city in the United States. Easton Town Center is consistently ranked in the Top 10 Busiest Malls (Placer.AI), along with Rockefeller Plaza (New York City), Mall of America (Bloomington, Minnesota), and the Grand Canal Shops (Las Vegas, Nevada).

DESIGN, ACTIVATION, AND DEVELOPMENT

The Easton Town Center expansion, consisting of approximately 140,000 square feet (1.3 ha), was designed and positioned on undeveloped parcels between the Easton's Fashion District (Phase 2, circa 2001) and Easton Gateway (2015). The comprehensive master plan anticipated the phased development, allowing earlier phases to remain open and unimpaired by new construction. For example, parking for the expansion consists of a vertical addition to an existing adjacent parking garage. The additional floors were added in phases, which allowed the garage to remain at least 50 percent open throughout construction.

The expansion was designed so that on either side of the retail and restaurants, the pedestrian spaces transition into a sequence of smaller courtyards that offer multiple opportunities for customers to explore. Instead of channeling customers along storefronts in the expected linear fashion, the expansion offers a flexible, complex series of immersive experiences influenced by the Xintiandi area in Shanghai and the old streets of Europe. This strategy continues with the architectural language of a postindustrial development adopting former utilitarian structures to new uses; it layers traditional and contemporary forms and materials to create the perception of urban renewal and revitalization.

The most urgent question facing any commercial development today is how to compete with the online world. The expansion focuses on activating public space, since experiences are the most decisive advantage the physical environment may claim in its competition with the online world. Thus, an already successful mixed-use center has been able to expand in a complementary manner while efficiently utilizing minimal amounts of additional land.

STEINER + ASSOCIATES

Steiner created a Community Art program involving local artists to foster a connection with the community. Easton's "Art Evolution" showcases the work of Columbus's diverse talents through murals, architectural installations, open spaces, and digital elements. The art installations, which are located throughout the urban district, were all created by local artists. They continue to play a critical role in the evolution of Easton's public spaces and reinforce its strong relationship with the community.

Easton Town Center was designed to appear as if it had evolved naturally over time, and now, 21 years after its inception, it has done so. The expansion reinforces proven concepts but also applies lessons learned from previous phases. Most important is the connection with the customer, both visually and functionally, through a vibrant mix of art and architecture, united by public plazas, animated sidewalks with intimate patios, creative programming, community events, and the encouragement of pedestrian and cyclist traffic.

To promote a pedestrian-friendly environment, the expansion has a total of 1,937 parking spaces, including on-street, surface, and integrated structured parking options in two parking decks. The parking decks are connected via stairs, bridges, and elevators to the retail, office, and hotel properties. Each deck is also equipped with electric vehicle charging stations and restrooms.

MERCHANDISING, MARKETING, AND MANAGEMENT

One challenge in planning the expansion was to create a merchandising plan/approach that complemented rather than competed with the existing tenants established in earlier phases. To achieve this objective, the leasing team emphasized integration of larger-format home furnishing tenants, including RH Columbus (Restoration Hardware) and Arhaus. These retailers offer a gallery-like experience and extended shopping-visit durations, a key indicator of cross-shopping potential, particularly for specialty and discretionary shopping purchases.

The flagship Restoration Hardware store anchors the expansion phase of Easton Town Center. It includes landscaped decks and a rooftop restaurant.

With a well-defined and differentiated merchandising plan, the leasing team successfully integrated 14 retailers and restaurants, including Beeline, Crimson, True Food Kitchen, Forbidden Root Brewery, LemonShark Poké and Makai Grill, Slurping Turtle Ramen, and Ivan Kane's Forty Deuce Night Club & Café. Incorporating these smaller, more unique uses created interest, giving customers a sense of exploration in the alleys connecting the various blocks within the expansion. Steiner's ultimate strategy was to prioritize long-term flexibility, diversification, and densification of uses; the arrangement of the new uses around larger and more plentiful public space of various scales creates the engaging sense of place they were looking for.

STEINER + ASSOCIATES

The urban district of the expansion attracted many small, unique tenants that were exclusive to the center or new to Ohio, including Beeline Bar.

The success of the expansion, despite the COVID-19 pandemic, has been demonstrated by the quick lease-up (99 percent leased as of this writing), strong tenant sales, and continual demand from local and national tenants seeking a location at Easton Town Center.

ACTIVATION AND NONTRADITIONAL AMENITIES

In addition to the targeted merchandising mix and unique design elements, the expansion offers a number of nontraditional amenities. These include same-day delivery and curbside pickup options, reserved VIP parking, and a real-time parking availability map; new LED screens that promote all the center's tenants by tapping into their Instagram feeds, which customers can view from the Yard; benches, public seating, fire pits, and an abundance of natural gathering places; and the award-winning "MyEaston" app (a mobile concierge system).

SUSTAINABILITY AND ENVIRONMENTALLY FRIENDLY EFFORTS

With its emphasis on sustainability and environmentally friendly development strategies, the Steiner team incorporated several concepts into the expansion:

- Electric-car charging stations are located in the new parking deck and throughout the expansion.
- All potted plants are pollinator-friendly.
- The landscape design makes use of drought-tolerant/native plant material.
- Smart irrigation controllers improve water use efficiencies in the landscape.
- The base of the "urban chimney" in the Beer Garden was built using reclaimed antique brick.
- The art and sculpture throughout the expansion are the work of local artists and fabricators.
- The project prioritized the use of locally sourced materials to reduce the carbon footprint.

SUMMARY

The expansion unites community space, public art, and visitor experiences with a curated collection of restaurant and retail offerings and boutique hospitality, along with integrated office and residential buildings. It further establishes Easton Town Center as a true mixed-use community, while continuing to innovate and develop cutting-edge solutions that will help transform the retail industry. One way to measure success is by examining visitation. Shopping centers generally show a large disparity between midday and evening traffic. However, Easton Town Center, while still seeing a peak in the evening, experiences a much more consistent pattern of visitation throughout the day. The difference is largely due to the center's focus on architectural detail, a dynamic merchandising mix, activated public spaces, and engaging art installations.

Easton Town Center has become one of the industry's standards as a retail and entertainment destination. The expansion further reinforces the Easton Town Center brand and has influenced the construction of dozens of secondary developments in the immediate area, while also significantly increasing adjacent land values.

Easton Town Center's layout has constantly evolved, with new elements added to ensure the center's continued appeal. Each new phase remains connected by the conceptual thread that has made Easton a regional destination. The expansion is a genuine extension of Easton Town Center and, ultimately, the new hub of the surrounding community it serves.

Project Data

Type of project	Super-regional center, fashion/specialty center, lifestyle center, mixed use
Number of levels	5
Project's trade area	Suburban
Population of primary trade area	1.3 million
Population of secondary trade area	5 million
Annualized percentage of shoppers from outside of trade area (e.g., tourists, conventioneers)	30
Total retail space	1,553,818 square feet (144,354 sq m)
Number of retail stores (excluding anchors)	14
Major tenants	RH Columbus The Gallery at Easton (Restoration Hardware), Arhaus Furniture, True Food Kitchen, Forbidden Root Brewery, LemonShark Poké and Makai Grill, Slurping Turtle Ramen, and Ivan Kane's Forty Deuce Night Club & Café. (Many of the expansion's retail brands are exclusive and new to Ohio and/or central Ohio, including the Urban District's newest additions listed here.)
Original project opening date	June 1, 1999
Current renovation/ expansion opening date	June 1, 2020
Development company	Steiner + Associates
Owner	Steiner + Associates, The Georgetown Company, L Brands
Design	Architect Design 3 International
Production or executive architect	M + A Architects
Landscape architect	MKSK

Cambridge Marketplace is a 20,000-square-foot (1,860 sq m), Target-anchored project located in Cambridge, Minnesota, a northern suburb of Minneapolis/St. Paul. This project illustrates how creative owners/developers can leverage the established traffic patterns of existing big-box retailers to add gross leasable area (GLA)—typically small shops (also known as a shadow center)— thereby increasing operating income and overall project value.

DEVELOPMENT BACKGROUND

The Target in Cambridge, Minnesota, is one of the dominant anchor store destinations in the region. As the community grew, Cub Foods, Aldi, Fleet Farm (formerly Mills Fleet Farm), and Kohl's opened stores adjacent to this Target location. In addition, a Walmart Supercenter and Menard's Home Improvement opened stores across the street on Highway 95, further establishing this location as a retail hub within the trade area.

Given this established retail node, a national retain chain asked a local developer, Timber Development Corporation (TDC) to identify a site in Cambridge. Upon review of the market, TDC found a 2.5-acre (1 ha) site adjacent to Target as well as a vacant pad site in front of Target, which represented an excellent shadow center development opportunity.

PREDEVELOPMENT APPROVALS, FINANCING, LEASING, AND CONSTRUCTION

Given this two-parcel condition, the project would comprise two separate single-story retail buildings. The first building (14,000 square feet or 1,300 sq m) would be physically attached to the existing Target; the second building (6,400 square feet or 595 sq m) would be situated on the pad site, which offered great visibility from Highway 95. Both would house multiple small shops.

Upon reviewing all relevant entitlement and related documentation, TDC discovered that the Target reciprocal easement agreement (REA) not only allowed development of additional retail space, as proposed; it also allowed easement rights to access the Target stormwater management pond, permitted cross traffic within the Target parking lot, and shared the use of curb cuts granted to Target. In addition, the existing parking lot and site lighting, developed by Target, were sufficient to support the additional development. All told, TDC would save a substantial amount of money on grading, site utilities, and installation of the parking lot and site lighting.

LAND PURCHASE AGREEMENT

After multiple discussions, a comprehensive document review, and a personal visit with the property owner, a land purchase agreement was executed, providing TDC a 120-day period to perform its due diligence on the property. The due diligence included a survey, title report, Phase 1 environmental report, soil samples, utilities study, grading design of the property, review of the existing storm-

DOUG BERKU

The formal merchandising plan leveraged the existing Target to attract complementary junior anchors, Maurice's and Famous Footwear. They in turn attracted smaller tenants that wished to be in adjacent locations. Because these tenants shared the same type of shoppers, the arrangement created a cross-shopping pattern.

water management design, review of the existing Department of Transportation report, parking lot inspection, site lighting inspection, review of the Target REA agreement, the city's zoning letter, letters from all utility companies, and the development agreement between the city and TDC. Following the 120-day period, TDC posted a land deposit, security deposit, and downpayment, which was applicable to the purchase price. In addition, the development team devised a site plan that laid out both parcels with an optimal design for ease of leasing. The civil engineer presented all plans to the community, and TDC formally hired an architect and general contractor who had experience in retail development.

CONSTRUCTION LOAN AND PERMANENT FINANCING

Parallel to the design and municipal review process, TDC created a pro forma and tightened its budget as the predevelopment phase matured and true numbers were submitted to the contractors, architect, and engineers. TDC also approached a local bank to obtain a construction loan, utilizing an income-based approach for financing. Due to significant predevelopment tenant interest, this approach resulted in a favorable cap rate relative to the anticipated net operating income (NOI). When construction was completed and the project had stabilized (fully leased), TDC obtained a takeout loan to pay off the construction loan and place more favorable, long-term financing rates on the property.

LEASING AND TENANT MIX

TDC handles all its leasing in-house and implemented an aggressive leasing program. The first step was to devise a formal merchandising plan (tenant mix) based on having the established Target location as an anchor, the needs and demographics of the community, and the customers the junior anchors would potentially attract. The merchandising plan placed Maurice's, a women's clothing store, in close proximity to Target and located Famous Footwear adjacent to Maurice's. This early momentum established the leasing theme, and Sally Beauty Supply, Totally Tan, and Fantastic Sam's Hair expressed interest in being immediately adjacent to these specific junior boxes—they share the same type of shoppers, and the arrangement created a cross-shopping pattern. Interest in the out-pad building was also significant and now consists of Kay Jewelers (which wanted an end-cap with high visibility), a nail salon, Jimmy John's, Cricket Wireless, and a T-Shirt Lab store. TDC delivered a design that includes full plate glass storefronts, a flat sign band that provides retailers optimal exposure, and small shop spaces designed with the dimensions (depth and width) the desired retailers were seeking.

EXPERIENCE GAINED

Based on the partners' understanding of the Cambridge, Minnesota, retail trade area, the limited supply of adequate retail space, and the expressed retail demand, TDC identified and developed a shadow retail center immediately adjacent to, and in front of, an established Target anchor store. This example highlights how develops/owners can create value-add opportunities when they embrace an outside-the-box approach.

In completing this shadow center, TDC learned the following lessons:

- Remember that the numbers are very tight on small shopping center developments. It is important to watch your land and building costs, as these will be the biggest variables that will make or break your budget on the development.
- Be sure to review all relevant documentation and verify whether a favorable easement is in place. You will save money on your utilities, stormwater management pond, and Department of Transportation costs if the existing anchor tenant owns the excess property and an easement is in place and paid for by the anchor.
- Design your small shops with a clean sign band and full plate glass storefronts. Control your signage to maintain uniformity.
- Always review the REA; it will describe use restrictions and architectural guidelines on the property.
- Use a local bank for both the construction loan and the permanent loan. Local banks are easier to work with and save you money on closing costs.
- Although an existing big-box anchor can help solidify your leasing, understand that on a small development, if you have three vacancies, your return will be very tight. Work hard to be 100 percent leased.

Pro Forma

Tenant	Size	Rate	Rent	CAM
INCOME ANALYSIS				
Maurice's	5,000	$13.50	$67,500.00	$20,750.00
Famous Footwear	5,000	$14.00	$70,000.00	$20,000.04
Sally Beauty	1,600	$13.00	$20,800.00	$6,664.00
Vacant	1,600	$13.00	$20,800.00	$6,640.00
Vacant	1,200	$15.00	$18,000.00	$4,980.00
Subtotal	14,400	$13.69	$197,100.00	$59,034.04
Outparcel				
Kay Jewelers	1,750	$24.00	$42,000.00	$7,262.50
Verizon	1,400	$18.00	$25,200.00	$5,810.00
Real Estate Office	850	$14.00	$11,900.00	$3,527.50
Vacant	1,400	$16.00	$22,400.00	$5,810.00
Nail Salon	1,600	$14.00	$22,400.00	$6,640.00
Subtotal	7,000	$17.70	$123,900.00	$29,050.00
Total Income	**21,400**	**$15.49**	**$321,000.00**	**$88,084.04**
	Percent	Sq Ft		
Less: Shop Vacancy	5%	1,070	$16,575	
EFFECTIVE GROSS INCOME			**$392,509**	
Expenses				
Management Fee	4%		$12,198	
Reserves	$0.10		$2,140	
CAM Tax and Ins Exp	$3.50		$74,900	
Total Expenses			**$89,238**	
NET OPERATING INCOME			**$303,271**	

Note: All tenants except Maurice's have a lease wherein they reimburse the landlord for a pro rata management fee and 15% administration fee. Common area maintenance (CAM), taxes, and insurance collections for those tenants will exceed cost, providing additional income to the landlord.

8 Trends and Issues

RICHARD B. PEISER AND DAVID HAMILTON

Effective real estate professionals are responsive to change. Changes in markets, consumer preferences, and supply chains can happen quickly, as they did during the COVID-19 pandemic, but the development process is typically slow. Developers, planners, and investors, therefore, are always building for a world that may be different when their product arrives. They must look forward, and wherever possible they must maintain flexibility.

This chapter begins by reviewing long-term structural changes in the field and highlighting the market conditions and the types of opportunities and pitfalls beginning developers may encounter during their careers. A variety of industry leaders and innovators then offer their advice on key trends and development issues that they are currently grappling with, or that they anticipate will be important over the next decade. The consensus view of contributors includes the following key themes:

- The adoption of environmental, social, and governance (ESG) goals, as a way of evaluating investment in addition to economic targets, is accelerating.
- A related movement is demanding a voice for more stakeholders, and more diverse teams, in community decision-making and in development firms.
- The application of technology through every step of development, from envisioning through sales and operations, is broadening, and can accelerate the adoption of other trends.
- Patterns of work, shopping, and dwelling are changing unusually quickly along with demographic and technological trends, and this rapid change is affecting multiple property types.
- Affordability, inclusion, and social justice are increasingly seen as issues that should be addressed by development, land use regulation, and finance.

- Even for smaller developers, the "typical" project is becoming more complicated. Multiuse projects on infill and redevelopment sites are increasingly the best opportunities.

Historical Cycles

For many developers, weathering their first recession is a formative experience. Along with incentives, land use regulations, and demographic change, the repetitive but seldom predictable cycle of expansion and recession is the most important determinant of how and when to invest. Each downturn imparts new lessons to those who survive it. As Don Killoren of Celebration Associates puts it, "Each time seems to be just different enough."[1]

Hedging the double-digit inflation of the late 1970s and early 1980s made real estate a preferred investment, relative to stocks or bonds. This increased investor demand for the tax advantages of real property, and development outpaced absorption. Savings and loan associations (S&Ls) overinvested in real estate often to accommodate investment flows

The Helios Education Campus in Phoenix, Arizona, is a build-to-suit contemporary revision of the garden office for a nonprofit organization and its partners. Environmentally and economically sustainable, it incorporates building materials and systems, such as chilled-beam ceiling cooling and in-floor warming systems, plus natural stone and exterior materials that do not require finishes to limit maintenance needs.

seeking high yields rather than to satisfy market demand. The subsequent crash of the late 1980s and early 1990s catalyzed dramatic structural changes in the real estate industry, some of which are still reverberating today.

INDUSTRY RESTRUCTURING IN THE 1990s

The early 1990s crash and recovery led to several fundamental changes in the development industry. Real estate finance followed commercial banking into a thorough restructuring, with more multiproduct financial service providers offering an increasingly homogeneous and national menu of services. Investment-grade real estate became an asset class comparable to tradeable securities, attracting new types of investors who demanded more institutional organizations. At the same time, financial innovation greatly increased the amount of capital flowing to real estate, through new types of debt instruments collateralized by real estate assets and traded on secondary markets. Foreshadowing future crises, some critics pointed out that a downside to this new liquidity—increased distance between asset management and secondary investors—would obscure the relationship of capital to projects.

CHANGE DURING AND AFTER THE GREAT RECESSION OF 2008

The international financial crisis that followed the bursting of the early 2000s housing bubble took many observers by surprise. As the crisis spread beyond subprime mortgages to impair global debt markets, major lenders, investment banks, and government-sponsored entities (GSEs), unprecedented actions were taken to mitigate systemic risks. Looking back on this episode, the relative importance of causes is still debated, but the key sequence of events is clear. Financial innovation, applied to increasing flows of international capital, increased the volume and complexity of investment in real estate. This liquidity flowed through systems to substantially increase credit availability for buyers and boosted demand across most sectors of real estate. For-sale housing and commercial space were the primary beneficiaries of these liquidity-driven value gains. Investors, and the bankers and analysts who serve them, underestimated the risks of this rapid sectoral inflation. The subsequent crash led to many changes that helped to drive the sustained improvement in the real estate market from 2010 to 2020.

Owen Thomas, chief executive officer of Boston Properties in New York City, observes that the world is less leveraged today. "Even highly leveraged guys are at 70 percent versus 90 percent before. Banks are more disciplined. Real estate used to be [a] dirty word. The Great Financial Crisis was a crazy case because leverage fueled all that growth."[2] He says that during the COVID-19 pandemic, leverage was not really tested because so much money was injected into the system.

Jeff Hines says they were trying to raise money for emerging markets (China, Brazil, Russia, and India), but the price tag was too high.[3] No one investor wanted that much concentration of risk in emerging markets. Hines notes, "By necessity, we had to create a fund with multiple investors, which in the end was very successful. We learned the real benefit of having discretionary capital available at a moment's notice."

Benjamin Cha, chief executive officer Asia Pacific at Grosvenor, believes that while the past 20 years saw the world becoming more and more global, it is now going the other way—there is a decoupling of capital between China and the West.[4] He does not foresee the same freedom of capital flows. He believes there will be more separation of supply chains. However, Cha does not believe the pendulum will swing all the way to the other side—50 years of globalization will not turn back. Instead, a new equilibrium will be reached. Cha notes that Grosvenor is very global; the company is looking at hedging risk in China, Japan, and the United States. He asks, "How do we do business in China? Accusations are very serious about [the] bad behavior of government—labor practices, job sites, construction sites. A generation ago corruption was a huge worry. While the government has been on an anticorruption campaign for a decade, outside investors as well as Chinese developers have to be very careful." Cha adds that a generation ago, demand was insatiable. "China is a more level playing field today—not just colonels going into development 25 years ago, when things were very opaque. Today it is more transparent, but a lot more competitive."

Changing Market Conditions

Few industries have as broad an impact or draw on as many disciplines as real estate. Every quarter brings changing market conditions, but the changes that have occurred since the previous edition of this book in 2012 have been dramatic. This section highlights some of the most significant changes—in particular, the impacts of COVID-19, new technology, and public engagement—as they affect the market and the development industry.

THE COVID-19 PANDEMIC

The global spread of a novel virus is not on most developers' due diligence checklist, but the COVID-19 pandemic, and governments' responses to it, have revealed new issues for owners and developers. At the onset of the pandemic, patterns of work and living were disrupted almost immediately across many markets simultaneously because of an unanticipated risk. Retail and restaurant operations in most cities ceased, and they remained impaired for more than a year, first by public health rules and then perhaps more enduringly by individuals' changing perceptions of risk. Retail center owner Christopher Kurz says he was "struck by what didn't change. Local merchants pivoted quickly to new business models," such as takeout dining.[5] "National chains with more fixed business plans demanded concessions, and local restaurants shifted to percentage rent, but the spectrum of what can be in a shopping center broadened, as it does in every downturn. We see public tenants like courthouses, health, and wellness businesses, and quickly we got back to basic criteria for evaluating tenant quality."

The long-term impact of pandemic changes on work and commuting patterns is still unclear. For two decades before the pandemic, the atomizing effect of telepresence was predicted and consistently failed to materialize. Highly productive firms rediscovered the value of locating in dense regions of highly qualified workers, interacting in environments of synergy and innovation. That increasing concentration of talent has been—for at least a moment—rolled back, as technology made it possible, and public health made it necessary, at least for many white-collar workers, to work from home (WFH). In 2020, the temporary impairment of the cultural, dining, and economic benefits of city living, and the need for more domestic space, spurred over one-quarter of a million New Yorkers to leave the city. While there was less of an impact on Austin, Raleigh, and Nashville, older gateway markets were severely affected. How many of those who left will be lured back remains to be seen, but the flight to lower-density areas has already spurred an affordability crisis in many exurban areas of metropolitan statistical areas (MSAs). This trend coincides with the preferences of millennial suburbanites, who Charles Adams calls "surban."[6] According to Adams, these recent arrivals "want more space, they want a school district, but they want to bring some experiences of the city out with them. Coffee, dining, and culture need to become part of these places to succeed." Of

EV635 in Mexico City, a building offering diverse commercial spaces, incorporates windows that open along its four sides, allowing access to natural light as well as providing ventilation to all areas of the building. The capture of rainwater and its reuse throughout the building creates a sustainable alternative that is both cost-efficient and ecologically favorable.

course, residents of urban and rural areas also want goods, and the incredible growth of online shopping and fulfillment has placed increased pressure on data and distribution centers, particularly "last mile" and urban facilities.

The immediate effects of the COVID-19 pandemic were dire for both office and residential markets. Tim Rowe of Cambridge Innovation Center observes that "our priority of making the office a productive and innovative place, we realized, had very suddenly become second to just making people confident it was safe to go to work."[7] Rowe's team pivoted to address testing and other public health priorities, eventually becoming a standalone company. For apartments, the early pandemic was a massive stress test as tenants' incomes were interrupted, and a flurry of federal programs attempted to support unemployed workers and simultaneously subsidize rental assistance to landlords. "It was like a hurricane disaster response, but in all of our markets at once," noted one apartment manager. Many local jurisdictions passed temporary moratoria on eviction, while a federal effort to do so nationally was discontinued by courts. However, apartment owners abruptly became aware that their assets could be thought of, in an emergency, as essential public health infrastructure. However, Daryl Carter, chairman and chief executive officer of Avanath Capital Management in Irvine, California, says not being able to evict bad tenants (such as drug dealers) during the COVID-19 pandemic made many communities less safe.[8] According to Carter, when Avanath Capital Management renovates buildings, it tries to keep tenants in place and to raise rents only 2 to 3 percent after the renovation. He notes that keeping a tenant equates to a 10 to 11 percent premium if Avanath must get a new tenant.

The shape of postpandemic life is still far from clear, but most contributors agree that the experience has encouraged several trends that seem likely to persist:

- demand for integrated home workspaces and infrastructures because WFH will persist for many people;
- an emphasis on access to outdoor spaces, public or private, from apartment balconies to porches; and
- a general theme of health and wellness, in office as well as residential development.

EFFECT OF COVID-19 ON APPROACHES TO DEVELOPMENT

A survey of development professionals conducted in 2020 and 2021 reveals a variety of opinions and perspectives as to how the pandemic has changed their approach to development in the short, intermediate, and long term.[9]

In the short term, respondents note that they have considered or implemented some or all of the following in their projects:

- HVAC alterations to enhance air circulation and filtration;
- more home offices in unit floorplans;
- more parking for more residents staying at and working from home;
- more public indoor and outdoor space;
- safe on-site construction protocols for laborers;
- use of local supply chains;
- touchless restrooms and keypads for tenants;
- clean environments and increased property maintenance; and
- increased building safety and disinfection.

Several responses reflect a middle-term approach in considering COVID-19's effect on development. Tyler Higgins, managing partner at Orchard Partners, advises, "Make sure that 'pandemic' is part of force majeure definition." Scott E. Shapiro, managing director of Eagle Rock Ventures LLC, recommends that developers "stay disciplined and prepare for the long term." In considering underwriting and financials, John Oharenko of Real Estate Capital Investors says, "Expect more occupancy and income collections variability. Be patient and work with tenants [to insure] long-term viability [as opposed to] short-term profitability." In

that same vein, Kacey Cordes, vice president at U.S. Bancorp Community Development Corporation, states, "We have adjusted our underwriting to account for the ongoing economic recession/depression and its impacts on rental revenue and overall rent/expense growth projections. We know that there has never been more of an urgent need for housing, so the demand is unquestionable. We are concerned about potential project shortfalls on existing deals and how that will impact developers' liquidity."

Others are taking a longer-term view, believing that the changes will be less significant over time.

David Farmer of Keystone Development Advisors states, "Things will be different but not as different as some are predicting." "I am not sure there are any real long-term changes," says James D. Klingbeil, chair of KCM LLC. Chuck Schilke, director and professor at the Center for Real Estate and Urban Analysis at George Washington University, echoes that sentiment, stating, "Mostly, I think that developers should keep their heads about them. This too will pass, although COVID does have an impact." Dan Rosenfeld, director of land use solutions at Community Partners, similarly says, "I think most markets will return to their previous trends."

This range of perspectives—the perceptions, mindsets, and predicted outcomes—points up the difficulty of analyzing the effects of the pandemic on development while it is ongoing. Viewpoints considered and acted upon in the short term may or may not prove to be true or beneficial in the long term. It is always easier to critique a belief, decision, and action in hindsight. Ronald Altoon of Altoon Strategic LLC, summarizes the difficulty well, stating, "COVID-19 has certainly altered physical real estate in the short term, with an emphasis on fresh air, filtration, spacing, surfaces, and so forth, but it has also implanted a desire to return to normalcy. When confidence returns, the need for social spaces, cultural and recreational experiences, and educational opportunities will surge."

FINANCING

Historically, the perception of real estate was as a low-volatility, inflation-hedged, steady cash flow asset class, with the perceived ability to dramatically improve returns on these assets with leverage. The introduction of REITs, securitization, and commercial mortgage–backed securities changed real estate finance. Valuation of assets became more volatile, and the complexity of some of the financial structures overlaid on assets made understanding risk allocation more difficult.

Although beginning developers' initial projects will likely be financed through small banks and local lenders, they should understand the bigger picture of financing real estate deals. Owen Thomas observes that funding is becoming more and more institutional.[10] Data and rents are more readily available—they used to be very opaque. Capital markets have expanded with better information. Thomas worries that too much money is going into property technology, creating applications that are not particularly useful. The abundance of capital makes it easier for small developers to get started. He notes, "If you have a creative idea and can find a great site or great piece of real estate, you can get financing. Real estate is still a local business and local sharpshooters have a role to play." Opportunities for cheap permanent mortgage money may come from different sources at any given time: from insurance companies or banks, or through mortgage brokers representing conduit loans (prepackaged pools of mortgages that Wall Street sells to investors). At times, capital may come on favorable terms from global investors. And although developers will need to find equity for their initial projects from friends and family, they should position themselves to be able to find institutional equity partners as soon as their track record permits.

PAYING FOR INFRASTRUCTURE

Fiscal problems have increasingly forced localities to rely on real estate development to balance local budgets and help pay for new infrastructure. Before 1980, most municipal services and infrastructure, such as schools, public safety, roads, and utilities, were paid for out of general revenues and general obligation bonds. Today, residents view crowded roads and schools as impacts of growth, and in fast-growing regions these costs can be a contentious issue. Virtually every major city and many small cities across the country have adopted comprehensive systems that include impact fees, exactions (payments made to receive a permit to develop),[11] community facilities districts, and adequate public facilities or "concurrency" ordinances (requirements that facilities or plans for new facilities be in place, or at least financed and bonded, before new development is approved)[12] to address these issues. Based on the theory that development should pay its own way, communities impose impact fees—usually charged per dwelling unit or per square foot—on developers to fund roads, intersections, schools, and public safety improvements. In many jurisdictions, the rezoning process includes evaluation

of "proffers," specific off-site improvements like parks or roads that may be "voluntarily" performed by the developer, with benefit to both the development and to the larger community.

The trend toward higher impact fees and exactions is likely to continue as cities try to maximize revenue without raising taxes. Some of the best opportunities for beginning developers lie in working with cities on government-owned land or in targeted redevelopment areas. If developers are willing to tolerate red tape and bureaucratic delays, cities and their redevelopment agencies can support, and sometimes streamline, the approvals process. These types of deals, sometimes with explicit public/private partnership, are available to smaller developers as cities motivated by "smart growth" ideas push development toward more complicated infill sites. Often, developers are able to tie up city-owned property for extended periods without having to close on it while problems are worked out.

REGULATORY CHANGE

In many jurisdictions, the increasing cost of approvals has been accompanied by a reevaluation of government's role in development. For most landowners, this is an erosion of development rights. Because concerns about fiscal health and quality-of-life issues have become tied to development, pressure has built for increased regulatory control. Municipal strategies range from the blunt instrument of downzoning (reduction of allowed density across a zoned area) to a set of more finely tuned incentives to locate and shape allowable development where political opposition will allow it, or where infrastructure better supports it. The affordable housing crisis is creating development opportunities for "mother-in-law" and accessory dwelling-unit additions to existing dwellings.[13]

Developers can do little to influence blunt regulatory actions like moratoriums, so it becomes very important to understand the exact process by which development rights (typically outlined in zoning as a set of allowed uses and a density) become vested (the moment at which these rights cannot be taken away by regulatory change).

One way for developers to hedge against the risk of losing development rights is to buy land subject to an "entitlement contingency," essentially making the seller a partner whose equity will be paid out when permissions are received. Developers pay for this consideration, but the higher price is often worth the reduced risk. Aside from the obvious benefit of delaying payment for the land, the alignment of sellers' and developers' interests can be advantageous, particularly because sellers of desirable tracts often have deep roots in the community, and sometimes political power. It is worth noting that in extremely hot markets, often such contingencies will be off the table. Also, in some cases, to outbid others with deeper pockets, smaller developers with good local relationships feel they can make an offer without such a clause by taking on more entitlement risk. Developers of larger projects can deal with the risks of vesting by negotiating "development agreements" that require them to build certain facilities in exchange for a city locking in existing zoning and development rights.[14]

The pace of government involvement has quickened, and its scope has expanded, as concerns about ecology and climate have gained support. In addition to basic considerations such as density and setbacks, developers must navigate a web of rules for water rights, stormwater, wildlife habitat, traffic, and other issues including subjective items like "viewshed" and "neighborhood character." Still, the blanket disgust expressed by some developers toward regulation is misplaced. Historically, zoning and other forms of regulation have been supported by developers as a means of protecting the neighborhood character and sense of place that make their assets more valuable.

It is not regulation per se but the uncertainty about new regulation that can be the greatest risk to developers. With this in mind, recent trends are troubling. Matt Kiefer of Goulston & Storrs suggests, "As the public sector pulls back financially . . . we are in a period of regulatory experimentation. Rather than issue commands, or regulate simple metrics like density, the trend is toward setting goals and performance standards, and leaving it to the developer to figure out how to get there."[15] This trend is particularly apparent in green building, where a third-party standard, such as LEED (Leadership in Energy and Environmental Design), may be required, but the approach to meeting the standard might allow an à la carte selection of construction practices that are more or less appropriate in different types and climates.

Tax increment financing districts are one way to finance infill development, and the transfer of development rights markets, which allow shifting of density to targeted growth areas, brings another set of tradable real estate assets to the market. Kiefer notes that "changes in regulation lag social change," so developers with long project timelines need to watch today's hot-button issue because it may be a condition of a building permit in a few years. Just as zoning can

benefit the conscientious developer, new conditions can serve as a bar that ultimately supports projects that contribute to a desirable shaping of the urban fabric.

Technology

The implications of technology for real estate are dramatic, and new tools have transformed how real estate professionals conduct many areas of the business, from acquisition, design, and construction to marketing, brokerage, property management, community operations, and financing. Predicting the outcome of any given technology in the years to come is nearly impossible, but some of the changes currently afoot can be analyzed.

ACQUISITION AND DUE DILIGENCE

New tools such as geographic information system–based technologies, websites that provide access to property tax databases, real estate listing services, and even free aerial mapping databases like Google Earth have revolutionized the "pursuit and feasibility" phase of development. An initial investigation of a property can now be performed quickly, remotely, and with virtual anonymity using such tools. In this way, developers are able to move quickly toward the acquisition of properties (and discard unsuitable candidates) while delaying the expense and involvement of consultants like surveyors and planners. Free or inexpensive tools are available that offer the ability to generate preliminary yield plans and criteria for valuation, from the most basic of available data sets. Already, it has become nearly as easy for a developer three states away to take a first pass at a property as it is for an in-town professional. "Proptech" companies are real estate startups that employ property-related technology, including sharing platforms, construction technology, smart buildings and cities, asset and property management, and property valuation tools. Proptech companies are organizing and placing at developers' fingertips enormous amounts of data on all aspects of the market, regulations, demographics, physical constraints, infrastructure, and other critical information for upfront due diligence. Accelerated in part by the COVID-19 pandemic, proptech and "fintech" (finance-related technology) companies are making it possible to find development opportunities remotely, to raise debt and equity money, and to close transactions entirely online.

MARKET STUDIES AND BROKERAGE

The quarterly or annual market report has given way to a continuously updated stream of data on sales and leasing that is available from a variety of private plat-forms. Therefore, development teams are hiring the expertise of marketing consultants to make sense of the data and to develop strategy. In fact, the predic-tive conclusions offered by market professionals may, in the coming decade, be outperformed by predictive algorithms using artificial intelligence (AI). Altus is among the firms using machine learning to process data—not only from real estate, but from all man-ner of consumer purchasing and behavior—to make predictions. Changes in markets might be predicted by analyzing a hundred or more variables from as many data sets. James Chung with Altus explains that the uncanny volume of data available is offset by the relative blindness of models to seemingly obvious con-straints like zoning, or exogenous shocks to employ-ment, so he advocates a partnership of professional and machine. He states, "A second-tier human with a good machine beats the best of either."[16] Although brokers are not disappearing, buying, selling, and leas-ing real estate has been transformed forever. Everyone starts with internet searches to gather information, check on comps, or obtain sale/buy leads.[17] Albert Saiz writes, "Integrated commercial real estate services companies effectively bundle brokerage with mar-keting, PR, research, financing, investments, asset management, custodial, technology, site selection, planning, consulting, and advisory."[18]

STAKEHOLDER ENGAGEMENT AND APPROVALS

The ever-increasing importance of community stake-holders demands more time and attention of devel-opment teams. Though the community meeting and charrette (design session with public input) are still important elements, new platforms enable more con-tinuous and deep connection to stakeholder interests. Bill Massey, principal at Sasaki, and James Miner, chief executive officer at Sasaki, use mapping technology to gather data on public-space use and preferences; they spend "lots of time on data visualization, before [showing] anyone the project design."[19] Kurt Culbert-son, chairman emeritus at Design Workshop, terms the process "co-creating with communities." The essential components are surveys, or even project-specific apps that can reach the people who do not often engage in the process—at least until a contentious hearing. Project teams are thinking of residents as "ambassadors" and attempting to equip ordinary citizens to communicate with their neighbors about projects.

DESIGN AND CONSTRUCTION

Easy communication using the internet is changing how property is developed. Networks that facilitate the ex-change of information—including plans, specifications, and financial data—are widely used in the design phase of development and are increasingly used during con-struction.[20] Building information modeling (BIM) allows team members, clients, and contractors to manipulate and reference the same base drawings for their special-ties. These tools create an operational model—a "digi-tal twin" of the building as design proceeds. The model links to relevant databases, budgets, and schedules to streamline the development process across multiple roles; for example, a change order might be delineated by an architect and automatically priced, shared, and presented for approvals. Other construction-related technology ("contech") applications link construction team members to nearly real-time information in the field or in markets. Extensive use of three-dimensional imaging and virtual reality allows clients and stakehold-ers to visualize the project, and photorealistic imaging is now almost a required component of public approv-als processes. General connectivity of team members has shortened the time required to revise drawings and other documents and has greatly expanded the geographic range of participants in the development process, allowing specialty engineers to work effectively across many jurisdictions. The long-promised evolution of BIM technology is becoming commonplace.

In addition to changes in the development process, smart developers and landlords anticipate future technology needs and plan accordingly to install wiring, backup generators, and other infrastructure in above-ground locations that might "future-proof" the asset.[21] Proptech firms are facilitating real-time reporting of energy usage, automatic sensors to adjust comfort and lighting in every room and at every desk, monitoring of building systems, and other aspects of construction and building operations.

PROPERTY MANAGEMENT

A plethora of software packages and apps are avail-able to assist in increasing the productivity of individu-als managing ever-larger portfolios. Those platforms can be tailored for any type of property and can inte-grate tenant records, lease management, maintenance scheduling, checks, taxes, profit and loss reports for one unit or an entire portfolio, payroll, and work orders. In addition to office tasks, innovative technol-ogy is causing rapid change in energy management, security and access control, real-time space reservation and allocation, and building-systems monitoring, any of which might now be as easily handled from Bangalore as from the boiler room. More importantly, access and control of key systems may be partially in tenants' hands, and the expectations and users' experience of a building may be as dependent on an app as they are on personnel. As in any business, owners should understand that technology represents an initial investment, not just in products, but in training personnel and in the replacement and maintenance of systems. The excitement over proptech solutions is real, but as of this writing it can appear that there is "an app for everything." Owners should understand both sides of these investments and should ensure that the "cool factor" does not supplant a real cost-benefit analysis.

FINANCING

The greatest penetration of technology in real estate finance has been in those areas serving the largest number of consumers—home mortgage originations and servicing. Still, with web-based platforms taking over substantial portions of Americans' financial lives, purely digital real estate transactions—digital transaction processing, information disclosure, financing, and closing transactions—are happening. The number of online mortgages, equities, leases, and sales transactions is increasing dramatically, and web-based appraisal services are edging into an important transactional role. In addition, as online appraisal services improve, companies with asymmetrical data are exploring using these data to make blind offers on property based on algorithmic evaluation of potential value. The COVID-19 pandemic accelerated exclusive use of online mortgages and sales transactions as buyers consummate deals without ever meeting in person. The winding down of Zillow's iBuying program is not likely the end of the use of AI to determine offer prices because even a few misses can be tolerated if the scale and transaction costs work. If one lesson has been learned, it is to avoid being the first to adopt an innovation, as many new tools fail or are supplanted as industry standards shake out. A successful developer will, however, stay abreast of technological developments and will be ready to invest in appropriate tools when they offer improvement to productivity, marketing success, and profitability of the enterprise.

Trends

Opportunities abound for developers that are able to capitalize on the many changes taking place. Demographic trends, such as the aging of the American population, the influx of immigrants, and the impact of new technology on work and leisure, are creating demand for innovative types of living environments. Some developers will find success providing these new kinds of places for work, home, and leisure pursuits. Historically, though, the safest bet on the future is usually that it will look more like the recent past. Developers must be cautious not to innovate beyond what their target market can afford and accept.

DEMOGRAPHIC AND GEOGRAPHIC CHANGE

Results of the 2020 census show that demographic factors will have a profound effect on the nation's economy and population distribution over coming decades. The combined growth rate for both cities and suburbs in the 100 largest metropolitan areas dropped to little more than half that of the 1990s due to an aging population and sluggish economy. The white population fell by more than 1 million people from 2016 to 2020 while the number of Latino or Hispanic Americans increased by almost 1 million per year and the number of Asian Americans increased 300,000–500,000 per year.[22] As the baby boom generation enters retirement, the United States is moving toward a population with a roughly equal number of people in each major age group, with slight bumps at the boomer and millennial age bands. At the same time, Americans are becoming a substantially more diverse group. By 2042, non-Hispanic whites will no longer be a simple majority. As planner Elizabeth Plater-Zyberk points out, relative increases in single-parent households, blended households, and singles mean that two-parent households with children—the historical driving force behind U.S. housing markets—now make up only one-quarter of all households.[23] Developers must consider a variety of housing types to attract buyers from these diverse households. In addition, multigenerational living and age-in-place solutions are becoming an important part of designing for this changing demographic makeup.

According to demographer William H. Frey, new regional demographic divisions will be created that will be as important as our current distinctions between cities and suburbs, rural and urban. These divisions will encompass entire metropolitan areas and states, distinguishing "multiple melting pot regions," "suburban-like new Sun Belts," "heartland regions," and "new minority frontiers."[24] The multiple melting pots—California, Texas, southern Florida, the eastern seaboard, and Chicago—will become increasingly younger, multiethnic, and culturally vibrant. Heartland regions will become older, more staid, and less ethnically diverse and will encompass growing parts of the Sun Belt, economically healthy states of the new West, and declining areas of the Farm Belt and Rust Belt.

The new immigrants and their children, primarily Latinos and Asians, will contribute 1 million people annually to the U.S. population, accounting for more than half of the 50 million additional residents during the next 25 years. As a result of current immigration laws, it is expected that incoming immigrants will choose to live in a handful of metropolitan areas spread across the country from California to Texas to Florida. Two key constituencies continue to drive expansion in some of the fastest-growing cities: the young—particularly the professionals known as "the creative class"—and the old (empty nesters and early retirees).

Advice on Opportunities

Owen Thomas, chief executive officer at Boston Properties, believes that building renovations are a great opportunity.[a] With the carbon footprint of steel and concrete for new buildings, he sees a future with many more rehabs and more attention to repurposing buildings. Thomas asks, "Can you take out every other floor if you can buy it for little money?" Jeff Hines agrees. He says his father, Gerry Hines, resisted buying existing buildings at first. "Why would we want to buy a building that someone else developed? By definition it is inferior."[b] But Hines notes that their development mindset and property management allow them to determine if a building has the right footprint, the right floor plan, and efficient window systems. "How is it operating? Is it a good location, in the path of growth? Can we improve operations? A lot of our skill sets are very applicable to re-envisioning other people's buildings," says Hines.

Daryl Carter, chairman and chief executive officer at Avanath Capital Management, believes that underserved markets offer great opportunities. His firm emphasizes building a sense of community. "When people know their neighbors, they feel safer. It also helps to reduce turnover."[c] Avanath has 20 percent turnover versus 40 to 60 percent across the industry.

Jeff Hines says there is a blurring of lines between product types. The office is becoming much more like hospitality; apartments and homes are taking on some office aspects because people want to work from home. Tom Bozzuto, chairman and chief executive officer of the Bozzuto Group, states, "We are creating more amenity space in our buildings—semipublic space. Sixty percent of our residents live alone. The need for amenity space is reinforced by people working from home. Apartments will need to offer social opportunities equal to what people had when they went into the office."[d]

Mixed use is also more popular. People like the sense of gathering that good retail used to provide. It works well with residential but must be built to scale to support entertainment and food and beverage—things for families to do. Mackenzie Makepeace, director of development at RMS Investment, says the key to mixed use is building an experiential place—creating a hub for the community.

Bozzuto notes that proptech is changing how people shop for apartments. "We used to walk through every apartment; today it's all done online. How do we retain whatever made us different if people would prefer to do all their shopping online? There will be people who prefer to be Walmart shoppers, while others prefer more personal treatment. How can we be leaders in technology while retaining a high-touch personality? This is our biggest strategic challenge."

Jeff Hines says, "Data and the digital world are becoming a huge part of our business. We are trying to harness all the data we have access to in our vertically integrated role. We are just scratching [the] surface of value. Digitization of our industry will take us through profound changes. Real estate used to be a stodgy industry but not anymore. How can we build a better product, or new kinds of companies? Can we sell decarbonization services?"

Roy March, chief executive officer at Eastdil Secured, adds that his firm can now underwrite a company based on its talent score—that is, invest in a company that evaluates talent. March asks, "Does a company have the right talent to succeed?"[e] Edward Walter, global chief executive officer at the Urban Land Institute, says proptech companies that affect revenues will have the biggest impact. A lot of focus now is on how to improve service and reduce cost. "You don't need a leasing agent in multifamily. Prospects can see apartments on their own."[f]

Owen Thomas says the definition of uses has changed a lot. "The growth is in high tech and life sciences as well as big new users like Google and Amazon. Now industrial is on fire (it used to be a secondary asset class). New uses, driven by technology, include cell towers, medical offices, self-storage, and data centers. Well-located retail centers with inherent assets like parking that are no longer working as retail will be ripe for redevelopment—to be converted to medical facilities, production studios, and apartments." Thomas believes that conversions and rehabbing older buildings will offer enormous opportunities.

[a] Owen Thomas, interview by Richard Peiser, November 17, 2021.
[b] Jeff Hines, interview by Richard Peiser, December 7, 2021.
[c] Daryl Carter, interview by Richard Peiser, January 12, 2022.
[d] Tom Bozzuto, interview by Richard Peiser, November 11, 2021.
[e] Roy March, interview by Richard Peiser, November 18, 2021.
[f] Edward Walter, interview by Richard Peiser, August 2, 2021.

The requirement that development take increasing diversity into account means also that developers should look to build diversity in their project teams. Firms report that this is not just an issue with the executive team, but may involve supplier and subcontractor diversity. Pressure comes from requests for proposal (RFPs), particularly municipal briefs, and from investors, particularly pension funds with ESG mandates. Ultimately, building a more diverse firm can make the firm more effective on the ground, working in an increasingly diverse country.

Diversity, equity, and inclusion are top priorities in this diverse environment. Increasingly, integrating racial equity in the development life cycle is becoming a high priority, and the industry is recognizing that an elevated focus on equity can have benefits for financial and social returns.[25] "Diversity feeds diversity. Every young African American will find me," says Daryl Carter. "I have a very diverse team. You need more diverse leaders who are visible. We get very positive feedback from residents who see us using diverse contractors and suppliers."[26] In Carter's company, Avanath Capital Management, people who started out in property management are encouraged to cross over into acquisitions and development. Carter says that having their input on the acquisition side is helpful. He notes that the service side has a lot of diversity, but the other side not so much. Crossing

The dozen individual "micro-projects" within the Plant-Riverside Redevelopment in Savannah, Georgia, exemplify how each site's existing conditions, infrastructure, and advantages can be studied to great effect. Advantages are maximized and the whole is unified with landscape and street improvements.

over provides upward mobility into other areas of the company.

Adam Weers of Trammel Crow has led efforts to diversify his firm's professional staff and leadership. He notes, "There are two sides, attraction and retention, and retention is the hard one, because you have to think about culture: Can a young employee see someone who looks like them? Do they feel they have agency and appropriate autonomy?"[27] Weers recommends instituting a formal program of diversity and inclusion at the firm level but planning for plenty of room for the specifics to spring up organically. Weers says, "We'll have a working group that's talking about hiring and assigning, but then there might be affinity groups that support historically underrepresented people. We might have a semiformal sponsorship program, where senior executives take on mentees."

Mackenzie Makepeace, director of development at RMS Investment, states that more people will be entering real estate from different perspectives. Developers will need to differentiate their buildings so that prospects are not just comparing rents. Makepeace states, "Make it a seamless experience. Bring whimsy—something that is unexpected."[28] She adds, "Being a woman—when I started going to national meetings—it felt like I was one of the only women in the room. It can be more challenging to find your circle and your comfort zone. I've had many champions both female and male who have helped me. Seeing others in leadership roles was great. If people have many organizations to choose among, they will go where they feel comfortable and see themselves represented."

CHANGING LIFESTYLES

Driving demographics since the 1950s, the aging baby boom generation continues to determine many market trends. This generation is already redefining retirement and semiretirement and making substantially different market choices from those of their parents' generation. With increased life span and good health, baby boomers expect to have an active lifestyle and to spend greater amounts on experiences rather than goods. Higher wealth accumulation and fewer children than previous generations will permit many to define retirement on new terms, allowing them to stay busy with volunteerism, second careers, and travel. Their demographics will determine where they retire and their preference for different types of housing. To cater to this market, more homes will offer accessible features such as first-floor master suites and accessible or convertible fixtures to facilitate aging in place.

Ten years ago, much was made of the potential reurbanization of baby boom retirees. Although preference surveys indicate that a portion of this cohort might be interested in a downtown area with ample amenities, so far the data show these people are remaining largely in suburbs, with a roughly equal proportion of them moving into city centers as are moving out to exurban locales. Many people of this generation chose to live their working lives in suburban metropolitan areas, and most can be expected to retire in those locations, or similar locations in other states, often moving to be near their children and grandchildren. As with previous generations, their retirement choices will be influenced by the quality of nearby health care facilities, and a greater share of new housing construction will likely be nontraditional types of smaller single- and multifamily residences, following a consistently expressed preference for minimizing home maintenance and upkeep.

Because of seniors' continued full- or part-time involvement in the workforce and their diverse lifestyles, traditional "active adult" communities are likely to be less attractive than more connected and authentic environments. Unlike past decades, seniors are not expected to relocate in large numbers to the Sun Belt. Except for the wealthiest elderly boomers who can search the country and select high-amenity locations, most are expected to age and retire near their families and other lifelong connections. Although many age-restricted communities remain focused on physical fitness, new ones are being developed around access to lifelong learning opportunities or outdoor amenities with an environmental or agricultural theme. For 20 years running, survey respondents have raised "walking/hiking trails" to the top preferred amenity in new community construction, and Helen Foster, an expert on "mature markets" suggests that "wellness is what we're going to hear about. Not just physical health, but indoor-outdoor integration, amenities designed to foster a 'joiner' mentality that connects people to community, a desire to live well."[29] Foster identifies coming opportunities in the translation of this thinking to the full spectrum of communities, from vertical urban towers to exurban agrihoods and housing with services and medical care. She identifies attainability as the biggest challenge, as numerous designers and developers are working to make these lifestyles attainable to middle-income buyers and tenants.

Along with demographic and technological trends, patterns of work, shopping, and dwelling are changing unusually quickly, affecting multiple property types. From 2010 to 2020, in addition to increased telecommuting and coworking, office buildings saw a stark increase in open floor plans and hot desks and fewer private offices. The COVID-19 pandemic may have reversed that trend, with a return to private offices and more space per employee—while companies grapple with the space implications of employees' preferences to work at home two to three days per week. Similarly, while online shopping increased sharply during the pandemic, e-commerce is still only 21 percent of total retail sales, and traditional retail is recovering quickly.[30]

At the same time, mixed-use environments are increasingly in demand, especially in densifying urban subcenters. Walkable neighborhoods with restaurants and bars close to residential and office space, with intensive landscaping, water views, and open space are commanding some of the highest rents. That said, beginning developers are wise to avoid mixed-use development because of the complications in design, construction, and financing. Nonetheless, office and residential buildings with ground-floor retail present attractive infill opportunities, although one must be careful not to provide more ground-floor retail than the market will absorb.

CITIES VERSUS SUBURBS

The extent to which cities are on the rebound is entering the third decade of a fiery debate. Urban history during the last half of the 20th century was largely about the migration of people from cities to suburbs and the decentralization of residences and, later, workplaces. Census data indicate that the draw of recent immigrants to urban cores is weakening. Preferences are shifting, particularly those of Latino and Asian immigrants, who are increasingly choosing suburbs.[31] Suburbs are becoming much more like central cities, with larger nonwhite populations, higher percentages of retired residents, and greater poverty, but also with increasing moments of vibrant urban activity. Crime, which had been dropping throughout metropolitan areas since the 1990s, is ticking up again. Affordable housing is the most critical issue, especially for Latino immigrants, who are projected to be drivers of growth, as they cluster in areas where land and housing costs are rising and developers have difficulty providing new housing at an affordable price.

Although immigrants are increasingly moving to the suburbs, urban living has been on the upswing in some cities, particularly among affluent, or at least upwardly mobile, high-tech-oriented young people. The conversion of older downtown and near-downtown offices and warehouses to loft housing, apartments, and condominiums signals the resurgence of urban life. Although a statistically significant increase in building in center cities is documented for some of the nation's largest MSAs, the shift is uneven. The trend is undetectable, and even reversed, in many second-tier cities. During the pandemic, the trend was reversed as many urbanites left the city for the countryside, where they could work from home in a natural setting. To maintain the interest in urban living, cities need successful downtown housing programs with several elements: committed public officials, aggressive marketing, creative financing, a flexible regulatory environment, a developer-friendly business climate, parking, amenities, and, most important, good product and urban design. Renting is the key for young professionals and minority households to live in the city. Although the average renter has an annual income of under $50,000, the fastest growing segment of renters is higher-income households, and the growth of this sector is remarkable in expensive major cities. More than 40 percent of householders ages 25 to 44 are renters, compared with around 20 percent of householders ages 45 to 64 and fewer than 20 percent age 65 and older.[32] The majority of center-city minority householders are renters.

Development Issues

In the coming years, a number of issues will continue to be of concern to developers. More sustainable development will be a way to address environmental, economic, and social problems.

SMART GROWTH

Although growth has benefits, it is widely recognized that it can result in unintentional fiscal, environmental, health, and lifestyle consequences for the larger community and for regional and national interests. As Matt Kiefer describes it, "The postwar view was of development as an engine of growth. The 21st-century view is of development as a generator of impacts."[33] Recent census and other data indicate strong growth will continue, and the challenge for many municipalities is how best to accommodate development while maintaining community identity and protecting the environment. Stepping into the unproductive "economic development versus no growth" debate is a powerful and simple concept: smart growth, also referred to as "sustainable growth" or "quality growth." It refers not to a single solution but to a set of principles promulgated by organizations like Smart Growth America that promote a higher quality of growth that accommodates and directs development activity in a way that supports the economy by encouraging investment and job creation, raising property and tax values, providing incentives for a variety of housing and transportation alternatives, preserving the environment, building healthy communities, advancing racial equity, and enhancing quality of life and a sense of place. Smart growth provides an intelligent counter to NIMBYism (the not-in-my-backyard syndrome) by encouraging higher-density development adjacent to public transportation.

Policies derived from smart growth principles have been promoted by states, and the federal government has promoted similar goals through interagency partnerships between the EPA, the Department of Transportation, and the Department of Housing and Urban Development. With that kind of support, it is likely that smart growth will continue to have a strong influence on development decisions, and developers should be able to frame their proposals in terms of those goals.

Despite planners' and policymakers' efforts, the job of implementing better growth ultimately falls to developers, who introduce proposals and invest capital to do the actual placemaking. As such, in the hands of entrepreneurs, these models must satisfy

The AT&T Discovery District in Dallas, the product of a public/private partnership, transformed an underused corporate campus into an immersive mixed-use urban environment. With offerings like purposeful outdoor spaces, free public wi-fi and 5G access, dining, retail space, and entertainment, it has become an active gathering spot for employees, the community, and visitors to the city.

not just civic ambition but also financial metrics, and the underlying principles must be able to survive the "sausage-making" process of public approvals and regulatory review. Public opposition to growth can deter even high-quality projects that incorporate smart-growth principles, and the "smarter" plan often exacerbates the rancor of abutters and environmental groups because these principles, when applied to a given site, typically result in higher densities and mixed uses where growth is desired, to minimize sprawl, impact, and infrastructure provision in other areas designated for protection. Advocates for these projects should not expect an easier ride through approvals, unless the jurisdiction offers an explicit fast track or public partnership for appropriate projects. Developers should, however, heed one of the key principles: planning should involve community stakeholders. At the mercy of local politics, developers may be loath to admit outside voices into project planning, but when these plans succeed, they do so with coalitions behind them.[34]

When conceiving a project, developers must not conflate desires of the public at large with individual buyer decision-making. A well-conceived smart-growth project may put all the parts together in an innovative way, but demand for individual product types should be well established in the market.

PLACEMAKING

Nearly everyone agrees on the need to preserve a *sense of place*. A sense of place gives residents and workers in a community a feeling of belonging. It is achieved through a combination of policy, planning, design, marketing, and the evolution of a set of social structures and local organizations over time. Design plays a critical role, helping define boundaries, public spaces, places where people meet and have fun, character, and landmarks that people identify with that community.

Why should developers care about streetscapes and public places? Such concern is part of good citizenship, but it also translates into long-term value. Streets and plazas that are pleasant to experience, durable, and accommodating of change, rather than requiring demolition, will appreciate more and hold their value over time. Developers, however, cannot improve streetscapes by themselves. They are often constrained by zoning and engineering standards that mandate the width of streets, setbacks, and building heights;

AQUAFOR BEECH LIMITED

Saigon Park in Ontario, Canada, is a model for 21st-century open space design, providing a multifunctional public area that includes recreational amenities and green stormwater infrastructure near the city of Mississauga's downtown core. The park, located within a highly urbanized area 6.2 miles (10 km) from Lake Ontario at the headwaters of Cooksville Creek, is ideally situated to treat runoff and mitigate flood risk.

by lenders' impulses, such as mandating front-door rather than backdoor parking; or by standards that require overbuilt roadways in pedestrian districts. On the other hand, early 20th-century planning principles favoring the separation of uses have given way to new trends favoring mixed-use development. Many planning commissions now actively encourage mixed-use development with offices, shopping, and residences on the same or adjacent sites. Developers of dense office and residential projects may be required to allocate ground-level space to public-facing uses, which can be infeasible when retail markets are weak. Urban designers have developed a variety of strategies for "activating" street-level spaces with limited retail need. These strategies range from stretching the definition of retail to include health care and semipublic office, to allocating building amenities in retail formats. Supporting an active street life is sometimes just design, and investment in street furniture, public art, landscape, or even programming, and in mechanisms such as business improvement districts can help provide funding for these sorts of improvements and coordination of disparate property owners.

ENVIRONMENTAL CONCERNS AND CLIMATE CHANGE

Environmental concerns are of central importance to the general public and to policymakers and, therefore, to real estate developers who must work with

all these parties. Increasingly, developers recognize that a sensitive approach to the environment is good not only for the community but also for business. Although external pressure for environmental responsibility may be uneven, with some clients and investors more or less compelled by the issues, developers must look at the big picture. There is no longer any doubt that the environmental impact of land and building development is important to society at large, and from large-scale climate change to indoor air quality, careful attention to environmental factors is a feature of forward-looking development.

Owen Thomas observes that having projects that address climate change are important to tenants and capital providers. He notes, "The trend will get more intense. The sustainability footprint will be increasingly important. Customers will ask what the carbon footprint of a building is. You must have a carbon footprint strategy. Everyone was focusing on how to reduce energy consumption because it put money in our pocket. The focus now is much more on the source of the power."[35]

Professional Real Estate Development

Edward Walter, global chief executive officer at the Urban Land Institute, says climate change is a much bigger issue when cap rates are going up. It affects insurance rates and cities are recognizing that they will have to take expensive measures. Walter asks, "Who will pay for that? Real estate will. Not that those issues weren't there before, but now they are a much bigger part of everyone's underwriting."[36]

Site contamination is a major problem for developers, but the industry has adopted methods for dealing with it. Both developers and lenders are slowly becoming more accustomed to dealing with brownfield sites, partly because the majority of urban sites—and even undeveloped farmland—have some contamination that must be mitigated, or at least suspected problems that must be investigated. As always, new problems generate new opportunities. Some investment and development firms now specialize in rehabilitating properties contaminated, or suspected of contamination, by toxic materials. Because the properties can usually be purchased at significant discounts, careful analysis of the removal costs and appropriate actions can generate large profits. Although lenders have been extremely wary of loans on such properties, federal and state governments have established grant and loan programs to partially underwrite remediation costs, and knowledge of the intricacies of these programs can improve the profitability of a project. Nonetheless, developers that fail to perform adequate due diligence before purchasing new properties risk financial disaster.

Water availability and quality issues increasingly determine where and how much development can occur. In addition, communities are concerned about the preservation of hillsides, wetlands, canyons, forests, and other environmentally fragile areas. Jim DeFrancia, principal of Lowe Enterprises in Steamboat Springs, Colorado, observes that one of the biggest impacts of climate change has to do with water, especially out West. According to DeFrancia, "All desert country is impacted. Growth pressures make it even more important. You can't have a lawn like you would in New England. It affects character of development."[37]

Developers that address these concerns in planning and designing their buildings will find communities more receptive to their projects. A related matter, habitat preservation, can touch nearly any land development project and can trigger unsustainable delays as field science is scoped and as preservation and mitigation plans are prepared and approved. Of considerable

frustration to landowners is the perception that time, the enemy of the developer, often seems to hold little interest for the regulator, whose goal is to prevent a detrimental project from being developed, not just to approve good projects. As in so many other areas, the best defense against uncertainties is twofold: negotiating appropriate approval contingencies in acquisition and performing solid due diligence. Modest, early expenditures with reputable and experienced consultants can help owners foresee, if not forestall, such problems.

Stormwater management is one of the most common pitfalls facing developers, particularly in suburban and exurban settings. As environmental science has advanced understanding of nonpoint source pollution of waterways, regulatory attention has shifted from the stereotypical factory pipe discharging PCBs into a river to a focus on limiting sedimentation and the low-level but constant runoff of nutrient- and contaminant-laden stormwater.

Rapid changes are afoot with regard to climate, particularly as ESG requirements trickle down into asset-level decisions. Investment guidelines may soon require minimum efficiency standards, or complete nonreliance on fossil fuels. Greenhouse gas (GHG) emissions are clearly moving the planet toward irreversible climate change, with impacts that cannot yet be reliably predicted. European nations have begun voluntary trading of GHG credits, and in the United States, while national policy is being negotiated, California is implementing a regulatory scheme to rein in emissions. This scheme, likely to become a model for other states, directly addresses GHG and energy impacts deriving from land use change, which puts developers in the driver's seat. This leadership role is appropriate, as the largest forests, farms, utilities, industry, and building construction and operation are all touched by real estate development, though few developers active today would consider themselves qualified to make decisions in the field of planetary energy balance. At the same time, stricter regulations on GHG emissions from existing buildings are creating opportunities for developers who focus on renovating older buildings.

Judi Schweitzer, founder and president of Schweitzer & Associates in Lake Forest, California, advises developers of long-timeline projects to jump into energy-related issues, with appropriate consultants to help navigate the process. She notes, "These constraints are coming, and they will be complex, and it will pay to be familiar with the terms and players early. . . . In addition to regulation, funding sources increasingly have portfolio requirements that will further motivate developers following capital to address these issues."[38] Rather than recoil at the thought of accounting for carbon and methane in a land use plan, developers should delineate the constituencies that must be satisfied, and treat energy like any other approvals issue. According to Schweitzer, "A checklist, or even a series of checklists, is insufficient. Rather than tick off points toward LEED or other certification, developers will, over the coming years, have to become familiar with the emissions profile of various land use decisions they make, in the aggregate, and working as a system." Steve Kellenberg, retired principal of AECOM, states it differently: "What's happening now, and going forward, is a shift from qualitative (add bike lanes, preserve a wetland) to quantitative (carbon accounting, energy modeling) understanding of environmental impacts. This is good. It means, with the right tools, we are going to start making smarter and more informed decisions. . . . We think we can knock 25 percent off carbon emissions, just by using models and adjusting land uses accordingly."[39]

Climate change is having enormous impact on location and real estate value as the public and insurance companies become increasingly aware of flooding and wildfire risk. As climate change increases the number and severity of storm events, flood insurance is becoming a costly requirement in many areas where it was not a concern before. Sea-level rise of two to three feet by 2050 and six to seven feet by 2100 threatens vast areas of coastal development, rendering some of the most valuable oceanfront real estate increasingly vulnerable. Even today, parts of Miami Beach are under water two weeks a year during King Tides, and those areas will become uninhabitable as flooding becomes more frequent.

Separate from the effects of climate change is the trend of real estate as an energy producer. Increasingly, as the costs of renewable energy sources come down, and the costs of nonrenewables go up, real estate can have an important asset in the ground (geothermal heat) or on the roof (solar or wind power). Fortunately for the bewildered developer, many of the recommended—or legislated—land use solutions to climate change already closely follow principles of smart growth: colocation of jobs and housing, transit orientation, and compact and efficient buildings. As is often the case, developers that pay attention to areas of concern today will have a leg up on future issues.

THE NEED FOR OPEN SPACE

Preservation of open space consistently ranks among the top concerns of both urban and suburban residents. The increasing interest in ecological function of even highly urbanized areas portends only greater focus on this issue in the coming decades. Open space comes in many different forms, from manicured golf courses to permanently wild forests and wetlands. These spaces might allow a wide range of uses, from farming and passive recreation to structured facilities, such as ball fields. Ownership and protection of these spaces can range from public ownership, in the case of city parks, to quasi-public service districts within planned communities, to privately held easements across individually owned land, or public/private funding initiatives to rent or ease specific assets of ecological or cultural value or other ground maintenance. Each type of open space is critical for the enjoyment of different people who make up a community, and many of these spaces perform important—and sometimes economically valuable—ecological functions, such as filtering runoff and carbon sequestration. One trend worth watching is the attempt to monetize these "ecosystem services" and to establish markets that will pay landowners for their stewardship of these values by mechanisms like credit trading. Although municipal parks and other small-scale breaks in the dense urban fabric often generate the most intense public feeling and interest, environmental science has prioritized the protection of large, unfragmented spaces, where water and wildlife can more closely approximate their predevelopment functions.

Open space must be specifically protected, either by zoning, tax policy, or rolling rent payments on a long-term agreement or by a permanent legal reduction of development potential. If it is not, incremental urban development will eventually consume potential sites and cut up habitat areas. Since the Tax Reform Act of 1976, developers have been able to generate charitable tax deductions by donation of land, or by donation of an easement reducing development potential to a nonprofit easement holder. These returns can be attractive to investors and have spawned their own niche product: conservation development. States have responded to this relatively inexpensive method of conservation by offering their own suite of credits, which in some states are tradable on open markets for cash, to sweeten conservation deals. This response has greatly accelerated land conservation and has created an infrastructure of local and national land trusts qualified to accept and monitor these easements and to develop plans that prioritize parcels for conservation.

The importance of equitable and socially responsible practices in the field of development has increased in recent years. Referring again to the 2020 and 2021 surveys of development leaders, several responses are worth noting.[a] Anne Cummins at Gattuso Development Partners says, "As a partner in [public/private partnerships], we spend a lot of time trying to increase [our] local/minority workforce; maximize contracts to minority, women, and disadvantaged persons' business enterprises; and maximize positive impact to the community through creative partnerships with the schools."

Investing in early education is another practical and realistic way to facilitate greater racial and social equity in development. "Mentor the next generation of developers with more diverse backgrounds," says Mike Powers of McNellis Partners, while Joe Pazdan at McMillan Pazdan Smith Architects states, "The architecture/engineering industry as well as the professional real estate and development businesses need to support the education and advancement to provide social equality and professional advancement of our diverse society." Linda Congleton of L.S. Congleton & Associates also mentions the importance of increasing opportunities for women in the field of real estate; she says, "Encourage young women to go into the field, no matter what race, and serve as functioning mentors. Recruit on campuses with business and real estate programs."

In a similar vein, some leaders point out the importance of more professional training for women and persons of color. "Take a risk and hire young people of color and provide them with constant mentorship and project ownership opportunities," says Jerry Rappaport of New Boston Fund. Steve Marker at Brightview Senior Living states, "Hire, train, retain, and build succession planning to provide opportunity for racially diverse candidates to lead development projects." Fred Cooper at Toll Brothers also makes the point that increased social and racial equity can be achieved in development with "well-organized hiring, training, and mentoring of young employees of diverse backgrounds; investment funds providing equity to developers of diverse backgrounds; [and] pairing of minority and women-owned developers with experienced nonminority developers."

Stuart Margulies of Ascent Real Estate says, "Encourage [joint ventures] between minority/diverse firms and larger, more traditional firms." Another suggestion is to lower the barrier to entry by reducing bid package values to enable small businesses—especially those that are WBE (women business enterprises) or MBE (minority business enterprises)—to compete for parts of large projects. And another method is to incorporate mixed-income units (for example, at ranges of 20 percent to 80 percent of area median income) in multifamily projects. Trinity Hart of Storie Co. Development notes that the makeup of a developer's own team is significant as well; she states, "Choose companies on your team that have diverse ownership. . . . If you can't

incorporate racial and social equity into your team, you aren't providing it in your project."

Kacey Cordes at U.S. Bancorp Community Development Corporation summarizes just how integral incorporating increased racial and social equity into the field of real estate development is: "Racial equity must be baked into the entire life cycle of real estate development, beginning with the foundational principles of the development firm all the way to the exit strategy of the project."

Jeff Hines believes that real estate has seen more changes in the past two to three years than in the past 30 to 40 years and that change has been super accelerated by the COVID-19 pandemic. He notes, "ESG is everything in our industry. It is a huge focus for us. It is important to investors and to tenants who are trying to recruit young people who really care about it. It is important to our employees. It is so important to have a firm that has purpose beyond just making money. And it is the right thing to do."[b]

Roy March, of Eastdil Secured, says being sensitive to carbon neutrality, governance issues, and one's social role in society will be central to successful operations. He notes that Europe is six years ahead of the United States in terms of measuring and reporting ESG. He also believes that the definition of real assets will be much broader including cold storage, Amazon verticals with automated robotics, and nontraded REITs.

Daryl Carter observes that ESG has fueled Avanath Capital Management's business for raising capital. According to Carter, "Our affordable housing funds are big on social. When you talk about affordable and workforce housing, U.S. investors think it is public housing. They have very outdated views. They are scared of Section 8 vouchers. But under the 1994 entitlement reform, there is a work requirement that most people don't know about. U.S. investors are not as focused on that."[c] Carter notes that German investors invest heavily in affordable housing back home. Many countries outside the United States provide housing subsidies to people who make less than a certain threshold of income. He is a big proponent of mixed-income communities. "You don't know who's paying full rent and who isn't." Carter adds that ESG has tangible benefits. Avanath tracks ESG carefully in projects it buys or builds, including energy and water use savings. Carter says, "For our after-school programs, we bring in a nonprofit to manage the number of kids who attend and even track test scores. Your ability to track and measure the impact you say you're having is really important."

[a]Julian Huertas, "How Developers Got Started," Survey, Urban Land Institute, 2021.

[b]Jeff Hines, president and CEO, Hines, Houston, Texas, interview by Richard Peiser, December 7, 2021.

[c]Daryl Carter, chairman and chief executive officer, Avanath Capital Management, Irvine, California, interview by Richard Peiser, January 12, 2022.

At the national level, organizations like the Nature Conservancy and the Trust for Public Land provide mechanisms for developers and communities to set aside land for open space. The organizations serve as stewards of such land, providing various levels of access to the public while preserving natural amenities and wildlife habitats. Such organizations are needed because the timeline of preservation covenants is extremely long, often "perpetual." In some states, easements held by these groups are "backstopped" by state-chartered corporations, such as the Virginia Outdoors Foundation, which receive easements on their own, and when small land trusts can no longer serve as conservators.

For land developers, a familiarity with local land trusts is critical because they are often key stakeholders in community decision-making. A working knowledge of the mechanisms of open-space preservation will increasingly become part of the necessary toolkit for many developers, as municipalities respond to the contradictory challenge of constituents who want open space but cannot or will not pay for it from general funds.

TRANSPORTATION AND CONGESTION

Transportation has always been a major source of real estate value because of its effect on location—but solving the problem of overburdened roads and parking continues to be one of the development industry's principal concerns. Congestion—or merely the perception of congestion—can undermine a property's value and motivate new and existing development to continue its move outward to more accessible locations. Idling and inefficient operation waste tremendous fuel resources and contribute to GHG emissions, airborne particulates, and ozone.

The most direct method of reducing traffic congestion is to decrease the length and number of vehicle trips. One major unknown is whether commuting patterns will materially change as patterns of work and living change. Working at least partially from home is more than a temporary pandemic adjustment, and if it becomes widespread in white-collar fields, it has the potential to change assumptions about housing and traffic. Even without this change, some jurisdictions now require proof of a compact development plan for approval, but in other jurisdictions minimum lot sizes and performance requirements are working against this goal. Developers can assist in achieving these reductions by offering development in a dense, compact form with a mix of land uses accessible to mass transit. Though it generates controversy, many progressive jurisdictions may incentivize density near transit nodes. The inclusion of residential development, offices, retail uses, and entertainment venues in a convenient and accessible location reduces vehicle trips, spreads peak-hour flows on arterial roads, makes transit more feasible, and allows more people to live closer to employment and services. To achieve this scenario, federal and state agencies must work with the cities and counties that control land use. Developers, who will shoulder much of the burden for improving inadequate transportation in suburbs, would be well advised to support coordinated, collective efforts to plan transportation in their communities. Otherwise, they will be forced to pay a disproportionate share of the cost, and what they do provide will be inadequate to hold congestion constant, let alone reduce it.

Social Responsibility

Developers hold special responsibilities because their activities involve large public commitments and last for decades if not centuries. Growth policies and development also affect individual and group economic status, and they should be equitably deployed with input from many stakeholders. This imperative has too often been ignored, and in many American cities the history of redlining—racial zoning, discriminatory lending, and top-down infrastructure decision-making—has created conditions that require remedial action. Redlined neighborhoods, many of which were home to Black Americans and other minorities, have been linked to severe asthma, adverse birth outcomes, cancer, urban heat, and food deserts. Developers have a special role to play in redressing the discrimination of the past. Understanding and addressing implicit bias is an important pillar. In the survey of development leaders, Kacey Cordes notes, "We . . . have strived to educate ourselves as an institutional investor in regards to the implicit biases we might exhibit in our decision-making. This is a challenge for our entire industry." Implicit bias can have a considerable impact on how an investor or developer selects project sites, raises or awards financing, considers agreements and contracts, and selects employees, contractors, vendors, or tenants. Because development tangibly affects local communities and the built environment, it is incumbent upon professionals in the field to understand the role of implicit bias in how communities and space are considered, financed, planned, designed, and built.

At the same time, developers must be sensitive to concerns about gentrification: although reinvestment in deteriorating neighborhoods is essential for their restoration, rising rents drive out the most vulnerable residents and can reduce the supply of affordable housing. The problem of affordable housing has been exacerbated, according to Ron Terwilliger, chairman of Terwilliger Pappas Multifamily Partners in Atlanta. He says it costs $230,000 to build a unit in Charlotte—a cheap place to build. Terwilliger states, "Only one in five families is on Section 8 certificates, which should be dramatically expanded. The solution has to come from the supply side. Bring back tax-exempt bonds. We have to do a better job at preservation."[40] James DeFrancia adds that there needs to be a broader range of housing that can be broadly afforded. "NIMBYism is a form of social prejudice that hurts our industry and raises costs," he believes.[41]

In many communities, developers actually build most of the urban infrastructure, including roads, sewer, water treatment facilities, and drainage. They may also provide civic facilities, such as schools, hospitals, and police and fire stations. As the public sector pulls back from financial commitments, this trend is likely to continue. Developers are the intermediaries through which growth and change occurs and they must take responsibility for the equitable use and diversity of ownership in cities. This can include responsibilities far from land use and construction, such as economic development and supporting local enterprises.

Communities have a right to expect the highest possible quality of design, construction, and implementation from developers. They should expect developers to be sensitive to community concerns, to the streetscape and landscape, traffic, and other dimensions of development that affect the civic environment. This extends to concerns about displacement, and to affordability and issues that entangle development and larger economic forces. Developers should uphold their promises—delivering buildings on time and with appropriate attention to quality. Developers are also expected to be ethical citizens of the community, concerned with protecting its long-term interests.

What do developers have a right to expect from communities? They have a right to be treated fairly and consistently and for decisions to be made on the basis of merit and law. The community should honor its commitments to build promised infrastructure on time and to properly maintain public facilities and services. Developers have a right to expect the community to exercise foresight and good planning judgment in setting public policy—to ensure that new regulations are handled efficiently and do not impose unnecessary costs or delays on the development process.

THE DEVELOPER'S PUBLIC IMAGE

Developers as a group suffer from a negative public image. That image is often undeserved—as when developers are mistakenly identified as causes of, rather than responders to, demographic and economic change. Sometimes, however, the image is deserved—for example, when they build shoddy products, they impose costs on the community for which they should have taken responsibility, or they ignore clearly articulated community concerns.

Developers should understand the sources of the distrust that they will encounter. Many communities and neighborhood groups have relied on developers' promises that were never kept or on inaccurate predictions, such as a new office building that would not increase congestion. Developers are the standard-bearers for the real estate industry as a whole, even though architects, real estate brokers, property managers, and even public planners may also be to blame for these failings.

UNDERSTANDING AND INTEGRATING STAKEHOLDERS IN DEVELOPMENT

Community opposition to growth can be one of the most difficult challenges developers face. Debates often begin with the question of how the land is currently used. Although vacant land choked with weeds may seem to builders like a prime opportunity for development, surrounding neighbors may consider this open space a recreational area, dog park, parking area, or view corridor. Failing to acknowledge these existing, very low-intensity uses can make it difficult for a developer to reach consensus with neighbors about future land uses. The situation is different when the land is already intensively used. Then parties must explore the more complex question of whether the proposed land use is more or less desirable than the existing uses.

The analysis of citizen opposition to development proposals has spawned its own vocabulary, with terms like *NIMBY* (not in my backyard) and *LULU* (locally unwanted land use) often used interchangeably. A significant amount of opposition to development proposals is based on citizens' misperceptions, lack of information, or exaggerated fears of project impacts. Common areas of misinformation about new projects include consistency with zoning and general plan criteria; impact on property values, views, traffic, types of residents or commercial tenants; and changes in community character. The developer can minimize opposition spawned from a lack of information by providing clear, credible data about the project. Aside from misinformation, however, Matt Kiefer notes a substantial change in the etiquette of land use debates over the past 20 years. "Opponents who are impacted by projects used to feel a need to hang their hat on an external, objective concern. Traffic maybe, or environmental concerns. Social mores have changed, in that it is now seen as acceptable to oppose a project based merely on the personal impact of the proposal."[42] An assumption that ownership connoted rights to determine use is no longer a given, and developers that do not understand this end up in litigation.

Developers and planners must address a variety of different constituencies: local residents, including historically marginalized populations; local merchants; preservation and arts groups; city officials; and public agency officials. Michael Converse of AECOM says, "Winning or approving a project is no longer just the project, but proving how the team will be good custodians of stakeholder interests. We demonstrate how we use interviews, events, modeling, even virtual reality, to communicate, and we spend a lot of time thinking about equity and inclusion."[43] Displacement is now commonly expressed as a fear of neighbors, even when presented with appealing projects. In fact, the more appealing the project, the greater the fear that a changing neighborhood will price out residents or change valued neighborhood norms. Woo Kim of WRT cautions, "When you work in affordable housing, there's often so much to do in these neighborhoods. Too much gets put on a project, trying to solve too many problems. Our solution is to start with agreed principles, in a Memorandum of Understanding that sets goals. Here's what we're trying to do . . . preserve affordable housing, create a community space, then we're always checking back to see that we're achieving that goal, or we're getting distracted on something outside the project brief."[44]

The late Gerald Hines emphasized the role that community acceptance plays in marketability. "We look at each city as a different culture, and if we don't know the culture, we're going to have an unsuccessful project. Conferring with community boards and neighborhood associations has become a part of a project's market analysis and its later acceptance by the market."[45] Because the civic contribution of a development project is not always apparent, developers can benefit from regular civic involvement, such as

KEVIN SCOTT

The Liberty Bank Building is a mixed-use affordable housing development in Seattle's Central District with 115 affordable units. The project is located on the site of the former Liberty Bank, the first Black-owned bank in the Pacific Northwest. The project honors a rich cultural history while maximizing community empowerment to address gentrification and displacement.

serving on boards and working with nonprofits and schools. The presumption by opinion leaders of good civic intentions can be a great asset to developers who will, at some point, find themselves asking for the community's trust. Community leaders should remember that most of their goals for community improvements will be attained only with the participation of developers. The delicate balance between the interests of communities and of developers must be maintained if communities are to grow sensibly and sustainably.

Conclusion

Our understanding of how to shape development to create better, more equitable cities and neighborhoods is far from complete, but we are making progress. Among the greatest problems facing planners and public policymakers are how and where to invest scarce public funds so that the investment will do the most to enhance areas that are improving or to halt the fall of areas that are declining. Too often, massive public and private expenditures are made to rejuvenate one section of town, only to pull businesses and homebuyers away from another section. Similarly, land use, building, and engineering regulations are too often imposed with thought only of curbing the excesses of bad actors, and with insufficient understanding of unintended consequences.

Our recent performance in developing cities has been mediocre at best. Our cities fall short of their potential. Often, spaces are poorly planned and boring, and repetitive designs are deployed. Once-beautiful neighborhoods as well as urban infrastructure are falling into disrepair. Developing new greenfield sites is easier and cheaper than maintaining or redeveloping older areas. The development community must exercise stronger leadership, not only in constructing and renovating American cities but also in correcting the harmful aspects of the present development system. By looking after the interests of the community at large, developers serve their own interests.

ULI former president Robert Nahas summarized the attraction of development when he stated, "The great developers whom I've been privileged to know never worked for money per se. . . . I think these developers want to leave a footprint in the sand. It's their particular kind of immortality."[46] All developments must pass the test of serving current market needs or they will fail. But most developments also have a future clientele. Although individual homes and buildings may be replaced, the basic fabric of the community that developers create—street layout, parks, urban design elements—will last for hundreds of years. Indeed, one of development's greatest rewards—and the source of its greatest responsibilities—is its effect on future generations.

NOTES

1. Don Killoren, principal, Celebration Associates LLC, Hot Springs, Virginia, interview by author, 2010.

2. Owen Thomas, interview by Richard Peiser, November 17, 2021.

3. Jeff Hines, president and CEO, Hines, Houston, Texas, interview by Richard Peiser, December 7, 2021.

4. Benjamin Cha, chief executive, Asia Pacific, Grosvenor, Hong Kong, interview by Richard Peiser, November 22, 2021.

5. Christopher Kurz, president, Linden Associates, Baltimore, Maryland, interview by author, 2021.

6. Charles Adams, ThriveWell Advisors, interview by author, 2020.

7. Timothy Rowe, chief executive officer, Cambridge Innovation Center, Cambridge, Massachusetts, interview by author, 2020.

8. Daryl Carter, interview by Richard Peiser, January 12, 2022.

9. Julian Huertas, "How Developers Got Started," Survey, Urban Land Institute, 2021.

10. Thomas, interview.

11. Harvey S. Moskowitz and Carl G. Lindbloom, *The New Illustrated Book of Development Definitions* (New Brunswick, New Jersey: Center for Urban Policy Research, 1993).

12. Alvin L. Arnold, *The Arnold Encyclopedia of Real Estate*, 2nd ed. (New York: Wiley, 1993).

13. See the California Department of Housing and Community Development (website), Accessory Dwelling Units (ADUs), accessed March 3, 2022, https://www.hcd.ca.gov/policy-research/accessorydwellingunits.shtml.

14. See Rita Fitzgerald and Richard Peiser, "Development (Dis)Agreements at Colorado Place," *Urban Land*, July 1988, pp. 2–5; and Douglas R. Porter and Lindell L. Marsh, *Development Agreements: Practice, Policy, and Prospects* (Washington, DC: Urban Land Institute, 1989).

15. Matthew Kiefer, partner, Goulston & Storrs, Boston, Massachusetts, interview by author, 2020.

16. James Chung, Strato-Analytics/Altus Group, interview by author, 2022.

17. See Albert Saiz, "Bricks, Mortar, and Proptech: The Economics of IT in Brokerage, Space Utilization and Commercial Real Estate," *Journal of Property Investment and Finance* 38, no. 4 (2020): 327–47.

18. Ibid., 331.

19. Bill Massey and James Miner, interview by Richard Peiser, 2010.

20. Joint Center for Housing Studies of Harvard University, *America's Rental Housing 2017* (Cambridge, MA: Joint Center for Housing Studies, Harvard Graduate School of Design, Harvard Kennedy School, 2017).

21. Elizabeth Hayes, "Radical Changes as Worlds of Tech, Real Estate Merge," *Los Angeles Business Journal*, January 24, 2000, p. 36.

22. William H. Frey, *All Recent US Population Growth Comes from People of Color, New Census Estimates Show* (Washington, DC: Brookings Institution, 2021).

23. Elizabeth Plater-Zyberk, founding principal, Duany Plater-Zyberk & Company, Miami, Florida, interview by author, 2010.

24. William H. Frey, "Metro Magnets for Minorities and Whites: Melting Pots, the New Sunbelt, and the Heartland," PSC Research Report no. 02-496, Population Studies Center, University of Michigan, Ann Arbor, February 2002; and William H. Frey and Ross C. DeVol, "America's Demography in the New Century," Policy Brief no. 9, Milken Institute, Santa Monica, California, March 8, 2000.

25. Diana Schoder, *10 Principles for Embedding Racial Equity in Real Estate Development* (Washington, DC: Urban Land Institute, 2022).

26. Carter, interview.

27. Adam Weers, chief operating officer, Trammell Crow, Washington, D.C., interview by author, 2022.

28. Mackenzie Makepeace, director of development, RMS Investment Corporation, Shaker Heights, Ohio, interview by author, January 7, 2021.

29. Helen Foster, principal, Foster Strategy, New Orleans, Louisiana, interview by author, 2021.

30. It is expected to grow to 24.5 percent by 2025. Statista, "E-Commerce as Percentage of Total Retail Sales Worldwide from 2015 to 2025," accessed May 3, 2022, www.statista.com/statistics/534123/e-commerce-share-of-retail-sales-worldwide/.

31. Interview with Joel Kotkin, author of *The Next Hundred Million: America in 2050* (New York: Penguin Press, 2010).

32. NMHC tabulations of 2020 American Community Survey microdata, US Census Bureau, July 2022, accessed August 26, 2022, www.nmhc.org/research-insight/quick-facts-figures/quick-facts-resident-demographics/renters-and-owners/.

33. Kiefer, interview.

34. David Goldberg, communications director, Smart Growth America, Washington, D.C., interview by author, 2010.

35. Thomas, interview.

36. Edward Walter, interview with Richard Peiser, August 2, 2021.

37. James DeFrancia, interview with Richard Peiser, November 17, 2021.

38. Judi Schweitzer, president, Schweitzer & Associates, Lake Forest, California, interview by author, 2009.

39. Steve Kellenberg, principal, AECOM (formerly EDAW), Irvine, California, interview by author, 2010.

40. Ron Terwilliger, interview with Richard Peiser, December 2, 2021.

41. DeFrancia, interview.

42. Kiefer, interview.

43. Michael Converse, senior vice president, AECOM, Los Angeles, California, interview by author, 2021.

44. Woo Kim, principal, WRT, interview by author, 2021.

45. Gerald Hines, founder, Hines real estate organization, Houston, Texas, interview by Richard Peiser, August 2010.

46. Robert Nahas, former general partner, Rafanelli and Nahas, Orinda, California, quoted in Ed Micken, "Future Talk: The Next Fifty Years," *Urban Land*, December 1986, p. 16.

Index

Italicized page numbers indicate figures, photos, and illustrations.
Bold page numbers indicate feature boxes.

A

Absorption: industrial development and, 299, 304; land development and, 77, 78, 97–98, 116; market analysis estimates of, 10; multifamily residential development and, 152–54; office development and, 255; real estate cycles and, 16

Accelerator office space, 241

Accessibility: of industrial development, 298; of multifamily residential development, 159, 198–99; of office development, 257, 263, 264; of retail development, 349, 353, 355

Accrued return balance, 214–15

ACI. *See* American Concrete Institute

Action plans, 37, **38**

Activity-based work, 251, *251*

ADA. *See* Americans with Disabilities Act of 1990

Adams, Charles, 61–62, 375

Adaptive use. *See* Redevelopment/rehabilitation

Advertising agencies, 60, 227. *See also* Marketing

Aerial photographs, 51, 79, 115, 229

Affordable housing, 124, 152, 235, 345, 377, 384, 391–92

Agglomeration, 298

Aging populations. *See* Older adults

Agrihoods, *139*, **139–41**, 383

AI. *See* Artificial intelligence

AIA. *See* American Institute of Architects

Airports, 298

Air quality, 49, 161–62, 202, 247, 386

ALTA. *See* American Land Title Association

Altoon, Ronald, 376

Altus, 379

Amazon, 290, 291, 332–33, 342–43

Amenities: development industry trends and, 383; industrial development and, 313; multifamily residential development and, 199, 201; office development and, 251–52

American Concrete Institute (ACI), 312

American Institute of Architects (AIA), 43, 45

American Land Title Association (ALTA), 52–53, 58, 115

American Society of Heating, Refrigerating and Air-Conditioning Engineers (ASHRAE), 264

American Society of Landscape Architects, 46

Americans with Disabilities Act of 1990 (ADA), 263, 355

Anchor tenants, 353, 355, 360–64

A.O. Flats at Forest Hills [Jamaica Plain, Massachusetts], *153*

Apartment development: condominium development versus, 203–4; garden, **5**, **144**, 145, 195–98, **197**, 209, 225, 232; high-rise, **5**, 97, **144**, 145, **196**, 225; low-rise, **144**; mid-rise, **144**, *164*, **197**, 225; pre-leasing in, 64; timeline for, 17, 20, *20*, 25. *See also* Multifamily residential development

Appraisers and appraisals, 20, 56–57

Approvals: advice regarding, **22**, **26**; challenges related to, 6; of industrial development, 304–6; in land development, 93, 94; of multifamily residential development, 204–5; of office development, 265; in retail development, 350–51; technology and, 379. *See also* Regulatory issues; Zoning

Architects: advice for working with, **205**; carbon footprint and, 246, *247*; compensation for, 45; energy efficiency and, 245; landscape, 45–46; lighting and, 262; multifamily residential development and, 163; role of, 42–45, 55, 56; signage and, 262. *See also* Design

ARCOS apartments [Sarasota, Florida], **148–49**, *148–49*

Arterial streets, 116

Articles of incorporation, in homeowners associations, 135, 136

Artificial intelligence (AI), 225, 252, 379, 380

Asbestos abatement, 53–54, 357

As-built surveys, 52

ASHRAE. *See* American Society of Heating, Refrigerating and Air-Conditioning Engineers

Assessment districts, 92

AT&T Discovery District [Dallas, Texas], *385*

Atelier [Dallas, Texas], **196**

At-risk capital, 24–25

Attorneys: condominium conversion and, 164; in contract preparation, 86; in development process, **40**, 57; for land acquisition, 81; land use, 49, 50, 88–89; with lease experience, 267, 361

Automation, 252, 289–90, 297, 298, 323

Azola South Tampa [Tampa, Florida], **197**

B

Baby boomers, 143–45, 156, **218–19**, 235, 247, 380, 383

Back-of-the-envelope analysis. *See* Simple capitalization

Balance sheets, 211

Banks: commercial, 65; permanent loans from, 70; relationship building with, 11. *See also* Financing; Lenders; Loans

Barnes, Joe, 76

Base maps, 113–16

Bascom Group, **218–19**

Base maps, 113–16

Bay depths, *259*, 259–60, 353

Beneficiaries, in surety bonds, 58

Bidding by contractors, 54, 55, 130

Big-box stores, 336, 339, 340, 358

BIM. *See* Building information modeling

Biodiversity, 91

Bioretention basins, 119, *121*

Bjorson, Kris, 291

Blossom Plaza [Los Angeles, California], *233*

Bonds, 58

Bonuses, 37, 55, 59, 131–32

Boundary surveys, 21, 52, 115

Bozzuto, Tom, **22**, **27**, **381**

Bram, Steve, 70

Brick construction: multifamily residential development and, 200; office development and, 262; retail development and, 357, 358

Brokers. *See* Mortgage bankers and brokers; Real estate brokers

Brownfield sites, 51, 91, 301, 387

Budgets: for construction stage, 54; land use, *97*, 97–98; marketing, 131–32, 225, 364; for office development, *259*

Building codes: for multifamily residential development, 144, 163–64; for office development, 244, 246, 257; for retail development, 363

Building development versus land development, 75–76

Building information modeling (BIM), 252, 379

Building permits, 49, 79, 86, 90, 153, 162, 265, 362

Building shells/skin systems, 260, 357

Build-to-suit approach, 241, 269, 287, 292, 363

Bulk warehouses, 290, *290*

Bullet loans, 267

Bureau of Labor Statistics, 346, 347

Burns, John, **148**

Business parks, 242, 294, 299–300, 304–7, 313, 315, 321–22

Buy/sell clauses, 319

Bylaws, in homeowners associations, 135, 136

C

CAD. *See* Computer-aided design

California: coastal land development in, 88; condominium conversions in, 164; demographic trends in, 380–81; design controls in, 135; environmental issues in, 387; impact fees in, 165; industrial development in, 304, 305; neighborhood redevelopment in, *72*; property taxes in, 136; regulatory issues in, 88–90; security systems in, 203; site acquisition process in, 81, **84**; subdividing land in, 74, 89; on transit-oriented development, 163; vesting of development rights in, 90

Capital accounts, 33

Capital costs of retail development, 351, **352**

Capitalization, simple. *See* Simple capitalization

Capitalization rates, 56, 111, 172–74, 194, 235, 258, 268

Capture rates, 77, **86**, 153, 155

Carbon footprint, 243–46, *247*, 252, **381**, 386

Carrying costs, 11, 16, 96, 99, 300

Carter, Daryl, **26**, 375–76, **381**, 382, **389**

Casa Arabella [Oakland, California], *79*

Cash distribution priorities, 127

Cash flow: for development firms, 13, 14; industrial development and, 315, 318; multifamily residential development and, *182–85*, 190–91

Cash flow analysis: land development and, 95; in predevelopment period, 20. *See also* Discounted cash flow analysis

Category-killer retailers, 336, 339, 340

CDEs. *See* Community Development Entities